Mike Nagy
517-792-3072
365-86-4326

MICROCOMPUTER HARDWARE DESIGN

D. A. Protopapas

Unisys Networks
and Polytechnic University

PRENTICE-HALL, INC.
Englewood Cliffs, New Jersey 07632

Library of Congress Cataloging-in-Publication Data

PROTOPAPAS, D. A. (DIMITRIOS A.), 1939–
    Microcomputer hardware design.

    Bibliography: p.
    Includes index.
    1. Microcomputers—Design and construction.   I. Title.
TK7888.3.P774 1987   621.391'6   87-8638
ISBN 0-13-581869-9

Editorial/production supervision and
    interior design: Richard Woods
Cover design: Edsal Enterprises
Manufacturing buyer: S. Gordon Osbourne

Printed in the United States of America

10 9 8 7 6 5 4 3

ISBN 0-13-581869-9 025

PRENTICE-HALL INTERNATIONAL (UK) LIMITED, *London*
PRENTICE-HALL OF AUSTRALIA PTY. LIMITED, *Sydney*
PRENTICE-HALL CANADA INC., *Toronto*
PRENTICE-HALL HISPANOAMERICANA, S.A. *Mexico*
PRENTICE-HALL OF INDIA PRIVATE LIMITED, *New Delhi*
PRENTICE-HALL OF JAPAN, INC., *Tokyo*
PRENTICE-HALL OF SOUTHEAST ASIA PTE. LTD., *Singapore*
EDITORA PRENTICE-HALL DO BRASIL, LTDA., *Rio de Janeiro*

To Lena, Alexander, and Anthony

CONTENTS

3 Example Microprocessors

4 Memory

5 Input/Output

6   Peripherals   417

References   498

Index   500

Contents

PREFACE

Not long ago, microcomputer componentry amounted essentially to 8-bit CPUs, RAM and ROM devices, and I/O ports. In fact, it was possible to treat in a single volume both hardware and software design. The spectrum of today's microcomputer components is much broader: It includes 8-bit CPUs, 16-bit CPUs, 32-bit CPUs, and support devices ranging from error correction and memory management devices to speech synthesizers and disk controllers. Such components can be used as building blocks to design a wide range of microcomputer-based systems. At the same time, these powerful components increase the need for designers who understand their characteristics and are able to employ them effectively. It is this need that provided the motivation to write this book.

The objective of this book is to help the reader develop the capability of designing the hardware of microcomputer systems. It addresses the spectrum of today's microcomputer building blocks (including microcomputer peripherals) in terms of

- types of building blocks
- underlying principles
- their functional and electrical characteristics
- how building blocks relate to each other
- how they are put together to design microcomputer systems

Functional and electrical characteristics are explained first in general terms to provide a common base for understanding the specifications of commercially available devices. Then, we examine specific (real) devices as examples and show how we can apply them in the design of a microcomputer. Design alternatives, trade-offs, and the rationale behind design decisions in real practice are discussed when appropriate. Most chapters include at their end design examples in addition to those scattered throughout. In these examples we take the opportunity to address important design issues and deal with more complicated designs.

The book is beyond the introductory level and is organized as a textbook. It is intended for:

- Design engineers and engineering managers engaged in the development of microcomputer-based products.
- Senior and graduate students in electrical engineering and computer science.

No prior knowledge of microcomputers is necessary. However, the reader should have some knowledge of programming, logic design, and basic computer organization. Special attention should be given to the examples we provide in the text in the form of solved problems. Some are intended to enhance understanding of the material presented in that section. Others extend the material of a section. Collectively, these examples provide the background for the solution of the problems given at the end of each chapter. Each problem is labeled with its specific subject to facilitate selection for assignments. Problems whose subject is associated with the same section in the text are usually listed in ascending order of difficulty. A solution manual for all problems is available for instructors through the publisher. References are provided at the end of the book for those interested.

The book is organized into six Chapters. Chapter 1 gives an overview of the organization of a computer and discusses the tasks of the microcomputer hardware designer in the course of product development. This treatment is limited to the block diagram level. It sets the stage for the subject of the book. The next two chapters deal with CPUs. Each of the remaining chapters is dedicated to one of the three other sections of a microcomputer (and generally a computer): memory, input/output, and peripherals.

Chapter 2 concerns the principles and characteristics of microprocessors. Emphasis is given to the external interface, which is what the designer deals with in real designs. Limiting oneself to dealing with a specific CPU, or even one family of CPUs, always represents a problem in a book of this nature. We have chosen to use a "generalized" CPU model to explain the organization of a microprocessor and the functions of each group of its external interface lines. Addressing modes and instruction formats are discussed before proceeding to the important section on CPU timing.

In Chapter 3 we address the spectrum of real microprocessors and discuss categorization on the basis of the width of their external data bus. Then we examine a number of selected real devices. The examined devices are members of established microprocessor families and thus serve to describe the main features of each family. Yet these are not full descriptions. Our main objective is to demonstrate the different approaches employed for implementation of similar functions and their impact on CPU performance.

Chapter 4 discusses the principles and interface characteristics of dynamic and static random access memory devices. A similar treatment follows for read-only memories and programmable read-only memories, including EEPROMs. Emphasis is given to the subjects of error-detection-and-correction and memory management. In this chapter we have the opportunity to deal with the design of operational processors comprised of a CPU and memory.

In Chapter 5 we explain how input/output is organized in microprocessors. Then we discuss and compare the employed I/O techniques in conjunction with design examples. In the course of doing so we examine I/O interface, interrupt, and DMA controllers. A good part of this chapter's material is dedicated to I/O support devices, including those employed for serial communication. Serial communication deserves special attention because the marriage between computers and communications is now a fact. The last part of the chapter concerns the organization of microcomputer buses and discusses one of the standards associated with their implementation.

Chapter 6 addresses the hardware of microcomputer peripherals. The peripheral devices we discuss include keyboards, CRT displays, printers, and floppy disks. For each type of peripheral device we explain its principles of operation and its I/O control circuits. We also examine integrated peripheral controllers such as those intended for video and floppy disk control.

Our overall emphasis in *Microcomputer Hardware Design* is on microcomputer systems designed around a single, general-purpose CPU. Multiprocessors, computer networks, special-purpose microprocessors, and other advanced topics (such as speech I/O, computer graphics, and hard disks) are treated in a companion volume entitled *Advanced Microcomputer Hardware Design*.

I would like to thank Professor Lance A. Leventhal and Dr. Wing N. Toy for their valuable comments and suggestions throughout the development of the manuscript. Thanks are also due to Dr. Greg E. Masterson for his comments on the final version of the manuscript.

DIMITRIOS A. PROTOPAPAS

1

INTRODUCTION

What is a microcomputer? Why such a phenomenal interest in microcomputers? What is microcomputer hardware design all about? Before we start answering these questions we will review the basics of computer organization and discuss how computers are classified. This is very appropriate because microcomputers are organized and operate the same way computers in general do.

1.1 ORGANIZATION OF A TYPICAL COMPUTER

Digital computers are electronic machines capable of performing arithmetic and logical operations. These operations are specified by instructions which the computer recognizes and executes. A **program** is a sequence of instructions telling the machine how to execute a specific task. Execution of a user's program involves both hardware and software components within the computer. The hardware components (which are collectively known as "**hardware**") include electronic circuits, power supplies, cables, racks, and other physical entities. The software components are internal programs which

1. Monitor and coordinate all internal operations of the system
2. Simplify the interface between people and the computer

Software components of category 2 include, for example, language translators. A translator allows users to write programs in a compact form using an easier-to-handle "high-level" language. When the program is submitted to the computer,

1

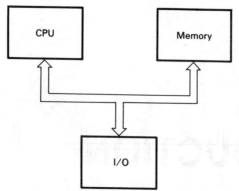

Figure 1-1. The organization of a typical computer.

it is first converted by the translator into the language the machine understands and then is executed.

Figure 1-1 shows the organization of a typical computer in simplified form. Programs and any data on which the programs will operate are entered through the input/output (I/O) subsystem. They may be stored temporarily in one of the storage devices of the I/O subsystem or brought directly into the memory for processing. The central processing unit (CPU) accesses a program and its data from memory. It may also use the memory to store intermediate results. The final results become available from memory via the I/O subsystem.

The CPU

A CPU, often called simply **processor**, consists of three main sections:

- Registers
- Arithmetic/logic unit
- Control unit

Registers are high-speed memory locations used to store important information during CPU operations. The **arithmetic/logic unit (ALU)** performs operations on operands, that is, data which have arithmetic or logical meaning. For example, it may add two numbers or complement a single logical quantity. The **control unit** generates the control signals which control the flow of information within the CPU. Data transfers between CPU, and memory and I/O are also controlled by this section. Exception to this are high-speed I/O controllers which may read and write into the computer memory without CPU involvement.

We will use Figure 1-2 to show how a CPU functions in simple terms. All the registers and the output of the ALU share a common set of signal lines for information exchange. This is the internal CPU bus. A CPU may have more than one internal bus to allow overlapping operations. Communication with the memory and I/O is through the external bus. In some computers the CPU has

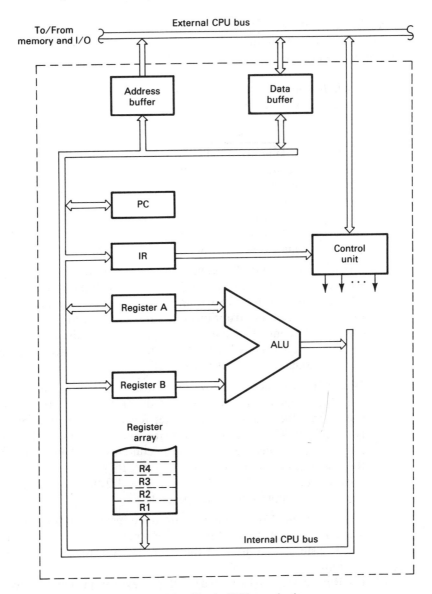

Figure 1-2. Simple CPU organization.

two separate external buses: one for memory and another for I/O. In either case an external bus includes address, data, and control lines. The address signals determine the memory (or I/O) location which the CPU is to access in order to read or write data. These data are carried over the data lines of the bus. The control lines determine the purpose of the operation, for example, to read or write.

Execution of an instruction starts from the **program counter** (**PC**), which contains the address of the instruction, and ends with the placement of the result in the appropriate location.   Next we describe the phases involved in the execution of an instruction and the sequence of steps during each phase.

1. *Fetch Instruction:* The instruction is read from memory and placed in the **instruction register (IR)**.   The sequence of steps are:
   (a) Transfer the address of the instruction from the PC into the **address buffer** (register).
   (b) Load the contents of the address buffer on the address lines of the external bus and generate a read signal to the memory.
   (c) The memory reads the instruction and places it on the data lines of the external bus.
   (d) Load the instruction from the external bus into the **data buffer** (register).
   (e) Transfer the contents of the data buffer into the IR.
   (f) Increment the PC so that it points to the next instruction.

2. *Decode Instruction:* The control unit decodes the instruction to determine what control signals to generate next.   A small number of instructions does not involve operands.   Such an instruction, for example, may be one that enables program interruptions by events external to the CPU.   In this case, appropriate control signals may perform the required action directly.   The instruction cycle ends here.   If the instruction involves operands, we have the additional phases that follow.

3. *Determine Operand Addresses:* The location of an operand is determined by the CPU from the address part of the instruction.   It may, for instance, specify that the operand is in register R1, or that the address of the operand is in register R2.   In other addressing modes the instruction may provide a number which must be added to the contents of a CPU register to calculate the operand's memory address.   Many CPUs have a separate ALU for address calculations.   In the CPU of Figure 1-2 the sequence is similar to that of adding or subtracting two operands.

4. *Fetch Operands:* We assume the decoded instruction specifies two operands. The addresses of the operands are assumed to be in registers R1, R2:
   (a) Transfer the address of the operand from register R1 into the address buffer.
   (b) Repeat steps 1(b) to 1(d) with the exception that now we deal with an operand rather than an instruction.
   (c) Transfer the contents of the data buffer into register A.
   (d) Transfer the address of the second operand from register R2 into the address buffer.
   (e) Repeat steps 1(b) to 1(d) for the second operand.
   (f) Transfer the contents of the data buffer into register B.

5. *Operate on Operands:* The first operand is now held in register A and the

second operand in register B. Control signals from the control unit activate the ALU so that the operation specified by the instruction is performed. The result of the operation is transferred via the internal bus into register A. This completes the execution of the instruction. Another instruction may store the result in memory or use it as an operand. In some CPUs, instructions specify where to store the result itself. For such instructions the execution cycle includes one more phase.

6. *Store the Result:* We assume that the decoded instruction specifies that the result be stored in the memory address contained in register R3. The sequence of steps is:

   (a) Load the contents of R3 into the address buffer.
   (b) Transfer the result from register A into the data buffer and generate a write signal to the memory.
   (c) The memory stores the result in the specified location, and the execution cycle of the instruction ends.

The Memory

Computer memories are organized into locations. Each location consists of the same number of cells. A memory cell can store only one of two different values. These values are the binary digits 0 and 1, which are commonly known as bits. So, the quantity contained in a location, whether this is an instruction or a piece of data, is in binary form. The same is true about information that flows over buses or information stored in other parts of a computer.

Usually a memory location stores one byte, that is, a group of eight bits. **Words** are larger groups of bits consisting generally of two or more bytes. Each location has a unique address which itself is a binary number. Figure 1-3 shows the functional units of a computer memory. Like the CPU, the memory includes an address buffer and a data buffer. The control circuits receive read/write signals sent by the CPU or I/O over the external bus. On the basis of these inputs the control circuits generate other signals which control internal memory operations.

The I/O

The I/O subsystem allows a computer to exchange information with the external world. In addition, it provides a computer with the means of storing information on disks and tapes. It consists of **I/O controllers** and **peripherals**. A peripheral may be an input device, an output device, or both. Examples are printers (output), and display/keyboard terminals (input and output). An I/O controller controls the operation of a peripheral according to commands received from the CPU. It provides the CPU with information about the status of the device and coordinates the flow of data between the external bus and the device. Two or more peripherals may share the same I/O controller, as shown in Figure 1-4. In slow-speed pe-

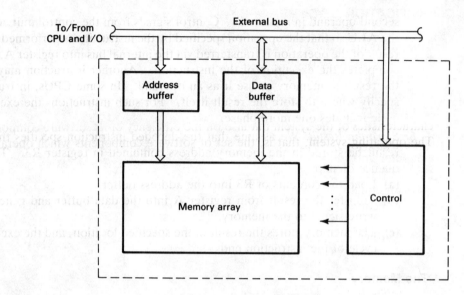

Figure 1-3. Memory organization.

ripherals, a data transfer amounts to sending or receiving from the CPU one byte of information. High-speed peripherals, like tapes and disks, transfer data in blocks of many bytes. The controllers of such devices are usually capable of reading and writing data into the computer memory on their own—that is, without CPU intervention.

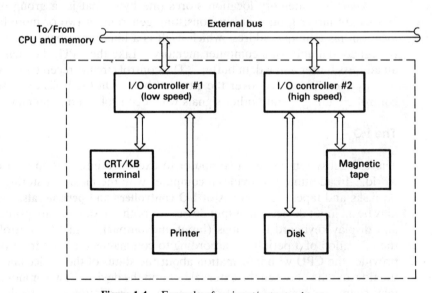

Figure 1-4. Example of an input/output subsystem.

1.2 CLASSIFICATION OF COMPUTER SYSTEMS

Computers are usually classified in terms of how fast they can process information. Processing speed may be quantified by using a mix of programs which is representative of the typical load of the system. By measuring the processing time we can then determine the average instruction processing rate. This rate is expressed in millions of instructions per second (**MIPS**). It depends not only on the hardware characteristics of the system but also on the efficiency of its software components. The operating system, that is, the set of software components which operate the computer, introduces overhead. In a well-designed operating system this overhead is minimized. If the system includes high-level language translators, their efficiency plays an equally important role. Efficiency here relates to translating speed and the production of a "translation" which can be executed by the computer relatively fast.

Hardware characteristics of importance in achieving high processing speed follow.

1. *Logic family:* Determines the switching speed of the digital circuits within the computer.

2. *Word length:* The number of different types of instructions (instruction set) is directly related to the word length. Word length is the number of bits treated by the computer as a unit. When the instruction set is small, we use combinations of instructions to perform operations for which there are no instruction types. This may reduce the average instruction processing rate.

3. *Width of internal CPU buses:* Wider data paths speed up CPU operations, since more information is transmitted in a single transfer.

4. *Overlapping of CPU operations*: Fetching from memory the next instruction while the CPU is executing the current instruction is a common form of overlapping. The extent of overlapping has a major impact on the effective length of the instruction cycle.

5. *Memory bandwidth:* The maximum continuous data rate supported by a memory is determined by its cycle time and the width of the memory bus. **Cycle time** is the time required to complete a single read or a single write operation. The width of the memory data bus determines how many bytes can be read or written in a single operation. Memory bandwidth is expressed in megabytes per second (MB/s).

6. *I/O bandwidth:* This is the maximum aggregate I/O traffic which can be handled by the I/O subsystem(s). It is mainly dependent on the speed of peripheral devices and the capabilities of the I/O controllers.

On the basis of their processing speed, computer systems can be classified into large, medium-size, and small computers. This differentiation of course is not strict. For example, low-end models of a family of large computers and high-end models of a family of medium-size ones have comparable capabilities. Each of the three classes serves different types of applications.

Large computers are better known as mainframe computers, or simply mainframes. Their high speed and their large capacity memories and peripherals are geared to match the demands of business data processing and scientific computing applications. Their manufacturers provide sophisticated operating systems supporting various operating modes (like timesharing of the machine by a large number of users or remote job entry). Since there are a number of language translators, the machine can be programmed using different high-level languages. Many other software components are made available to help the user and increase the productivity of the machine. As a consequence of their general-purpose capabilities and their processing speed, mainframes are expensive. A typical mainframe computer consists of several cabinets or enclosures (including peripheral devices). It is usually stand-alone or plays the role of the central machine in a multi-computer environment.

Medium-size computers (often known as minicomputers) are conservatively designed systems. Their CPUs have longer instruction cycles. Word lengths and data buses do not usually exceed 32 bits. Also, their memories and peripherals are of medium performance in terms of speed and capacity. The same conservative philosophy applies to minicomputer operating systems and the other software components they offer. Minicomputer makers aim at applications which require less processing power and lower cost. Some of these applications are at the low-end of the spectrum of business and scientific computing applications. Most, however, are specialized applications for laboratories, process control, manufacturing, and so on. In these applications, users have to interface their own (external) hardware to the computer, so medium-size computers are generally equipped with flexible I/O characteristics to facilitate such interfacing. Typically a medium-size computer occupies about one equipment rack.

Small computer systems are intended for applications where cost is a critical factor while performance is of secondary importance. Word lengths and data buses are typically 16-bit wide. I/O capabilities range from a keyboard and a television receiver adaptor to small magnetic tape peripherals and disks. They are equipped with a relatively simple operating system and at least one high-level language translator. Small computers are used mainly as personal computers, both in homes and at work. In homes they are used for education, entertainment, word processing, business management, and so forth. At work they are used in accounting, engineering, research, inventory control, and many other applications. Because they are built from microcomputer components, small computers are commonly referred to as microcomputers; however, this name is somewhat misleading given that microcomputer components can be used to build medium-size computers as well. The physical size of small computers allows tabletop accommodation. Very often, the CPU and most of its peripherals are packaged in a single enclosure.

1.3 MOTIVATION FOR USING MICROCOMPUTERS

Up to this point we overviewed computer systems in general. Now we will discuss what microcomputers are and why they are so important.

Microcomputers (μCs) are the result of the marriage between semiconductor and computer technologies. The μC era started in the early seventies when it became possible to fabricate the circuits of a simple 8-bit CPU on a silicon chip. Such a miniaturized CPU is now widely known as **microprocessor** (microelectronic processor or in short **μP**). With the gradual improvement of fabrication processes, chip complexity has been steadily increasing. Today it is possible to fabricate on a single silicon chip even 32-bit CPUs. Naturally, the same LSI (large scale integration) and VLSI (very large scale integration) techniques were applied to other parts of a computer. The result is memory and memory control chips, I/O and peripheral control chips, and a variety of other support devices (see Figure 1-5). **Microcomputers** are the computers we build from these building blocks. Such building blocks are "glued" together by means of ordinary SSI/MSI logic elements. In this book we will refer to these building blocks collectively as **microcomputer components.**

Like other integrated circuits (ICs), microcomputer components are produced using batch manufacturing processes. These processes make possible simultaneous fabrication of many identical chips on a single silicon slice known as a wafer. Thus, as long as the production volume is substantial, they cost significantly less than the SSI/MSI devices they replace. In addition, they consume less power and are more reliable. As we will see next, these advantages have a great impact on digital systems.

Advantages of Microcomputers

The benefits we gain with microcomputer (μC) components are better understood if we overview the approach employed in packaging computers and other digital systems in general (see Figure 1-6). Integrated circuits (ICs) and whatever discrete components we use in a design, for example, resistors or capacitors, are mounted on **printed circuit boards**. Each board provides the interconnections required among the components it accommodates. Printed circuit boards themselves plug into connectors which are mounted on another board called a **backplane**. Power distribution and interconnections among the printed circuit boards are provided through the backplane. If a system is small enough to need only one backplane, then the whole backplane assembly can be mounted directly in an enclosure with power supplies (and possibly some peripherals). Another way is to mount the backplane assembly on a metallic card cage which, in turn, mounts inside the enclosure. If the system needs two or more backplanes, we usually employ one card cage for each. Then, we mount the card cages one beneath the other in a cabinet or **rack**. In this case card cages are also called **subracks**. Large systems require two or more full-size racks.

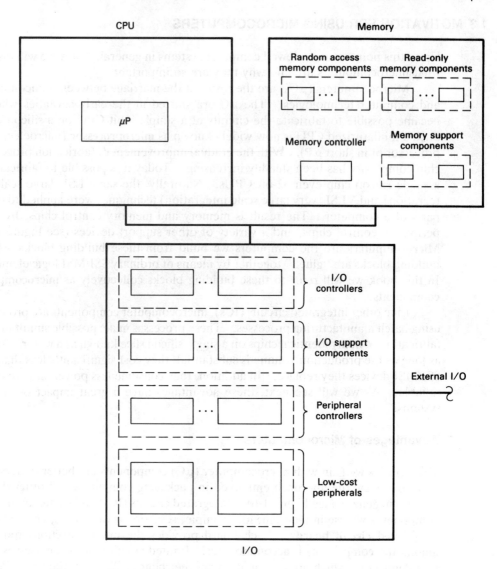

Figure 1-5. Miniaturization of the circuits of the digital computer.

Microcomputer components have three major effects on the product:

1. *Cost:* The purchasing cost of a μC component is less than that of the SSI/ MSI devices it replaces. Besides, since we deal with a smaller number of components, we also reduce the costs associated with component handling, including inventory and testing. The lower chip count reduces drastically the number of circuit boards we need in a system. As a result we achieve reduction of the number of subracks and racks. Most often the savings in

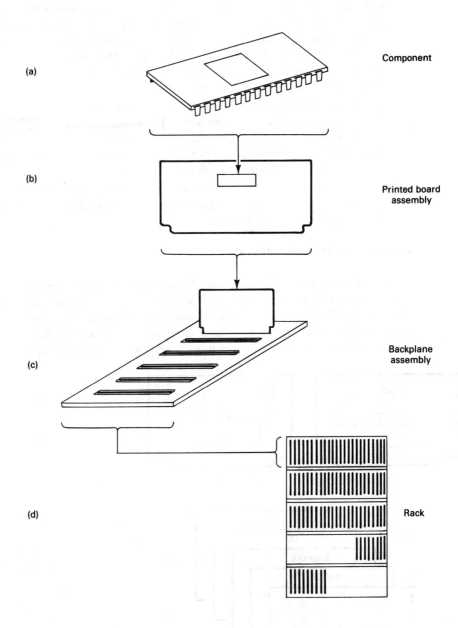

(a)

Component

(b)

Printed board
assembly

(c)

Backplane
assembly

(d)

Rack

Figure 1-6. Packaging approach for electronic systems. (a) Packaged integrated circuit (IC). (b) Printed board assembly accommodating many ICs. (c) Backplane assembly for accommodation of printed boards. (d) Equipment rack.

physical hardware exceed significantly those associated with components. For example, a multilayer printed board can cost more than the components we mount on it. Similarly, the cost of a rack (before we plug in any circuit boards) may be in the thousands of dollars. The lower power consumption of μC components is another factor to consider. It decreases both, the cost of the power supplies and the space they take.

2. *Reliability:* Systems built from μC components are more reliable. One of the reasons is that a μC component fails less often than the set of SSI/MSI components it replaces. Another reason is the drastic reduction of interconnections within the system (total number of soldering joints, circuit board connectors, inter-subrack connections, and so on).

3. *Development Time:* Designing a system with large building blocks saves development effort, so μC components reduce project costs and can shorten the product development cycle.

Microcomputer Applications

The factors we have just listed make the power of the digital computer available in an inexpensive, compact, and reliable form: the μC. Furthermore, the variety of commercially available components allows us to match the processing power of the μC to the needs of the particular application. Figure 1-7 reflects three representative levels of μC processing power. At the lowest level the μC is available

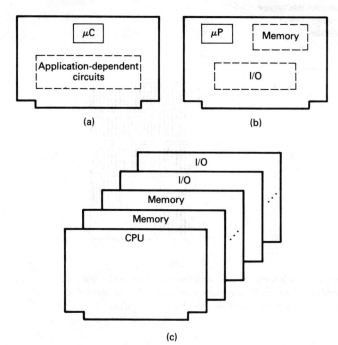

Figure 1-7. Typical levels of μC power. (a) Microcomputer chip. (b) Microcomputer board. (c) Microcomputer with multiple boards for memory and I/O.

in a single device called a microcomputer chip. Here CPU, memory, and I/O are all fabricated on a single silicon chip. For example, the "intelligence" built into some appliances and simple instruments comes from a 4-bit μC chip. Such a device includes (in addition to CPU and memory) I/O circuits capable of driving directly a small display and accepting inputs from keys or switches. At this level the capability of a μC is very limited, especially in terms of memory and I/O. Yet, it suffices for simple applications. The next level is a more powerful μC built from a μP, memory components, and I/O controllers—all on a single circuit board. Memory capacity and I/O capability are now much larger. At the third level the μC includes additional circuit boards enhancing further its memory and I/O capabilities. Naturally, at each level, processing power will also depend on the specific set of μC components we employ (8- versus 16-bit μP, and so on).

When supplemented with peripherals, a μC can be used as a general-purpose computer. Equally important, though, is its use in the implementation of a wide range of computer-based systems, in which case the "embedded" μC controls other circuits and/or electromechanical components of the system (see Figure 1-8). The μC may or may not include such peripherals as printers or disks. A system may employ multiple μCs controlling different parts of it. In this case the μCs are interconnected through some means so that they can exchange information. Now let us take a look at some application areas in which μCs are used.

The first application area concerns **general-purpose computing** (see Figure 1-9). μCs are used to build both medium-size and small computer systems for general-purpose use. Such systems contribute to the proliferation of computing power in business, design, research, education, and so on. Small computer systems are based on 8- and 16-bit μPs. They require only one to a few circuit boards which can be accommodated in a tabletop enclosure. This compactness and low cost, in conjunction with the development of inexpensive peripherals, have made personal computing a reality.

The second area involves **computer-based products** designed for specific applications. Here the μCs are used to implement the control and/or computational capability needed in a particular product. For example, a large telecommunication system may employ hundreds of μCs with each μC dedicated to a specific function, for example, control of a specific group of telephone lines. Another example is an engineering work station used for electronic design. Here the μC is equipped with high-resolution graphics capability and includes programs for entering schematic diagrams and simulating logic circuits. Typically, such a system needs one CPU for general tasks and another for generation of the graphics. The manufacturers of such products may employ commercially available μC boards. Usually, when the volume is sufficiently large to amortize the development costs, they design their own. In doing so they may achieve savings by designing only what is needed in the product. At the same time they may add to the value of the final product by accommodating special features not available in off-the-shelf μC boards.

The third application area is **logic design**. Here we do not really need a computer. What we do is take advantage of the flexibility of μC components to

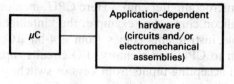

(a)

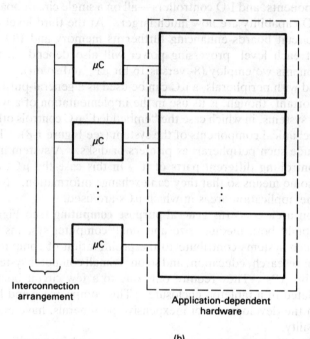

Interconnection
arrangement   Application-dependent
                               hardware

(b)

Figure 1-8.   (a) Computer-based system employing a single μC.   (b) System employing multiple μCs.

replace large numbers of ordinary logic elements, including gates, flip-flops, and counters. The required timing sequences are simply generated by a μC executing a suitable program. Interestingly, what is considered to be the first μP (the Intel 8008) evolved from a custom LSI chip implementing part of the logic of a CRT terminal. However, while the primary motive is cost reduction, this approach brings the additional benefits of higher reliability and flexibility. Fixing a problem or adding some new capability will most likely amount to changing software programs rather than hardware. So a change takes less time and effort. It is also easier to include features enhancing further the value of a product. For example, in the case of an instrument, you could add self-test capability. This new approach to logic design is used widely for implementation of the control logic in peripheral devices and instruments.

The fourth area includes **applications that became a reality thanks to the μCs**. Some of these applications were earlier simply not possible. Implanted heart

APPLICATION AREAS	EXAMPLES
GENERAL-PURPOSE COMPUTER SYSTEMS	
● Medium Size	32-bit microprocessor-based system capable of handling multiple users on a time-sharing basis
● Small	Personal computer
	Small business system
SPECIAL-PURPOSE (COMPUTER-BASED) SYSTEMS	
● Large Scale	Telecommunications system with many embedded microcomputers for the handling of thousands of telephone lines
● Medium/Small Scale	CAD engineering workstation
	Data terminal
REPLACEMENT OF LOGIC ELEMENTS	
● Terminals	Point-of-sale terminals
	CRT terminals
● Peripheral Controllers	Printers
	Disks
	Magnetic tapes
● Medical Systems	
● Avionics	
NEW APPLICATIONS	
● Health Aids	Pacemakers
● Appliances	Air conditioners
● Automotive Controllers	
● Smart Instruments	
● Robots	
● Electronic Games	

Figure 1-9.   Representative applications of microcomputers.

pacemakers, for instance, are the result of the miniaturization offered by μC componentry.   Some other applications could not justify computer control or even ordinary digital logic before.   For example, today we can afford precise control of automobile functions (for emission control and fuel economy) thanks to μCs.   Similarly we can afford to incorporate μCs in many simple instruments where no form of logic was justifiable in the past.

1.4 THE MICROCOMPUTER HARDWARE DESIGN TASK

Microcomputer hardware design is part of the overall hardware design task in a project.   Hardware design is itself one of the stages in the product development process.

The Product Development Process

Figure 1-10 illustrates the major stages involved in the development of a typical product. The process begins with marketing, where new products are identified and justified through marketing studies, contacts with customers, discussions with engineering, and so on. A product requirements specification is prepared by marketing describing what the product should be capable of doing from the customer's viewpoint. The same document specifies physical and other characteristics (such as compatibility to some other product), desired cost, and desired availability date.

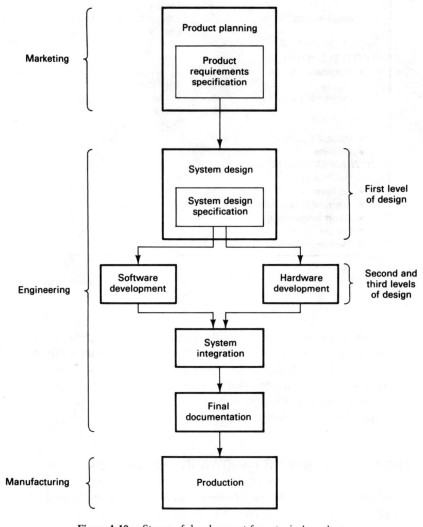

Figure 1-10.   Stages of development for a typical product.

A systems design group analyzes the product requirements to ensure that such a product is feasible and then proceeds to make the first critical design decisions. This activity can be considered the first level of design. The questions listed in Figure 1-11 are indicative of the kind of decisions we face at this early design stage. Our decisions must be constantly guided by the goal of developing a product which is:

1. Functioning and performing according to the agreed-upon product requirements
2. Cost competitive
3. Simple in concept
4. Reliable
5. Easy to maintain

Some of these **design objectives** affect others. For example, conceptual simplicity facilitates development and manufacturing but also contributes to easier maintenance. On the other hand, reliability may necessitate use of more expensive components which increase the product cost. Similarly, maintainability may re-

---

1. What component technology shall we use?
2. Which μP (or μPs) should we select?
   - One already used in another product (if suitable)?
   - One which is compatible with software and/or hardware we plan to use from another product?
   - A new one?
     - Are compatible μC components (I/O controllers, etc.)   available?
     - How about development support tools?
     - Are the μC components second sourced?
3. What operating system shall we use?
   - A commercially available one?
   - One we have been using in another product?
   - Design a new one?
4. What programming languages shall we use?
5. How should we go about software structuring?
6. How are we going to package the product?
   - Circuit board size?
   - Connector type(s)?
   - Subrack, etc.?
7. Should we use off-the-shelf μC boards rather than developing our own?
   - Which ones?
8. Does the product have to be compatible with some other product(s)?
9. How about future needs?
   - Should the product be expandable?
   - Is it going to be the basis for a product family?
10. What will be the architecture of the product?

Figure 1-11.   Questions at the early design stage.

quire additional software and built-in circuits which again increase the cost. In this case the designers make tradeoffs.

It turns out that the concept of **modularity** is a key to achieving some of the listed design objectives. At this early design stage, modularization is conceptual and is carried out along functional boundaries. The idea is to partition the system into smaller functional units each of which performs a specific set of functions in a semi-autonomous fashion. Such well defined units are understood better and can be developed to a large extent separately. They also facilitate troubleshooting in case of breakdown and provide flexibility for changes and system expansion. In large systems these functional units are often called subsystems. Examples are a subsystem controlling several I/O peripherals or one controlling a set of communication links to other remote systems.

The way we allocate the system functions among subsystems and the manner in which subsystems relate to each other define the **architecture** of a system. All first-level design decisions (including the architecture) are documented in a system design specification used by both the hardware and software design groups as a guideline.

Hardware and software are developed to a large extent in parallel but are tested by the design groups separately. At a certain point we are in a position to construct a model or prototype of the system so that we can integrate and test hardware and software together. This stage gives us the opportunity to verify that hardware and software interact properly and that the system performs according to requirements. Design corrections are made and we test again as necessary. Meanwhile we update and finalize the documentation for production purposes.

The product development process is an iterative one which necessitates interaction among the participating groups for design tradeoffs and resolution of problems relating to both technical issues and scheduling. In reality the specific tasks performed by each group, as well as the number of groups, depend on the size of the system and the particular company you are working with. For example, in the case of a large-scale system, the systems group must also contact performance analyses to determine if it is reasonable to expect that the system will be able to handle the anticipated load at the required speed. On the other hand, if the development task amounts to adding µC-based intelligence to a small instrument, a small group of designers will suffice for all design activities.

The Microcomputer Hardware Design Process

Even in large projects it is possible to begin hardware design while the system design is still in progress. Usually we start by drawing a hardware block diagram of the system or, if the system is large, a block diagram of each subsystem. Each block represents either one LSI/VLSI µC component (such as a µP or an I/O controller) or a group of SSI/MSI logic elements implementing a particular function (for example, buffering of the data lines of a bus). These diagrams help us to carry out modularization at the next level. The idea is to partition each subsystem into functional subunits which are implementable on separate circuits boards. A subunit represents a well-defined subset of functions, for example, interfacing and digitization of analog signals arriving over sixteen input lines. The design objectives are best met by holding to the following criteria:

1. *Minimize the total number of signal paths among circuit boards:* By doing so we economize connector pins and buffering circuits, while at the same time we simplify the layout of the backplane. The result is improved cost and reliability. Usually such minimization is achieved by using a common set of signal lines (called a bus) for interconnection of all boards or groups of boards.

2. *Economize circuit boards:* Each functional subunit should be large enough to justify its own circuit board. Otherwise we waste space on circuit boards.

3. *Avoid complex circuit boards:* Overly large functional subunits may not fit easily on a single circuit board and may thus necessitate multilayer boards. The latter become problematic if a design correction requires additional components. Besides, an (unpopulated) multilayer board is typically four to five times the cost of a two-sided one.

The partitioning into circuit boards completes the second level of design in the total hardware development process. Figure 1-12 shows the stages of the latter assuming a system based on a single backplane. In large systems, of course, we apply the illustrated process to each subsystem separately.

Now we are ready to proceed to the third, and last, stage of the design process. At this stage we are doing the actual design of the circuitry of each circuit board. The task is more involved and takes longer but, as you will discover, is probably the most enjoyable. Since we have already defined interboard signal connections, the design of the circuit boards can proceed in parallel with (1) the design and construction of the backplane, (2) the design or selection of a power supply, and (3) the physical design of the card cage, enclosure, cabling, and so on.

As a μC hardware designer, you will be designing one or more of the circuit boards which either make up a μC or whose circuitry includes a μC. Special-purpose systems may include non-μC-based circuit boards for functions specific to the particular application the product is intended for. These boards may be designed by digital or analog designers who are familiar with the specific application. In Figure 1-13 we list some design objectives and guidelines on how to go about meeting them. Again, you can see that there are tradeoffs; for example, maintenance diagnostics and LEDs (light-emitting diodes) will certainly increase the cost. Similarly, low-power dissipation favors reliability and may also reduce power supply and cooling costs; however, low-power components are generally more expensive and could very well negate such gains.

Following the design of each circuit board, we breadboard its circuitry on an experimental board, usually employing wirewrapping. Then we test it using μC

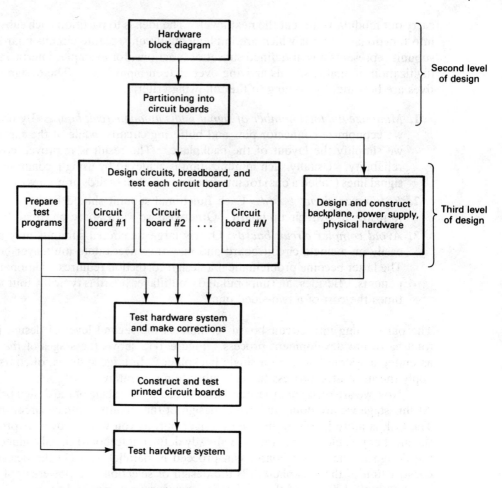

Figure 1-12.   Stages of hardware development for a typical product.

development aids and appropriate test programs.   Our intention is to verify that the circuits perform properly all the functions we designed them for.   After making design corrections we retest, and so on.   When all boards are ready, we begin testing a prototype of the hardware system.   Now we have the opportunity to verify that each board interacts properly with the remaining ones.   If necessary, we make design corrections again and then proceed to generate the circuit board layouts.   Subsequently, the printed circuit boards are fabricated, populated with components, and tested individually for layout (and possibly design) corrections. In the last stage we test a hardware prototype consisting entirely of printed circuit boards.

OBJECTIVES	GUIDELINES
1. The circuit board performs all the functions allocated to it at the required speed	• Understand fully what this circuit board must do and how it interfaces to other circuit boards • Do worst case timing analysis to ensure proper operation in the specified temperature/humidity range
2. Economy	• Minimize total component cost by reducing the chip count and by using components purchased for other products in high volume • Keep power dissipation down to reduce power supply costs and the need for fans or wider spacing of the circuit boards in the card cage • Reduce manufacturing costs by avoiding circuits requiring manual adjustment or selection of resistors and/or capacitors with precise values • Design according to the company's manufacturing practices and standards including means facilitating automated testing; also, avoid components that may become obsolete and secure second sources for all purchased components • Build in flexibility allowing board upgrading (e.g., memory expansion), and use in other subsystems and/or other products
3. Simplicity	• Keep it simple to facilitate debugging and ease understanding by others (for testing and maintenance purposes)
4. Reliability	• Do not use components having marginal reliability (e.g., lamps or relays) • Avoid using monostable circuits based on off-the-shelf one-shots; or SSIs, resistors, and capacitors • Keep power dissipation down (heat shortens the life of the components) • Lay out printed circuit boards properly and use adequate decoupling for noise reduction • Unless needed, do not use high-speed devices (they contribute to noise generation) • Buffer properly signals to/from other circuit boards
5. Maintainability	• Include means for easy maintenance through diagnostics, LEDs, etc.; also test points to facilitate testing during development and in manufacturing

Figure 1-13.   Circuit board design objectives and how to go about meeting them.

The Subject of this Book

In order to achieve the objectives listed in Figure 1-13, the μC hardware designer
has to know:

1. How μCs (and computers in general) operate, and what techniques are available for accomplishing the various kinds of operations
2. The functions performed by the basic μC components and how such devices interface to the external world
3. How μC components are interconnected to perform specific tasks
4. The possible choices and their impact on the design objectives

This book focuses on providing such a background. The organization into
chapters follows very much that of a computer. Chapters 2 and 3 are dedicated
to CPUs and the remaining three chapters to memories, I/O, and peripherals. The
text provides for each of the four areas:

1. The underlying principles and techniques employed
2. The types of μC components which perform functions related to that area and their organization
3. Descriptions of representative and actual devices for each type
4. Examples illustrating how these specific devices work with other μC components and how they can be integrated to build a μC

Design alternatives and tradeoffs are examined both while discussing principles
and techniques and in the course of presenting specific design examples. The
numerous examples throughout the text and the problems at the end of each chapter
provide another forum for examining choices and tradeoffs. In this volume we
are primarily interested in the basic μC components, whether such components
involve 8-, 16-, or 32-bit systems. Thus, the presented material should be suitable
for most of the applications listed in Figure 1-9.

When appropriate, we take the opportunity to reexamine issues relating to
the second level of design. The subject of buses, and how we interface to them,
is treated in a separate section.

2

CENTRAL PROCESSING UNIT

As with other computers, the central processing unit (CPU) constitutes the heart of a microcomputer (μC). It performs arithmetic/logic operations and controls memory and I/O. Yet, in μC systems the CPU is just one of the LSI/VLSI building blocks. Its circuits are fabricated on a silicon chip which is usually encapsulated in a plastic or ceramic package for protection. The package is surrounded by pins or terminals connected to the electrical inputs and outputs of the chip. We call the packaged device a microprocessor (μP).

This chapter is about μPs in general. We discuss how they are organized and what signals they employ to communicate externally with other μC components. Then we examine timing sequences and electrical characteristics as "seen" by the designer at the terminals of the device. The objective is to develop the background needed for understanding how a μP works together with other external components. Such a background is essential in learning how to design μCs. We also present an overview of instruction formats, addressing modes, and instruction sets. These topics are important in understanding the principles of I/O later on. At the end of the chapter we deal with the design of some of the auxiliary circuits surrounding a CPU. Examples of actual μPs are discussed in Chapter 3.

2.1 CPU ORGANIZATION

The basic principles of operation of a μP are similar to those of minicomputer and mainframe central processors. Although many μPs are equipped with advanced features, their basic organization may still be described in terms of an arithmetic/logic unit (ALU), a control unit, and registers (see Figure 2-1).

ALU

The ALU performs arithmetic and logic operations on operands. The operands are held temporarily in registers. After an operation, the ALU also places the result in a register. In some μPs the result is placed in a specific register called an **accumulator**. The type of operation is determined by the control unit which decodes the fetched instruction and then feeds the ALU with the appropriate control signals.

Besides binary arithmetic, the ALU may be capable of performing decimal

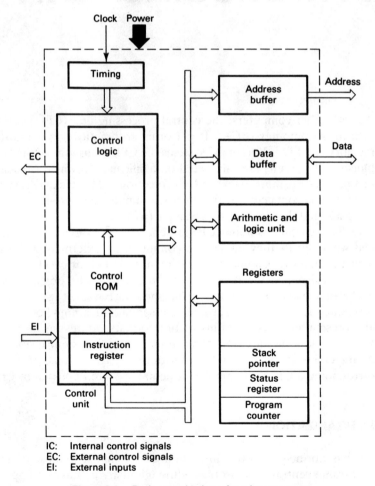

IC: Internal control signals
EC: External control signals
EI: External inputs

Figure 2-1.   Basic organization of a microprocessor.

arithmetic—and sometimes double-precision binary arithmetic.   Usually when an application requires fast, high-precision arithmetic, we attach to the main μP a special-purpose (slave) arithmetic μP.

Registers

Registers exchange information through one or more internal buses.   Multiple internal buses allow overlapping of certain operations and therefore increase CPU speed.   The length of each register—that is, the number of bits it can hold—is usually equal to the width of the internal data buses.   Figure 2-1 shows six registers dedicated to special functions.   The remaining are general-purpose registers used to hold addresses and temporary data during CPU operations.   Some of the special-purpose registers were dealt with briefly in Chapter 1.   Now we discuss their functions in greater detail.

1. *Program Counter:* Prior to the execution of a program, the program counter (PC) is loaded with the starting address of that program.   Thereafter it is incremented every time a new instruction is fetched such that, since the instructions of a program occupy contiguous ascending addresses, it always points to the location of the next instruction.   This sequential order is broken, however, when the CPU executes an instruction specifying it to jump to another program or to another part of the same program.   In this case, the instruction specifying the jump forces a new address in the PC, and the sequential order resumes again.

2. *Instruction Register:* Program instructions consist of an operation code part, commonly known as an **opcode**, and address fields.   The instruction register (IR) extracts from the data buffer register only the opcode part of an instruction.   Subsequently the control unit decodes the contents of the IR and generates the control signals which activate the actions specified by that instruction.

3. *Buffer Registers:* The address and data buffer registers isolate the external bus of the CPU from its internal buses.   Some μPs emit addresses and data directly into the external bus.   In such cases the buffer registers are simply replaced by buffering gates.

4. *Status Register:* The status register stores the program status word, which consists of **flag bits** and **control bits**.   Flags are set automatically by certain events during arithmetic and logic operations.   An example of a common flag is the zero flag, indicating that the result of an operation is 0.   Control bits are set by the program in order to enable certain modes of CPU operation.   For example, when set, the interrupt enable bit allows interruptions of a program by events external to the CPU.   Program status should not be confused with CPU status.   This second type of status information is provided on the external interface lines of the CPU and is discussed in the next section.

5. *Stack Pointer*: Stack is a set of contiguous memory locations where information items are added or removed in a stack-like fashion. The **stack pointer (SP)** points to the top of the stack. In other words, it holds the address of the item currently occupying the top. A stack may grow upwards or downwards, like the one pictured in Figure 2-2. To add (push) a new item onto the shown stack, we decrement the SP so that it is pointing to the next lower address. The new item is then written in this address which has now become the top of the stack. If we want to remove (pop off) an item, we read the item from the top of the stack and then increment the SP to point to the new top. The stack mechanism becomes very useful in situations where items must be retrieved on a Last-In-First-Out (LIFO) basis. As we will see later, such a situation is the one associated with the handling of program interrupts.

Control Unit

The control unit generates predefined signal sequences timed by pulses derived from a clock. The type of a signal sequence depends upon the opcode and inputs fed from sources external to the CPU. Such external inputs may be a request to interrupt the program—an interrupt request—or a request to surrender the external bus—bus request. As you can see from Figure 2-1, the control unit generates two groups of signals:

1. Internal control signals for activation of the ALU and the opening/closing of data paths between registers, and

2. External control signals destined for the memory and the I/O. These are sent either for activation of data transfers or as a response to interrupt and bus requests.

Very often the control units of μPs employ microcoding. Recall from the description of the simple CPU in Figure 1-2 that every instruction is executed in an orderly sequence of steps. **Microcoding** refers to the use of binary patterns to encode the control signals for each step. Each such pattern occupies one location of a read-only memory (ROM) and is called a **microinstruction**. A sequence of microinstructions constitutes a **microprogram**. Notice that the μP of Figure 2-1 is a microcoded (or microprogrammed) one. Each time a new opcode is loaded in the instruction register, it is examined for determination of the starting address of the respective block of microinstructions. In the so-called horizontal microprogramming approach there is a dedicated bit position for each control signal. Thus, control signals are simply enabled according to the bit settings of the microinstruction. In vertical microprogramming, a microinstruction is divided into fields which must be decoded separately to determine what control lines should be activated. Naturally, the horizontal technique is faster, but there are more bits per microinstruction.

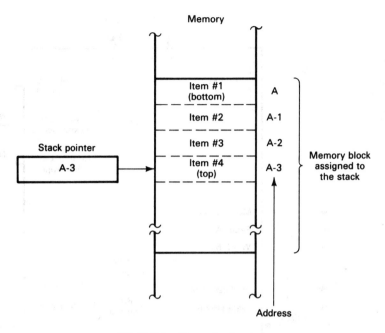

Figure 2-2.   Example of a stack.

2.2 THE EXTERNAL INTERFACE

Microprocessors interface to the external world through their pins or terminals. These terminals carry

1. Power
2. The clock
3. The signals by means of which the μP intercommunicates with memory, I/O, and possibly other μPs

The paths provided by the terminals constitute the **external interface lines** (or, in short, the external interface) of a device.

Unfortunately the external interface lines vary from μP to μP. Their makers employ a variety of interfacing schemes and signal names. Such differences may also be dictated by cost considerations. For example, the same line may be shared by two different signals. This economizes pins and may reduce packaging costs.

Instead of describing the lines of an actual μP, we will invent a hypothetical one (see Figure 2-3). We will assume a dedicated line for each signal. The groups and types of signals of our hypothetical device are typical of those found in actual μPs. In this section we are primarily interested in the functional aspects of the external interface. We will discuss each group of lines separately.

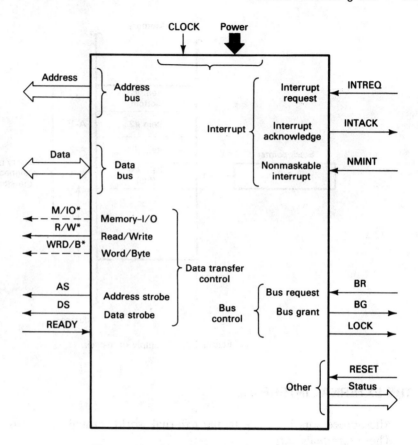

Figure 2-3.   External interface of a microprocessor.

Power and Clock

Typically, 8-bit μPs have one ground pin and one voltage pin (referenced to the ground).   Some 16- and 32-bit μPs have two or more ground pins and an equal number of voltage pins.

Like the CPUs of most computers, μPs are **synchronous machines** which depend on clock pulses to synchronize their operations.   Both the activation and deactivation of control signals (inside and at the external interface) relate to the edges of the clock.   Usually the clock pulses are supplied from an external source through the *CLOCK* line.

Address Bus

This set of signal lines identifies the location which is to be accessed by the CPU during a read or write operation.   Such a location can be a memory location or an I/O location. It stores one byte of data. The set of different addresses we can specify over the address bus constitutes the **direct address space** of a μP. If we assume N address lines, then the address space is 2^N byte locations. The lowest address is 0 and the highest 2^N-1. In 16-bit μCs, byte locations are usually paired into 16-bit word locations. Figure 2-4 depicts an often used pairing scheme. The even address byte constitutes the upper half of a word. The odd address byte immediately following constitutes the lower half. Words are usually addressed by using the address of the upper byte and a control signal indicating that this is a word, not a byte, address. In 32-bit μCs, byte locations may be grouped four at a time to form 32-bit word locations.

Example 2-1

A particular 16-bit μP has 23 address lines. Determine its memory address space in megabytes (MB). Up to how many 16-bit words can we possibly store in its memory?

Solution. The memory address space is equal to 2^{23}, which is calculated to be about 8,000,000 bytes or 8 MB. To store a 16-bit word we need two byte locations. Thus, if the μP is equipped with all of the memory it can possibly address, we can store 8,000,000 / 2 = 4,000,000 16-bit words.

Some CPUs have a single address space for both memory locations and I/O locations. Others have two separate address spaces: a **memory address space** and an **I/O address space**. In this case, the memory address space is again 2^N byte locations, while the I/O address space is much smaller, so only the low-order address lines are used to transmit I/O addresses.

Example 2-2

The address bus of a 16-bit μP consists of 23 lines. However, when addressing I/O locations, it employs only the 16 low-order address lines. Calculate ιne I/O address space of this CPU. What is the highest I/O address?

Solution. Since only 16 address lines are used in I/O operations, 'ιe I/O address space is 2^{16} = 65,536 bytes, or approximately 64 Kilobytes (KB). The highest I/O address is 65,536 − 1 = 65,535. The lowest I/O address is, of course, 0.

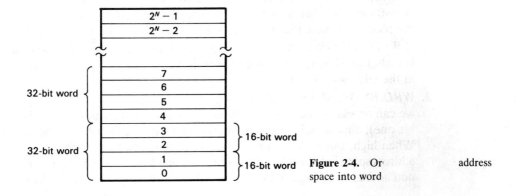

Figure 2-4. Or   address space into word

Data Bus

These lines carry the data to be written or read from the location identified through the address lines. Unlike address lines, which are unidirectional, data lines may transmit information in either direction. The number of data lines determines the maximum amount of information we can transfer during a single write or read operation. In fact, it constitutes the basis for categorization of CPUs. For example, if the data bus is eight bits wide, then the CPU is considered to be an 8-bit μP.

Data Transfer Control Lines

Suppose the CPU is about to transfer one byte of data. How would the memory know if the transfer is for it or for the I/O? How do memory and I/O know that the operation is for reading or writing? In the case of 16- and 32-bit μPs, how do memory and I/O know if the transfer involves one, two, or four bytes? Furthermore, how do they know that the CPU has placed over the address bus a new address, or over the data bus new data? What if the memory or the I/O are slow? How does the CPU know when they are ready to accept or provide data?

All of this information is communicated by means of the data transfer control lines. Our hypothetical μP uses six signal lines for this purpose. Three of these signals are meaningful whether in their true or false state. The other three are meaningful only when true. We will examine them in the order they are shown in Figure 2-3.

1. *M/IO* (Memory-I/O)*. This signal is required only if a μP has a separate I/O address space. For example, our hypothetical CPU has a separate I/O address space of 2^M byte locations (see Figure 2-5). If the CPU intends to perform a memory access, it brings the *M/IO* signal to a high. The memory takes notice of the fact and starts monitoring other data transfer control signals for more information about the intended operation. Meanwhile the I/O ignores such signals. When the *M/IO* signal is at a low, the described roles of memory and I/O are reversed. (Throughout the book we will be using an asterisk after the signal name to indicate an active low.) I/O addresses are placed by the CPU over the M low-order lines of the address bus.

2. *R/W* (Read/Write)*. The *R/W* line indicates the direction of a data transfer. If high, the μP reads data from the addressed location. If low, it writes data in the addressed location.

3. *WRD/B* (Word/Byte)*. Such a signal is not required in 8-bit μPs, where all we can access is one byte at a time. In our hypothetical μP (which is a 16-bit one), this signal indicates whether a byte or a word is to be accessed. When high, our CPU accesses two bytes simultaneously: one from the even address specified over the address bus and one from the immediately following odd address (see Figure 2-4). This type of access is often called **word access**

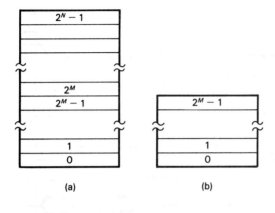

Figure 2-5. The case of separate address spaces. (a) Memory address space. (b) I/O address space.

mode. The even address byte is transferred via the eight high-order data lines, and the odd address byte via the eight low-order data lines. A low on the WRD/B^* line specifies **byte access mode**. Now only the single data byte specified over the address lines is to be transferred. A 32-bit μP may require two control lines of this type in order to differentiate among four modes: byte, full 32-bit word, lower half of 32-bit word, upper half of 32-bit word. Notice from Figure 2-3 that lines not applicable to all μPs are shown dashed.

4. *AS* (*Address Strobe*): Every μP uses some kind of address strobe. The CPU activates *AS* to indicate it has placed over the address bus a new address.

5. *DS* (*Data Strobe*): This signal plays a dual role. In write operations it indicates that the CPU has placed information over the data bus. In read operations it indicates to memory (or I/O) when to place information on the data bus. The situation gets somewhat complicated when the addressed part is not ready to provide or accept data. The actions of the CPU under such conditions are explained in the following.

6. *READY:* All data transfer control signals we have seen so far are generated by the CPU. This one is generated by external circuits to indicate memory and I/O readiness in the process of a data transfer. Following activation of the *DS* signal, our CPU monitors the *READY* line in order to determine its subsequent actions. If *READY* is true, it deactivates the *DS* line after a predetermined duration of time. At this point the data transfer is considered complete. However, if false, the CPU suspends the course of its operations at the external interface until *READY* changes to true. A very common expression for this event is to say that the CPU entered a **wait state**. Eventually, when *READY* goes from false to true, the CPU deactivates *DS* and the data transfer ends.

The transitions of the signals involved in a data transfer must occur in an orderly sequence. For now we are interested in the sequencing of the discussed signals only in qualitative terms, as shown in Figure 2-6. Later (in Section 2.6) we will see how signal transitions relate to the clock and to each other in quantitative

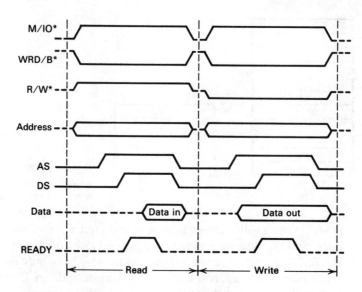

Figure 2-6. Memory read and write sequences at the external interface.

terms. Next we go through the steps of a read sequence assuming the CPU is about to read one byte of data from memory. Note that intervals in which signal states are either undefined or "don't care" are shown in Figure 2-6 by broken lines.

1. The CPU raises to a high the *M/IO** and *R/W** lines to indicate this is a memory read operation. At the same time it brings *WRD/B** to a low to indicate a byte transfer and emits the address of the desired memory location into the address bus.

2. Some time later, the CPU activates *AS* indicating that the address bus carries a valid address. At this point the memory initiates its own internal operations which will result in retrieving one byte of data from the specified address.

3. The CPU raises to a high *DS*, notifying the memory to load onto the data bus the retrieved byte of information.

4. Shortly after activation of *DS*, the CPU samples the state of the *READY* line. Since *READY* happens to be true (see Figure 2-6), it assumes the memory will respond with the data on time. Otherwise sampling would be repeated periodically until transition of *READY* to a high.

5. The data are loaded by the memory on the data bus.

6. The CPU reads the data and deactivates *DS*. A designer should remember that this occurs at a fixed time interval after a successful check of *READY*. Thus, although the memory is not required to provide the data immediately upon activation of *DS*, it must do so before the falling edge of *DS*.

7. Following deactivation of *DS*, the CPU deactivates *AS* and the remaining data transfer control lines, and the memory removes itself from the data bus.

The sequence involved in writing one byte of data into memory is similar except for the state of *R*/*W** line.   Also, data would originate from the CPU rather than memory.

Interrupt Lines

Because of its role as a central control point, the CPU must be constantly aware of events taking place in other parts of the system.   One way of accomplishing this is to perform a survey for such events every so often.   That, however, would take a sizable portion of CPU time which is needed to process the events and take appropriate actions.   To conserve CPU time, we need some means to alert the CPU automatically when important events take place.   This is precisely the purpose of the interrupt signal lines.

The group of interrupt lines you see in Figure 2-3 is typical for most μPs. First of all, there is an interrupt request (*INTREQ*) line, which we use to draw the CPU's attention to external events.   Peripheral devices activate this line to report the availability of a new block of data or the existence of a failure condition. This line is maskable—that is, a program may choose to inhibit interruptions of the CPU by turning off the interrupt-enable bit of the status register.   The masking mechanism allows us to prevent disruption of the CPU by events whose priority is lower than the one of the task currently being processed.   Following acceptance of an interrupt request, the CPU activates the interrupt acknowledge line (*INTACK*) to indicate the fact.

In our hypothetical μP the steps of an interrupt sequence go like this:

1. An interrupt source (say, a peripheral) activates *INTREQ*.
2. If the program the CPU executes currently has higher priority, the interrupt request is ignored.   Otherwise the sequence proceeds as follows.
3. The CPU completes execution of the current instruction in order to bring the interrupted program to an orderly stop.   Then it signals to the peripheral device acceptance of the request by activating *INTACK*.
4. Upon receipt of the acknowledgment, the peripheral device loads on the data bus a specific code and drives *INTREQ* back to a low.
5. The CPU accepts the address code presented in the previous step and deactivates the *INTACK* line.
6. In order to be able to resume execution of the interrupted program, the CPU saves certain information from its registers.
7. At this point the CPU makes use of the specific address code to determine the starting address of the routine, that is, subprogram, which will service the peripheral device.

Certain critical events should not be masked by any program.   For example, the servicing of an interrupt generated from detection of a forthcoming power loss should take precedence over anything else. Our hypothetical μP (and most real ones) have a separate nonmaskable interrupt (*NMINT*) line for this purpose. Interrupts through this line are honored unconditionally—that is, they cannot be. masked through the status register. The mechanism of program interruption remains the same except that the starting address of the service routine is determined by the CPU internally.

Bus Control Lines

As we will see later, some I/O devices are capable of transferring data to/from memory on their own. To do so, however, they must gain temporary control of the address bus, the data bus, and some of the data transfer control lines. Thus, we need some means of transferring bus control from the CPU to the I/O device and back to the CPU. Our CPU has three lines for this purpose: a bus request line (*BR*), a bus grant line (*BG*), and a *LOCK* line. *BG* serves to acknowledge a bus request. *LOCK* indicates to I/O devices whether the CPU allows bus requests at the present time.

Next we go through the steps associated with bus control transferring. As a typical case we assume a disk which is about to request the bus in order to transfer a block of data directly to memory.

1. The disk examines the *LOCK* line of the CPU to find out if bus requests are allowed at this time. *LOCK* is activated by the CPU during the execution of certain special instructions. These instructions are intended to prevent others from accessing the memory while some other operation goes on. If *LOCK* is false, the disk proceeds to activate the *BR* line.

2. In response, the CPU completes any read or write operation that may currently be in progress over the bus. Then it "disconnects" its outputs from the bus, leaving the corresponding bus lines in a floating state (in the electrical sense). The only exception to this is the *BG* line, which is brought by the CPU to a high, indicating acknowledgment of the bus request.

3. Following activation of the *BG* line, the disk becomes bus master. It then proceeds to transfer the desired block of information to memory.

4. Upon completion of its data transfers, the disk removes itself from the bus and drives *BR* back to a low.

5. The CPU deactivates the *BG* line and "connects" its outputs to the floating bus lines. It has regained bus mastership.

Other Lines

The last group includes lines for miscellaneous functions. Most important is the **RESET line**. Its purpose is to force into various CPU registers and control flip-flops predetermined contents such that we can start up the CPU from a known state. Thus, when *RESET* is switched back to a low, the program counter contains a predetermined fixed address. It is through this address that the CPU finds its way to the initialization routine when we turn the power on.

Many µPs have also **status lines**, which reveal information about CPU states and possibly other internal events. They may, for instance, indicate whether the CPU is currently fetching an operand, performing an internal operation, or is in a halt state.

2.3 INSTRUCTION FORMATS

In the two previous sections we saw how a CPU is organized internally and how its external interface lines function. As a next step we would like to examine the various types of timing sequences as seen at the external interface. These timing sequences are directly related to each and every instruction the CPU executes. However, before we examine CPU timing, it is appropriate to discuss three important topics on instructions: their formats, the addressing modes they employ, and their types. These topics are essential to understanding the principles of I/O in Chapter 5. We begin with the instruction formats.

Every instruction includes an opcode (operation code) field which specifies to the CPU what type of operation to perform. In a few cases the opcode alone provides the CPU with adequate information for the required action. For example, the instruction to halt the CPU need not include anything more than an opcode. However, most types of instructions specify some kind of operation involving one or more operands, in which case the instruction must include either the operands themselves or sufficient information to allow the CPU to locate them. Such information may be carried explicitly in the operand fields of an instruction or it may be implied by the opcode. Sometimes instructions with no operand fields are called **zero-address instructions**. Those with one operand field are called **one-address instructions**, and so on. The length of an instruction depends on

1. The number of operands it involves
2. The way it specifies each operand

Usually µP instructions specify one or two operands. Instruction lengths vary from one to many bytes. We will discuss some examples from two specific µPs—the Intel 8085 and the Zilog Z8001.

Figure 2-7 illustrates some representative instruction formats of the 8085 µP. The 8085 has an 8-bit-wide data bus and a memory address space of 64K bytes. Memory is organized into byte locations each of which is identified by a unique 16-bit address. In Figure 2-7(a) we show the format of the "complement accumulator" instruction. This instruction certainly operates on an operand—the one held in the accumulator which is to be complemented. Yet no explicit operand

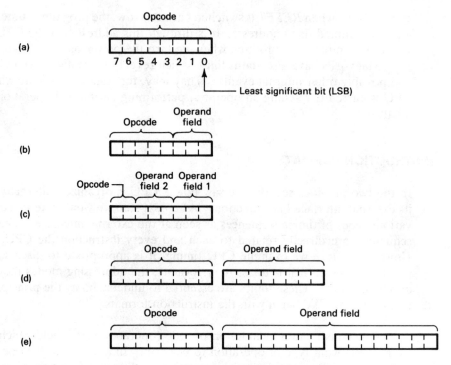

Figure 2-7. Some instruction formats of the Intel 8085. (a) Single-byte zero-address instruction. (b) Single-byte one-address instruction. (c) Single-byte two-address instruction. (d) Two-byte one-address instruction. (e) Three-byte one-address instruction.

field is necessary because the location of the operand (that is, the accumulator) is implied by the opcode. The instruction is considered to be a zero-address one.

Another instruction whose opcode implies one of the operands is the "add register to accumulator" instruction [Figure 2-7(b)]. Here the content of the register specified in the single operand field is added to the accumulator which, again, is implied by the opcode. Figure 2-7(c) shows a two-address instruction. This one moves the content of the register specified in operand field 1 to the register specified in operand field 2. Both operands are specified explicitly in this case.

Example 2-3

The opcode field of an 8-bit μP is fixed to eight bits. Two-address instructions employ a second byte which accommodates two 4-bit-long operand fields. What is the total number of available opcodes? Up to how many registers can we encode in each operand field?

Solution. If we assume that the opcode field is always limited to eight bits, then the total number of available opcodes is $2^8 = 256$. Each operand field is four bits long. Hence, we can encode up to $2^4 = 16$ different registers in an operand field.

In all three examples given so far, the instruction takes only one byte. Some instructions expand into additional bytes to accommodate the size of operand fields. An example is the "compare immediate" instruction of the 8085 [Figure 2-7(d)]. This two-byte instruction compares the accumulator with the operand contained in the second byte of the instruction so that the operand field provides the operand itself (rather than information about its address). Another example is the "store accumulator direct" instruction [Figure 2-7(e)], in which the operand field specifies the memory location at which to store the accumulator. Since 8085 addresses are 16 bits long, we need two bytes for the operand field. Note that multi-byte instructions occupy sequential memory addresses. The byte address containing the opcode is considered to be the address of the instruction.

The remaining examples are from the Z8001. This one is a 16-bit μP with an address space of 8M bytes. Its memory is organized into 16-bit words aligned in the fashion discussed in Section 2.2. An instruction consists of an integral number of words stored in sequential memory locations. The formats of Figure 2-8 apply also to the Z8002 (a smaller version of the Z8001 having an addressing capability of 64K bytes). Notice that the general format shown in Figure 2-8(a) includes two additional fields—a *mode* field and a W/B field. The *mode* field specifies to the CPU how to locate the operands from the information contained in the operand fields. For some instructions of the Z8001, however, this is not determined solely by the *mode* field, but also depends on the opcode and bits 4 to 7. The W/B bit is used in certain instructions to specify whether the operands are bytes or 16-bit words. In 8-bit CPUs, the *mode* and W/B fields are usually combined with the opcode, which is not the case in most 16-bit CPUs. In the latter the opcodes encode the nature of an operation but provide no information about the operands. As a result, many instructions have a number of variations determined from the values of *mode* and W/B type fields.

Figures 2-8(b) and (c) represent the formats of two single-word instructions— "clear register" and "add words from registers," respectively. In both cases an operand field designates the particular CPU register holding an operand. Figure 2-8(d) represents the format of an "add words" instruction in which the length of the second operand field necessitates expansion of the instruction by one additional word. In Figure 2-8(e) the expansion is due to a different reason: There are now three operands. This instruction specifies through registers:

- An I/O location
- A memory location to which the content of the I/O location is to be transferred
- A register which is to be incremented in order to keep track of the number of transferred words.

Clearly, the deviations from the general format are influenced by the manner in which operands are specified.

Inspection of the formats illustrated in Figures 2-7 and 2-8 leads to an inter-

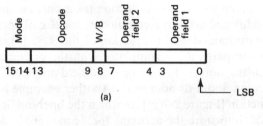

(a)

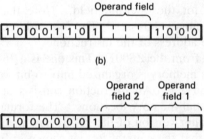

(b)

(c)

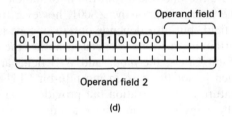

(d)

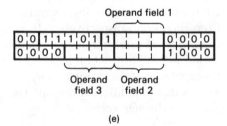

(e)

Figure 2-8. Some instruction formats of the Zilog Z8001. (a) General format. (b) Single-word one-address instruction. (c) Single-word two-address instruction. (d) Two-word two-address instruction. (e) Two-word three-address instruction.

esting observation. Notice for the case of the 8085 that only the two most significant bits of an instruction are always part of the opcode. Any additional bits in an opcode are contributed by unused operand fields. Similarly, in the Z8001, unused operand fields contain binary codes which extend the 5-bit-long opcode field of the general format. Very often we refer to opcodes extending into other unused fields as **expanding opcodes**. The aim is to allow the encoding of more instructions without having to increase the size of the dedicated opcode field. For example, in the case of the Z8001, the dedicated opcode field allows only $2^5 = 32$ different instructions.   Yet the actual number of instructions is much larger thanks to expanding opcodes.

Example 2-4

In the format of Figure 2-8(d) the opcode field expands into what is ordinarily operand field 2 (see the general format in the figure).   Up to how many additional opcodes can we economize by doing so?   Could we economize even more?   What is the tradeoff?

Solution.   First let us consider the general format shown in Figure 2-8(a).   The 5-bit opcode field provides up to $2^5 = 32$ different opcodes.   Operand field 2 may specify any one of the 16 general-purpose registers of the Z8001, except register 0 (R0). When operand field 2 is all zeros [as in Figure 2-8(d)], each of the original opcodes takes on a new meaning.   The result is 32 additional opcodes.

Suppose the format of Figure 2-8(d) employs, in addition to the all zeros pattern, the pattern 0001 as well.   This would provide another 32 additional opcodes.   The penalty, though, is that when we use other formats [like the one of Figure 2-8(c)] operand field 2 is not allowed to specify register 1 (R1).   In other words, the extra opcodes would be gained at the expense of programming flexibility.   This is an example of the kinds of tradeoffs made by CPU designers.

2.4 ADDRESSING MODES

During our discussion of instruction formats, we have seen that an instruction may include one or more operand fields specifying to the CPU how to locate the operands.   Often an operand may be located in one of the CPU registers.   Such an operand may, for instance, be the result of executing a previous instruction.   When this is the case, the operand field simply specifies the register containing the operand.   More often though, the operand is located in memory.   Now the operand field could specify the address of the memory location containing the operand. However, this direct approach makes instructions much longer.   For example, even in a μP having an address space of 64K bytes, we would need two bytes per operand field.   Besides, when we write a program, we may not know the memory address of an operand or even the memory addresses our program will occupy during its execution.   Instead, we can specify the operand address in some other way.   For example, the operand address could be specified using as a reference the PC or the contents of some other register.   The different ways we employ to specify the address of an operand are called **addressing modes**.

The CPU determines the applicable addressing mode by examining the opcode and the *mode* field (if there is one).   Then it proceeds to derive the operand address accordingly.   For some addressing modes, the CPU may have to perform calculations in the process.   We will see when and why while explaining some of the addressing modes used in μPs.

Implied Mode

Sometimes the address of an operand is implicit in the opcode field of the instruction. Implied addressing is used to access certain specialized CPU registers like the PC, the status register, or a stack pointer. The accumulator, used with the ALU in some μPs, is another example of a special-purpose register. In the previous section we encountered four instructions of the 8085 in which reference to the accumulator was implicit (see Figure 2-7).

Immediate Mode

In this addressing mode the operand is part of the instruction and is therefore immediately available. All other addressing modes specify the address of an operand either directly or in some indirect manner.

In order to demonstrate how this and other addressing modes apply, we will use as an example the "load word into register" instruction of the Z8002. This instruction transfers a 16-bit operand from some location into a register. It follows the general format shown in Figure 2-8(a). Very often the location from which an instruction retrieves an operand is called the source of the operand. Similarly, the location where an instruction is to store an operand is called the destination of that operand. In our example the destination of the operand is always a general-purpose CPU register specified in the 4-bit field Rd. However, the source of the operand depends upon the addressing mode indicated in the instruction. Figure 2-9(a) shows the "load word into register" instruction when the operand's source is specified using the immediate addressing mode. The operand is simply contained in the second word of the instruction.

Direct Address Mode

In this mode the instruction provides the operand address in a direct way. The CPU uses this address to fetch (or store) the operand. In contrast, the immediate mode does not require any access. While immediate addressing constrains the operand within the instruction and does not require any access, direct addressing— sometimes called absolute addressing—allows an operand to be located anywhere in memory. Figure 2-9(b) shows the format of our example instruction when using direct addressing for the source of the operand.

Register Direct Mode

The register direct mode is similar to the direct address one, except that the operand field specifies a register rather than a memory address. This register is one of the general-purpose registers of the CPU. Since the number of such registers is generally small, the length of operand fields designating registers is comparatively short, which in many cases allows the designer to accommodate the operand fields

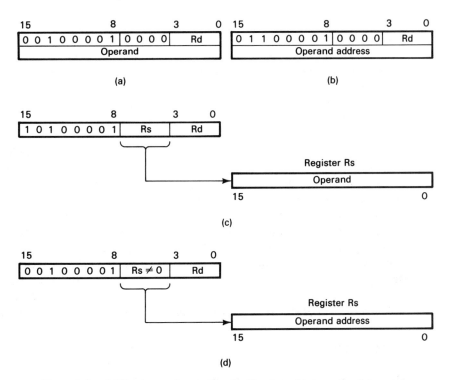

Figure 2-9. Addressing modes used by the "load word into register" instruction in Z8002. (a) Immediate. (b) Direct address. (c) Register direct. (d) Register indirect.

in the same byte (or word) with the opcode. Naturally, keeping instructions short conserves memory space. Besides, registers can be accessed by the CPU much faster than memory. Some intermediate results produced during program execution and stored in registers are accessed by subsequent instructions using the register direct addressing mode. In the example given in Figure 2-9(c) the source of the operand is one of the 16 general-purpose registers of the CPU. The 4-bit Rs field specifies which one. Notice that the destination of the operand is specified in register direct mode as well.

Register Indirect Mode

The register specified by the instruction contains the address of the operand, not the operand itself. Because it holds the operand address, such a register may be viewed as pointing to the operand. For this reason it is frequently called a **pointer**. Note again from Figure 2-9(d) the compactness of the instruction. However, a disadvantage of the register indirect mode is that the CPU has to retrieve the operand from memory.

Indexed Mode

In the remaining addressing modes the instruction specifies the operand address in terms of its distance from some other address. In other words, an operand address is specified in terms of two components, not as a whole. The instruction provides directly one of the two components and indicates a CPU register containing the other. Subsequently the CPU determines the full address by adding these two components.

In indexed addressing, the instruction provides an address and indicates which register holds the index. The index determines how far the operand is from the address provided in the instruction. This mode is frequently used when the same operations must be performed on a block of operands occupying contiguous memory locations. The idea is to execute the very same subprogram on one operand after another by simply advancing the index every time we finish with an operand. Figure 2-10(a) shows how the "load word into register" instruction of the Z8002 specifies indexed addressing for the source operand. In this particular μP we can use any of the general-purpose registers, except register 0, as an index register. Some μPs employ a dedicated register for indexing purposes. When this is the case, the index register is usually implied rather than being indicated explicitly.

Based Mode

Also known as base relative mode, this type of addressing specifies an operand address in terms of its distance (or displacement) from a base address held in a register [Figure 2-10(b)]. Although this is somewhat similar to indexed mode, no assumptions are made about sequential order of operands in memory. Note also that now the instruction provides the displacement, not a base address.

Based addressing permits items of a data structure to be accessed using only their displacements from the base of the structure. The length of the displacement field is generally shorter than the length of a full memory address. This in turn makes instructions more compact and thereby reduces memory space requirements. Some CPUs allow indexing in the based mode. Such a mode is known as **based indexed addressing**. Here the instruction also specifies an index register, which contributes a third component to the formation of the operand address.

Example 2-5

Assume an instruction employing indexed based addressing for one of its operands. The instruction specifies a displacement of 1970. Both the base and the index registers are implied by the opcode. Currently these registers contain the numbers 48022 and 8, respectively. What is the address of the operand?

Solution. The CPU calculates the address of the operand by adding to the displacement the contents of the base register and those of the index register. Consequently the operand memory address is $48022 + 1970 + 8 = 50000$.

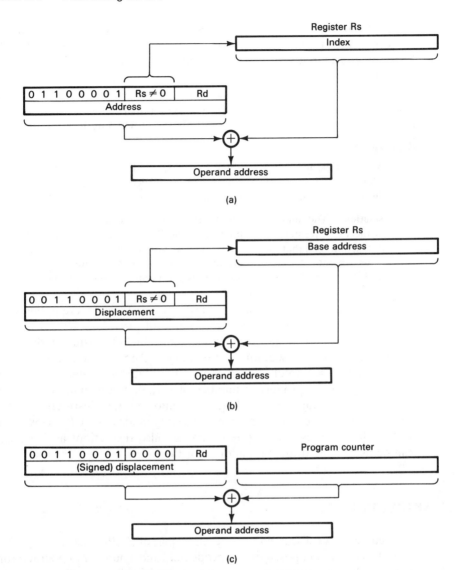

Figure 2-10. Other addressing modes used by the "load word into register" instruction in Z8002. (a) Indexed. (b) Based. (c) Relative.

Relative Mode

Programs employ jump type of instructions to transfer control to another program or to another part of the same program. Very often it is convenient to specify the "jump address" in terms of its distance from the address of the jump instruction.

Since this address can be determined from the PC, we are basically specifying an address relative to the PC. Such an addressing mode is called relative addressing. It can be considered a special case of base addressing where the role of the base register is played by the PC. In order to permit addressing of locations upwards and downwards (relative to the instruction address), we specify the displacement as a signed number [see Figure 2-10(c)]. When the relative addressing mode allows indexing as well, it is referred to as a **relative indexed addressing mode**.

Example 2-6

A jump type instruction is three bytes long and employs relative addressing. The address of the instruction itself is 256028. Calculate the jump address if the signed displacement specified in the instruction is -31.

Solution. The jump address is determined by adding the displacement to the contents of the PC. Remember, though, that the PC is incremented right after fetching an instruction, and that the process is such that the PC points to the following instruction. Thus, when the CPU starts the address calculation, the contents of the PC are already $256028 + 3 = 256031$. Consequently the jump address is $256031 - 31 = 256000$.

The number of addressing modes in 8-bit μPs is generally limited. On the other hand, 16- and 32-bit μPs are capable of providing most of the addressing modes we have discussed. Usually the applicable addressing mode is indicated in a separate *mode* field [see, for example, Figure 2-8(a)]. Sometimes the *mode* field is not decoded separately but in conjunction with other fields of the instruction. Addressing modes produce a number of variations for many instructions. See, for instance, variants of the "load word into register" instruction in Figures 2-9 and 2-10. However, the available addressing modes in a CPU may not be usable with all instructions. Very often there are also restrictions as to which registers can be used to hold the base address or the index.

2.5 INSTRUCTION SET

In Section 2.3 we discussed the overall format of a CPU instruction. We saw that an instruction is composed of an opcode field and a number of operand (or address) fields. Then we concentrated on the operand fields. We discussed the different ways they are utilized to specify operand addresses, in other words, the addressing modes of a CPU. An instruction may include additional fields indicating to the CPU which addressing mode applies to an operand and thereby how to locate the operand. In some μPs this indication is built into the opcode field. After locating the operand(s), the CPU proceeds to perform on them the operation specified by the opcode. In this section we examine the different types of operations we can specify through opcodes in a typical μP.

The set of available opcodes determines what basic operations a CPU can be instructed to do. These basic operations define collectively the **instruction set** of a CPU. Any other operations are performed in terms of the basic ones. Some of the considerations affecting the choice of an instruction set are:

1. There should be instructions for operations performed very frequently.

2. Other simple operations for which there are no instructions should be possible with relative ease, that is, using a small combination of CPU instructions.

Usually, the power of an instruction set is judged on the basis of the number of instructions we need to perform a specific complex task. Fewer instructions mean generally less memory space for the program and shorter task execution times. Hence, the instruction set is considered more powerful.

Instruction sets may differ not only in the type of operations they specify, but also the types of data on which such operations are performed:

- In 8-bit μPs, operations are usually performed on bytes and sometimes on 16-bit words.
- In 16-bit μPs instructions operate on bytes, 16-bit words, and sometimes 32-bit words.
- Instructions of 32-bit μPs operate on bytes, 16-bit words, 32-bit words, and usually 64-bit words.

From the viewpoint of operation type, instructions can be divided into three major classes: data transfer, data manipulation, and control instructions. **Data transfer instructions** move data between locations without doing any operation on the data themselves. **Control instructions** do not perform operations on data either. Their purpose is to provide means for controlling the program and the state of the CPU. Actual data operations are performed by the **data manipulation instructions**. These produce new results through data transformations. They may also process data in order to search for a specific item or a particular condition. Two of the classes may be subdivided further into categories as follows:

1. Data transfer instructions

2. Data manipulation instructions
   (a) Arithmetic
   (b) Logical
   (c) Shift/rotate
   (d) Bit manipulation
   (e) String processing

3. Control instructions
   (a) Program control
   (b) CPU control

Next we examine data transfer instructions and each category of the two other classes separately. While doing so we will have the opportunity to see representative examples. In these examples we use mnemonic names for opcodes and "labels" for operand fields. Such an approach to expressing instructions is commonly referred to as **assembly language**. Generally all μP makers provide an assembly language for writing programs. Prior to their execution, of course, such programs must be converted into machine code, that is, a binary representation of the instructions. This is accomplished by another program known as an **assembler**.

Data Transfer Instructions

This type of instructions transfers one byte or one word of data from one location to another. A word may be two, four, or even eight bytes, depending on the particular μP. Some typical examples are:

MOVE	R,MEM	load register from memory
MOVE	MEM,R	store register into memory
MOVE	R2,R1	transfer register R1 to register R2

The first instruction transfers the content of memory location MEM into CPU register R. The second one moves data in the reverse direction. In the third example the instruction transfers the content of CPU register R1 into CPU register R2. When R1 or R2 specifies an I/O register (rather than a CPU one), the instruction is called an I/O instruction. Note that these data transfers leave the content of the source location unchanged. What is actually transferred is a copy of the original data.

Another common type of data transfer instructions involves moving items between a specific or implied location and a stack. Also, in some μPs a set of CPU registers can be stored into (or loaded from) memory using a single instruction. This powerful form of data transfer becomes valuable when CPU registers must be saved or restored during program interruptions.

Data Manipulation Instructions

Arithmetic

All μPs have instructions for adding and subtracting binary integers, and often decimal numbers as well. Using these two basic arithmetic instructions, we can write programs to perform multiplication and division. In such cases we say that an operation is performed in software rather than hardware. Usually, 16-bit μPs have multiply and divide instructions. On the other hand, 32-bit ones are capable of supporting floating point arithmetic as well. In this kind of arithmetic a number is represented by a fractional part and an exponential part. Examples of arithmetic instructions are:

ADD	LOC2,LOC1	add numbers stored in locations LOC1 and LOC2
SUB	LOC2,LOC1	subtract numbers stored in locations LOC1 and LOC2
MUL	LOC2,LOC1	multiple numbers at locations LOC1 and LOC2
DIV	LOC2,LOC1	divide numbers at locations LOC1 and LOC2
COMP	LOC2,LOC1	compare numbers at locations LOC1 and LOC2
INC	LOC	increment the content of location LOC by 1
DEC	LOC	decrement the content of location LOC by 1

The first two instructions add or subtract the numbers stored in locations LOC1 and LOC2. Both store the result in location LOC2. In some CPUs the destination location LOC2 is always the accumulator. In others it can be any general-purpose register or even a memory location. The sign of a number is stored in the most significant bit position of the location. A 0 indicates a positive number and a 1 a negative number. Usually multiply and divide instructions store the result in CPU register pairs. Note that in multiplication the result is twice the length of each of the operands, while in division we need one register for the quotient and one for the remainder.

Another action resulting from the execution of an arithmetic instruction is the updating of the flags in the CPU status register. The four commonly used flags are:

1. *Carry:* Set when a carry occurs out of the most significant bit of the result (or a borrow into it).
2. *Zero:* Set when the result is zero.
3. *Sign:* Set when the result is negative.
4. *Overflow:* Set when the result exceeds the capacity of the destination location.

In many cases the result of the execution of an instruction is determined solely from the flag settings. Take, for instance, the COMP LOC2,LOC1 instruction. It subtracts the content of LOC1 from that of LOC2 and updates the flags accordingly. Subsequent instructions of the program find out about the result of the comparison by examining the zero and sign flags. The number coming out of the subtraction is itself of no use. If the zero flag is set, then the compared numbers are equal. If neither the zero nor the sign flags are set, then the content of LOC2 is larger than that of LOC1. When the carry bit is set, the opposite is true.

Very often a program needs to maintain a count of certain type of actions or events. This is facilitated by the last two instructions of the list which allow incrementing or decrementing by 1 the content of a location.

Logical

Most μPs perform Boolean operations using the following instructions:

```
AND       LOC2,LOC1
OR        LOC2,LOC1
EXOR      LOC2,LOC1
NOT       LOC
```

With the exception of the last one, these logical instructions operate on two operands. All store the result in the destination location LOC2.

The first instruction ANDs two operands on a bit-by-bit basis; that is, each bit position of the result is set to a 1 only if both operands have 1s in the corresponding bit positions. See an example in Figure 2-11(a). In the OR case, a 1 is posted in the result when at least one of the operands has a 1 in that bit position. The EXOR (exclusive or) operation posts a 1 in the result only if the corresponding operand bits are inverse. Finally, the last instruction inverts each bit position of the single operand. It is also known as a complement instruction. Figures 2-11(b), (c), and (d) illustrate examples of the above types of instructions.

Shift/rotate

This category of instructions shifts or rotates the bits of an operand in either direction. In some μPs the operand can be shifted or rotated only one place. So, for multiple places, we have to execute the respective instruction repeatedly. Other

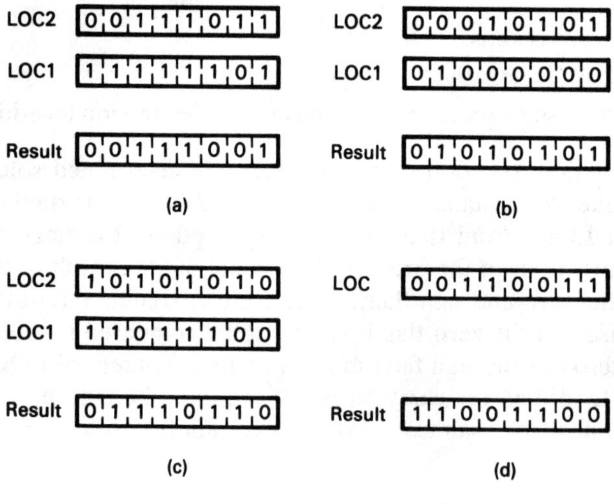

LOC2   `0 0 1 1 1 0 1 1`   LOC2   `0 0 0 1 0 1 0 1`

LOC1   `1 1 1 1 1 1 0 1`   LOC1   `0 1 0 0 0 0 0 0`

Result `0 0 1 1 1 0 0 1`   Result `0 1 0 1 0 1 0 1`

(a)   (b)

LOC2   `1 0 1 0 1 0 1 0`   LOC   `0 0 1 1 0 0 1 1`

LOC1   `1 1 0 1 1 1 0 0`

Result `0 1 1 1 0 1 1 0`   Result `1 1 0 0 1 1 0 0`

(c)   (d)

Figure 2-11. Examples of logical operations. (a) AND. (b) OR. (c) EXOR. (d) NOT.

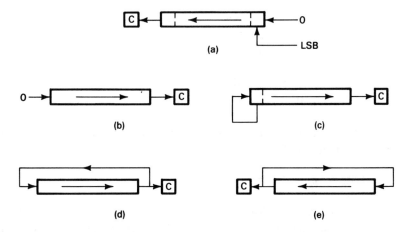

Figure 2-12. Shift and rotate operations. (a) Shift left logical or arithmetic. (b) Shift right logical. (c) Shift right arithmetic. (d) Rotate right. (e) Rotate left.

μPs provide a separate field specifying the desired number of shift/rotate places. Figure 2-12(a) depicts a "shift left" operation. Notice that a bit shifting out on the left is stored in the carry flag position of the status register. At the same time, 0s enter from the right. However, when it comes to "shift right" operations, there are two types:

1. Logical, where 0s enter from the left [Figure 2-12(b)].
2. Arithmetic, where the sign bit preserves itself by reentering [Figure 2-12(c)].

In rotate operations, bits shifted out are not lost. Instead, they reenter from the other side [Figures 2-12(d),(e)].

Notice from Figure 2-12 the involvement of the carry flag in all instructions. It permits isolation of a bit such that it can be tested by a subsequent instruction(s). Shift/rotate instructions are also useful in packing and unpacking groups of bits. They may serve in performing multiplication and division too.

Bit manipulation

Some μPs have instructions for testing, setting, or clearing a bit within a byte (or word). Such an instruction specifies both the address of the location and the desired bit position. The so-called "bit test" instruction sets or clears the zero flag to reflect the value of the tested bit. On the other hand, "bit set" and "bit clear" modify the operand. They insert in the specified bit position a 1 or a 0, respectively.

If the instruction set does not provide such instructions, bit manipulation is accomplished by means of logical and shift/rotate instructions. For example, bit setting can be done by ORing the operand with a number containing a 1 in the appropriate bit position and 0s in all other positions.   Similarly, a selected bit can be reset by ANDing the operand with a number containing:

1. A 0 in the corresponding bit position
2. 1s in all other positions.

It is for this reason that logical and shift/rotate instructions are sometimes referred to as bit manipulation instructions.

String processing

Recall from Section 2.4 that some addressing modes, such as indexing, allow the same sequence of instructions to execute repeatedly on different data.   In other words, the instruction sequence loops back for reexecution until some condition is met.   Usually this is called a **software loop**.   Some iterative operations are used frequently enough, however, to justify doing them in hardware rather than software.   The string processing instructions available in some μPs represent such cases.   We will briefly discuss examples of three basic types:

SEARST	OF1,OF2,OF3,OF4	search string
COMPST	OF1,OF2,OF3,OF4	compare strings
MOVEST	OF1,OF2,OF3	move string

The first instruction searches a sequence of bytes (or words) for the specific value held in the register specified in operand field OF1.   Operand fields OF2 and OF3 are used the same way in all three examples.   OF2 specifies the register containing the starting address of a string.   OF3 specifies the register indicating how many times the operation is to be repeated (count register).   The steps involved in the execution of the "search string" instruction are:

1. Fetch from memory the first item of the string.
2. Compare the value of the item against the specific value held in the register.
3. Increment the register holding the starting address to point to the next item. Decrement the count register.
4. Repeat steps 1 to 3 until the flag conditions encoded in field OF4 are met (equal to, greater than, etc.) or the repetition count becomes zero.

In the "compare strings" instruction the comparison is made against items of another string.   OF1 now represents the register holding the starting address of the second string.   This address is also incremented at the end of each comparison. The last example concerns movement of a string to another memory area.   Here

OF1 specifies the starting address of the destination.   Moving data in this fashion is often referred to as a **block transfer mode**.

Control Instructions

Program control

Instructions in this category change the content of the program counter (PC). This in turn causes transfer of control to another part of a program.   Examples of program control instructions are:

JUMP LOC	jump to location LOC
CALLSUB LOC	call subroutine at LOC
RETSUB	return from subroutine
RETINT	return from interrupt
JUMP LOC,OF2	jump to LOC if condition met
LOOPBCK R,LOC	loop back until condition met

The first instruction causes loading of the PC with the address assigned to LOC.   CALLSUB is a more elaborate form of JUMP in the sense that program control is transferred to a subprogram from which we expect to return at a later time.   In order to be able to do so, we must save the PC in the stack.   "Return from subroutine" (RETSUB) is usually the last instruction in a subprogram.   When executed, the PC is restored from the stack and execution of the main program resumes.   RETINT is used in the special case of returning from an interrupt service subprogram.   This instruction restores from the stack not only the PC, but also the CPU status which was saved when the interrupt occurred.

The two remaining instructions cause a jump only if the specified conditions are met.   Such conditions are either implied by the opcode or are encoded in an operand field.   Thus, JMP LOC,OF2 causes a jump to LOC only if the flag condition(s) encoded in the OF2 field are met.   LOOPBCK is a special case of conditional jump.   It is provided in some µPs to facilitate software loops.   Here, LOC specifies the start of the loop.   The program loop keeps reexecuting until the iteration count held in register R becomes zero.

CPU control

Most CPU control instructions involve operations on the CPU status register. Such instructions set/clear the flags, the interrupt enable bit, and possibly other control bits.   Examples are

SETC	set the carry flag
CLRC	clear the carry flag

ENINT   enable interrupts
DISINT   disable interrupts
HALT   halt instruction execution
NOP   no operation

ENINT and DISINT provide to a program the means of enabling/disabling interruptions from external events. Nonmaskable interrupts are, of course, an exception. A HALT causes the CPU to stop instruction execution indefinitely. The CPU remains in the halt state until its RESET input is activated or until an interrupt occurs. Execution of a NOP produces no action on the CPU's part. It simply proceeds into fetching the next instruction of the program. Note that some μPs also provide CPU control instructions for multiprocessing applications.

2.6 CPU TIMING

How does the CPU go about fetching and then executing an instruction? In what sequence does it activate/deactivate the external interface signals to accomplish this? The answers to these questions will bring us one step closer to understanding how we deal with a CPU in μC hardware design.

Our first objective is to discuss the kinds of steps we go through in the course of fetching and executing an instruction. Having done so, we will then examine the timing sequence associated with each kind of step. We are primarily interested in the timing sequences seen at the external interface, the ones we normally deal with as designers.

2.6.1 Instruction Cycle

The sequence of steps involved in fetching and executing an instruction is known as an **instruction cycle**. In μPs, these steps are grouped into smaller predefined sequences called **machine cycles**. Thus, although an instruction cycle can be very complex, it can be described (generally) in terms of a small number of machine cycles. For example, the instruction cycle pictured in Figure 2-13 is composed of only five machine cycles. The number of different types of machine cycles is limited. Some common types are:

- Memory Read
- Memory Write
- Internal Operation
- Interrupt Acknowledge
- Bus Grant

Recall that μPs are synchronous CPUs, so the actions taking place during a

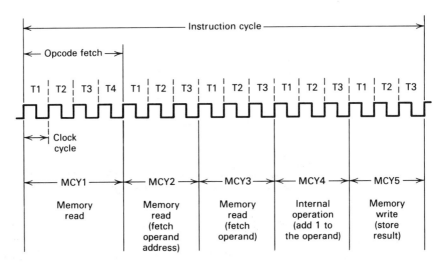

Figure 2-13.   CPU timing for "increment memory direct" instruction.

machine cycle are synchronized by the clock.   Typically a machine cycle consists of three to four clock cycles—that is, clock periods.

Example 2-7

A μP is clocked at the rate of 5 MHz.   How long is a clock cycle?   What is the duration of a particular type of machine cycle consisting of three clock cycles?

Solution.   The clock period T is equal to $1/f$, where f is the frequency of the clock. Hence, the duration of a clock cycle is $1/(5 \times 10^6) = 0.2 \times 10^{-6}$ s, or 200 ns (1 ns $= 1 \times 10^{-9}$ s).

The duration of the type of machine cycle in question will be $3T$.   Thus, substituting $T = 200$ ns we get for the duration of the machine cycle $3 \times 200 = 600$ ns.

Very often a CPU is stepped by its clock in a direct fashion; that is, a clock cycle represents the smallest step of processing activity.   Complementing the content of a CPU register may, for instance, proceed like this:

1. The content of the register is transmitted to the ALU during clock cycle $T1$.
2. During the following cycle ($T2$) the ALU is activated to produce the complement.
3. The result is returned to the register during the third clock cycle $T3$.

Sometimes we use the term ***T* state** to denote a clock cycle.

In some μPs, each clock cycle is divided into subcycles which are used to walk the CPU through a small sequence of substeps.   Such subcycles can be generated by combining multiple clock phases provided externally or produced from a single clock input.   As an example we show in Figure 2-14 a two-phase

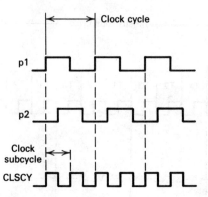

Figure 2-14. Example of a two-phase clock, and clock subcycles.

clock having a phase difference of 90 degrees. Here phases $p1$ and $p2$ can be combined logically to permit two subcycles. This in turn allows a sequence of two substeps per clock cycle. A typical case of activity corresponding to a substep is the reading of a microinstruction out of the control ROM of a microprogrammed CPU (see Section 2.1).

Example of an Instruction Cycle

Let us go back to Figure 2-13. The pictured instruction cycle is the one for the "increment memory direct" (INC) instruction of our hypothetical CPU. INC is a two-word instruction specifying to increment by 1 the content of a memory location. The result is returned to the same location. This instruction cycle is composed of five machine cycles (MCY1 to MCY5). Three of them are Memory Read cycles. We will examine what is accomplished during each machine cycle.

1. Machine cycle 1 (MCY1) uses the content of the PC to read the first word of the instruction. This is accomplished by the end of clock cycle $T3$. However, unlike the two subsequent Memory Read cycles, MCY1 is extended by one additional clock period ($T4$). This extra clock cycle gives the CPU the chance to decode the opcode and the address mode fields of the instruction. At the end of MCY1 the CPU knows that the instruction includes one more word (containing the address of the single operand). It also knows what type of operation is required. Thus, at this point, the sequence of the remaining machine cycles is fully determined.

2. Machine cycle 2 (MCY2) uses the content of the PC to read the address of the operand from memory. (Remember the PC was incremented after fetching the first word of the instruction.)

3. With the operand address now available, we can proceed to fetch from memory the operand itself. This is accomplished during MCY3.

4. After fetching the operand the CPU enters an Internal Operation cycle

(MCY4). During this cycle it performs the required operation—it adds 1 to the operand.

5. MCY5 is a Memory Write machine cycle. It stores the result back into memory.

Example 2-8

Assume a clock frequency of 8 MHz for our hypothetical CPU. How long does it take to fetch and execute an INC instruction? Up to how many INC instructions can the CPU execute per second?

Solution. The total length of the instruction cycle is 16 clock cycles (see Figure 2-13). A clock cycle takes $1/(8 \times 10^6)$ s or 125 ns. So a whole instruction cycle takes $16 \times 125 = 2000$ ns, or 2 µs (1 µs $= 1 \times 10^{-6}$ s $= 1000$ ns).

Our hypothetical CPU can execute up to $1/(2 \times 10^{-6}) = 500,000$ INC instructions/s.

The length of an instruction cycle depends on

- *The kind of operation:* For example, multiplication may require multiple Internal Operation cycles. On the other hand, addition is performed in one such cycle.
- *The addressing modes:* Addressing modes determine the number of Memory Read cycles required to fetch operand addresses as well as the operands themselves. They may also determine if Internal Operation cycles will be necessary for address calculations.

In direct address mode, INC requires:

1. One machine cycle to fetch the address of the operand (MCY2).
2. One to fetch the operand itself (MCY3).
3. One to store the result back into memory (MCY5).

In register direct mode we would need none of the above three machine cycles. Consequently, the instruction cycle would be composed of only two machine cycles. On the other hand, in based mode, the CPU would have to perform an extra Internal Operation cycle for calculation of the operand's address.

Program and Instruction Cycle Disruptions

The normal succession of one instruction cycle by another, during program execution, may be broken because of an external interrupt. Interrupt request lines may be activated at any time. However, most CPUs acknowledge interrupts only at the end of an instruction cycle. At that time, the CPU compares the priority of the interrupt(s) against that of the program it executes. If higher, the CPU postpones the next instruction cycle for an indefinite period of time. Then it enters an interrupt response sequence. If lower, the CPU ignores the interrupt(s) and proceeds to the next instruction cycle.

We can easily conclude that the worst case delay (between activation of an interrupt and its acknowledgment by the CPU) is determined by the longest instruction cycle. Some applications demand very fast response to interrupts, so they place a limit on this delay. The delays introduced, for instance, by string manipulation instructions are unacceptable in many applications. For this reason, they are very often interruptible.

Example 2-9

A μP is equipped with an instruction capable of moving a string of bytes from one area of memory to another. The fetching and initial decoding of the instruction takes ten clock cycles. Thereafter it takes 15 clock cycles to transfer each byte. Calculate the length of the instruction cycle for the case of a 64-byte-long string, given the μP is clocked at 10 MHz. What is the worst case delay to acknowledging an interrupt if the instruction is noninterruptible? Redo your calculations if the instruction can be interrupted at the beginning of each byte transfer.

Solution. The length of a clock cycle for the given clock rate is 100 ns. Consequently, the length of the instruction cycle is $(10 + 15 \times 64) \times 100 = 97,000$ ns, or 97 μs. If the instruction is noninterruptible the worst case delay to acknowledging an interrupt will also be 97 μs. However, if the instruction is interruptible at the beginning of each byte transfer the above delay is only $15 \times 100 = 1500$ ns, or 1.5 μs.

While interrupt requests do not break an instruction cycle, bus requests do. A bus request may, again, occur at any time. It is not acknowledged, though, until the current machine cycle is brought to completion. Then the CPU postpones completion of the instruction cycle and enters a Bus Grant cycle. The instruction cycle resumes later when the CPU regains bus mastership. Some μPs do not allow breaking of certain special instructions. Such "indivisible" instructions are important in multiprocessing applications.

Example 2-10

A CPU takes five clock cycles to complete its longest machine cycle. Determine the worst case delay to acknowledging a bus request if the CPU is clocked at 5 MHz.

Solution. The longest delay is experienced when a bus request arrives right after initiation of a machine cycle five clock cycles long. Since the clock period is 200 ns, this delay is equal to $5 \times 200 = 1000$ ns, or 1 μs.

2.6.2 Machine Cycles

In order to perform a machine cycle the CPU must activate/deactivate the external interface signals in a predefined sequence. This is done by the control unit of the CPU. The generated signal sequence is unique for each type of machine cycle.

Such sequences are described by means of timing diagrams showing how the signals relate to each other in terms of time.

We will examine in detail the timing sequence associated with each of the five common types of machine cycles. Once again we will use as a vehicle our hypothetical CPU, whose timing sequences are typical for most μPs. While examining machine cycles, we will have the opportunity to discuss wait states and their design implications. Finally, before concluding the section, we discuss the Reset sequence, which is not really an ordinary machine cycle in that its purpose is to bring the CPU to a known state.

Memory Read

Every instruction cycle starts with a Memory Read machine cycle which fetches the instruction itself. Additional Memory Read cycles may be included to fetch operand addresses and operands.

Figure 2-15 pictures the timing sequence of a Memory Read cycle in the case of our hypothetical CPU. Notice the use of clock transitions as reference points. Such an approach is very natural since all CPU operations are synchronized by the clock. For simplicity, though, we do not show all of the external interface signals. Those not shown are Memory-I/O (M/IO^*), Word/Byte (W/B^*), Read/Write (R/W^*), and status (see also Figure 2-3). Like address signals, the transitions of these lines occur early in the $T1$ cycle. From there on they remain stable until the whole machine cycle is over. Before going any further, let us examine the role of these lines as far as machine cycles are concerned:

1. *M/IO^*:* Recall that this type of line is found in μPs having separate memory and I/O address spaces. Such CPUs have two additional types of machine cycles: **I/O Read** and **I/O Write**. Generally, however, the timing sequences for memory and I/O machine cycles are the same; the only exception is the state of the M/IO^* signal, which indicates whether a cycle involves memory or I/O. Therefore we will not treat I/O machine cycles separately.

2. *WRD/B^*:* The state of this line has no influence on the timing of a machine cycle either. Consequently we will not consider it further at this point.

3. *Status:* Status lines may provide information concerning not only the type of machine cycle but also its purpose. They may, for instance, indicate if a Memory Read cycle is to fetch an instruction or to read an operand.

4. *R/W^*:* This signal is at a high during a Memory Read cycle and at a low during a Memory Write cycle.

We now return to Figure 2-15. First we consider the timing sequence of a "normal" Memory Read machine cycle [Figure 2-15(a)]. Such a cycle takes three clock periods corresponding to T states $T1$, $T2$, and $T3$. The signal transitions occurring during each of the three T states follow:

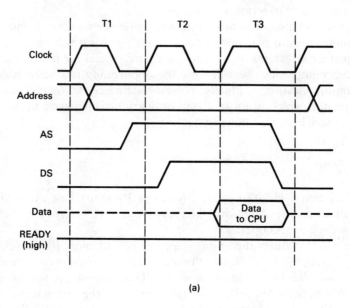

(a)

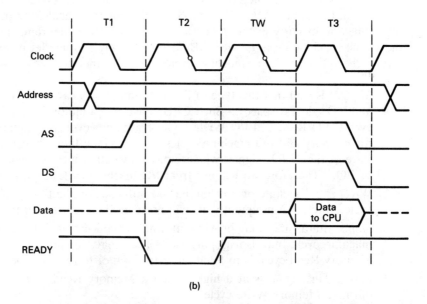

(b)

Figure 2-15. Memory Read machine cycle timing. (a) Without wait states. (b) With wait state insertion.

$T1$: The purpose of a Memory Read machine cycle is to read the contents of a memory location, so, during the early part of $T1$, the CPU places over the address lines the address of the desired memory location. The transitions of the lines we listed earlier also occur at this time. Now the CPU waits a short interval for the signal transitions to settle and then raises the address strobe (AS) to a high, which tells memory to begin initiating its own internal operations. Memory does so on the basis of the valid address and control information presented to it. Hence, the CPU activity during $T1$ amounts to simply transmitting to memory all signals required for the read operation.

$T2$: During the first half of $T2$ the CPU raises the data strobe (DS) to a high. This is an indication to memory that the CPU expects the read data before the end of $T3$. However, at this point, it is not known if the memory will be able to provide valid data at that time. This is determined by the CPU upon the falling edge of $T2$ when it samples its $READY$ (input) line. In Figure 2-15(a), $READY$ is true at that time. Thus, the CPU is certain that memory data will indeed be available before the end of $T3$. In summary, the CPU activity while in state $T2$ amounts to transmitting to memory DS and sampling the $READY$ line.

$T3$: The memory places on the data bus the information read from the addressed location. This is in turn read by the CPU on the falling edge of DS. Subsequently AS goes inactive. Then the address and other data transfer control lines do likewise. The memory removes itself from the bus following the falling edge of DS. Note that data lines go back to a floating state (indicated by a broken line). Hence, the activity in $T3$ is to read the data and terminate the timing sequence.

Example 2-11

Memory must place the read data on the bus sufficiently ahead of the falling edge of DS to allow for signal settling. Assume our hypothetical μP is clocked at 10 MHz and that DS falls in the middle of the second half of $T3$. Determine the length of its Memory Read machine cycle. How long after the beginning of the latter does the CPU check the $READY$ line? When (at the latest) should memory data be placed on the bus? Allow 20 ns for the settling of data lines. Ignore rise and fall times.

Solution. From the clocking frequency we calculate that the clock period is 100 ns. The length of a Memory Read cycle is then $3 \times 100 = 300$ ns. $READY$ is sampled by the CPU in the middle of $T2$, which is 150 ns away from the beginning of the machine cycle.

The falling edge of DS occurs $100 + 100 + 75 = 275$ ns from the beginning of the machine cycle. Thus, to allow for signal settling, memory must place the data over the bus $275 - 20 = 255$ ns after the start of the cycle—in other words, 55 ns from the rising edge of $T3$ at the latest.

What if memory is not fast enough to provide the data on time? In this case, we have to pull the $READY$ line down to a low prior to the falling edge of $T2$.

Now the CPU must stretch the machine cycle somehow to give memory more time for completion of the read operation. This stretching is accomplished by inserting **wait states**, that is, clock cycles during which the CPU takes no action. It simply waits for memory (or I/O) to complete an operation. The sequence we described for the normal case is still valid, but with the following exceptions:

1. On the falling edge of $T2$ the CPU takes notice of the fact that $READY$ is at a low.

2. Upon completion of $T2$ the CPU does not proceed to $T3$. Instead, it enters a wait state TW.

3. Still, the CPU does not know if insertion of one wait state is adequate. To find out it again samples the $READY$ line on the falling edge of TW. If $READY$ is now at a high, the CPU enters $T3$ upon completion of TW. Otherwise, it inserts another wait state, and so on.

Figure 2-15(b) pictures insertion of a single wait state in the case of our hypothetical μP. Notice that, with the exception of $READY$, signal transitions (during $T1$, $T2$, $T3$) remain unchanged. However, the machine cycle is now four clock cycles long. Naturally, longer machine cycles mean longer instruction cycles, which in turn slows down program execution.

Example 2-12

Consider a μP having Memory Read timing identical to that shown in Figure 2-15(a). After some analysis a designer determines that the memory falls short of providing read data on time by about 180 ns. How many wait states need be inserted for proper system operation if the clocking rate is 8 MHz? At what time interval must we keep $READY$ at a low in order to force the CPU to insert the required number of wait states?

Solution. The clock period is 125 ns. Hence, each wait state will stretch the Memory Read machine cycle by 125 ns. Since we need to stretch the machine cycle by 180 ns, we must insert two wait states. Actually the latter will lengthen the machine cycle by 250 ns, providing a margin of $250 - 180 = 70$ ns.

In order to force the CPU to insert two wait states, we must force $READY$ to a low prior to the falling edge of $T2$. Thereafter we should continue keeping $READY$ at a low until after the falling edge of the first wait state. The falling edge of $T2$ occurs $125 + 62.5 = 187.5$ ns from the start of the machine cycle. The falling edge of the first TW state occurs $187.5 + 125 = 312.5$ ns from the start of the machine cycle. Hence, $READY$ should be brought to a low a short while prior to the 187.5 point to satisfy setup time requirements, and should stay so until a little while after the 312.5 ns point (to satisfy hold time requirements).

Memory Write

When the CPU is to write information into a memory location it employs a Memory Write machine cycle. For example, if an instruction stores the result of an op-

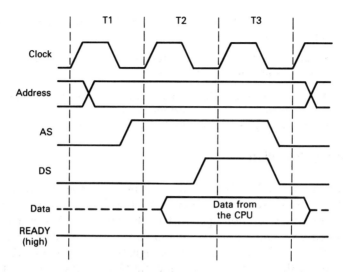

Figure 2-16.   Memory Write machine cycle timing.

eration in memory, then the instruction cycle includes a Memory Write machine cycle (see, for instance, MCY5 in Figure 2-13).

Figure 2-16 pictures the timing sequence of a Memory Write machine cycle for our hypothetical μP.   A comparison with the sequence of Figure 2-15(a) reveals some similarity with the Memory Read timing sequence.   The differences are that

1. The R/W^* signal (not shown in Figure 2-16) is now at a low, indicating a write operation.   Similarly, status lines reflect that this is a memory write operation.
2. Data are placed over the bus by the CPU (not by memory).   This is done at the beginning of state $T2$.   The data are presented to memory for the remaining part of the machine cycle.
3. In order to allow for signal settling, the CPU delays activation of the data strobe (DS).   The latter is now activated toward the end of $T2$.

What if memory is not fast enough in accepting and storing the data presented to it?   Here, again, we employ wait state insertion.   Sampling of the $READY$ line and subsequent CPU actions are like the case of a memory read operation.

Example 2-13

A particular μP has a Memory Write timing sequence identical to the one shown in Figure 2-16.   Its manufacturer specifies that the width of DS (data strobe) can be determined from the expression $T - 50$, where T is the clock period in ns.   What width should we expect for the DS if we decide to use a 5 MHz clock?

The data sheets of the μP specify that data remain valid for another 20 ns after the falling edge of DS.   What is the total duration of valid data presentation to memory?

How many wait states should we insert if memory requires valid data presentation for at least 190 ns?

Solution. A 5 MHz clock corresponds to a clock period of 200 ns. Hence, the expected width of DS is $200 - 50 = 150$ ns.

The data remain valid for a total of at least $150 + 20 = 170$ ns. If memory requires (at minimum) 190 ns, we must insert one wait state. This will increase the interval of valid data presentation to $170 + 200 = 370$ ns.

Internal Operation

After the operand(s) is fetched, a μP may enter an Internal Operation machine cycle (or even a series of such cycles). It is during this type of cycle that the CPU performs the operation specified in the opcode. No exchange of information between CPU and memory, or I/O, takes place in this case. In fact, with the exception of AS and status, the bus signals are undefined. AS goes active simply to indicate the beginning of an Internal Operation cycle. Status reflects the fact that the machine cycle is an Internal Operation one.

In contrast, all other types of machine cycles use the external CPU bus to transfer data or exchange some kind of control information. When a machine cycle (like the ones for Memory Read and Memory Write) involves data transfers over the bus, it is also referred to as a **bus cycle**.

Example 2-14

Consider again the instruction cycle of the INC instruction (Figure 2-13). By what amount (in percent) will the length of the cycle increase if we have to insert two wait states in each bus cycle? Repeat assuming the Internal Operation machine cycle takes 51 clock periods.

Solution. Normally, the instruction cycle takes a total of 16 T states. Insertion of two wait states per Memory Read and Memory Write machine cycle increases the length of the instruction cycle by eight T states, which amounts to 50 percent. If we assume 51 T states for the Internal Operation cycle, the normal length of the instruction cycle becomes 64 T states. Now the eight wait states represent an increase of only $8/64 = 0.125$, that is 12.5 percent.

This example indicates that the negative impact of wait state insertion depends on the length of the Internal Operation cycle. Some arithmetic instructions (like multiply and divide ones) have long Internal Operation cycles, so in the case of computationally intensive applications the impact is relatively small. On the other hand, in applications where the CPU spends most of its time moving data, the impact can be very large.

Interrupt Acknowledge

An instruction is usually a mix of two, or all three, types of machine cycles we have examined thus far. The Interrupt Acknowledge and Bus Grant machine cycles do not constitute parts of an instruction cycle. Instead, they are entered

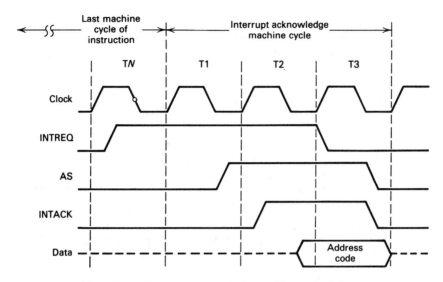

Figure 2-17.   Interrupt Acknowledge machine cycle timing.

by the CPU as a result of acceptance of an interrupt request or a bus request. Such requests are generated by sources external to the CPU.   First we describe an Interrupt Acknowledge machine cycle.

Figure 2-17 pictures the timing sequence associated with the Interrupt Acknowledge cycle of our hypothetical CPU, a sequence that is, however, typical of many actual μPs.   It is assumed that interrupts are allowed by the currently running program—that is, that they are not masked.   The events leading to and during such a cycle are:

1. The CPU samples the interrupt request line (*INTREQ*) on the falling edge of the last clock period (*TN*) of the current instruction cycle.   *INTREQ* must be active prior to the falling edge of *TN* to satisfy setup time requirements.
2. Upon detection of an active *INTREQ* signal, the CPU decides to enter an Interrupt Acknowledge machine cycle.   It does so, though, only after completion of the current instruction cycle.
3. The shown Interrupt Acknowledge cycle consists of three *T* states (*T*1, *T*2, *T*3).   The objective of the CPU is to read the address code provided by the interrupting device.   It is this address code that leads to the starting address of the interrupt service subprogram.   The signal transitions during each *T* state are:
   T1: Only the address strobe (*AS*) is activated during *T*1.   The state of address and other data transfer control lines carry no significance.
   T2: The CPU activates the interrupt acknowledge (*INTACK*) line.   This is seen by the interrupting device, which proceeds to place a specific address code on the data bus.   It also brings *INTREQ* to a low.

T3: Toward the end of *T*3, the CPU reads the address code presented over the data bus and brings *INTACK* to a low. Then the interrupting device removes itself from the bus.

Nonmaskable interrupts do not require an Interrupt Acknowledge cycle. For such interrupts, the starting address of the service subprogram is determined by the CPU internally.

Example 2-15

A keyboard activates *INTREQ* while our hypothetical CPU initiates fetching of the operand of an INC instruction (refer to Figure 2-13). After how long does the CPU enter the Interrupt Acknowledge machine cycle? How long does it take to complete the latter? Assume a clocking rate of 10 MHz.

Solution. The CPU needs another nine clock cycles to complete the instruction cycle. Thus, the Interrupt Acknowledge machine cycle will start after $9 \times 100 = 900$ ns. Since the Interrupt Acknowledge cycle consists of three *T* states it will take $3 \times 100 = 300$ ns to complete.

Bus Grant

This type of machine cycle serves the purpose of transferring control of the bus to an I/O device or another μP. Recall that bus requests can disrupt an instruction cycle but not a machine cycle. The CPU samples the bus request (*BR*) input line on the falling edge of the very last clock cycle (*Tn*) of the current machine cycle. If active, as in Figure 2-18, the initiation of the next machine cycle of the current instruction is postponed. The CPU enters a Bus Grant cycle instead. Any activity on the interrupt lines is ignored. In other words, bus requests have higher priority

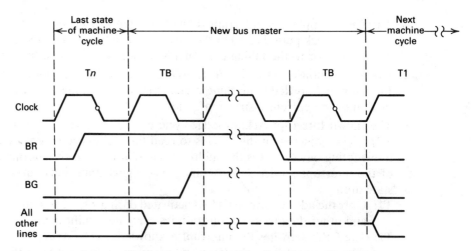

Figure 2-18. Bus Grant machine cycle timing.

than interrupt requests. The actions of the CPU after detection of a bus request
are:

1. During the following clock cycle (that is, the first *TB* clock period), the CPU
   brings to a floating state all output bus lines. The only exception is the bus
   grant (*BG*) line which is brought to a high. Unlike our hypothetical CPU,
   some μPs may require one or more clock cycles to do so.
2. From this point on, the bus is under control of the requesting device. Typically such a device proceeds to do its own data transfers to/from memory.
3. The CPU keeps sampling the state of the *BR* line on the falling edge of every
   subsequent *TB* state.
4. When the new bus master completes its data transfers, it drives *BR* back to
   a low. This, in turn, is detected by the CPU on the falling edge of the
   immediately following clock cycle.
5. At this point the CPU deactivates the *BG* line and takes over control of the
   bus again.

Not shown in Figure 2-18 is the *LOCK* line (see Section 2.2). A bus requester
may proceed into generating a request only when *LOCK* is at a low. Nevertheless,
during a sequence of *TB* states, *LOCK* itself remains in a floating state.

Example 2-16

The Bus Grant timing sequence of a μP is identical to the one pictured in Figure
2-18. A new bus master takes over the bus in order to transfer to memory a block
of 256 bytes. Each byte transfer takes two *TB* states. What is the duration of the
time interval taken by the chain of consecutive *TB* states if the clock frequency is 8
MHz?

Solution.   At the rate of 2 *TB* states per byte, the new bus master will take 2 × 256
= 512 *TB* states for its data transfers. Hence the total number of *TB* states is 514.
The corresponding time interval is 514 × 125 = 64250 ns, or 64.25 μs.

The Reset Sequence

The Reset sequence is not really a machine cycle. Its purpose is to bring the CPU
to a known state. The sequence shown in Figure 2-19 for our hypothetical CPU
is typical of the one employed by many μPs.

The CPU samples its *RESET* input on the falling edge of each and every
clock cycle. Thus there is no concern about completing the current instruction or
machine cycle, and *Ti* in Figure 2-19 can be any state of a machine cycle. When
the CPU detects that *RESET* is at a high, it enters the Reset sequence upon the
start of the following clock cycle. The subsequent actions are

1. As soon as it enters the first *TR* state, the CPU activates an internal reset

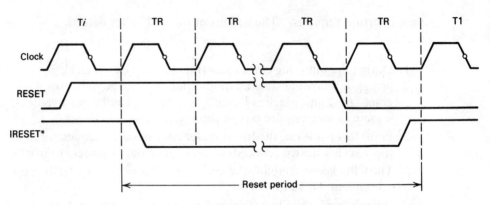

Figure 2-19. Reset sequence.

signal (*IRESET**). This signal terminates all internal activity and drives the output lines of the CPU to an inactive or (floating) state.

2. While *RESET* continues to be at a high, the CPU keeps entering one *TR* state after another. At the same time it keeps sampling *RESET* upon the falling edge of every *TR* state.

3. When the CPU detects the return of *RESET* to a low, it deactivates *IRESET**. This is done prior to the rising edge of the next clock cycle. Meanwhile it forces predetermined contents into certain registers and control flip-flops. The idea is to start up the CPU from a known state. The PC itself is loaded with a fixed address. This address is used in the first machine cycle following the Reset sequence to start execution of the initialization subprogram.

The length of a Reset sequence depends on how long we keep the *RESET* input at a high. If the CPU is in operation or in a halt state, the activation period may be only several clock cycles long. However, when power is turned on, we need a much longer duration (sometimes up to a fraction of a second). This is to allow certain CPU circuits to reach a stable state.

2.7 PHYSICAL CHARACTERISTICS

Up to this point we dealt with the functional aspects of a CPU. In the real world a CPU looks just like other ICs do. It comes encapsulated in a package surrounded by pins (or terminals). These terminals connect to the electrical inputs and outputs of the chip, so, to a hardware designer, the CPU is also an electronic component. Therefore, like we do with other components, we are also interested in its physical and electrical aspects—for example, the size of the package, how it mounts on a circuit board, and what choices we have. Similarly, we need to know the driving capabilities of the output lines, what voltage/current we need to drive the input lines, and the overall power dissipation. In this section we focus on physical characteristics of importance to the hardware designer. First we discuss in brief the constraints applying to the general characteristics of μPs.

Any CPU, whether a μP or one built out of other components, is influenced by technological and economical constraints. In the case of μPs the constraints are peculiar because the whole CPU is fabricated on a single silicon chip. In fact, these limitations apply to LSI/VLSI devices in general. How complex can such a device be? Generally, complexity is a function of chip size and the area taken for fabrication of a single transistor. There are of course limits to both. The larger the chip, the higher the chance of a manufacturing defect. This decreases the fraction of good chips (**yield**) per wafer and thereby increases the cost per chip. Thus, beyond a certain size, a chip can no longer be produced economically. Before reaching this limit, though, we may hit another one: **power dissipation**. This one may lead to unacceptable temperatures inside the chip. Power consumption goes hand in hand with speed. Bipolar devices, for instance, are faster, but at the expense of high power consumption. On the other hand, low-power CMOS (complementary metal-oxide semiconductor) chips consume very little power, but they operate at slower speeds. NMOS (N-type metal-oxide semiconductor) is at present a widely used technology because it offers a good balance of density, speed, and power characteristics. Power consumption has a significant impact on chip packaging which is our next subject.

Packaging

Encapsulation of a chip in a package may appear trivial; however, from a cost point of view it is not. Indeed, sometimes the cost of the package may represent a major fraction of the overall device cost. Why package a chip? Here are some reasons:

1. A chip is too small and delicate to handle in the environment of equipment manufacturing.
2. The package protects the chip from adverse environmental effects like moisture and surface contamination.
3. It plays the role of a sink for the heat generated during the operation of the device.

The physical size of a packaged chip is a function of the package type and the number of pins (or terminals).

Figure 2-20(a) illustrates an example of the **dual in-line package (DIP)** which is used widely for μP (and other) chips. Naturally, the physical size of the package grows rapidly with the pin count. As a result the space required for mounting on a circuit board increases considerably. There is also another concern. The larger the package, the greater the impact on the electrical characteristics of a device. Thus, when the total number of pins exceeds 40, we generally resort to more space-efficient types of packages.

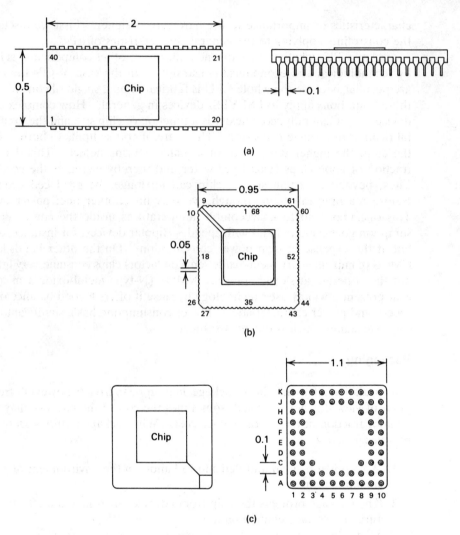

Figure 2-20. Representative types of packages. (a) Top and side view of a typical 40-pin dual in-line package (DIP). (b) Top view of a 68-pin leadless chip carrier (LCC). (c) Top and bottom view of a 68-pin pin-grid array (PGA). Indicated dimensions represent approximate values in inches.

Example 2-17

The impact of the package on the electrical characteristics of a device stems from the fact that the larger the package, the longer the leads connecting the chip to the external world. This in turn means that input/output signals will experience greater resistance and inductance. Consider a typical DIP where all leads have identical width/thickness characteristics. Which leads present higher resistance? In actual devices the power leads typically have resistances in the range of 30–50 milliohms while those of signal leads are between 100 and 500 milliohms. Why?

Solution. The longest leads will be the ones presenting the highest resistance. From Figure 2-20(a) we can see that the longest leads are those connecting to the four corner pins. For the package shown it is the leads connecting to pins 1, 20, 21, and 40.

The power leads carry the supply currents, which are much higher than the signal currents. Consequently, voltage drops across them can be much higher. The lower resistance of the power leads compensates for the higher currents passing through them.

Figure 2-20(b) shows an example of the so-called **leadless chip carrier (LCC)**— a more space-efficient package. Notice that this package is equipped with pads rather than pins. They are placed closely along all four sides of the package. Mounting on a printed circuit board is usually accomplished by means of sockets. Typically this type of package is employed when the number of required terminals falls between 40 and 84. See how close the periphery of the chip is to the surrounding pads. The shorter distances permit making leads narrower while still meeting lead resistance requirements. This type of package has also a leaded version.

Example 2-18

Assume a 68-pin DIP. How much extra space does it take compared to the LCC shown in Figure 2-20(b)? Suppose all leads of the LCC have the same width and thickness. How can we reduce further voltage drops along the power leads?

Solution. The board area occupied by the 68-pin DIP is (assuming dimensions per Figure 2-20) about $0.5 \times 3.4 = 1.7$ in^2. The LCC occupies $0.95 \times 0.95 = 0.9$ in^2. Hence, the extra space taken by the DIP amounts to 0.8/0.9, that is, about 90 percent.

By using multiple pins for power, we can reduce the supply current passing through each power lead. Such an approach is used in practice very often.

Further space efficiency can be achieved with **pin-grid arrays (PGAs)**. An example of such a package is shown in Figure 2-20(c). Like DIPs, this package is equipped with pins. However, the pins come out of the bottom of the package in an array formation. PGAs permit 132 pins and beyond. In addition to space savings, PGAs have better electrical characteristics.

Example 2-19

As LCC pad-to-pad distances decrease, the capacitance between leads increases. Why? For what type of devices would capacitive effects be more critical?

Generally PGAs offer better electrical characteristics than LCCs. Explain why it is so.

Solution. As pad-to-pad distances decrease, adjacent leads get closer to each other. Thus, interlead capacitance increases. Some CMOS devices can supply only limited current when they switch to a high. Hence they are more sensitive to capacitive loads.

The distances between the points where the pins of a PGA are soldered and the chip are shorter, so lead resistance and inductance are now lower. Also, adjacent pins are 0.1 in. apart so that lead-to-lead capacitances are also lower.

Very often manufacturers offer packaging choices. For example, a CPU may be available in DIP, LCC, or even PGA type of packages. The main selection criteria are:

1. *Cost:* LCC and PGA type packages are more expensive.
2. *Size:* DIP packages are the largest of all. The board space economized by using LCCs or PGAs will depend on the total number of terminals and the terminal-to-terminal spacing.
3. *Electrical characteristics:* The clocking rate of the CPU is certainly affected by the electrical characteristics of its package. Do you anticipate upgrading the product with a faster version of the CPU? If this is the case, you must select a package allowing operation at rates higher than the current one.
4. *Board Mounting:* Investigate the mounting requirements of the package. For example, some LCC packages may require special (and thus possibly un-available) soldering techniques.

How about the package material? Plastic is used very often because of its low cost. Better protection from environmental effects (and therefore better re-liability) is achieved with ceramic-based materials. Sometimes you may also have a choice of variants of plastic and ceramic packages. Another factor to be con-sidered in your selection are the thermal characteristics of the package.

Example 2-20

The temperature difference between the circuit elements of a semiconductor device and the surrounding (ambient) air depends upon the power dissipation of the device and the thermal resistance of the overall package. This is expressed by the equation

$$T_j - T_a = \theta P_d$$

where T_j is the transistor (junction) temperature in degrees centigrade (°C), T_a the ambient temperature (also in °C), P_d the power dissipated by the device in watts (W), and θ the thermal resistance of the package in °C/W. Naturally, there is a limit as to how high T_j can be. Besides, keeping the junction temperature low increases the reliability of a device. From this equation, it is evident that the lower the θ, the lower the T_j. Hence, it is desirable to have a package with low thermal resistance.

The power dissipation of a μP is 1.2 W, and the thermal resistance of the package 100 °C/W. What is the junction temperature if the ambient one is 40 °C? Assume the μP has an operating temperature range of 0 °C to 70 °C. What is the maximum allowable thermal resistance of its package, given that T_j must not exceed 150 °C?

Solution. The junction temperature is $T_j = 1.2 \times 100 + 40$, that is, 160 °C.

From the given equation we have $\theta = (T_j - T_a)/P_d$. Therefore, the maximum allowable thermal resistance is $(150 - 70)/1.2 = 66.7$ °C/W.

Pin Reduction Through Signal Multiplexing

Let us go back to our hypothetical CPU (Figure 2-3). Assume a 16-bit-wide data bus, a 1 MB address space (that is, 20 address lines), and eight status lines. Counting the total number of external interface lines, we conclude that the package must have 60 pins. Such a package is, however, not an industry standard and thus we have to resort to a 64-pin one. Sometimes a package with that many pins is not cost effective. So, μP makers try to minimize the total number of package pins.

A very common approach to pin count reduction is using a subset of lines for both address and data. Usually this approach is referred to as **signal multiplexing**. The common subset of lines is called **address/data bus**.

Example 2-21

Suppose we multiplex address, data, and status signals. How many pins could we save in the hypothetical CPU we just described? Is it possible to reduce the number of status lines by any other means (besides multiplexing)?

Solution. Sharing of the 16 low-order address lines by address and data signals saves 16 pins. High-order address lines could be shared by both address signals and status signals. This would save another four pins. Such a multiplexing scheme would then reduce the pin count to $60 - 16 - 4 = 40$.

Another way of reducing the number of status lines is encoding. The eight status lines, for instance, can be reduced to three at the expense of some external decoding circuits.

Inevitably, signal multiplexing impacts on CPU timing. As an example we will see how the Memory Write timing sequence of Figure 2-16 changes when we multiplex address and data signals. The new sequence is illustrated in Figure 2-23. Notice that the change involves essentially only the address strobe (AS), data, and address signals. Early during the machine cycle, the CPU places the address over the address/data bus. Shortly after the end of $T1$ the CPU removes the address from the address/data bus. Then it places over the bus the data which are to be written into memory. Observe that AS is now much shorter. It goes to an inactive state toward the end of $T1$. At that time, the memory must latch— that is, store—the address presented by the CPU. This is necessary since, unlike the case of Figure 2-16, addresses are not presented over the bus through the end of the machine cycle. In other words, memory (and I/O) will have to **demultiplex** (that is, separate) address signals from data signals.

2.8 ELECTRICAL CHARACTERISTICS

In this section we concern ourselves with the electrical characteristics of μPs. These characteristics describe the electrical behavior of a μP as seen by the designer at its terminals or pins. We are interested in the load presented to external circuits by input lines and the driving characteristics of output lines. Such characteristics are examined under both static and dynamic conditions. The electrical behavior of a device under static conditions is described by its **DC characteristics**. Those describing its behavior under dynamic conditions are called **AC characteristics**. Before discussing these two sets of characteristics we examine the ones associated with power and the clock.

2.8.1 Power and Clock

Typically, LSI/VLSI devices (including μPs) require a single +5 V voltage source (referenced to the ground pins). The supply voltage (V_{cc}) tolerance is usually either ±5 percent or ±10 percent. Some CMOS μPs can operate in a wide range of supply voltages. Such a range can be as wide as +3 V to +12 V.

Power Dissipation

Recall from Section 2.7 that power dissipation is a function of the fabrication process and the complexity of the device. As we will see later, the power dissipation (P_d) of a specific device is also a function of the clocking frequency. For NMOS μPs, P_d falls generally in the range of 0.5 to 1.5 W. A low-power CMOS device of comparable complexity may dissipate one or more orders of magnitude less.

Example 2-22

Two μPs, one NMOS and the other CMOS, operate at the same supply voltage (V_{cc}) of 5 V ±10 percent. However, the supply currents (I_{cc}) of the two devices are 200 mA (milliamperes) and 5 mA, respectively. Calculate the nominal and maximum power dissipation of each device.

Solution. The dissipated power is determined from the relation

$$P_d = V_{cc} I_{cc}$$

For the NMOS μP the nominal power dissipation is 5 × 200 = 1000 mW (milliwatts). The CMOS μP dissipates only 5 × 5 = 25 mW.

Both devices have a maximum operating voltage of 5.5 V. Hence, the maximum values of dissipated power for the two devices are 5.5 × 200 = 1100 mW and 5.5 × 5 = 27.5 mW, respectively.

Low power dissipation brings with it several advantages. First of all, it implies lower junction temperature which, in turn, makes a device more reliable (see Problem 2-18). At the system level, it reduces the size and cost of power supplies. It may also reduce the costs associated with heat removal (cooling fans and so on). The very low power dissipation of some CMOS devices makes practical battery powering. This is a significant advantage when it comes to portable systems. In order to capitalize on these advantages, NMOS μPs are often available in CMOS as well.

Example 2-23

The thermal resistance of the two μPs we dealt with in Example 2-22 is 50 °C/W. Calculate the junction temperature of each device at an ambient temperature of 25 °C. What is the maximum junction temperature of each μP for an operating range of 0 °C to 70 °C?

Solution. At the nominal value of V_{cc}, the junction temperature of the NMOS μP is 50 × 1 + 25 = 75 °C (see Example 2-20). At the same ambient temperature of 25 °C, the CMOS μP will have a junction temperature of only 50 × 0.025 + 25 = 26.25 °C.

The maximum values correspond to an ambient temperature of 70 °C. Hence, all we have to do is increase the already calculated values by 70 − 25 = 45 °C. This yields a maximum of 120 °C for the NMOS device and a maximum of 71.25 °C for the CMOS one.

The Clock

Because of their peculiarity, the characteristics of the clock input are examined separately from those of the other signal lines. Most CPUs do not buffer the clock signal we supply externally. Instead, they distribute the clock directly to many circuits within the CPU. Consequently the clock input is more demanding than other input lines. What justifies the absence of an on-chip clock buffer? The larger the driving capability of a buffer, the more silicon area it occupies and the higher its power dissipation. So most CPUs do not include on-chip a clock buffer in order to conserve silicon area and power dissipation.

Figure 2-21 indicates the usual parameters associated with the waveform we must supply to the clock input. These parameters are specified in terms of minimum and/or maximum allowable values.

V_{ILCL} represents the voltage at the clock input when the clock signal is at a low. This parameter is specified by the μP manufacturer in terms of both a minimum and a maximum. For example, in the case of a typical NMOS μP, it is required that

$$-0.3 \text{ V} \leq V_{ILCL} \leq 0.5 \text{ V}$$

The bound of −0.3 V is an absolute maximum rating not only for the clock but for all input signals. Voltages lower than this may destroy or impair the useful

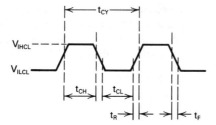

Figure 2-21. Clock waveform specification.

life of a device. On the other hand, the limit of 0.5 V is more stringent in the case of the clock. As we will see later, the rest of the input lines allow up to 0.8 V.

V_{IHCL} is the voltage at the clock input when the clock signal is at a high. Now the requirement for a typical NMOS μP is

$$3.5 \text{ V} \leq V_{IHCL} \leq V_{cc} + 0.3 \text{ V}$$

The upper limit is common for all input lines. However, the lower limit of 3.5 V is much higher than the one for other input signals. The latter allow this voltage to be as low as 2.0 V.

All remaining parameters (shown in Figure 2-21) concern timing. Such parameters are specified by all manufacturers. The voltage points they use for their definition vary. We will assume the low and high voltage points at 1 V and 3 V, respectively. The clock timing parameters of interest are:

t_{CY}: Clock Cycle Time

t_{CH}: Clock High Duration

t_{CL}: Clock Low Duration

t_R: Clock Rise Time

t_F: Clock Fall Time

The first three parameters are specified in terms of maximum and minimum values. These limits correspond to those of the clock frequency. Why a lower frequency limit? In NMOS μPs such a limit is dictated by the need to refresh CPU registers. Refreshing must be performed at an adequately fast rate so that no information is lost. It is a consequence of the CPU registers being dynamic rather than static circuits. On the other hand, bipolar and (usually) CMOS devices are static. Hence, there is no lower limit to the clock frequency. As a matter of fact, the clock may even be stopped for an indefinite period of time.

Rise and fall times are very often required to be 10 ns or less. The capacitance of the clock input line is itself typically in the range of 30 to 40 pF. To charge/discharge such a substantial capacitance within a very short time, we need equally substantial currents. In other words, the clock input represents a comparatively large dynamic load to the source of the clock.

Example 2-24

The clock input line of a μP has a capacitance of 40 pF. Its data sheets specify that rise and fall times must not exceed 8 ns. What current drive is needed during clock transitions given the latter are approximately linear? Assume that the voltage points associated with the definition of rise and fall times are 1 V and 3 V.

Solution. The required current is determined from the relation

$$I = C \left(\Delta V / \Delta t \right)$$

where C is the input capacitance, $\Delta V = 3 - 1 = 2$ V, and $\Delta t = 8$ ns. Substituting the numerical values we get $I = 40 \times 10^{-12} [2/(8 \times 10^{-9})] = 10 \times 10^{-3}$ A, or $I = 10$ mA. Hence, to meet the rise time requirements we need a driver capable of supplying at least 10 mA of current during low-to-high clock transitions. The same driver must be able to sink 10 mA during high-to-low transitions.

Clock transitions account for part of the overall power dissipation. This part is consumed in charging and discharging internal capacitances. Very often we reduce the clock frequency in order to decrease power dissipation and thereby gain reliability. Our criterion here is CPU processing speed. Will the slowed down CPU still satisfy the requirements of our application?

Example 2-25

A particular NMOS 16-bit μP can be clocked at a rate as high as 12.5 MHz. Its manufacturer provides data indicating a power reduction of about 0.3 W at 8 MHz. How cooler will the device run if we derate the clock to 8 MHz? Assume a thermal resistance of 50 °C/W.

Solution. First, let us apply the equation $T_j = T_a + \theta P_d$ for the two different clock frequencies. The junction temperature corresponding to the maximum clock frequency will be $T_{j2} = T_a + \theta P_{d2}$, where P_{d2} is the power dissipation of the μP when clocked at 12.5 MHz. The power difference of 0.3 W is independent of the ambient temperature. Hence T_a can be any temperature in the specified ambient temperature range, usually between 0 °C and 70 °C. At a frequency of 8 MHz, the junction temperature will be $T_{j1} = T_a + \theta P_{d1}$, where T_a is the same ambient temperature we assumed above and P_{d1} the power dissipation at 8 MHz. Subtracting the two equations, we obtain $T_{j2} - T_{j1} = \theta(P_{d2} - P_{d1})$. After substitution of the numerical values we get $T_{j2} - T_{j1} = 50 \times 0.3 = 15$ °C. Thus by lowering the clock frequency to 8 MHz, we reduce the junction temperature of the μP by 15 °C. This in turn reduces the failure rate of the μP.

In some CMOS μPs, transistor currents are very small even in the ON state. Consequently dissipation is determined entirely in terms of the clock frequency. Clock derating has now a far larger impact on dissipation (see Problem 2-21).

Some CPUs require a nonsymmetrical clock waveform for their operation. For example, a μP may require the clock high duration (t_{CH}) to be one-third of the clock cycle time (t_{CY}). Very often this is referred to as **clock duty cycle**.

Designing your own clock generator is not a trivial task. However, most μP makers offer such circuits, simplifying greatly the clock generation problem. In Chapter 3 we will have the opportunity to see examples of such off-the-shelf devices. In fact, some μPs include on-chip the clock generation circuitry as well. All that is necessary is adding externally a crystal and a few other discrete components. Use of crystals for control of the clock frequency (whether the latter is generated on-chip or externally) is a standard practice in μC systems. Aside from keeping the frequency within the required range, crystals provide the necessary accuracy for timing of processing tasks through software.

2.8.2 DC Characteristics

Semiconductor manufacturers provide two types of electrical characteristics for μPs:

  1. DC characteristics describing the behavior of a μP under static conditions.
  2. AC characteristics describing the behavior of a μP under dynamic conditions.

Such characteristics are usually given in terms of maximum and/or minimum values. These values are specified over the operating range of supply voltage (V_{cc}) and temperature. For example, a typical NMOS device operates in a voltage range of 4.75 V to 5.25 V and an ambient temperature range of 0 °C to 70 °C.

    DC characteristics, also known as **static characteristics**, concern input and output signals after they reach a stable high or a stable low level. In the previous section we saw such parameters for the clock. Here we discuss some DC parameters for the rest of the signal lines. The numeric values, given as examples, are for typical NMOS devices. To better understand such parameters, we show in Figure 2-22 the types of input and output circuits employed in NMOS devices.

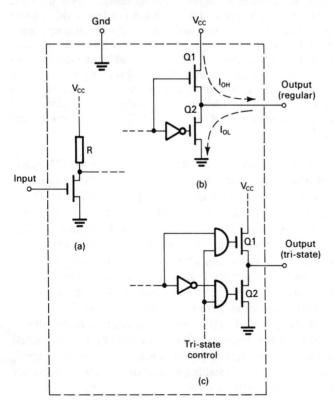

Figure 2-22. Simplified NMOS interface circuits. (a) Input circuit. (b) Regular output circuit. (c) Tri-state output circuit.

Input Voltages

To bring an input line to a high we must apply an input voltage (V_{IH}) such that

$$2.0 \text{ V} \leq V_{IH} \leq V_{cc} + 0.3 \text{ V}$$

The lower limit of 2.0 V ensures that the input MOS transistor of Figure 2-22(a) turns and remains fully on. The upper limit is the same maximum rating we have seen for the clock input.

In order to bring an input line to a low we must apply an input voltage (V_{IL}) satisfying the condition

$$-0.3 \text{ V} \leq V_{IL} \leq 0.8 \text{ V}$$

Now the upper limit of 0.8 V ensures that the input MOS transistor turns and remains completely off. The -0.3 V again represents a maximum rating.

Recall that the values of 0.8 V and 2.0 V are the same with those of the corresponding parameters in TTL (transistor–transistor logic). In fact, the circuits of Figure 2-22 are in reality more complex in order to achieve compatibility with TTL circuits.

Output Voltages

Before dealing with numeric values, let us examine how a regular (two-state) output circuit operates. Such an MOS circuit is shown in Figure 2-22(b). When the signal fed by another internal circuit of the CPU is high, transistor Q1 turns on. This provides a low impedance path to the voltage source (V_{cc}). At the same time the feeding signal is inverted to a low, turning Q2 off. This ensures a high impedance path to the ground. Under these conditions the output voltage level is at a high. So the circuit becomes a current source for the external circuits it drives.

Since the voltage maintained at the output terminal depends on the current drawn by the external circuits, it is specified for a specific current value. Usually, the condition satisfied by the output high voltage (V_{OH}), and the output high current (I_{OH}) at which it is specified, are

$$2.4 \text{ V} \leq V_{OH} @ I_{OH} = -250 \text{ } \mu\text{A}$$

That is, V_{OH} is guaranteed to be at least 2.4 V, provided the current drawn by the external circuits does not exceed 250 μA (microamperes). Notice that the supplied current is by convention designated by a minus sign.

What if the signal feeding the output circuit of Figure 2-22(b) is at a low? Now Q1 is turned off. Hence the impedance of the output terminal to V_{cc} is maintained high. On the other hand, Q2 sees a high. Thus it turns on, providing a low impedance path to the ground. Under these conditions the circuit plays the role of a sink for current coming from the driven circuits. The output low voltage (V_{OL}) is (again) specified at a specific value of the output low current (I_{OL}). For a typical NMOS device the condition is

$$V_{OL} \leq 0.4 \text{ V} @ I_{OL} = 2.0 \text{ mA}$$

In other words, as long as the output circuit does not have to sink more than 2.0 mA, the output voltage is guaranteed to stay below 0.4 V.

Example 2-26

Assume a μP whose output signal lines have the typical driving capabilities given in this section. How many TTL loads can they handle?

Solution. Standard TTL circuits require an input current of 40 μA when driven to a high. Hence in the high state, each output line of an NMOS μP can drive up to 250/40, or 6 TTL loads. However, when a standard TTL circuit is driven to a low, it supplies back to the driver 1.6 mA. Since each output line of a typical NMOS μP can sink only 2.0 mA, it can maintain at a low no more than a single TTL load. Consequently, each of the output signal lines of the CPU can handle only one TTL load.

Why is the driving capability of CPU output lines so modest? Like in the case of the clock, the reason is twofold: to conserve silicon area and power dissipation. When we need more drive than that provided by an output line, we resort to external buffers.

Let us go back to Figure 2-22(b). Since the states of transistors Q1 and Q2 are mutually exclusive, the output impedance is high to either V_{cc} or ground. Tri-state circuits allow a third state where the output impedance is high to both V_{cc} and ground. A circuit of this type is shown in Figure 2-22(c). When the tri-state control input is at a high, this output circuit behaves the same way a regular (two-state) one does. The situation becomes different when the tri-state control input is brought to a low. Now both transistors are turned off through the AND gates. Under this condition the output of the circuit is "disconnected" from both V_{cc} and ground. Another way of expressing such a condition is to say that the output is in a floating state. What is the advantage? While floating, a tri-state circuit does not interfere with some other circuit that may attempt to drive the very same bus line. Recall that the CPU brings most of the bus lines to a floating state prior to surrendering the bus to an I/O device (or another μP). From there on, the latter can drive bus lines without any interference from the CPU circuits.

Other DC Parameters

Other DC parameters of interest are the input and output leakage currents. Maximum values are usually in the range of ± 5 to ± 10 μA. They are of particular interest for tri-state signal lines. Some manufacturers specify the maximum value of the supply current (I_{cc}), rather than power dissipation. Typically I_{cc} falls between 100 and 300 mA. Another parameter of interest is the capacitance of input and output lines. This one has implications for the switching characteristics of a device and is usually around 10 picofarads.

One thing to bear in mind is that DC parameters are not always the same for all input and output lines.   A particular output line, for instance, may not be capable of sinking the same amount of current other output lines do.   Sometimes the μP manufacturers offer additional versions permitting a wider operating range for temperature.

2.8.3 AC Characteristics

This type of characteristics concern the switching of the external interface signals from one state to another.   Hence they are also known as **dynamic characteristics**. The parameters we deal with here are time intervals measured between signal transitions.   Data sheets define such parameters on timing diagrams.   They also tabulate maximum and/or minimum values over the operating range of the device. To this point we have used timing diagrams to demonstrate signal relationships in qualitative terms.   Now we examine such relationships quantitatively.

Examples of Timing Parameters

As examples we discuss the timing parameters associated with the Memory Write cycle pictured in Figure 2-23.   Recall from Section 2.7 that such a timing diagram is fairly typical of μPs with a multiplexed address/data bus.   Signal names are similar to those we employed in our hypothetical μP.   Assume that time intervals are defined between 1.5 V points (as is frequently the case in reality).   A list of the ten parameters defined in Figure 2-23 follows.   For each one it is indicated whether we need its maximum or minimum value.

1. *Rising Clock to Address Valid Time (t1 ; max):* This parameter specifies how long, after beginning the cycle, the address presented by the μP (on its pins) will be valid.   According to Figure 2-23, *M/IO**, *R/W**, and *WRD/B** also become available at that time.   The earlier a valid address becomes available the better.   Consequently we are interested in the maximum possible value of *t1* over the operating range of a device.
2. *Rising Clock to Rising Address Strobe Time (t2 ; max):* This determines the beginning of the address strobe (*AS*) pulse using, again, as a reference the start of the cycle.
3. *Address Strobe Width (t3 ; min):* Memory and I/O devices use the falling edge of *AS* to latch the address into their own circuits.   If *AS* is too short, its waveform may suffer enough degradation to present problems at the destination.   For this reason, manufacturers guarantee minimum durations for strobe pulses.
4. *Address Valid to Falling Address Strobe Time (t4 ; min):* This one specifies how long the presented address is valid prior to the trailing edge of *AS*.   It

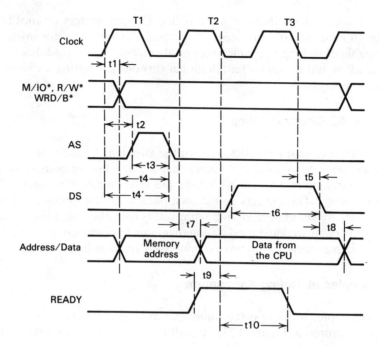

Figure 2-23. Typical Memory Write timing characteristics of a microprocessor with multiplexed address/data bus.

constitutes a key parameter because it determines the time allowance for address settling at the destination.

5. *Falling Clock to Falling Data Strobe Time (t5 ; min, max):* t5 determines the duration of the data strobe (*DS*) beyond the falling edge of state *T*3.

6. *Data Strobe Width (t6 ; min):* This one specifies a guaranteed minimum for the width of the data strobe (*DS*).

7. *Rising Clock to Data Out Valid Time (t7 ; max):* It indicates when, at the latest, we should expect valid data to be available after the start of state *T*2.

8. *Falling Data Strobe to Data Out Valid Time (t8 ; min):* t8 guarantees a minimum time data will remain valid after *DS* goes inactive.

9. *READY to Falling Clock Setup Time (t9 ; min):* In our hypothetical µP, *READY* is sampled on the falling edge of *T*2. This important parameter indicates how long prior to its sampling (by the CPU) the *READY* line should be switched to its appropriate state.

10. *READY to Falling Clock Hold Time (t10 ; min):* Usually the CPU requires *READY* to remain in its valid state for some short time after its sampling. *t*10 specifies the minimum duration of this time.

Setup and Hold Times

Going back to Figure 2-23, we observe that (aside from the clock) the only input signal is *READY*. Thus, the CPU represents for this signal a destination. Let us examine again the two timing parameters associated with *READY*. The first one specifies that the *READY* signal must arrive and settle at least $t9$ ns prior to its sampling. This type of timing parameter is very common for input signals and is called **setup time**. Failure to meet setup time requirements means unpredictable results. For example, if *READY* goes to a high less than $t9$ ns prior to the falling edge of $T2$, the CPU may see a low rather than a high level. Yet meeting the setup time requirements is not enough. *READY* must also continue being at a high for $t10$ ns (at minimum) past the sampling point, a timing parameter known as **hold time**.

The situation is similar for memory and I/O which constitute the destinations for the rest of the signals seen in Figure 2-23. Take for instance the address signals. Memory samples address signals upon the falling edge of *AS*. So, prior to the latter, it requires some setup time interval for the address signals. Usually, $t4$ is long enough to provide allowance not only for setup time (at the destination), but also settling time. One, of course, may argue that *AS* will suffer similar delays and undergo some settling time too. However, transmission delays over bus lines and propagation delays through logic elements are never the same in practice.

Example 2-27

Assume both address signals and *AS* are transmitted to memory through buffers over equal length bus lines. The propagation delays experienced through the buffers are unequal even when they belong to the very same package. Similarly, although of equal length, the bus lines do not have identical capacitance (inductance, etc.) characteristics. Hence, transmission delays through them are not identical. Take the case of a maximum difference of up to 7.5 ns for propagation delays and up to 2.5 ns for transmission delays. What should be the value of $t4$ if it is to account for signal settling imbalances and an address setup time (at the memory) of 45 ns?

Solution. The worst case imbalance in terms of delays amounts to $7.5 + 2.5 = 10$ ns. $t4$ must compensate for this plus a setup time of 45 ns. Therefore, $t4$ should have a value of at least 55 ns.

Setup and hold times are generally given explicitly in the data sheets of a device. Sometimes their values can be deduced from other given parameters. For example, in Figure 2-23 $t4 = t4' - t1$. Thus, the minimum value of $t4$ might be found by using $t4'$ min and $t1$ max. On the other hand, circuits of the same chip are tracking each other in terms of parameter variations due to temperature and manufacturing tolerances. Consequently, it is very unlikely that $t4'$ will be minimum and $t1$ maximum at the same time. This explains why most manufacturers give certain AC parameters which could otherwise be calculated from others. When such is the case, explicit values override those calculated.

Timing Parameter Variations

Some of the timing parameters may change values as a result of

1. Wait state insertion
2. Clocking rate changes
3. Excessive AC loading

Insertion of wait states, for instance, would lengthen the width of the data strobe (parameter $t6$). If a μP is available in versions of differing clocking rates, timings are given separately at each frequency. It is also possible that you may find in the data sheets equations for calculation of (clock) cycle-dependent parameters.

The capacitive load presented to an output line is also referred to as **AC load** or **dynamic load**. Such AC loads influence the slopes of waveforms and thereby the duration of timing parameters. Very often timing parameters are given assuming a load capacitance on the order of 100 pF.

Example 2-28

The AC parameters of a particular μP are given assuming a maximum AC load of 110 pF on each of its output lines. The circuits driven by one of the output lines have an input capacitance of 10 pF each. However, interconnecting wires add another 5 pF of capacitance per driven circuit. Determine how many capacitive loads this line can handle.

Solution. Each driven circuit presents to the output signal line of the CPU a composite capacitive load of 10 + 5 = 15 pF. Hence, we can drive up to a total of 110/15, or 7 AC loads. Very often the total number of loads we can drive is limited by AC loading rather than DC loading. When the actual capacitive load exceeds the specified one, then the given values of the timing parameters do not hold any more. Under such conditions we employ buffers (see Problem 2-20).

2.9 DESIGN EXAMPLES

In this section we will see how to go about designing the circuits associated with CPU reset and wait state generation. Such circuits are necessary in most μC systems.

Reset Circuit

Every μP must be initialized when we turn power on. This is accomplished by providing at its reset input a pulse of appropriate duration. A reset pulse is also necessary if for some reason the CPU must be reinitialized while power is on.

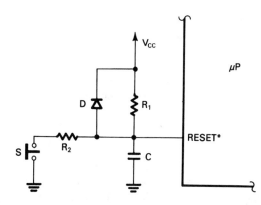

Figure 2-24.   Reset circuit of a typical microprocessor.

Figure 2-24 shows a typical circuit for CPU reset.   Notice that unlike our hypothetical μP, this one is initialized by bringing its reset input to a low.   When the power goes on, capacitor C (which is initially discharged) starts charging through resistor R_1 toward V_{cc}.   The R_1C time constant determines how long it takes to reach the switching threshold of the reset input.   Hence, it determines the duration of the reset pulse.

Usually, the internal CPU circuit driven from the reset input has **hysteresis characteristics** (Schmitt trigger) in order to prevent the internally generated reset signal from oscillating.   Such oscillations can be caused by noise on the reset input while the exponentially rising voltage across the capacitor passes near the switching threshold.   When the reset input circuit of a μP does not introduce hysteresis, we place a Schmitt trigger circuit between the RC network and the reset input.   Diode D allows capacitor C to discharge rapidly (through the output impedance of the V_{cc} supply) when the power goes off.

While power is on, we can reinitialize the CPU by pressing pushbutton switch S.   This causes C to discharge via resistor R_2, which is typically a few hundred ohms.   Resistor R_2 serves the purpose of limiting the discharge current which could otherwise damage or shorten the life of the capacitor.

Example 2-29

The switching threshold of the reset input in Figure 2-24 is 1 V.   How long should the R_1C time constant be to ensure a 100-μs-long reset pulse following the release of pushbutton switch S?   Assume R_2 is much smaller than R_1.

Solution.   First, let us see how we should interpret the assumption about the value of R_2.   Upon pressing S, the capacitor starts discharging very quickly.   At the same time there is current flowing from V_{cc} to ground via R_1 and R_2.   This current contributes a constant voltage drop across R_2.   The capacitor stops discharging when the voltage across it becomes equal to the voltage drop in question.   However, since $R_2 \ll R_1$, the voltage drop across R_2 can be assumed close to 0 V.   In other words, the capacitor is discharged completely.

When we release S, the capacitor starts charging again toward V_{cc}. The voltage (V_c) across it increases with time (t) according to

$$V_c = V_{cc} [1 - e^{-t/(R_1C)}]$$

Solving the latter in terms of R_1C, we arrive at the expression $R_1C = t / \ln[V_{cc} / (V_{cc} - V_c)]$. The duration of the reset pulse is determined from the time taken to reach the threshold of 1 V. Substituting $t = 100$ μs, $V_{cc} = 5$ V, and $V_c = 1$ V we get $R_1C = 448$ μs.

Example 2-30

The time constant we calculated in the previous example satisfies CPU reset requirements while the power is on. However, for proper resetting when we turn the power on, we need much longer time constants. This is because when we turn the power on, V_{cc} takes a relatively long time to reach its nominal value. Thus, R_1C must be long enough to ensure that V_c does not reach the threshold of 1 V until after V_{cc} reaches a specified value. A μP may, for instance, require the reset pulse to last 100 μs beyond the point where V_{cc} reaches a value of 4.5 V.

After some experimentation (with an oscilloscope), a designer has selected 100 KΩ and 15 μF for R_1 and C, respectively. These values provide a very comfortable margin for proper reset when we turn the power on. What will be the duration of a manual reset after we release the pushbutton switch S?

Solution. Solving the equation we used in Example 2-29 in terms of t, we obtain $t = R_1C \ln[V_{cc} / (V_{cc} - V_c)]$. Substitution of the numeric values yields 335 ms (milliseconds).

Wait State Generation Circuits

Because the memory and/or I/O cannot usually provide or accept data within the time interval dictated by a machine cycle, we have to insert wait states. The decision as to whether wait states are to be inserted is made by the CPU. It does so on the basis of the status of its *READY* input line. The external logic employed for deactivation and subsequent activation of the *READY* line is called a **wait state generator**.

Figure 2-25(a) illustrates an example of a circuit generating a single wait state. It consists of two D type flip-flops (FFs). Its output is connected to the *READY* input of the CPU. The first FF is clocked by one of the signals generated by the CPU at the beginning of a read or write machine cycle. Such a signal, for instance, might be the address strobe and will cause the Q output to switch to a high. The second FF is clocked by the very same clock which feeds the CPU. Normally this one is in a reset state so that its Q^* output is at a high. Let us assume now that the first FF is set. Then, the second one will also do so upon the following rising edge of the clock. As a result Q^* will switch to a low, deactivating the *READY* input of the CPU. Observe that the same signal feeds the reset input (*R*) of the

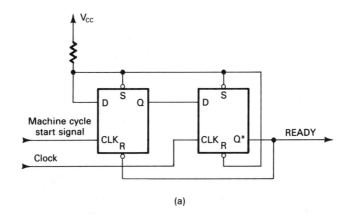

(a)

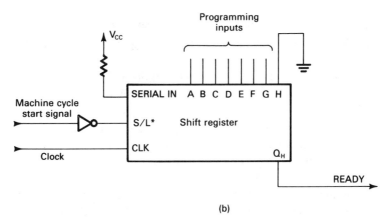

(b)

Figure 2-25.   Examples of wait state generation circuits.   (a) Circuit generating a single wait state.   (b) Programmable wait state generator.

first FF.   Hence, the latter resets.   Consequently, on the next rising edge of the clock, the *READY* output of the circuit switches back to a high.   By now, however, *READY* has been kept at a low long enough to be sensed by the CPU as such.

We can see how this circuit operates in the case of the Memory Write machine cycle shown in Figure 2-23.   *AS* is the proper signal for clocking of the first FF. The second FF sets at the beginning of state *T*2, bringing *READY* to a low.   This gives *READY* plenty of setup time until its sampling by the CPU on the falling edge of *T*2.   Realizing that *READY* is at a low, the CPU will insert a wait state (TW) after completion of state *T*2.   At that time also the second FF resets, bringing *READY* back to a high.   Notice that this again provides plenty of *READY* hold time.   While in a wait state, the CPU samples and finds out that *READY* is at a high.   It therefore proceeds to state *T*3.   Only a single wait state has been inserted.

A single wait state may not give memory (or I/O) enough extra time for presenting or accepting data. In such cases two or more wait states must be inserted. Figure 2-25(b) shows a circuit suitable for generation of multiple wait states. It is based on a parallel-in/serial-out shift register. This register is loaded with parallel data at the beginning of a read or write cycle. Such data correspond to the number of wait states we want the CPU to insert. Loading is accomplished by bringing the register's shift/load (S/L^*) input to a low. The address strobe may serve this purpose. As seen, the contents of the register are shifted out one position during each clock cycle. In fact a 1 enters via the *SERIAL IN* input every time the register is clocked.

As an example let us assume we load 0s in the three high-order bit positions (F to H) and 1s in the remaining low-order positions (A to E). We will examine what happens in the case of the machine cycle of Figure 2-23.

1. The register goes into shift mode upon the trailing edge of *AS*.
2. Since we have loaded a 0 in the most significant bit position, the serial output (Q_H) is already at a low.
3. Upon the start of $T2$ the most significant bit is shifted out. *READY*, however, will continue being at a low because bit position G was originally loaded with a 0. At the conclusion of $T2$ the CPU inserts a wait state.
4. The register is clocked again upon the start of the wait state. Now *READY* reflects the content we loaded originally in bit position F. Since the latter was also a 0, *READY* stays at a low. Thus, at the conclusion of this wait state the CPU will insert a second one.
5. When the register is clocked again (at the start of the second wait state), *READY* switches to a high. This reflects the content of bit position E, which was originally a 1. Thereafter, *READY* remains at a high because all subsequent bits are 1s. Hence no additional wait states are inserted. The state of *READY* may change only after loading new parallel data.

The preceding discussion indicates that insertion of N wait states requires setting of the $N + 1$ high-order bits to a 0.

When the number of wait states per read or write cycle is fixed, the parallel inputs of the register may be strapped to permanent high and low levels. However, we can also feed the register from a latch which is loaded under program control. Furthermore, it is possible to supplement the shown circuit with additional logic, permitting insertion of a variable number of wait states. This can accommodate memory and I/O devices of varying speeds. Take, for instance, a system whose memory is implemented with both static and dynamic devices. Insertion of wait states may be needed only when a memory cycle involves the dynamic section of the memory.

PROBLEMS

2-1. External Interface. Although μPs appear to be very different from the external interface viewpoint, they are actually very similar. With a few exceptions, all fit the model of the hypothetical CPU of Figure 2-3, which separates external interface lines into several functional groups. Use block diagrams to indicate which groups of external interface lines connect to

(a) Memory
(b) Low-speed I/O devices with no interrupt capability
(c) Low-speed I/O devices having interrupt capability
(d) High-speed I/O devices with direct memory access (DMA) capability

Justify your answer in each case.

2-2. Instruction Formats. Consider a 16-bit μP with single-word instructions consisting of an opcode field and two operand address fields. Assuming each operand field is four bits long and may take any value, determine the maximum possible number of

(a) Two-address instructions
(b) One-address instructions
(c) Zero-address instructions

Now, assume that an all-zeros value in the upper operand address field (that is, the one occupying bit positions 4 to 7) indicates its use for opcode expansion. Similarly, when the lower operand address field has an all-zeros value, that too serves opcode expansion purposes. Would the previous results change? If they do, calculate the new numbers.

2-3. Addressing Modes. Compare the addressing modes discussed in Section 2.4 in terms of

(a) Number of additional memory accesses (after the whole instruction is fetched) until the operand is retrieved by the CPU.
(b) Number of arithmetic operations required (if any).

Tabulate the results of the comparison.

2-4. Static and Dynamic Frequency of Instructions in a Program. Instruction set designers try to keep short the types of instructions which are used more frequently in a typical program. Static frequency refers to how often a particular type of instruction appears within the program in memory. Dynamic frequency refers to how often a particular type of instruction is executed by the CPU.

(a) Explain why these two frequencies are usually not equal.
(b) Assume the instruction set of a μP employs three different formats: short single-word formats, two-word formats, and long three-word formats. In a particular program, 50 percent of the instructions are short, 35 percent are two words long, and 15 percent represent three-word instructions. Quantify the impact on program compactness (and thereby memory space requirements) if all types of instructions had a uniform two-word format.
(c) While the above program is running it is monitored by another program which counts the number of times each type of instruction is executed. After monitoring the program for a sufficiently long time interval, we analyze the results of the

measurements to determine the dynamic frequency of instructions (in terms of their length). It is found that short instructions account for 60 percent of the total number of executed instructions, while two-word instructions account for only 30 percent. What would be the penalty in terms of extra instruction fetch cycles if the μP was employing a uniform two-word format?

2-5. Generation of Clock Subcycles. Use logic gates to show how you can derive the clock subcycles illustrated in Figure 2-14 (*CLSCY*), from clock phases $p1$ and $p2$.

2-6. Timing. The "jump to location at address LOCATION" instruction of the 8085 has the format shown in Figure 2-7(e). The operand field contains the address of the instruction to which control is to be transferred. In the 8085 a Memory Read (or Write) machine cycle takes three clock cycles. However, when an opcode byte is fetched, the machine cycle is stretched by one additional clock cycle to allow decoding of the opcode by the CPU. On the other hand, no extra clock cycles are required for loading of the jump address into the program counter.

(a) Sketch the instruction cycle in terms of machine and clock cycles.

(b) If a clock of 2.5 MHz is used, how long does it take to fetch and execute the above instruction?

2-7. Timing. The instruction set of the 8085 provides two input/output instructions for I/O devices: "input port" and "output port." Both instructions have the format shown in Figure 2-7(d). The operand field specifies the I/O address to/from which one byte of data is to be transferred by the CPU. The 8085 uses its accumulator to hold data read from I/O devices or data destined for I/O devices.

(a) What is the size of the I/O address space of the 8085?

(b) Sketch the instruction cycles for the "input port" and "output port" instructions in terms of machine cycles and clock cycles. (Take into consideration that the only difference between a Memory and an I/O machine cycle is the state of the *IO/M** line which is activated following the decoding of the opcode byte.)

2-8. Impact of Clock Frequency on Instruction Processing Speed. A designer upgrades a system with a CPU with a clocking rate twice as fast.

(a) Explain why instruction execution times will be shorter by one half.

(b) Will memory cycles become shorter too? Discuss.

(c) Under what conditions would the new CPU be able to process (that is, fetch and execute) instructions twice as fast?

(d) For what types of tasks would the instruction processing rate be insensitive to memory speed?

2-9. Impact of Addressing Modes on the Length of an Instruction Cycle. Figures 2-9 and 2-10 illustrate seven of the addressing modes employed by the "load word into register instruction" of the Z8002. Assume that instruction decoding, as well as loading of a fetched address or operand into a specified register, does not necessitate extra clock cycles. Assume also that memory cycles and internal operation cycles (like those associated with address calculations) take three clock cycles each.

(a) Sketch the instruction cycle in terms of machine cycles for each addressing mode.

(b) Construct a histogram depicting the length of the instruction cycle in each addressing mode for a clock frequency of 4 MHz.

2-10. Performance of CPUs Clocked at Different Rates. The maximum clock frequency of an 8-bit μP, which we will designate by X, is 3 MHz. Another 8-bit μP, Y, has a maximum clock frequency of 5 MHz.

(a) Is this information sufficient for determining which of the two μPs will fetch and execute instructions at a faster rate?

(b) A designer decides to reduce the clocking rate of μP Y to 3 MHz for reliability purposes. Will this impact on its instruction-processing speed?

2-11. Interrupt Acknowledge. Consider an 8-bit μP whose memory and I/O machine cycles are three clock cycles long. The data tabulated in the user's manual indicate that the longest instruction cycle takes 32 clock periods. On the average, though, an instruction is three bytes long and specifies one additional memory access for a single operand. The CPU requires (on the average) two clock cycles to perform the operation specified by the opcode.

(a) Calculate the worst case delay in acknowledging an interrupt, assuming a 2 MHz clock.

(b) What is the average time between occurrence of an interrupt and its acknowledgment?

2-12. Response to a DMA Request. In most μPs bus requests are honored at the end of the current machine cycle.

(a) Explain why this is not possible with interrupts which instead must wait for completion of the current instruction cycle.

(b) Does the CPU always go into an idle state after surrendering the bus to a DMA device? Under what conditions would the length of the current instruction cycle be unaffected despite its disruption by a DMA request?

(c) If most machine cycles require six clock periods and the clocking rate is 3 MHz, what is the average response time to DMA requests?

2-13. Wait States. μP manufacturers provide, among other technical data, the total number of clock cycles (N) and the number of memory cycles (M) taken by each instruction. Naturally, the furnished data assume no wait states.

(a) Suppose we have to insert W wait states per memory cycle. What will be the actual total number of clock cycles per instruction?

(b) Derive a formula allowing calculation of the actual length of an instruction cycle in terms of N, M, W, and the clock frequency f.

2-14. Impact of the Package on the Electrical Characteristics of a Device. The higher the speed of a device, the more critical the inductance of signal leads. Why? Would power dissipation itself have any impact on the criticality of lead inductance?

2-15. Physical Characteristics. An NMOS μP has an operating temperature range of 0 °C to 70 °C and a maximum power dissipation of 800 mW.

(a) What is the thermal resistance of its package given that the junction temperature (T_j) does not exceed 150 °C?

(b) Suppose we use the same package for a CMOS μP having a maximum power dissipation of 100 mW. What is the maximum value of T_j over the same temperature range?

2-16. Extension of the Operating Range of Temperature by Derating. The maximum power dissipation of a CMOS μP over the 0 °C to 70 °C range is 480 mW. In order to meet certain reliability objectives it is required that T_j does not exceed 130 °C.

(a) What should the thermal resistance of the package be?

(b) The manufacturer of the device indicates that the operating temperature range may be extended beyond 70 °C by derating—that is, reducing—power dissipation.

A designer has determined that by reducing the supply voltage and the clock frequency, power dissipation can be dropped to only 80 mW. Calculate the maximum allowable ambient temperature under these conditions.

2-17. Impact of Air Flow on Thermal Resistance. The effect of heat removal means, such as cooling fans, is equivalent to reducing the thermal resistance of a package. As an example consider a μP whose package has a thermal resistance of 70 °C/W. For an air flow of 3 m/s (meters per second), its equivalent thermal resistance may drop to only 40° C/W. Assume this to be the case for a μP having a power dissipation of 800 mW and answer the following questions.

(a) By how many degrees would T_j be reduced as a result of the air flow?

(b) What additional power would the cooling fans allow us to dissipate without any further increase of T_j?

2-18. Impact of Temperature on Failure Rate. The failure rate (R) of a μP, and semiconductor devices in general, can be determined from the equation $lnR = -E/(kT) + B$. The first term represents the temperature contribution to failures. E is the activation energy of the failure process, k is Boltzmann's constant, and T the absolute temperature in °K. The second term (B) accounts for failure-causing stresses other than temperature.

(a) Draw a graph showing how R varies with T (in qualitative terms).

(b) Ignoring B and assuming E to be constant, we can deduce easily the relation $lnR_2 / lnR_1 = T_1 / T_2$, where R_2 and R_1 are the failure rates at temperatures T_2 and T_1, respectively. Failure rates are usually expressed in terms of the probability the device will fail within a time interval of 1000 hours. For example, at a junction temperature (T_j) of 130 °C, a μP may have a failure rate of 0.01 percent per 1000 hours of operation. Alternatively, we may consider a time interval of one hour and express the failure rate as a power of ten. Suppose a μP has a failure rate of 10^{-7} when operating at a T_j of 130 °C. By what factor will the failure rate increase if we elevate T_j by 20 °C?

2-19. DC Loading. The DC load presented to a driving source by a logic circuit depends on the type of logic involved. For LSTTL (low-power Schottky) the maximum values of input current in the high and low state are 20 μA and 400 μA, respectively. On the other hand, a single MOS load requires an input current of 10 μA (at maximum) in either state. Consider a particular output line (of a μP) capable of providing an I_{OH} of −250 μA and an I_{OL} of 2.0 mA.

(a) How many LSTTL or MOS loads can be driven?

(b) When the presented load exceeds the driving capability of an output line, we resort to external buffers. If we have to drive a combination of 8 LSTTL loads and 4 MOS loads, what are the minimum driving requirements placed upon such an external buffer?

2-20. AC Loading. When the driven circuits are MOS (that is, NMOS, CMOS, and so on), the limiting factor is AC (rather than DC) loading. The AC load presented to an external interface line is the sum of:

• The input capacitances of all driven lines
• The distributed capacitance of interconnecting wires (or etched lines, in the case of printed boards)
• Stray capacitances

If the composite capacitive load exceeds a specified value, the values of the timing parameters provided by a manufacturer may no longer hold. In such cases the designer has to determine the new values of the timing parameters. This is done on the basis of the extra amount of driven capacitance. However, large capacitive loads decrease noise immunity. They also increase switching currents, which in turn impact on the reliability of the device. Thus it is advisable to use external buffers instead of driving directly the excessive AC load.

As an example consider the case treated in Problem 2-19 where the number of MOS DC loads that can be driven was determined. Calculate how many MOS AC loads can be handled. Assume each driven input has a capacitance of 10 pF and the total capacitive load is not to exceed 120 pF. Include (for each driven input) the distributed capacitance contributed by 12 in. of wiring (at 2.5 pF/in.).

2-21. Power Consumption versus Clock Frequency in CMOS μPs. In low-power CMOS, most of the power is dissipated in charging and discharging capacitances. This is in contrast to other logic families where most of the consumed power is dissipated as heat in ohmic resistances. The total power consumption (P_w) of a low-power CMOS device may be determined from the expression $P_w = K_1 V_{cc}^2 f + K_2 C_L V_{cc}^2 f + I_l V_{cc}$ where K_1 and K_2 are constants, V_{cc} the supply voltage, C_L the external capacitive load, and I_l the leakage current.

The first term represents AC power dissipated in charging and discharging internal nodal (gate) capacitances during clock transitions. It also accounts for power dissipated by current spikes between V_{cc} and ground during the transition of a CMOS circuit from one state to another. Such spikes materialize while both the P-channel and the N-channel transistors are on (see Figure P2-21). The second term represents AC power dissipated in charging/discharging load capacitances driven by output signal lines. Finally, the last term accounts for DC power dissipation due to leakage currents.

(a) Explain why the power dissipation associated with the charging/discharging of a capacitor has the form $KV_{cc}^2 f$.

(b) Show that the total supply current (I_{cc}) drained from the power supply varies linearly with f and V_{cc}.

(c) Since internal capacitances account for most of the consumed power, the total power consumption can be approximated by $K_1 V_{cc}^2 f$. Use this relation to calculate the power consumption of a μP for $V_{cc} = 5$ V and $f = 100$ KHz given that for $V_{cc} = 5$ V and $f = 1$ MHz the power consumption of the device is 15 mW. Repeat

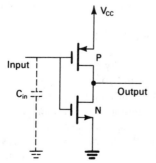

Figure P2-21.

the calculation for $V_{cc} = 3$ V. Plot P_w as a function of f (using logarithmic scales) with V_{cc} treated as a parameter (3 and 5 V).

2-22. Reset Generation with an RC Network. Consider the simple circuit of Figure 2-24 where the required pulse for CPU reset is generated using an RC network. When power is turned on, the capacitor starts charging toward V_{cc} (through R_1). The internal reset circuit does not change state until the voltage across the capacitor reaches the switching threshold specified in the data sheets of the μP. However, the switching threshold is specified in terms of a minimum (V_{IL}) and a maximum (V_{IH}). That is, the *RESET** input will never switch before the voltage across C reaches V_{IL}. However, it is guaranteed to switch prior to reaching V_{IH} (see Figure P2-22). The manufacturer of a particular μP specifies that for proper CPU reset upon power on, the *RESET** input must remain at a low a minimum of 100 μs after V_{cc} reaches 4.5 V.

(a) Determine the minimum acceptable value of the R_1C constant given that V_{IL} is 1 V and V_{IH} 2.6 V. Ignore the time taken by V_{cc} to reach 4.5 V, and the charge accumulated in the capacitor in the mean time.

(b) In what range could the duration of the reset pulse vary for the calculated value of R_1C?

(c) Actually, V_{cc} takes a considerable amount of time to reach 4.5 V after power is turned on. Consequently the time constant of the RC network must be much longer to account for it. Recalculate the value of the R_1C time constant given V_{cc} takes 250 ms to reach 4.5 V. If you select a 15 μF capacitor for C, what is the required value for R_1?

(d) What is the purpose of diode D?

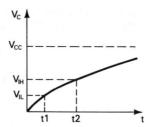

Figure P2-22.

2-23. Manual Reset. The pushbutton switch S shown in Figure 2-24 permits reinitialization of the CPU while power is on. Assume $R_1 = 100$ KΩ, $C = 15$ μF, $V_{cc} = 5$ V, and the V_{IL} and V_{IH} values given in Problem 2-22.

(a) How low does the voltage across C get when S is depressed? Express it in terms of R_1, R_2, and V_{cc}.

(b) What will be the length of the manually generated pulse (at minimum) if $R_2 = 200$ Ω?

(c) Suppose you are asked by the reliability engineer about the maximum current through C. How would you calculate it?

2-24. Reset Generation with a Constant Current Source. Figure P2-24 shows a transistor-based circuit for reset pulse generation upon power on. If we represent the emitter current by I_e, then the voltage between points a and b is $I_e R + V_{eb}$, where V_{eb} is the emitter-to-base voltage of PNP transistor Q. This voltage will be equal to the voltage drops through diodes D1 and D2. Hence, assuming 0.7 V for V_{eb} and for each diode

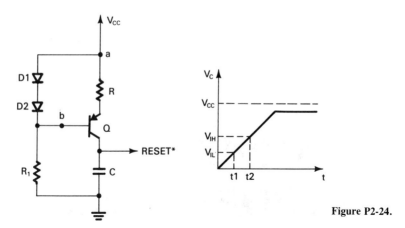

Figure P2-24.

drop, we get $I_e = 0.7 / R$.   When we turn power on, capacitor C is charged by the collector current I_c.   The latter, however, is approximately equal to I_e.   Thus, C is charging at a constant rate as determined by the value of R.

(a) Express the voltage across C in terms of the RC constant and time (t).

(b) Assume the minimum and maximum values of the switching threshold of the reset input are 1 V and 2.6 V, respectively.   What should be the minimum value of RC to ensure a reset duration of at least 100 μs?

(c) In what range could the duration of the reset pulse vary for the calculated value of RC?   Compare the result with the one obtained in Problem 2-22(b).

3

EXAMPLE MICROPROCESSORS

In the previous chapter we dealt with the characteristics of μPs in general—that is, their basic organization, representative instruction formats and addressing modes, the kinds of instructions they provide, and their physical and electrical characteristics. We also examined the external interface and CPU timing, employing as a vehicle a hypothetical CPU. In this chapter we discuss some real μPs. We are interested in

1. Their external interfaces.
2. Their internal organization.
3. Characteristics which are important to a user from a programming viewpoint. The latter include CPU registers, instruction formats, addressing modes, and the instruction set as seen directly by a programmer. Usually, these characteristics are said to define collectively the **architecture** of a CPU.

We make no attempt to provide details which can be found in data sheets and user's manuals available from manufacturers. Instead the objective is to

- Demonstrate the diversity of existing μP designs.
- Provide the basis for realistic design examples.
- Emphasize special device features and take the opportunity to explain some additional concepts.

First we discuss μP categorization and what types of μPs are available.   Then we examine representatives from two popular μP families:

- The Intel 8086 family
- The Motorola 68000 family

Toward the end of the chapter we deal with CPU support components for clocking and bus interfacing.

3.1 MICROPROCESSOR CATEGORIES

Microprocessors are grouped according to the width of their external data bus. On this basis they are categorized into:

- 8-bit μPs
- 16-bit μPs
- 32-bit μPs

Some μPs have an internal data bus wider than the external one.   For example, in the Intel 8088 the widths of the external and internal data buses are 8 and 16 bits, respectively.   However, it is the external data bus that determines the number of bits transferred during a memory or I/O machine cycle.   Besides, such cycles usually take the largest part of an instruction cycle, so the impact of the external data bus width is generally much greater.   Consequently, a device like the 8088 is still considered an 8-bit μP.

General-Purpose μPs

Figure 3-1 depicts how some of the representative, general-purpose μPs evolved. Arrowed lines reflect the chronological order of device development; however, the members of each evolutionary branch are not always compatible.   They may be different from the external interface and/or software viewpoints.   Usually the same μP (or a compatible version of it) is available from two or more sources.   Only the primary manufacturer is indicated in Figure 3-1.

Early μPs were all 8-bit CPUs with limited capabilities.   The advancements brought about by semiconductor technology made possible the development of faster and architecturally more powerful μPs.   However, as the achievable circuit complexity motivated the design of new and more powerful μPs, it also made the cost of developing a new device much higher.   Another important consideration is the cost of software.   For users, software development represents a sizable investment.   Thus they are reluctant to switch to another type of μP unless they can still make use of existing programs.

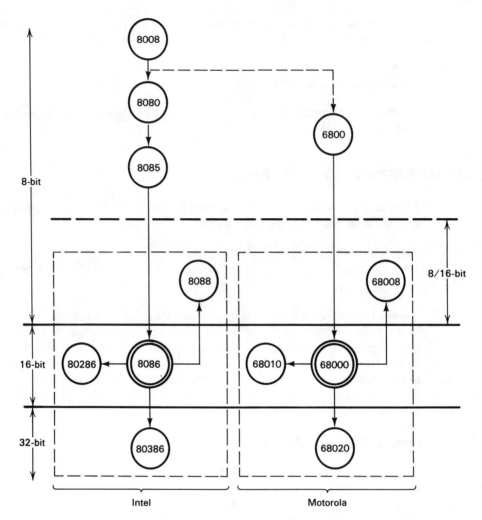

Figure 3-1. Evolution of microprocessors.

These and other constraints led to the contemporary **μP families**; that is, instead of being completely different, new μPs are architecturally compatible with existing ones. In fact, compatibility often extends to hardware as well (external interface lines, timing, and so on). Figure 3-1 shows two such families (see broken line boxes). Family roots are doubly circled. For example, the members of the Motorola 68000 family are all architecturally compatible descendants of the 16-bit 68000 μP. Observe the three types of variants that evolved from the root of each family. They are:

1. 8-bit μPs (68008, 8088). The essential difference between these CPUs and the respective roots is their 8-bit-wide external data bus. For example, the 68008 is essentially a 68000 with an 8-bit-wide external data bus.

2. **Enhanced 16-bit CPUs** (68010, 80286). In general, this type of variant offers virtual memory and other memory management capabilities. Otherwise, they are like their respective family roots. We will come back to this variant in Chapter 4 when we discuss memory management.

3. **32-bit μPs** (68020, 80386). These ones have 32-bit-wide buses and other features beyond those of their family roots. In general, they do not preserve interface compatibility but have upwardly compatible architectures. For example, the external interface of the 68020 differs from that of the 68000. Yet the two CPUs are upwardly compatible; in other words, programs written for the 68000 can also run on the 68020, but not necessarily the other way around.

Special-Purpose Microprocessing Components

Before examining some of the members of major μP families, we discuss briefly two kinds of special-purpose microprocessing components: μC devices (or chips) and special-purpose μPs.

μC chips

A μC chip is essentially a μP equipped (on-chip) with read-only memory (ROM), random access memory (RAM), and I/O circuits. Such components are intended mainly for control type of applications in industrial and consumer products. Here the processing speed demands placed upon the CPU are usually very modest. On the other hand, it is important to keep the component count and power consumption quite low. For this reason such devices may also include circuits that directly drive displays, analog-to-digital converters, and so on. Most μC chips have 4- or 8-bit data buses with limited address space and I/O capabilities. This is in contrast to μPs which are designed to be flexible for general-purpose applications.

Special-purpose μPs

As the name implies, these CPUs are specialized in the execution of certain specific tasks. Typical examples are:

- Arithmetic processors designed to handle floating point and other arithmetic operations.
- I/O processors designed to handle I/O data transfers.

Such μPs are "attached" to a main CPU. Hence, the name **attached** (or **slave**) μPs. Very often they are also referred to as **coprocessors**. The objective is to perform functions the main CPU cannot perform as fast, if at all. Besides, by offloading the main CPU, such μPs economize time for other tasks the main CPU has to perform. Coprocessors are treated by the CPU much like peripheral devices.

Next we consider each category of general-purpose μPs separately. We discuss the characteristics of each category and one or two representative CPUs.

3.2 8-BIT MICROPROCESSORS

The Intel 8008, which is considered as the first μP had an address space of 16K bytes and only two addressing modes. It was followed by the Intel 8080 and the Motorola 6800 (see Figure 3-1). Both devices are still in use and represent the first general-purpose μPs. Yet their capabilities are limited in terms of number of registers, speed, power of the instruction set, and so on. Subsequent μPs evidenced improvement in speed and architecture, but they were still limited to a 64K bytes addressing space.

Many of the new 8-bit μPs have a 16-bit-wide organization internally. Often they are also referred to as 8/16-bit μPs. These devices evolved either as upward versions of true 8-bit μPs or as downward versions of 16-bit ones. Figure 3-1 shows two representatives of this subcategory: the Intel 8088 and the Motorola 68008. Typically, members of this class have address spaces much larger than 64K bytes. They also have features supporting more complex applications, such as multitasking, which is the ability of a CPU to handle multiple tasks in a concurrent fashion.

Because of its wider external data bus, a 16-bit μP has higher processing speed than the corresponding 8/16-bit one. At the same time, the cost difference between two such devices is generally small (if any). Thus, even though we may not need the extra processing speed of a 16-bit μP, there seems to be no apparent advantage in choosing an 8/16-bit one. However, there is a real advantage when considering overall costs:

1. An 8-bit-wide data bus reduces the number of bus buffers and the number of required connections (on printed boards, backplanes, connectors, cables, and so forth). It also simplifies memory interface circuits and those used in peripheral subsystems.
2. The same advantage comes into play when we need upgrading of an existing system which is based on an older 8-bit μP. By using an 8/16-bit μP we may avoid major hardware modifications.

We now discuss the characteristics of one of the major representatives of 8-bit μPs: the 8088.

3.2.1 Intel 8088

The 8088 is a descendant of the Intel 8086 16-bit μP (see Figure 3-1). Internally the two devices are essentially identical. However, the external data bus of the 8088 is only eight bits wide. We will discuss the characteristics of the 8088 focusing on those pertaining to its external interface, internal organization, and architecture. The rest of the μPs we will see in this chapter are dealt with in the same terms.

Emphasis will be given to certain special features, which in turn will lead us into a discussion of some new topics and concepts. We will see

1. What **pipeline organization** is about
2. How a CPU can handle a large address space even though its data paths may be only 16 bits wide
3. What **segmented addressing** is about
4. Examples of instructions for applications involving multiprocessing

External Interface in Minimum Mode

One of the interesting aspects of the external interface of the 8088 is the dual definition of some of its interface lines. The objective is to increase the flexibility of the device by permitting its use in two different configurations named

- Minimum mode, and
- Maximum mode

Figure 3-2 shows the external interface line definitions in both modes. Lines with a single signal mnemonic name play the same role in either configuration. Doubly defined lines are labelled with two names—an ordinary one applying to minimum mode and a parenthesized name applying to maximum mode. The applicable definition for such lines is determined from the state of an input line called MN/MX^* (minimum/maximum). When the latter is at a high, the 8088 is configured in minimum mode. If at a low, then the maximum mode is selected. We start with the external interface functions in minimum mode.

The 8088 employs 20 lines to send addresses to memory and I/O. These lines are numbered from 0 (least significant) to 19 (most significant). Hence, its memory address space is 1 MB (2^{20}). For pin economy, address lines are also used to transmit data and status information, so the eight low-order address lines play the role of an address/data multiplexed bus. They are labeled $AD0$–$AD7$. Similarly, the four most significant address lines are used as status lines—$S3$–$S6$— to convey the status of the interrupt enable bit of the flag register and the currently used segmentation register. Only lines $A8$–$A15$ are dedicated to transmitting address signals.

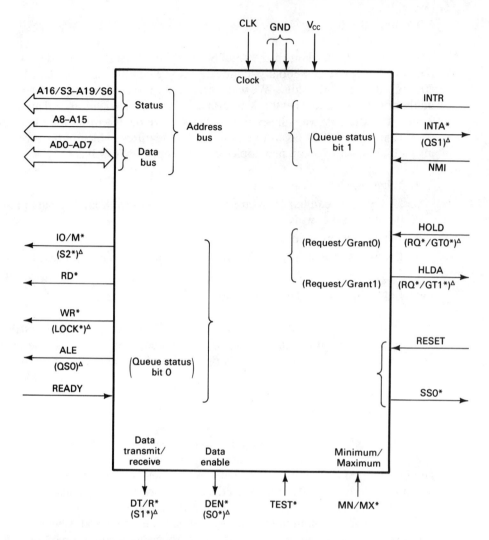

Figure 3-2. External interface lines of the 8088.

△ **Maximum mode definitions**

In place of the *R/W** (read/write) and *DS* (data strobe) lines of our hypothetical μP, the 8088 uses two strobe lines. A read data strobe (*RD**) and a write data strobe (*WR**). The roles of the *IO/M** (I/O-memory) and *ALE* lines are analogous to those of *M/IO** and *AS* in the hypothetical μP. The same holds true for the *READY* and interrupt related lines. *HOLD* and *HLDA* (hold acknowledge) act as bus request and bus grant lines. Unlike lines *S3–S6* which convey internal status, *SS0** indicates the status of the external bus. That is, when decoded (in conjunction with *IO/M** and *DT/R**), it indicates whether the current bus cycle is to read memory, write memory, read I/O, acknowledge an interrupt, and so on. In 8088 terminology, a bus cycle is essentially a machine cycle involving the external bus.

At the bottom side of the diagram we see three special-purpose lines (in addition to the *MN/MX** one). *DT/R** (data transmit/receive) and *DEN** (data enable) are auxiliary lines. They carry signals facilitating control of CPU support components such as the Intel 8286/8287 transceivers. The latter are bidirectional buffers for the address/data bus of the 8088. *DT/R** may be used to control the direction of data flow through the transceivers, while *DEN** is used to enable/disable the outputs of the buffers. *TEST** is used by a special instruction named "wait for test." When such an instruction is executed, the CPU samples the state of the *TEST** line. If active, then program execution continues. Otherwise, the CPU waits until this line goes active.

As an example of an 8088 machine cycle, Figure 3-3 illustrates a Memory Read machine cycle. Its timing is the same as that of an I/O Read machine cycle. The only difference between such cycles is the state of the *IO/M** line. Collectively, these two types of machine cycles are called Read bus cycles. Notice that clock

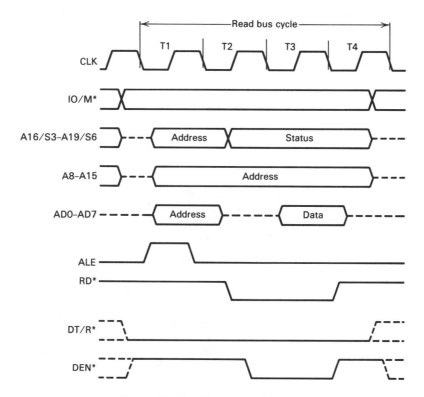

Figure 3-3.   Read bus cycle of the 8088.

cycle boundaries here are defined by negative (not positive) clock transitions. Also, a Read cycle takes four T states. *READY* is sampled by the CPU on the rising edge of $T3$. If *READY* is at a low, the CPU inserts one wait state between $T3$ and $T4$. Lines $A16/S3$ to $A19/S6$ carry address signals for most of $T1$ and part of $T2$. For the remaining part of the bus cycle they carry status information. In contrast, address bits A8 to A15 are presented by the CPU over the whole duration of a bus cycle. Lines $AD0–AD7$ carry address signals $A0–A7$ during the first part of the cycle, but later they carry data. Memory latches address signals $A0–A7$ and $A16–A19$ upon the trailing edge of the *ALE* (address latch enable) strobe. I/O devices need not latch $A16–A19$ because in such cycles only the lower 16 address lines are used. The 8088 I/O address space is 64K bytes, so lines $A16–A19$ are at a low. Data are read by the CPU at the end of state $T3$.

Example 3-1

Assume you clock an 8088 at a rate of 8 MHz. What is the data transfer rate if bus cycles follow one another? Repeat if you have to insert one wait state per bus cycle.

Solution. A clock cycle is 125 ns long. Therefore, a bus cycle has a duration of 125 $\times$ 4 = 500 ns or 0.5 μs. If bus cycles repeat one after another we can transfer data at the rate of 2 MB/s. Insertion of one wait state extends a bus cycle by 125 ns. Thus its duration becomes 625 ns. The corresponding maximum data transfer rate is now 1 / 0.625 = 1.6 MB/s.

External Interface in Maximum Mode

When the MN/MX^* line is grounded, then eight of the external interface lines carry signals different from those we discussed earlier. The names of these signals are shown in Figure 3-2 within parentheses. Lines that used to carry DEN^*, DT/R^*, and IO/M^* now carry status signals $S0^*$, $S1^*$, and $S2^*$, respectively. Toward the end of a bus cycle, these lines switch their states to reflect the type of bus cycle following next. The idea is to feed these signals to an external chip which, in turn, generates signals compatible to another bus. Such a chip is the Intel 8288 bus controller, which generates the memory and I/O control signals required by Intel's standard μC bus known as "Multibus."

Lines *HOLD* and *HLDA* now become two bidirectional, independent request/grant lines. The latter serve multiprocessing applications. When another μP needs to become bus master, it sends to the (main) 8088 CPU a bus request through one of the RQ^*/GT^* lines. Such a request is communicated by means of a single, one-clock-period-wide pulse. In response, the (main) CPU sends to the requester a similar signal over the same RQ^*/GT^* line. Finally, when the bus requester is to return bus mastership, it informs the (main) CPU by means of another pulse. This scheme is functionally equivalent to the one employed by our hypothetical CPU. It differs, though, in that signals are communicated by means of fixed width pulses rather than DC levels. Such an approach permits time–

sharing of a line by bus request and bus grant signals.   This, in turn, economizes one pin which is employed for provision of the second RG^*/GT^* line.   What if two μPs connecting to the bus control lines of the (main) CPU request the bus at the same time?   In such a case, the requester connecting to the $RQ^*/GT0^*$ line has a priority over the one connecting to the $RQ^*/GT1^*$ line.

Another signal provided for multiprocessing applications is $LOCK^*$.   This signal is under software control.   While active, it indicates that no bus requests are allowed.   In maximum mode the 8088 provides two more new signals: $QS0$ and $QS1$.   As we will see shortly, the 8088 prefetches instructions which are waiting in a queue for execution. $QS0$ and $QS1$ encode the status of events at the instruction queue on a clock cycle by clock cycle basis.   They indicate whether the byte taken out of the queue was the first, or a subsequent byte of an instruction; whether the queue was empty; or whether there was simply no activity.

The 8088 represents an interesting case of intensive pin count reduction by means of multiplexing and strapping techniques.   Multiplexing economizes eight pins for data, four pins for status ($S3$–$S6$), and two pins for bus control signals. Redefinition of a number of pins (by means of strapping MN/MX^* to a low or high) allows further pin reduction.   Combined together, these techniques make it possible to accommodate the CPU in a 40-pin package.   On the other hand, there is some negative impact on the neatness of the external interface and the simplicity of timing relationships.   However, the alternative would be a considerably more expensive 64-pin package.

Internal Organization

One way of increasing the instruction processing rate of a μP is to clock it at a higher frequency.   Another way is to employ the so-called **pipelining technique**, as does the 8088.   What is pipelining?   Recall from Section 1.1 the tasks involved in processing an instruction, including fetching, decoding, determination of operand addresses, and so on.   Ordinarily a CPU performs these tasks serially on a one-at-a-time basis.   Now, assume we organize the CPU into specialized stages such that:

1. Stage 1 fetches an instruction which it passes to stage 2.   Then it goes on to fetch another one.
2. Stage 2 decodes the instruction received from stage 1 and informs stage 3 of the required actions.   Then it proceeds to decode the next instruction arriving from stage 1.
3. Stage 3 performs part of the required actions and informs the next stage to take over, and so on.   If stage 3 performs all required actions then it constitutes the last stage of the pipeline.

Alternatively we may visualize instructions flowing one behind the other through

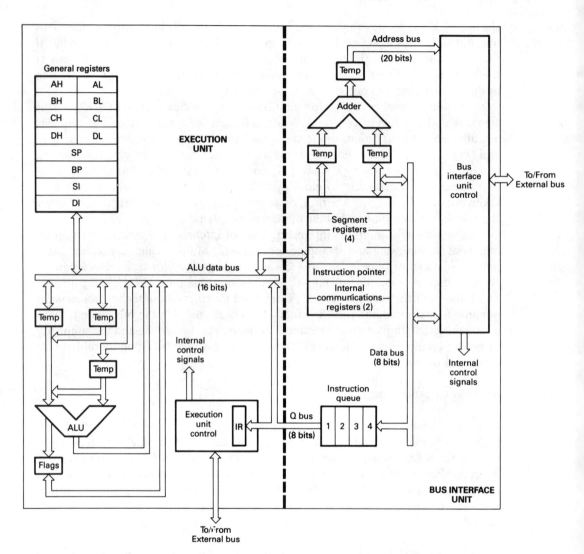

Figure 3-4. Internal organization of the 8088.

Alternatively we may visualize instructions flowing one behind the other through a series of stages, where each stage performs a particular function. Because of its analogy to a physical pipeline, such an organization is called a **pipeline organization**.

The 8088 consists of a Bus Interface Unit (BIU) and an Execution Unit (EU). Together they form a two-stage pipeline (Figure 3-4). Each unit is dedicated to performing certain of the tasks associated with instruction processing. The BIU fetches instructions, while the EU decodes and executes them. What makes the 8088 organization different from a strict two-stage pipeline is that the BIU does not wait to pass to the EU a fetched instruction before reading from memory another one. Instead, it builds a reserve of up to four bytes into a First-In-First-Out (FIFO) buffer called an **instruction queue**. In addition to fetching instructions, the BIU participates in address calculations, fetches operands, and writes results in memory as requested by the EU. However, if no such requests are outstanding and the bus is free, the BIU proceeds to fill any vacancies created in the instruction queue. Similarly, when the EU completes execution of an instruction, it passes to the BIU any results (destined for memory or I/O) and proceeds to the next instruction. The latter is, of course, very likely to be already waiting in the queue. What if (after execution of a jump instruction) the EU determines that the next instruction must be fetched from elsewhere in memory? Now the advantage of filling the queue with prefetched instructions is lost. However, this is not likely to be the case for the majority of instructions from a typical program. Thus, the ability of the two separate units to perform certain tasks simultaneously allows the 8088 to achieve a higher instruction execution rate.

Example 3-2

Suppose the tasks performed by the BIU and the EU take about equal time. By what factor does pipelining increase the performance of the 8088? What if those performed by the EU take twice as long?

Solution. If the tasks performed by the two units take equal time then the instruction processing rate increases by 100 percent—that is, by a factor of 2. In the second case, performance increases by only 50 percent—that is, by a factor of 1.5.

From Figure 3-4 we see that the main parts of a BIU are:

- The instruction queue
- A register array
- An adder
- A control unit

The register array serves addressing purposes. It includes four segment registers, an instruction pointer (equivalent to a PC), and two other registers for internal communication purposes, all of which are 16 bits long. This particular adder is used only for address calculations. It does not possess the full arithmetic/logic capabilities of the main ALU of the EU. Three temporary registers (shown with the adder) hold either address components (prior to an address calculation) or the results. Notice that each unit of the 8088 has its own independent control section. The control section of the BIU is responsible for all data transfers over the external CPU bus. Incoming data flow via the internal bus of the BIU to the instruction queue or its register array. Addresses flow from the temporary register, at the output of the adder, to the external CPU bus via a 20-bit address bus.

When a program jump must take place (following execution of a jump type of instruction), the EU informs the BIU. Then, the BIU empties the queue and fetches the next instruction from a new address. Discarding queue contents means wasting time on unnecessary fetch operations. If excessive, this may impact on system performance in two ways:

1. Although EU requests to the BIU have priority over prefetch operations, the EU will have to wait longer if the BIU is already engaged in a prefetch.
2. The external bus is overutilized at the expense of other bus users (such as I/O devices and possibly other μPs).

It is for these reasons that the capacity of the instruction queue is kept small.

Example 3-3

Assume an 8088 is executing a program in which the probability of program jumps (resulting from execution of unconditional and conditional jump instructions) is 10 percent. For simplicity, also assume that all instructions are two bytes long. What fraction of instruction fetch bus cycles could be wasted? Repeat if the instruction queue were eight bytes long.

Solution. The occurrence of a program jump means wasting up to four bus cycles (corresponding to the four bytes already contained in the queue when the jump is encountered). For 100 instructions the number of nonwasted bus cycles is (on the average) $90 \times 2 = 180$. Those wasted can be as high as $10 \times 4 = 40$. Hence the fraction of wasted cycles can be up to $40/(180 + 40) = 18$ percent. If the capacity of the instruction queue were twice as big, the wasted fraction of bus cycles could amount to $80/(180 + 80)$—that is, about 30 percent.

The main parts of the EU are:

- The array of general registers
- The main ALU
- A flag register
- A control section

There are again three temporary registers holding operands during data manipulations by the ALU. Employed in most CPUs, such registers are generally inaccessible and transparent to a programmer. Note from Figure 3-4 that all registers of the EU connect to a common 16-bit-wide bus for data exchanges. Results from the ALU flow to registers through this bus as well. The control section of the EU is more complex than that of the BIU. Some of the control lines of the external bus, as, for example, bus control and interrupt lines, are handled by the control section of the EU. However, all data transfers are via the BIU. Opcodes flow from the instruction queue into the instruction register (IR) for decoding. Operands flow to appropriate registers via the ALU data bus. Notice also a 16-bit bidirectional data path between the BIU register array and the ALU data bus.

Address components for final address calculations at the BIU, as well as data destined for the external bus, flow from the EU via this path.

Architecture

The remainder of this section deals with the architecture of the 8088 in terms of its

- Register model
- Instruction formats and addressing modes
- Instruction set

which is a format we will also use for discussing the architecture of the other μPs in this chapter. Before looking at its register model, we see how the 8088 manages to address up to 1 MB of memory.

Memory segmentation

When the EU of the 8088 decodes an instruction, it determines (among other things) the applicable addressing modes. Then it manipulates each operand field accordingly to derive a 16-bit address. Since internal paths are 16 bits wide, the EU is generally limited to handling quantities up to 16 bits long. A 16-bit address allows unique identification of 64K (2^{16}) byte locations. If the address space of the 8088 was 64 KB, such a 16-bit address would be used in a direct manner for memory addressing, but since the 8088 has a 1 MB address space, the 16-bit address must be augmented somehow to 20 bits to make possible unique identification of 1 million byte locations (more precisely 1,024,000).

Here is exactly where the role of the BIU comes into play (in address calculations). The BIU takes the 16-bit address derived by the EU and adds it to the contents of a register. This register can be any one of the four so-called **segment registers**. Before the addition, the contents of the segment register are shifted four positions in the direction of the MSB, that is, to the left. Thus, the adder produces a 20-bit quantity (see Figure 3-5). This quantity is used for identification of physical memory locations and is therefore called a **physical address**. Addresses presented over the external bus are always physical addresses. You can see that the segment register plays essentially the role of a base register. However, the address component it contributes is named a **segment address** rather than a base address. On the other hand, the address provided by the EU is treated as a displacement (or offset).

What is the lowest physical address within a segment? Clearly this corresponds to an all-zeros offset and thus coincides with the segment address (SA) itself. Note that due to the 4-bit shift, segment addresses are always multiples of

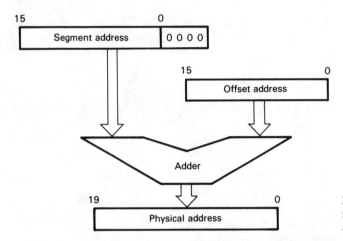

Figure 3-5. Physical address generation in the 8088 from a segment address and an offset address.

16.   The highest possible physical address (within a segment) corresponds to the maximum possible value of the offset—that is, SA + 64K.   Since the 8088 has four segment registers it can address up to a total of 4 × 64 = 256 KB at any given time.   By loading different segment addresses in the segment registers, any location in the 1 MB address space may be accessed.

Many other μPs employ addressing schemes similar to that of the 8088.   Such an approach to managing a large address space is known as **memory segmentation** or **segmented addressing**.

Register model

Figure 3-6 depicts which of the 8088's registers are accessible and thereby "visible" to a programmer.   Collectively, such registers are said to comprise the **register model** of a CPU.

As part of the EU, the general registers include a data group, used mainly to hold data, and a pointer and index group, used for address components.   Each of the 16-bit registers of the data group may also be addressed as two separate 8-bit registers.   Take, for instance, the top register shown in Figure 3-6(a).   It can be addressed as a 16-bit register named AX.   Alternatively, its lower half may be addressed individually as an 8-bit register named AL and its upper half as another 8-bit register named AH.   The addresses held in the registers of the pointer and index group are mainly offset addresses.   For example, the SP points to the top of the stack relative to the beginning of the stack segment.   The base pointer (BP) supports the based addressing mode.   On the other hand, source index (SI) and destination index (DI) hold the offsets associated with the source and destination operands during string operations.

The segment registers define the four memory segments to which the CPU has access at a particular time.   While there is no restriction as to their position

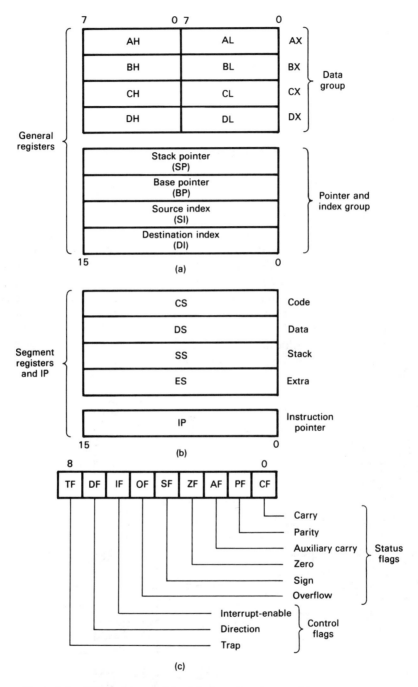

Figure 3-6. 8088 register model. (a) General registers. (b) Segment registers and instruction pointer. (c) Flag register.

within the physical address space (except for starting on 16-byte boundaries), each segment is assigned a specific role.

Code Segment (CS): Program instructions are stored in this segment.

Data Segment (DS): This segment contains program variables which are commonly referred to as data.

Stack Segment (SS): Memory locations comprising the stack used by a program fall in this segment.

Extra Segment (ES): Usually this segment is employed for data as well.

Remember, again, that since we have access to the segment registers, we may address memory locations beyond the four currently defined segments. See Figure 3-7 for an example of segment mapping into the physical memory space.

In addition to making possible expansion of the address space, memory segmentation permits relocation of programs dynamically. Assume, for instance, we are about to load into memory program #*n* for execution. Let us suppose the only available portions of memory are the nonshaded ones in Figure 3-7. Then, all the operating system has to do is load the segment registers such that they point to the beginnings of the vacant portions of memory. It is, of course, required that users' programs do not change the contents of the segment registers thereafter. Being able to relocate programs dynamically is especially important in multiprogramming systems where a CPU executes two or more programs concurrently. In

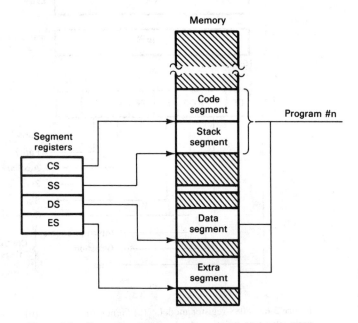

Figure 3-7. Example of program segments placement in 8088 memory.

such systems a program may be moved to disk in order to make room in memory for other programs. Later on, when that program is brought back for continuation of its execution, it can be placed anywhere in memory; that is, dynamically relocatable programs may share memory in a very flexible manner. The same feature becomes important in multitasking systems.

Last we see the instruction pointer (IP) and the flag register. IP essentially plays the role of a program counter; however, its contents do not specify a physical memory address but an offset. The BIU adds this offset to the code segment register to determine the address from which the next instruction is to be fetched. Flag register is simply another name for status register. Figure 3-6(c) shows the associated status and control flags. Recall the meaning of some of these flags from Sections 2.1 and 2.5. Here we discuss the remaining types.

PF (parity flag) is set to indicate that the result produced by the ALU has an even number of 1s (even parity). It is intended for transmission error-checking purposes. AF (auxiliary carry flag) indicates a carry from the lower 4-bit group of an 8-bit quantity into the upper 4-bit group of the same quantity. Such 4-bit groups are often known as nibbles. This type of carry (or borrow) is important in decimal arithmetic. DF (direction control flag) determines whether item addresses are to increment or decrement during the execution of string type of instructions. When TF (trap control flag) is set, it interrupts the CPU automatically after the execution of an instruction. It can be used to operate the CPU in step mode. Although they are called flags, IF, DF and TF are actually control bits which are set by a program to enable the respective actions.

Instruction formats and addressing modes

In the 8088, instruction lengths vary from one to six bytes. For example, the instructions that set/clear the interrupt enable bit of the flag register are single-byte ones. Figure 3-8(a) illustrates a typical short instruction format consisting of two bytes. Besides the opcode, the first byte includes two single-bit fields: a D field and a W field. The D (direction) field indicates whether the REG field in the second byte applies to the source operand or the destination operand. The W (word/byte) field indicates whether the operation specified by the instruction is to be performed on a 16-bit word or on a byte.

Addressing information is provided in the second byte of the instruction. The latter is divided into three fields:

MOD (address mode field): Indicates whether the second operand represented by the R/M field is located in a register or in memory. If in memory, it indicates how long is the offset contained in subsequent bytes of an instruction.

REG (register): This is the first operand field. It specifies a CPU register.

R/M (register/memory): The interpretation of this field depends on the MOD field. If MOD indicates the second operand is in a register, then R/M specifies the particular register. If MOD indicates the second operand is in

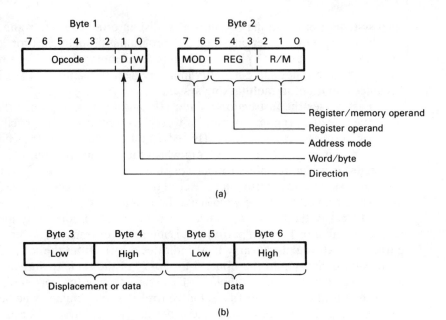

Figure 3-8. Instruction formats of the 8088. (a) Typical short instruction format. (b) Instruction extension format.

memory, then R/M specifies to the EU how to go about determining the offset address of the operand.

When an instruction is more than two bytes long, the extra bytes contain an address component for a memory-located operand and/or an immediate operand. Either one may be eight or 16 bits long. Figure 3-8(b) illustrates the format of the extension part in such instructions. Note that in this instance low and high refer to the lower and upper halves of 16-bit quantities.

The 8088 supports a variety of addressing modes, including all modes discussed in Section 2.4. With a few exceptions these modes apply to all types of instructions. Sometimes this kind of property is called **orthogonality**.

Instruction set

The instruction set of the 8088 includes special-purpose instructions such as those for control of software loops and string processing instructions. It also includes multiply/divide instructions for integers and decimal numbers and instructions supporting multiprocessing. Two examples from the latter follow:

Escape: When the 8088 executes an "escape" instruction it gives another μP the opportunity to pick up an instruction code and/or an operand from its program. The idea is to have another μP perform a special function which the 8088 cannot perform as fast or perhaps at all.   For example, it may request an 8089 "I/O processor" to transfer a block of data to a particular I/O device. Or it may request an 8087 "numeric data processor" to perform a floating point operation.

Lock the Bus: This is not really an instruction by itself but a "prefix" in front of ordinary instructions.   When used in front of an instruction it activates the synonymous bus interface line ($LOCK^*$) until execution of that instruction is completed.   The activated $LOCK^*$ line, in turn, prevents other μPs from getting hold of the external bus.   Such a feature is key to synchronizing accesses to common resources in a multiprocessing system.

Many of the instructions of the 8088 apply equally to operands (whether they are bytes or 16-bit words).   For example, the opcode of the "add" instruction is the same for both bytes and words.   What clarifies the length of an operand is the W bit.   Another way of expressing this property is to say that instructions are symmetrical as far as operand lengths (or data types) are concerned.   Orthogonality represents another aspect of symmetry.   This one concerns the degree to which addressing modes apply to all instructions.

An instruction set with symmetry properties regarding various operand aspects (such as length and addressing modes) is often called a **symmetrical instruction set**.   Symmetry frees the (assembly) programmer from having to know which data types and addressing modes apply to every instruction.   It is also very important to compiler writers.   Generally, instruction sets are not truly symmetrical.   Thus, what we are really interested in is the degree to which an instruction set is symmetrical.

3.3 16-BIT MICROPROCESSORS

What distinguishes 16-bit μPs from 8-bit ones is their 16-bit external data bus.   An immediate advantage of this is that information to/from the CPU can be transferred two bytes at a time, so the number of bus cycles required for fetching instructions and operands, or writing results, is reduced significantly.   However, the number of bus cycles is not reduced exactly by half, because some operands (and often some instructions) are only one byte long.   In any case, since bus cycles are the most frequent ones, it follows that a wider external data bus shortens instruction cycles.   Hence, the instruction processing rate of the CPU increases.

Example 3-4

Consider two μPs having 8- and 16-bit-wide external data buses.   The two CPUs are identical otherwise and their bus cycles take just as long.   Suppose all instructions and operands are two bytes long.   By what factor do their maximum data transfer rates differ?   What if 50 percent of the operands and instructions are single-byte ones?

Solution.   During a single bus cycle the 8-bit μP transfers only one byte while the 16-bit one transfers two.   Hence the 16-bit μP has a twice as fast transfer rate.

Let us consider 100 operands (and/or instructions), of which 50 are one byte long and 50 are two bytes long. The 8-bit μP requires $2 \times 50 + 50 = 150$ bus cycles for their transfer. The 16-bit one requires $50 + 50 = 100$. Thus their transfer rates are now differing by a factor of only 1.5.

The internal data paths, ALUs, and CPU registers of 16-bit μPs are at least as wide as their external data bus. In fact, some devices have 32-bit-long registers and even 32-bit-wide internal buses and ALUs. When compared to ordinary 8-bit μPs—that is, those where both internal and external buses are eight bits wide— there are additional differences. They have more powerful instruction sets, larger CPU register space, ability to address and manage large memories, and so on. These capabilities, in conjunction with their higher processing speed, make 16-bit μPs suitable for more complex applications.

Usually such applications involve concurrent handling of multiple tasks in a single user environment. For example, in a real-time control system the CPU may have to

1. Scan input ports for detection of changes.
2. Convert signals from analog to digital form.
3. Keep the time of day.
4. Communicate with another CPU, and so on.

Naturally, the CPU can handle only one task at a time. It has, however, to handle all of its tasks fast enough such that it gives the appearance of executing them simultaneously. Another typical characteristic of multitasking applications is the large size of the software, necessitating large-size memories to accommodate it and high-level languages (HLL) to develop it. Certain characteristics—such as a high degree of symmetry in the instruction set—make a CPU more efficient in the handling of HLLs. Here efficiency is expressed in terms of the average number of CPU instructions corresponding to one HLL statement.

As examples of 16-bit CPUs we examine the Intel 8086 and the Motorola 68000. Both are family roots of two widely used μP families (see Figure 3-1).

3.3.1 Intel 8086

The 8086 is very much like the 8088. In fact, from the programming viewpoint they appear identical. However:

1. Since the 8086 has a 16-bit-wide bus, it can read from (or write into) memory a 16-bit quantity by performing a single bus cycle. A 16-bit word consists of a pair of bytes stored in two contiguous (byte) addresses. The question is whether there are any restrictions about the "alignment" of a word. That is, does the lower byte address have to be an even or an odd one? Can the

CPU accommodate either case?   Moreover, does word alignment have any impact on the performance, or some other aspect, of a system?

2. The instruction set of a 16-bit μP may be either **byte-oriented** or **word-oriented**. In the case of the 8086 it is byte-oriented.   The question is what implications these two approaches have.

Before we consider word alignment and byte- versus word-oriented instruction sets, we discuss some (small) differences between the 8086 and the 8088.

Differences from the 8088

The external interface of the 8086 should differ from that of the 8088 in at least two respects:

1. Eight additional lines are used for data.

2. We need a signal indicating to memory and I/O if a transfer involves a 16-bit word or a byte.

A comparison between Figures 3-2 and 3-9 shows that this is indeed the case.   The differences are illustrated in Figure 3-9 using broken lines.   What used to be the $A8-A15$ address lines become now address/data lines $AD8-AD15$.   The latter are combined with lines $AD0-AD7$ to form the 16-bit multiplexed address/data bus of the 8086.   Similarly, the $SS0^*$ status line of the 8088 becomes now line $BHE^*/$ $S7$ to serve word/byte indication purposes.   This line multiplexes one additional status bit ($S7$) with a BHE^* (byte high enable) signal. BHE^* plays a role analogous to that of the WRD/B^* (word/byte) signal of our hypothetical CPU.   Notice also the line used to distinguish a memory data transfer from an I/O one.   In the 8088 the name and polarity of this signal (IO/M^*) were chosen to be compatible with those of the 8085 μP.

Internally the 8086 and 8088 are very much alike.   There are two differences as a consequence of the width of the external data bus.   In the 8086, the internal data bus of the BIU is 16 bits wide (see Figure 3-4).   This has no impact on the path feeding the instruction queue where instruction bytes are still packed one behind another.   On the other hand, data paths from the control section of the BIU to its registers are now 16 bits wide.   The second difference concerns the capacity of the instruction queue.   In the 8086 its size is six bytes.   Recall the reason for limiting the capacity of the 8088 instruction queue to four bytes: to reduce the number of wasted bus cycles when program jumps occur.   However, because of its wider data bus, the 8086 needs fewer bus cycles to fetch an equal number of instructions so that the capacity of its instruction queue can be increased (provided the 8086 BIU will not attempt to prefetch unless the queue has enough space for at least two bytes, which is precisely the algorithm employed in the 8086).

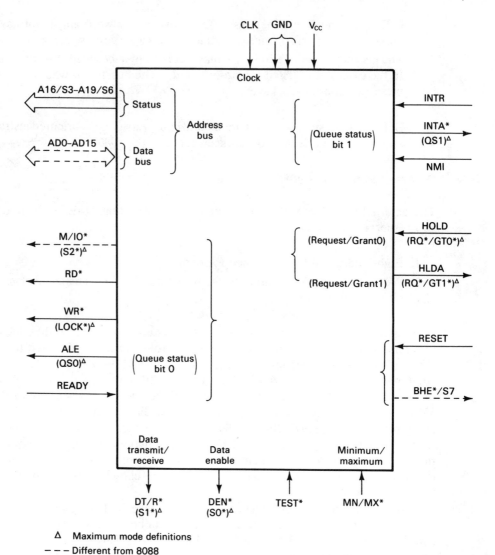

Figure 3-9. External interface lines of the 8086.

Memory Organization and Word Alignment

In the 8088 (and other 8-bit μPs), memory addressing is straightforward. The CPU simply places on the bus a byte address identifying uniquely a byte location. Things are somewhat complicated in 16-bit CPUs. Now the CPU is capable of accessing a pair of bytes from two contiguous locations at addresses A and A + 1. (Very often, a 16-bit CPU is also capable of accessing single bytes.) Let us see how this works.   Usually, in order to access a word, the CPU places on the bus the lower address A.   When A is even, the word is said to be aligned to an even address or (for brevity) **even-aligned**.   If A is odd, then the word is said to be **odd-aligned** [see Figure 3-10(a)].

The 8086 allows both even- and odd-aligned word operands.   Figure 3-10(b) depicts how memory connects to the CPU bus.   Memory is split into two sections:

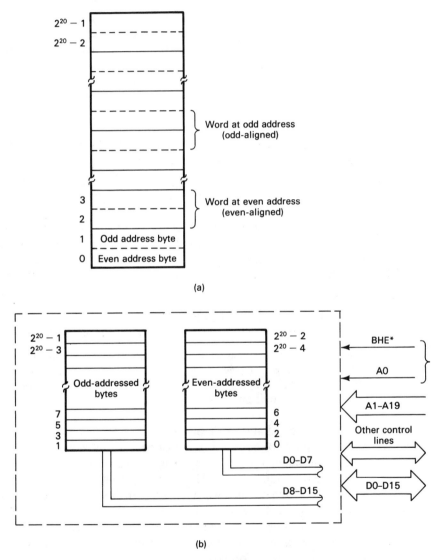

Figure 3-10.   Memory organization in the 8086.   (a) Logical address space.   (b) Physical organization.

one with all even-addressed byte locations (even section), and one with all odd-addressed byte locations (odd section). As seen, the even section connects to the lower half of the external data bus. The odd section connects to the upper half. Two signals determine which memory section is to be accessed—BHE^* and $A0$. This is done during the early part of a cycle. It may also be determined that both sections must be accessed simultaneously in order to read or write a word. Notice, however, that the latter is possible only if the accessed word is even-aligned [Figure 3-10(b)]. The problem with odd-aligned words is how to get the byte at address A (where A is now odd) into the lower half of the bus.

   This problem is solved in the following way. The 8086 performs two memory cycles. One for the odd-addressed byte and one for the even-addressed one. Routing of each byte to the appropriate half of the data bus is accomplished internally. Although transparent to the programmer, this approach necessitates one extra bus cycle whenever we access odd-aligned words. For instructions the penalty is small, since

1. A longer fetch cycle may not delay the EU thanks to the prefetch mechanism.
2. When a program jump occurs, the BIU may have to fetch the first byte of an instruction from an odd address. Thereafter, though, instruction bytes are fetched two at a time from even-aligned locations.

The impact can be significant when operands are fetched by the BIU at the request of the EU. This suggests that operands—that is, program data—should be even-aligned for higher processing speed. Such alignment is particularly important in the stack, where access speed has a direct effect on interrupt processing times.

Example 3-5

   A particular instruction of the 8086 involves two 16-bit operands. How long does it take to fetch the operands? Assume a clocking rate of 4 MHz and no wait states.

   Solution. A bus cycle takes $4 \times 0.25 = 1$ µs. If both operands are even-aligned it will take only 2 µs. However, if only one of them is even-aligned, the fetching of the two operands will take 3 µs. The worst case corresponds to both operands being odd-aligned. In that case it will take 4 µs.

   Since they take longer to read and write, why do we consider odd-aligned words at all? Why not employ even alignment for all words? The answer is that by allowing odd-aligned words we can pack information in memory more densely. This is demonstrated in Figure 3-11. Observe what happens if we align words at even addresses. Every time we encounter an instruction consisting of an odd number of bytes we waste one byte location. Naturally, this does not hold for CPUs having word-oriented instruction formats. In such CPUs an instruction always includes an even number of bytes. However, it does apply to CPUs having byte-oriented instruction formats.

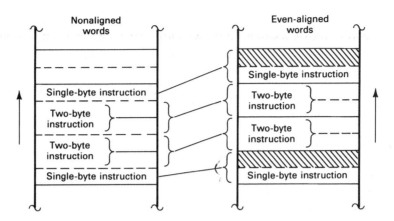

Figure 3-11. Example of program packing in a nonaligned and an even-aligned fashion.

Byte- versus Word-Oriented Instruction Sets

The 8086 has the same instruction set as the 8088.   However, in a 16-bit CPU the instruction set may be either byte-oriented or word-oriented.   The 8086 has a byte-oriented instruction set.   Although it introduces some complications (like those associated with odd alignment), a byte-oriented instruction set has also advantages. In this section we examine what those are.   We also consider the 8086 instruction set relative to that of a typical 16-bit μP.

As in the 8088, instruction lengths in the 8086 vary from one to six bytes. In fact, a substantial number of instructions are only one byte long.   Examples include those specifying operations on single registers.   Generally, keeping instructions short economizes memory space and reduces fetch time.   In the case of the 8086, byte orientation also allows a certain degree of software compatibility with older CPUs like the 8085.

A major reason for the compactness of 8086 (and 8088) instruction formats is the assignment of specific functions to certain CPU registers.   This approach permits implied addressing.   Take, for instance, the case of operations involving strings.   The source index (SI) and destination index (DI) registers always hold the offsets for the source and destination operands.   Such instructions then need not carry operand addresses.   Consequently, they are very short.   Another example is the segment registers.   All instructions imply that the required segment address is to be found in the appropriate segment register.   If, for instance, an instruction involves stack manipulations, the segment address is to be found in the stack segment register.   Again, by relieving instructions from having to specify segment addresses we keep them shorter.

Specializing certain CPU registers affects instruction lengths in another way too. The number of (remaining) general-purpose registers is now smaller. Hence, we need shorter fields to specify such registers in an instruction. On the other hand, this approach reduces the register space available to the CPU during operations. Thus, the above advantage does not really come quite free. The property of short instructions (on the overall) in an instruction set is often referred to as **encoding efficiency**. Such a property allows the 8086 to reduce further memory space requirements.

3.3.2 Motorola 68000

As another example of a 16-bit μP we discuss the Motorola 68000. This one is also a family root (see Figure 3-1). Like other typical 16-bit μPs it has a large address space (16 MB). However, it differs from the 8086 in many respects. Some of the differences are:

1. The 68000 does not multiplex address and data signals.
2. Instead of separate maskable and nonmaskable interrupt lines it uses a set of priority encoding lines.
3. The 68000 does not employ the memory segmentation approach.
4. Its instruction set is word-oriented.

We are primarily interested in characteristics different from those we have seen thus far for other μPs. Some of them will give us the opportunity to discuss new concepts. We will see

- An alternative to using a *READY* line for data transfers
- How a CPU can provide separate address spaces for the user
- How we can inform a CPU about certain abnormal conditions and what it does about them
- What read-modify-write machine cycles are about
- Two variations of the register indirect addressing mode
- How we can prevent user programs from taking actions out of their domain by disallowing execution of certain "privileged" instructions.

External Interface

We begin with the external interface lines.

Address, data, and data transfer control lines

Figure 3-12 illustrates the external interface lines of the 68000. There is an address bus and a separate data bus. This simplifies interfacing but at the expense of a higher pin count (64). Lines $A1$ to $A23$ constitute the 23-bit-wide address

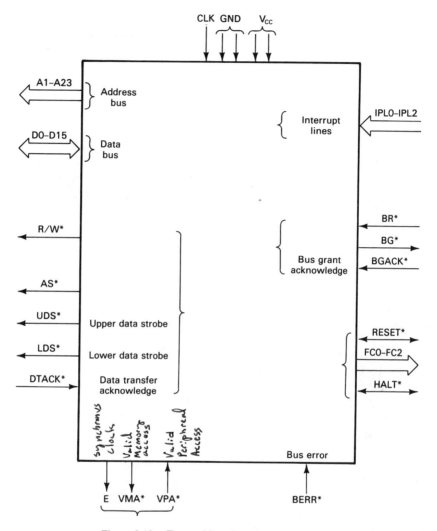

Figure 3-12.   External interface lines of the 68000.

bus. The CPU places on these lines a word address—not a byte address. Hence, its addressing capability is 2^{23} = 8M words or 16 MB.

The group of data transfer control lines does not include a *M/IO** (memory-I/O) type of line. Consequently, the 68000 does not have separate memory and I/O address spaces. Another way of expressing this is to say that the address space is unified. Notice the two separate data strobe signals: an upper byte data strobe (*UDS**) and a lower byte data strobe (*LDS**). The 68000 activates one of these signals to access the respective byte of the addressed word. To access a whole word it activates both signals. Such an approach eliminates the need for a line differentiating between byte and word accesses. It also makes unnecessary the least significant address line $A0$ (which is indeed missing).

Instead of a *READY* line, the 68000 has a so-called data transfer acknowledge (*DTACK**) line. Functionally, it is somewhat similar to the *READY* line of most μPs, but its handling is more straightforward. For example, in our hypothetical CPU, *READY* is normally active. Unless memory is fast enough, the *READY* line must be deactivated shortly before the falling edge of $T2$ (see Figure 2-15). Later on, when the memory is ready to accept/provide data, *READY* is activated again. On the other hand, *DTACK** is normally inactive and may be activated at any time. Memory, for instance, activates *DTACK** when it places data over the bus. A fast memory will do so early. A slow one will do so after a longer time interval. In write operations, memory and I/O activate *DTACK** to indicate they have accepted the data placed on the bus by the CPU.

Interrupt lines

The interrupt mechanism of the 68000 differs from that of our hypothetical CPU (and the other μPs we have seen thus far). All three lines of the interrupt group are input lines. Collectively, they encode the priority level of the interrupting device. Hence, they are named **interrupt priority level lines** (*IPL0–IPL2*). The state of the latter is continuously compared with a 3-bit mask contained in the status register of the CPU. Level 7—that is, when all lines are at a high—has the highest priority. However, level 0 does not exist since there is no signal indicating to the CPU when to sample the *IPL0–IPL2* lines.

An interrupt is honored when its level exceeds the level defined by the 3-bit mask. In such a case the CPU waits until the end of the current instruction cycle. Then it proceeds to acknowledge the interrupt:

1. First the CPU saves the contents of its status register in another register. Then it modifies the control bits of the status register as follows:
   (a) The S bit is set to supervisor state to allow interrupt processing.
   (b) The T (trace) bit is reset to prevent interference with the interrupt process.
   (c) The interrupt mask is set equal to the level of the interrupt we are about to acknowledge.

   As we will see shortly, the 68000 operates in one of two states: a supervisor state and a user state. When set, the T bit generates an internal interrupt at the end of the execution of each instruction. Hence, the reason for keeping it reset while processing an interrupt. The new setting of the mask ensures that only higher level interrupts will be honored by the CPU while servicing this one.

2. Next the CPU starts an interrupt acknowledge timing sequence. In the first phase it places the present interrupt level over address lines $A1$ to $A3$ and performs a read cycle. The interrupt source identifies that this is an interrupt acknowledge cycle by decoding the status lines of the CPU. At the same

time, it recognizes its priority code. In the second phase the interrupt source places an 8-bit code (known as a **vector**) on the lower half of the data bus. This code is then read by the CPU.

3. The CPU saves the copy of the original contents of the status register and the PC in the supervisor stack. Subsequently it enters the interrupt service routine via the location pointed to by the 8-bit vector.

Priority level 7 represents an exception in the sense that it cannot be inhibited by the interrupt mask. In other words, interrupts at this level are not maskable, so there is no need for a separate nonmaskable interrupt line.

Bus control lines

Bus control signal sequencing is somewhat more involved when compared to that of other CPUs we have seen so far. First of all, there is no line equivalent to the $LOCK$ line of Figure 2-3. A bus request (BR^*) may be sent to the CPU at any time. Activation of the bus grant (BG^*) line by the CPU does not constitute permission to gain bus mastership immediately. It is simply an indication to the requesting device to do so after the bus becomes free. The requesting device determines when the bus goes free by monitoring certain bus signals such as AS^*, $DTACK^*$, and $BGACK^*$. When the condition is met, the requesting device activates the bus grant acknowledge line ($BGACK^*$) indicating it is the new bus master. It also brings to a false the BR^* line. Then, the CPU does likewise for the BG^* line. $BGACK^*$ is kept by the new bus master in an active state until ready to relinquish bus control.

Other lines

Before examining the special-purpose lines shown at the bottom of Figure 3-12, we discuss the functions of the $RESET^*$, $HALT^*$, and $FC0-FC2$. The function of the $RESET^*$ line is somewhat different in the 68000. It still provides the means for CPU reset. For this to happen, though, it is necessary for the $HALT^*$ line to be active at the same time. Notice also that the $RESET^*$ line is bidirectional. As an output line it becomes active when executing the RESET instruction provided in the 68000. This permits resetting of external devices without affecting CPU operation.

The $HALT^*$ line plays a dual role. As a status line, it indicates whether the CPU is in a halt or running state. When activated externally (as a control line), it brings the CPU to a halt state at the conclusion of the current bus cycle. Later, when $HALT^*$ is deactivated again, the CPU resumes instruction execution starting with the next bus cycle. Hence, with proper manipulation of the $HALT^*$ line, one can step through an instruction cycle on a one-bus-cycle-at-a-time basis. Such a capability can be very useful in debugging.

CPU status (in terms of cycle activity) is conveyed by the three **"function**

code" lines FC0–FC2.   These lines indicate (through encoding) whether a cycle involves:

- User data
- A user program
- Supervisor data
- A supervisor program
- An interrupt acknowledge

As the list suggests, memory cycles are separated into two categories—those involving instructions and those involving operands.   In the 68000, memory read operations associated with instruction fetching are named **program references**.   The ones associated with operands are named **data references**.   On the other hand, while performing such operations, the CPU may be either in supervisor state or in user state.   This yields the first four classes of memory cycles.   Such categorization of read/write operations is often known as **reference classification**.   Interrupt acknowledge cycles are also considered a reference class.   Being able to distinguish memory reference classes externally makes possible a separate 16 MB address space for each class.   This raises the overall address space of the 68000 to 64 MB.

The lines shown at the bottom of Figure 3-12 serve special purposes.   *BERR** (**bus error**) indicates to the CPU the existence of some abnormal event about the current bus cycle.   For example, an external memory management unit has detected an illegal access attempt to some protected memory area, or a peripheral device does not respond.   This second possibility is particularly important due to the asynchronous nature of the 68000 bus.   Recall that memory and I/O devices are not constrained to provide (or accept) data within some predefined time interval.   As a result, failure to receive a *DTACK** causes the CPU to wait for an indefinite period of time, because the CPU has no way of knowing when to abort the current, abnormally long, bus cycle.   Such malfunctions can be detected by using circuits external to the CPU.   These circuits are designed to generate timeout signals activating the *BERR** input when memory or I/O do not respond within a certain time period.

When *BERR** goes active, the CPU starts an interrupt-like sequence.   It enters the appropriate error-handling routine through a fixed vector address.   However, unlike ordinary interrupts, the CPU saves in the stack additional information which aids later error analysis.   Such information includes

1. The first word of the currently executed instruction.
2. The address of the location being accessed when the bus cycle was aborted.
3. The state of the *R/W** and *FC0–FC2* lines.
4. A single bit indicating if the bus cycle was a part of an instruction cycle.

If *BERR** goes active again, while the CPU is placing in the stack the above information, then the CPU halts. Occurrence of a second bus error prior to executing the first instruction of the error-handling routine is referred to as a **double fault**. Another situation causing a halt is occurrence of a single bus error when the CPU is in the process of entering the initialization routine—that is, after external activation of the *RESET** line. Halts caused under such circumstances are quite different from those forced through external manipulation of the *HALT** line. Here the only way to bring the CPU out of the halt state is to activate externally the *RESET** line.

The 68000 provides a second alternative to bus error handling—that is, bringing the defective bus cycle to an end and then attempting to rerun it. When this option is chosen, we must activate both *BERR** and *HALT** upon occurrence of a bus error. This action terminates the inconclusive bus cycle and brings the CPU to a halt state. Next we deactivate *BERR** and then do the same for the *HALT** line. At this point the CPU repeats the aborted bus cycle in exactly the same way—that is, using the same control signals, address, function code, and data (if the cycle involves a write operation). Any type of bus cycle may be rerun in this manner except the read-modify-write cycles which are discussed shortly.

The three remaining signals (*E*, *VMA**, and *VPA**) are provided to ease interfacing with support components developed in the past for the 6800 μP (see Figure 3-1).

Bus cycle timing

Let us now examine some representative bus cycle timings. Figure 3-13 depicts the timing relationships in a read bus cycle of the 68000. Notice the succession of CPU states in half clock cycle intervals. This is in contrast to most μPs, where CPU states succeed one another in intervals equal to one clock period. During *S0* (state 0) the *R/W** line switches to a high, indicating a read operation. Address and function code lines switch at the beginning of state *S1*. The CPU allows about one-half of a clock period for stabilization of the address signals. Then it activates the address strobe (*AS**) around the beginning of *S2*.

If the instruction specifies a byte operation, the CPU examines internally the least significant address bit A0 in order to determine which address strobe line it should activate during this bus cycle. Recall the 68000 places word addresses on the external bus. However, internally it deals with full 24-bit addresses. If A0 is a zero, the CPU activates the upper data strobe (*UDS**). Otherwise it activates the lower data strobe (*LDS**). When the instruction specifies a word (or double word) operation, both data strobes are activated.

Beyond this point the CPU takes no further action. It waits until memory (or I/O) responds by activating the *DTACK** line. Activation of *DTACK** is an asynchronous event. In other words, there is no AC timing parameter specifying the distance between the leading edge of *DTACK** and some other bus signal. When data become available, they are placed by memory on the bus. Then the

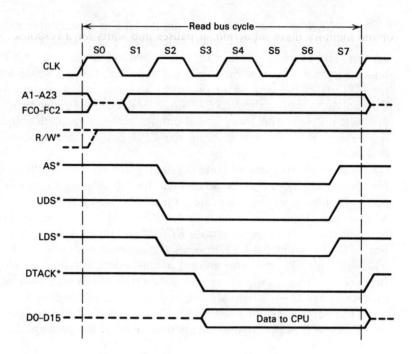

Figure 3-13. Memory Read cycle of the 68000.

memory activates *DTACK**. The CPU starts monitoring for the arrival of *DTACK**
at the beginning of *S5*. Data are not read until two states later, however. Thus,
if *DTACK** goes active at the start of *S5*, data are latched by the CPU at the end
of *S6*. Subsequently the CPU deactivates the strobe lines. The memory "sees"
this and responds by bringing *DTACK** to a high and removing itself from the
data bus.

Example 3-6

If the clocking rate of a 68000 is 10 MHz, what is the duration of a state? How long
is a read bus cycle (at minimum)? Repeat the last question if *DTACK** goes active
shortly after the start of *S5*.

Solution. The duration of a clock period is 100 ns. Therefore a state lasts for 50
ns. A read bus cycle includes at least eight states. So its minimum duration is 8 ×
50 = 400 ns.

Despite the asynchronous nature of its external bus, the 68000 is internally synchronous. *DTACK** is sampled for the first time at the beginning of *S5*. If not at a low
then, the CPU does not enter *S5*. In fact, *DTACK** must meet preset time requirements prior to the leading edge of *S5*. The given condition does not meet these
requirements. Thus, instead of entering *S5*, the CPU inserts two wait states (of 50
ns each) and samples *DTACK** again after one clock period. Consequently the
duration of the bus cycle will be now 400 + (2 × 50) = 500 ns.

A distinct characteristic of the described sequence is that each time the CPU or the memory takes an action, it pauses and waits for a response. It does not proceed further until the required response arrives. For example, after the CPU has generated all necessary signals for initiation of a read cycle, it does not proceed further until the memory responds with data. Similarly, the memory presents data and takes no further action until the CPU indicates acceptance (through deactivation of its data strobes). This approach to data transfer control is commonly known as **handshaking**. Buses employing the handshaking technique (where responses are generated asynchronously) are said to be **asynchronous buses**.

Example 3-7

Assume a 68000-based design. Would you wait for memory or I/O data to become available and then activate $DTACK^*$?

Solution. Doing so would force the CPU to insert unnecessary wait states. Since data are sampled by the CPU two states later, we can activate $DTACK^*$ earlier (that is, before data become available). What we have to ensure is that data meet preset time requirements relative to the trailing edge of S6 (where their sampling by the CPU takes place).

In addition to ordinary read and write cycles, the 68000 has a third type of memory cycle, a **read-modify-write cycle**, depicted in Figure 3-14. During the first part of the cycle, the CPU reads a location following the steps we have seen for a read bus cycle. The CPU processes the information retrieved from memory during the middle part of the cycle. It then uses the last part of the cycle to store the processed information back into memory. Notice that address, function code, and address strobe lines do not switch state throughout the entire cycle. On the other hand, half way through the cycle, R/W^* switches to indicate a write operation. The CPU generates a separate set of $DTACK^*$s and data strobes for each operation.

Why such a cycle? After all, the operation we just described can be accomplished with an ordinary read cycle followed by an ordinary write cycle. The difference is that when performed by means of a read-modify-write cycle, the operation becomes **indivisible**; that is, the operation cannot be disrupted since a bus cycle is an unbreakable timing sequence. Such a property is instrumental in synchronizing accesses to shared resources (in multiprocessing applications). In the 68000 this cycle is used by the TAS (test and set) instruction which is intended for such applications.

Internal Organization

The 68000 has two types of internal registers:

1. Address (A) registers used for addresses.
2. Data (D) registers used for data.

Both types allow storage of 32-bit addresses or data words. As seen in Figure

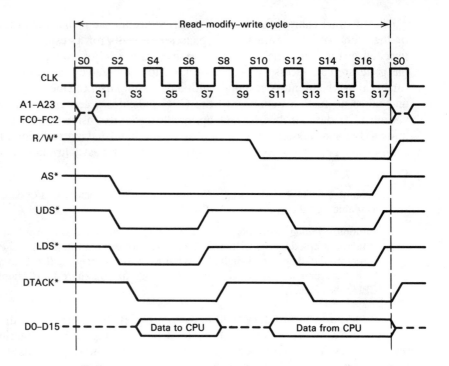

Figure 3-14. Read-Modify-Write cycle of the 68000.

3-15, each type consists of a "high group" and a "low group," which correspond to the upper and lower 16-bit halves, respectively. The four groups are interconnected by means of two 16-bit-wide internal buses: an address bus and a data bus. However, either bus can be configured dynamically into isolated segments. Such a capability permits separation of the execution unit into three independent sections. Each section employs one address bus segment and one data bus segment.

The top section includes the ALU, the status register (SR), the low group of D registers, and a special functions unit. One set of inputs to the ALU connects to the top segment of the data bus. The other connects to the top segment of the address bus. Results from the output of the ALU may flow to either one of these segments. The special functions unit performs specialized functions such as long shifts and bit manipulations. It can be considered as an extension of the ALU.

The middle section of the execution unit includes the low group of the A registers and an adder for address calculations. Finally, the bottom section includes the high group of D registers, the high group of A registers, and a second adder also employed for address calculations. The ability to isolate bus segments permits simultaneous operation of the sections of the execution unit. For example, while one adder adds the 16 LSBs of two address components, the other adder may add the remaining high-order bits. Yet, at the same time, the ALU may perform some other operation.

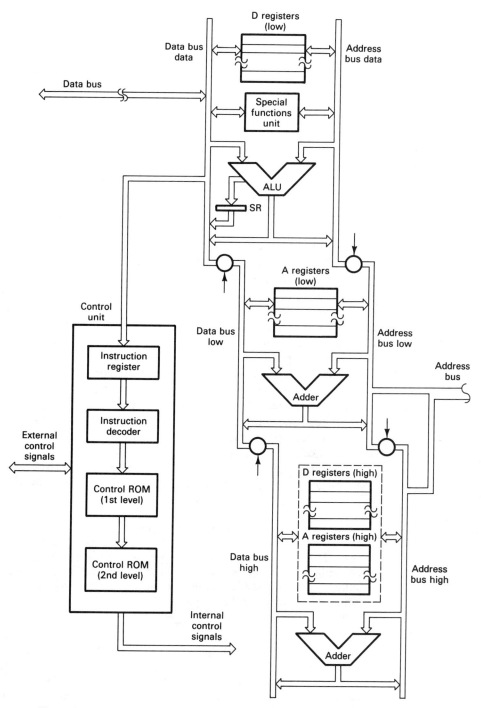

Figure 3-15.   Organization of the execution and control units of the 68000.

Although the 68000 has full 32-bit internal capability, only 23 address lines are provided in order to keep the package small. Address bits A1–A15 flow from the low group of the A registers or from the PC. Bits A16–A23 flow from the high group of the A registers or (again) from the PC. Unlike many other μPs, the 68000 does not employ a memory segmentation approach. Instead, it has a **linear address space** and treats all addresses uniformly. If the capability of program relocation and memory protection are necessary, an (external) memory management unit must be used. Word locations in memory are even-aligned. The byte at address A constitutes the upper half of a 16-bit word. The byte at address A + 1 constitutes the lower half. Long (or double) words are organized in a similar fashion. That is, if the upper 16 bits are stored at address A, then the lower 16 bits are stored at address A + 2.

The control unit of the 68000 is entirely based on microcode. In fact, in order to reduce the size of the control ROM, the 68000 employs two levels of microcode. As usual, instructions flow to the instruction register via the data bus (Figure 3-15). The instruction decoder determines from the opcode the address of the appropriate microsubroutine. The latter is stored in the first control ROM. Unlike the conventional approach, however, control words of the microsubroutine are not really microinstructions but addresses of the actual microinstructions. Microinstructions are stored in a second control ROM which employs the horizontal microprogramming technique for derivation of the various control signals.

To see how this approach economizes ROM space, consider the second-level ROM. Here all we need is to store the control word corresponding to each type of machine state. Consequently, its size is relatively small. That means a small number of address bits and thereby a small width for the first ROM. In other words, since we replicate short addresses instead of lengthy microinstructions, the overall size of the first ROM is reduced. The gains, in terms of total ROM bits, are significant considering that the number of locations in the first ROM is much higher. On the other hand, since it is necessary to perform two ROM accesses per microinstruction, there is some negative impact on execution speed.

Example 3-8

Suppose you design a CPU using bit-slice components. The microcoded control unit is to employ horizontal microprogramming, where each microinstruction is to be 16 bits long. The total number of different type microinstructions is 16. Preliminary estimates indicate the need for a 1K × 16 control ROM with an access time of about 80 ns. Determine the saved ROM capacity if you employ the two-level control ROM approach. What should be the access times of the ROMs if execution speed is to remain unaffected?

Solution. The second-level ROM will store the 16 types of microinstructions. Hence its capacity has to be 16 × 16 or 32 bytes. The first-level ROM stores microinstruction addresses rather than the microinstructions themselves. Since the second-level ROM has only 16 locations, addresses are four bits long. Thus, the first-level ROM need only be 1K × 4, a reduction of approximately 75 percent in total ROM space.

If we are to maintain the same level of execution speed, the sum of the access times of the two ROMs should not exceed 80 ns.

Architecture

Register model

Figure 3-16 illustrates the register model of the 68000. The eight data registers can hold up to 32-bit-long operands during data manipulations. Byte operands occupy the eight LSBs of the respective register. When an operand is 16 bits long, it occupies the lower half of a register. In operations involving bytes or 16-bit words, the contents of the unused portions of a register remain intact. However, unused 8- and 16-bit portions cannot be used independently, a feature that would provide additional storage space and flexibility during byte and 16-bit word operations.

The seven address registers and the stack pointers can hold full 32-bit addresses. Any one of them may serve as a stack pointer or as a base register. Besides, any of the 17 registers may also be used as an index register. Register A7 serves as a user stack pointer. Its duplicate, A7′, serves as a stack pointer in supervisory mode.

Figure 3-16(b) illustrates the 16-bit status register. Status flags occupy the lower half of this register. In the 68000, this portion is referred to as the **user byte**. Such a name is appropriate given that the state of the flags is under control of the user program. In contrast, the state of the control bits can be changed only by the operating system. Hence they are collectively referred to as **system byte**. Except for the X bit, the meaning of the flags is the same as in other CPUs we have discussed. The X (extend) bit is used in precision arithmetic operations. I0 to I2 comprise the 3-bit mask against which external interrupt priority levels are compared. The S bit setting determines whether the CPU is in user or supervisory mode. When set, the T (trace) bit generates an internal interrupt (trap) at the end of the execution of every instruction. This permits tracing of a program on an instruction-by-instruction basis. The objective of such a facility is to aid software debugging.

Instruction formats

Next we see some instruction formats of the 68000. Instruction lengths vary from one to five words depending on addressing modes. The first word contains the opcode and a number of short fields. In 68000 terminology it is known as the **operation word**. Subsequent instruction words extend one or both operand address fields. Figure 3-17(a) shows the operation word format for the MOVE instruction. MOVE simply transfers an operand from a specified source address to a specified destination address. The **size field** encodes the length of the operand. It indicates

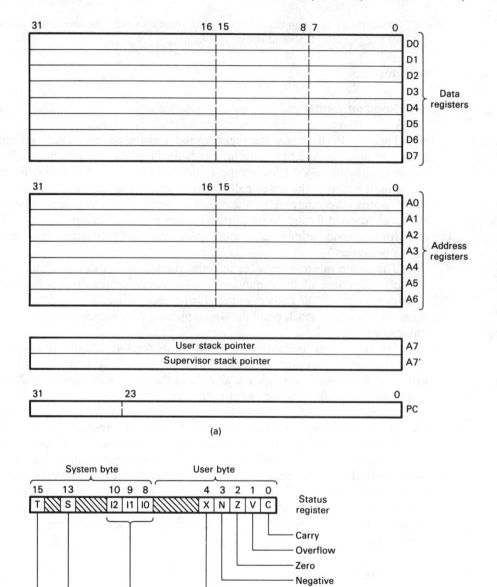

(a)

(b)

Figure 3-16.   Register model of the 68000.   (a) Data registers, address registers, stack pointers, and program counter.   (b) Status register.

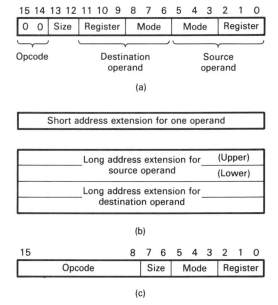

(a)

Short address extension for one operand

(b)

(c)

Figure 3-17. Some instruction formats of the 68000. (a) Operation word format of the MOVE instruction. (b) Examples of address extension formats. (c) Typical operation word format for one-address instructions and two-address instructions when one of the operands is immediate.

whether the operation is to be performed on bytes, words, or long words. Each operand address field is divided into two subfields: a *register* subfield and a *mode* subfield. The latter determines the applicable addressing mode. The former determines the register involved in the formation of the operand address. When an addressing mode does not involve registers, the *register* subfield is utilized as an extension of the *mode* subfield.

Address fields extend into additional instruction words in the case of modes specifying a displacement, immediate addressing, or direct addressing (referred to as absolute addressing in the 68000). Figure 3-17(b) shows two examples of address extension formats. The first specifies a short (16-bit-long) address extension for one operand. In the "absolute short address" mode, this word specifies a 16-bit address. In immediate mode it specifies an 8- or a 16-bit operand. In other modes it may specify a 16-bit displacement.

The second example illustrates the format of the longest possible extension. It applies to two-address instructions when both operands have long addresses. In the "absolute long address" mode the two extension words are combined to form a 24-bit direct address. In immediate mode they contain a 32-bit-long operand.

Figure 3-17(c) shows a typical one-address instruction format. The same operation word format though is applicable to some two-address instructions. Such are those in which the opcode encodes the fact that the source operand is immediate.

Addressing modes

In the 68000, all addressing modes involving registers imply one of the eight address registers. The "data register direct" mode is of course an exception. In

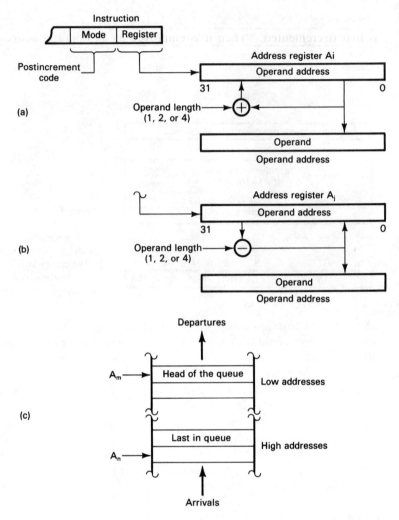

Figure 3-18. (a) Operand address determination in postincrement mode. (b) Operand address determination in predecrement mode. (c) Implementation of a queue (in memory) using the postincrement addressing mode.

addition to the addressing modes we have discussed in Section 2.4, the 68000 has two very useful variations of the register indirect mode.

The first variation is called **address register indirect with postincrement**. It is illustrated in Figure 3-18(a). In this mode, the process of address determination is the same as in the register indirect mode. The difference is that afterwards the register is incremented by one, two, or four to point to the subsequent memory address. Figure 3-18(b) shows the second variation called **address register indirect**

with predecrement. As the name implies, the operand address held in the register is first decremented. Then it is employed as an operand address by the CPU. The decremented value is also fed back to the address register itself. In both modes the size of the increment/decrement depends on the length of the operand specified in the instruction. Size is one for bytes, two for words, and four for long words. There is one exception. If the register happens to be the stack pointer (SP), it is incremented/decremented by two even for byte operations. This is necessary in order to preserve the alignment of the SP to word boundaries.

Figure 3-18(c) demonstrates one of the many useful applications of these two addressing modes. Two address registers (Am and An) are used in the postincrement mode to implement a queue in memory. Unlike stacks, where items are pushed in or pulled out through the top, queues have two active ends. Arriving items are added through one end, while departing ones are pulled out through the other. Register Am points to the location of the item which is to depart next— that is, the head of the queue. After this item is pulled out, Am is incremented. Hence it points to the next item which has now become the new head of the queue. Similarly, register An points to the location where the first arriving item is to be stored. Following such an arrival, An is incremented and points to the next higher address where a new item will be stored.

The flexibility to specify any of the address registers as a stack pointer, in conjunction with the two described addressing modes, permits the 68000 to maintain multiple stacks in memory.

Modes of operation

The 68000 has two modes of operation: a **user mode** and a **supervisory mode**. In user mode, the CPU is prohibited from executing certain **"privileged" instructions**. The idea is to prevent user programs from taking any actions which are out of their domain. For example, a user program may not be allowed to gain access to a disk in order to prevent it from accessing, and possibly modifying, information which does not belong to it. A user program may instead request such an access through the operating system, which determines whether the requested access should be honored or denied. By doing so, accesses to various parts of a system can be performed in a controlled and thereby more secure way. Another example is the halting or reinitialization of some part of a system. Such system operations should be kept out of the domain of users' programs.

In the 68000 the privileged instructions are

1. Those affecting the system byte of the status register.
2. The MOVE USP instruction which transfers data between the user stack pointer and one of the address registers.
3. The RTE (return from exception) instruction, which is equivalent to a return from interrupt instruction.

4. The STOP instruction, which stops the CPU from fetching and executing instructions.

5. The RESET instruction.

The CPU is forced into supervisory mode after disruption of normal program execution by an external or internal event. Return to user mode can be accomplished either by clearing the S bit in the status register or by executing an RTE instruction.

Exception processing

Normal program execution may be disrupted by a variety of external or internal events. In the 68000, such events are called **exceptions**. The actions taken by the CPU for their servicing are collectively referred to as exception processing. A list of the sources which generate exceptions in the 68000 follows:

1. External Sources
- Interrupts (*IPL0–IPL2* lines)
- Reset (*RESET** line)
- Bus error (*BERR** line)

2. Internal Sources
- Hardware
  - Address error
  - Illegal instructions
  - Privileged instruction violation
  - Spurious interrupt
  - Divide by zero
  - Unimplemented instructions
- Software
  - TRAP instruction (16 vectors available)
  - TRAPV (trap on overflow) instruction
  - CHK (check register against bounds) instruction
  - Trace mode

The CPU steps associated with exception processing are essentially the same for all types of exceptions. They are similar to those we described for external interrupts. However, vectors are provided externally only in the case of external interrupts. All other types of exceptions are serviced through fixed vector addresses. Very often exceptions caused by internal sources are called **traps**. Those caused by abnormal internal conditions are usually referred to as **hardware traps**. The ones caused by trap-related instructions, or special modes of operation (like the trace mode), are referred to as **software traps**. We have already dealt with all three external sources of exceptions. Here we examine in brief the internal sources.

First, let us consider the internal sources associated with hardware.   An address error exception is generated when the CPU attempts to use an odd address while accessing a 16- or a 32-bit word.   Recall that, in the 68000, words are always even-aligned, so an attempt to use an odd address is indicative of some kind of internal error.   When such a condition arises, the CPU aborts the current bus cycle and initiates exception processing immediately.   Address errors are treated like bus errors.   That is:

1. Additional information is saved in the stack for error analysis.
2. Double errors cause a CPU halt.

Illegal instructions are simply bit combinations which do not represent valid operation words.   A privileged instruction violation exception is caused when the CPU attempts execution of a privileged instruction while in user mode.   A spurious interrupt exception occurs if the bus error input ($BERR^*$) goes active while the CPU presents the priority code to an interrupting device.   Recall that this process takes place in the course of an interrupt acknowledge cycle.   A divide-by-zero exception occurs when attempting execution of a divide instruction with a divisor equal to zero.   In contrast to illegal instructions, unimplemented ones represent valid operation words.   Such undefined instructions may be used by the system for detection of programming errors.

Software traps (caused by the TRAP, TRAPV, and CHK instructions) are a result of normal instruction execution.   TRAP causes an unconditional trap.   TRAPV and CHK do so only if the associated condition is met.   By being able to specify 16 different vectors, the TRAP instruction provides the flexibility of up to 16 trap service routines.   Finally, trace mode exceptions occur at the end of the execution of every program instruction as long as the T bit is set.

Instruction set

The instruction set of the 68000 includes bit manipulation and multiply/divide instructions (but not string processing ones).   It also provides some uncommon types of instructions such as

1. Instructions incrementing/decrementing an operand by a value in the range of 1 to 8
2. Instructions moving multiple registers to/from memory
3. Instructions for support of high-level languages

Unlike the 8086, the 68000 has a word-oriented instruction set.   Because of this, and the fact that some addressing modes need one long word per operand address, instructions are rather long.   For this reason the 68000 provides short, single-word versions of some addressing modes, as well as "quick" versions of some instructions.   For example, the "move quick" instruction loads a data register with an 8-bit immediate operand which is part of the operation word.   Thus, no extension word is necessary.

The "test and set" instruction and the read-modify-write cycle are provided for support of multiprocessing applications.   The trap mechanism associated with unimplemented instructions may be also used for other purposes.   For example, it can provide the means to execute certain types of instructions (such as floating point arithmetic ones) with the aid of specialized μPs.   The same trap mechanism may be employed to execute such instructions in software by means of a subroutine.

In addition to operating on bytes and single words, most instructions also operate on 32-bit words.   This gives the instruction set a high degree of symmetry relative to operand lengths.   With some exceptions, instructions can use most (or all) of the available addressing modes, so the instruction set has a high degree of symmetry relative to addressing modes as well.

3.4 32-BIT MICROPROCESSORS

Most 32-bit μPs are descendants of 16-bit ones.   Figure 3-1 shows two such CPUs which evolved from their respective 16-bit family roots.   32-bit μPs are higher complexity chips (100K transistors and beyond) and are classified as VLSI devices. They are used in more demanding applications such as those involving computer-aided design (CAD), robotics, and speech recognition.   In this section we examine some of their typical characteristics and discuss pertinent design considerations. Then we go on to look at the Motorola 68020 and the Intel 80386 as examples.

Many of the capabilities we have seen in 16-bit CPUs are more extensive in the case of 32-bit ones.   For example, 32-bit μPs implement fully a two- or three-stage pipeline.   In 16-bit μPs the pipeline is usually a partial two-stage one.   Similarly, characteristics supporting HLLs are more extensive in 32-bit CPUs, and capabilities appearing only in certain 16-bit CPUs become typical in 32-bit ones. For example, they provide memory management and virtual memory support (on- or off-chip) and are also geared to handle coprocessors for floating point arithmetic and other tasks.

The main characteristics distinguishing 32-bit μPs from their 16-bit family roots are

1. Their 32-bit external data buses
2. Their larger address spaces
3. On-chip implementation of barrel shifters for fast execution of shift/rotate instructions
4. Use of the cache approach for faster instruction processing
    They either provide a cache on-chip or short (typically two clock periods long) bus cycles for cache implementation off-chip.

Barrel shifters

In 8- and 16-bit CPUs, shift/rotate instructions include generally a count field specifying how many bit positions the operand is to be shifted/rotated. Such operations are performed one bit at a time. Consequently, the execution time of a shift/rotate instruction depends on the number specified in the count field.

A faster alternative is using a network of gates which shifts/rotates an operand in a single step, regardless of the value of the count field. The network has two sets of inputs. One set serves to feed the operand. The other set applies the control signals determining the type of operation (shift left, shift right, and so on) and the shift/rotate count. Such networks are commonly referred to as **barrel shifters** and are implemented in 32-bit μPs. Typically, a barrel shifter takes only one clock cycle for generation of the final result.

The cache

Often a 32-bit μP is equipped on-chip with a small capacity, high-speed buffer known as a **cache**, in which is stored the currently executed block of instructions (and possibly operands) for faster access by the CPU. This approach improves performance because typical programs have the so-called **property of locality**. That is, over a short period of time, the CPU accesses mostly a small group of neighboring memory locations. Examples are short program loops involving repetitive operations (like those associated with string processing), table look-up routines, small subroutines, and so on.

The cache, which consists of a "data" buffer and a "tag" buffer, is "located" between CPU and main memory. The tag buffer stores the addresses of the memory locations whose content is currently resident in the data buffer of the cache. When the CPU is to access a location, the address is compared to those currently stored in the tag buffer in order to determine whether or not the contents of that memory location are already in the cache. If they are, the needed information is fetched from the cache. Such a condition is referred to as a **cache hit**. Otherwise, the CPU will have to access the (main) memory, a case referred to as a **cache miss**.

Actually, a cache is employed to store many blocks rather than a single block. Each tag identifies the starting memory address of a particular block. The notable benefit from the use of a cache is the reduction of the "effective" memory access time seen by the CPU. Besides, since the CPU now utilizes the memory and the bus less frequently, contention with DMA controllers (and possibly other μPs) is reduced. Naturally, to capitalize on the benefits of the cache technique, both the data buffer and the tag buffer must be much faster than memory. While discussing the 68020 we will have the opportunity to see a cache example.

The wider external data bus of 32-bit μPs has a direct impact on instruction processing speed. Long words are now accessed in a single bus cycle. The actual benefit will, of course, depend on what fraction of the instructions and the operands is 32 bits long. If most instructions and operands are eight or 16 bits long, the benefit may not be impressive at all.

Example 3-9

Consider a 32-bit μP whose bus cycle has the same duration as that of a 16-bit one. It has been determined that (on the average) 20 percent of the operands and instructions are 32 bits long, 40 percent are 16 bits long, and 40 percent are only eight bits long. Calculate the improvement factor when fetching instructions and operands with the 32-bit μP.

Solution. Let us consider a mix of 100 instructions and operands. On the average they represent 20 long words, 40 words, and 40 bytes. The number of bus cycles required for their fetching by the 16-bit μP is $2 \times 20 + 40 + 40 = 120$. The 32-bit μP will have to perform for their fetching $1 \times 20 + 40 + 40 = 100$ bus cycles. This amounts to an improvement factor of (120 − 100) / 120 or only about 17 percent.

The gain could be just as modest (if any at all) for I/O operations. I/O paths (and peripherals) are usually eight bits wide. Thus, the availability of a 32-bit-wide bus may have no appreciable impact. In fact, if the application is such that the CPU spends most of its time in I/O operations, overall system performance may improve very little with a 32-bit μP. The faster bus cycles of 32-bit μPs may not represent a significant advantage either. Unless the memory is fast enough, we have to insert wait states which slow down memory accesses anyway. Therefore, before you decide to design (or upgrade an existing system) with a 32-bit μP, you should consider carefully the advantages justifying it.

3.4.1 Motorola 68020

Our first example of a 32-bit CPU is the Motorola 68020. The 68020 is a descendant of the 68000 16-bit μP we examined before. In fact, its basic architecture and many other characteristics are the same as those of the 68000. This will be seen as we examine the external interface, the organization, and the architecture of the 68020. The 68020 will give us the opportunity to see:

1. How a 32-bit CPU deals with variable-width data transfers. The ability of a CPU to handle such transfers is often referred to as **dynamic bus sizing**.
2. How a cache is implemented and how it operates in a real CPU.

External Interface

Like the 68000, the 68020 does not multiplex data and address signals on the same lines. This accounts for the large number of its pins. Indeed, the 68020 comes in a pin-grid array (PGA) of 114 pins. Yet, thanks to the high pin density of PGAs, the overall package is only 1.36 in. $\times$ 1.36 in. (see Figure 2-20). Both the address bus and the data bus are 32 bits wide, so the 68020 can address directly up to 4 GB (1 gigabyte equals 1×10^9 bytes—that is, 1000 MB of memory).

Most of the external interface lines of the 68020 shown in Figure 3-19 are identical in name and function to those of the 68000. Only the lines whose full name appears within the box are different from the ones we have seen in the 68000.

First, let us examine the differences in the data transfer control group of lines (lower left side in Figure 3-19). Unlike the 68000, which has a separate data strobe for the upper and lower bytes of a 16-bit word, the 68020 has a single data strobe line (DS^*). The number of data bits involved in a transfer can be eight, 16, or 32. In the 68020 this is indicated by means of a separate pair of lines named SIZ0 and SIZ1. In other words, these lines indicate to the addressed device whether the data transfer which is about to take place involves a byte, a word, or a long

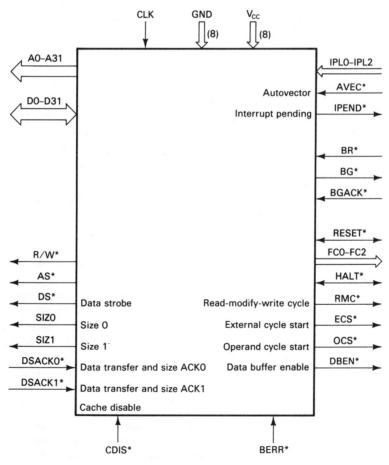

Figure 3-19.   External interface lines of the 68020.

word.   To determine which specific byte or which word of a 32-bit entity is to be transferred, the addressed device must also decode address bits A0 and A1.   (Note that in the 68020, address bit A0 is available at the external interface.)   A second difference concerns the data transfer acknowledge lines.   While the 68000 has a single $DTACK^*$ line, the 68020 has two such lines.   They are called **data transfer and size acknowledge** ($DSACK0^*$ and $DSACK1^*$) lines because of the additional role they play.   They are also used by an addressed device to indicate the width of the data port it employs during each bus cycle.

The interrupt scheme of the 68020 is not any different from that of the 68000. However, the group of interrupt lines includes two additional auxiliary ones: $AVEC^*$ (autovector) and $IPEND^*$ (interrupt pending).   Recall from the 68000 what an interrupting device does during an interrupt acknowledge cycle: It places over the data bus an 8-bit vector leading the CPU to the respective interrupt service routine. The $AVEC^*$ line provides to the interrupting device an alternative, so that instead of supplying the CPU with a vector, the device may simply activate $AVEC^*$.   When this happens, the 68020 generates automatically a predetermined vector address. Hence the name autovector. $IPEND^*$ is essentially a status line.   When active, it indicates that some interrupt is currently pending.

Besides these additional lines the 68020 offers greater flexibility when it comes to vectored interrupts.   The vector furnished by an interrupting device is treated by the CPU as a relative rather than an absolute address.   Actual vectors are determined by adding a base address contained in the "**vector base register**" of the CPU.   Such a facility permits placing the vector table in whatever memory area it is desired.   Therefore it supports **multiple vector tables**.

Three status lines indicate certain events relating to bus cycles (see the lower right-hand side in Figure 3-19). RMC^* (read-modify-write cycle) goes active when a read-modify-write cycle is in progress. ECS^* (external cycle start) indicates the beginning of a bus cycle.   On the other hand, OCS^* (operand cycle start) goes active only during the beginning of the first bus cycle of an operation involving the transfer of an operand. $DBEN^*$ (data buffer enable) can serve as an enable signal for external buffers.   Finally, the $CDIS^*$ (cache disable) line permits disabling of the on-chip cache of the 68020.

Timing relationships during a bus cycle are quite similar to those of the 68000, but the length of a cycle is shorter.   For example, a read bus cycle normally takes three clock cycles versus four in the 68000.   Faster cycle times increase the processing speed of the CPU.   They also reduce bus utilization and thereby free the bus for use by DMA devices (and possibly other μPs).   On the other hand, such gains can be negated if we have to insert wait states in the bus cycles.

Example 3-10

Suppose you clock a particular version of the 68020 at a rate of 16.67 MHz.   Calculate the durations of clock cycles, states, and read bus cycles.   Now assume an instruction has on the average the following characteristics: It takes 80 ns to fetch (thanks to the cache), one clock cycle to execute (thanks to pipelining), and involves two operand accesses. Determine the instruction processing rate of the 68020 in MIPS.

Solution. The period of the clock is $1/16.67 = 0.06$ µs, or 60 ns. Hence a clock cycle takes 60 ns. As in the 68000, a state takes half a clock cycle (see Figure 3-13). Therefore, the state duration is 30 ns. A read bus cycle takes $3 \times 60 = 180$ ns (assuming no wait states).

As we will see shortly, the 68020 employs the cache only for instructions—not for operands. Consequently, the two operand accesses add to each instruction cycle $2 \times 180 = 360$ ns (assuming again no wait state insertion). The average length of an instruction cycle is then $360 + 60 + 80 = 500$ ns. This is equivalent to an instruction processing rate of $(1/500) \times 10^9 = 2 \times 10^6$ instructions/second, or 2 MIPS.

Example 3-11

Assume that the memory speed does not match the speed of the above version of the 68020. In fact the CPU has to insert six wait states in each bus cycle. What is the duration of each bus cycle? Under what conditions would you consider derating the clock frequency?

Solution. A bus cycle takes now $180 + (6 \times 30) = 360$ ns, which is twice the duration of a normal bus cycle.

If the application is such that the CPU spends most of its time executing instructions, then the high clocking rate is certainly advantageous. What if most of the CPU time is taken by data movements (to/from memory and I/O)? Moreover, what if we have to insert wait states in bus cycles because memory and I/O are not fast enough? Under such circumstances the (normally) faster bus cycle of the 68020 will have very small impact on overall system performance. Thus, it may be advisable to decrease the clocking rate to the point that no wait state insertion becomes necessary. By derating the clock frequency we reduce power dissipation and thereby gain reliability. Besides (as we will see later), the higher the clock frequency, the more precautions we have to take for suppression of the noise generated during clock transitions.

Internal Organization

Internally the 68020 is considerably different and much more complex than the 68000. The internal buses and the various functional units are 32 bits wide. Thus all three ALUs employed in the three sections of the execution unit are 32 bits wide. The simplified block diagram of Figure 3-20 reveals the presence of a new functional unit—the cache—which is used only for instructions. It includes a cache tag buffer and a 32-bit-wide cache data buffer.

The 68020 is equipped with separate paths for instructions and operands such that the three sections of its execution unit can work independently in an overlap fashion. Thus, while the instruction address section calculates the address of a new instruction, the operand address section calculates and may even initiate a memory access for an operand and the data section carries on data manipulation

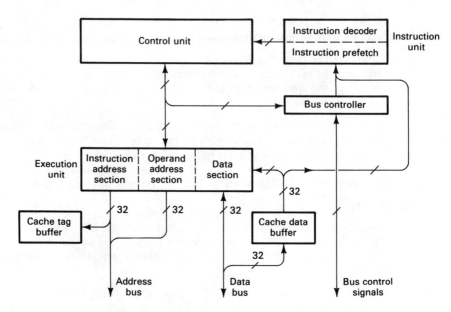

Figure 3-20. Internal organization of the 68020.

operations as dictated by the currently executed instruction. However, while they are capable of operating independently, the three sections of the execution unit are also interlinked. This allows them to perform together and thereby speed up certain operations such as multiplication.

As a whole, the execution unit can function independently of the other units. In fact, the instruction unit, the control unit, and the execution unit can be viewed as the three stages of a pipeline. While the execution unit executes instruction i, the control unit works on the generation of the appropriate control signals for instruction $i + 1$, and the instruction unit prefetches and decodes instruction $i + 2$.

The cache itself increases further the degree of overlapping. When the instruction address section of the execution unit derives a new instruction address, it takes two actions:

1. It presents the derived address to the cache tag buffer, which proceeds to search for a match to one of the stored tags.
2. It prepares for presentation of the same address to memory.

A memory access is initiated only if the tag buffer indicates a no-match condition. However, if a match is indicated, the instruction is fetched from the cache data buffer and no memory access is initiated for that instruction. The point is that while the instruction is fetched from the cache data buffer the execution unit may proceed to fetch or write an operand in memory. Notice the two paths at the output of the cache data buffer. One of them serves the flow of operand fields to the execution unit; the other serves the flow of the opcode field to the instruction unit. Aside from decoding opcode fields, the latter initiates loading of the cache with a new block of instructions from memory. It also maintains within itself an instruction queue having a capacity of three 16-bit words.

Such an extensive degree of overlapping reduces drastically the time required to fetch and execute an instruction. As a matter of fact, since the CPU may continue executing instructions one after another while performing an operand access, certain instructions may be executed in a totally transparent manner. This is equivalent to saying that certain instructions are executed in zero time. In addition to the performance improvements resulting from its organization, the 68020 permits higher clocking rates; so its overall performance is much higher when compared to that of the 68000. Another advantage of the 68020 is the support of virtual memory (page-based scheme). That is, when a bus error signals a page fault, this CPU is capable of suspending execution of an instruction until the missing page is loaded into memory from the disk (see Section 4.4 on memory management).

Organization of the cache

We now proceed to examine how the cache of the 68020 is organized. The cache of the 68020 accommodates up to 64 four-byte-long blocks of instructions at the same time (Figure 3-21). For each of the stored blocks there is one entry in the **tag buffer** and one entry in the **data buffer**, so that the tag buffer and the data buffer have 64 entries each. As in any cache, the idea is to divide the address space into blocks of consecutive addresses and bring in blocks independently of one another as they are needed. In the case of the 68020, where the address space

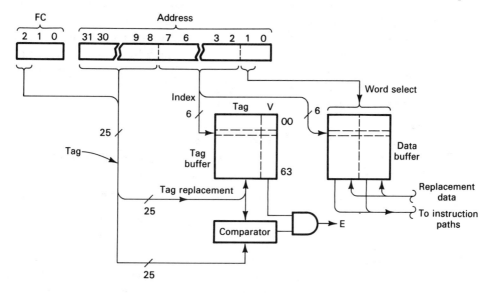

Figure 3-21.   Organization of the cache in the 68020.

is four GB, there are 1G—1×10^9—blocks. However, since there are separate address spaces for user and supervisory programs, we actually have a grand total of 2G blocks.

Which entry of the cache do we use for an arriving block? The 68020 determines this from address bits A2–A7 of the block brought in. These bits are treated as an index pointing to the cache entry we should be using for that block. Bits A8–A31, in conjunction with FC2 (which indicates either user or supervisor program space), serve as a tag of the block. This tag is stored in the location of the tag buffer pointed to by the index. The block of data is itself stored in the cache data buffer as specified by the same index. Thus, if the tag of a block is stored in entry 50 of the tag buffer, the block of data is stored in entry 50 of the cache data buffer.

Figure 3-21 illustrates how the 68020 goes about determining whether an instruction is already in the cache on the basis of the address of the instruction. First, the index is presented to both the tag buffer and the data buffer. The tag contained in the location designated by the index is then read and fed to a comparator. The second set of inputs of the comparator is fed with the tag comprised of bits A8–A31 and the associated FC2 bit. If the comparator indicates a **match** and the "valid" bit at the read location of the tag buffer is on, then E goes active, enabling the data buffer. Subsequently, the latter emits the data (from the location pointed to by the index) into the instruction paths. From there on, the data find their way to the instruction and execution units. Bit A1 indicates whether one or both words stored in that entry of the data buffer are to be read. If the comparator indicates **no-match**, the CPU proceeds to fetch the instruction from memory. Note that the **valid (V) bits** serve to indicate whether blocks contain valid information or not. For example, if (as a result of program execution) the operand field of one of the instructions of a block changes, the valid bit of that block is turned off to indicate the fact. The memory is, of course, updated accordingly.

The 68020 permits control of its cache only by the operating system. This is accomplished by means of two on-chip registers: the **cache control register** and the **cache address register**. Through control of the settings of various bit positions in the cache control register, it is possible to

1. Enable or bypass the cache (*enable* bit)
2. Clear all V bits and thereby force the CPU to refill the cache (*clear* bit)
3. Prohibit the CPU from replacing the contents of the cache (*freeze* bit)
4. Turn off the valid bit of a specific block (*clear entry* bit in conjunction with the cache address register)

One of the limitations of this caching scheme is that a new block must always be stored in the location pointed to by the index. This scheme is known as the **direct mapping approach**. More elaborate schemes permit greater flexibility by allowing a new block to occupy any one of a set of consecutive entries or even any of the entries of the entire cache. Having a choice means that it is not necessary to replace a block which may shortly be needed again by the CPU (see Problems 3-23 and 3-24). Despite the simple replacement algorithm it employs, the small block size of only four bytes, and the fact that only instructions are accommodated, the 68020 cache contributes significantly to the performance of this CPU.

We have already seen that the cache makes possible overlapping of instruction fetches and operand accesses. In general, though, the major advantage of a cache is the fact that it reduces the number of CPU accesses to memory. If an instruction is in the cache, the CPU does not perform a memory cycle; instead it fetches the instruction from the cache. Since the cache is faster, the "effective" length of a bus cycle becomes shorter. The latter can be determined from the relation

$$t_{effective} = H \, t_{cache} + (1 - H) \, t_{memory}$$

where t_{cache} and t_{memory} represent the length of a machine cycle when accessing the cache and the memory, respectively. H is the so-called **hit ratio**. It represents the probability that the new instruction we need will be found in the cache.

Example 3-12

In the case of the 68020, a cache access takes two clock cycles. A bus cycle, however, takes three clock cycles even in the case of no wait state insertion. Calculate the effective length of a memory cycle (as far as instruction fetches go), given a hit ratio of 0.9 and a clocking rate of 16.67 MHz. Then repeat your calculations assuming insertion of four wait states per memory cycle.

Solution. For the given clocking rate, a clock cycle takes 60 ns. Hence, the machine cycles corresponding to a cache access and a memory access take 120 ns and 180 ns, respectively. The effective length of a memory cycle is then $(0.9 \times 120) + (0.1 \times 180) = 126$ ns. This represents an improvement of 30 percent over the length of an actual memory cycle—that is, over 180 ns.

If we have to insert four wait states, a memory cycle is extended to $180 + (4 \times 30) = 300$ ns. The effective length of a memory cycle (as seen by the CPU) is now $(0.9 \times 120) + (0.1 \times 300) = 138$ ns, and the improvement factor is 54 percent. Observe that although an actual memory cycle was lengthened by 120 ns, the effective length was increased only by 12 ns. So the slower the memory, the greater the impact of the cache.

Since the cache decreases the number of memory cycles, it also decreases bus utilization. Consequently, the bus becomes more readily available to DMA devices (and possibly other μPs).

Example 3-13

Assume a CPU having a memory cycle time of 300 ns and an instruction processing rate of 1 MIPS. On the average, each instruction requires one bus cycle for its fetching and one bus cycle for the operand it involves. Calculate the utilization of the bus by the CPU. Suppose the CPU is equipped with an instruction cache and the associated hit ratio is 0.5. Determine the impact on bus utilization.

Solution. The given instruction rate implies that each instruction takes (on the average) 1000 ns (to fetch and execute). During this time the CPU performs two memory cycles: one to fetch the instruction itself and one to fetch or store the operand associated with the instruction. Therefore, over a period of 1000 ns the CPU utilizes the bus for 600 ns (on the average). In other words bus utilization amounts to 60 percent.

As a result of the cache, bus utilization decreases to $(150 + 300) / 1000 = 0.45$, or 45 percent. This in turn reduces the waiting time for bus requesters (such as DMA devices and other μPs).

Architecture

The 68020 has the same architecture as the 68000. Such is generally the case with new CPUs. Their manufacturers preserve the architecture of older family members to allow use of software developed by users for older CPUs. In fact, the 68020 maintains full object code compatibility with other members of the 68000 family of CPUs. At the same time, it provides certain architectural extensions for performance enhancement, which we now discuss.

Except for a few special-purpose registers, the register model of the 68020 remains the same as that of the 68000. Such special-purpose registers are the vector base register and the registers associated with the cache.

While the 68020 utilizes all addressing modes we have seen in the 68000, it also provides other modes to facilitate the use of HLLs. Remember that a flexible set of addressing modes is key to expressing easily the structures associated with HLLs. Besides, they allow compilers to produce more efficient object code. In the 68020, indexed addressing modes are expanded to permit displacements of up to 32 bits. They also permit **index scaling** (by 2, 4, or 8) and variants such as memory indirection, which refers to the addition of the contents of a base address register to one of the A registers for derivation of an indirect address. The CPU then fetches a long word from this address and uses it for determination of the effective address.

The 68020 provides all of the instructions of the 68000 and more. First, all instructions are extended to permit handling of 32-bit operands. For example, the multiply and divide instructions can operate on 32-bit operands too. In addition, instructions can operate on a number of new data types, such as 64-bit operands and packed BCD numbers (that is, two BCD numbers per byte).

Some new types of instructions are provided. Among them is a set of instructions permitting manipulation of variable-width bit fields up to 32 bits long. Such bit fields need not be aligned and may span across as many as five byte locations in memory. Instructions of this class allow setting/resetting, scanning, extraction, and complementing of specified bits within a bit field, and they become important in applications involving serially packed information—that is, serial communications and graphics.

A second class of instructions used by the 68020 provides for coprocessor support. An example is the Motorola MC68881 floating point coprocessor.

Other instructions of the 68020 are the CALLM (call module) and RTM (return from module) instructions, both of which support modular programming. There is also the BKPT (breakpoint) instruction for debugging purposes.

3.4.2 Intel 80386

Our second 32-bit μP example is the Intel 80386, a descendant of the 8086 16-bit μP we discussed earlier (see Figure 3-1). Its capabilities are a superset of those of the 8086 and other members of the same family, such as the 8088 and the 80286. At the same time the 80386 preserves the basic architectural characteristics of the previous 8086 family members to achieve object code compatibility with them.

Unlike the 68020, the 80386 does not provide an on-chip cache. Its bus cycle, however, is only two clock periods long, making possible implementation of a cache off-chip. On the other hand, the 80386 provides on-chip extensive memory management capabilities. During our discussion of the 80386 we will have the chance to see

1. Another approach to dynamic bus sizing for support of interfaces to mixed-size ports
2. What the pipelined address mode is about
3. Testability and other features facilitating system debugging

External Interface

Unlike the 8086, the 80386 does not multiplex data and address signals on the same lines. There are 32 lines for data and a separate set of lines for address signals. The 32-bit-wide address bus permits the 80386 to address directly up to 4 GB (2^{32}) of memory. Despite its complexity (which is equivalent to 275,000 transistors) the 80386 is implemented on a single chip. The latter comes in a 132-pin PGA package.

Notice that only address signals $A2$ to $A31$ are actually carried over the address bus (Figure 3-22). The two least significant address bits (A0 and A1) are decoded to generate four **byte enable** signals ($BE0^* - BE3^*$). These signals indicate which of the four bytes of a 32-bit word are involved in the current bus cycle. $BE0^*$ corresponds to the lowest byte—that is, data bits $D0-D7$. $BE1^*$ corresponds to the next higher byte (data bits $D8-D15$), and so on. This approach eliminates the need for external byte decode circuits.

Some of the remaining external interface lines of the 80386 are the same as those of the 8086. Others—whose full name appears within the box of Figure 3-22—differ from the 8086. There are also three special-purpose lines intended for interfacing to a numeric coprocessor (bottom right). We start with the data transfer control group of interface lines.

The 80386 employs a single line (W/R^*) to differentiate between read and

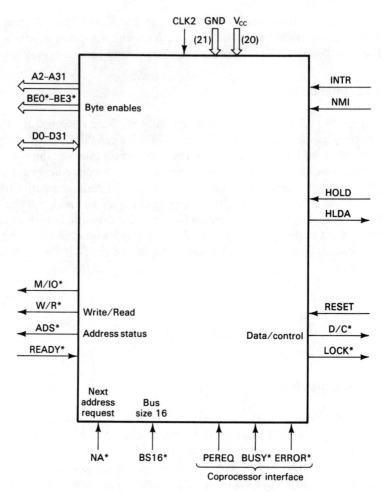

Figure 3-22. External interface lines of the 80386.

write bus cycles.   This is unlike the 8086 which has an RD^* line and a WR^* line.
On the other hand, the function of the ADS^* (address status) line is similar to that
of the ALE line of the 8086.   That is, it indicates that a valid address and valid
bus cycle definition signals (such as M/IO^* and W/R^*) are presented over the bus.

Note the lack of an interrupt acknowledge line.   Instead, such and other bus
cycles not involving data transfers are indicated by means of the D/C^* (data/control)
line.   When at a high this line indicates that the current bus cycle involves a data
transfer.   If at a low it may indicate an interrupt acknowledge cycle, an instruction
fetch, a **Halt Indication** bus cycle, or a **Shutdown Indication** bus cycle.   The differentiation is made by decoding the M/IO^*, W/R^*, and $BE0^*-BE3^*$ lines.   A
Halt Indication bus cycle is the result of execution of a "halt" instruction.   It is

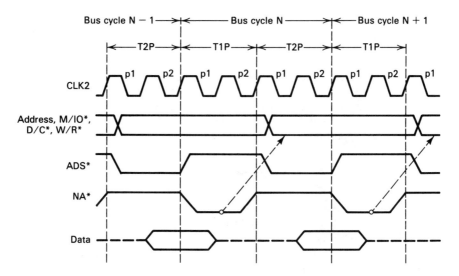

Figure 3-23. Read bus cycle timing relationships of the 80386 in pipelined address mode.

employed by the 80386 as a means of signaling its entry into the halt state. A Shutdown Indication bus cycle signals entry of the CPU into the shutdown state. The 80386 is driven to such a state under certain fault conditions. Exit from the shutdown state is accomplished by activating either *RESET* or *NMI*.

The *BS16** (bus size 16) line allows direct connection of the 80386 to 16-bit data buses. When *BS16** is at a low, the current bus cycle uses only the 16 low-order data lines. Otherwise it may use part or all of the 32 data lines (depending on the state of the byte enable signals). This feature makes possible "sizing" of the data bus on a cycle by cycle basis (dynamic bus sizing), so the 80386 can accommodate at the same time both 16- and 32-bit-wide ports in a way transparent to the software. The *BS16** input may be controlled through address decoding or by the device connecting to the port.

Normally a read or write bus cycle of the 80386 takes only two clock periods. The CPU divides by two the frequency of the externally supplied clock signal (*CLK2*) to generate the internal clock. In fact, a period of the internal clock is partitioned into two phases (*p1* and *p2*). Each phase corresponds to one period of *CLK2* (see Figure 3-23).

Example 3-14

Assume you operate a particular version of the 80386 at a clocking rate of 16 MHz. Determine the duration of each phase and the frequency of the required *CLK2* signal.

Solution. The frequency of CLK2 must be twice the operating clocking rate (that is, the internal clock frequency). So *CLK2* must have a frequency of $2 \times 16 = 32$ MHz. Each phase of the internal clock has a duration of $1/32$ μs. That is about 31 ns.

Example 3-15

Calculate the maximum bus bandwidth of an 80386 μP operating at a clocking frequency of 16 MHz.

Solution. The normal duration of a read or write bus cycle equals two periods of the internal clock. Hence, if we run bus cycles back to back, the CPU can perform 8,000,000 bus cycles per second. Assuming each bus cycle involves a 32-bit word, we would be able to transfer a total of $4 \times 8 \times 10^6$ bytes per second. Thus the CPU can support a maximum data transfer rate of up to 32 MB/s.

Pipelined address mode

The short length of a normal bus cycle is of no benefit if memory (and I/O) cannot keep up with the speed of the CPU. A special mode of operation of the 80386 can be very helpful in this regard. It is called the **pipelined address mode**. This is where the role of the NA^* (next address request) interface line comes into play.

Figure 3-23 depicts the read bus cycle timing relationships when operating in pipelined address mode. They are similar to those of an ordinary bus cycle except that the CPU presents the address of the next bus cycle (and activates ADS^*) during the second half of the current bus cycle. For example, observe that the CPU presents the address of cycle $N + 1$ before the data for cycle N become available. Thus bus cycle $N + 1$ is starting essentially at the beginning of the second clock cycle (state $T2P$) of bus cycle N. This kind of overlapping increases the time allowance given to memory by an extra clock cycle without having to lengthen the bus cycle itself. The 80386 can be switched to the pipelined address mode of operation dynamically—that is, on a bus cycle by bus cycle basis. To do so, we activate (externally) the NA^* line during the first half of the current bus cycle.

Early availability of the address of a forthcoming bus cycle means that the address presented to memory (or I/O) when that cycle starts is already stable. Besides, the memory may decode this address while the current cycle is still in progress to economize additional time. Consequently, after completion of the access required by the current bus cycle, the memory could start another access immediately.

Example 3-16

Consider an 80386 μP operated in the ordinary (nonpipelined) address mode at a clocking rate of 16 MHz. Assume that ADS^* and address signals become valid 40 ns (at maximum) after the beginning of a bus cycle. In the case of a read bus cycle, data must be available no later than 10 ns before the end of the bus cycle. How fast should the memory be in order to avoid wait state insertion?

Solution. At the given clocking rate a bus cycle normally takes 125 ns. Let us take as a reference the beginning of a bus cycle—that is, the leading edge of $p1$ of state $T1$. The memory is presented with a stable address at time 40 ns (at the latest).

Read data must be provided to the CPU by time $125 - 10 = 115$ ns (at the latest). Thus, the memory must be capable of providing data within $115 - 40 = 75$ ns following presentation of a stable address by the CPU.

Example 3-17

The 80386 finds out if memory (or I/O) is to provide read data on time by sampling the $READY^*$ line shortly before the end of state $T2$. When $READY^*$ is not asserted, the CPU repeats state $T2$ and tries again shortly before the end of the inserted $T2$ state. If this time $READY^*$ is at a low, the CPU proceeds to read the data and terminates the bus cycle. If $READY^*$ is still inactive, the CPU inserts another extra $T2$ state, and so on. Assume the memory of the system in the previous example falls short of meeting the speed requirement by 35 ns. How many wait states would the CPU have to insert per bus cycle?

What if we operate the CPU in pipelined address mode?

Solution. Each wait state—that is, each of the extraneous $T2$ states—provides an extra time allowance of $125/2 = 62.5$ ns. Therefore, one wait state will be more than adequate.

When operating in the pipelined address mode we save at a minimum the time required for stabilization of the address signals—that is, 40 ns. The latter exceeds the shortfall of 35 ns and thus no wait state insertion becomes necessary.

Internal Organization

The internal organization of the 80386 is different and far more complex than that of the 8086. Besides its 32-bit-wide internal buses and functional units, the 80386:

1. Is organized into an eight-stage pipeline achieving a higher degree of overlapping during instruction processing
2. Implements on-chip sophisticated memory management and protection capabilities (see Section 4.4)
3. Is equipped with **self-test** and other features facilitating system debugging

Figure 3-24 illustrates the five major functional units of the 80386. The bus unit receives and prioritizes bus requests from the other functional units. It then proceeds to perform the requested bus transactions on their behalf. In the pipelined address mode, the bus unit presents the address of the next bus cycle before completion of the current one.

The prefetch unit maintains a queue of prefetched instructions in a 16-byte buffer. When there is adequate space in the latter, the prefetch unit requests the bus unit to fetch the next 32-bit word from the instruction stream. However, such requests are given lower priority than those of other functional units, such as those associated with the fetching or storing of an operand during the execution of an instruction.

The decode unit prepares instructions for processing by the execution unit.

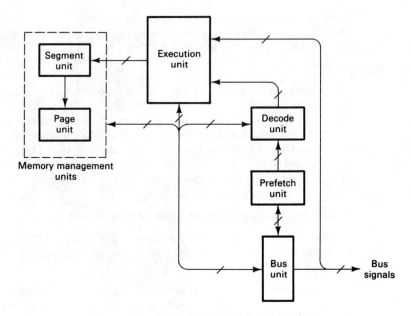

Figure 3-24. Internal organization of the 80386.

It takes one instruction at a time from the prefetched instruction queue and decodes it fully, deriving the starting address of the microcode implementing the instruction, operand addresses, and so on.   (Note that the control unit of the 80386 is micro-coded.)   All this information is stored as a single "word" in a "decoded instruction queue."   The latter is three words deep, so that it can accommodate up to three fully decoded instructions.

Since each instruction is already fully decoded, the execution unit, including an ALU and a barrel shifter, can proceed directly into instruction execution.   The execution unit itself is organized into three subunits such that some of the execution tasks can overlap.   The segment and page units are for memory management.

The three subunits of the execution unit, in conjunction with the five other units, form an eight-stage pipeline for instruction processing.   (Remember it is because of the pipelined organization that the CPU knows in advance the address of the next bus cycle prior to the completion of the current one.)   The characteristics of the 80386 we have just discussed—its wider data bus, higher clocking rate, shorter bus cycle, eight-stage pipeline, and so on—permit an instruction processing rate much higher than that of the 8086.

Example 3-18

Consider an 80386-based system where the CPU is operated at a clocking rate of 16 MHz.   In a particular application it is found that each instruction takes (on the average) about 4.4 clock cycles.   Determine the achieved instruction processing rate in MIPS.

Solution.   Since the (internal) clocking rate is 16×10^6 the average instruction processing rate is $(16/4.4) \times 10^6 = 3.6 \times 10^6$ instructions/second—that is 3.6 MIPS.

Testability

The 80386 is equipped with test circuits allowing self-test of

1. All large PLAs (programmable logic arrays) employed in its implementation
2. The control ROM and certain other parts of the execution unit

In addition the CPU includes instructions, microcode, and test circuits for testing of a special (on-chip) buffer. This buffer is used by the memory management units in the translation of virtual addresses into physical addresses (see Section 4.4).

Self-test is activated when the following two conditions are satisfied:

- The *BUSY** input of the CPU is held at a low.
- The *RESET* input of the CPU goes from a high to a low.

The duration of the self-test depends on the clocking rate (why?). For example, if the CPU is operated at 16 MHz, self-test takes about 30 ms. The AX and DX CPU registers reflect the results of the self-test after its completion. If the contents of these registers are zero, the CPU passed the test successfully. If nonzero, then the CPU is faulty. The all-zeros bit pattern (indicating successful completion of the self-test) is also referred to as the **self-test signature** of the 80386. Generally such "signatures" are derived by means of techniques similar to those employed for CRC generation (see Section 6.5). They serve to detect errors in a data block and thereby determine if a device (or system) malfunctions. Furthermore, it is possible to localize the faulty part of a system (**signature analysis**).

Architecture

The register model of the 80386 is somewhat similar to the register model of the 8088 (see Figure 3-6). However, the registers of the 80386 are 32 bits wide. Also, the 80386 has a number of additional registers, among them six **debug registers** (DR0–DR3, DR6, and DR7). These registers provide the means for setting up to four **code** or **data breakpoints** and thereby facilitating system debugging. For example, assume we find out (while debugging new software) that the contents of a particular memory location are modified due to some kind of error. The debug registers allow us to set up the system so that a trap occurs the moment the CPU attempts to write data into that location. This may lead us to the cause of the problem.

Registers DR0–DR3 store the desired breakpoint addresses—that is, the addresses of those locations containing instructions or data we are interested in. DR6 serves as a breakpoint status register. By setting a particular bit, it indicates, for instance, that the breakpoint associated with DR0 has occurred. DR7 plays the role of a breakpoint control register. It specifies conditions such as:

- For what type of memory access do we want the breakpoint to occur? For example, only when a data write access is attempted—or for both read and write accesses to the specified location?
- How do we want to handle the occurrence of a breakpoint? Is it to generate a trap or do we simply want the event recorded in the breakpoint status register?

The 80386 supports the addressing modes we have seen for the 8088 plus more. Effective addresses are generally calculated from the expression

$$[\text{Base Reg}] + [\text{Index Reg}] \times (\text{Scale}) + \text{Displacement}$$

The first term represents the contents of a base register. The second term represents the contents of an index register scaled by a factor of 1, 2, 4, or 8. Any of the general-purpose registers of the CPU can serve as a base register or as an index register. The third term represents an immediate value (or displacement) and is contained in the instruction itself. The addressing modes we have seen for the 8088 are derivatives of the above expression. Beyond those, however, we see that the 80386 supports index scaling and based indexed mode with displacement.

Unlike the 8088 and the 8086, the 80386 has a set of bit manipulation instructions. Generally instructions permit specifying any one of the general-purpose CPU registers. Besides, operands may be eight, 16, or 32 bits long, or they may even consist of bit strings.

Modes of operation

The 80386 can operate in either one of two modes:

1. A Real (Address) Mode: In this mode the 80386 operates as if it were a very fast 8086.
2. A Protected (Virtual Address) Mode: This mode makes available the extensive memory management and protection capabilities of the 80386.

3.5 CPU SUPPORT COMPONENTS

Before concluding this chapter we will examine the additional components we need in the design of an operational processor. These "auxiliary" components fall into two categories:

1. Components required for clock generation.
2. Interface circuits placed between the CPU and memory or I/O.

3.5.1 Clock Components

The circuitry needed for the clock depends on how much is already included on the CPU chip. Some μPs include a clock generator on-chip. In this case only discrete components need be added externally for selection of the desired frequency. Information on how the discrete components interconnect, and the range of their values, is provided by the μP manufacturer. Other μPs require an external clock generator to supply the precise clock waveforms specified by the CPU manufacturer.

In either case we need a crystal, especially when the clock is used to time critical software tasks. Otherwise, the clock frequency may vary widely within the operational range of supply voltage and temperature. Besides, it would drift with time as a result of gradual changes in component values.

First we discuss crystals. Then we consider external clock generators, including an example of such a device.

Crystals

Crystals capitalize on the piezoelectric phenomenon—that is, on the fact that application of mechanical stress on a quartz crystal generates a voltage at its terminals (and vice versa). Generally the frequency of a crystal depends on the way it is "cut" and its thickness.

Figure 3-25(a) depicts the equivalent electric circuit for a crystal. The values of L, C, and R relate to the properties of the crystal. C_s represents the shunt capacitance contributed by its package—that is, the crystal holder and its leads. Manufacturers specify their crystals as being either **series resonant** or **parallel resonant**. The frequency of a series-resonant crystal is determined from the values of L and C. On the other hand, parallel-resonant crystals are sensitive to the input capacitance of the circuit to which they connect (see Problem 3-20).

The series resistance of a crystal determines what driving capability we need from the oscillator circuit to which it is connected. Other parameters of importance are the frequency tolerance and the frequency stability (in terms of time and temperature). In most μP applications the requirements placed upon such parameters are comparatively modest. For example, tolerances of 0.002 percent to 0.005 percent are common in crystals. Yet, in a μC system, a tolerance of 0.01 percent is usually satisfactory. Given that the cost of a crystal depends on its frequency tolerance and stability, such parameters should not be needlessly overspecified. Note, though, that frequency stability may be a problem if the oscillator delivers to the crystal more power than it can dissipate.

Figure 3-25(b) shows an arrangement used very often in μPs having on-chip

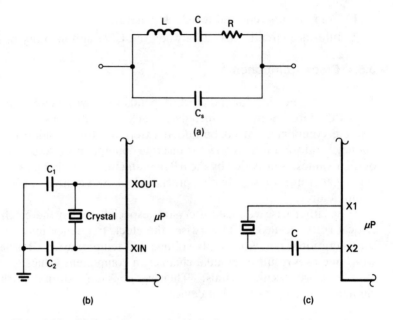

Figure 3-25. (a) Equivalent electric circuit of a quartz crystal. (b) Use of a crystal for control of the frequency of the on-chip oscillator of a μP. (c) Use of a series capacitor to de-bias the crystal.

clock oscillators. Typically, each capacitor is 20 pF. They ensure that the crystal will oscillate at the appropriate frequency when the power goes on. Figure 3-25(c) shows another arrangement employing a series capacitor which prevents DC biasing of the crystal from the internal circuits. It also serves for fine tuning of the oscillator frequency.

Extra care should be exercised for all clock components in the layout of the printed board. In order to minimize stray capacitances, the crystal (and other discrete components) should be placed as close to the respective CPU pins as possible. Connections to the ground should be made very near the ground pin of the CPU. This reduces noise effects on the clock oscillator. For the same reason, coupling with other signal lines must be avoided. When possible, surround the crystal and associated discrete components with a ground island extending under the crystal holder.

Often, μP manufacturers suggest specific crystals for their μPs. Such information should be taken into consideration along with any other information they provide about clock requirements.

External Clock Generation

When the CPU is not equipped (on-chip) with an oscillator, the clock has to be generated externally.

A simple solution consists of an SSI-based design where a few inverters and discrete components are interconnected to function as an oscillator whose output is then fed to the CPU. This is done through a buffer providing the required drive at the specified voltage levels. Such a solution is acceptable in very few applications, however. The problem is that over the operational range of the supply voltage and temperature, the clock frequency may vary as much as several percentage points. The next step is to use a crystal. Frequency variations are now reduced by two or more orders of magnitude.

However, despite improving frequency stability, this solution may still be inappropriate for most CPUs because of the tight timing requirements specified by their manufacturers. Meeting such requirements necessitates a not so trivial solution in terms of development and number of components so that there is motivation to use a commercially available clock oscillator.

Clock oscillators come in single DIP packages. They may or may not include a crystal. For example, the Motorola MC6870 clock oscillator includes on-chip a crystal. On the other hand, the Intel 8284 clock generator requires adding a crystal externally; however, it does include timing logic for the CPU *RESET* and *READY* inputs. Clock oscillators are also available from independent manufacturers offering

- Symmetrical square wave oscillators for general use
- Oscillators for specific μPs
- High-stability oscillator modules for special applications

A μP may permit clocking by an external source, even when equipped with an on-chip oscillator, as is illustrated in Figure 3-26(a). Here the μP pictured includes on-chip an oscillator. All we need is a crystal connected to the *XIN*, *XOUT* terminals of the CPU. However, we also have the option to use a more accurate external oscillator. In this mode, the on-chip oscillator is simply bypassed. Figure 3-26(b) shows the clocking arrangement for the 8088 and 8086 CPUs. This one is typical of μPs which are not equipped with on-chip clock oscillators.

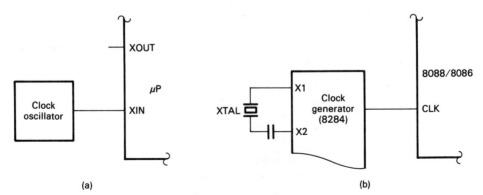

(a)   (b)

Figure 3-26. Examples of off-chip clock configurations. (a) A μP fed from an external clock oscillator. (b) The 8088/8086 fed from the 8284 crystal-controlled clock generator.

Example of a Clock Generator

As an example of a clock generator we describe the Intel 8284. It is intended for the 8088 and 8086 CPUs. First we examine the clock waveform requirements of these two CPUs. Observe from Figure 3-27(a) that the required duty cycle is about 33 percent. In the 8088/8086 the minimum allowable clock frequency is 2 MHz. The maximum allowable clock frequency depends on the particular version of the device. For example, the 8086-4 permits a maximum clock frequency of 4 MHz, while the 8086-2 permits 8 MHz. Naturally, except for certain timing parameters, these two versions are identical. Figure 3-27(a) indicates the ranges for high and low voltage levels as well. Note that when the clock is at a high, the clock input must be at least 3.9 V. Rise and fall times are defined between the 1 V and 3.5 V points. They are required to be less than 10 ns.

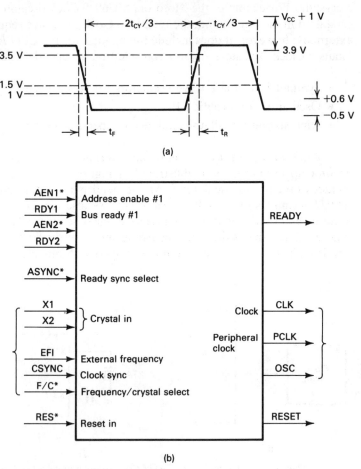

Figure 3-27. (a) Clock waveform of the 8088 and 8086. (b) External interface lines of the 8284 clock generator.

All these requirements are met by the 8284 clock generator. Its external interface lines are shown in Figure 3-27(b). Notice that the device involves more signals than one would expect for a clock generator. This is typical of clock generators designed by μP manufacturers. The objectives are to make the device more versatile for diverse applications and also to add functions which would otherwise necessitate additional SSI components for their implementation. Only the lines indicated by brackets in Figure 3-27(b) have direct association with the clock oscillator. The remaining lines concern auxiliary logic functions.

The 8284 has two modes of operation: a **crystal mode** and an **external frequency mode**. When line *F/C** (frequency/crystal select) is strapped high, the clock is generated from an external source feeding the *EFI* (external frequency input) line. If *F/C** is strapped low, the clock is generated by the internal oscillator of the 8284. This local oscillator is controlled by a series-resonant crystal connecting to the *X*1, *X*2 terminals of the 8284.

In either mode the 8284 divides the frequency by three to produce the frequency supplied to the CPU over the *CLK* output line. Thus, if our CPU is an 8086-2 and we decide to clock it at its specified maximum of 8 MHz, we must use a 24 MHz crystal or an external 24 MHz signal. At such high frequencies it is critical to minimize stray capacitances. As you may suspect, the divide-by-three approach facilitates achieving the objective of a 33 percent duty cycle. The auxiliary *PCLK* (peripheral clock) output has a 50 percent duty cycle and a frequency equal to one half the frequency of the *CLK* output. The *OSC* (oscillator) line makes available the output of the internal oscillator in crystal mode. Finally, the *CSYNC* (clock synchronization) input serves applications where multiple 8284s are employed.

All other lines serve auxiliary logic functions. For example, the two sets of *AEN** (address enable) and *RDY* (ready) inputs permit activation of the CPU *READY* line from two different sources. Each *AEN** signal is simply gating its corresponding *RDY* signal. The 8284 includes circuitry for synchronization of the *RDY* input signals, so that setup and hold time requirements at the *READY* input of the CPU are met. *ASYNC** allows the choice of synchronizing on a rising or on a falling clock edge. *RES** (reset) is used to generate the *RESET* signal for the CPU and other system components. The 8284 synchronizes generation of the *RESET* output on the next falling edge of *CLK*. An external RC network determines the duration of the *RESET* pulse.

Figure 3-28 pictures a typical configuration of the 8284. The *F/C** input is strapped to ground, placing the device in the crystal mode of operation. Input *AEN1** is grounded, unconditionally enabling the *RDY1* input line.

3.5.2 Bus Interface Circuits

The need for bus interface circuits in microcomputer design stems from three reasons.

1. *Limited Driving Ability of the CPU:* In the course of examining the electrical

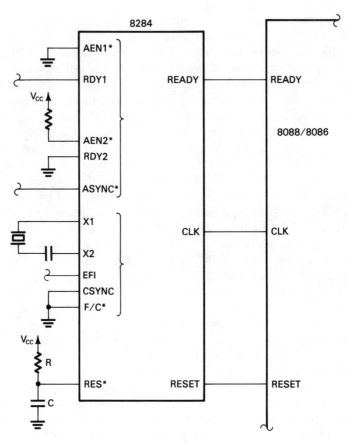

Figure 3-28. Typical interconnection diagram of the 8284 clock generator.

characteristics of μPs, we have seen that their driving capabilities are generally limited. The large capacitance presented to the CPU over its bus poses a particular problem. This capacitance is contributed by the inputs of the various (memory and I/O related) components attached to the bus and the distributed capacitance of the bus lines themselves which often must be extended beyond the CPU board.

2. *Need for Isolation of Signal Paths:* When the CPU drives the bus, other parts of the μC system must be prevented from causing any interference. The same applies when another part of the system—for instance, an I/O device—drives the bus. Now the CPU must be prevented from presenting to the bus any signals. For example, when a DMA device addresses the memory, the address lines of the CPU must be isolated from the memory address inputs and vice versa.

3. *Address/Data Demultiplexing:* Many CPUs employ a multiplexed address/

data bus. When such is the case, we have to use external circuits to separate the address signals from the data signals.

These needs are satisfied by commercially available buffer and latch circuits. Bus buffers are classified into:

1. Unidirectional buffers or simply **buffers**. As their name implies, such circuits buffer signals only in one direction.
2. Bidirectional buffers or **transceivers** (transmitters–receivers). These buffer signals in both directions.

Latches are used for address/data demultiplexing. The idea is to store the address during the early part of a bus cycle. Thereafter, the latched address is presented to memory and I/O for the entire duration of the cycle.

Bus interface circuits are designed to handle the DC and capacitive loads encountered in μC systems. Most are 74LS series devices with a typical current sinking ability of 24 mA and a current sourcing ability of around 12 mA. Some are available in the 74S series for applications having higher drive and speed requirements. CMOS versions are also available for low-power consumption designs. For each type of interface circuit, the designer often has the choice of selecting either an inverting or a noninverting device.

Example 3-19

The large capacitive loads presented to bus interface circuits result in large transient currents. Such current spikes in turn may cause large voltage spikes on V_{cc}. Unless filtered, this "noise" propagates to other circuits and may cause false transitions. Thus, it is advisable to connect between the V_{cc} pin of a bus driver and ground a decoupling capacitor. The latter is generally a ceramic disk one and has (typically) a value of 0.1 μF.

In order to appreciate the magnitude of such transient currents, consider an octal bus buffer having a composite dynamic load of 250 pF per output line. Calculate the transient current when all outputs switch at the same time. Assume that rise and fall times are about 25 ns.

Solution. Let us assume that all eight lines switch simultaneously from a low to a high state. The transient current is the result of the currents charging the capacitances seen by all eight output lines. Charging currents can be determined from the relation $i = C \, (dV/dt)$. Rise and fall times are usually defined between the 10 percent and 90 percent of the amplitude of a transition. For simplicity we will assume that they correspond to 0.5 V and 2.5 V, respectively, and also that the transition from the 10 percent to the 90 percent point is linear so that dV/dt is constant. Using the above relation we have for the total transient current $I = 8 \times (250 \times 10^{-12}) \times [(2.5 - 0.5)/(25 \times 10^{-9})]$, or $I = 160$ mA!

Regardless of the logic family they belong to, bus interface circuits are usually octal (that is, a circuit can handle eight bus lines). They also have tri-state outputs, which is a key to achieving isolation between portions of a system. By driving the outputs of a circuit to a high impedance state, we virtually "disconnect" the circuit from the bus so that only a selected source will drive the bus at any particular time. Each "disconnected" circuit does, of course, contribute some small load to the bus because of leakage currents. However, this may be of concern only when the number of circuits attached to the bus becomes large.

Another common feature of bus interface circuits is their hysteresis characteristics. This means that input switching thresholds for high-to-low and low-to-high transitions are different, at least for control lines. Typically, the introduced hysteresis improves noise rejection by about 0.4 V. This reduces the potential for signal oscillations due to noisy inputs at the output lines. Remember that conventional inputs—that is, those without built-in hysteresis—have about the same threshold regardless of the direction of the transition. Next we examine examples of bus interface circuits.

Bus Buffers

An example of a bus buffer is the 74LS244 shown in Figure 3-29. This device is split into two quad groups having separate output enable lines ($OE1^*$, $OE2^*$). It is a noninverting circuit whose logic symbol is shown in Figure 3-29(b).

Figure 3-29(c) demonstrates its use in the buffering of the address bus of a μP, for instance, a 68000 whose data and address lines are not multiplexed. Notice that all output enable lines of the buffers are grounded, so the buffered address bus lines reflect the state of the CPU address lines on a continuous basis. What if other devices (such as I/O ones) can also drive the buffered address bus? It is clear that in this case the output enable lines must be controlled on a dynamic basis. For example, in the case of a 68000, one might invert the bus grant acknowledge ($BGACK^*$) signal and use it for disabling of the address buffers.

Bus Transceivers

Bus buffers are appropriate for the buffering of address (and sometimes control) lines because of their unidirectional nature. They are not suitable for the buffering of data buses, however, since the latter are usually bidirectional. Data buses are buffered with transceivers which permit two-way communication. Figure 3-30(a) shows the logic diagram of an octal transceiver—the 74LS245. As seen, internally there is a separate buffer for each direction (per line). However, because they are tri-state, the two opposite direction circuits can be connected together.

A transceiver has two types of control lines—one for directional control and one for output enabling. In the 74LS245, the former is accomplished through the DIR (direction) input. Observe that when DIR is at a low, only the B side outputs are enabled. Hence data flow is from A to B. When DIR is at a high, only the A side outputs are enabled and thus data flow from B to A. In both cases the

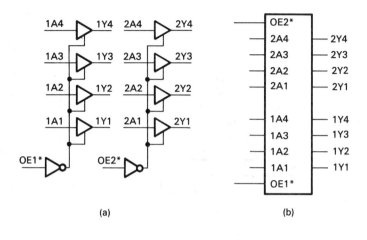

(a)   (b)

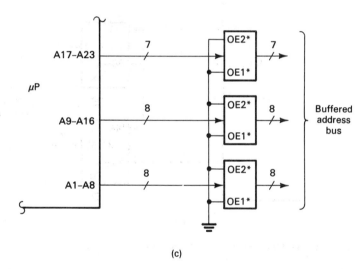

(c)

Figure 3-29.   74LS244 octal bus buffer.   (a) Logic diagram.   (b) Logic symbol.
(c) Application example.

enable (EN^*) input must be active.   If not, both sides remain in a high impedance
state.

Figure 3-30(c) shows two octal transceivers buffering the data bus of a 16-bit
μP.   The *DIR* control lines of both transceivers are driven by the R/W^* line of
the CPU.   Thus, during a write cycle (when R/W^* is at a low) data will flow from
the CPU toward memory and I/O devices.   During a read cycle data will flow in
the opposite direction.   In this example, the grounding of the enable lines implies
that there are no DMA devices.   Otherwise the enable lines would have to be
deactivated whenever such a device performs a bus cycle.

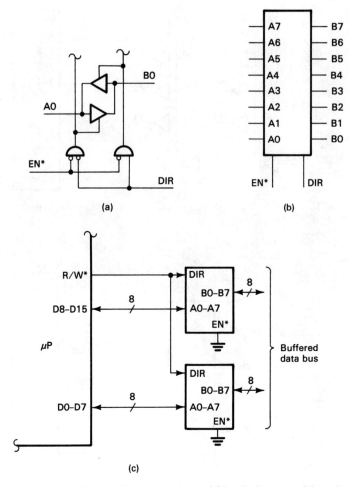

Figure 3-30. 74LS245 octal bus transceiver. (a) Logic diagram. (b) Logic symbol. (c) Application example.

The 74LS245 happens to have the same driving capability in both directions, but this is not always the case. When employing a nonsymmetrical transceiver, we normally connect the CPU to the lower drive side because the CPU side usually represents a light load. In contrast, the buffered data bus side (to which memory and I/O circuits attach) sees a much higher composite load.

Latches

If the CPU has a multiplexed address/data bus, we need latching circuits. This is necessary because the address is presented by the CPU only during the early part of a bus cycle. Leaving it up to memory and I/O to do address latching individually,

would be less economical.   Besides, we would normally have to buffer the address
lines anyway.   The latches employed in μC design combine storage and buffering
in the same circuit.   To store the address we use the address strobe generated by
the CPU.

Figure 3-31(a) illustrates the logic diagram of an octal "transparent" latch—
the 74LS373.   It has a separate D type flip-flop and tri-state buffer for each line.
On the other hand, the latch enable (*LE*) and output enable (*OE**) control lines
are common to all eight sections of the latch.   The term *transparent* refers to the
fact that as long as *LE* remains high, the output lines reflect the state of the input
ones.   Latching takes place upon *LE* going low.

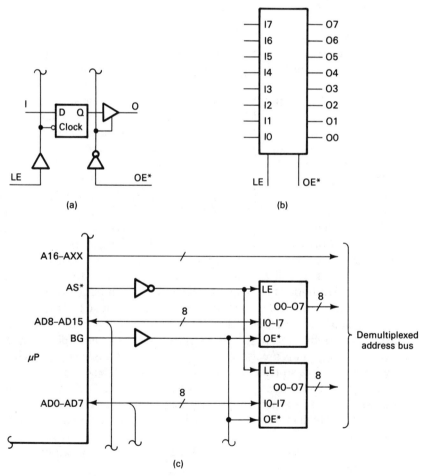

Figure 3-31.   74LS373 octal transparent latch.   (a) Logic diagram.   (b) Logic
symbol.   (c) Application example.

A typical application of an octal latch is shown in Figure 3-31(c). Notice that only the lower 16 address bits need be latched. Because higher-order address lines are dedicated to carrying address signals exclusively, they do not require latching—but may require buffering. If the system includes DMA devices, we must disable the latches while a DMA device has bus mastership. This can be accomplished with one of the signals generated when the CPU relinquishes bus mastership. In Figure 3-31(c) we assume that the μP generates a bus grant (*BG*) signal similar to the one of our hypothetical CPU. High-order address lines would also have to be buffered (for isolation purposes) during DMA bus cycles.

3.6 DESIGN EXAMPLE

In this chapter we have discussed several CPUs and the support components we need for a μP. We will conclude the chapter with a design example which is illustrated through the simplified schematic shown in Figure 3-32. The CPU is an 8088.

The *MN/MX** pin of the 8088 is connected to a permanent high which places the CPU in the so-called minimum mode of operation. Hence all signal names seen in Figure 3-32 are those corresponding to the minimum mode. Unused output lines are shown disconnected. However, unused input lines are either grounded or connecting to a permanent high.

The clock is supplied by an 8284 clock generator which is compatible with the 8088. In addition to the *CLK* input, the 8284 drives the *RESET* and *READY* inputs of the CPU. Here the RC network required for generation of the reset pulse is connected to the 8284—not to the CPU. In this example we assume no wait state insertion; hence there is no wait state generation logic. Instead, *AEN1** and *RDY1* are connected to permanent active levels securing the *READY* output to the CPU always at a high. The crystal connecting to the X1, X2 terminals of the 8284 determines the frequency of the 8284 (on-chip) oscillator.

In this example we assume a total memory capacity of no more than 64 KB. Consequently we need only the 16 low-order address bits. The eight least significant address bits (A0–A7) are extracted from the multiplexed address/data bus *AD0–AD7*. This is precisely the purpose of the 74LS373 octal latch. It is enabled by *ALE* and thus stores the address carried on the *AD0–AD7* bus lines during the early part of a bus cycle. The upper address bits (A8–A15) are provided directly by the CPU on its synonymous set of address lines. No buffers are employed for these lines, which implies that the load presented by the memory devices is relatively small.

We will come back to this design example in Chapter 4 after discussing memories.

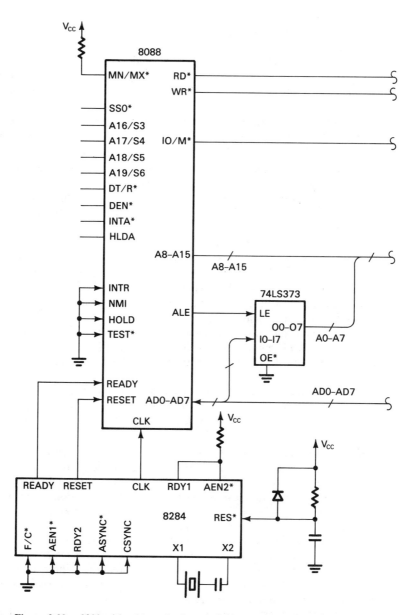

Figure 3-32. 8088 with address latch and clock generator (minimum mode configuration).

PROBLEMS

3-1. Timing. Suppose you have in the laboratory an operational prototype of an 8088-based μC. What will happen if, while the CPU executes an instruction, one of the following occurs:
  (a) The *READY* line shorts to the ground.
  (b) The connection between the *READY* pin and the external circuits breaks.
  (c) The connection between the *ALE* pin and the external circuits shorts or breaks.
  (d) The *IO/M** line shorts to the ground.

3-2. Wait State Generation. Consider the wait state generation approach pictured in Figure 2-25(b). Show how you would use such a circuit to generate wait states for an 8088 or an 8086. Indicate what CPU signals feed the shift register.

3-3. Wait State Insertion. In the course of designing an 8088-based μC we find out that we have to insert two wait states in each bus cycle.
  (a) Redraw the timing diagram of Figure 3-3 to reflect the insertion of two wait states (disregard signals *DT/R** and *DEN** but include *READY*).
  (b) Quantify the impact of the wait state insertion on the duration of a read bus cycle in terms of percent increase.
  (c) Naturally, longer bus cycles mean longer instruction cycles. However (in the case of the 8088), an increase of, say, 100 ns in a bus cycle does not necessarily mean an equal increase in the instruction cycle. Why?

3-4. 8-Bit versus 16-Bit μPs. In the 8088 and 8086, memory and I/O bus cycles normally take four clock cycles.
  (a) What is the maximum possible rate (R) at which data can be transferred between each CPU and memory or I/O? Express it in terms of the clock frequency f.
  (b) Determine the new expressions for R if n wait states must be inserted per bus cycle.
  (c) Assume insertion of two wait states per bus cycle and a clock frequency of 5 MHz. How fast will each CPU read data from memory?
  (d) Under what conditions would the data transfer rates of the two CPUs be about equal?

3-5. 8-Bit versus 16-Bit μPs. Consider two CPUs differing only in the width of the external data bus. CPU A has an 8-bit-wide external data bus, while CPU B has a 16-bit-wide one. Since the two CPUs have identical execution units they take equal amounts of time to execute an instruction once operands become available. However, the rate at which CPU B can process (that is, fetch and execute) instructions is higher because of its wider external data bus.
  (a) Assume instructions are three bytes long and require one additional bus cycle for a single 8-bit operand. Plot the percent improvement in instruction processing rate when using CPU B as a function of instruction execution time. Use the length of a memory cycle as a unit of instruction execution time and include execution times up to eight units long.
  (b) Repeat if instructions are four bytes long and require one additional access for a single 16-bit operand.
  (c) Interpret and assess the results obtained in (a) and (b).

3-6. Number of Wait States in Terms of Clock Frequency. Examination of the timing diagram of Figure 3-3 indicates that the 8088 and 8086 present a valid address to memory at about the middle of the first half of state $T1$. Memory must respond with valid data by the end of state $T3$. In other words, the memory access time should not exceed about 2.75 clock cycles if no wait states are to be inserted. If we assume a fixed memory access time, then the number of wait states we have to insert will depend on the chosen clock frequency. To see this, assume an 8086-based design where memory access time is 680 ns. The clocking rate depends on the CPU employed version as follows:

CPU version	Clock frequency (MHz)
8086-4	4
8086	5
8086-2	8
8086-1	10

(a) Plot the number of wait states (n) we must insert in each memory read bus cycle in terms of the clock frequency (f).

(b) Plot the length of the memory read bus cycle (L) as a function of the clock frequency.

3-7. Wait State Insertion in the 68000. Consider a 68000-based design where $DTACK^*$ goes active five states after the end of state S4. Redraw the timing diagram of Figure 3-13 showing the inserted wait states. How long is the machine cycle? When (at the latest) should memory data be available?

3-8. Context Switching. The process of saving and restoring the contents of CPU registers is often referred to as context switching. Saving registers' contents becomes necessary when the execution of a program is interrupted by a higher priority event. Remember that the information contained in CPU registers changes dynamically in the course of program execution. For example, the PC is incremented after each instruction fetch. Also, the status register flags change constantly to reflect various conditions concerning the results produced by the ALU. Similarly, intermediate results held in general registers may undergo constant change. In the course of summing up the terms of a series, for instance, the partial sum held in the accumulator will change every time we add a new term. All such time-varying information associated with a program is often referred to as its context. If we are to be able to correctly resume execution of an interrupted program we must save its context. Likewise, to start up the interrupt service routine we need its context (new PC contents, status register control bits that enable higher priority interrupts, and so forth). In other words, after saving the context of the suspended program, we must bring into the CPU registers the context of the new one (hence context switching). Fast context switching allows a CPU to respond faster to external events. This is particularly important in real-time applications where events external to a μC system may impose strict limits on response time. Suspension of a program, though, is not always the result of external events. Very often the CPU may do so on the basis of internal events. The procedure is very similar to the one for interrupts and again involves context switching. Besides its impact on real-time response, context switching represents an overhead. In multitasking applications, where the CPU switches from task to task frequently, such overheads may amount to a significant fraction of CPU time.

In order to speed up context switching, the 68000 provides a "move multiple registers" (MOVEM) instruction which makes possible to save or restore a specified set of registers. In the register indirect addressing mode, the MOVEM instruction takes 8 + 4N clock cycles to save N 16-bit registers. To restore N 16-bit registers from memory it takes 12 + 4N clock cycles (assuming no wait states).

(a) Consider an application where the context of task i involves eight registers, while that of task j involves four registers. Suppose the 68000 is clocked at 8 MHz. How long it takes to switch from task i to task j and vice versa?

(b) Besides the clock, what else could slow down task switching significantly?

(c) Without an instruction like MOVEM we would need a separate instruction (taking eight clock cycles) for saving and restoring each register. Determine the speed improvement (on a percent basis) when using the MOVEM instruction to save and restore N registers.

3-9. 32-Bit versus 16-Bit μPs. Among other advantages, 32-bit μPs are capable of handling high-level languages (HLLs) more efficiently. As an example consider the compiled code produced by the 68020 and the 68000 for a particular HLL statement. The code produced by the 68000 takes 79 clock cycles to execute and requires 15 bus cycles. In contrast, the code produced by the 68020 takes only 24 clock cycles for execution and requires only two bus cycles. What makes a big difference here is the extended addressing mode capabilities of the 68020.

(a) Assume both CPUs are clocked at a rate of 8 MHz and determine how long it takes each to execute this particular HLL statement (ignore the time taken by bus cycles).

(b) Repeat if the 68020 is clocked at the rate of 16 MHz.

3-10. External Interface. Compare the address bus, data bus, and data transfer control lines of the 8086 (in minimum mode) with those of the 68000. Use the model of the hypothetical μP as a reference. Tabulate all functional differences you identify.

3-11. External Interface. In the 8088 (minimum mode), the data transfer control lines include a read strobe (RD^*) and a write strobe (WR^*). On the other hand, other μPs employ a read/write (R/W^*) line and a single data strobe (DS^*). Functionally, these two pairs of signals are, of course, equivalent.

(a) Write the boolean equations and use NAND gates to show how we can derive each signal pair from the other.

During read/write operations the 68000 uses two separate strobes: an upper data strobe (UDS^*) and a lower data strobe (LDS^*). Other μPs employ a single data strobe and a byte/word (B/W^*) line indicating whether the access involves a byte or a 16-bit word. If the CPU specifies a byte access, the memory control circuits examine address bit A0 to determine the specific byte.

(b) Write the boolean equations and use NAND gates to show how we can derive from each set of signals the other.

3-12. External Interface. An examination of the external interfaces of the μPs we treated in this chapter reveals two alternative structures for the interrupt group of lines.

(a) Identify the two alternative structures.

(b) Discuss any differences among CPUs employing the same structure.

3-13. External Interface. Compare the bus control groups of external interface lines of the 8088 (minimum mode) and the 68000. Discuss any common characteristics and differences. What additional advantages are provided by the 8088/8086 bus control signals in maximum mode?

3-14. 16/32-Bit versus 32-Bit μPs. Consider two members of a μP family having external data bus widths of 16 and 32 bits. The two CPUs are otherwise identical and are clocked at the same rate.

(a) Would instruction execution times be identical for both CPUs?

(b) How about instruction and operand fetches?

(c) Suppose the CPUs perform highly computational types of tasks involving very little in terms of data movements. How different would you expect the instruction processing speeds of the two CPUs to be?

(d) Now assume the opposite—that is, the two CPUs perform tasks involving data movements (between CPU and memory) almost exclusively. How would their instruction processing speeds compare in this case?

(e) Which CPU is likely to use the external bus less often and thereby leave more time for bus use by other devices?

3-15. Pipelined Organization. A μP employs a four-stage pipeline for instruction processing. The tasks associated with instruction processing are divided such that all stages perform their tasks at approximately equal times.

(a) Compare the processing speed of the above μP with the speed of a conventional single-stage CPU which performs serially all the tasks associated with fetching and executing an instruction. Assume the same clocking rates for the two CPUs.

(b) Under what conditions would the processing speed of the two CPUs be the same?

(c) Because of difficulties in dividing equally the instruction processing tasks among the four stages, one stage takes on the average 25 percent longer in performing its task. What is the impact on the processing speed of the pipelined CPU?

3-16. Pipelined Organization. In the course of designing a new CPU it is determined that its clocking rate cannot exceed 10 MHz. In order to achieve higher performance the designers are considering pipelining.

(a) How many stages are needed (at minimum) to achieve the same performance we would get at a 40 MHz clocking rate?

(b) The CPU designers estimate that if memory is fast enough the fetching and execution of an instruction will take on the average 2.5 T states. Calculate the achievable processing speed in MIPS.

3-17. Impact of Internal CPU Organization on Hardware Design. Although it may not appear obvious, the internal organization of a CPU has important implications on hardware design. To see this, consider two alternative CPU organizations: one employing a four-stage pipeline and a cache and a second conventional, single-stage one. The former is clocked at 5 MHz, the latter at 20 MHz. Bus cycles are three clock cycles long in both CPUs. From the instruction execution viewpoint (that is, if we disregard instruction and operand fetching) the two CPUs have about the same performance. Yet, unless we employ in our design very high-speed memories, which could be prohibitively expensive, the single-stage CPU may yield a much lower overall instruction processing rate.

(a) Determine the length of the bus cycle for each CPU. Discuss the implications on memory speed.

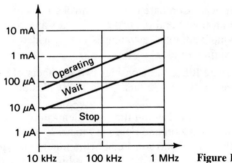

Figure P3-18.

(b) Explain why the four-stage CPU can tolerate slower memory without severe impact on its instruction processing speed.

3-18. Further Reduction of Power Consumption in CMOS μPs. Many CMOS μPs permit switching from the normal operating mode to a power save mode when the CPU is idle. While in such a mode, only the on-chip oscillator (and possibly a few other circuits) is running, so the power associated with the charging/discharging of internal capacitances is saved. Transition from one mode to the other is accomplished either by hardware or by software. For example, in certain μPs it is an externally driven input that determines whether the CPU is in the operating or the power save mode. On the other hand, others switch themselves into a power save (or wait) mode when executing a special "wait" instruction. Some also provide a "stop" instruction, in this case shutting off the clock oscillator and thus reducing power consumption to a minimum (see Figure P3-18). Here, however, there is a penalty: When the CPU is restarted, instruction execution cannot resume until thousands of clock cycles later. This time interval is necessary for the clock oscillator to reach a stable state. Such power save features become very important in certain applications where power consumption must be reduced to an absolute minimum.

(a) Consider a portable battery-powered system where the CPU periodically samples certain inputs. Subsequently it takes the required actions and then remains idle until sampling time comes again. In such an application it is very desirable to switch into a power save mode as soon as the CPU completes the processing tasks. However, the proper choice for the clocking rate (f) is not obvious. It appears that if f is relatively high, the CPU will complete the processing tasks faster and will therefore remain in the power save mode for a longer time. The problem is that higher f means higher power dissipation in both operational and power save modes. If we choose a low f, power dissipation will be low in both modes but the CPU will be in the operational mode for a longer time. You are asked to determine the optimum value of f (f_{opt}) to minimize the average power consumption P_{avg}. The sampling period is t and the CPU takes n clock cycles to sample and process the inputs. Assume an expression of the form $P = K V_{cc}^2 f$ for the power dissipated in either mode, where V_{cc} and the respective values of K are known.

(b) Suppose the CPU has a stop mode with given constant power consumption P_s. What is the value of f_{opt} and P_{avg}?

3-19. Instruction Execution Times. Sometimes CPU manufacturers claim that execution of

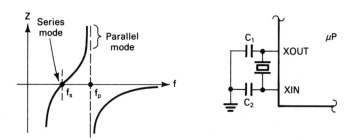

Figure P3-20.

certain instructions takes zero clock cycles.   Naturally, there is no such thing as zero
execution time.   What they mean is that execution of these instructions overlaps fully
with some other operation, for example, the operand storing of the previous instruction.   Consider a particular instruction whose execution normally takes three clock
cycles.   However, during the execution of a program it has been determined that
execution of this instruction very often overlaps with the execution of some other
instruction.   Specifically, there is a 60 percent chance of overlapping by one clock
cycle and a 20 percent chance of overlapping by two clock cycles.   Calculate how
many clock cycles it appears to take (on the average) for the execution of this instruction.

3-20. Crystals.   Figure P3-20 pictures the reactance (Z) of a crystal in terms of frequency.
f_s and f_p represent the frequencies at which a crystal oscillates when operating in series
and parallel mode, respectively.   In series mode the frequency of a crystal is deter-
mined by its own inductance (L) and capacitance (C) from the relation $f_s = 1/(2\pi\sqrt{LC})$.   In parallel mode the frequency also depends on the external capacitance
across the crystal terminals.   Such is the stray capacitance (C_s) due to the leads and
the holder (see equivalent circuit in Figure 3-25).   The total capacitance (C_L) seen
by the crystal at its terminals is calculated by adding:

- C_s
- The capacitance between the ($XIN/XOUT$) terminals of the μP
- The capacitance contributed by any externally added capacitors
- Any additional non-negligible stray capacitance across the crystal

The series combination of C_L with C and L determines the frequency of oscillation:
$f_p = \sqrt{(1/C + 1/C_L)/L} / (2\pi)$.   Thus, when selecting a crystal we must take into
consideration (or specify to the vendor) C_L as well.   Typically, C_L is in the range of
20 to 40 pF.   Often it is also known as correlation capacitance.

(a) Determine f_p/f_s in terms of the ratio C/C_L.

(b) What value of C_L would you specify to the vendor if the external capacitors are
$C1 = C2 = 20$ pF and the $XIN/XOUT$ input capacitance is 4 pF?   Assume a
typical value of 6 pF for C_s and an additional stray capacitance of 5 pF (due to
interconnections and other factors).   Assume the circuit of Figure 3-25(b).

3-21. Impact of Cache Hit Ratio on CPU Throughput.   The performance we gain with a
cache depends very much on the cache hit ratio—that is, on the probability that the
next item to be accessed can be found in the cache.   Consider a particular μC system
where a cache read cycle takes 60 ns, while a memory read cycle takes 480 ns.

(a) Calculate the average fetch time if the hit ratio is 90 percent.

(b) What improvement (in percent) do we gain with the cache as far as the "effective" length of a read cycle goes?

(c) Determine the improvement in the instruction processing rate given that without a cache the CPU would consume 60 percent of its time on memory cycles.

(d) Repeat parts (a), (b), and (c) if the hit ratio is only 60 percent. Compare the results with those obtained previously.

3-22. Cache and Clocking Rate. The cache access machine cycle of a CPU takes two clock cycles. Memory machine cycles take three or more clock cycles depending on the number of inserted wait states. That in turn depends on both the clocking rate and the memory speed. The cache hit ratio is about 90 percent.

(a) Suppose you use a 5 MHz version of this CPU and memory speed is such that you have to insert one wait state per memory cycle. Calculate the effective length of a memory read cycle as "seen" by the CPU.

(b) Assume you upgrade the system with a 16 MHz version of the CPU. After careful analysis you determine that now you have to insert nine wait states per memory cycle. Calculate the new effective length of a memory cycle. By what amount (in percent) has the effective length of a memory read cycle improved in the upgraded system?

(c) Suppose the 5 MHz CPU version was consuming 50 percent of its time for instruction and operand references. What percent improvement can we expect in the instruction processing rate with the faster CPU?

3-23. Fully-Associative Cache. Recall how the 68020 cache is organized: Each of the 64 four-byte blocks is assigned a dedicated "location" of the tag buffer. For example, block 00 is always associated with the first location of the tag buffer. Hence, the tag part of a new address need only be compared with the contents of a single location of the tag buffer (see Figure 3-21). Although easier to implement, this simple direct-mapping approach has a drawback. It gives us no choice as to which of the cache-resident blocks we can replace with a new one, so even when there is a high probability that the block under replacement may be needed by the CPU again shortly, we have no alternatives.

This problem can be solved by permitting each location of the tag buffer to be associated with any of the blocks. Such a cache is referred to as a fully-associative one. The least significant bits of a (CPU-generated) address are again employed to specify bytes within a block. Now, however, all the other bits are employed as a tag; that is, no part of the address is used as an index (and that makes tags longer). To determine if the desired block is already in the cache, the tag field of an address has to be compared with all the tags stored in the tag buffer. Thus, an associative cache is more costly to implement.

(a) Suppose you were to implement the cache of the 68020 as a fully-associative one. How many additional bits would you need per tag location (in the tag buffer)?

(b) How many comparisons are involved when the tag buffer is searched for a match?

(c) Would the size of the cache data buffer be affected?

Consider the design of an on-chip fully-associative cache for a μP employing 32-bit addresses. The cache must be capable of accommodating simultaneously up to 16 blocks of 16 bytes each.

(d) What should the capacity of the tag buffer be?

(e) In addition to data, the cache data buffer must store one validity bit per 16-bit word. This bit indicates if a word is a valid copy of the contents of the corresponding memory location. What is the total capacity of the data buffer? Show how it is organized.

3-24. Set-Associative Cache. The cost of a fully-associative cache can be reduced by associating each block to a specific set (rather than any) of the locations of the tag buffer. As is the case with the direct mapping approach we have seen in the 68020, part of the CPU-generated address is employed as an index. Now, though, the index points to a set of tag locations, not to a single location. Consequently, the tag part of an address is compared to the contents of the set of tag locations pointed to by the index. Such a cache is called a set-associative cache.

Consider the design of an off-chip set-associative cache for a μP employing 32-bit addresses. The cache must be capable of accommodating simultaneously up to 256 blocks of 16 bytes each. Each block is to be associated with any one of 16 contiguous tag locations.

(a) How many bits of the CPU-generated address do we need for indexing purposes?

(b) What should the capacity of the tag buffer be?

(c) How many comparisons are involved when the tag buffer is searched for a match?

(d) What would be the answers to parts (b) and (c) if the cache had to be a fully-associative one?

4

MEMORY

The last two chapters were about CPUs. We also dealt with CPU support circuits for

- Clocking
- Reset
- Wait state generation
- Address latching
- Bus buffering

Figure 3-32 pictures an example of a CPU surrounded by support circuits. Yet a CPU with its associated support circuits is not capable of producing any useful work. To see this, let us consider the sequence of events after we turn the power on:

1. The reset circuit activates the synonymous input of the CPU. This initiates the reset sequence.
2. Meanwhile, as V_{cc} approaches the operational range, the clock generator starts feeding the CPU with clock pulses.
3. At the end of the reset sequence the program counter (PC) is loaded automatically with a fixed address.
4. The CPU places this fixed address over the bus and proceeds to perform a memory read machine cycle. The objective is to read the addressed location and thereby find its way to the initialization routine.

5. If the *READY* input of the CPU is inactive, the attempted machine cycle will
be endless. The CPU will keep inserting one wait state after another until
power is turned off. If *READY* is active (as in the example of Figure 3-32),
the course of events is different. The CPU will sample the data bus and
conclude the machine cycle. It simply assumes that the data lines carry the
contents of the addressed memory location. Naturally (since they are not
connecting to any memory or I/O circuits), the state of the data lines is
undefined. At the time of their sampling they are floating, so the CPU—
or any in-between buffers—may interpret the state of a data line as a 1 or
as a 0. Unaware of the situation, the CPU will attempt to execute the
instruction corresponding to the read bit pattern. This generally leads either
to a meaningless program loop or to a CPU halt.

Clearly, our CPU (with its surrounding support circuits) cannot go any farther
without memory. After all, we need memory to store the program(s) we want to
process. Once equipped with memory, our CPU indeed becomes an operational
entity. From here on we will refer to a CPU equipped with support circuits and
memory as an operational processor or simply **processor**.

This chapter is about memory. We examine the characteristics of memory
devices and how they are interfaced to CPUs, the choices and tradeoffs involved,
and the problems we face in the course of designing a memory subsystem. Memory
errors are critical in many applications and can be catastrophic in some. In Section
4.3 we discuss how to detect and correct such errors. On the other hand, some
applications require large memories whose management becomes quite a task.
This subject is dealt with in Section 4.4. At the end of the chapter we will see
design examples involving operational processors.
First we discuss some important characteristics common to all memory devices.

Memory Devices

Memory devices are LSI/VLSI chips just like μPs. In fact, memory chips usually
have higher levels of complexity because iterative circuits can be packed more
densely. Depending on the desired overall memory size, the memory of a μC
may consist of a few to many such chips.
There are two families of memory devices: **read/write memory** devices, and
read-only memory devices. The characteristics we discuss next are those of key
importance from the design standpoint. They apply to both families.

Speed

Speed is expressed in terms of an **access time** and a **cycle time**. Usually,
access time is defined as the time elapsing from the moment we present a stable
address until the memory responds with stable data. The cycle time determines
how fast we can access memory on a continuous basis. Cycle time is not always

the same as access time, because some memories need additional time for "recovery" after an access.

Density

How many bits can we store per memory chip? Generally, this determines how many chips we need for implementation of the memory of a μC. Fewer chips mean less circuit board space for component accommodation, which in turn reduces system cost.

Power dissipation

In memory devices, power dissipation is specified in terms of an **operating power** and a **standby power**. Low standby power represents a very important advantage. What if we operate memory on a continuous basis? Even then, standby power is important since only a fraction of the total number of memory chips is usually active at a given time. Power dissipation has reliability implications (a device running hot is less reliable), as well as cost implications (power supply and possibly heat removal costs).

Component cost

Usually the cost of the overall memory subsystem is dominated by the cost of the employed memory devices. However, do not overlook the cost of other additional components such as memory control circuits. When memory size is small, such costs may become critical.

Other factors

How about memory device reliability—or compatibility with other memory devices? How is memory organized in terms of bits per location? These aspects are also important from the design standpoint.

Our guide (in selecting a device) is the set of design objectives discussed in Chapter 1. Tradeoffs must be made in accordance with the requirements of the particular product we are designing. For example, if our application does not require fast devices, we can trade off speed for lower cost.

4.1 RANDOM ACCESS MEMORY

We begin with the first family of memory devices: read/write memory devices. As the name implies such devices allow both read and write operations. In fact, the time to read from or write into a location is independent of which location was accessed previously—that is, locations can be accessed randomly and independently of each other.   Access time is the same for all locations in contrast to other types of memories such as sequential ones in which the time needed to access a location depends on its "distance" from the currently accessed location.   It is for this reason that semiconductor memory devices are called **random access memories (RAMs)**.

The circuit elements employed by a RAM device can be either dynamic or static, so that we have **dynamic RAMs (DRAMs)** and **static RAMs (SRAMs)**.   We will consider each type separately, starting with DRAMs.

4.1.1 Dynamic RAM

Most common among RAMs are the DRAMs.   The main reasons for their popularity are:

1. Their high capacities
2. Their relatively modest power requirements

DRAMs are usually organized for storing a single bit per location, which is referred to as the $\times$ 1 (times one) organization.   Examples of devices organized in this fashion are:

- 64K $\times$ 1 DRAMs
- 256K $\times$ 1 DRAMs

Figure 4-1 pictures the internal organization of such DRAMs.   The main part of the chip is an array of cells storing information in terms of 1s and 0s.   Each cell includes one or more transistors and a small capacitor.   The state of the latter (that is, charged or discharged) corresponds to storing a 1 or a 0.   A cell is addressed by means of a **row address** and a **column address**.   These two addresses may be thought of as being the coordinates of a cell.   In order to reduce the number of external interface lines, these two address components are multiplexed on the same input lines ($A0-AN$).   First we place over these lines the row address.   Then we activate the row address strobe (RAS^*).   The DRAM responds by storing the presented address in the row latch.   Next we remove the row address and load the $A0-AN$ lines with the column address.   This time we activate the column address strobe (CAS^*).   The DRAM stores the presented address in the column latch.   Subsequently, it decodes the two stored addresses to locate the addressed cell.   The write enable (WE^*) line indicates whether an access is for reading or writing.   *DIN* and *DO* are the data input and data output lines, respectively.

The same lines are seen in Figure 4-2(a) which depicts the industry standard external interface for $\times$ 1 DRAMs.   This is unlike the case of μPs where no such standard exists.   As a matter of fact, the package for $\times$ 1 DRAMs is itself an industry standard.   It is the 16-pin DIP shown in Figure 4-2(b).   Note that the latter reflects the address lines required in the case of 64K $\times$ 1 DRAMs.   In 16K

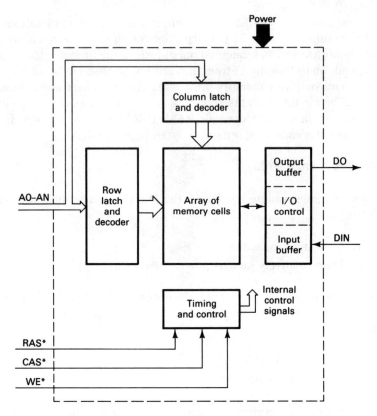

Figure 4-1.   Organization of a typical dynamic RAM.

× 1 DRAMs address line A7 is not needed and so pin 9 is unassigned.   On the other hand, in 256K × 1 DRAMs we need an extra address line, A8, which is assigned to pin 1.   Naturally, standardization of the external interface and package does not imply the same electrical characteristics.   For example, the AC parameters of two 64K × 1 DRAMs produced by different manufacturers are generally not the same.   In fact, a device may be available from a manufacturer in two or more versions differing in speed and hence having different timing parameters.

In standby mode, DRAMs dissipate ten or more times less power.   This reduces significantly average power consumption.

Example 4-1

Consider two 256K × 1 DRAMs—one NMOS and one CMOS.   Both devices have an operating power dissipation of 200 mW.   However, in standby mode the NMOS DRAM dissipates 30 mW while the CMOS dissipates only 0.5 mW.   Calculate the average power dissipation of each device given a duty cycle of 25 percent.

Solution.   CPUs spend part of their time executing instructions and performing I/O operations.   Thus, they do not access memory all the time.   Besides, the CPU may

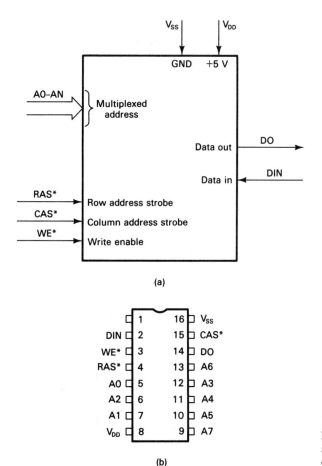

Figure 4-2. External interface lines and standard pinout of a × 1 (times one)-organized DRAM.

access different memory devices at different times. Hence in practice the duty cycle of a memory chip is considerably less than 1. Here the NMOS DRAM spends 25 percent of its time performing memory cycles. While doing so it consumes 200 mW. The rest of the time it switches (automatically) to standby mode where power consumption is only 30 mW. Consequently its average dissipation is (200 × 0.25) + (30 × 0.75) = 72.5 mW. This is less than half of its operating power consumption. Similarly we calculate for the CMOS DRAM (200 × 0.25) + (0.5 × 0.75) = 50.4 mW. The latter figure is indicative of the impact of standby power on overall power dissipation. Standby power becomes an important criterion in the selection of a DRAM. The problem, of course, is that DRAMs having very low standby power are likely to be more expensive so that we again have to make tradeoffs.

The number of DRAMs needed for implementation of the memory of a μC depends on:

1. The width of the external data bus of the CPU

2. The desired total memory capacity

3. The capacity of the DRAM and how it is organized

In the case of the × 1-organized DRAMs we need, at minimum, a number equal
to the width of the CPU data bus because each DRAM contributes only one bit
per memory word. For example, if our CPU is an 8-bit μP we need at least eight
DRAMs (Figure 4-3). With 64K × 1 DRAMs, the resulting memory capacity
would be 64 KB. For a larger memory capacity we would have to add a second
"bank" of 8 DRAMs, and so on. Higher capacity DRAMs do not necessarily
consume more power. A 64K × 1 DRAM and a 256K × 1 one, for instance,
have comparable power figures. This, plus the savings in circuit board space,

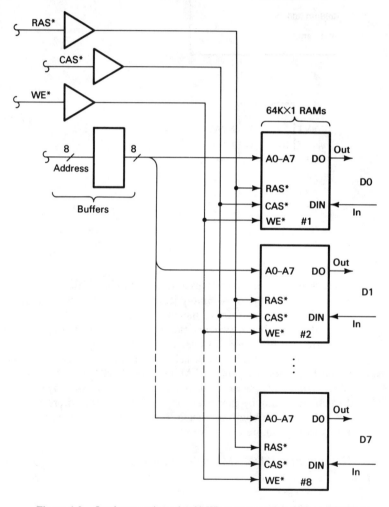

Figure 4-3. Implementation of a 64 KB memory using 64K × 1 DRAMs.

points to higher capacity DRAMs. On the other hand, lower capacity devices permit finer **granularity** in memory capacity; that is, the size of the increments in which we can add memory capacity is smaller.

Example 4-2

How many 64K $\times$ 1 DRAMs do you need to implement a 256 KB memory for an 8-bit μP? What is the smallest size increment in memory capacity? Repeat with 256K $\times$ 1 DRAMs.

Solution. The smallest size capacity corresponds to the one obtained with 8 DRAMs. In the case of 64K $\times$ 1 devices it is 64 KB. With 256 $\times$ 1 devices it is 256 KB.

For implementation of a 256 KB memory with 64K $\times$ 1 DRAMs we need four banks of eight devices each; that is, a total of 32 DRAMs. The same capacity can be obtained with only eight 256K $\times$ 1 devices. Thus with higher capacity DRAMs we gain in power consumption and board space. We also gain in reliability (because of the small number of employed devices) and component costs (since the cost of a 256K $\times$ 1 DRAM is significantly less than four times the cost of a 64K $\times$ 1 one).

The problem (in the case of 256K $\times$ 1 DRAMs) is granularity. If all we need is 64 KB of memory, implementation with 256K $\times$ 1 DRAMs is inappropriate. Memory capacity cannot be upgraded in increments smaller than 256 KB.

Other DRAM Organizations

A DRAM device may be organized for storing more than one bit per location. For example, a 64 Kb (Kilobit) DRAM may be organized as a 16K $\times$ 4 cell array storing four bits per location or as an 8K $\times$ 8 array storing one byte per location. Similarly, 256 Kb DRAMs are available in 64K $\times$ 4 and 32K $\times$ 8 organizations. These alternatives to the $\times$ 1 organization are often called **wide-word organizations**. Such organizations become advantageous in the design of small capacity memories. For example, in the case of an 8-bit μP we need only two 16K $\times$ 4 DRAMs to implement 16 KB of memory (see Figure 4-4). With 64K $\times$ 1 DRAMs we need eight devices (see Figure 4-3). We also gain in granularity since we can add memory capacity in increments of only 16 KB. Besides, since we activate fewer devices per memory access, there are power savings as well.

However, as memory capacity increases, the required number of wide-word DRAMs approaches that of $\times$ 1-organized ones. Moreover, $\times$ 4-organized devices require an 18-pin package and thereby take more board space. The situation is worse with $\times$ 8-organized DRAMs which require a 28-pin package (see Problem 4-2). Consequently, wide-word DRAMs are limited to applications needing small memory capacities.

Example 4-3

A designer considers employing 256 Kb DRAMs in the design of the 512 KB memory of an 8-bit μP. How many 256 $\times$ 1 DRAMs are needed? What if DRAMs are $\times$ 4-organized? Compare the two implementations in terms of power dissipation and board space.

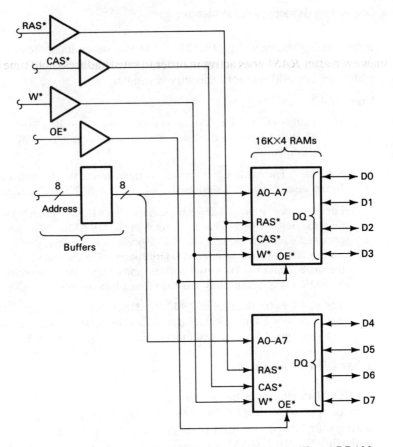

Figure 4-4. Implementation of a 16 KB memory using two 16K × 4 DRAMs.

Solution. Eight 256K × 1 DRAMs provide 256 KB of memory. Hence, we need two banks of eight DRAMs each—that is, a total of 16 devices. On the other hand, two 64K × 4 DRAMs provide 64 KB of memory. Thus, we need eight banks of two DRAMs each. Again, we need a total of 16 devices. The conclusion is that for such a large size memory the number of devices remains the same regardless of DRAM organization.

We still have the advantage of finer granularity (64 KB) with 64K × 4 DRAMs. Power dissipation is also lower because each bank consists of only two devices. The drawback, however, is board space. 64K × 4 DRAMs come in 18-pin packages and therefore will take more space on the circuit board (see Problem 4-2 for additional considerations).

Timing

Let us now look at the timing relationships among the external interface signals of a DRAM. Figure 4-5(a) depicts those associated with a read cycle. Prior to activating *RAS** we must present a stable row address satisfying the setup time requirements of the device. The row address must be maintained over the input lines even after RAS^* goes active in order to satisfy address hold time requirements. RAS^* itself is governed by timing restrictions. It must remain at a low for a specified time interval (at minimum). Afterwards it has to stay at a high for a certain minimum time interval on account of internal precharge operations. The sum of the minimum values associated with these two intervals defines the read cycle time (t_{CY}) of a DRAM (see Figure 4-5).

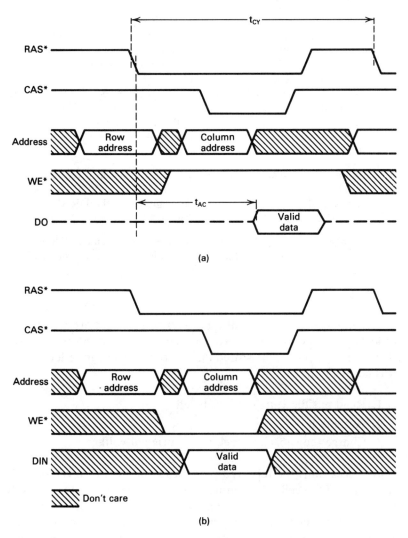

Figure 4-5. The basic timing relationships in a typical DRAM. (a) Read cycle timing. (b) Write cycle timing.

Similar setup/hold time and pulse width restrictions apply to column addresses and the *CAS**. The access time (t_{AC}) is defined relative to the leading edge of *RAS**. Notice how the precharge time interval lengthens the cycle time beyond the point that valid data become available.

Signal sequencing is similar for write cycles. However, *WE** is now active, indicating a write operation. Also, the DRAM is now presented with data to be written. Another type of cycle is the read-modify-write cycle. During such cycles, *RAS** and *CAS** remain active until the modified data are written back into memory.

Example 4-4

Consider an 8086-based μC system employing DRAMs. *RAS** is activated by the trailing edge of *ALE*. However, due to propagation and other delays, *RAS** does not go active until 50 ns after *ALE* returns to a low. The latter occurs in the middle of the second half of state $T1$. Data are read by the CPU at the end of state $T3$. For timely presentation to the CPU, though, data must be provided 60 ns earlier by memory. This interval accounts for propagation delays along the data paths (from memory to CPU) and CPU data hold time requirements. How fast should the DRAMs be if no wait states are to be inserted? How many wait states do we have to insert per bus cycle if the access time of the DRAMs is 150 ns? Assume a clocking rate of 10 MHz.

Solution. The length of a state is 100 ns. Take as a reference the beginning of a read bus cycle. *ALE* returns to a low at time 75 (ns). *RAS** goes active 50 ns later, that is, at 125. Data must become available by the DRAMs at time $300 - 60 = 240$. Hence, t_{AC} must be at least $240 - 125 = 115$ ns.

A single wait state will change access time requirements to $115 + 100 = 215$ ns. This can be met easily by the DRAMs which have an access time of 150 ns.

Refresh

The charge stored in the small capacitors of a DRAM array dissipates fast because of leakages. As a result the voltages across the capacitors drop to the point that they no longer reflect the stored information. Thus, in order to avoid loss of data it is necessary to

1. Read out the voltage of each cell
2. Amplify it
3. Charge the capacitor back to the original voltage

This process must be repeated periodically and is called **refresh**. DRAMs allow refreshing of the cells of an entire row in a single operation. Usually they require refreshing of 128 rows every 2 ms, or 256 rows every 4 ms.

What we need is a timer generating refresh requests periodically and a counter keeping track of row addresses. Figure 4-6 depicts the basic principles. When the control logic receives a refresh request:

1. It gates the contents of the refresh address counter to the address inputs of the DRAMs. This is accomplished through a multiplexer.
2. It generates the memory control signals which are sequenced as required for a refresh cycle.
3. After completion of the refresh cycle, the control logic advances the counter. The new contents reflect the address of the row to be refreshed next.

For ordinary memory cycle requests the process is simpler. Now the control logic gates through the multiplexer the row address corresponding to the addressed location. Usually we employ as such the lower part of the address placed over the bus by the CPU. The generated memory control signals are those appropriate for ordinary memory cycles.

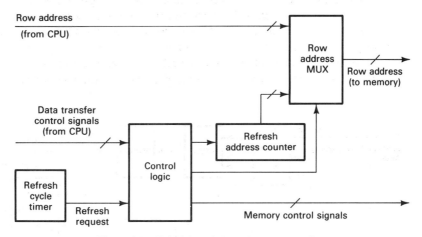

Figure 4-6. Principles of dynamic memory refresh.

What if the control logic receives a refresh request and an ordinary memory cycle request at the same time? Clearly one of the two will have to be put on hold. The design of the circuits performing the **arbitration** function is not a trivial task. If not properly designed, they can cause unpredictable behavior and lead to problems which are difficult to trace. Another objective is to design these circuits such that they do not introduce significant delays during arbitration. Fortunately, as we will see shortly, you will seldom have to design the refresh circuitry.

Example 4-5

The memory of a particular μC is built from 64K × 1 DRAMs. According to the data sheets, the cell array of the DRAM is organized into 256 rows. Each row must be refreshed at least once every 4 ms. Suppose we refresh the memory on a strictly periodic basis. What is the time period between successive refresh requests? How long a refresh address counter do we need?

Solution. The refresh period (from row to row) must be at maximum $4000/256 = 15.625$ μs. Since we deal with a total of 256 rows—that is, row addresses 0 to 255—we need an 8-bit counter ($256 = 2^8$).

Memory Interface Circuits

Figure 4-7 pictures the additional circuit blocks needed to interface the memory to the CPU (buffered) bus. A second multiplexer is used to multiplex row and column addresses. Also, prior to their distribution to the DRAMs, the address signals are buffered. This becomes necessary because of the dynamic load presented by the array of DRAMs. In the particular case shown in Figure 4-7, for instance, the address signals are distributed to 16 DRAMs. There are two banks of × 1-organized devices. Each bank consists of eight DRAMs (implying an 8-bit μP application). Both the *DIN* and the *DO* lines connect to the CPU bus.

How do we employ the address provided by the CPU over the bus? The lower part of the address is split into two parts. One of the parts is employed as a row address. The other is employed as a column address. The high-order address bits—those beyond the lower part we use for row/column addressing—

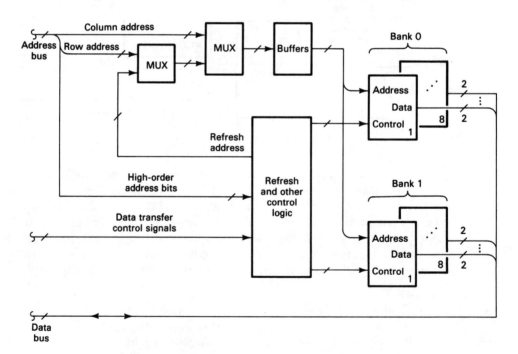

Figure 4-7. Simplified diagram of memory interface circuits.

are employed for bank selection.   The decoding is done by the control logic which generates the control signals for the selected memory bank.

Example 4-6

Assume the memory devices of Figure 4-7 are 64K $\times$ 1 DRAMs and the CPU bus has 20 address lines.   How would you employ a bus address for row/column selection? Up to how many memory banks can be handled?

Solution.   A 64K $\times$ 1 DRAM represents a 256 $\times$ 256 cell array.   Hence, we need eight (256 = 2^8) address bits to locate a row and another eight to locate a column. Ordinarily we would use address bits A0–A7 as a row address and address bits A8– A15 as a column address.   High-order bits A16–A19 can be used for bank selection purposes.   Decoding of these four most significant address bits allows distinguishing up to 2^4 = 16 memory banks.   In the example of Figure 4-7 we need only decode bit A16.   When a 0, we select bank 0.   When a 1, we select bank 1.

Dynamic Memory Controllers

The design of memory interface circuits is simplified greatly by using a **dynamic memory controller (DMC)**.   Such a device replaces most (if not all) of the memory interface circuits pictured in Figure 4-7.   The resulting component cost savings and board space conservation make this solution more cost effective as well.   As an example we describe the Intel 8203 DMC.

The 8203 is intended for 64K $\times$ 1 (and other lower capacity) DRAMs.   Its simplified block diagram is shown in Figure 4-8.   Timing signals are derived by means of an on-chip oscillator or an externally supplied clock.   Optionally, refresh requests can be initiated externally via the *REFRQ* (refresh request) line.   Whether external or internal, refresh requests are given lower priority by the arbitration and synchronization logic.   Ordinary read/write memory requests are given higher priority.

In addition to internal signals, the timing generator of the 8203 receives two external bank select signals (*B0*, *B1*).   Normally, these are fed from two of the bus address lines and are decoded for activation of one of the *RAS0*–RAS3** lines. *SACK** (system acknowledge) indicates start of a memory access cycle.   On the other hand, *XACK** (transfer acknowledge) is a strobe indicating valid data during a read or write operation.   In the course of a refresh cycle the timing generator activates all of the *RAS** lines.   For ordinary cycles it activates only one, plus the *CAS** line.   *WE** reflects the states of the *RD** and *WR** input lines.

The 8203 (and other DMCs) provides on-chip address drivers capable of handling capacitive loads on the order of hundreds of picofarads (lines *OUT0*– OUT7**).   In some DMCs the drivers include series resistors to reduce undershoot and dampen signal ringing.   We will come back to this subject later.   The 8203 has some additional options and operating modes which are selected by strapping the appropriate input pins.

Figure 4-9 illustrates a typical application of the 8203 in an 8088-based system. The DRAMs are 64K $\times$ 1 ones.   Each bank contributes 64 KB of memory.   Hence,

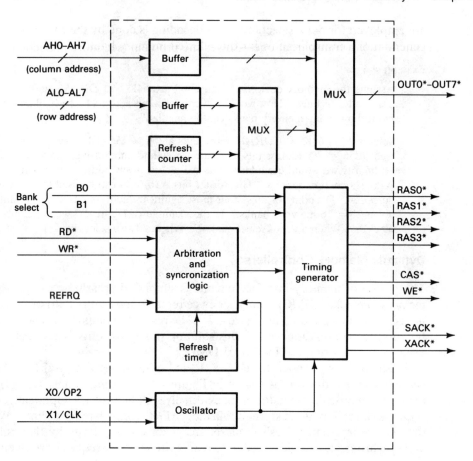

Figure 4-8. Simplified block diagram of the 8203 dynamic memory controller.

the total memory capacity is 128 KB. Notice that lines $OUT0^*-OUT7^*$, CAS^*, and WE^* connect to each and every DRAM chip. In contrast, each RAS^* output line drives only the eight DRAMs of the respective memory bank. The RD^* and WR^* inputs of the 8203 are driven directly from the synonymous outputs of the CPU.

A latch is employed for demultiplexing the eight least significant (CPU) address bits from data. The latched address bits play the role of a row address feeding the $AL0-AL7$ inputs of the 8203. Address bits A8–A15 are fed directly from the CPU and play the role of a column address. Address bit A16 is used for bank selection purposes.

A second latch is employed to store data read from memory, but for an entirely different reason. The 8088 reads data at the beginning of state $T4$. However, it is not known if memory keeps presenting valid data until then. This second latch—not a transparent one—solves the problem (see more in Section 4-5). As seen, the *DO* lines of DRAMs corresponding to same bit positions are bused together. This poses no problem because they are tri-state and only one of them can be active at any particular time. Also, no transceivers were used since each of the (*AD0–AD7*) bus lines connects only to two DRAMs. Read data are stored in the data latch using the *XACK** signal. The output of the latch is disabled as soon as *RD** goes back to a high. In this example we assume that no wait states are necessary.

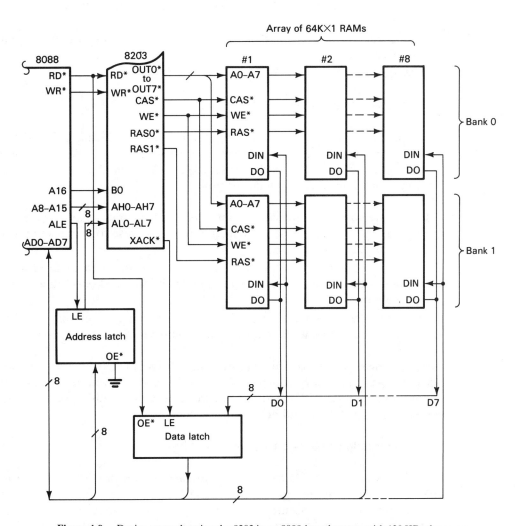

Figure 4-9.   Design example using the 8203 in an 8088-based system with 128 KB of memory.

How do we go about selecting a DMC?   Here are some of the characteristics we should consider carefully:

1. Which DRAMs does it support?   For example, does it support both 64K × 1 and 256K × 1 DRAMs?
2. Does it provide on-chip drivers?   Up to how many DRAMs can we drive without external drivers?
3. How many memory banks can be selected?
4. What is the length of the propagation delays introduced by the DMC?   Such delays increase the memory access time seen by the CPU and may necessitate insertion of wait states.
5. Does the DMC accommodate byte accesses?   This is important in 16-bit μP applications.
6. What alternatives does it offer as far as refresh goes?

Putting it All Together

At this point we have dealt with the criteria involved in selecting a DRAM and a DMC, the main components in a dynamic memory subsystem.   We have also seen how we go about producing a design on paper.   Yet, on the road to a properly working product we face a number of problems:

1. The memory interface circuits introduce propagation delays.   Such delays lengthen the memory access time and may have a serious impact on overall system performance.
2. Our paper design may work marginally, or not at all, when implemented with real devices.   We must perform timing analysis to find out if there is such a possibility.
3. Real-world phenomena, like noise, can cause improper operations and memory errors.   Other nasty realities, like ringing, may even damage components.

These are the same kind of problems we generally face in digital design.   However, when it comes to memory design, such problems become far more serious because of the large number of DRAM devices we usually deal with.   We will examine some of these problems and how we get around them.

Propagation delays and signal skewing

The signals generated by the CPU propagate through several logic elements before they appear on the input lines of the DRAMs.   For example, address signals propagate through two or more multiplexers and buffers before they arrive at their destination.   Data read from memory are themselves buffered and therefore delayed.   All such delays lengthen the memory access time and may necessitate insertion of additional wait states.

Another factor we have to consider when doing timing analysis is the skew introduced by multiple signal paths.   Take, for instance, the case of Figure 4-10(a) where address signals $A1$ and $A2$ propagate via similar logic paths.   Data sheets guarantee only minimum and maximum delay values for a logic element.   Consequently, we cannot predict the exact delay experienced by either address signal. The difference between the delays introduced by these two seemingly identical logic paths is known as **skew**.   Its maximum value is

$$\sum_i d_{i,max} - \sum_i d_{i,min}$$

where $d_{i,max}$, $d_{i,min}$ represent maximum and minimum delays through stage i of a logic path.

Figure 4-10(b) pictures another hypothetical chain of gates.   This one involves generation of RAS^* from the CPU's $READ$ strobe.   Recall that prior to activating RAS^* we must allow for a row address setup time.   Clearly, the shortest setup time corresponds to the case where address signals suffer maximum delay while RAS^* suffers minimum.   For worst case design, we must make sure that even then we meet the setup time requirement.   This may imply delaying further RAS^* on purpose.

Example 4-7

Assume for simplicity that all types of logic elements of Figure 4-10 have the same delay characteristics.   The values of maximum and minimum delays are 15 and 10 ns.   Calculate the maximum possible skew between $A1$ and $A2$.

Suppose that $READ$ goes active 35 ns after address signals do.   The DRAMs require an address setup time of 10 ns at minimum.   Do we meet this timing requirement?

Solution.   At worst, the delay experienced by address signals is $5 \times 15 = 75$ ns.   At best, it is $5 \times 10 = 50$ ns.   So the skew between $A1$ and $A2$ can be as large as $75 - 50 = 25$ ns.

Let us use as a reference the time $A1$ and $A2$ assume their new states at the inputs to the gate chains. $READ$ is delayed by at least $4 \times 10 = 40$ ns.   Hence RAS^* goes active at time $35 + 40 = 75$ ns at the earliest.   Since address signals may be delayed by up to 75 ns, we have no guarantee of meeting the setup time requirement.   To ensure this, we have to delay $READ$ by another 10 ns.   Addition of one more gate to the chain will accomplish this.

Reduction of the delays and skew introduced by logic elements is achieved in a number of ways:

1. Minimize the number of logic elements involved in each signal path.   You may also select their type for small propagation delays.

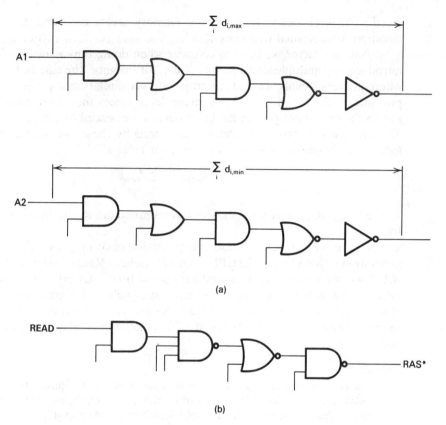

Figure 4-10.   Examples of logic paths for timing analysis.   (a) Two address signals.
(b) A control signal.

2. Use logic elements for which the gap between minimum and maximum delays
   is small.   This reduces skewing.
3. The skew between two critical paths can be decreased further by using logic
   elements from the same IC package, since propagation delays of circuits of
   the same chip track each other closely—typically, to within 2 ns.

Usually, manufacturers specify delays at a temperature of 25 °C.   To account
for higher temperature effects such values may have to be increased, typically by
30 percent or so.   Also, they may specify typical instead of minimum values.   In
the latter case we may use one half of the typical value as a minimum.   Naturally
the use of a DMC simplifies timing analysis considerably.   Besides, such devices
are designed with delay minimization in mind.

Capacitive loads constitute another source of delays.   When excessive, they
increase significantly rise and fall times and thereby signal path delays (see Problem

4-25). This situation is encountered in the buffers driving the DRAMs. Very often we reduce such delays by splitting the load between two or more buffers. Usually, the propagation delays of the latter are given assuming a specific load. If the actual load is higher, we must increase the listed values of the delays. For example, for Schottky buffers we add 0.05 ns/pF of the excess load. Load calculations should include the capacitance contributed by printed circuit board (PCB) traces (about 2 pF/in.).

Example 4-8

> The effect of PCB trace capacitances can be significant. To see this, assume a design similar to that of Figure 4-9 for a 16-bit μP. How much capacitance does the trace of the *CAS** line contribute? Devices are spaced about 0.5 in. from one another.
>
> The *CAS** input of each DRAM presents a capacitance of 10 pF. Calculate the composite dynamic load seen by the driver of the *CAS** line. Suppose we employ a driver whose propagation delay is specified at 150 pF. By what amount should we increase its delay in our analysis?
>
> **Solution.** Each memory bank now requires 16 DRAMs, so the total number of devices is 32. The *CAS** line connects to all 32 DRAMs. Since the latter are on a 0.5 in. grid, the length of the traces associated with *CAS** is about $32 \times 0.5 = 16$ in. At 2 pF/in. they contribute $16 \times 2 = 32$ pF.
>
> The total capacitance presented by the DRAM *CAS** inputs is 320 pF. Hence, the composite dynamic load is $320 + 32 = 352$ pF. The specified delay of the driver should be increased by $(352 - 150) \times 0.05 = 10.1$ ns (assuming a Schottky one). We will come back to the topic of timing analysis in Section 4.5.

Ringing

Etched PCB traces do not contribute only capacitance. They also contribute inductance. A consequence of this is that the overall signal path (along a PCB) can be modeled as a transmission line. The situation is pictured in Figure 4-11(a). As seen, the transmission line is open at the far end, so it will reflect the signal back toward the driving end (on the left). The problem is that such reflections result in ringing right after signal transitions.

Figure 4-11(b) shows the kind of ringing resulting from a high-to-low signal transition. When the signal transition is reflected back (primary reflection), it can produce an **undershoot** on the order of -2 V. Such a voltage can damage the DRAMs which are often able to withstand only -0.5 V. This undershoot propagates itself toward the open end of the line. Like the original signal transition, it is reflected back, producing an **overshoot** (secondary reflection). The overshoot itself is reflected, producing a second undershoot, and so on. This sequence of undershoots/overshoots constitutes what we call **ringing**.

Aside from its potential to damage DRAMs, ringing can cause other problems. For example, if the overshoot is far enough from the falling edge [Figure 4-11(b)], it may be interpreted as another ordinary transition. Thus, it can cause

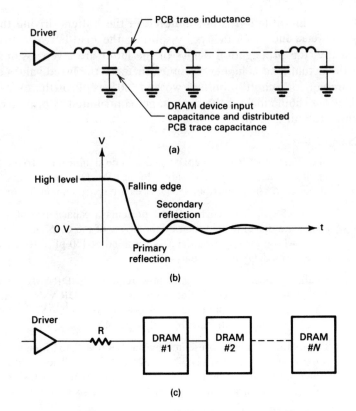

Figure 4-11. Transmission line effects in memory design. (a) The load presented by the address and control inputs of the DRAMs, and the associated PCB traces, are modeled as a transmission line. (b) Ringing after a high-to-low signal transition. (c) Use of a damping resistor to reduce or eliminate the undershoot.

circuits to switch. The duration of ringing (and thereby the distance of the overshoot from the falling edge) depends on the length of the transmission line. A solution to this problem is allowing a signal extra setup time until ringing dies out.

Example 4-9

Suppose the length of the equivalent transmission line is 6 in. How long (after the falling edge) does the reflected signal arrive at the driver? By what amount should we increase the setup time of a signal to ensure the secondary reflection has died out? Assume signal propagation over the line takes 4 ns/ft.

Solution. Our original transition travels to the end of the line and back, a total of 12 in. Hence, the signal resulting from the primary reflection arrives after 4 ns. The signal resulting from the second reflection arrives after another 4 ns, and so on. Thus to ensure the latter has died out we need an extra setup time of about $3 \times 4 = 12$ ns. Note, however, that the effects of signal reflections depend also on the rise and fall times of the original signal. Take, for instance, the case when fall times are 15 ns. Now, by the time our original signal reaches a low, the secondary reflection has died out.

The consequences of ringing are more critical for clock signals. A clock edge may look like multiple signals, resulting in additional (faulty) clock steps. Such a situation may be encountered in the process of upgrading an existing product with a faster CPU. Usually, a faster clock implies shorter rise and fall times, so the signals resulting from the reflections may not overlap with the ordinary clock transitions any more.

Let us go back to the problem of the undershoot in memory design. Figure 4-11(c) demonstrates a widely used solution to this problem. It consists of a **damping resistor** placed in series at the output of the driver. This resistor is generally from a few to several tens of ohms. The higher its value, the lower the amplitude of the undershoot. At the same time, though, we get a greater increase in rise/fall times and therefore lengthening of signal delays. Very often, DMCs include on-chip damping resistors, eliminating the need for external ones.

Noise

The considerations that generally apply to noise in digital systems hold for memories as well. However, the situation is more severe in dynamic memories. This is due to the amount of capacitance charged/discharged during memory operations (especially refresh ones where all banks are activated at the same time). Large capacitances mean large charging/discharging currents and hence large current spikes over the V_{cc} lines, which generate faulty transitions.

Like other digital circuits, the amplitude of such transients is kept under control with decoupling capacitors. For high frequency (HF) decoupling we need ceramic (or other monolithic) capacitors having low inductance. Though not always mandatory, using one such capacitor per DRAM constitutes a good practice. The connection points to the leads of each capacitor should be very close to the V_{cc} and ground terminals of the DRAM. Our goal is to minimize the total inductance between V_{cc} and ground terminals. The lower the inductance, the easier the passage of spikes to the ground. Typical capacitor values are 0.047 and 0.1 µF.

Larger capacitors needed for low frequency (LF) decoupling are usually of tantalum type with values in the range of 15 to 47 µF. Their purpose is to prevent V_{cc} from dropping below acceptable levels. Such a situation could arise especially during refresh. In general we use one capacitor per V_{cc} input from the backplane. The capacitors are placed close to the edge of the PCB. For large PCBs, however, it is advisable to distribute additional capacitors throughout the PCB (see Problem 4-19).

Noise cannot be reduced adequately without proper PCB layout. The general rules applying to the layout of digital PCBs hold for memories too. Observing such rules becomes more critical in memories where capacitive loads and the physical size of the DRAM array are usually large. For example, crosstalk can be more severe due to higher amplitude current spikes (see Problem 4-16). The following rules are keys to reducing noise, ringing, and propagation delays:

1. Pack DRAMs as close as possible. Drivers must be placed very close to the array. Each row (or column) of DRAMs should connect to the driving point individually (rather than being chained). Consider splitting large arrays into two or more subarrays. Place the memory control circuits close to the center of the board.

2. A multilayer board is preferred with one internal plane dedicated to V_{cc} and another to ground. The need for such a design increases with the physical size of the array and the speed of DRAMs. If only one of the internal planes is available for power, use it for ground. Avoid discontinuities on the internal planes. This keeps their inductances low.

3. If you have to employ the ordinary (two-sided) PCB approach, use a "grided" power busing scheme. Lay out a V_{cc} grid on one side and a ground grid on the other so that traces of the two grids are directly above/below each other. This minimizes the impedance between them. The more massive the power distribution grids, the lower their inductance.

4.1.2 Static RAM

DRAMs are widely used in the implementation of μC memories. Even though they require refresh and other support circuits, they remain cost effective for most applications. A single DMC, for instance, may suffice for control of a 1 MB memory. Yet there are applications where the cost effectiveness of dynamic memories becomes questionable. Consider for example the case where the μC plays the role of a microcontroller as a substitute to random logic. Such a μC may serve as a controller to a printer, a terminal, or a small disk. Here a small RAM of (say) 4 KB may suffice. All we need to accommodate is some small program(s) and a limited amount of data.

Using a DMC and associated support circuits for such a small size DRAM is clearly not cost effective. This motivated the development of DRAM devices integrating on-chip refresh and other support circuitry. Such devices are often referred to as **integrated RAMs**. Because of the fact that they hide refresh (and thereby their dynamic nature) these devices are also called **pseudostatic** RAMs.

What if we still need a small memory but also a high-speed one? Such a memory may store pointers indicating what part of main memory is to be accessed, for instance. The video look-up tables employed in graphics is a case in point. What if we design a cache? For this type of applications the main problem is speed, and DRAMs cannot provide the required access and cycle times.

Under such circumstances we resort to another type of memory device: **static RAMs (SRAMs)**. In a SRAM a bit cell amounts to a flip-flop built from several transistors, so bit capacity per device lags that of DRAMs. On the other hand, SRAMs have the following advantages:

1. No refresh necessary
2. Simplified timing requirements
3. Higher speeds (in general)

These characteristics reduce the cost of memory interface circuits and thus make SRAMs good candidates for instruments and other applications needing small memories. Besides, those with fast access times can serve as high-speed buffer memories.

External Interface

SRAMs are available in various organizations, but most popular are the byte-wide ones. Figure 4-12 illustrates the external interface of such a SRAM.

Notice that in SRAMs row and column addresses are not multiplexed. There are no address strobes either. Instead the device is equipped with a chip select (CS^*) input. It is through the latter that the device is activated for initiation of a memory cycle. When CS^* is at a high, the bidirectional data lines $DQ1–DQ8$ are forced to a floating state. Furthermore, any input data placed over these lines by external logic are ignored. The role of the write enable (WE^*) input is the same one we have seen for DRAMs.

The output enable (OE^*) line affects data lines $DQ1–DQ8$ only as far as output goes. When inactive, the data lines are brought to a high impedance state from the SRAM device side. However, they can still serve as input lines. This type of control input is very useful when using two or more SRAMs. It provides the means of ensuring that only one SRAM drives the data bus at a given time. We will come back to this shortly.

Usually, the pinouts of byte-wide SRAMs are compatible with those of ROMs and EPROMs (see Section 4.2). This allows us to debug a system using SRAMs in place of ROMs or EPROMs. Later on, when the software becomes stable, we store it on pin-compatible ROMs or EPROMs. For example, the standard pinout shown in Figure 4-12(b) is similar to that of 2K × 8 EPROMs. Only the parenthesized pins carry different signals in the case of EPROMs. To accommodate either device type, then, we make connections to these pins through jumpers. The SRAMs must be, of course, at least as fast as the ROMs or EPROMs they are going to be replaced with.

Timing

SRAM timing relationships are much simpler than those of DRAMs. As an example we show in Figure 4-13 the read cycle timing of a typical byte-wide SRAM. The chip select (CS^*) signal is derived by decoding high-order address bits. Thus,

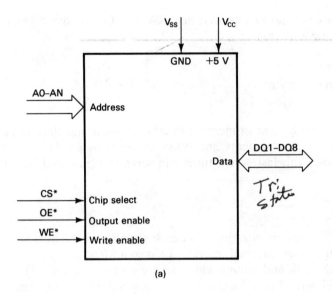

(a)

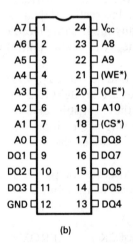

(b)

Figure 4-12. (a) External interface lines of a byte-wide static RAM. (b) Standard pinout of a 2K × 8 static RAM. This pinout is compatible with that of EPROMs except for parenthesized pins which may be assigned different functions.

it goes active shortly after the beginning of a memory machine cycle. Following the end of such a cycle, CS^* goes back to the inactive state. Note the "guard" time interval between CS^* and OE^*. It ensures that the DQ data lines remain in a floating state during the front part of a cycle. This is precisely what OE^* is all about.

Without the additional control provided through the OE^* input, we face a problem known as **bus contention**. Consider, for instance, having two SRAMs. Assume the DQ outputs of both devices connect to the same data lines. The problem arises when we access one device right after the other. Under such

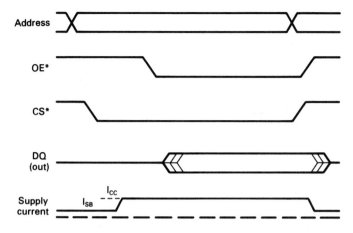

Figure 4-13.   Read cycle timing relationships in a byte-wide static RAM.

conditions it is possible that the newly selected device may start driving the data bus while the previously selected one is still doing so.   Consequently, a data line may be pulled by one device toward ground and by the other toward V_{cc}.   This kind of contention generates sizable noise spikes.   It also has the potential of damaging the SRAM devices.   What if a SRAM is not equipped with an OE^* control line?   We can still get around the problem by introducing a guard time interval between successive memory cycles.   However, this makes the effective length of memory cycles longer.

SRAMs usually dissipate less power while in standby mode—that is, while CS^* is at a high.   This is seen in Figure 4-13 which shows how the supply current (I_{cc}) varies in the course of a memory cycle.   In SRAMs, there is no essential difference between access and cycle times.   This is in contrast to DRAMs, which necessitate a precharge time interval following each access.

The example of Figure 4-14 demonstrates how much easier it is to interface to SRAMs versus DRAMs.   The pictured system is based on an 8088 and employs two 2K × 8 SRAMs.   Address lines $A0$–$A10$ connect to both SRAMs.   They select one out of the 2,048 byte locations within each device.   High-order address lines $A11$–$A13$ are decoded for generation of chip select signals.   The decoder is enabled only during memory cycles (see more about address decoding in Section 4.5).   In the 8088, RD^* is inactive during the front part of a read bus cycle.   Hence, it can be used directly as an OE^* signal (see Figure 3-3).   Although the OE^* signal is common, only the data lines of one SRAM are enabled (from the device side) at any particular time, because enabling of the DQ lines requires both CS^* and OE^* to be active at the same time.

Example 4-10

SRAM access times are usually specified in terms of two parameters: access time relative to address valid and access time relative to the leading edge of CS^*.   A third

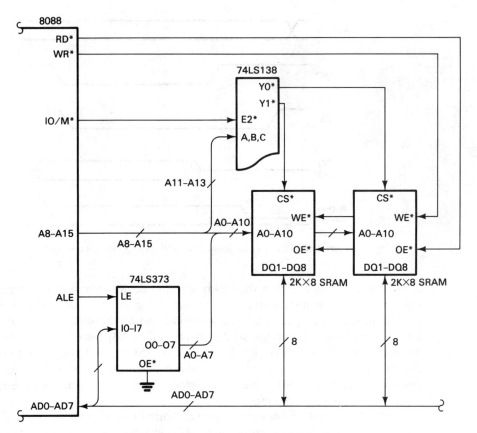

Figure 4-14. Example of static RAM interfacing.

parameter of importance is the OE^*-to-valid-data delay time. Assume a SRAM for which the above parameters have the values 80, 80, and 20 ns, respectively. The CPU is an 8088 and interfaces to the SRAMs as shown in Figure 4-14. The data-to-output delay of the latch is 32 ns, and the address-to-output delay of the decoder 39 ns. For simplicity you can assume the address signals stabilize 50 ns after the start of $T1$, RD^* goes active in the middle of the first half of $T2$, and the clocking rate is 10 MHz. Which timing parameter determines the access time of the static memory? Do we need any wait states?

Solution. Let us take as a reference point the instant address signals become stable at the CPU pins. The valid address access time requirement is satisfied after $32 + 80 = 112$ ns. The access time requirement relative to CS^* is satisfied after $39 + 80 = 119$ ns. RD^* goes active at time $50 + 25 = 75$ ns. Hence the data lines are enabled after a total of $75 + 20 = 95$ ns from our reference point. Thus, the memory access time is determined by the CS^*-related access time parameter (which is the longest of the three).

The CPU samples the data bus at the end of state $T3$; that is, $300 - 50 = 250$ ns from our reference point. Consequently no wait states are necessary.

SRAMs for Low-Power Designs

The advantages we have seen for CMOS μPs hold for CMOS SRAMs as well. For example, the power consumption of the latter may be ten times lower compared to that of their NMOS counterparts. As a result, CMOS SRAMs play a key role in portable equipment and other applications having low-power requirements.

Some devices are designed for operation at a fixed V_{cc} voltage of 5 V. Others permit a wide range of supply voltages. Employing higher (than 5 V) supply voltages can be advantageous in applications demanding high noise immunity. Remember, though, that the selected supply voltage has a major impact on the speed and power dissipation of a CMOS device (see Problem 2-21). Such impacts must be determined before we finalize a design. We may also have to use level shifters when interfacing to devices operating at a V_{cc} of 5 V.

Minimization of power consumption is always a design objective. However, in the case of μC systems with battery power or battery backup, this becomes a must. First, let us examine how power is dissipated in CMOS memories.

Most operating power is consumed while the chip select (or chip enable) inputs switch from one state to another. To see this, consider the typical inverter structure employed in CMOS devices (Figure 4-15). When the input voltage (V_i) is lower than the threshold (V_1) of the N-channel transistor, only the P-channel transistor is conducting. Hence, the output voltage (V_0) is close to V_{cc}. Likewise, when V_i is higher than the threshold (V_2) of the P-channel transistor, only the N-channel transistor is conducting. In this case V_o is close to ground voltage.

What if V_i has values between V_1 and V_2? Now both transistors are conducting. This introduces a low impedance path between V_{cc} and ground. As a consequence, the supply current (I_{cc}) increases. Figure 4-15(b) illustrates this in qualitative terms. Notice that when V_i is sufficiently close to V_{cc} or ground, I_{cc} reduces to a very small value representing leakage current. A direct consequence of this behavior is that CMOS inputs should not be driven by devices having valid

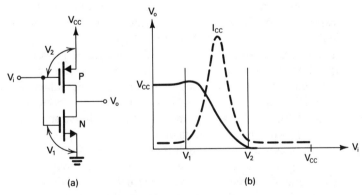

Figure 4-15. Basic CMOS inverter. (a) Circuit structure. (b) Output voltage and supply current in terms of the input voltage.

logic levels between V_1 and V_2. In such cases it may be necessary to use pull-up resistors. This way CMOS inputs are kept above the V_2 threshold.

Power consumption can be reduced further by

1. Avoiding floating conditions on CMOS inputs. Take, for instance, the case of a system employing battery backup only for the memory devices. If power is lost, the outputs of the memory interface circuits will be floating. Then the inputs of the CMOS SRAMs will be floating too. The result is increased power consumption. To prevent this we may use both pull-up and pull-down resistors.

2. Keeping devices in idle mode when appropriate. While in that mode, input lines should be driven to their respective inactive state (held at a voltage close to V_{cc} or ground). Maintaining logic levels close to V_{cc} or ground is especially critical for devices operating at reduced supply voltages.

3. Using CMOS rather than LSTTL (low-power Schottky TTL) drivers. Reduction of the capacitive loads driven by the drivers is also conserving power.

Nonvolatile Memory

SRAMs are often used in the design of nonvolatile memories. The idea is to switch the memory (or a portion of it) to battery power whenever the primary power is lost. This allows us to preserve its contents until primary power is restored. CMOS SRAMs are favored in such applications for two reasons:

1. Their low power consumption (which is particularly important when long periods of power loss must be tolerated)

2. The ability of some devices to retain data at voltages as low as 2 V

The choice of batteries is not a trivial problem in applications involving temperature extremes, condensation, and so on. Among other characteristics you should consider carefully the temperature range, the shape of the discharge curve, physical size, leakage rate, recharging features, and cost.

There are many approaches to the design of power supplies with battery backup. For example, some schemes are based on simple diode isolation. More elaborate ones employ a separate winding in the secondary of the transformer for direct detection of AC loss. Figure 4-16 illustrates a battery backup arrangement in simplified form. Under normal conditions the supply current is provided by the primary power supply through diode D1 (which is forward biased). In contrast, diode D2 is backward biased such that no current flows into or out of the battery. When main power is lost, the supply current is provided by the battery. The supply current flows via protective resistor R and diode D2 which is now forward biased. D1 is now backward biased, inhibiting battery current flow toward the power supply. Capacitor C serves the usual filtering purposes.

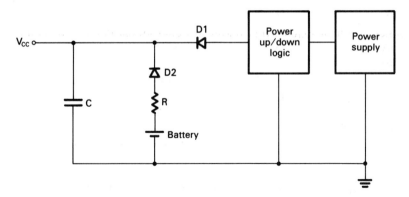

Figure 4-16. Simplified diagram of a power supply with battery backup.

We will discuss in brief some of the problems we face and what considerations we should keep in mind when we design systems with battery backup.

1. The design of the circuitry which senses power loss and power restoration needs special attention. Ensure the sensing circuits will not be mistriggered by noise spikes.
2. During power up/down sequences
   - Input voltages to CMOS devices should not exceed V_{cc} or go below ground.
   - V_{cc} should stay always above 2 V.
   - Memory devices must be protected from transients which can cause loss of stored data.
3. A forthcoming power loss must be detected early enough to allow completion of any memory cycle that may currently be in progress. Some applications require saving in the CMOS SRAMs data contained in CPU registers or volatile memory. In this case we need longer times for completion of the data transfers before switching to the battery.
4. Deactivate the enable inputs of the CMOS SRAMs before switching to the battery. Maintain such inputs in an inactive state until AC power is again restored.
5. After switching to battery power, the control lines of the CMOS devices must not be left floating. Otherwise we may have loss of memory data.

4.2 READ-ONLY MEMORY

The memory devices we examined so far permit the CPU to read or write into any memory location. As a matter of fact, read cycle times are about equal to write cycle times. However, memory portions containing programs are usually accessed by the CPU in read-only mode. The same holds true for certain permanent data. This suggests that very often programs (and even data) could be stored permanently in read-only memory. Read-only memories have the important advantage of being nonvolatile. Their content does not change as a result of some erroneous operation or when power is lost. In fact, most µCs require some kind of nonvolatile memory to store the program which starts up the system when power is turned on or when power is restored following an interruption. The software we store permanently in read-only memory is commonly known as **firmware**.

Read-only memory devices employ a byte-wide organization. They also share the same standard packaging and (with some exceptions) the same pinout with byte-wide SRAMs. The types of read-only memory devices are categorized into:

1. Nonprogrammable read-only memories (**ROMs**)
2. Programmable, nonerasable, read-only memories (**PROMs**)
3. Programmable, ultraviolet erasable, read-only memories (**UV EPROMs**)
4. Programmable, electrically erasable, read-only memories (**EEPROMs**)

ROMs are not user-programmable. Instead, the seminconductor manufacturer "wires in" the contents specified by the user. This is accomplished using a mask process during the final stage of the fabrication of the device. Programmable read-only memories allow users to program the desired contents after the devices are purchased. Nonerasable memories can be programmed by the user only once, but erasable ones can be erased and reprogrammed whenever necessary. The latter are further classified into UV EPROMs and EEPROMs on the basis of the means utilized for erasing. Next we discuss each category of read-only memory devices and its applications separately.

4.2.1 ROM

The external interface and read cycle timing of ROMs are similar to those we have seen for byte-wide SRAMs. Most are available in 24-pin or 28-pin packages (depending on the required number of address lines and hence capacity). Usually, higher capacity devices preserve (to a certain degree) pinout compatibility with lower capacity ones. It is therefore advisable to lay out the circuit board for a 28-pin package. This will permit easy accommodation of a larger capacity ROM if future upgrading becomes necessary.

Because they are simpler, ROMs allow higher bit densities than other memory devices. As a result, the cost per bit is lower compared to RAMs and EPROMs of comparable capacities. Remember, though, that since ROMs are programmed during their fabrication, they represent custom devices. Consequently they must be produced in high volume to become economical. **Programming** refers to storing the user-specified program (or data) using a mask process (which is why ROMs are often referred to as **mask-programmable**).

A second significant consideration has to do with the fact that ROMs are truly permanent memories whose contents cannot be altered. Although this makes the devices more reliable, it also has a serious drawback. It does not permit corrections of software errors or program modifications. If we must do so, we have to discard the original parts, repay a mask charge, and wait for months for the new devices. To minimize the risk we use initially EPROMs or even SRAMs. Later on, when the software matures we may use ROMs for higher reliability.

4.2.2 PROM

Programmable, but nonerasable, read-only memories are known as PROMs. They consist of cell arrays interconnected by means of **fusible links**. The latter can be "burned away" or "shorted" (depending on the type of fuse), to store the desired data permanently. Since the process is based on electrical means, it can be performed in the laboratory. So, in contrast to ROMs, PROMs are available as general-purpose parts which can be purchased in advance and be programmed later as needed.

PROMs are primarily used for storing microcode in microprogrammed designs. Usually such applications require high speed, which is why most PROMs are bipolar devices. Hence, their power consumption is higher and capacities are lower than those of other (MOS-based) read-only memory devices.

The external interface and timing of PROMs are similar to those of ROMs. Many of the PROMs fabricated by different manufacturers have very similar electrical characteristics (including those relating to programming). Such devices are often referred to as **generic PROMs**. PROMs have the disadvantage of not allowing reprogramming. This limitation is overcome by EPROMs which are examined next.

4.2.3 UV EPROM

In ROMs and PROMs, the storage mechanism is based on permanent circuit alterations. EPROMs employ an entirely different mechanism. They store information by trapping charge in the array cells.

The transistors forming the cells of an EPROM differ from ordinary MOS transistors. The former include underneath the regular gate an extra **floating gate**. As implied by the name, this gate does not connect to any element external to the transistor, yet it constitutes the storage node. The floating gate is charged by applying to the regular gate a relatively high voltage (typically 21 V). This causes injection of electrons through the junction area of the transistor. A fraction of these electrons is captured by the floating gate and continues to remain there even after the high bias voltage is removed. The trapped charge changes the threshold of the transistor and thus allows us to determine whether the cell contains a 1 or a 0. Since the floating gate is insulated from its surroundings it can preserve the charge for years. Over this period, the cell can be read reliably millions of times.

Information stored in a cell can be erased by discharging its floating gate. Thus, EPROMs can be erased and subsequently reprogrammed for a practically unlimited number of times. Such flexibility is valuable in the design of μC systems since it makes reusable existing parts when a program change becomes necessary. On the basis of the approach employed for erasing, EPROMs are categorized into UV EPROMs and EEPROMs.

UV EPROMs are erased when exposed to ultraviolet (UV) light. For this purpose the package is equipped on the top with a UV-transparent **quartz window** allowing complete exposure of the cell array. UV light is simply giving the trapped electrons enough energy to return to the substrate of the cell transistor. UV EPROMs are primarily intended as a design tool during system development (when program changes are frequent and must be made quickly). Because of the flexibility they offer for future program changes, they are often used in production equipment. They are also used when the production volume is not large enough to justify use of ROMs.

External Interface and Timing

Figure 4-17 shows the external interface lines of a typical UV EPROM. Observe the similarity to those of byte-wide SRAMs, shown in Figure 4-12. Naturally, there is no write enable line. On the other hand, there is a V_{pp} line for programming purposes. The chip enable (CE^*) input plays the same role chip select does in SRAMs. Generally, the manufacturers maintain pin compatibility between their UV EPROMs and ROMs. This permits plugging in the same socket a UV EPROM (prototype units) or a ROM (production units). Such compatibility extends to different capacity EPROMs even when they have different numbers of pins. As an example Figure 4-17(b) shows the pinout of Intel's 2732A (4K × 8) and 27256 (32K × 8) UV EPROMs. You can see that a 28-pin socket would accommodate either one of these two devices. It can also accommodate members of the compatible 2300 series of Intel's ROMs.

Read cycle timing is like that of byte-wide SRAMs. In Figure 4-18 we show the timing relationships associated with the programming of the 2732A. This device goes into programming mode when the OE^*/V_{pp} input is at 21 V. Data are presented to the device through the data output pins which in this mode play the role of input lines. A program pulse is required for each location we program. Note from Figure 4-18 that right after programming, a location may be read back for verification. In the case of the 27256, programming is accomplished by holding V_{pp} to a DC level of 12.5 V and CE^* to a TTL low level. In addition to lower programming voltages, some devices are designed such that they can be programmed very fast. Furthermore, they may contain an identification code (often known as **electronic signature**) indicating their manufacturer and type. This code is read by the programming equipment which then chooses the appropriate programming algorithm.

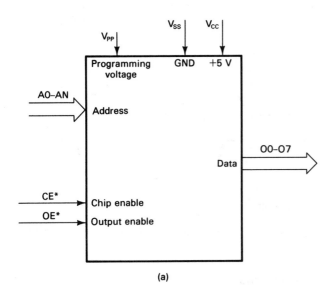

(a)

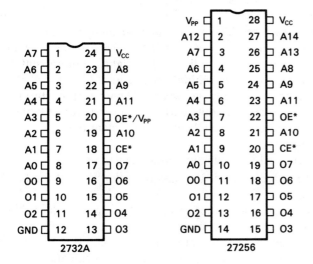

2732A   27256

(b)

Figure 4-17.   (a) External interface lines of a typical UV EPROM.   (b) Pinouts of the 2732A (4K × 8) and 27256 (32K × 8) UV EPROMs.

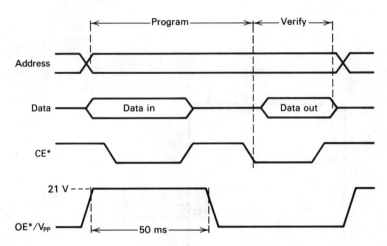

Figure 4-18. Program and verify cycle timing of the 2732A UV EPROM.

Interfacing to the CPU is just as easy as in the case of byte-wide SRAMs (see Figure 4-14).

Data Retention and Other Concerns

Besides the usual key characteristics such as access time and power dissipation, we are interested in how well a UV EPROM retains data over its lifetime. Typically, **retention times** amount to many years. They are usually given by the manufacturer at a specific temperature—for example, 15 years at 55 °C. This assumes the device will not be exposed for long to sources radiating UV light. Fluorescent room lighting, for instance, may erase a device within three years. Direct sunlight can have the same effect within approximately one week. Device manufacturers provide opaque labels which are placed over the quartz windows to protect them from unintentional erasure. Data retention may become a problem only if:

1. The UV EPROMs are used in production equipment
2. The life cycle of the product exceeds the data retention time of the devices

When this is the case, you must plan either to reprogram or to replace the UV EPROMs (with newly programmed ones) prior to the elapse of the specified retention times. What if the devices are reprogrammed or replaced, say, every two to five years in order to incorporate firmware changes? In this case data retention will never become a problem.

The decoupling practices discussed for RAMs also apply to UV EPROMs. If a device employs high-voltage pulses for programming, you should decouple the V_{pp} pin as well. This prevents the noise spikes, generated during programming, from damaging the device. UV EPROMs (as well as PROMs) are programmed in the laboratory or the factory using special equipment known as **PROM programmers**.

4.2.4 EEPROM

UV EPROMs fall short of providing the ideal alterable memory characteristics. Reprogramming necessitates their removal from the system. Besides, they cannot be erased selectively. Once exposed to UV light, the entire device is erased and needs to be wholly reprogrammed. Both problems stem from the fact that their electron injection mechanism is not reversible, so we have to resort to optical means of erasing.

In EEPROMs, electrons are injected to the floating gate using a tunneling (rather than an avalanche) mechanism. This mechanism is bilateral, permitting electron injection from the floating gate to the substrate by reversing the bias conditions. It is this capability that allows erasing of array cells electrically. As a consequence, EEPROMs (also designated as E^2PROMs) do not have the two problems we mentioned in connection with UV EPROMs:

1. Reprogramming does not necessitate removal of EEPROM devices from the system. The erase/write circuits are themselves part of the system. Thus such operations can be performed "in-circuit."
2. EEPROMs can be erased and reprogrammed on a location-by-location basis. This saves time and makes patching of programming errors practical.

These characteristics eliminate the field service expenses associated with the removal of the devices from the equipment, their reprogramming at a service facility, and their reinstallation. Instead, product changes can be done on-site. In fact, reprogramming can be accomplished even remotely by transmitting the information over a communication link. For example, this approach could be used to update from a central location data in point-of-sale terminals (such as product code, pricing, and so on).

Erase/Write Operations

Before writing new data in a byte location, the old information must be erased. Erasing and writing are accomplished by means of programming pulses much like in UV EPROMs. However, since such operations are performed in-circuit, EEPROM-based designs must include circuitry for generation of the programming pulses. Typically, the length of a write cycle (including erasing) is 10 ms or more, so direct interfacing to a μP would impose on the CPU a very long chain of wait states. This problem is solved by supplementing the erase/write circuitry with logic, which

1. Receives and stores the information associated with a write cycle (that is, address, data, and even control signals)
2. Proceeds on its own to perform the write cycle
3. Notifies the CPU upon completion

Such an arrangement frees the CPU during the long time intervals taken by EEPROM write cycles.

EEPROMs place a limit on the total number of write cycles over the lifetime of the component (**write endurance**). For example, a device may have a write endurance of 10,000 write cycles per location (erasing and writing does not affect adjacent byte locations). EEPROMs are used to store programs, as well as parameters whose values do not change very often. Thus, write endurance does not pose a problem in real systems. How about data retention times? As in UV EPROMs, they amount to many years; however, we can make a firmware change without having to reprogram the entire device. When firmware is updated in this mode, we must consider data retention for locations we never reprogrammed. This should be done prior to the elapse of the specified data retention time; better yet, the entire device can be reprogrammed when firmware is updated. After all, this can easily be accomplished in-circuit.

Example of an EEPROM

Figure 4-19 shows the external interface lines of a representative EEPROM—the Intel 2817A (2K × 8). This device includes on-chip all of the erase/write support circuits discussed earlier. Such is the case with other EEPROMs as well, a fact which considerably simplifies interfacing EEPROMs to CPUs.

Notice the similarities with the external interface of a typical UV EPROM as seen in Figure 4-17. There is, however, no V_{pp} input. On the other hand, there are two additional control lines: WE^* (write enable) and $RDY/BUSY^*$ (ready/busy). When WE^* is activated, the 2817A latches the location address and the new data. Then it goes on to initiate and complete automatically all actions associated with an erase/write operation. Meanwhile it maintains the $RDY/BUSY^*$ line to a low to indicate its busy state. Upon completion of the write cycle, the device informs the CPU by switching its $RDY/BUSY^*$ line back to a high.

Read cycles are like those of UV EPROMs and SRAMs. In fact, the schematic of Figure 4-14 continues to hold if we replace the two SRAMs by two 2817As. The $RDY/BUSY^*$ line would connect to interrupt circuitry to notify the CPU about the completion of a write cycle.

Example 4-11

A particular version of the 2817A takes 10 ms per write cycle. It is employed in a robot to hold calibration constants. Suppose we have to modify the table of calibration

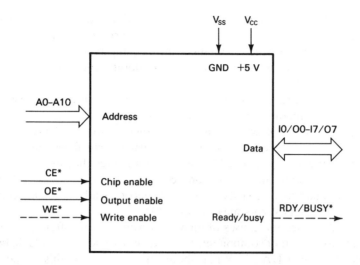

Figure 4-19.   External interface of the 2817A (2K × 8) EEPROM.

constants. How long it will take to do so, given that a total of 180 bytes need to be changed?

Compare an EEPROM to a nonvolatile RAM (implemented with CMOS SRAMs) from the applications viewpoint.

Solution. The updating of the table will take (at minimum) 180 × 10 = 1800 ms, that is, 1.8 s.

EEPROMs have the significant advantage of not requiring batteries. Unfortunately, when it comes to write operations, they are too slow. This fact makes them unsuitable in saving information when power is lost. Assume, for instance, that V_{cc} remains within the operational range for 3 ms after detection of a forthcoming power loss. For the EEPROM described here, this time interval will not be sufficient to save even one byte. On the other hand, SRAMs (with battery backup) would permit us to save hundreds of bytes.

4.3 ERROR DETECTION AND CORRECTION

The motivation for error-detection-and-correction (EDAC) in memories stems from two reasons:

1. The probability of occurrence of a memory error is quite considerable. This is especially true in large dynamic memories.
2. The consequences of a memory error can be very serious.

Consider, for example, a single bit inversion in the opcode part of an instruction. This will change the original instruction into some other type of instruction, which, when executed by the CPU, will cause an unintended operation. In fact, if the original instruction changes into a jump type one, the CPU is likely to start execution of some other program. Generally this eventually leads to a "**system crash**."

Such situations are unacceptable in most applications. Instead memory errors must at a minimum be detected and brought to the attention of the CPU. Many applications, of course, require that such errors not only be detected but also corrected. This is accomplished by using **error-detection-and-correction codes**, commonly known as EDAC codes. Sometimes they are also referred to as ECC (error checking and correction) codes. EDAC reduces system downtime and lowers maintenance costs. Hence, it becomes advantageous even in applications where memory errors may be tolerable.

What are the causes of memory errors? How often do memory devices fail compared to other components? What approaches are available for error detection and possibly EDAC? What about components for this purpose? How do we apply them? The objective of this section is to address these and other related concerns.

Types of Errors and Their Causes

Memory errors are classified into hard errors and soft errors. A **hard error** represents a permanent failure due to some physical defect—for example, a short within a memory chip causing a data bit to get "stuck" to a permanent 1 or 0. Such errors necessitate replacement of some part of the hardware for their elimination. The part we replace is typically a printed board assembly.

In contrast, **soft errors** are not related to hardware failures. They are random and unpredictable in nature. For example they can be caused by noise due to poor board layout, out-of-range voltage or temperature, sensitivity to some data pattern, and so on. However, in dynamic memories the major soft error contributor is alpha particles. These particles are emitted by traces of radioactive materials present in the package which encapsulates the chip. Recall that the storage mechanism of a DRAM cell is based on a small capacitor whose state determines whether a 1 or a 0 has been stored. An alpha particle causes ionization and thereby neutralizes part of the charge stored in a cell capacitor. This, in turn, affects the critical charge on the basis of which a 1 is differentiated from a 0. Hence, a cell may appear containing the inverse of its original content. Naturally the device itself is not affected. In fact, such an error can be eliminated by correcting and then rewriting the data. Note that SRAMs, PROMs, and EPROMs are not employing a capacitor-based mechanism. Consequently they are not affected by alpha particle radiation.

Most manufacturers express the **failure rate** of their devices in terms of the percent probability that the device will fail over a time interval of 1000 hours. Let

COMPONENT TYPE	TYPICAL FAILURE RATE (FITs)
Resistor	1
Diode	1
SSI	10
Ceramic capacitor	10
Tantalum capacitor	20
MSI	50
Printed board	500
64K × 1 DRAM	1200

Figure 4-20. Typical failure rates of some common components.

us take, for instance, a 64K × 1 DRAM. The meaning of a failure rate of 0.12%/1000 hours is that over 1000 hours of operation the probability the device will fail is 0.0012. Alternatively, failure rates are expressed in **FITs (failures in time)**. One FIT represents one failure over a time interval of 10^9 hours. For example, the failure rate of 0.12%/1000 hours is equivalent to $0.0012 \times 10^6 = 1200$ FITs. Regardless of how we express them, failure rates reflect how reliable devices (or assemblies) are.

Failure rates are additive, so if we assume the above failure rate for a 64K × 1 DRAM, the failure rate of a 64K × 16 memory array will be $1200 \times 16 = 19200$ FITs. Similarly, in order to determine the (composite) failure rate of a DRAM device we add its hard and soft failure rates. In general, soft failures exceed hard ones. For example, a 64K × 1 DRAM having a hard failure rate of 200 FITs, may have a soft failure rate of 1000 FITs. Furthermore, to calculate the overall reliability of a memory, we must add the failure rates of the rest of the components employed in its design. In Figure 4-20 we tabulate typical failure rates for some common components. Notice the magnitude of DRAM failure rates compared to those of other components. This, plus the fact that a memory may include many DRAMs, justifies why we are so concerned about detecting and possibly correcting memory errors.

Example 4-12

The 512 KB memory of a 16-bit μP is implemented with 64K × 1 DRAMs on a single PCB. In addition to the memory chips, it includes 11 MSI and 25 SSI devices. Calculate its failure rate assuming that there are ten resistors, 100 ceramic capacitors, and four tantalum capacitors. Assume the typical failure rates listed in Figure 4-20.

Solution. Each memory bank requires 16 DRAMs and provides 128 KB. For a total of 512 KB we need four banks; that is, 64 DRAM devices. The failure rate of the memory array is $1200 \times 64 = 76800$ FITs. That of the remaining components is $(11 \times 50) + (25 \times 10) + (10 \times 1) + (100 \times 10) + (4 \times 20) + (1 \times 500) = 2390$. Therefore the failure rate of the entire memory board is $76800 + 2390 = 79190$ FITs. Note that the memory devices account for about 97 percent of the failures.

Another measure of the reliability of a device is the **mean time between failures (MTBF)**; which indicates how long, on the average, we can operate a device (or an assembly) without an error. MTBF is simply the reciprocal of the failure rate.

Example 4-13

Calculate the MTBF of the 64K × 1 DRAM we discussed above. Repeat for the 512 KB memory board we dealt with in Example 4-12.

Assume a large-scale system employing 32 μCs. Each μC is equipped with one such memory board. What is the mean time between memory failures in this system?

Solution. The MTBF of a DRAM is $1/(1200/10^9) = 10^9/1200$ hours, or about 830,000 hours—that is, 95 years. For the memory board we have $10^9/79190 = 12600$ hours, or $12600/(24 \times 30) = 17$ months. In other words, we should expect (on the average) a memory board failure about every 1.5 years.

The memory of the entire system amounts to $512 \times 32 = 16$ MB (32 memory boards). Its failure rate will be 32 times that of a single memory board. Equivalently, its MTBF will be shorter by a factor of 32. That is, $12600/32 = 394$ hours, which is equivalent to $394/24 = 16.4$ days only. Hence, we should expect a memory failure somewhere in the system about every two weeks!

Error Detection

Both error detection and EDAC techniques employ the same principle. They add redundant information bits to data words before they are written in memory. These extra bits provide the means for error detection or EDAC when a data word is read from memory. As you might suspect, the number of detectable (or detectable and correctable) errors depends on how many redundant bits we add per data word. Before considering EDAC techniques we discuss a very common approach to error detection: parity.

The **parity technique** requires adding only one bit—called a parity bit—to a data word. A parity bit may take the value of 1 or 0 depending on:

1. The number of 1s in the data word
2. The employed parity scheme

The **even parity** scheme requires the total number of 1s (including the parity bit itself) to be even. Thus, if the data word has an even number of 1s, the parity bit is assigned the value of 0. If the data word contains an odd number of 1s, the parity bit is assigned the value of 1. The **odd parity** scheme requires the total number of 1s to be odd. Some examples in which the data word is assumed to be one byte long are shown in Figure 4-21.

Prior to writing a data word in memory, we generate its parity according to the adapted parity scheme. The generated parity bit is stored in memory with the data. Subsequently, when the data word is read from memory, we again determine

Parity Scheme	Data Bits	Number of 1s in Data Byte	Parity Bit
even	10100011	4	0
even	00101100	3	1
odd	10111010	5	0
odd	10001000	2	1

Figure 4-21. Examples of parity generation in the case of single-byte words.

its parity. The latter is compared with the original parity bit read from memory. If they are different, then an error has occurred.

This simple technique permits detection of single errors. It can also detect multiple errors as long as the number of bits in error is odd. However, double errors (and other multiple ones having an even number of bits in error) cannot be detected. Still, parity is a very useful error detection mechanism because the most common errors are single ones. Double errors, for instance, are 50 to 100 times less frequent. If data words consist of two or more bytes we can increase the detection capability further by employing one parity bit per byte. Take, for example, the case of 16-bit words. Use of a separate parity bit for each byte allows detection of double errors (as long as they occur in different bytes).

The circuitry for generation of the parity bit before a memory write, and checking after a memory read, is available in a 14-pin device called a **parity generator/checker**. An example of such a device is the 74280. Figure 4-22(a) shows the external interface of a parity generator/checker. The device generates both even and odd parity over eight bits of data. Figure 4-22(b) depicts its function as a parity generator and as a parity checker. The illustrated case involves an application where data bytes are transferred from a source to some kind of destination.

Input $P9$ allows selection of either odd or even parity. In applications where parity must be generated over a data field longer than eight bits, $P9$ can serve as an expansion input (fed from the output of another parity generator/checker). When active, the *INHIBIT* input disables both parity outputs. At the destination (where parity is checked), $P9$ is fed from the parity bit generated at the source. If the parity output of the checker is high, one of the bits arrived in error. However, it is not possible to determine which bit is in error unless additional cycles are performed and the error happens to be a hard one (see for example Problem 4-12). What then? Usually we simply restart the system. The system may even be shut down to prevent it from entering an unknown state and thereby cause additional "damage."

Example 4-14

A system employs an 8-bit μP with 128 KB of memory, implemented with 64K × 1 DRAMs having a failure rate of 1200 FITs. The nature of the application is such that failures are tolerated as long as they are detected on time and the system is brought to a halt. Hence, it is decided to add one parity bit per byte for error

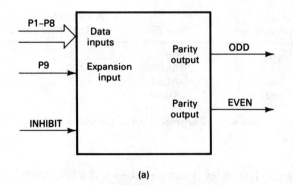

(a)

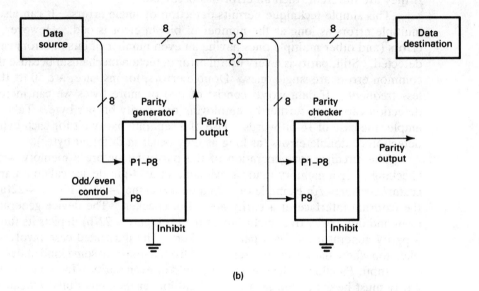

(b)

Figure 4-22. Parity generator/checker. (a) External interface. (b) Application
of the device as a parity generator and as a parity checker.

detection. How often would the memory fail before we add parity? Assume all
failures involve single errors. How often will the system stop because of a memory
failure? Ignore failures caused by other components such as memory interface circuits.

Solution. In Example 4-13 we calculated that the MTBF of one such DRAM is 95
years. For a total of 128 KB we need 16 DRAMs organized into two banks. Therefore, the MTBF of the memory is reduced to 95/16; that is, about six years. To
answer the second question we must take into consideration the number of added
DRAMs for parity implementation, which requires one 64K × 1 DRAM per bank.
Thus the total number of DRAMs is 18, so the MTBF of the memory decreases to
95/18, or about five years. The advantage of course is that memory errors are now
detectable. Since all failures are assumed to involve single memory errors, they are

all detected. Consequently, memory errors will halt the system (on the average) every five years.

Error Detection and Correction

The error-detection-and-correction (EDAC) techniques are an extension of the simple parity method just discussed. They are usually modified versions of a technique invented by Hamming based on multiple parity bits which are generated over certain subsets of bits in a data word. These parity bits are called **check bits** and are stored with the data in memory. When the data word is read from memory, new check bits are generated which are compared with those read from memory. The result of the comparison is known as **syndrome** and identifies which bits are in error. Furthermore the syndrome may be used to correct some or all detected errors.

How many errors can be detected in a data word? From those detected, how many can be corrected? The answers to these questions depend on:

1. The number of data bits per word
2. The number of check bits

The most widely used EDAC scheme detects double errors and allows correction of single ones. This is satisfactory for most applications because single errors are the most common (soft errors occur only one at a time). Usually, double errors happen when a soft error remains uncorrected in memory and another soft error occurs later. Such occurrences can be prevented by

- Substituting corrected data in a location whenever a single soft error is detected
- Error scrubbing

Error scrubbing refers to the scanning of the entire memory for correction of any detected soft errors. Naturally error scrubbing consumes system time, but it might be done as a low priority software task.

Figure 4-23 lists the number of required check bits (for double error detection and single error correction) in the case of 8-, 16-, and 32-bit words. We see that for 8-bit data words we need more than 60 percent additional memory capacity for

Length of Data Word	Number of Check Bits	Overhead
8	5	62.5%
16	6	37.5%
32	7	21.9%

Figure 4-23. Required number of check bits per data word for detection of double errors and correction of single ones.

accommodation of the check bits. The overhead drops to about 40 percent for 16-bit data words and keeps dropping further as data words get longer.

Example 4-15

The 1 MB memory of a 16-bit μP is implemented with 256K $\times$ 1 DRAMs. Calculate its MTBF assuming 2000 FITs for each DRAM.

Suppose we use EDAC for correction of single errors. What improvement are we going to gain in reliability given that 98 percent of the failures involve single bits?

Solution. Each bank requires 16 DRAMs and provides 512 KB of memory. Hence, the required total number of devices is 32. The composite failure rate (ignoring components other than DRAMs) is 2000 $\times$ 32 = 64000. This corresponds to an MTBF of 10^9 / 64000 = 15625 hours, or 15625 / (24 $\times$ 30) = 22 months.

Each memory bank requires six more DRAMs for storing check bits. Thus, the total number of devices becomes 22 $\times$ 2 = 44. The failure rate is now 2000 $\times$ 44 = 88000 FITs. However, only multiple errors constitute failures (single errors are corrected), so the effective failure rate of the memory is reduced to 88000 $\times$ 0.02 = 1760. This corresponds to an MTBF of 10^9 / 1760 = 568,180 hours, or about 790 months. Hence reliability improves by a factor of 790 / 22 = 36. This result is indicative of the dramatic improvement we gain even with single error correction.

Besides the additional memory capacity, EDAC requires extra logic to perform the operations associated with error detection and correction. Such operations can be very complex, yet the design of EDAC-equipped memories is relatively simple thanks to the availability of EDAC "units." These are LSI/VLSI devices performing the operations just discussed and certain useful additional ones. They are our next subject.

EDAC Devices

First we examine how an EDAC device relates to the CPU and the memory from the functional point of view. Then we discuss the functions provided in typical EDAC devices.

Figure 4-24 illustrates the basic interface lines. Observe that the memory does not connect directly to the CPU data bus. When a byte or a word of data is to be written, the data go through the EDAC unit for generation of the check bits. Data and check bits are then sent out to memory via the *data out* and *check bits out* buses. The check bits section represents the additional DRAMs we add to each memory bank for accommodation of the check bits. In other words, the data and their associated check bits are read or written as one "word."

For read operations we have two alternatives:

1. Read the data over the *data in* bus and send them to the CPU (via the *DI/DO* lines) unchecked. At the same time start data checking for any errors.

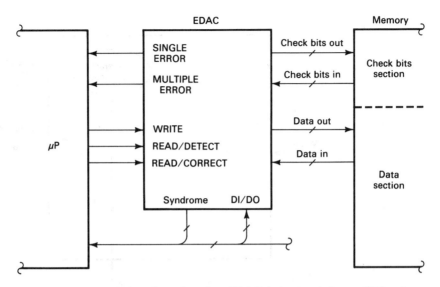

Figure 4-24. Typical configuration of an EDAC device in relation to CPU and memory.

If an error is detected a short time later, alert the CPU via the *SINGLE ERROR* or *MULTIPLE ERROR* lines.

2. Check the read data for errors, correct them if necessary, and then send them to the CPU.

The operating mode of the EDAC device is determined from the CPU by means of the *WRITE, READ/DETECT,* and *READ/CORRECT* control lines.

Figure 4-25 pictures the internal functions of an EDAC during memory operations. It is assumed that a data word is 16 bits long and that six check bits are generated. In the write mode, the situation is fairly straightforward. The device simply generates the check bits for the data we are going to write in memory. Such data are received over the CPU data bus either from the CPU itself or from a (DMA) peripheral device.

In the **read/detect mode** the 16 bits of data bypass the internal logic of the EDAC and become immediately available to the CPU or I/O device. However, the EDAC unit proceeds into generating the new check bits which are then compared with the six check bits read from memory. The results of the comparison are reflected in the syndrome. If any of its bits are 1s, then one or more of the read bits are in error. This is brought to the attention of the CPU through the error flags. The syndrome itself is latched and may be read by the CPU via the data bus.

Notice that in this mode the device does not exercise its error-correcting capabilities. The objective is to avoid the time delays introduced in a memory

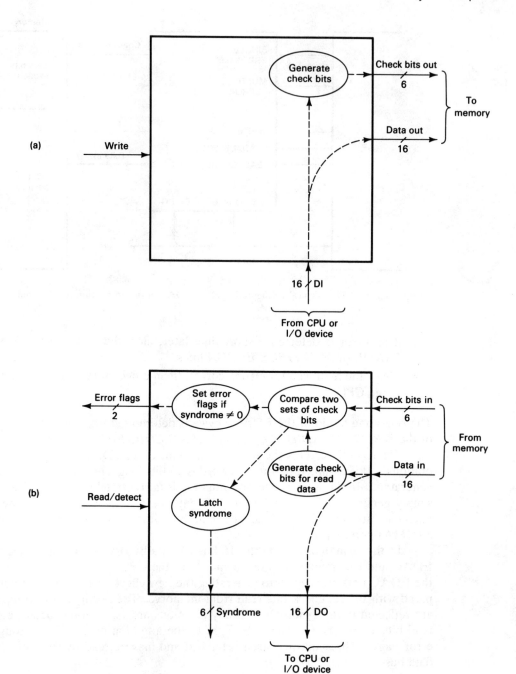

Figure 4-25. Functions of an EDAC device during memory operations. (a) write mode. (b) read/detect mode. (c) read/correct mode.

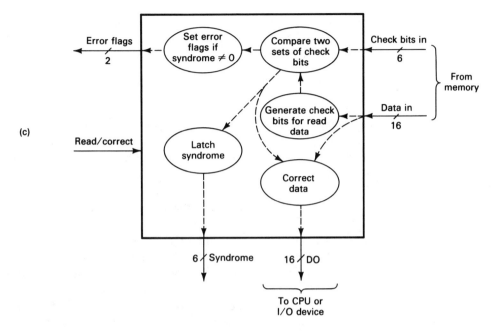

Figure 4-25. (*cont.*)

read cycle by the error detection and correction circuits. On the other hand, if an error is detected, the CPU must be prevented from executing the associated instruction. This implies alerting the CPU through a mechanism other than interrupts. Such a mechanism, for instance, is provided in μPs capable of supporting virtual memory. It allows them to abort and then to restart an instruction cycle or even a machine cycle. Another possible alternative would be to alert the CPU of a detected error(s) prior to the completion of a memory cycle. The CPU would then have to lengthen the cycle to permit error correction and presentation of corrected data by the EDAC.

The **read/correct mode** differs in that data are withheld by the EDAC unit until checked and corrected of any single error. Data correction is accomplished by decoding the syndrome for identification of the erroneous bit, which is subsequently complemented.

Example 4-16

EDAC affects power dissipation and (usually) system speed. Assume a 16-bit μP with 1 MB of memory. By what amount would power dissipation increase if we add double error detection/single error correction capability? Suppose a CPU state is 100 ns long and the memory access time provides a 20 ns margin. How many wait states would the CPU have to insert per memory cycle given the employed EDAC introduces a delay of 40 ns?

Solution. Power dissipation increases because of the additional memory capacity we need. Since we deal with 16-bit words, the increase amounts to 37.5 percent (see Figure 4-23). Data become available to the CPU 20 ns prior to the time they are sampled. However, this margin will not compensate for the additional delay of 40 ns when we add EDAC capability. As a result, the CPU must insert one wait state per memory cycle. This amounts to a lengthening of a memory cycle by an extra 100 ns.

Although EDAC devices are usually designed to handle 16-bit words, they can also operate on individual bytes. Besides, it is possible to cascade two or more units for handling of 32- or even 64-bit words. Other typical characteristics of EDAC devices are:

1. *Detection of All 1s and All 0s:* Such patterns are usually indicative of some major failure.

2. *Error Flags:* EDAC devices provide on two separate lines indications about the nature of an error (that is, whether single or multiple). If there is a double error while in the read/correct mode, or even a single error while in read/detect mode, the CPU must be alerted to prevent the execution of the associated instruction. If there is a single error while in the read/correct mode, the CPU may simply be interrupted to take notice of the event some time later. At that time, the CPU reads the syndrome and the location address.

3. *Syndrome Accessibility:* Most devices make available the syndrome bits at the external interface. These bits become important in the case of errors involving a single bit. By reading and then decoding the syndrome, the CPU determines which bit is in error. In this way the CPU can log information on errors for preventative maintenance purposes. For example, a hard error can be identified from its consistent pattern in the log. Similarly, a high rate of soft errors is indicative of a forthcoming permanent failure. Thus, if the error log shows so, we may replace a memory board before the hard failure occurs.

Example of an EDAC Device

As an example of an actual EDAC device we discuss the AMD Am2960 EDAC unit (Figure 4-26). While doing so we will have the opportunity to see how check bits are derived and how we deduce which bits are in error from the syndrome.

This device employs a common set of lines ($DATA0$–$DATA15$) for both data to/from memory and data to/from the CPU. The *syndrome/check bits* lines multiplex the check bits generated during write cycles with the syndrome derived during read cycles. Notice the use of two 16-bit latches and the separate byte controls. Another 7-bit latch is used to store the check bits read from memory. The seventh check bit allows direct handling of 32-bit words by cascading two devices.

Input control lines *GENERATE** and *CORRECT*, correspond to the write

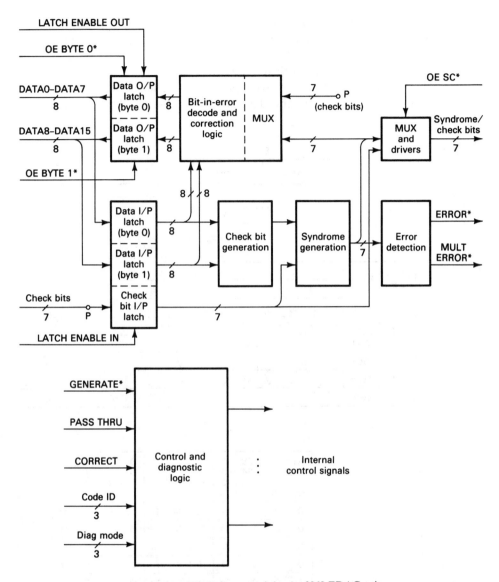

Figure 4-26. Block diagram of the Am2960 EDAC unit.

and read/correct modes of operation discussed before.   In generate mode, the data stored by the CPU in the data input latch are fed to the check bit generation logic. The derived check bits pass (transparently) via the syndrome generation logic and the multiplexer.   They appear over the *syndrome/check bits* outputs when the *OE SC** output enable line goes low.   In the meantime the data are transferred unchanged from the data input latch via the block representing the correction logic. Note that the contents of the data output latch are continuously updated as long as the *LATCH ENABLE OUT* line remains at a high.   With the check bits now available, we activate the output enable lines for presentation of the write data to memory.

In correct mode, both the data and the check bits are read from memory. They are stored in the respective input latches by activating the *LATCH ENABLE IN* line.   Subsequently, the data are fed to the check bit generation logic for

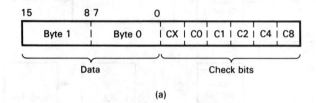

(a)

Check bits	Parity	Data bits															
		0	1	2	3	4	5	6	7	8	9	10	11	12	13	14	15
CX	Even	✓	✓	✓		✓				✓	✓		✓		✓		
CO	Even	✓	✓	✓		✓		✓		✓		✓		✓			
C1	Odd	✓			✓	✓			✓	✓	✓				✓		✓
C2	Odd	✓	✓				✓	✓	✓				✓	✓	✓		
C4	Even			✓	✓	✓	✓	✓	✓							✓	✓
C8	Even									✓	✓	✓	✓	✓	✓	✓	✓

(b)

			S8 S4 S2							
SX	S0	S1	000	100	010	110	001	101	011	111
0	0	0	NE	C8	C4	D	C2	D	D	M
0	0	1	C1	D	D	15	D	13	7	D
0	1	0	CO	D	D	M	D	12	6	D
0	1	1	D	10	4	D	0	D	D	M
1	0	0	CX	D	D	14	D	11	5	D
1	0	1	D	9	3	D	M	D	D	M
1	1	0	D	8	2	D	1	D	D	M
1	1	1	M	D	D	M	D	M	M	D

(c)

Figure 4-27.   (a) Memory word format of the Am2960 in 16-bit data word configuration.   (b) Generation of the check bits from the values of data bits.   (c) Identification of bit(s) in error from the value of the syndrome.

derivation of new check bits. See from Figure 4-26 that the latter are compared with the read check bits by the syndrome generation logic. The syndrome is then fed to

1. *The error detection logic.* If any of the syndrome bits is set to a 1, this logic activates the *ERROR** output line. If an error involves more than one bit, it also activates the *MULT ERROR** output.
2. *The multiplexer and drivers for access by the CPU.*
3. *The bit-in-error decode and correction logic*, which corrects the data by simply inverting the erroneous bit.

The corrected data are then fed to the data output latch for transfer to the CPU. However, for multiple errors, the outcome of the correction process is unspecified.

The Am2960 is used in the read/detect (or check-only) mode by simply ignoring the contents of the data output latch. In this case, the CPU (or DMA device) reads the same data fed from memory to the data input latch. The *pass thru* and *code id* lines are utilized in wider word applications. Finally, this device has a diagnostic mode (*diag mode* signals) whereby it can be exercised by the CPU for correct operation.

Figure 4-27(a) illustrates the memory word format (including check bits) for the standard 16-bit word configuration. The table of Figure 4-27(b) depicts how the check bits (CX, C0, C1, C2, C4, C8) are generated by the Am2960. Each check bit is the parity bit for the data bits indicated by $\sqrt{}$ in the respective row. Observe that all check bits are generated on the basis of the values of eight data bits. Two check bits are generated using the odd parity scheme. The remaining are derived using even parity.

A second table, shown in Figure 4-27(c), reflects the meaning of each of the 64 possible values of the syndrome. Only when all syndrome bits are 0 there is no error (NE). All other 63 values of the syndrome indicate some kind of error condition. When the error is single, the table indicates the bit in error using either a number (for data) or a check bit designation. Double errors are indicated by D. Finally, triple and higher order ones are indicated by M.

4.4 MEMORY MANAGEMENT

In some applications the µC system has to serve many users. However, even when it serves a single user, it may have to handle concurrently multiple tasks. This kind of applications raises a number of serious issues:

1. How do we allocate memory to multiple users or multiple tasks? Allocation of a portion of memory (to each user or each task) on a static basis would be unacceptable. It would require a very large memory. Besides, not all programs need reside in memory at the same time. Those executed infre-

quently may reside in a less expensive storage device and may be brought into memory only when they are to be executed. These considerations suggest allocating memory on a dynamic (rather than static) basis. How do we manage such an allocation scheme?

2. How do we prevent users from causing any modifications (and possibly destroying) system software or programs of other users?

3. How do we prevent users from illegal access to each other's data? For applications (like those dealing with financial transactions) where confidential data must be protected, this is a must.

4. How do we protect a program from other programs of the same user? What about separation of a program from its data?

5. Yet, most often we want to allow sharing of certain data, and even certain programs, among users and tasks. How can we isolate users and tasks from each other and allow such flexibility at the same time?

These questions reflect the type of issues we deal with in memory management. First, we examine the foundations on which memory management is based. Then, we discuss how it is done in practice. At the end of the section we will see an example of a memory management device.

Segmented versus Linear Addressing

Let us start with the two common addressing schemes employed in μPs: segmented addressing and linear addressing. The motivation stems from the fact that one of them lends itself to some form of memory management.

A good representative of **segmented addressing** is the scheme employed by the 8088/8086 CPUs. Recall that the address specified by a programmer in an 8088/8086 instruction does not really constitute an effective logical address. Instead, it is treated as an offset which must be added to a segment address. Though not straightforward, this scheme facilitates considerably program relocation and memory protection.

The **linear addressing** scheme treats the entire memory in a uniform, structureless manner. Here, no effective logical address calculations are necessary. CPUs of the 68000 family employ such a scheme. Clearly, the linear addressing scheme lacks the relocatability advantage of segmented addressing. On the other hand, it facilitates applications involving large data structures where segment size limitations could pose problems.

Translation of Logical Addresses into Physical Addresses

Physical addresses are the addresses of physical memory locations. Ordinarily they are derived directly from the logical addresses specified in the instructions of a program. Take, for instance, the case of an 8-bit μP having a 64 KB address

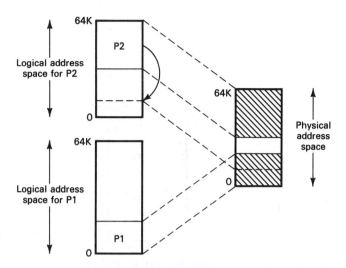

Figure 4-28. Programs can interfere directly with each other when the logical address space coincides with the physical address space.

space. The operand address specified by an instruction (through the various addressing modes) can be anywhere between 0 and 64K, so two programs, say P1 and P2, can have access to any memory location. This means that the logical address space of each program is one and the same thing with the physical address space. The result is possible interference between the two programs, as seen in Figure 4-28. Notice that the two hypothetical programs are allocated separate memory regions. Yet an addressing error in program P2 may modify program P1. What we need is to separate the logical address spaces (used by programs) from the physical address space, a process that also provides the capability of dynamic memory allocation.

The separation of logical and physical address spaces necessitates translations in the course of program execution. We have to translate the logical addresses referenced in the program into physical addresses, a process commonly known as **mapping**. It provides the means of assigning a logical address to any physical one. As an example, see how three programs are mapped into a single physical address space in Figure 4-29. The logical address space of each program is mapped into a separate region of the physical address space. Now programs cannot interfere directly with each other. Besides, they can be located anywhere in memory and thereby we can utilize memory more efficiently. The price is the additional step we introduce during a memory access. Other than that, mapping is transparent to a program.

Figure 4-30 illustrates another mapping approach. A logical address space is not mapped as a whole. Instead, it is divided into fixed size portions (called **pages**) which are mapped individually. The advantage is that a program need not be allocated a single set of contiguous memory locations. It may be accommodated

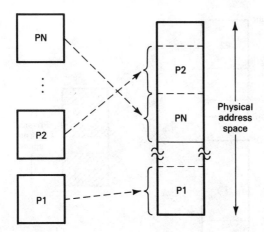

Figure 4-29. Mapping of separate logical address spaces into a single physical address space.

in a number of sets, making memory utilization even more efficient. In the case of μPs employing memory segmentation, the mappable entities are the segments themselves. That is, each memory segment is mapped into the physical address space individually.

Memory management involves more than dynamic memory allocation and prevention of interference among programs. To achieve adequate protection we must check every memory access requested by a program. This checking is done against the **access rights** of the program to the segment or page to which the location belongs. Such checks are performed while the logical address is being translated into a physical one. When necessary, the CPU is alerted to a **protection violation**

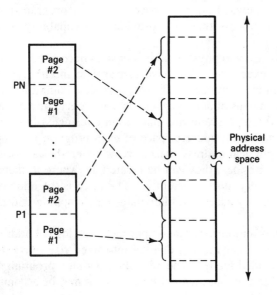

Figure 4-30. Mapping of logical address spaces into the physical address space on a page basis.

or some other kind of inconsistency. Next we discuss virtual memory. Very often, this is another function that must be supported by memory management.

Virtual Memory

All mapping cases we have seen thus far have a common characteristic. The size of the logical address space was smaller (or at the most equal) to the size of the physical address space. The term **virtual memory** refers to the case where the logical address space is much larger than the physical one. Here, programmers have the illusion of a very large memory when in fact the size of the real memory may be smaller by many orders of magnitude.

Virtual memory implies the use of a more economical storage medium which has enough capacity for all programs and data. This medium is usually a disk. From there, pages or segments are brought into main memory on a demand basis. Virtual memory involves more than translation of logical addresses, which are now called **virtual addresses**. The CPU has to determine whether the page or segment the address belongs to is in memory. When it is not, the CPU follows one of the following two courses of action:

1. If there is spare space in memory, the CPU transfers the desired page from disk.
2. If no spare space exists, the CPU transfers to disk one of the pages currently residing in memory. Once it makes room, it transfers from disk the desired page.

The process of replacing in memory one page by another is referred to as **swapping**. The criterion used in choosing which page will be replaced is called **replacement algorithm**. A very often employed algorithm is replacing the least recently used (LRU) page. If the page under replacement was not modified while in memory, transferring to disk is not necessary. Its old copy (in disk) remains valid. Reading a page from disk takes quite some time (say 30 to 50 ms). However, in the meantime, the CPU is free to perform other tasks.

Depending on whether the entities we deal with are pages or segments, we have two virtual memory schemes:

- A page-based virtual memory scheme
- A segment-based virtual memory scheme

Figure 4-31 depicts how a physical address is derived from a virtual one in the case of the page-based scheme. The logical address specified in the program— that is, the virtual address—is partitioned into two parts. The upper part identifies the page where the desired information is. The lower part determines the address of the word within the page. First of all, the page number is used to locate information pertaining to the addressed page. Such information is contained in a

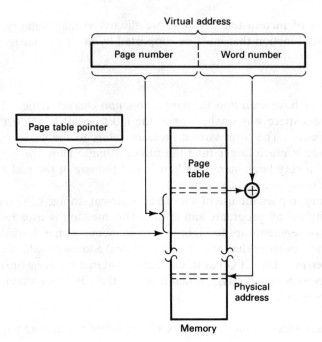

Figure 4-31. Page-based virtual memory scheme.

memory resident **page table**. The latter is pointed to by the **page table pointer**. As seen from Figure 4-31, the page number provides the displacement for locating the pertinent information within the table. This information indicates:

1. Whether the addressed page is already in memory or not
2. The starting address (if the page is already in memory)
3. Its location on disk (if the page is not currently in memory)
4. The access rights of the program on this particular page

The physical address is then determined by adding the starting address of the page (in memory) to the word number. Typically the size of a page is a few kilobytes.

Example 4-17

Assume the page table pointer contains 4096 and the page number is 128. What is the starting address of the block which specifies the information for page #128? Suppose the page is already in memory and has a starting address of 65536. What is the physical address given the word number is 32? How many pages of 2048 bytes each can we accommodate in a 256 KB memory bank?

Solution. The sought address (within the page table) is 4096 + 128 = 4224. The physical address (corresponding to the given page number and word number) is 65536 + 32 = 65568. The bank in question can accommodate a total of 256/2 = 128 pages.

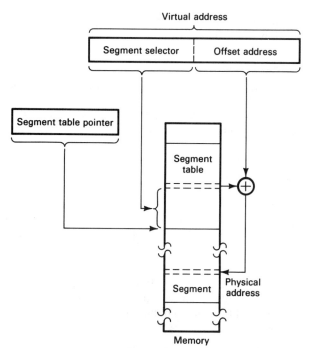

Figure 4-32. Segment-based virtual memory scheme.

In the segment-based scheme, the virtual address space is divided into segments of variable length. Otherwise, the mechanism of physical address generation is similar, as can be seen in Figure 4-32. A virtual address is, again, partitioned into two parts. The upper part locates the corresponding **segment descriptor**, while the lower part provides the address of the word within the segment. Segment descriptors are contained in a **segment table**. This table is stored in memory and is pointed to by a register. It provides the same type of information as page tables, plus the segment length. Sometimes descriptors are stored in registers to eliminate the extra memory accesses needed for their fetching.

Example 4-18

The virtual memory of a μC is implemented by means of a hard disk having a formatted capacity of 16 MB. Up to how many segments can the system handle, given an average segment length of 64 KB? The real memory has a capacity of 1 MB. What is the approximate number of segments it can accommodate at any particular time?

Solution. Assuming all 16 MB serve as virtual memory, the system can handle up to about 16000/64 = 256 segments. The physical memory, however, can handle only about 1000/64 = 16 segments.

Both schemes may employ a cache storing newly derived physical addresses. The objective is to save translation time for virtual addresses whose translation was done recently (and is therefore available in the cache). In any case, virtual memory appears (and is) slower for two reasons:

1. The virtual address translation overhead
2. The time taken for transfer of a page or a segment from disk to memory

On the other hand, virtual memory is valuable in large software systems involving large numbers of users and tasks. Otherwise, such systems would not be economical.

Example 4-19

Consider a μC employing a page-based virtual memory scheme similar to the one pictured in Figure 4-31. Determine how long it takes to fetch an (already memory-resident) operand in terms of memory cycles. Suppose we use a cache to store recent virtual memory translations. It is estimated that the probability of finding the physical address in the cache is about 0.84. What improvement do we gain with the cache given its cycle time is twice as short compared to that of the memory?

Solution. To fetch an operand we need two memory cycles—one for access to the page table and another for access to the operand itself. This duration does not include the time required for derivation of the physical address—that is, address calculations and such. We also assume that transferring of the information needed from the page table takes only one memory cycle.

Whenever we find the translation of a virtual address—that is, the corresponding physical address—in the cache, we save the access to the page table. On the average, an operand fetch takes $t + 0.16t + 0.84t/2 = 1.58t$, where t is the length of a memory cycle. The gained speed amounts to $(2t - 1.58t) / 2t = 0.21$, that is, 21 percent. The translation itself is sped up by $(t - 0.58t) / t = 0.42$, that is, 42 percent.

Memory Management Implementation

In μPs, memory management capabilities vary widely. Some 8-bit μPs have no such capabilities at all because the applications they are intended for do not usually need them. On the other hand, 32-bit CPUs are supported by comprehensive schemes offering a high degree of protection and virtual memory capability.

Generally, 16-bit μPs provide on-chip some limited memory management features. Most provide separate logical address spaces and in some cases the ability to relocate programs as well. For example, the 68000 has a system (or supervisory) mode and a normal (or user) mode. This permits separation of system software from user's programs. In addition, in each mode there is a program space and a data space. Hence, programs and data can be separated. On the other hand, the 8086 permits definition of four separate segments which can be mapped anywhere within the physical address space of 1 MB for program relocation.

However, these limited built-in features may not meet the requirements of some applications. For this reason, μP makers offer specialized devices known as **memory management units (MMUs)**. With such devices we can add externally extensive memory management capabilities.

Some MMUs support virtual memory as well. A word of caution, though, when designing a virtual memory system: The CPU must have certain special features such as instruction cycle or machine cycle **abort/restart** capability. To see why, consider the case of an addressed page not currently in memory, known as a **page fault**. This "fault" is detected while translating the virtual address associated with, say, one of the operands of the instruction—that is, in the course of an instruction cycle. Clearly, the instruction cycle cannot be completed until the CPU brings from disk the page associated with the missing operand. Meanwhile it has to abort the instruction cycle and jump to some other task. Later on (say after 30 ms), when the missing page is brought to memory, the CPU restarts the instruction cycle. Enhanced versions of 16-bit µPs, such as the 68010, do support such a capability (see Figure 3-1).

Another approach to providing memory management is integrating the required circuitry on the same chip with the CPU. Representatives of this approach are the Intel 80286 and 80386 which we discuss next. Before concluding this section we will also discuss the Motorola MC68451 as an example of MMU.

Examples of CPUs with Integrated Memory Management

First we examine the memory management capabilities provided on-chip by the Intel 80286 16-bit CPU. Then we discuss in brief how these capabilities are extended in the Intel 80386 32-bit CPU.

80286 µP

The 80286 is an enhanced version of the 8086 (see Figure 3-1). It has two modes of operation:

1. A "**real address mode**" identical to that of the 8086.
2. A "**protected virtual address**" mode. While in this mode, the 80286 provides extensive memory management capabilities. It supports a 16 MB physical address space and a 1 GB virtual address space per task [1 GB (gigabyte) = 1000 MB = 10^9 bytes].

Figure 4-33(a) shows the block diagram of the 80286. The address unit of the CPU performs both address calculations and the checking functions associated with memory protection. This unit constitutes one of the stages of the four-stage pipeline employed in the 80286. Notice the two separate adders for address calculations. The offset adder does the ordinary address calculations as dictated by the addressing modes specified in the instructions. For example, if the instruction specifies based mode for an operand, the offset adder receives:

1. The displacement from the instruction unit (via the main internal bus)
2. The contents of a base register from the execution unit

These quantities are added to produce the offset address. The latter represents one of the components feeding the physical address adder.

When operating in protected mode, the 80286 employs a segment-based scheme similar to the one shown in Figure 4-32. However, only the offset part (16 bits) of a virtual address is specified in an instruction. The segment selector part of a virtual address is contributed by one of four segment registers. These registers are loaded by separate instructions. As in the 8088/8086, they hold the addresses of the four segments which are accessible at any particular time (code segment, data segment, stack segment, and extra segment).

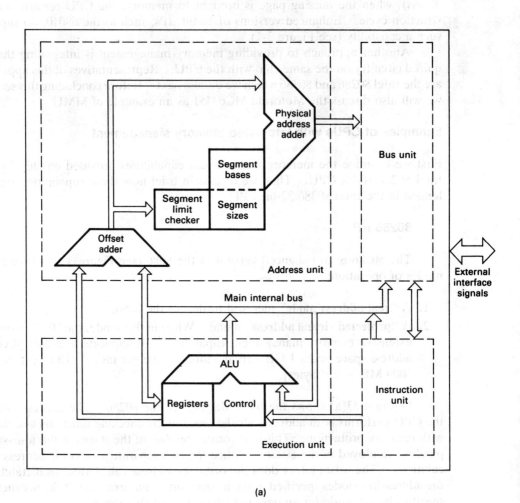

(a)

Figure 4-33. 80286 microprocessor. (a) Simplified block diagram. (b) Segment selector fields. (c) Segment selector registers and segment descriptor registers.

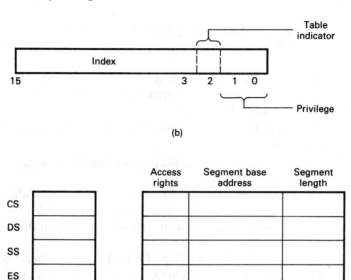

(b)

(c)

Figure 4-33. (*cont.*)

Figure 4-33(b) illustrates the format of a segment selector. As seen, not all bits are used as a straight address to the segment table (see Figure 4-32). Bits 0 and 1 indicate one of four possible privilege levels (recall the meaning of super-visory/user levels of privilege in the 68000). Bit 2 indicates whether the segment descriptor is to be provided from a **local descriptor table** or a **global descriptor table**. The descriptors stored in these two tables are the only ones accessible to a task at any given time. Note that the local descriptor table contains descriptors which can be private to a task. Those stored in the global descriptor table are available to all tasks. Two registers are associated with each table: one containing a pointer to the table and another specifying the size of the table (for checking purposes). Each pair of registers is loaded by special instructions. Finally, the index portion of the segment selector specifies the location of the segment descriptor within the selected table. A virtual address is composed of the 16 offset address bits and the 16 selector bits. Since two bits are dedicated to privilege indication, however, the virtual address space of the 80286 is actually 2^{30}.

Let us now see what the segment descriptors are about. Segment descriptors are fetched automatically during the execution of the instructions loading the seg-ment selector registers. They are stored in the four segment descriptor registers (one for each type of segment) provided in the 80286 address unit. See the format of the descriptors in Figure 4-33(c). They consist of three parts:

1. An access rights part providing accessibility-related indicators (that is, whether the segment is currently mapped into physical memory, if it can be accessed in write mode, and so on)
2. A segment base address part supplying the starting address of the segment in memory
3. A segment length part indicating the length of the segment in bytes

Physical addresses are generated by the physical address adder which adds the 16-bit offset address (produced by the offset adder) to a 24-bit segment base address. The resulting 24-bit address is then fed to the bus unit of the 80286 for presentation to memory.

In parallel, the address unit performs the various checks pertaining to memory protection. For example, it checks the offset address against the length of the segment to ensure that access is within the bounds of the segment. It also verifies that the type of attempted access complies to the access rights specified in the descriptor. Failure to pass any of the checks prevents the memory cycle and generates a high priority internal interrupt, which leads to a service routine to determine the type of memory protection violation. Another condition causing an internal interrupt is the "segment not present" one. This interrupt provides the mechanism for requesting the transfer of the particular segment from disk. Once the segment is transferred, the "failing instruction" can be restarted.

80386 μP

More extensive memory management capabilities are provided by the Intel 80386 μP (see Section 3.4.2), which permits segments as large as 4 GB. In addition to supporting paging (see Figure 3-24), the 80386 permits a choice among the following schemes:

1. **Unsegmented/Unpaged Memory.** No address translations are performed. Effective addresses are always physical ones.
2. **Unsegmented/Paged Memory.** Memory management and protection are accomplished through paging.
3. **Segmented/Unpaged Memory.** Memory is organized into one or more segments which vary in size. A segment can be as large as 4 GB.
4. **Segmented/Paged Memory.** This is the most comprehensive of the four memory management schemes. Memory is again partitioned into segments. However, memory allocation and management within each segment is accomplished through paging. Pages are 4 KB in size.

The 80386 includes on-chip a cache storing the physical addresses of the 32 most recently used pages. This permits mapping of up to 128 KB (4 KB × 32) of memory at any particular time. Such a cache is often referred to as a **translation lookaside buffer (TLB).** The TLB enables the 80386 to translate most addresses on-chip and thereby avoid the delays associated with the access of memory-resident page tables.

The overall virtual address space of the 80386 amounts to 2^{46} bytes, or about 64 TB [1 TB (terabyte) equals 1 trillion bytes, that is, 1×10^{12} bytes].

Example of a MMU

In the remaining part of this section we discuss a memory management device designed for the 68000—the Motorola MC68451. We will refer to it simply as the 68451 MMU. The same device provides virtual memory support as well, provided it is used in conjunction with a CPU having instruction cycle or machine cycle abort/restart capability. Such a CPU is the Motorola 68010, an enhanced version of the 68000. Figure 4-34 shows the external interface lines of the 68451 and how it relates to a 68000 and to memory.

External interface

The 68451 MMU translates the upper 16 bits (A8–A23) of a logical address into a 16-bit physical segment address. A logical address may be supplied by the CPU or by a DMA device. Bits A1–A7 bypass the MMU, directly becoming the lower portion of the physical address. Notice that the generated upper portion of a physical address is stored in an external latch, because the same lines are used to read and write data in the MMU registers. The bidirectional (data) buffer is enabled by the ED^* (enable data) signal. HAD^* does likewise for the address latch. A valid memory address is indicated by means of the MAS^* (mapped address strobe).

Function code lines $FC0$–$FC2$ connect to the synonymous outputs of the CPU. $FC3$ indicates to the MMU whether a cycle is initiated by the CPU or by a DMA device (in Figure 4-34 we assume no DMA). It is through these lines that the CPU identifies the separate address space to which the addressed segment belongs. IRQ^* (interrupt request) plays a dual role. As an output line it carries interrupts from the MMU. During an interrupt acknowledge cycle it plays the role of an input line and is activated at the same time that $IACK^*$ (interrupt acknowledge) is.

Indication of a memory protection violation or any attempt to access an undefined segment is provided via the $FAULT^*$ line. WIN^* (write inhibit) gives the means of protecting a write-protected segment in the course of a read-modify-write cycle. CS^* and $RS1$–$RS5$ are employed to address the on-chip registers of the MMU. GO^*, ANY^*, and ALL serve special purposes in applications employing multiple MMUs. So does MAS^* as an input line. $MODE$ determines

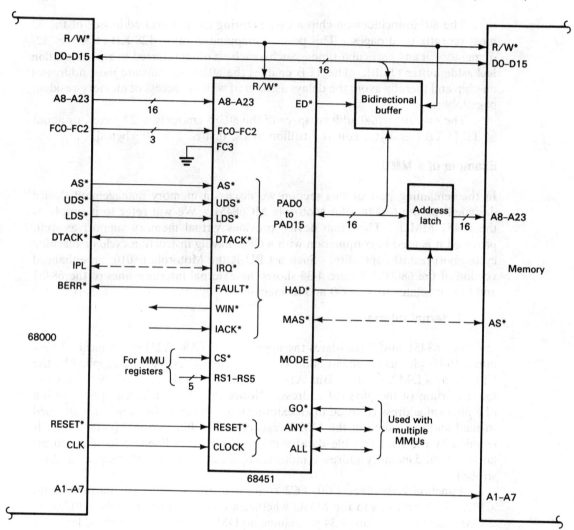

Figure 4-34. External interface of the MC68451 MMU and its functional relations to CPU and memory.

whether *MAS** is to be generated asynchronously or synchronously (on the rising or falling edge of the clock). The three possible modes correspond to connecting the line to V_{cc}, ground, or leaving it floating. All other interface lines have the same meaning the synonymous lines of the 68000 have.

Organization

The 68451 has a large number of internal registers. It can store up to 32 sets of segment descriptors. Figure 4-35(a) depicts the registers associated with each set of descriptors. A physical address is formed from the logical address fed to the MMU in conjunction with the physical base address and the logical address mask.   In parallel, the CPU performs the following checks:

1. The incoming logical address and the logical base address are checked against the logical address mask for matching.

2. The address space number, in conjunction with the address space mask, are checked against the cycle address space number obtained from the address space table shown in Figure 4-35(b).   There is one such table per MMU.   It is addressed through the FC0–FC3 bits provided to the MMU during a particular memory cycle.

3. If the attempted cycle is a memory write one, a check is made to ensure the addressed segment is not write-protected.

Failure to pass any of these checks will activate the *FAULT** line alerting the CPU of the fact.

Figure 4-35(c) indicates the format of the segment status byte in each segment descriptor.   When bit E (enable) is set, the segment is allowed to undergo the matching process mentioned previously.   Bit WP (write protect) indicates the segment is write-protected, and any attempt to perform a write cycle when WP is set is considered a memory violation.   Bit M (modified) is set by the MMU to reflect the fact that at least one write operation has been performed on the segment since the time of its definition.   The I (interrupt) bit is set when we want to interrupt the CPU whenever this segment is accessed.   As soon as such an access occurs, the IP (interrupt pending) bit is set to reflect this event.   Finally, when set, the U (used) bit indicates that the segment has been accessed at least once since the time of its definition.

Multiple MMUs can be interconnected for applications requiring more than 32 segments.   Also, the device can support a page-based scheme by simply fixing the size for all segments.   The required number of segments is usually large in the case of virtual memory systems.   Here are some other features of the 68451 which are intended to aid the design of such systems.

1. When the MMU activates the *FAULT** line (as a result of an address mismatch or a write protection violation), it stores in its registers information pertinent to the faulty cycle.   After the CPU is alerted, it examines the status byte of the segment to determine the cause of the fault.   First, the CPU examines the write protect bit.   If not set, the CPU deduces that the fault was due to an address mismatch.   This in turn implies that the addressed segment is not available in memory (page fault).   Having determined this, the operating system proceeds to bring from disk the missing segment.   Once this is accomplished, the CPU repeats the faulty cycle on the basis of the information saved when the cycle failed.

2. The E (enable) bits of the status bytes serve a very important role.   Collec-

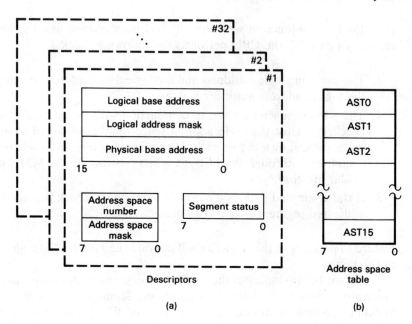

Descriptors

(a)

Address space
table

(b)

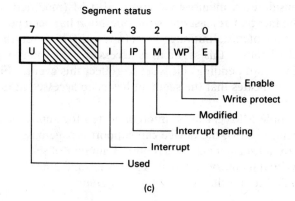

(c)

Figure 4-35.   Registers of the 68451 MMU.   (a) Segment descriptor registers.   (b)
System registers storing the entries of the address space table.   (c) Segment status
byte.

tively, they allow the operating system to determine if there is room (in
memory) for the segment (or page) it intends to bring from disk.

3. What if the E bits of all 32 descriptors are set? That means no room for the
new segment. Thus, one of the segments currently present in memory must
be replaced. The U (used) bits are intended to aid in implementing an LRU
(least recently used) replacement algorithm.

4. If the segment (or the page) we intend to replace has been modified (during its stay in memory), its old disk copy is not valid any more. Hence, it must be saved on disk prior to bringing in the new segment. The decision is made on the basis of the M (modified) bit. Recall that the latter indicates if a segment has experienced any write operations during its stay in memory.

Virtual memory processors

The features just outlined are not sufficient for implementation of a virtual memory system. The CPU, for its part, must be capable of aborting and later restarting either the whole instruction cycle or the failed machine cycle of that instruction. Recall that the 68000 aborts the current machine cycle when its $BERR^*$ (bus error) input is activated (see Figure 4-34). It also saves enough information for repetition of the faulty machine cycle. However, the saved information is not adequate for continuation of the instruction cycle (or repetition of it) after the missing page is brought from disk.

An enhanced version of the 68000 has instruction continuation capability. This is the 68010 "**virtual memory processor**," which is pin-compatible with the 68000. The 68010 saves additional information when a bus cycle is aborted. Such information includes temporary registers as, for example, the microprogram counter. This enables the 68010 to return later to the very same state it was when the instruction cycle was suspended. In the specific case of a page (or segment) fault, the MMU supplies all necessary information for the missing page (or segment). The latter is of course brought from disk prior to initiating the recovery process.

Let us go back to the problem we face when employing an EDAC unit in check-only mode. Data are passed to the CPU as they arrive from memory (unchecked). Meanwhile the EDAC unit examines their correctness and informs the CPU (via the error flag lines) accordingly. What if the error flag lines indicate incorrect data? Could the CPU be stopped from going any further with them? Typical CPUs do not permit this. However, the 68010 does. That is, the memory may have activated $DTACK^*$ (data transfer acknowledge) indicating valid read data. Yet, data will be disregarded by the CPU, provided $BERR^*$ is activated no later than half a clock period after the activation of $DTACK^*$. Such a time allowance may be sufficient for error detection in many applications. In contrast, the 68000 will not ignore read data once $DTACK^*$ has been asserted.

Example 4-20

Consider a 68010-based design employing memory error correction. The CPU is clocked at a rate of 10 MHz. How fast should the EDAC unit be if we are to be able to use it in check-only mode? What if the EDAC unit takes 60 ns for error detection?

Solution. Ordinarily, the memory activates $DTACK^*$ as soon as data become valid. At the same time, the valid data become available to the EDAC unit. The clock period is 100 ns long. Consequently, the EDAC unit should be able to check the data within 50 ns following activation of $DTACK^*$. If the EDAC unit takes any longer than that, we must delay issuance of $DTACK^*$ accordingly. For the given case, $DTACK^*$ will have to be delayed for at least 10 ns. This delay does not necessarily imply wait state insertion (see Example 3-7).

4.5 DESIGN EXAMPLES

In this section we discuss some design examples. All are intended to demonstrate further how CPUs interface to memory devices. The first example concerns an 8-bit CPU with static RAM and EPROM. In this example we discuss how we do address decoding (and thereby generate memory select signals) with an octal decoder. Our second example involves a 16-bit CPU with dynamic RAM. First we derive a simplified schematic for the associated circuits. Then we proceed to perform worst case timing analysis. In the last example we overview the design of a 16-bit CPU equipped with memory management and EDAC capabilities. This example permits us to look at how we go about calculating the power dissipation of a memory.

8-Bit CPU with Static RAM and EPROM

The first design example is a continuation of the one we discussed in Section 3.6 (Figure 3-32). The CPU is an 8088. We have seen how we equip it with support components, and now we go on to look at interfacing it to static memory and EPROM. Let us assume the design calls for 2 KB of read/write memory and 2 KB of read-only (program) memory.

Our modest memory capacity requirements can be satisfied with a single 2K × 8 static RAM (SRAM) and a single 2K × 8 EPROM. Consideration of DRAMs for such a small capacity read/write memory is completely out of the question (why?). Thus, our design task amounts to interfacing the two byte-wide memory devices to the CPU. For further simplification we will assume that no wait states are necessary. In other words, the memory devices are fast enough for the clocking rate of the CPU.

In Section 4.1.2 we considered the case of an 8088 equipped with two SRAMs (Figure 4-14). The case of one SRAM and one EPROM is very much the same (Figure 4-36). Naturally, the EPROM need not connect to the WR^* line of the CPU. What we have not discussed, though, is the generation of the select signals for the memory devices. That is, the generation of the CS^* signal for the SRAM and the CE^* signal for the EPROM. Device selection can be accomplished by means of the next high-order address bit A11. For example, CS^* may be connected to address line A11. The same signal may be inverted for selection of the EPROM. While address decoding becomes trivial in our simple design case, we will consider the general approach to it.

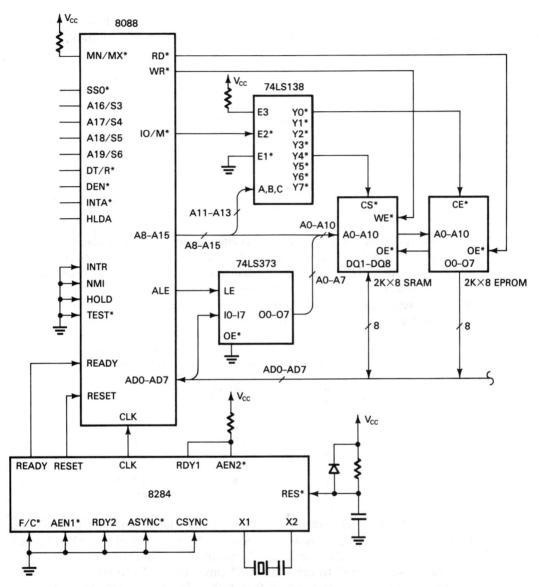

Figure 4-36.   Minimum mode 8088 configuration with 2 KB of EPROM and 2 KB of static memory.

What if the number of memory devices was larger?   What if we have to differentiate between memory address space and I/O address space?   The common approach is employing an MSI decoding device.   Such is the 74LS138 decoder pictured in Figure 4-36.   The 74LS138 has three enable inputs (*E1**, *E2**, *E3*), three select or address inputs (*A, B, C*), and eight outputs (*Y0** to *Y7**).   When all three enable inputs are satisfied, one of the eight outputs is activated. The particular output going active depends on the state of its select inputs:

CBA	Active output
000	$Y0^*$
001	$Y1^*$
010	$Y2^*$
011	$Y3^*$
100	$Y4^*$
101	$Y5^*$
110	$Y6^*$
111	$Y7^*$

Such a decoder is called a **3-to-8 decoder** or simply an **octal decoder**. In our example, $E1^*$ and $E3$ are always satisfied. $E2^*$ is satisfied only when IO/M^* is at a low. Consequently, the decoder is enabled only if a bus cycle involves memory. The three select inputs A, B, and C connect to high-order address bits A11, A12, and A13, respectively. The correspondence between blocks of addresses and activated decoder outputs follows:

A13	A12	A11	Address block	Active output
0	0	0	0–2K	$Y0^*$
0	0	1	2K–4K	$Y1^*$
0	1	0	4K–6K	$Y2^*$
0	1	1	6K–8K	$Y3^*$
1	0	0	8K–10K	$Y4^*$
1	0	1	10K–12K	$Y5^*$
1	1	0	12K–14K	$Y6^*$
1	1	1	14K–16K	$Y7^*$

Actually, address blocks are not exactly on 2 KB boundaries. For example, the lowest address of the 2K–4K address block is $2^{11} = 2048$ and its highest address $2^{12} - 1 = 4095$. So, the size of an address block is 2048, not 2000.

Since we use $Y0^*$ to drive the CE^* input of the EPROM, the latter will respond only to addresses between 0 and 2K. In other words, the EPROM is assigned the 0–2K block of addresses. On the other hand, the SRAM is assigned the 8K–10K block of addresses. This might be done in order to reserve addresses 2K–8K for additional EPROMs we may need later. EPROMs would then be assigned contiguous address blocks.

Example 2-21

Consider an 8088-based design where the CPU is configured in maximum mode. The memory is to consist of a 512 Kb (64K × 8) EPROM (assigned addresses 0–64K) and four 8K × 8 SRAMs (assigned contiguous addresses from 64K and up). How would you go about generating the select signals employing a single octal decoder?

Solution. The address inputs of the EPROM would connect to the 16 low-order lines of the CPU address bus ($A0$–$A15$). The next higher order address bit ($A16$) can serve device select purposes. If no I/O addresses are employed, $A16$ may be used to drive the CE^* input of the EPROM in a direct fashion. Otherwise, A16 must be ORed with IO/M^* for derivation of the enable signal.

The octal decoder generates the select signals for the four 8K × 8 SRAMs. Since they are assigned addresses beyond 64K, the decoder should be enabled only when $A16$ is at a high. For example, $A16$ might be connected to the $E3$ input of the decoder (see Figure 4-36). The address inputs of the SRAMs would connect to lines $A0$–$A12$ of the CPU address bus. Higher order lines $A13$–$A15$ may be connected to the select inputs (A, B, C) of the decoder. The CS^* inputs of the four SRAMs will connect to outputs $Y0^*$–$Y3^*$ of the decoder.

16-Bit CPU with Dynamic RAM

We now discuss a design example where memory is implemented with DRAM devices. Figure 4-37 shows the circuit schematic in simplified form. After discussing the circuitry we will consider worst case timing analysis, which is far more involved when a design employs DRAM devices.

Two designers are given the task of developing an 8086-based μC with 128 KB of memory. After doing some estimates they conclude that SRAMs would not allow them to meet product cost objectives. Consequently they decide to use DRAMs. In fact, they are instructed to use 64K × 1 DRAMs which are purchased in volume for another product. The memory array will thus consist of 16 DRAMs organized into a single 16-bit-wide bank. The next concern the designers have is whether they should design their own memory refresh and control circuits or use a dynamic memory controller (DMC). Following a short discussion they agree that the DMC will simplify the design considerably at very little additional cost and decide on an 8203. At this point the designers draw a diagram depicting the componentry in terms of blocks—one block for the address latches, one for the 8203, and so on. Starting from this they proceed to identify all the components they will need (including SSI ones):

1. Three latches are needed to store all address bits and the BHE^* signal. Remember the 8086 multiplexes address signals and BHE^* with either data or status signals. Thus, it is necessary to demultiplex all of them during the early part of a bus cycle. For this purpose they use the ALE (address latch enable) signal. $A0$ is decoded in conjunction with BHE^* to determine if the low byte, high byte, or both bytes of a word are to be accessed. This is necessary for write operations only (why?). Decoding gates O1 and O2 are enabled from the WE^* output of the 8203, and address lines $A1$–$A16$ are split into two groups. $A1$–$A8$ drive the row address inputs ($AL0$–$AL7$) of

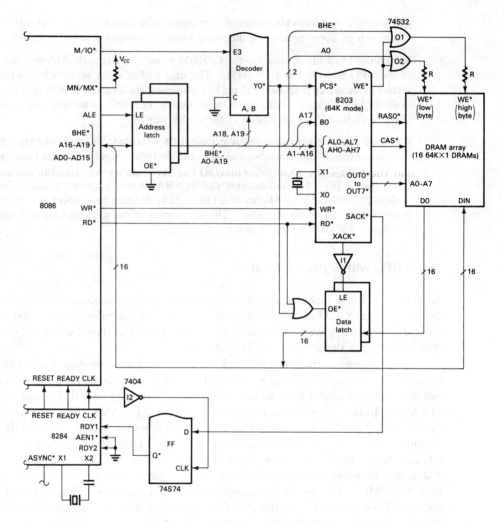

Figure 4-37. Simplified schematic of an 8086-based (minimum mode) system with dynamic memory.

the 8203. $A9-A16$ drive the column address inputs ($AH0-AH7$) of the 8203. Line $A17$ drives the bank select input ($B0$) of the DMC. Therefore, $A17$ determines which row address strobe ($RAS0^*$ or $RAS1^*$) is activated. The memory bank shown in Figure 4-37 is driven by $RAS0^*$ and thus requires $A17=0$ for its selection. $RAS1^*$ would allow implementation of a second 128 KB memory bank. More than one 8203 would necessitate decoding of high-order address bits for their selection. Here, the PCS^* (protected chip select) input of the single 8203 is driven from $Y0^*$. Hence, the 128 KB memory bank will respond to addresses 0–128K. The decoder is enabled only while M/IO^* is at a high.

2. The *RD** and *WR** lines of the CPU connect directly to the synonymous inputs of the 8203. It is on the basis of these inputs that the 8203 decides whether it should activate its *WE** output or not. The crystal connecting to the *X*0, *X*1 inputs of the DMC is needed for its on-chip oscillator. The *RAS0**, *CAS**, and *OUT0*–OUT7** outputs of the 8203 must be connected to all 16 DRAMs.

3. Each of the DRAMs contributes a single bit in every one of the 64K 16-bit words. The multiplexed address/data bus of the CPU can be connected directly to the *DIN* (data in) pins of the DRAMs. The designers determine that the composite load presented to the *AD* bus by the address latch and the memory array does not exceed the driving capability of the 8086. Hence, no transceivers are employed.

4. The situation is not as straightforward for the *DO* (data out) lines. Some kind of buffer is necessary for isolation of the *DIN* and *DO* pins of the DRAMs. It is also necessary to retain data in the event that memory does not maintain them on the bus for the duration required by the CPU. Consequently, it is decided to use two positive-edge-triggered octal latches. Later on we will see that timing analysis also indicates the need for such buffers. The data latches are enabled when both *RD** and *Y0** are active—that is, when the address placed on the bus is in the range of 0–256K and the bus cycle specifies a read operation. Data are latched in on the leading edge of the *XACK** (transfer acknowledge) signal provided by the DMC.

5. An 8284 clock generator is used for provision of the clock and *RESET* signals and also to manipulate the *READY* line of the CPU for insertion of wait states. The designers have figured out that the ability to insert wait states is necessary even if the DRAMs are fast enough for the CPU. As an example, assume that the 8203 initiates a refresh cycle and the CPU follows immediately with a request for a read cycle. Clearly, the DMC will not be in a position to generate any control signals such as *RAS** or *CAS** until the refresh cycle is over. In the mean time the CPU will have to wait. This is communicated by means of the *SACK** signal of the 8203. *SACK** (system acknowledge) remains inactive for the duration of the refresh cycle and until the requested data are forthcoming. In fact it is decided to make use of *SACK** for insertion of wait states in bus cycles. The state of *SACK** is monitored by means of a 74S74 D-type flip-flop (FF) which is clocked through inverter I2 at the beginning of every clock cycle. While *SACK** remains at a high, FF stays set, *Q** is at a low, and the *RDY*1 input to the clock generator is kept inactive. When *ASYNC** is left open (and hence high via an on-chip pull-up resistor), the 8284 samples its *RDY*1 and *RDY*2 inputs at the start of state T3 (see Figure 4-38). Within 8 ns (at maximum) it then updates its *READY* line toward the CPU. Since neither *RDY*1 nor *RDY*2 is active, *READY* will either stay at a low or be driven to a low. Thus, when the CPU samples its *READY* input (at the beginning of the second half of *T*3), it finds this input inactive and, upon completion of *T*3, enters a wait state *TW*. The sampling

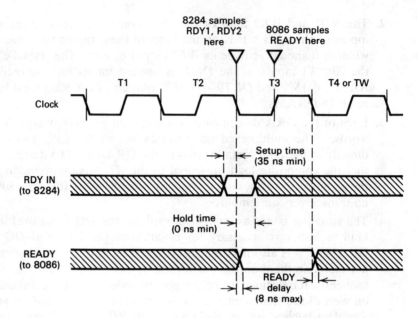

Figure 4-38. *READY* signal generation by the 8284 clock generator when *ASYNC** is inactive. The 8284 samples its *RDY1* and *RDY2* inputs at the beginning of state *T3* and at the beginning of each wait state (if any) thereafter. For a change in the state of *RDY1* and *RDY2* to be sensed though, it must be setup for at least 35 ns prior to the sampling instant. From there on, the *READY* output of the 8284 will reflect the condition sensed on the *RDY1* and *RDY2* inputs for the duration of an entire clock cycle.

process is repeated and new wait states are inserted as long as *RDY*1 stays at a low. When the 8203 finally activates *SACK**, FF resets at the beginning of the clock cycle immediately following. *RDY*1 is now at a high, but it does not meet the minimum setup time requirement of 35 ns (Figure 4-38). As a result the 8284 will miss *RDY*1 but will sense it at the beginning of the next clock cycle. After completion of that cycle, no more wait states are inserted. Instead, the CPU enters *T*4 and the memory cycle ends. The one-clock-cycle-long delay between FF setting and the sensing of *RDY*1 by the 8284 is specifically designed to ensure an adequate number of wait states given that, unlike *XACK**, *SACK** is activated by the 8203 prior to obtaining valid data from memory. On the other hand, the reason 8284 samples *RDY*1 and *RDY*2 half a cycle ahead of the CPU is to ensure that setup and hold time requirements (at the *READY* input of the 8086) are met.

Example 4-22

Consider a similar design employing 256K × 1 DRAMs. Assume a DMC having for such DRAMs the same capabilities the 8203 has for 64K × 1 ones. How many address lines would connect to this DMC? What address decoding circuits do we need if we are to implement a 1 MB memory?

Solution.   Each of the RAS^* signals of the (new) DMC will be handling a bank of 16 256K $\times$ 1 DRAMs—that is, 2 $\times$ 256 = 512 KB.   Thus a single DMC will suffice for a full 1 MB memory.   Now, address lines $A17$ and $A18$ connect to the address inputs of the DMC. $A19$ connects to the bank select input of the DMC.   There are no other decoding circuits as far as memory goes.

At this point, the designers have arrived at the simplified schematic shown in Figure 4-37.   Very often, as a next step the designer adds the rest of the details— for example, all interface lines for the DRAMs—and proceeds to prototyping. Yet, this may not yield a sound design—that is, one functioning properly over the operating temperature and V_{cc} range of the product.   What we need is a worst case timing analysis.   As an example we will perform such an analysis on the design we just discussed.

Timing analysis

For the purposes of our example, we assume the standard version of the 8086 clocked at a rate of 5 MHz.   Assume 64K $\times$ 1 DRAMs having a maximum access time of 200 ns.   Generally, timing analyses are based on information furnished by manufacturers in the pertinent device data sheets.   Among other data, such information includes tabulated values of AC parameters and timing diagrams.   Very often, data sheets provide relationships among AC parameters as well.   In our case, the key device is the 8203.

1. The data sheets of the 8203 express most of its AC parameters in terms of the period (t_p) of its own clock.   These expressions have the general form $Nt_p + K$, where N is usually a small integer and K is a constant between 10 and 100.   In order to reduce the overheads imposed on memory accesses, we must keep AC parameters short.   That means clocking the 8203 at its maximum allowable rate.   At the same time, however, we must ensure that the resulting values remain compatible with those of the DRAMs.   Take, for instance, the width of the CAS^* pulse.   Its minimum value is determined from the expression $5t_p - 10$.   If we clock the 8203 at its maximum rate of 25 MHz, then $t_p = 40$ ns, so the guaranteed minimum CAS^* pulse width will be 190 ns.   Let us assume that the data sheets of the DRAM indicate that the CAS^* pulse width must be at least 120 ns.   Then this particular require-ment is met even when clocking the DMC at its maximum rate.   We will assume that this is true for the rest of the parameters of the 8203 so that the 8203 can be clocked at 25 MHz.   What if one or more of the parameters were incompatible?   We would have to decrease the clocking rate of the 8203 until we meet all the requirements of the employed DRAMs.

2. Compatibility verification, though, gives us no assurance that the overall system will work properly.   Take, for example, the case of the row address setup time $\tau 1$ shown in Figure 4-39.   This is the interval between activation

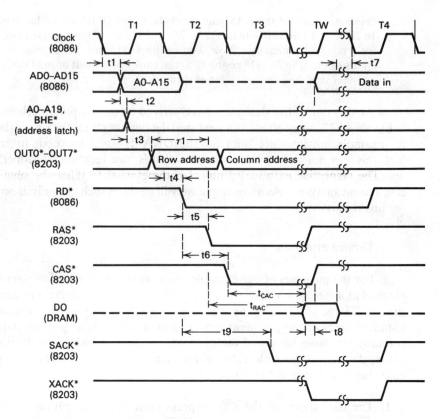

Figure 4-39. Timing diagram used for worst case analysis of an 8086-based system employing the 8203 dynamic memory controller.

of the $OUT0^*-OUT7^*$ lines (for flow of a row address) and RAS^* generation. The 8203 may be compatible with the DRAMs in the sense that $\tau1$ is guaranteed to exceed the row address setup time they require. However, if a valid address is not presented to the 8203 on time, the row address provided to memory may be invalid. Thus, to ensure proper system operation we must check timing from end to end—from the CPU to the memory array and back—under worst case conditions.

3. Let us now see how we can determine the address setup time in the case of a read access. As a time reference we will use the leading edge of the first clock cycle $T1$. From Figure 4-39 we see that it takes time $t1$ to obtain a valid address at the CPU output, $t2$ for its propagation through the address latches, and $t3$ for its propagation through the 8203. Hence, a valid address is available to the memory array at time

$$T_{ADDR} = t1 + t2 + t3$$

The 8203 takes time $t5$ to activate a RAS^* line after receiving RD^* from the

CPU. RD^* itself is generated by the CPU $t4$ ns after the leading edge of the second clock cycle $T2$. Hence a RAS^* strobe is generated at time

$$T_{RAS} = 200 + t4 + t5$$

where the 200 ns represent the CPU clock period. Clearly, the shortest value of the row address setup time is:

$$T_{RAS(MIN)} - T_{ADDR(MAX)}, \quad \text{or}$$

$$200 + t4_{(MIN)} + t5_{(MIN)} - t1_{(MAX)} - t2_{(MAX)} - t3_{(MAX)}$$

The respective extreme values of parameters $t1$ to $t5$ can be obtained from the AC parameter tables of the 8086, the 8203, and the latch (we assume a 74LS373). Substitution of the numeric values yields for the worst case address setup time 110 ns. Assuming the DRAM specifies 0 ns for this parameter, the above value provides a very comfortable margin.

4. The 8203 does not activate a RAS^* line unless its PCS^* input is also activated. Specifically, PCS^* must switch to a low at least 20 ns prior to the arrival of a RD^* or WR^* strobe. Following the same approach, we conclude that the worst case value for the PCS^* setup time is

$$200 + t4_{(MIN)} - t1_{(MAX)} - t2_{(MAX)} - tD_{(MAX)}$$

where the last term represents the delay introduced by the decoder. If we assume a 74LS138 decoder with a maximum propagation delay of 40 ns, and substitute numeric values for all parameters, we obtain 40 ns. Hence, our worst case safety margin for the PCS^* setup time is 20 ns.

5. Next we determine how many wait states are required to give memory sufficient time for reading and presentation of stable data. Recall that DRAMs have two access time parameters: access time from RAS^* (t_{RAC}) and access time from CAS^* (t_{CAC}). The maximum values of these parameters in the case of the particular DRAM we have assumed are

$$t_{RAC(MAX)} = 200 \text{ ns}$$

$$t_{CAC(MAX)} = 120 \text{ ns}$$

Although the access time from CAS^* is shorter, we do not yet know which of the two parameters determines the overall access time of our memory, because RAS^* and CAS^* are activated at different times. In order to find out we use as a reference point the leading edge of the RD^* strobe. As seen from Figure 4-39, the corresponding maximum memory access times relative to the reference point are

$$t5_{(MAX)} + t_{RAC(MAX)}, \quad \text{and}$$

$$t6_{(MAX)} + t_{CAC(MAX)}$$

Substitution of numeric values yields 350 ns for the RAS^*-based parameter and 365 ns for the CAS^*-based one, which is therefore our worst case access time. When does the 8086 expect valid data? If wait states are inserted, data are sampled at the end of the last TW. Otherwise, data are sampled at the end of state $T3$. In either case the data must satisfy the data setup time $(t7)$ requirements. Using again as a reference point the leading edge of RD^*, we see that the earliest time the CPU would expect valid data is:

$$400 - t4_{(MIN)} - t7_{(MIN)} = 360 \text{ ns}$$

This is shorter than the worst case access time. Therefore, we need insertion of one wait state during memory read cycles. (Actually our shortfall is more than 5 ns since we have not taken into consideration the delay $t8$ introduced by the data latch.)

6. The insertion of a single wait state is guaranteed even under worst case conditions. That is, even if we assume that $SACK^*$ goes active immediately after RD^* does $(t9 = 0)$, FF does not reset until the end of $T2$. Thus $READY$ will be inactive during $T3$ and a wait state is inserted. As a matter of fact, device parameter variations may result in the insertion of two wait states per memory read cycle. This can be seen when considering that the maximum value of $t4$ is 165 ns and the maximum value of $t9$ is given by the expression $2t_p + 47$ (Figure 4-39).

7. How about data hold time at the DO outputs of the DRAMs? Meeting the timing requirements here becomes quite problematic since the 8086 reads data long after the 8203 terminates the CAS^* pulse (and hence the DRAM cycle). A data latch solves the problem. The data are latched on the leading edge of $XACK^*$ and are preserved until read by the CPU. Note that this latch should not be a transparent type such as those used for address latching.

This completes the worst case timing analysis as far as read cycles go. A good part of the results derived also apply to write cycles. It is, however, necessary to calculate margins concerning write data setup and hold times.

16-Bit CPU with Memory Management and EDAC

The last design example involves a 16-bit CPU equipped with both memory management and EDAC, as shown in Figure 4-40. Unlike the two previous examples which we discussed in detail, we examine this case in general terms and complete the section with a detail analysis of power dissipation in memories.

A senior designer is asked to produce a block diagram of the CPU and memory sections of a new product. The objective is to identify the major components and picture the flow of address, data, and control signals. This diagram is to serve later on as a basis for the detail design.

The requirements call for multitasking capability, which necessitates memory management, and 512 KB of memory. They also specify single error correction for reliability reasons. The designer plans to use a μP and 64K × 1 DRAMs

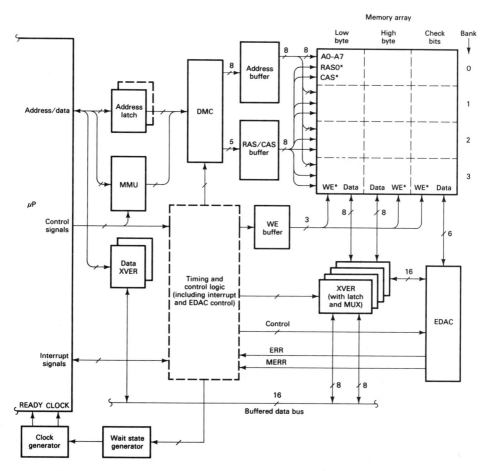

Figure 4-40.   Simplified diagram of a system with memory management and error-detection-and-correction capabilities.

employed in an earlier product. This μP has a multiplexed address/data bus. However, it lacks on-chip memory management capabilities and thereby requires an external MMU:

1. A latch is needed to demultiplex the low-order address bits from data. Since these bits are used directly as part of the physical address, they are directed to the dynamic memory controller (DMC). High-order address bits must flow to the (external) MMU. There they are translated for generation of the upper part of a physical address and are also directed to the DMC. The DMC can handle up to four banks of 64K × 1 DRAMs but lacks on-chip buffers for its output signals. Hence, it is necessary to use external buffers for *CAS**, *RAS**, and the multiplexed row/column addresses.

2. Each memory bank contributes 128 KB. Thus, a total of four banks is

necessary. In addition to the 16 data bits, each memory location must store the six check bits associated with that word, which yields a total of 22 DRAMs per memory bank. The 16-bit data words are themselves organized into low bytes and high bytes, yet all 22 bits of a memory word are accessed together. This means that even when the CPU specifies a single byte, it is necessary to access all 22 bits of the respective location, because the six check bits are derived over both bytes of a 16-bit word. Practically, the correctness of a byte cannot be checked unless the whole 16-bit word is read. A similar situation applies when writing a byte in a location. Again, it is necessary to read all 22 bits from that location, check them for correctness, insert the new byte into the word, derive the new check bits, and then write the new 22-bit word.

3. The designer's next concern is the data paths. First of all, it is necessary to provide a buffered data bus serving I/O devices as well. This suggests using ordinary transceivers for buffering of the CPU address/data bus. However, the designer recognizes that this is not enough—the flow of data between memory, EDAC unit, and the buffered data bus must also be controlled. The implication is that these additional transceivers should have both multiplexing and latching capabilities (why?). In fact, such (quad) devices are commercially available. They are often referred to as EDAC buffers.

4. The EDAC unit supports single error correction and double error detection. At this stage, the designer assumes its configuration in the read/correct mode. Read data flow to the EDAC unit from memory via the quad transceivers. The corresponding check bits flow to it directly from memory. Subsequently, the EDAC unit checks and (when necessary) corrects the data word. Then the latter flows via the quad transceivers to the buffered data bus and from there on to the CPU. The syndrome can be read by the CPU through the same path.

5. Additional logic is needed for control of the transceivers, the DMC, the EDAC unit, and so on. This part is implemented with common SSI and MSI circuits, shown collectively in Figure 4-40 as "timing and control logic."

Example 4-23

Assume implementation of the 512 KB memory of Figure 4-40 with 256K × 1 DRAMs. Determine how many DRAMs are required. Is there any impact on the memory buffer circuits?

Solution. A single memory bank requires, again, a total of 22 DRAMs, but it now provides a capacity of 2 × 256 = 512 KB. Thus the memory capacity requirements are satisfied with only one bank. The capacitive load of the buffer circuits is lower by a factor of about four. Therefore, the buffers need not be as capable as those shown in Figure 4-40 between the DMC and the memory array.

Example 4-24

The DRAMs employed in the design of Figure 4-40 have a device failure rate of 1200

FITs. What would be the reliability of the memory array without EDAC? How often will the memory array fail given that EDAC provides a tenfold improvement? What change would you expect in the derived results if you were using 256K × 1 DRAMs?

Solution. Without EDAC we need only 4 × 16 = 64 DRAMs. Their composite FIT rate amounts to 1200 × 64 = 76800 FITs. This corresponds to an MTBF of 10^9 / 76800 = 13021 hours, or 13021 / (24 × 30) = 18 months. That is, one failure over a time period of 1.5 years. EDAC will increase the MTBF to 15 years.

The failure rate of a DRAM device does not increase linearly with its capacity. In other words, the failure rate of a 256K × 1 DRAM is much less than four times that of a 64K × 1 DRAM. Besides, the number of support components (such as buffers, decoupling capacitors, and so on) decreases, as does the number of interconnections. Thus, overall reliability improves significantly with higher capacity DRAMs.

Power dissipation analysis

The power dissipated by a DRAM device is due to:

- The operating current (i_{op}) drawn while the device is being accessed
- Its standby current (i_{st})
- The current drawn in the course of a refresh cycle (i_{ref})

First we examine each of the contributing currents. Then we calculate the power dissipation of the memory array pictured in Figure 4-40. For the purpose of generality we assume a memory organized into B banks with N devices per bank.

1. The *DO* (data output) lines of DRAMs belonging to the same column of the array are tied together. As a result, an active DRAM has to support the leakage current (i_l) of each of the other DRAMs of that column. Moreover, an active DRAM provides the input current (i_{in}) required by the circuits driven from the data output lines of the array. Take, for instance, the case of the design pictured in Figure 4-40. Each active DRAM has to support the leakage current of three standby DRAMs plus the input current of a quad transceiver. Hence, considering that only one bank can be active at any given time, we have for the total operating current:

$$I_{op} = N[i_{op} + (B - 1)i_l + i_{in}]\,(t_{cy} / t_{bcy})$$

Notice the multiplication by the duty cycle of memory activity. Indeed, the length of a memory cycle (t_{cy}) may be considerably shorter than the length of a machine (or bus) cycle (t_{bcy}). Another important thing to note is that the derived expression assumes memory cycles succeeding one another immediately. However, not all machine cycles involve memory. A number of them involve internal operations and I/O, so that this expression should be multiplied by the fraction of bus cycles involving memory.

Example 4-25

Consider the system associated with the timing diagram shown in Figure 4-39. Assume insertion of a single wait state and that memory machine cycles immediately succeed one another. What is the duty cycle of memory activity?

If only 75 percent of machine cycles involve memory, what is the actual (composite) duty cycle of memory activity?

Solution. Since only one wait state is inserted, a memory machine cycle takes a total of five clock cycles. Memory does not go active until after the end of $T1$ and is always back to standby before the start of $T4$. Hence, the duty cycle is about $3/5 = 0.6$; that is, 60 percent.

Actually only 75 percent of the machine cycles are memory ones, so that the actual duty cycle is $0.75 \times 0.60 = 0.45$ or 45 percent.

2. The total standby current includes two parts—one contributed by the inactive banks and another drawn by the active bank during that part of a cycle when memory is not active ($t_{bcy} - t_{cy}$).

$$I_{st} = N(B - 1)i_{st} + Ni_{st}(1 - t_{cy}/t_{bcy})$$

3. In general, DRAMs require refreshing of 128 cell rows every 2 ms, or refreshing of 256 cell rows every 4 ms. In either case the row refresh period (T_{ref}) is the same. If we assume the time taken for refreshing a single row to be t_{rcy}, then the duty cycle of the refresh activity is t_{rcy}/T_{ref}. The total consumption due to refresh is then:

$$I_{ref} = NBi_{ref}(t_{rcy}/T_{ref})$$

Once we determine the values of the three contributing currents, we can calculate the total power dissipation of the memory array from the expression:

$$P_W = (I_{op} + I_{st} + I_{ref})V_{cc}$$

We are now ready to calculate the typical power dissipation of the memory array of Figure 4-40. The following typical values are assumed for the associated parameters:

Parameter	Typical value
i_{op}	30 mA
i_{st}	3 mA
i_{ref}	25 mA
i_l	10 µA
i_{in}	200 µA
t_{cy}	400 ns
t_{rcy}	300 ns
t_{bcy}	600 ns

Substitution of the numeric values in these formulas yields:

$$I_{op} = 443 \text{ mA}$$

$$I_{st} = 220 \text{ mA}$$

$$I_{ref} = 42 \text{ mA}$$

The typical power dissipation is then calculated to be about 3.5 W. Similarly, we may determine maximum power dissipation by using maximum values for the DC parameters and the value of $V_{cc,max}$. Depending on the allowable tolerance, the latter may be 5.25 V or 5.5 V.

PROBLEMS

4-1. Memory Implementation with DRAMs. Consider implementation of the memory of a 16-bit CPU having a 1 MB address space. Determine the smallest increment in which we can add memory capacity and the maximum possible number of memory banks if we employ

(a) 64K $\times$ 1 DRAMs

(b) 256K $\times$ 1 DRAMs

Answer the same questions assuming a 32-bit CPU having an address space of 16 MB.

4-2. Wide-Word versus $\times$ 1-Organized Memory Devices. Wide-word DRAMs present advantages when the needed memory capacity is relatively small. Assume, for instance, an 8-bit μP. A 16 KB memory takes only two 8K $\times$ 8 RAMs to implement, while with 64K $\times$ 1 RAMs we need eight devices. However, as memory capacity grows, this advantage disappears. In fact, $\times$ 1-organized RAMs become more advantageous due to other considerations. To see this, consider two alternative implementations for the 128 KB memory of a 16-bit μP—one with 8K $\times$ 8 DRAMs and one with 64K $\times$ 1 DRAMs.

(a) How many devices do we need in each case?

(b) Assume an 8K $\times$ 8 DRAM takes up twice the area required for a 64K $\times$ 1 DRAM and also that the spacing between devices remains the same in the layout of the respective arrays. Determine the percent gain in real estate (in terms of the space taken by the array), when using the 64K $\times$ 1 devices.

(c) Compare the two implementations in terms of the required number of connections between DRAMs and the data bus.

(d) Which of the two arrays presents a higher capacitive load over the data lines?

4-3. Page Mode of Operation. In the normal mode of operation, a DRAM is presented a row address and a column address. These two address components determine jointly which location is accessed. However, most DRAMs feature a page mode of operation as well. In this mode, data can be transferred to/from a set of contiguous locations much faster. A page cycle differs from an ordinary cycle in that only CAS^* is activated (for latching of a new column address). In contrast, RAS^* is maintained active cycle after cycle (for a limited duration) to indicate use of the same row address. In this context we refer to the set of contiguous locations we can access, using the same row address, as a page.

(a) What is the maximum possible size of a page in the case of 64K × 1 DRAMs?

(b) Does the capacity of a page depend on whether the CPU is an 8- or a 16-bit μP? Explain.

(c) Suppose you are developing a system which is to include a very fast DMA peripheral. Under what conditions would you consider employing the page access mode to speed up DMA transfers?

4-4. Refresh Overhead. In general, DRAMs require either refreshing of 128 cell rows every 2 ms or refreshing of 256 cell rows every 4 ms. The time required for refreshing of a single row constitutes the refresh cycle. In a particular μC system a refresh cycle takes 500 ns. Determine (on a percent basis) the fraction of time consumed by memory for refresh operations. Would this overhead reduce the processing speed of the CPU by the same amount?

4-5. Circuit with Battery Backup. Figure P4-5 shows a CMOS μP-based circuit with nonrechargeable battery backup. Notice that the battery is isolated from the circuit completely and is thus protected from current leakages. This is accomplished by means of a low profile (printed board mountable) relay. As long as the relay is energized, V_{cc} is provided from the power supply. When primary power is lost, the relay is deenergized and power is supplied from the battery. While the relay is in transition, we rely on capacitor C for current supply. The circuit draws 10 mA and requires the supply voltage to be at least 3.6 V (for proper operation).

(a) Determine the minimum acceptable value of capacitor C, given that switchover in either direction takes about 5 ms.

(b) Assume the battery has a rated capacity of 180 mA-hours. For how long can we sustain a power outage?

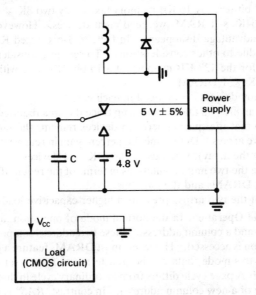

Figure P4-5.

4-6. EPROM Timing. Consider replacement of one of the SRAMs with a 2K × 8 EPROM in the interfacing example shown in Figure 4-14. The timing waveforms of the EPROM are similar to those shown in Figure 4-13. Specifically, the EPROM presents on its data lines valid data 450 ns (at maximum) after CE^* goes active or after the address becomes valid (whichever occurs last).   On the other hand, examination of the timing waveforms of the 8088 indicates that the interval between the time the CPU outputs a stable address and the time it expects valid data is (at minimum):

$$t_{acc} = 3T - 140 \text{ ns}$$

where T is the length of a clock cycle.   Assume a worst case propagation delay of 20 ns for the address latch and 30 ns for the decoder.

(a) Determine if the EPROM is compatible with the 8088 from the access time viewpoint when the latter is clocked at 5 MHz.

(b) Would such compatibility be achieved by inserting one wait state in each bus cycle?

(c) Consider lowering the clock frequency instead of inserting wait states.   What is the maximum clock frequency which would permit access time compatibility between the CPU and the EPROM?

4-7. Power Dissipation in SRAMs.   A particular 8K $\times$ 8 SRAM has an operating current of 30 mA and a standby current of 5 mA.   The CS^* input of the device is active for about half of the duration of a memory access machine cycle.   Given that 40 percent of the bus time is consumed for SRAM accesses:

(a) Calculate the average power dissipated in a device implementing all of the memory of a μP.

(b) What is the average power dissipation of an array of eight such devices in an 8-bit μP application?

4-8. Impact of Wait States on Instruction Processing Rate.   The memory cycle of a particular μP takes four clock cycles (without wait states).   On the average the CPU spends half of its time executing instructions and the other half accessing memory.   Suppose we have to insert one wait state per memory cycle:

(a) Determine the penalty in terms of reduction in instruction processing rate.

(b) Would your result change if the CPU is equipped with a separate subunit maintaining a queue of prefetched instructions?

4-9. Initialization of EDAC-Equipped Memory.   When power is turned on, the contents of a RAM are random.   Thus, if we attempt to perform a read operation in a system equipped with EDAC, the EDAC unit will generally detect multiple errors.   The same situation arises if we attempt a partial write operation, that is, writing one byte in a 16-bit word.   In either case we are not able to go any further since multiple errors are (in general) not correctable.   This problem is solved if we initialize the memory contents by writing, for instance, 0s in every memory location.   Yet, if the memory access width is larger than that of the CPU bus, things become complicated.   Take, for example, the case of a design based on an 8-bit CPU.   Assume we generate the check bits over 16 rather than eight bits in order to reduce EDAC overheads.   Here, prior to writing a byte the hardware reads the corresponding full 16-bit word.   The detected multiple errors will, again, prevent us from going any further.   What means would you incorporate in your design to overcome such a problem?

4-10. Memory Scrubbing for Soft Error Correction.   Unless corrected, soft errors accumulate over time and can cause occurrence of double errors in a word.   Hence it is advisable occasionally to scrub the memory for correction of any single errors we may detect.   This is especially important for infrequently accessed memory locations.   It amounts to reading one location after another for error checking. When an error is detected, the location in error is simply rewritten with corrected data.

(a) Consider a 16-bit μP having 1 MB of memory. A memory cycle takes 650 ns and the entire memory is scrubbed without interruption during "low system activity." How long does it take to scrub the entire memory? Disregard the extra time needed to rewrite corrected data into locations containing single errors. Assume the μP can perform memory cycles one right after another.

(b) Suppose that (on the average) 2 percent of the locations contain single errors. Repeat the previous question taking into account the time required to rewrite corrected data. Assume the memory does so automatically.

(c) It is most desirable to scrub memory gradually while the system performs some other regular function as, for instance, refresh. In this way we spread the associated overheads and secure memory scrubbing on a regular basis. In fact, some DMCs do just that. For example, the Intel 8207 replaces a *RAS**-only refresh cycle by a read cycle; that is, while refreshing the locations specified by a row address, it also reads the location specified by a full row/column address for checking. How long would it take to scrub the 1 MB memory when employing such a scheme? Again, disregard the time involved in rewriting corrected data.

4-11. Error-Detection-and-Correction. The 1 MB memory of a 16-bit CPU is implemented with 64K × 1 DRAMs. The manufacturer of the DRAMs specifies a soft error rate of 0.1% / 1000 hours and a hard error rate of 0.02% / 1000 hours.

(a) Calculate the composite failure rate of the whole memory in FITs.

(b) Determine the MTBF caused by hard errors and the MTBF caused by soft errors (for the entire memory). What is the MTBF caused by errors of either kind?

(c) The requirements of the application dictate that memory failures should not exceed more than one over a period of three years. Consequently, it is decided to employ an EDAC unit for correction of single errors and detection of double ones. This necessitates six additional bits per 16-bit word but will increase reliability by a factor of about 20. Calculate the rate of occurrence of single errors in the EDAC-equipped memory. How often do double and higher order errors occur?

4-12. Double Error Correction. Ordinarily a commercial EDAC unit corrects only single errors. Yet it is possible to correct double ones as well as long as one of them is a hard error. This can be accomplished using a comparatively short software routine initiated upon activation of the multiple-error flag of the EDAC unit. Recall that by examining the syndrome the CPU can determine (in the case of single errors) which bit is in error. It can also determine whether a multiple error involves two or more bits. Our first step is finding out whether or not one of the two errors is a hard one. If it is, we can determine the bit position it corresponds to and correct it by simply inverting it. This will leave a single (soft) error which can be corrected with the EDAC unit.

(a) Describe how you could find out if one of the errors is caused by a hard failure.

(b) Would the location with the hard failing bit be reusable? Discuss the risks.

(c) What if both errors are a result of hard failures? Would we be able to correct them?

4-13. Memory Management Overhead. A CPU is currently clocked at a rate of 4 MHz and operates without wait states (as far as memory cycles go). In fact, a worst case timing analysis indicates a 30 ns margin in the presentation of a valid memory address by the CPU. However, it is decided to add an MMU for memory management and protection. The MMU requires (at maximum) 120 ns for generation of a physical address from the logical address fed to it by the CPU.

(a) What is the impact of the MMU on memory cycle timing?

(b) Suppose the MMU has 32 descriptor registers and that context switching necessitates reloading of all registers from memory. What is the minimum time needed for context switching if a normal memory cycle (with no wait states) takes three clock cycles?

(c) Discuss how we could reduce context switching time by employing multiple MMUs.

4-14. Segment- versus Page-Based Virtual Memory Schemes. One of the disadvantages of segment-based virtual memory schemes is that prior to bringing a segment into memory, we have to economize an appropriately large block of contiguous memory locations. Thus, in order to accommodate a large segment we may have to swap many other segments. Naturally this increases system overheads. Besides, if segments are large, we may not be able to accommodate in memory at the same time the programs associated with many tasks. On the other hand, the fixed size employed by page-based schemes may result in wasting memory because of partially filled pages. Assume, for instance, that we employ 4-KB-size pages. Then, in the case of a program requiring 5.5 KB we will be wasting 2.5 KB of memory space. The amount of wasted memory space can be reduced by employing smaller size pages. However, that increases the required number of page descriptor registers and an MMU can provide only a limited number of such registers.

(a) A CPU has a virtual address space of 16 MB and employs a page size of 512 bytes. How many page descriptor registers (PDRs) do we need?

(b) What is the total capacity of the PDRs given we need four bytes for "description" of a page?

(c) A particular manufacturer uses a two-step approach for reduction of the number of required PDRs; that is, instead of a full set of PDRs the MMU provides a page table whose entries point to different "pointer tables" stored in main memory. Each entry of a pointer table, in turn, points to a physical page. Such a two-step approach reduces drastically the number of MMU-based registers but introduces another penalty. Explain what that penalty is.

4-15. Virtual Memory. The virtual address space (defined through descriptor registers) in virtual memory systems is much larger than the physical address space. For example, the 80286 μP has a virtual address space of 1000 MB, while its physical address space is only 16 MB. Assume a page-based virtual memory system where page size is fixed to 8 KB. The physical memory is 2 MB, of which 256 KB is occupied by permanently resident programs. The remaining memory space temporarily accommodates program pages brought from disk.

(a) Up to how many pages can we swap between disk and memory at any particular time?

(b) Suppose we upgrade the system with 1 MB of additional memory. Would this be transparent to the software? Would it make any difference in terms of system performance?

4-16. Crosstalk. The induction of unwanted signals from one signal line to another is commonly referred to as crosstalk. Such parasitic signals are due to the capacitive and inductive coupling between adjacent signal lines. This is illustrated in Figure

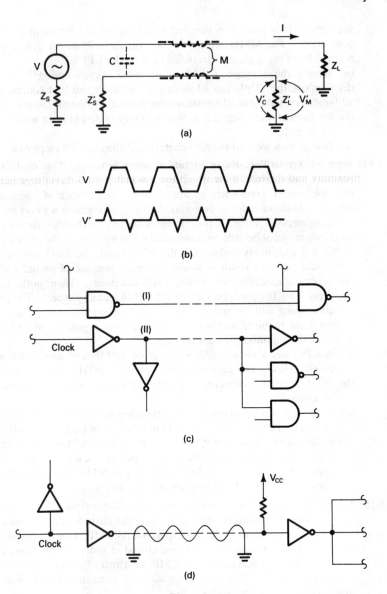

Figure P4-16.

P4-16(a). The two signal lines may represent etched lines on a printed circuit board or two common wires. Consider, for instance, the case when the upper line carries a square wave while the lower line is at a high level. Driven circuits are represented by their equivalent impedances (Z_L, Z'_L). Similarly, driving circuits are replaced by their source impedances (Z_S, Z'_S). For the upper line the equivalent representation includes the square wave voltage source (V) as well. As seen, signal energy flows to the lower line by means of capacitance C and the mutual inductance M between the two lines. An approximate expression for the voltage component contributed by C is:

$$V'_c = R'C(\Delta V/t_r)$$

where R' is the resistive part of Z'_L, ΔV the voltage difference between a high and a low level, and t_r the rise/fall time of signal V. On the other hand, the voltage component contributed by M may be expressed by:

$$V'_M = 2M(I/t_r)$$

where I represents the current in the upper line. Both, C and M increase with proximity and the length for which the associated lines travel together.

These relations justify the noise spikes induced into the lower line during signal transitions in the upper line [Figure P4-16(b)]. In fact, the amplitude of the noise depends on how fast such transitions take place.

(a) Explain why the noise induced by a clock line into an adjacent ordinary (logic) line can be particularly severe.

(b) Figure P4-16(c) shows a logic signal line (I) and an adjacent clock line (II). Clock rise and fall times are defined between 1 V and 3.8 V points and are 5 ns each. In contrast, logic signal rise and fall times are defined between 0.4 V and 2.6 V and are 15 ns each. Compare the V'_c noise induced on line I by the clock line with that induced if line II were a logic signal line.

(c) The fact that the clock line feeds four circuits will increase crosstalk on adjacent lines further [Figure P4-16(c)]. Why?

(d) Figure P4-16(d) depicts a more appropriate way of handling clock transmission. Note the use of a separate buffer for each destination and the buffering before driving multiple circuits. In fact, instead of etching clock lines (especially when they are long), we use a twisted pair of wires with one of them grounded at both ends. Explain why this is a better way to handle clock transmission.

(e) Explain why we may need a pull-up resistor at the destination and possibly a small series resistor.

4-17. Wait State Generation. Sometimes it is possible to insert a single wait state using only one flip-flop. Such is the case, for instance, when using an 8088 or an 8086 in conjunction with an 8284 clock generator. As seen from Figure P4-17, *ALE* (address latch enable) will always clear the JK flip-flop during state *T1* (see also Figure 3-3) and will thus activate *READY*. Now let us assume the system has two EPROMs which necessitate insertion of one wait state whenever accessed. The rest of the memory is RAM, access of which does not require insertion of wait states. *CS1** and *CS2** are the chip select signals generated by an address decoder when one of the EPROMs is addressed. The decision as to whether *READY* will be driven to a low or continue to be a high depends on the state of *CS1** and *CS2** at the middle of *T2* (that is, when the negative-edge-triggered flip-flop is clocked). If neither chip select is active, the output of the tri-state buffers will be floating, and because of the pull-up resistor both J and K are at a low. As a result the flip-flop preserves its state and *READY* remains at a high. However, if either chip select is active at that time, the corresponding tri-state buffer's output will be at a low and thus J and K will be at a high. Hence clocking will drive the flip-flop to the opposite state and *READY* goes to a low. Normally the latter connects to one of the *RDY* inputs of the 8284

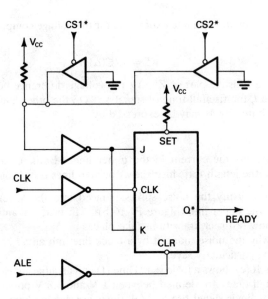

Figure P4-17.

which samples its ready lines at the end of $T2$ (see Figure 4-38). Subsequently, the 8284 drives the *READY* input of the CPU to a low for the duration of $T3$ and thus a wait state *TW* is inserted. Note that in the middle of $T3$ the state of the flip-flop will change again and *READY* will go back to a high. Therefore no additional wait states are inserted by the CPU. Draw a timing diagram depicting the transitions of the associated signals (T states, address, *ALE, RD*, CS*, READY, RDY*) during a Read bus cycle.

4-18. Insertion of a Variable Number of Wait States. Consider a system whose memory includes a static section requiring one wait state, a DRAM section requiring two wait states, and an EPROM section requiring four wait states per read cycle. Assume that a separate signal indicating when a particular section of memory is addressed is available, as well as an address strobe signal provided by the CPU during the first T state of a memory cycle. Design the wait state generation logic and indicate how the *READY* input of the CPU is to be driven.

4-19. Decoupling. Generally the current drawn by a device varies with time. Such variations are especially significant in DRAMs and other devices featuring a standby mode of reduced power dissipation. Decoupling capacitors cover short-term current requirements and thereby reduce the amplitude of the transients on the power distribution buses. Proper decoupling is critical for DRAMs because of refresh and the fact that all devices belonging to the same bank switch to operating mode at the same time. Decoupling is required at both device level and circuit board level. Each DRAM device is individually decoupled by a small capacitor satisfying the short-term "instantaneous" current requirements of the device. The small capacitors are recharged by larger (bulk decoupling) capacitors which are usually mounted in the periphery of the board. The larger capacitors are themselves recharged by the power supply. When properly designed, this power distribution hierarchy minimizes transients and maintains V_{cc} within the operating range.

The values of the capacitors can be determined from the relations:

$$\Delta Q = I\,\Delta t \quad \text{and} \quad C = \Delta Q/\Delta V$$

where ΔQ is the charge loss due to supplying current I for a duration Δt, ΔV the voltage change across the capacitor, and C the capacitance of the latter.   As an example let us assume a 64K $\times$ 1 DRAM having the following characteristics:

standby current	10 mA
operating current	60 mA
refresh current	50 mA
cycle time	500 ns
refresh cycle	400 ns
V_{cc} supply tolerance	$\pm 5\%$

We further assume that bulk decoupling response time (for recharging of the small capacitor) is 1.2 μs and that a memory access machine cycle takes about 800 ns. Clearly, the current demand placed upon the capacitor is maximum when an access cycle and a refresh cycle occur right after one another.   When a DRAM switches to operating mode it requires an extra current of $60 - 10 = 50$ mA for a duration of 500 ns.   This current is provided by the capacitor and corresponds to $50 \times 0.5 \times 10^{-9}$ Cb or 25 nCb.   Similarly we find for the refresh cycle a charge of 16 nCb.   Hence the total charge supplied by the capacitor is 41 nCb.   Now, from the second of the above relations we find that if V_{cc} is to drop no more than 250 mV below its nominal value, C must be at least $41 \times 10^{-9} / 0.25 = 0.16$ μF.   Bear also in mind that the equivalent series inductance L_s of the capacitor causes an additional voltage loss equal to $L_s(\Delta I/\Delta t)$, so it is important to select capacitors with good high-frequency charac-teristics.   This, in addition to minimizing the inductances introduced by the DRAM and capacitor leads and the etched connections.   Ceramic disk capacitors generally satisfy such requirements and are commonly used for high frequency (HF) decoupling.

(a) Calculate the amount of required bulk capacitance per device for the above 64K $\times$ 1 DRAMs.   Assume a 45 μs power supply response and that over this period a DRAM is not active for more than 20 percent of the time. V_{cc} is not to drop by more than 250 mV.   (Hint: Determine the average standby current over a 45 μs period.   Use as basis the current required for three refresh cycles and the standby current of a single device during that period.)

(b) How many 15 μF tantalum capacitors are required given there are four banks of 16 DRAMs each?

(c) Suppose you design a memory with 256K $\times$ 1 DRAMs drawing twice as much (standby, operating, and refresh) current and being equally fast.   Would you expect any problems if the board layout and the decoupling capacitors remain as for the 64K $\times$ 1 DRAMs mentioned earlier?

4-20. Error Detection Using Parity.   A system based on a 16-bit μP uses a single parity bit per byte for error detection.   When a parity error is detected, the CPU jumps au-tomatically to a diagnostic routine stored in EPROM.   Subsequently, the CPU ex-ecutes this routine which checks the entire dynamic memory for parity errors.   If no error is found it is assumed that the parity error detected originally was due to some noise spike. Hence, the system is reinitialized for normal mode of operation. If the diagnostic routine detects a parity error, the CPU jumps to a loading routine which is also stored in EPROM. This one reloads the dynamic memory from disk and restarts the system.

    (a) Discuss the complications we would face if we were to employ one parity bit per 16-bit word rather than one parity bit per byte. (Hint: Consider byte write operations.)

    (b) Assume memory is always accessed in the 16-bit word mode. Would you now consider using one parity bit per byte?

4-21. EDAC in Static Memories. The 64-KB memory of an 8-bit μP is implemented with 64 Kb SRAMs.

    (a) Draw the circuit schematic including pertinent buses and control signals assuming byte-wide SRAMs. Chip select signals are generated by an octal decoder.

    (b) How reliable is this memory compared to one of equal capacity implemented with 64K $\times$ 1 DRAMs? Assume the same hard failure rate for both types of devices.

    (c) Suppose you are to incorporate parity for detection of memory errors. Show how you would do it given that 64 Kb SRAMs are available in $\times$ 1 and $\times$ 4 organizations as well.

4-22. CPU Clocking Rate versus Memory Speed. Rather than inserting wait states in memory cycles, a designer decides to reduce the CPU clocking rate such that no wait states need be inserted.

    (a) Is this a good idea if (in this particular application) the CPU spends most of its time doing computations?

    (b) Assume clocking of the CPU at its maximum rate and insertion of one wait state per memory cycle. Under what conditions would a slight reduction of the CPU clocking rate be beneficial?

The CPU is clocked at its maximum clocking rate of 8 MHz, and the number of wait states per memory cycle is three. In fact, the third wait state provides a margin of 80 ns between the time memory data become available and the time data are sampled by the CPU. Later on, the designer considers employing a faster version of the RAM devices. The timing parameters of the new version are otherwise identical to those of the currently used devices.

    (c) What access time improvement should the new devices provide if they are to allow elimination of one of the wait states?

4-23. Upgrading with a Faster CPU. The μC imbedded in a particular product is currently operating without wait states. However, in order to improve the performance of the overall system, it is decided to upgrade it with a faster version of the CPU.

    (a) Explain why we should perform timing analysis before proceeding any further.

    (b) Under what conditions would the introduction of the faster CPU impose no wait state insertion?

    (c) How would you design a system to allow future use of faster memory devices?

4-24. Advance Generation of Memory Control Signals. Some μPs provide appropriate status information which can be decoded externally for fast generation of memory and I/O control signals. Examples are the 8088 and 8086 μPs whose status may be decoded to generate, for example, read/write strobes for memory. In fact, a special device, the Intel 8288 bus controller, is intended for this purpose. The signals generated by the 8288 provide an indication of the type of bus cycle earlier than the CPU does. Take, for instance, the *MRDC** (memory read command strobe) signal generated by

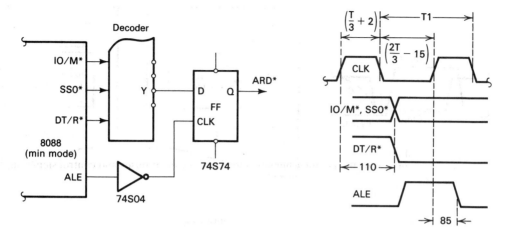

Figure P4-24.

the 8288. Its maximum delay from the start of $T2$ is 35 ns. In contrast, the corresponding delay of the $RD*$ strobe generated by the 8086 is 165 ns.

(a) Does this imply we will be able to initiate a RAM cycle 130 ns earlier (and thereby reduce or eliminate any wait states we would otherwise have to insert)?

(b) Assume a design where the address setup time requirements (relative to the start of the CPU $RD*$ signal) are exceeded by 50 ns. Discuss how you would take advantage of such a margin if advance $RD*$ and $WR*$ strobes are available.

(c) Figure P4-24 demonstrates another approach to generating advance memory control signals in the case of an 8088. Decoding of the three lines shown reveals the type of bus cycle when the 8088 is configured in minimum mode. Let us consider generation of $ARD*$ (advance read) only. The decoder output corresponding to a read cycle connects to the D input of a 74S74 flip-flop (FF), which is clocked at the trailing edge of ALE. That is, at a distance of $2T/3 + 70$ ns from the start of $T1$ (where T is the clock period). Determine how long in advance $ARD*$ is issued compared to the ordinary $RD*$ signal of the CPU. Assume a CPU clocking rate of 5 MHz and a maximum propagation delay of 4.5 ns for the inverter and 9 ns for the FF.

4-25. Propagation Delays and Signal Skewing. Figure P4-25(a) intends to illustrate the effects of capacitive loading on the delays experienced by a signal propagating through a circuit. As an example let us consider the propagation of a positive-going pulse through an inverting buffer. If the capacitance C presented at the output of the buffer is small (say, a few tens of picofarads), the output pulse edge delays are only those due to the internal circuitry of the buffer. However, if C is substantial, the leading edge of the output pulse will experience an additional delay resulting from the time taken by C to discharge from a high to a low logic level. Similarly, the trailing edge of the pulse will experience an extra delay because of the time taken by C to charge from a low to a high level.

Now, consider the system pictured in Figure P4-25(b) where the memory is accommodated on a printed board separate from that of the CPU. For simplicity, only the address signal paths are shown. Notice that the latter are buffered on the memory

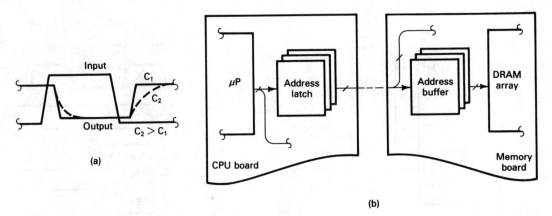

Figure P4-25.

board as well (even though the two boards may be plugging in neighboring slots of the backplane). The address latch is mounted very close to the μP and has the same delay characteristics as the address buffer. Assume address signals travel a total distance of about 25 in. (from the latch to the buffer). On the memory board, each address signal is fed to all 48 DRAMs of the memory array through etched connections of about 30 in. long. The following data describe delay characteristics of the latch and buffer devices (in terms of the capacitance C seen at their terminals, etc.):

Max delay for $C = 50$ pF: 30 ns
Min delay for $C = 50$ pF: 15 ns
Max delay difference between circuits of the same package: 3 ns

Assume that beyond $C = 50$ pF, propagation delays vary linearly with capacitive load at the rate of 0.06 ns/pF. The capacitance of a DRAM address input is 5 pF, and the etch contributes about 2 picofarads of capacitance per inch.
(a) Determine the skew between address signals (at the inputs of the DRAMs).
(b) What is the skew between address signals latched/buffered by circuits belonging to the same IC package?
(c) Calculate the worst case propagation delay suffered by an address signal during its travel from the μP to the input of a DRAM device.

4-26. **8-Bit CPU with Static RAM and EPROM.** Consider the design example pictured in Figure 4-36.
(a) Suppose this design works with no wait state insertion. Can this lead to any conclusions concerning the speed of the memory devices? Explain.
(b) Assume we decide to reduce the clock frequency drastically. How far can we go before we run into problems?
(c) Does the power dissipated in the memory devices vary with the clock frequency?
(d) How would you modify the pictured design if you have to replace the 2K × 8 EPROM with an 8K × 8 one?
(e) List the necessary modifications if the memory is implemented with one 128 Kb EPROM and eight 2K × 8 SRAMs. Redraw the modified schematic.

4-27. 16-Bit CPU with Dynamic RAM. Consider the design example shown in Figure 4-37.

  (a) Draw the layout of the memory array for a capacity of 128 KB and a capacity of 256 KB.

  (b) What purpose do resistors R serve? Why not show resistors on the rest of the input lines of the DRAMs?

  (c) Suppose we eliminate the decoder and employ directly the inverse of M/IO^*. Would this have any consequences?

  (d) The schematic implies that a read access always involves a full 16-bit word. How would you modify the design so that only the desired byte is read? Would such a modification have any impact on power dissipation?

4-28. Debugging. Assume a design similar to the one pictured in Figure 4-37. After breadboarding the circuitry, you find out (to your amazement) that you can successfully write and read back a memory location.

  (a) Subsequently you decide to run a diagnostic routine which does the following: Starting from the lowest address it stores sequentially in each 16-bit location the address of that location, and then goes back to read and verify the contents of each location. After running the diagnostic you discover that the lower half of the memory bank contains incorrect data. In fact, it contains the same patterns the upper one does. Now you decide to run another diagnostic routine. This one performs a similar test except it starts from the highest memory address. To your surprise, the results indicate the reverse problem; that is, the upper half of the memory bank seems to contain incorrect data—in fact, the same data patterns contained in the respective locations of the lower half. What conclusions do you draw from these symptoms? Did these tests really exercise the entire memory?

  (b) Suppose address lines $A1$ and $A2$ are somehow shorting together. What would you expect to find out after running each of the above tests?

  (c) After fixing the problems associated with the address lines, you satisfy yourself that both diagnostics run successfully. Now you run another diagnostic routine which stores in each location a randomly generated pattern. Then it resets the random pattern generator and goes back to read and verify the contents of each location. Unfortunately, the problems are not yet over! The results reveal frequent errors with no consistency as far as address or data bit positions go. List possible causes for such an erratic behavior of the memory.

4-29. Memory Equipped with EDAC. Figure 4-40 pictures a high-performance system with memory management and EDAC. Normally (when no wait states are inserted) a memory access machine cycle takes three clock cycles. On the average, an instruction cycle takes eight clock cycles and involves one operand fetch. However, the access speed of the employed DRAMs, in conjunction with the delays introduced by the MMU and the multiple buffers, imposes insertion of two wait states per memory cycle. Nonetheless, if we decide to use the EDAC unit in read/correct mode we will have to insert a third wait state.

  (a) Determine the introduced overhead (on a percent basis) if we operate the system in read/correct mode. Assume a nonpipelined organization for the CPU.

  (b) Because of the performance requirements of the application it is decided to operate the EDAC in read/detect mode. What specific feature should the CPU have in order to facilitate system operation in such a mode?

  (c) When an error is detected, the CPU discontinues the current instruction cycle and retries to read the same location. Suppose the second time the EDAC unit detects no error. How would you explain such a case? What do you think caused the error the first time the location was read?

(d) Let us assume that when the CPU retries, the EDAC unit again detects an error. Now the CPU reads and then examines the syndrome to determine the nature of the error (single, double, multiple) and the particular bit in error (if the error involves a single bit). In this specific case it turns out that the error does indeed involve a single bit. Hence, the CPU corrects it and then writes the corrected data back in the same location. Immediately afterwards, it reads the location once more and finds no error. What type of failure caused the original error? What if the error persisted after the CPU stored the corrected data in the location?

(e) The memory error log (maintained by the CPU) indicates bit 13 of bank #2 to be consistently in error; however, corrective action is not possible immediately. Thus, you decide to keep running until such action takes place. What aspects of system performance are affected during that interval—that is, before maintenance is performed?

4-30. Placement of the Cache. In Chapter 3 we had the opportunity to see an example of on-chip (with the CPU) cache implementation. Suppose the CPU is not equipped with a cache and you have to design an external one.

(a) Discuss the disadvantages of connecting the cache to the buffered CPU bus (to which memory and I/O circuits connect).

(b) Draw a block diagram depicting where you would place the cache relative to the CPU, memory, and I/O interfaces.

(c) Suppose the system is equipped with an (external) MMU as well. Would you place the cache before or after the MMU?

5

INPUT/OUTPUT

Up to this point we have seen how we can design a system consisting of a CPU—that is, a μP—and memory. Such a system might be thought of as an operational processor, in the sense that it can be initialized to start execution of a memory-resident program. It was implied the program was operating on memory-resident data and that any results derived in the course of program execution were also stored in memory. However, such a system raises some very serious questions:

1. How do we store the program in memory initially?
2. Even if we assume that the program is stored in some read-only memory devices, how do we present to the system the data we intend to process?
3. How does the system make available to the outside world the derived results?

The remaining part of the book deals with the means which permit a CPU and its memory to exchange information with the external world. Collectively, these means constitute the input/output part of a μC system. This part is also referred to simply as I/O.

In the first part of this chapter we examine the principles of I/O and the three basic I/O techniques (programmed I/O, interrupt-driven I/O, and DMA). We are interested in (1) the design of the interface circuits implementing each of these techniques, (2) the types of available I/O control devices, (3) how we apply these devices, (4) what problems we face and what alternatives we have, and (5) the criteria used in choosing an I/O technique.

The second part of the chapter is about common types of I/O support devices. Our main objective is to discuss typical characteristics of such components and how we employ them in the design of I/O interfaces for serial communication and visual displays.

I/O devices are not always interfaced to the (buffered) CPU bus. Very often they connect to a higher level bus known as the μC (microcomputer) bus. The last part of the chapter deals with such buses. We are interested in their structure and how we go about interfacing to them.

In Chapter 6 we discuss common I/O devices such as keyboards, CRT displays, printers, and floppy disks. Such I/O devices are better known as μC peripherals, and they are usually attached to a system via the μC bus. Peripherals supplement the means through which information is exchanged with the external world. They also provide additional space for storing programs and data.

5.1 I/O ORGANIZATION IN MICROPROCESSORS

How do we address I/O devices? How does a CPU communicate with them? What kinds of information does a CPU exchange with an I/O device? What do I/O instructions accomplish? How do we address I/O when the CPU has no separate I/O address space? The subjects of this section are these and other related topics.

Fundamentally, a CPU communicates with I/O the same way it does with memory. Information is again exchanged through the CPU data bus. The address bus identifies who is to receive or provide such information. However, because of the different roles played by I/O and memory, the design of I/O interfaces differs from the design of a memory interface. Let us examine some of the main differences between memory and I/O devices.

1. The memory stores programs and data for convenient access by the CPU. When the memory cannot read and write fast enough, the CPU waits. In any case, its speed is certainly comparable to that of the CPU. In contrast, the rate at which an I/O device can accept or provide data may be slower than that of the CPU by many orders of magnitude. Take, for example, a printer having a speed of 10 cps (characters per second). It can accept only one byte of data every 100 ms. Here insertion of wait states is ruled out because of the very long time intervals involved—unless, of course, the application allows dedication of the CPU to this task. The alternative is providing to the CPU some indication as to whether the I/O device is ready to send or receive information. Such an indication is provided in the **status word** of an I/O device. The status word is read by the CPU via its data bus like ordinary data. The status word may not indicate just the readiness of the I/O device for data. It may also convey information about certain operational conditions, or events, concerning the device. In the case of the printer, for instance, one status bit indicates if the printer is ready to accept

from the CPU the next character.   Another status bit may indicate if the printer is about to run out of paper, and so on.

2. Rather than presenting to the CPU its status in a passive manner, an I/O device may take the initiative for a data transfer.   This is accomplished by interrupting the CPU whenever the I/O device is ready to accept/provide data.   Moreover, I/O devices with DMA capability can transfer data to/from memory without any CPU intervention.   So, unlike memory (which never initiates a data transfer by itself), I/O devices may initiate, and even carry out, such transfers on their own.

3. Memory performs only two types of operations—reading and writing—and only reading in the case of read-only memory.   On the other hand, an I/O device may perform other operations as well.   A printer operation of this type could be the advancing of the paper to the next line.   Such operations are specified in the **control word** sent by the CPU to the I/O device.   The control word encodes the commands associated with the functions the I/O device can perform.   Like status, control words are sent over the CPU data bus.

I/O Ports

Figure 5-1 illustrates in simplified form the interface between an 8-bit CPU and a typical I/O device.   There is one register for each type of information exchanged between I/O device and CPU.   These registers constitute the backbone of the I/O interface.

1. *Command Register:* The CPU loads this register with a control word specifying to the I/O device one or more commands.   Usually, each bit of the control word indicates a specific command.   Thus, each of the parallel outputs of the command register drives one of the control inputs of the I/O device.

2. *Status Register:* This register reflects the status of the I/O device at any particular time.   The CPU reads the contents of the status register and then examines which bits are set.   From there it determines the operational conditions of the device—that is, whether it is ready to accept or provide data and so on.

3. *Data Output Register:* If the I/O device indicates readiness to accept data, the CPU proceeds to do so.   The new data are placed in the data output register.   The (parallel) outputs of the latter connect to the data lines of the I/O device.   In Figure 5-1 we assume a device with bidirectional data lines.

4. *Data Input Register:* What if the device is ready to provide new data?   Such data are stored by the device in the data input register.   At the same time it sets the appropriate bit of the status register to reflect that fact.   Subsequently, the CPU takes notice of the fact and reads the new data.

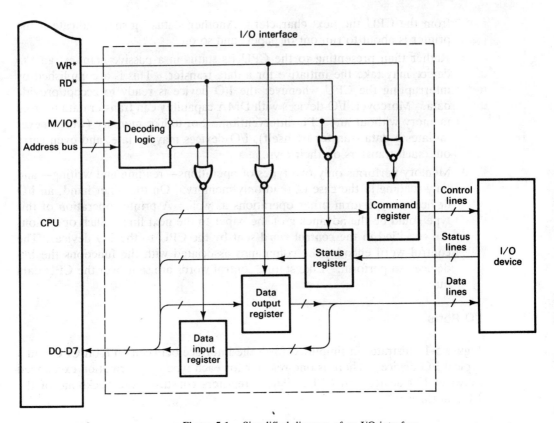

Figure 5-1. Simplified diagram of an I/O interface.

Notice from Figure 5-1 that all four registers connect to the CPU data bus. The command and data output registers are write-only registers. The status and data input registers are read-only registers. Hence, a total of two addresses is all we need. For example, the command register and the status register are selected using the same address (see Figure 5-1). However, the output of the address decoder is gated by the *WR** strobe in the case of the command register and the *RD** strobe in the case of the status register. Thus, only one of them responds during a bus cycle.

Because they are dedicated to I/O operations, the four registers are called **I/O registers**. Not all of them are always needed. For example, if the I/O device presents status information as DC levels, we do not need a status register. Instead, we may simply employ buffering circuits. The output lines of the buffer are enabled using the same select signals shown in Figure 5-1 for the status register.

Whether implemented with real registers or actually representing buffers, the four I/O registers are also known as **I/O ports**, because such registers can be viewed as gateways (or ports) through which the CPU exchanges information with I/O devices and thereby with the external world. An I/O port can be as wide as the

CPU bus itself—up to eight bits for systems based on 8-bit μPs, and up to 16 bits for systems based on 16-bit μPs. Both the needed number of ports and the number of bits per port depend on the particular I/O device. Take, for instance, the case of a light emitting diode (LED). All we need is a single, one-bit-wide output port to turn the LED on/off. At the other side of the spectrum we have complex I/O devices, like disks, which require many byte-wide I/O ports.

As examples we show in Figure 5-2 the actual I/O port configuration for a very simple printer and a keyboard. A printer is an output-only device, so no data input register is needed. Similarly, a keyboard is an input-only device. Hence, there is no data output register. Since both devices deal with 8-bit characters, the data registers are eight bits wide. Notice, however, that there is only one command bit and only one status bit. Consequently, each of the respective registers need be only one-bit wide.

First, let us examine a typical sequence of events in the case of a printer which is ready to accept a character:

1. The printer activates its *RDY* (ready) status line.
2. The CPU takes notice of the event by reading and then examining bit 0 of the status register.
3. Now the CPU proceeds to load a new character into the data output register. It also sets to a one the LSB of the command register.
4. The printer senses the activation of its *PNC* (print new character) control line. Hence, it proceeds to read the new character from the data output register.
5. In the meantime the printer deactivates its *RDY* status line. From here on, the printer appears to the CPU as being busy, a state which continues until it prints the new character. Then it activates its *RDY* status line to indicate to the CPU its readiness for the next character, and so on.

A similar procedure applies in the case of the keyboard (though in a somewhat reverse direction):

1. When a key is depressed, the keyboard loads the corresponding character code in the data input register.
2. At the same time it sets to a 1 the NCA (new character available) bit in its status register.
3. The CPU takes notice of the fact by reading and then examining the keyboard status register. Subsequently, it proceeds to read the new character from the data input register.
4. After doing so, the CPU sets to a 1 the CHA (character accepted) bit in the command register.
5. As a result of the previous action, the *CHA* control line of the keyboard goes active, having been informed of the acceptance of the character code.

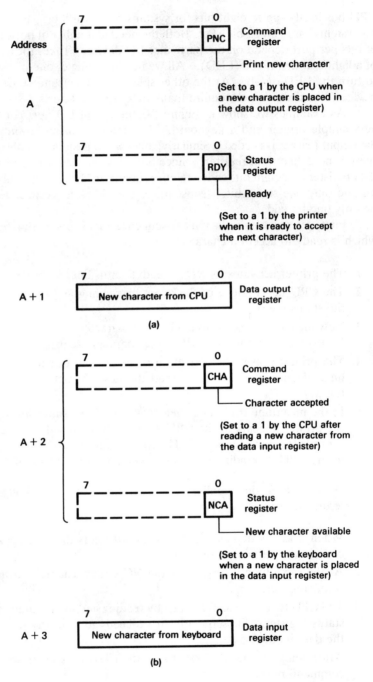

Figure 5-2. Examples of I/O register configurations. (a) I/O registers of a simple printer. (b) I/O registers of a keyboard.

Note from Figure 5-2 that command and status registers are assigned the same address. In fact, if both devices belong to the same system, we may go even further. We can use the same address for the data output register of the printer and the data input register of the keyboard.

Example 5-1

A system is based on an 8-bit μP and has two I/O devices. Both devices handle data on a one-byte-at-a-time basis. The first device has two status lines and three control lines. The second device has three status lines and four control lines. How many 8-bit I/O ports do we need for status reading and control of each device? What is the total number of needed I/O ports given the first device is an output-only one? How about the total number of needed addresses?

Solution. Each I/O device requires one output port for commands and one input port for status. The width of each port is determined from the corresponding number of status and control lines. For example, the status port of the first device need only be two bits wide. The first device requires only one port for data. The second device requires two ports for data (one for input and one for output). Therefore, the total number of I/O ports is seven. If we employ a separate address for each port we need a total of seven different addresses. However, we could employ the very same address for the status and control port of each device. Also, we could employ the same address for the data input and data output ports of the second device. Thus, the total number of addresses can be as low as four.

I/O Address Space

Some CPUs have a separate I/O address space (see Section 2.2). For example, the 8088 and 8086 μPs have a separate I/O address space of 64 KB. The state of an external interface line (such as the IO/M^* line of the 8088) determines if a read/write cycle is intended for memory or for I/O. Otherwise, I/O cycle timing is very similar to memory cycle timing.

The size of the I/O address space is usually small compared to the (ordinary) memory address space. Each I/O address specifies uniquely an 8-bit-wide I/O port—that is, one 8-bit-wide input port and one 8-bit-wide output port. The number of port addresses required per I/O device is generally small, so the size of the I/O address space (especially when 64 KB) is seldom a problem. Keeping the I/O address space small makes I/O instructions shorter (which is an advantage).

I/O Instructions

The movement of data between CPU and I/O ports is accomplished through execution of **I/O instructions**. Such instructions are provided in the instruction sets of CPUs having separate I/O address spaces. They belong to the class of data transfer instructions (see Section 2.5) and include

- An "input" instruction
- An "output" instruction

"Input" instructions move the data presented (by an I/O device) over a specified I/O port to a CPU register which is either implied by the opcode or specified explicitly in the instruction. An "output" instruction does the reverse. It moves data from a CPU register to the addressed I/O port.

How does an I/O instruction specify the desired I/O port? In general I/O ports are addressed employing one of two addressing modes:

1. *Direct Address Mode:* The instruction contains the address of the I/O port. Very often this mode is called the **direct port addressing mode**.
2. *Register Indirect Mode:* The address of the port is contained in a CPU register. This register is either implied in the opcode or specified in the instruction. Sometimes this mode is called **indirect port addressing mode**.

Some μPs implement a more powerful version of the indirect port addressing mode. The idea is to facilitate block transfers between CPU and I/O ports. In this mode the instruction specifies two additional registers:

1. The first register holds the address of the memory location which is to exchange data with the I/O port (through the CPU).
2. The second register holds the instruction repeat count.

Each time such an instruction is executed, the register holding the memory address is incremented (or decremented). This way it points to the next sequential address. Also, the register holding the repeat count is decremented. When the contents of this second register reach zero, the automatic reexecution of the instruction ends.

The largest address we can specify in an instruction depends on the size of the I/O address space. When the CPU decodes the opcode of an I/O instruction, it activates the *IO/M** (or some other functionally equivalent) external interface line. This line provides to memory and I/O circuits the means of distinguishing between memory addresses and I/O addresses. Next we examine examples of I/O instruction formats.

Figure 5-3(a) illustrates the format of the "input" instruction of the 8088 in direct port addressing mode. The first byte (of the two-byte instruction) specifies the opcode. The second byte specifies the address of the (input) port. Figure 5-3(b) shows the format of the same instruction in indirect port addressing mode. Now, the whole instruction takes only one byte. The opcode implies that the port address is contained in the DX register of the CPU. Hence we can vary the port address by manipulating the contents of the DX register. In either mode, the "input" instruction transfers the port data into the 8-bit AL register of the CPU. The formats are similar for the "output" instruction (Figure 5-3). However, the data are now transferred from the AL register to the output port.

Example 5-2

How many ports can the 8088 address in each I/O addressing mode?

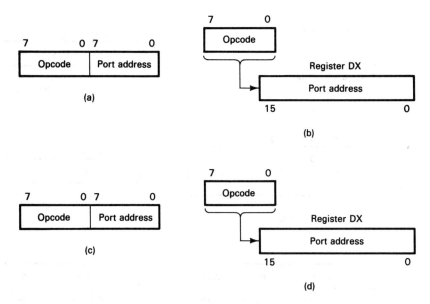

Figure 5-3. I/O instruction formats of the 8088. (a) "Input" instruction employing direct port addressing mode. (b) "Input" instruction employing indirect port addressing mode. (c) "Output" instruction employing direct port addressing mode. (d) "Output" instruction employing indirect port addressing mode.

Solution. First let us take the "input" instruction. In direct port addressing mode, the port address is contained in the second byte of the instruction. Therefore we can distinguish among $2^8 = 256$ input ports. In the same mode the "output" instruction can address just as many output ports. In indirect port addressing mode, the port address is contained in the DX register. The latter can store 16 bits. Hence we can address up to $2^{16} = 64K$ input ports (with the "input" instruction) and up to 64K output ports (with the "output" instruction).

The 8086 has identical I/O instruction formats except that a port can be also 16 bits wide, which means there is an additional "input" instruction opcode and an additional "output" instruction opcode. Another point is that an 8-bit port may connect to the lower or the upper half of the 16-bit data bus. An I/O instruction can handle either case by setting the LSB of the address (that is, A0) to the appropriate value (even/odd byte addressing). Finally, for 16-bit ports, the data are transferred to/from the CPU AX register which is 16 bits wide.

Figure 5-4 pictures another example, this time I/O instruction formats employed in the Z8000 CPU family. In direct port addressing mode, an "input" instruction requires two 16-bit words. The first word includes an opcode field, an opcode expansion (opex) field, and an Rd field. This last field indicates which CPU register is to receive the data read from the input port. The second word specifies the address of the input port. In indirect port addressing mode, the instruction specifies explicitly two registers—a register holding the port address

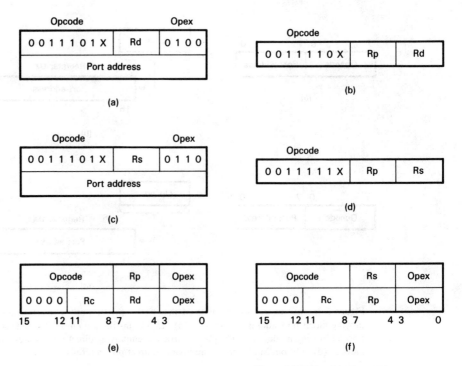

Figure 5-4. I/O instruction formats of the Z8001 and Z8002. (a) "Input" instruction using direct port addressing mode. (b) "Input" instruction using indirect port addressing mode. (c) "Output" instruction using direct port addressing mode. (d) "Output" instruction using indirect port addressing mode. (e) Format of instructions transferring data blocks from an input port to memory. (f) Format of instructions transferring data blocks from memory to an output port.

(Rp) and a destination register (Rd). "Output" instructions have a similar format with one exception: the Rd field is replaced with an Rs one. This new field specifies the source register from which data are to be transferred to an output port.

Example 5-3

How many ports can the I/O instructions of the Z8000 family handle?

Solution. Direct port addresses are 16 bits long. Hence, in direct mode, an I/O instruction can address up to 64K (8-bit-wide) ports. Rp can be any of the 16-bit general-purpose registers of the CPU. Thus, in the indirect mode, the I/O addressing capability of these CPUs is also 64K.

Figure 5-4(e) illustrates another type of "input" instruction format of the Z8000 family. Here the instruction specifies a port address register (Rp), a count register (Rc), and a destination register (Rd). Rd contains the memory address at which the first byte (or word) read from the input port is to be stored. After each execution the CPU increments (or decrements, as dictated by the opcode) the Rd for derivation of the next memory address. The size of the increment/ decrement is one for 8-bit ports and two for 16-bit ports. Also, before re-executing the instruction, the CPU decrements Rc by one and compares the result to zero. Automatic re-execution continues as long as the contents of Rc remain nonzero. Figure 5-4(f) shows the format of "output" instructions of the same type.

Such iterative I/O instructions remind us of string processing operations (Section 2.5) which are executed repeatedly until a certain condition is met. However, the block transfers accomplished with these instructions should not be confused with the DMA mode of I/O. As we will see later, in DMA mode, the CPU is completely bypassed. In contrast, when executing iterative I/O instructions, the data are transferred to/from memory via the CPU. For example, input data are first transferred to a CPU register and then stored in memory, so the I/O device is still dealing directly with the CPU.

Example 5-4

How large a data block can we transfer when employing the iterative type of I/O instructions shown in Figure 5-4?

Solution. Rc can be any one of the 16-bit general-purpose registers of the CPU. Hence, an I/O instruction can be executed repeatedly up to $2^{16} = 64K$ times when transferring bytes. If we transfer 16-bit words, the instruction can be re-executed up to 32K times. in either case the total volume of transferred data amounts to 64 KB.

Memory-Mapped I/O

What if a CPU lacks a separate I/O address space? In this case we treat I/O ports just as if they were memory locations, so for I/O data transfers we use the very same instructions we do for transfers between CPU and memory—that is, I/O ports are assigned addresses from the memory address space. In principle we can assign to an I/O port any memory address. Usually, however, we put aside one or more blocks of sequential addresses which are used exclusively for I/O purposes. Figure 5-5 shows an example of address space allocation. It is assumed that the CPU has a memory address space of 1 MB. Memory has been assigned the lower half of the address space (addresses 0 to 512K). For I/O ports we reserve a block of 4K byte locations, starting from address 512K. The use of memory addresses for I/O is commonly referred to as **memory-mapped I/O**.

Even when our CPU has a separate I/O address space, we may choose to employ memory-mapped I/O, which can be done for part or all of the I/O ports. The reasons behind such a choice can be seen by considering the differences between memory-mapped and separate I/O.

1. In memory-mapped I/O, the number of addresses assigned to I/O ports is up to the designer. Thus, it can be as large as necessary, as long as we have

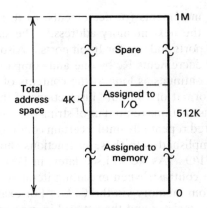

Figure 5-5. Example of memory address space allocation in memory-mapped I/O.

plenty of address space left for memory. On the other hand, separate I/O spaces generally have limited size. As a result, they may not be adequate in certain applications.

2. When employing memory-mapped I/O, all I/O operations are performed by memory reference instructions. This is an advantage because such instructions offer greater flexibility—first, because of the larger number of addressing modes they accommodate, and second, because of special operations they may allow. Example of the latter are bit manipulations facilitating the checking of individual bits in status registers. On the other hand, I/O instructions have shorter operand fields. Consequently, they are more compact and take less time to fetch and execute.

3. Memory-mapped I/O requires more elaborate address decoding (since I/O port addresses are now full-length ones). In contrast, separate I/O simplifies decoding because only a subset of the address bits need be decoded. In fact, when the number of I/O ports in small, the decoding logic becomes trivial.

I/O Techniques

Let us now go back to the I/O interface pictured in Figure 5-1. We have seen that before transferring a byte of data, the CPU examines the status of the I/O device to find out if the device is ready for a data transfer. In other words, the CPU has no direct way of knowing that the device is indeed ready. Instead, it has to read and examine the status word on a regular basis in order to find out. Such timed scanning of device status is performed by the CPU under control of internal programs. For this reason, this type of I/O scheme is very often called timed I/O or programmed I/O. Sometimes it is also referred to as CPU-initiated I/O because status scanning is performed entirely at CPU's initiative. In this book we have chosen the term **programmed I/O**.

Unless the device happens to be ready, the time spent for status scanning represents time wasted. The overhead can be very significant in the case of fast I/O devices which require scanning at a high rate. It would be far better if the

I/O device could inform the CPU when to look at its status. An I/O device may accomplish this by means of the external interface lines associated with interrupts. That is, instead of presenting its status passively via the status port, the device causes (in addition) an interrupt. It does so when ready for a data transfer, or because of some other event whose nature is indicated in the status word. The interrupt activates the appropriate internal program which examines the device status and follows up with the required actions. Such an I/O scheme is commonly known as **interrupt-driven I/O** or sometimes as device-initiated I/O.

A common characteristic of the two previous schemes is that the CPU is directly involved with the movement of each and every byte of I/O data. For I/O devices having high transfer rates this raises problems. Consider, for instance, the case of an 8-bit μP reading a block of data from a disk. Assume the latter has a data transfer rate of 1 MB/s (megabytes/second). Such a rate gives the CPU only 1 μs to

1. Read and examine the status of the disk
2. Transfer the byte of data into one of the CPU registers
3. Set the appropriate bit in the command register to indicate the input data were read
4. Transfer the read byte from the CPU register to memory

A typical CPU will be unable to complete all of the above within 1 μs. Then what?

The alternative is to bypass the CPU and transfer the data directly to (or from) memory, an approach known as **direct memory access (DMA)**. Remember, though, that the CPU still has direct control of the status and command ports. However, the information exchanged via these ports pertains to blocks of data rather than individual bytes or words. Hence, these ports need not be accessed very frequently. We will discuss each of the three I/O techniques separately.

5.2 PROGRAMMED I/O

The I/O scheme pictured in Figure 5-1 is actually one of programmed I/O. In fact, this scheme represents a particular form of programmed I/O known as **polled I/O**. The name stems from the fact that prior to performing a data transfer, the CPU "polls" the I/O device to check its readiness. On the other hand, status checking does not make sense in the case of very simple I/O devices (like switches or visual indicators). For example, if the CPU has to read the settings of a row of on/off switches, it may do so unconditionally. Here there is no concern about the status of the I/O device(s). This particular form of programmed I/O is called **direct I/O**.

In this section we discuss how we go about designing programmed I/O interfaces. We also examine (integrated) I/O interface controllers and their application in the design of such interfaces. We start with direct I/O—the simplest form of programmed I/O.

Direct I/O

Consider a μP-based instrument with panel switches and indicators. The switches serve for selection of the desired mode of operation by the operator of the instrument. The indicators are implemented with light emitting diodes (LEDs). They serve to indicate the status of the instrument, certain parameter values, and so on. Prior to taking a new measurement, the operator sets up the panel switches accordingly. Then a pushbutton switch is depressed for initiation of the measurement. At this point the μP proceeds to read the settings of the panel switches, from which it determines how it should go about performing this particular measurement. Here the panel switches play the role of an input device; in fact, the reading of the switch settings is done the direct I/O way—that is, without need for prior status checking.

Figure 5-6 illustrates how we can go about designing such a direct input interface. We assume an 8-bit μP with a separate I/O address space. First of all we need buffers for isolation of the switches from the data bus. An octal buffer, for instance, can accommodate up to eight switches. Each such buffer represents an 8-bit input port. We also need an address decoder, which is enabled only when the *M/IO** line of the CPU is at a low. Since the switches involve only read operations, we gate the respective output of the decoder with the *RD** strobe of the CPU.

Let us see now what happens when the CPU executes an "input" instruction. We assume that the operand address corresponds to the one assigned to the input port shown in the figure.

1. Some time during the early part of the I/O machine cycle the output of the decoder goes to a low.
2. Later on, *RD** is activated and *SEL1** also goes to a low. Subsequently, the outputs of the bus buffer are enabled.
3. Each buffering circuit drives the respective line of the CPU data bus to either a high or a low. This depends on the position of the corresponding switch. For example, when S0 is open, *D0* is driven to a high. When closed, *D0* is driven to a low.

What if the input port is memory-mapped? In this case the address specified by the instruction will be the memory address which has been assigned to the input port. The instruction itself will be a memory reference (rather than an "input") instruction. Regardless of the employed address space, however, the settings of the switches are read in terms of 1s and 0s. They are then examined by the CPU, which takes whatever actions are dictated by the program.

The panel indicators represent output devices. They, too, are treated the

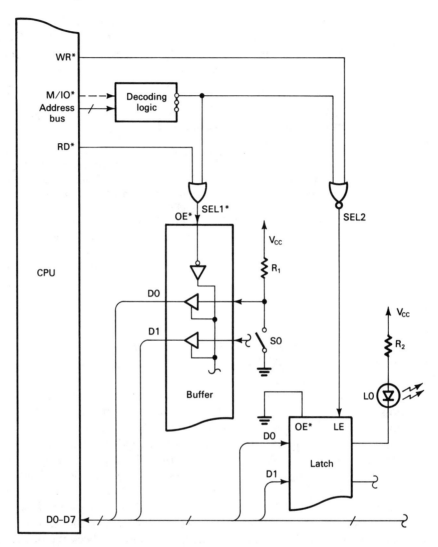

Figure 5-6. Example of direct I/O. The direct input port is used to read switch settings. The direct output port is used to control the state of solid-state lamps.

direct I/O way. Take, for instance, the case in which (LED) L0 indicates the readiness of the instrument. The CPU turns L0 off as soon as the pushbutton switch is depressed for a new measurement. Similarly, L0 is turned on (indicating a ready state) as soon as the results are derived. Both actions are taken by the CPU unconditionally—that is, status checking does not apply.

Now we need an output port. It is implemented with a latch storing the output data and thereby maintaining each LED in the desired state. The LEDs are connected to the outputs of the latch. An LED is turned on by setting to a

0 the corresponding bit position in the latch. When the loaded bit is a 1, the voltage difference across the terminals of the LED is very small. Hence the LED stays or switches off. Notice the sharing of the same address by the input and output ports. However, for the latter we use for gating purposes the WR^* strobe.

Example 5-5

Assume that while at a high state, each input of the buffer in Figure 5-6 requires 15 μA. What value would you suggest for resistor R_1?

Solution. If R_1 is very large, the input voltage may not be sufficiently high when S0 is open. For example, if $R_1 = 220$ KΩ, the input voltage will be $5 - (15 \times 0.22)$ $= 1.7$ V, assuming a V_{cc} of 5 V. For a device of the 74LS family, this value would be unacceptable. On the other hand, too low a value for R_1 increases power dissipation when S0 is closed. For example, if $R_1 = 100$ Ω, the supply current drawn via R_1 will be about $5/0.1 = 50$ mA, that is, a dissipation of $0.05^2 \times 100 = 0.25$ W. To maintain a sufficiently high input voltage of, say, 3.5 V, R_1 should not exceed $(5 - 3.5) / 15 = 0.1$ MΩ, or 100 KΩ. Choosing $R_1 = 10$ KΩ will more than satisfy such a condition. At the same time it will reduce the current drawn (when a switch is closed) to only 0.5 mA.

Polled I/O

In polled I/O it is necessary to first check the status of the I/O device. The flow diagram of Figure 5-7 depicts the sequence of associated actions. After the system is initialized, the pertinent I/O program, known as I/O driver, reads the status of the I/O device. Then it examines the status bits for determination of the operational condition of the device. If the device is not ready, the CPU may jump to other tasks. Later on, after some timed interval, it comes back to repeat the described process again. This timed interval depends on the speed of the device. For example, in the case of a character printer having a speed of 10 cps it is about 100 ms long. However, if no other tasks exist, the CPU loops back immediately to read and check the device status again. Eventually, when the device is found ready for data, the I/O program exits the "wait loop." Now the I/O program goes on to transfer such data and, as we usually say, service the device. Following a timed interval the I/O program returns once more to check the device status, and so on.

Example 5-6

Consider the 10 cps printer just mentioned. What will happen if its status is scanned every 200 ms? Next, consider a keyboard having a single character buffer. On the average, characters are entered at the rate of 10 cps. However, the time interval between two consecutive key depressions can be as short as 60 ms. At what frequency should the keyboard be scanned by the I/O program?

Solution. If the printer is scanned every 200 ms, printing is slowed down to only about 5 cps. The situation is different with input devices like the keyboard. Although characters are entered (on the average) every 100 ms, the device should be scanned

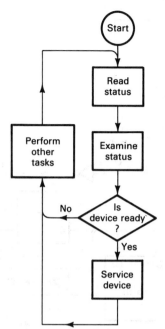

Figure 5-7.   Flow diagram of polled I/O.

at least every 60 ms.   Otherwise, we risk overwriting of the character buffer by a new character before reading the previous character.

In Section 5.1 we discussed the interface functions of a character printer and a keyboard.   Let us now see how we would go about designing a polled I/O interface for each.   First, the character printer.   Figure 5-8(a) shows the interface circuitry in simplified form.   The *RDY* (ready) is provided by the printer as a DC level signal, so it does not have to be latched.   It is simply buffered on the I/O device side by a common buffer and on the CPU side by a tri-state buffer.   The tri-state buffer constitutes the single-bit status port of the device.   A tri-state latch can serve for the output port.   Select signals for the two ports are derived the same way as seen in Figure 5-6.   *PNC* (print new character) is the only command line. Hence, the command register degenerates to a single D-type flip-flop (FF).   In fact, we can set the FF by the same select signal we use for data latching.   This eliminates the additional output operation we would need to set the *PNC* bit via a separate command port, so all port functions can be accomplished by means of a single address.

A separate clear (*CLR**) signal is needed to ensure that the *PNC* line is initially inactive.   This signal must be generated during initialization.   After transferring the status bit in a CPU register, the I/O program examines the LSB of that register.   If set, the I/O program proceeds to service the printer.   This amounts to transferring the next character into the octal latch.   At the same time, FF is set and thus *PNC* is activated.   The printer detects the transition of the *PNC* line,

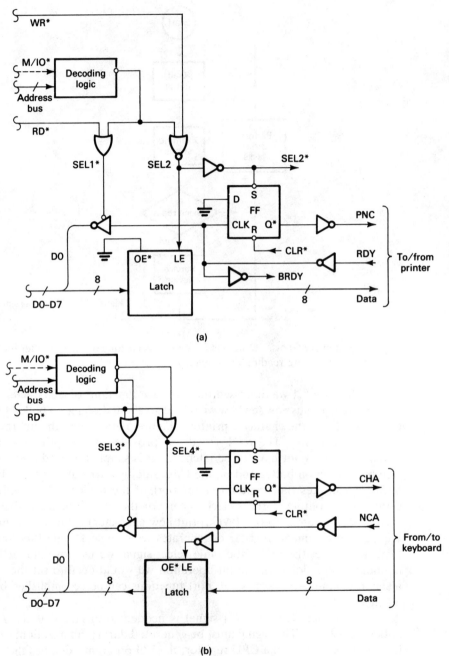

Figure 5-8. Examples of polled I/O. (a) Character printer interface. (b) Keyboard interface.

inputs the new character from the latch, and then deactivates its *RDY* line. Subsequently, FF clears and *PNC* goes back to the inactive state. Meanwhile the printer will stay busy for some time (until the received character is printed). The CPU takes no further action (except for status checking) until the printer raises its *RDY* line. After doing so, the printer itself does not proceed further until the CPU causes *PNC* to go active. Recall that this kind of interaction, in which each side signals the other and then pauses awaiting response, is referred to as handshaking. This approach is used widely for control of I/O data transfers.

Figure 5-8(b) pictures the keyboard interface circuitry. Again, two ports are needed: (1) A single bit input port for the *NCA* (new character available) status bit, and (2) an 8-bit data input port for the characters transmitted from the keyboard. However, since both are input ports we have to employ different port addresses. The *NCA* signal is used to alert the CPU about the availability of a new character. It is also used to enable the data latch. For the command port we follow the very same approach we did for the printer. The handshaking between CPU and device is now accomplished by means of the *NCA* and *CHA* signals.

Example 5-7

A μP scans the status of an I/O device every 20 ms. This is accomplished by means of a timer alerting the CPU every 20 ms. The interface of the device includes two ports—one for status and one for data output. How long does it take to scan and service the device given a clocking rate of 8 MHz? Assume for simplicity that all pertinent instruction cycles take 12 clock cycles.

Solution. Status reading requires fetching and execution of an "input" type of instruction. The whole instruction cycle (including memory machine cycles for instruction fetching and the input machine cycle) takes $12 \times 0.125 = 1.5$ μs. Status examination will require fetching and execution of at least one more instruction, that is, another 1.5 μs, so that status scanning takes 3 μs. If the device is ready to accept another data word, the CPU will have to execute an "output" instruction as well. This means 1.5 μs more (assuming the data word we are to transfer to the output port is already in a CPU register). Therefore, scanning and device service take a total of at least 4.5 μs.

Does polled I/O always imply transferring a single data word when the device is found ready? The answer is no. Take, for instance, the case of a line printer. Such a printer is capable of printing a full line (rather than a single character) at a time. It is equipped with a buffer capable of holding a full line of characters (usually 80 or 132). After printing a line, the printer indicates its readiness to accept another block of, say, 80 characters. Hence, device service amounts to filling the printer buffer with the characters of the next line. Data words are still sent one at a time, but there is no need to check status between transmissions of consecutive characters. This kind of data transfers is often referred to as **block I/O**. Such transfers are sped up greatly when the CPU has iterative types of I/O instructions. What if an I/O device cannot accept consecutive characters of a block fast enough? In this case we have to slow down the CPU through manipulation of its *READY* line (insertion of wait states in the I/O machine cycle).

Example 5-8

Consider a CPU having iterative types of I/O instructions. Following its first execution, such an instruction takes only five clock cycles to re-execute. However, if we employ a noniterative I/O instruction, it takes a total of 20 clock cycles for fetching and execution. Calculate the gained increase in speed with iterative instructions when transferring blocks of 128 data words.

Solution. With noniterative instructions, 128 data words take a total of $20 \times 128 = 2560$ clock cycles. If we employ an iterative I/O instruction it takes about $5 \times 128 = 640$ clock cycles to transfer the same block. The gained speed increase amounts to about $(2560 - 640) / 2560 = 0.75$, or 75 percent (ignoring the one-time fetching of the iterative instruction and its associated operands).

I/O Interface Controllers

The number of components required in the I/O design examples we have seen thus far is fairly small. However, for multiple and more complicated I/O devices, this number becomes quite substantial. Still, the design of programmed I/O interfaces remains simple thanks to the availability of LSI devices known as I/O interface controllers. Such devices support implementation of at least two 8-bit-wide I/O ports. They are usually programmable, so that users can select by software means the operating modes and port configurations that suit their needs.

Figure 5-9 depicts the organization of a typical I/O interface chip. On the left it connects to the CPU data bus and various CPU control lines. It is through the data lines that the CPU exchanges information with the two on-chip I/O ports and the control registers of the device. The fed CPU control signals include

1. Data transfer control signals (read strobe, write strobe, and so on)
2. A chip select and signals for selection of on-chip registers
3. Interrupt signals facilitating implementation of interrupt-driven I/O as well

On the right, the interface controller connects to one or more I/O devices via port A and port B. Typically, each port is equipped with ten I/O lines: eight for data and two for handshaking. From the latter one is for control and one for status. Data transmitted to an I/O device are stored in the data output register of the respective port. Data read from an I/O device are buffered (but usually not stored) at the port. The information stored by the CPU in the control registers determines operational characteristics such as:

1. Port direction. Is the port to be configured as an input, output, or bidirectional port?
2. Ability of a port to cause an interrupt.

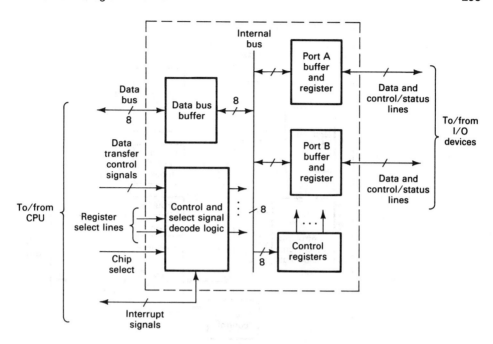

Figure 5-9. Typical organization of an I/O interface controller.

The capability to program these characteristics is key to the flexibility of I/O interface controllers.

Microprocessor manufacturers use various terms for their I/O interface controllers. For example, Motorola uses the term Peripheral Interface Adapter (PIA) for their 6820 I/O interface controller, which is compatible with the 68000 family of μPs. On the other hand, Intel uses the name Programmable Peripheral Interface (PPI) for their 8255A I/O controller.

Example of an I/O Interface Controller

As an example of an I/O interface controller, we examine the 8255A (Figure 5-10). This device was designed for the 8- and 16-bit Intel μPs. With the exception of CS^*, all other inputs (on the left) can connect directly to these CPUs. The CS^* (chip select) input is generally driven from the output of an address decoder, and address lines $A0$ and $A1$ permit the CPU to address any one of three 8-bit ports or the on-chip control registers. Notice that port C is split into two 4-bit sections. The upper section is grouped with port A, and the lower section is grouped with port B. The idea is to use ports A and B for data and the lines of port C for status and control. Although this is not the only way to use the lines of port C, this rationale does explain the reason behind the port groupings shown in Figure 5-10.

Next we see how we go about defining the mode of operation and port

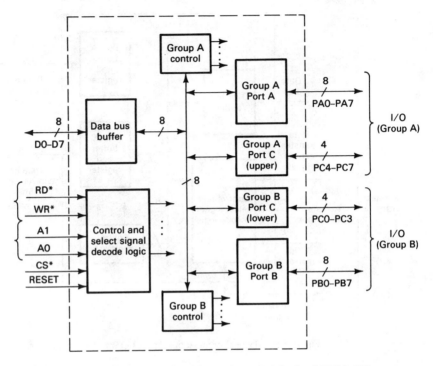

Figure 5-10. Simplified block diagram of the Intel 8255A PPI.

configuration. The 8255A treats CPU data as a control word when A1A0 = 11. Then, it examines D_7 for determination of the type of control word. If $D_7 = 1$, the 8255A interprets the control word according to the mode definition format seen in Figure 5-11(a). Depending on the defined mode, the 8255A may also permit setting/resetting of certain individual output lines of port C. This is accomplished by using the format shown in Figure 5-11(b), where $D_7 = 0$. In the mode definition format, the control word consists of two fields. The upper field (D_3–D_6) selects the operating mode for the I/O lines of group A. The lower field (D_0–D_2) does so for the lines of group B.

Mode 0

When $D_6 D_5 = 00$ and $D_2 = 0$, the 8255A is said to operate in mode 0. In this mode none of the lines of port C are dedicated to specific functions. Instead, each section of port C may be defined to act as a set of either four input lines or four output lines. Furthermore, these lines may be used for data or for handshaking signals. When used for handshaking, the user can take advantage of the bit set format of Figure 5-11(b) to activate/deactivate individually I/O control lines. However, the primary intention of mode 0 is to make available all 24 I/O lines of the 8255A for direct I/O applications (where handshaking signals are not required). Figure 5-11(a) reflects which bits of the control word define the

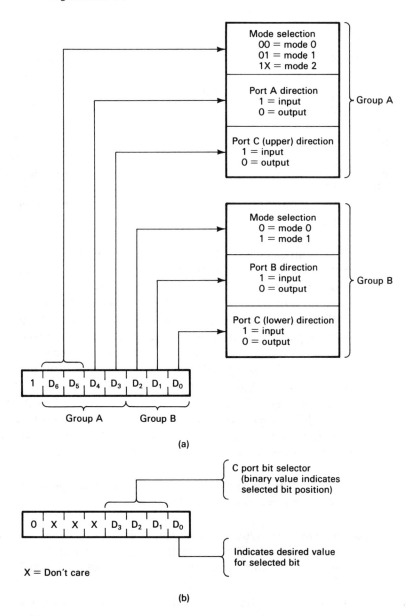

Figure 5-11. Control word formats of the 8255A PPI. (a) Mode definition format. (b) Bit set/reset format for port C.

direction of port A, port B, and each half of port C. Assume, for example, that we set $D_4D_3D_0 = 111$ and $D_1 = 0$. Then, 16 I/O lines of the 8255A (eight of port A and eight of port C) will act as data input lines, while eight I/O lines (those of port B) will act as data output lines.

Mode 1

When $D_6D_5 = 01$ and $D_2 = 1$, the 8255A is said to operate in mode 1. Here the 8255A dedicates (by itself) six lines of port C to handshaking signals (three on behalf of port A and another three on behalf of port B). In other words, mode 1 is intended for polled I/O. Besides, two of these dedicated lines perform interrupt-related functions, so this mode may also support interrupt-driven I/O. The bit settings in the control word define the direction of all but the six dedicated lines. In fact, the particular C port lines dedicated to handshaking signals depend on whether the respective data port (A or B) is defined for input or for output. Figure 5-12 illustrates the handshaking and interrupt-related signals for each case.

Figure 5-12(a) shows the handshaking and interrupt signals for data output. An explanation of their meaning follows.

1. *OBF** (output buffer full) indicates to the output device that the CPU has written data into the respective data output port. It goes active automatically as soon as the CPU completes the writing of such data. This line corresponds to the *PNC* (print new character) line of our simple printer.

2. *ACK** (acknowledge) plays the role of a status signal. It indicates acceptance of the output data by the output device—hence, readiness to receive the next byte of data. The 8255A uses this signal to deactivate the *OBF** line. Functionally, *ACK** corresponds to the *RDY* line of our printer.

3. *INTR* (interrupt request) can be used to interrupt the CPU in the case of interrupt-driven I/O. It is activated when *OBF** and *ACK** are both active, provided the respective INTE (interrupt enable) flip-flop of the 8255A has been set via one of the C port lines. The 8255A resets the *INTR* line when the CPU latches new data in the data port.

Figure 5-12(b) shows the handshaking and interrupt signals for the case of data input. Their meaning is as follows:

1. *STB** (strobe) is activated by the input device to indicate availability of a new byte of data. The 8255A uses this signal to latch in the input data. *STB** corresponds to the *NCA* (new character available) signal of our example keyboard.

2. *IBF* (input buffer full) is activated by the 8255A in response to the reception of a new character from the input device. It is reset when the CPU reads the new character from the data input port.

3. *INTR* (interrupt request) serves the same purpose it does in the case of data output. It is set when *STB** and *IBF* are both active, and the respective INTE flip-flop has been set. The 8255A resets *INTR* when the CPU reads the data from the input port.

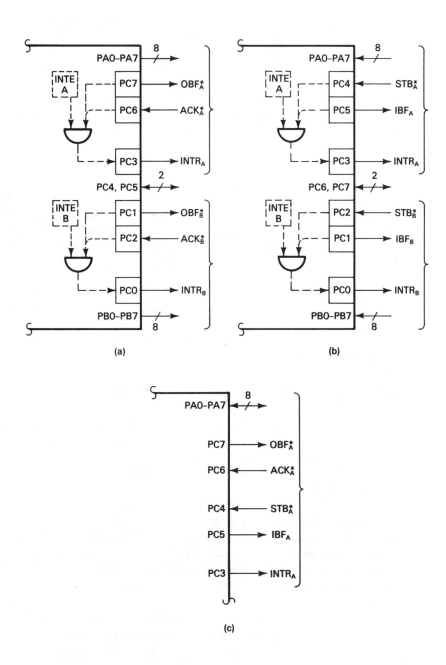

Figure 5-12. Functions assigned by the 8255A to the I/O lines of its C port. (a) mode 1, output. (b) mode 1, input. (c) mode 2.

Note that the CPU can check the status bits by reading all input lines of the C port in a single operation regardless of the direction of data flow. However, the control lines are activated by the 8255A automatically. This relieves the CPU from having to do so (recall the use of a similar approach in the design examples of Figure 5-8). Another point to be noted is that mode 1 does not require selection of the same direction for data ports A and B. For instance, one of them may be selected for input and the other for output. As a matter of fact, since the mode of each group (A, B) of I/O lines is defined separately, it is possible to mix modes.

Mode 2

A third mode of operation allows port A to function as an 8-bit bidirectional data bus (on the I/O device side). This mode is intended for devices where data flow in both directions. An example is a floppy disk where data may be transferred from the CPU to the disk, or from the disk to the CPU. Now the 8255A dedicates five lines of the C port to handshaking and interrupt-related functions. When port A is configured in mode 2, port B may be configured in either one of the two previously described modes. Figure 5-12(c) depicts which lines of port C are dedicated on behalf of port A. Observe that these signals are a combination of those we have seen for input and output in mode 1, since we have to be able to control data transfers in both directions. However, the interrupt request signal is common for both directions.

Design Example with an I/O Interface Controller

Earlier in this section we discussed the design of two polled I/O interfaces, one for a character printer and one for a keyboard. In both cases we used only SSI/MSI components (see Figure 5-8). In the remaining part of this section we see how we can design those interfaces using an 8255A I/O interface controller. We assume the CPU is an 8088 μP.

Both I/O devices involve polled I/O. Thus, the appropriate configuration mode for the two data ports of the 8255A is mode 1. The data port we will be using for the printer must be defined as a data output port. The one for the keyboard must be defined as a data input port. Let us choose data port A for the printer and data port B for the keyboard (Figure 5-10). Then the mode definition control word (Figure 5-11) should be as follows:

$D_7 = 1$ (indicates a mode definition control word)

$D_6D_5 = 01$ (selects mode 1 for the I/O lines of group A)

$D_4 = 0$ (defines port A as a data output port)

$D_2 = 1$ (selects mode 1 for the I/O lines of group B)

$D_1 = 1$ (defines port B as a data input port)

Recall that when we select mode 1 for a group of I/O lines, the 8255A automatically assigns six lines of the C port for handshaking. This satisfies our needs for the printer and the keyboard. Consequently, bits D_0 and D_3 need not be defined. At this point we have determined the control word with which we have to initialize the 8255A. After doing so (with software), the 8255A will configure itself as described above.

Since we selected port A as a data output port, the handshaking lines provided by the 8255A will be as shown in the upper half of Figure 5-12(a). Similarly, since we selected port B as a data input port, the handshaking lines will be those illustrated in the lower half of Figure 5-12(b). At this point we are ready to start drawing a simplified schematic for the overall I/O interface (Figure 5-13). First we see what we have to do on the side facing the printer and the keyboard.

Our first concern are the connections to the control/status lines of the printer and keyboard. Earlier in this section we noted the correspondence between these lines and the handshaking lines provided by the 8255A in mode 1. Figure 5-13 reflects that correspondence. However, examination of the meaning of the associated signals indicates that they must be inverted. Besides, all output signals (toward the printer and the keyboard) must be buffered in order to provide adequate drive to the cables connecting the processor board with the two I/O devices. We assume flat cables, say, 6 ft long with every other conductor grounded. The idea is to "sandwich" each signal line between two grounded conductors for reduction of crosstalk. (Figure 5-13 shows the ground conductor only for *PNC*.)

The responsibility for provision of adequate drive to input lines is left to the I/O device. Very often, though, a designer may have to use pull-up resistors at the receiving end. This speeds up the charging of cable capacitances and thereby improves signal waveforms. Such resistors are, of course, definitely required if the I/O device drives input lines through open collector circuits. Under certain conditions we may also have to use terminating resistors at the receiving end of each signal line. We will come back to this subject later.

What about the four unused I/O port lines? These are shown at the bottom of the schematic in Figure 5-13. Lines *PC0* and *PC3* play the role of interrupt request lines for the keyboard and the printer, respectively. If we were employing an interrupt-driven I/O scheme, they would be used as such. *PC4* and *PC5* are spare I/O lines. Their role depends on the setting of bit D_3 in the mode definition control word. They can be defined to act as a pair of data input lines or as a pair of data output lines. Consequently, they might be used for direct I/O purposes, as interfacing, for instance, to two switches or two LEDs.

Next we examine what we have to do on the side facing the CPU. The *RESET* input can be driven by the same signal feeding the synonymous input of the 8088. This signal initializes the 8255A which is placed automatically in mode 0. A 74LS138 octal decoder is used for generation of the *CS** signal. We assume that we will be using the I/O address space of the 8088, and so the decoder must be enabled only when *IO/M** is at a high. We also assume that the 8255A has

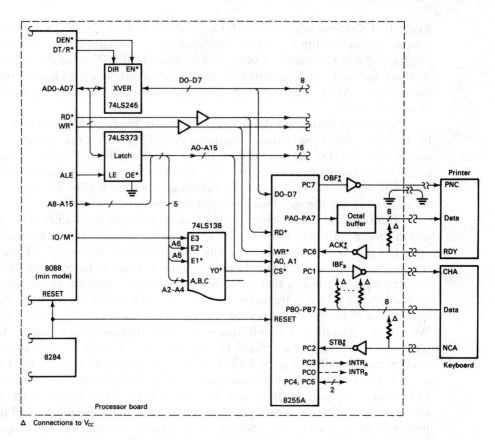

Figure 5-13. Simplified schematic of an I/O interface employing the 8255A controller.

been assigned the lowest I/O addresses. An octal latch and a transceiver are employed for demultiplexing and buffering of the CPU address/data bus.

How would we go about addressing the 8255A and handling the printer and the keyboard? A look at the address decoder leads to the conclusion that the 8255A is enabled when

1. An "input" or "output" instruction is executed (so that *IO/M** goes to a high)

2. Address bits A2 to A6 are all 0s

Address bits A0 and A1 determine which of the three ports (A, B, C) is to be accessed by the CPU and whether the intention is simply to write a control word into the 8255A. For example, if the instruction is an "output" and A1A0 = 00, the 8255A stores the data presented over its D0–D7 lines in the latch of port A (printer data). Similarly, if the instruction is an "input" and A1A0 = 01, the

8255A presents to the CPU the keyboard data already stored at port B. With an "input" instruction and A1A0 = 10, the 8255A presents to the CPU the states of all input lines of port C. As seen from Figure 5-13, this makes available to the CPU the states of status lines *RDY* and *NCA*. Subsequent examination of these lines permits the CPU to determine:

1. When to write into port A another character for the printer
2. When to read from port B keyboard data

The preceding example shows that I/O interface controllers simplify the design of I/O interfaces considerably. However, the gained advantages depend upon the degree to which we capitalize on their capabilities. Such gains may become marginal in cases of very simple I/O interfaces where SSI/MSI components will do just as well.

5.3 INTERRUPT-DRIVEN I/O

The problem with polled (programmed) I/O is that CPU time is wasted for status checks. Interrupt-driven I/O eliminates this problem. In this section we review the interrupt schemes employed in μPs and how a CPU goes about processing an interrupt. Then we deal with the design of interrupt circuits and integrated interrupt controllers. First an introductory discussion:

The basic data transfer mechanism employed in interrupt-driven I/O is the same one we have seen for programmed I/O—that is, the CPU is still exchanging data with an I/O device via some CPU register. Thus, the I/O interface has to provide (again) control, status, and data ports. The essential difference relates to who has the responsibility for initiation of a data transfer. In programmed I/O such responsibility rests with the CPU. In other words, the I/O program must scan the I/O device status frequently to determine if the device is ready for a data transfer. In interrupt-driven I/O, data transfers are initiated by the I/O device, which uses the interrupt mechanism to notify the CPU of its readiness. This eliminates the burden associated with status scanning. An I/O device may also use the interrupt mechanism for other purposes—for example, to draw CPU attention to the fact that the device is experiencing some failure condition, or to indicate completion of a local operation. Such conditions are encountered very often in peripheral devices (see Chapter 6).

Example 5-9

A particular system is controlled by an operator through commands entered from a keyboard. The CPU scans the keyboard about every 100 ms. Calculate the approximate number of keyboard status checks over a time period of eight hours.

The average number of commands entered over a time interval of eight hours is 60.

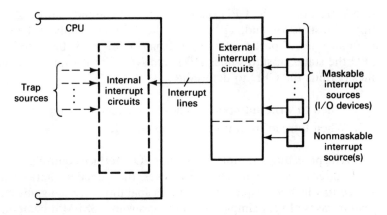

Figure 5-14. Sources of interrupts in a typical microprocessor.

A typical command involves about 48 characters. By what fraction would the number of CPU visits to the keyboard be reduced if we were using interrupt-driven I/O?

Solution. The CPU scans the keyboard ten times per second. Over a period of eight hours, the number of scans is $10 \times 60 \times 60 \times 8 = 288000$.

Interrupt-driven I/O implies that the keyboard interrupts the CPU whenever a key is depressed. The CPU proceeds to service the keyboard only after such an interrupt occurs. The total number of characters keyed in over a period of eight hours is only $60 \times 48 = 2880$. Therefore, the number of CPU visits to the keyboard is reduced by $(288000 - 2880) / 288000 = 0.99$, that is by 99 percent!

The interrupt mechanism is important not only for I/O, but for other purposes as well. This is seen in Figure 5-14 which pictures the various sources of interrupts in a typical µP. The interrupts caused by external sources (on the right) may be maskable or nonmaskable. Maskable are usually the interrupts caused by I/O devices. They are so called because they can be disabled through the CPU status register. Nonmaskable interrupts, which cannot be disabled, always have higher priority than maskable ones. Their primary purpose is to alert the CPU of a catastrophic event, such as a forthcoming power failure or a memory error. Usually, the sources of external interrupts do not drive the CPU interrupt lines directly. Instead, they do so through external circuits whose complexity depends on the type of CPU and the particular application. Interrupts may also be caused by events internal to the CPU. Such interrupts are known as traps. They are generated during program execution either as a result of some unexpected condition or intentionally.

Regardless of its type, an interrupt forces the CPU to take the same course of actions. Once it accepts an interrupt the CPU:

1. Postpones execution of the current program
2. Saves its status

3. Jumps to an interrupt service routine (ISR)

4. Returns later to resume execution of the interrupted program

Interrupt Structures in μPs

From the external interface viewpoint, most μPs employ one of the two schemes shown in Figure 5-15. The first scheme is based on two separate interrupt request lines, one for maskable (*INTREQ*) and one for nonmaskable (*NMINT*) interrupts. Usually *INTREQ* is paired with an interrupt acknowledge line (*INTACK*). Through the latter, the CPU acknowledges acceptance of the interrupt request and instructs the I/O device to place on the CPU data bus an address code. The address code leads the CPU to the ISR which transfers data or performs some other service on behalf of the I/O device. *INTREQ* and *INTACK* may be viewed as a pair of handshaking lines (see Figure 2-17). Some CPUs do not provide the interrupt acknowledge signal over a separate line, but instead encode the occurrence of such a cycle on their status lines. In this case we derive an *INTACK* signal by decoding the CPU status lines. Nonmaskable interrupts need not be acknowledged because they are always accepted and because no address code has to be provided externally. Hence, there is no acknowledge line for such interrupts. Example of μPs employing this scheme are the 8088 and the 8086.

The second scheme uses a set of lines for generation of an interrupt request. At first that may sound like a waste of lines, but it actually is not. The idea is to convey to the CPU not only the occurrence of an interrupt, but its priority level

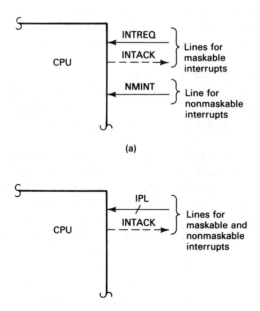

Figure 5-15. External interface signals for interrupts. (a) Separate lines for maskable and nonmaskable interrupts. (b) Common set of lines for both maskable and nonmaskable interrupts.

as well. For example, the 68000 has three such interrupt priority lines (IPL). These lines are monitored continuously by the CPU. When the binary number (defined by the combination of the states) of the IPL lines is higher than the 3-bit mask (contained in the CPU status register), the interrupt is honored (see Figure 3-16). Otherwise the CPU ignores the interrupt. Notice there is no signal indicating to the CPU when to sample the IPL lines. Consequently there is no priority level 0. On the other hand, an interrupt at level 7 will always be accepted, and there is no need for a separate nonmaskable interrupt line. Like the first scheme, a dedicated *INTACK* line may not be provided. For example, the 68000 uses its status lines to convey an interrupt acknowledge cycle.

The ability to prioritize interrupts is a significant advantage. It provides a program with the flexibility of establishing which interrupt levels will be inhibited during its execution. CPUs employing the first scheme do not offer this capability. Instead, our only option is to turn maskable interrupts on/off as a group by means of the single interrupt-enable/disable bit of the CPU status register (see, for example, the 8088 in Section 3.2.1). However, we do have the option of leaving the interrupt-enable/disable bit on and using external circuits for prioritization.

Let us now see the significance of the address code sent to the CPU by the interrupting device. This code is usually eight bits long. It constitutes the basis for generation of a full memory address. At this address the CPU finds the so-called **interrupt pointer** or **interrupt vector**, which is nothing but the starting address of the ISR. Interrupt vectors are stored in contiguous memory locations forming the so-called **interrupt vector table**. The set of memory addresses used by this table is often named **interrupt space**.

Figure 5-16 shows (as an example) the interrupt vector table of the 8088 and the 8086. It occupies addresses 0–1023 and includes trap vectors as well. Note from Figure 5-16(b) that in the 8088/8086 a vector requires four byte locations:

1. Two for the code segment (CS) part of an address.
2. Another two bytes for the instruction pointer (IP) part of the address. (Recall from Section 3.2.1 that the CS part is treated as a base address and the IP part as an offset in the formation of a full 20-bit address.)

These CPUs multiply by four the 8-bit address code (furnished by the interrupting device) to generate the respective vector address. Thus, each value of the 8-bit address code corresponds to a **vector number** and the total number of possible vectors is 256. From these, 224 are assigned to vectored interrupts, so such an interrupt could be vectored to any one out of a maximum of 224 ISRs. In contrast, nonmaskable interrupts (NMIs) are vectored to a common ISR. This is accomplished through the fixed address assigned to such interrupts. Another way of expressing this distinction is to say that maskable interrupts are vectored, while nonmaskable ones are nonvectored. The implication is that NMI sources need not provide the CPU with an address code. Instead, the CPU derives the NMI vector internally on its own.

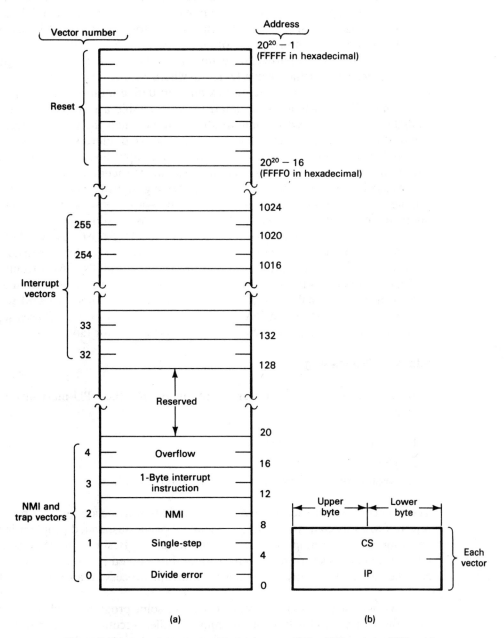

Figure 5-16. Interrupt vector table in the case of the 8088 and the 8086. (a) Addresses dedicated to interrupt vectors. (b) Composition of each vector.

Although the approach just described is widely employed, it is not the only one. Another approach is the one employed in the 68020 (Section 3.4.1). This CPU makes use of a special register (named vector base register) to specify the starting address of the interrupt vector table. Now the 8-bit address code is treated as an offset to locate a particular vector within the vector table. This approach permits placement of the vector table anywhere in memory. Furthermore, one may take advantage of the offered flexibility to define multiple vector tables.

Some CPUs include in the interrupt vector table a **reset vector**. This one leads the CPU to the system initialization routine when the power is turned on. It also does so when restarting the system. The fixed address of the reset vector is forced into the PC when activating the *RESET* input line. After *RESET* goes back to inactive, the CPU fetches and treats as an instruction the reset vector itself, which usually is a jump type instruction transferring control over to the initialization routine. Thus, although the reset vector fulfills a purpose similar to that of an interrupt vector, it does so as an instruction (not as an address).

Going back to Figure 5-16, we see that the 8088/8086 reserve the 16 top addresses of the memory address space for reset vectors. Here, *RESET* forces the CS part of the address to all 1s and the IP part to all 0s. As a result, when *RESET* goes back to inactive, the CPU fetches the first instruction from address FFFF0 (in hexadecimal). In general, reset vectors are stored in ROM while interrupt vectors are stored in RAM. Therefore, it is better if a μP uses separate memory areas for the reset vector and the interrupt vector table.

Interrupt Processing

Prior to entering the interrupt service routine (ISR), the CPU must save the following:

1. The program counter (PC)
2. The status register
3. Possibly other information about the interrupted program

The collection of all such time-varying information associated with a program is referred to as its **context**. Saving the context of the suspended program is key to ensuring correct resumption of its execution later. Besides, the ISR itself must take certain actions for proper return to the interrupted program. These actions and the rest of the steps pertaining to interrupt processing are shown in Figure 5-17.

We assume the CPU is currently executing some program which for distinction from the ISR we will call main program. While execution of the main program proceeds, the CPU hardware constantly monitors the state of the interrupt line(s):

1. First, the case of CPUs employing the scheme of Figure 5-15(b): If the priority of the detected interrupt is not higher than the one defined by the mask, the

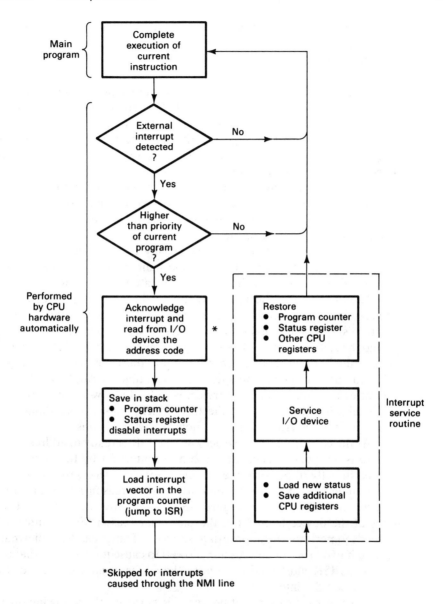

Figure 5-17. The sequence of events associated with the servicing of an external interrupt.

interrupt is ignored by the CPU. However, if the presented priority is higher than the one defined by the mask, the CPU proceeds to acknowledge the interrupt.

2. Now the case of CPUs employing a nonprioritized scheme: The decision is made on the basis of the state of the interrupt-enable bit (in the status register).

When that bit is reset, all maskable interrupts are ignored. However, if the interrupt-enable bit happens to be set, the CPU goes on to acknowledge the interrupt.

Remember, though, that interrupts are acknowledged between (not during) instruction cycles. Consequently, the CPU enters an interrupt-acknowledge cycle only after completion of the current instruction cycle.

At that time *INTACK* goes active and the I/O device presents the address code to the CPU. (For requests made via a separate NMI line this step is eliminated.) Then, the CPU stores in the stack the contents of the PC and the status register. It also disables any further interrupts in order to avoid complications while in transition to the ISR. The next step involves loading the PC with the interrupt vector, which is nothing but the starting address of the ISR, so that this step amounts to jumping to the ISR.

All steps (up to this point) are usually taken by the CPU hardware automatically. Once the transition from the main program to the ISR has been accomplished, the actions of the CPU are dictated by the ISR.

The objective of the ISR is to service the interrupting device. Yet it must take certain actions securing proper return to the main program. One such action might be saving additional CPU registers. Remember, the CPU saved only the PC and the status register. However, the context of the main program may involve additional CPU registers. Such information must then be saved (especially if the ISR is to utilize those registers during its run time). Another action taken by the ISR, prior to initiating device service, is to load a new status word from memory. This establishes the context of the ISR, which, among other things, determines if higher priority interrupts are to be honored while it runs.

At the conclusion of these actions, the ISR is ready to address the I/O device. If there is only one reason for cause of an interrupt by the device, the ISR may proceed directly to perform the required service. Take, for instance, the case of our example printer. There, the only possible reason for an interrupt would be the activation of *RDY* (see Figure 5-8). Otherwise, the ISR must first read the status of the device to find out the particular reason for this interrupt. Then it proceeds to perform the appropriate service. Things can be somewhat more complicated if two or more devices are allowed to cause interrupts at that priority level, so that the ISR must read and check the status of all such devices to determine which caused the interrupt.

Whatever the case might be, the ISR performs the following operations after service completion:

1. It restores any additional registers it saved previously.
2. It restores the PC and the status register (usually through execution of a return from interrupt instruction).

These operations reestablish the context of the main program so that execution

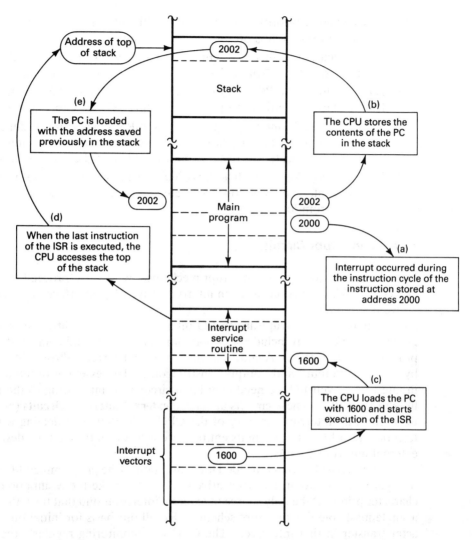

Figure 5-18.   Example of the flow of events following an interrupt by an I/O device.

can resume from the time the interrupt was acknowledged. Can the ISR itself be interrupted? Unless it is running with interrupts disabled, the answer is yes. In fact, the described sequence of steps applies to the ISR as well, when it is interrupted by a higher priority event. Any ISR may be interrupted by a higher priority event, a situation referred to as **nested interrupts**.

Figure 5-18 highlights the flow of events by means of an example. Assume the CPU has just fetched a two-byte instruction of the main program from location 2000.

1. While fetching the first operand (specified by the instruction), the CPU receives a higher priority interrupt. The CPU takes no action, however, until instruction execution is brought to completion.

2. After execution of this instruction, the CPU stores in the stack the PC and the status register. Notice that the contents of the PC are now 2002.

3. The CPU loads the PC with the interrupt vector, which happens to be 1600. Then it starts execution of the corresponding ISR from location 1600.

4. After servicing the interrupting device, the ISR prepares for transfer of control to the main program. Its last instruction is a return from interrupt one. When this is executed, it restores both the PC and the status register.

5. The PC is now loaded with address 2002. This is precisely what it contained when the interrupt was honored. Hence, execution of the main program continues from location 2002.

External Interrupt Circuits

Now that we know how the interrupt mechanism works, we proceed to our main objective. What functions does an interrupt-driven I/O interface perform? How do we design one?

Actually, an interrupt-driven I/O interface is not very different from a programmed I/O one. It includes I/O ports for data, status, and commands just like programmed I/O does. Again, information is transferred to/from CPU registers by means of "input" and "output" instructions. The essential difference is that in interrupt-driven I/O we need additional circuits for interfacing to the interrupt lines of the CPU. These circuits are called **external interrupt circuits** (as opposed to the on-chip interrupt circuitry of the CPU). Rather than dealing with an interrupt-driven I/O interface in its entirety, we will concentrate on the design of the external interrupt circuits.

Let us consider what is needed for conversion of the programmed I/O interface of Figure 5-8(a) into an interrupt-driven one. We make the assumption that the character printer is the only source of external interrupts and that the CPU employs a single maskable line interrupt scheme. Recall our basis for initiation of a character transfer in that interface. The CPU was monitoring regularly the state of the *RDY* line to determine when the printer was ready to receive a new character. Therefore, the appropriate time for generation of an interrupt request (to the CPU) is when *RDY* switches from a low to a high. Somehow we must record such a transition and activate the *INTREQ* input of the CPU. This can be accomplished with a D-type flip-flop as shown in Figure 5-19(a). *BRDY* is the buffered *RDY* signal seen in Figure 5-8(a).

Our interrupt circuits must also be able to inject into the CPU data bus an address code of, say, eight bits. This can be done with an octal tri-state buffer whose inputs are connected to a high or a low (depending on the desired value of the address code). This code is placed on the data bus when the CPU raises its

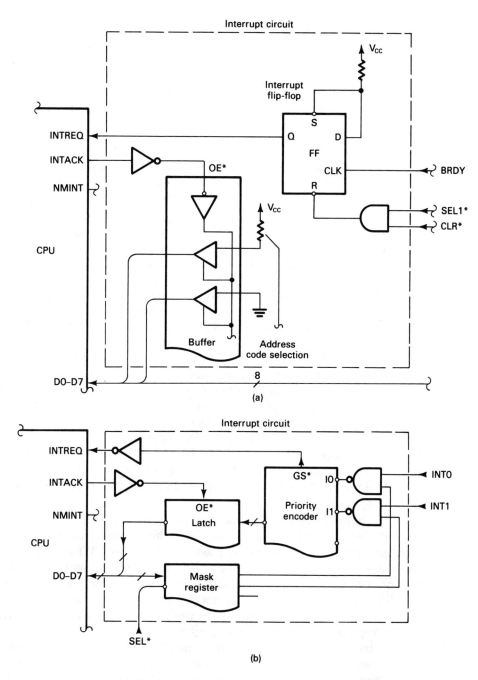

Figure 5-19.   (a) Simple interrupt circuit for a single source of interrupts.   (b) Interrupt circuit for prioritization and masking of multiple interrupts.

INTACK line. From there on, the CPU finds its way to the ISR of the printer. The ISR reads the status of the printer to confirm its readiness. Then it proceeds to sent a new character via the data output port. In fact, since the printer is the only source of interrupts, we may bypass status reading and proceed directly to send the new character. Notice that the interrupt flip-flop is reset by the *SEL1** signal generated during status reading (*SEL2** should be used if status checking is bypassed).

Example 5-10

Suppose the CPU is an 8088 and the vector address for the printer is to be 132. How would you configure the octal buffer of Figure 5-19(a) for injection of the proper address code during an interrupt acknowledge cycle?

Solution. The corresponding vector number is 132/4 = 33 (see Figure 5-16). Hence, the injected address code should be 00100001. This means that the inputs of the buffering circuits connecting to data lines *D0* and *D5* must be at a high. The inputs of all other buffering circuits must be grounded.

What if we have multiple sources of interrupts? For example, what if the same system must accommodate an interrupt-driven I/O interface for a keyboard? In this case there are two approaches. The simplest one (from the hardware viewpoint) is to OR interrupts from different sources and use a common address code for all of them. In terms of Figure 5-19(a) that would mean adding one interrupt flip-flop for each source of interrupts and using the address code injected through the octal buffer for all of them. Naturally, use of a common address code means a common interrupt vector which, in turn, implies a common ISR for all I/O devices. So, in order to determine which device caused an interrupt, the ISR has to check the status of all devices. This approach is often referred to as **polled interrupts** (as opposed to vectored interrupts). A basic disadvantage of this scheme is the software overhead associated with the polling of interrupts. On the other hand, it simplifies the interrupt circuits and thereby can be advantageous in small system applications.

The polled interrupts approach is the only solution in the case of μPs incapable of handling vectored interrupts. Such CPUs have a single interrupt vector (stored in a fixed memory address) for all maskable interrupts. What happens when two or more interrupts occur simultaneously? In the polled interrupts approach the task of prioritization is generally left to the software. In other words, it is up to the ISR to decide in what order to service interrupting devices.

The second approach uses more complex hardware for support of a truly **vectored interrupt system**. Figure 5-19(b) illustrates such a circuit in simplified terms. Its basic elements are a **priority encoder** and a tri-state latch. The priority encoder may be implemented using one or more MSI components like the 74148 eight-input priority encoder. This device is fed with eight parallel inputs and presents over three output lines the equivalent binary code of the highest order input.   For example, if inputs $I1$ and $I4$ are active at the same time, the state of the output lines will correspond to 100.   In order to encode more than eight interrupt request lines, one may use additional 74148s.   The GS^* (group signal) output goes active when any one of the eight input lines is activated.   Hence it is used to drive the *INTREQ* input of the CPU.   The derived code (which is three bits in the case of the 74148) is stored in the latch and represents the variable part of the address code.   The remaining bits of the address code are fixed to a 1 or a 0 as in Figure 5-19(a).

A **mask register** adds another important capability to the interrupt circuit. It permits the CPU (and thereby a program) selectively to inhibit interrupt signals (*INT0–INT7*) from causing an interrupt.   This flexibility is very important in CPUs employing the single nonmaskable line interrupt scheme.   Recall that such CPUs (like the 8088/8086) do not provide masking through the status register.   In Figure 5-19(b) interrupt sources are inhibited by setting to a 0 the respective bit of the mask register.   How do we address the mask register?   External registers are generally treated like I/O ports.   This is so whether they are MSI registers or on-chip registers of the integrated (LSI/VLSI) controllers surrounding the CPU.   Thus, programs (including an ISR) address the mask register as if it were a data output port.

Thus far we assumed that the CPU is equipped with a single maskable interrupt line.   What if it employs a prioritized scheme similar to the one shown in Figure 5-15(b)?   Here, again, we have a number of options:

1. We may use the approach of polled interrupts.   However, we do not have to OR and connect all interrupt request lines to a single IPL line.   Instead, we may OR them in groups and connect each group to a separate IPL line. The priority of each group will depend on that of the IPL line to which it connects.

2. We can employ a circuit similar to the one of Figure 5-19(b) for implementation of vectored interrupts.   However, now we drive the IPL lines from the output lines of the encoder (not from GS^*).   Also, no mask register is needed (as long as masking through the CPU status register mask bits is adequate).

Example 5-11

A particular (68000-like) μP has three IPL lines.   Suppose you are to implement a vectored interrupt scheme for 11 interrupt request lines of which five are to be non-maskable.   How would you go about doing so with a 74148 priority encoder?

Solution.   All five nonmaskable interrupts must be assigned the highest priority level— that is, level 7.   Consequently we OR all five and feed the resulting signal to input $I7$ of the 74148.   The remaining six (maskable) lines are connected to inputs $I1-I6$ of the encoder per desired order of priority.

Interrupt Controllers

Some µP manufacturers offer integrated interrupt controllers for their CPU families. These devices are usually intended for CPUs employing the single maskable line interrupt scheme. Generally, they are programmable and follow the structure we have seen in Figure 5-19(b). Most often they are named either **programmable interrupt controllers (PIC)**, or **priority interrupt controllers**. A typical PIC accommodates up to eight interrupt sources which are prioritized at eight levels. A separate vector is generated for each interrupt source. Also, an on-chip mask register permits the CPU to inhibit lower priority levels or individual interrupt sources.

Such devices can simplify greatly the implementation of vectored priority interrupts. Next we discuss some of the characteristics of a typical interrupt controller—the Intel 8259A PIC. Then we consider an application example.

Allows change of interrupt priority after hardware is completed.

Example of an Interrupt Controller

Figure 5-20 depicts the functional organization of the interrupt controller we will be discussing as an example—the 8259A. On the left it connects to the CPU data bus via a tri-state buffer. It is through this buffer that the CPU writes control words in the various on-chip control registers of the 8259A and reads its status. It also reads the address code during an interrupt acknowledge sequence. The *INTA**, *RD**, and *WR** inputs are driven by the synonymous outputs of the CPU— as, for example, in an 8088. *A0* serves control register addressing purposes. Interrupt requests to the CPU are made via the *INT* line. The control logic also accommodates cascading of multiple 8259s for applications where the number of interrupt request lines exceeds the number handled by a single 8259A.

The 8259A has eight interrupt request inputs (*IR0–IR7*). It is through these lines that I/O devices, and possibly other interrupt sources, place their requests for CPU interruption. The interrupt request register stores indiscriminately the levels of all active interrupt inputs (*IR0–IR7*). In contrast, the in-service register stores only the levels of interrupts which are currently being serviced. (Remember, it can be more than one since an ISR may itself be suspended by a higher priority request.) The priority resolver monitors these two registers and the mask register. On the basis of their contents it decides which interrupt input (if any) should be honored next. It then sets the respective bit in the in-service register and notifies the control logic for activation of the *INTR* input of the CPU. The 8259A is designed to handle the interrupt acknowledge sequence of the 8088/8086, which consists of two consecutive interrupt acknowledge cycles. The first *INTA** indicates acceptance of the interrupt request. The second one is used to read the address code for that interrupt.

The operating characteristics of the 8259A are controlled by the CPU through control words sent over the data bus. In 8259A terminology such words are named

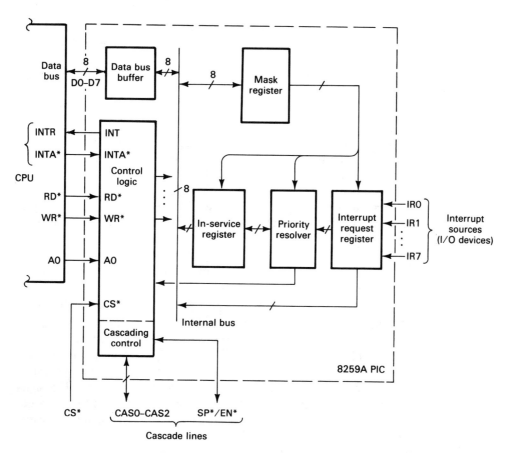

Figure 5-20. Simplified block diagram of the 8259A programmable interrupt controller.

command words. They are classified into two categories: initialization command words and operational command words.

Initialization command words (ICW) are issued as a sequence. They serve selection of particular modes and characteristics such as:

1. Is the 8259A alone or cascaded? In cascaded mode one of the 8259As plays the role of master. It is the only one driving the *INTR* input of the CPU. The *INT* outputs of the remaining 8259As connect to *IR* inputs of the master.

2. Do we want the *IR* inputs level-triggered or edge-triggered? Either mode has advantages and drawbacks. The level-triggered mode places certain responsibilities on the I/O interface circuits, which should not return an *IR* input to a low too soon or too late. In fact, an *IR* input should stay at a high until its respective *INTA* * is received from the CPU. On the other hand, it should

be back to a low by the time the respective ISR sends an "end of interrupt" command to the 8259A. The edge-triggered mode eliminates such requirements. It records low-to-high transitions and ignores signal levels thereafter. However, it is inappropriate to wire-OR two or more interrupt sources to the same IR level, because until a previous transition recording is cleared, any other transition goes unnoticed.

3. In what range should be the address codes employed for the interrupt vectors? For example, in the case of 8088/8086 applications the user specifies the five high-order bits. The three low-order ones are generated by the 8259A according to the particular IR input being acknowledged.

Operational command words (OCW) are individual commands issued by programs (including ISRs) as needed. Operations performed by means of such commands include:

1. Setting of the desired mask in the 8259A mask register.
2. Resetting of bits in the in-service register.
3. Selection of a priority scheme (which is possible on a dynamic basis). Normally the 8259A assigns fixed priority to each IR level. *IR0* has the highest and *IR*7 the lowest priority. This scheme supports a fully nested interrupt environment, which can be viewed as a general-purpose priority mode. Besides this mode, one may select either one of two priority rotation schemes. In the first one, rotation is automatic; that is, the 8259A automatically assigns the lowest priority to a serviced IR level. Hence, all interrupt sources get the same chance of being serviced. In the second rotation scheme the priorities are reassigned in a user-defined fashion.
4. Reading of the interrupt registers of the controller.
5. Polling of I/O devices through the 8259A. One of the options is to turn off the interrupt-enable bit of the CPU status register and utilize the so-called poll command of the 8259A to which the 8259A responds by indicating over the data bus whether any of the IR lines is active. It also provides the binary code of the highest priority active *IR* line. Such a "centralized polling" approach constitutes a more efficient alternative to the conventional approach of polling I/O devices individually.

Design Example with an Interrupt Controller

As an application example we consider the conversion of the programmed I/O interface of Figure 5-13 into an interrupt-driven one. We assume an application calling for 12 fixed-priority interrupt levels. We also assume that the printer and the keyboard are the lowest priority devices.

Since we need more than eight interrupt levels, we have to use two 8259A interrupt controllers (Figure 5-21). They are cascaded, providing a total of 15

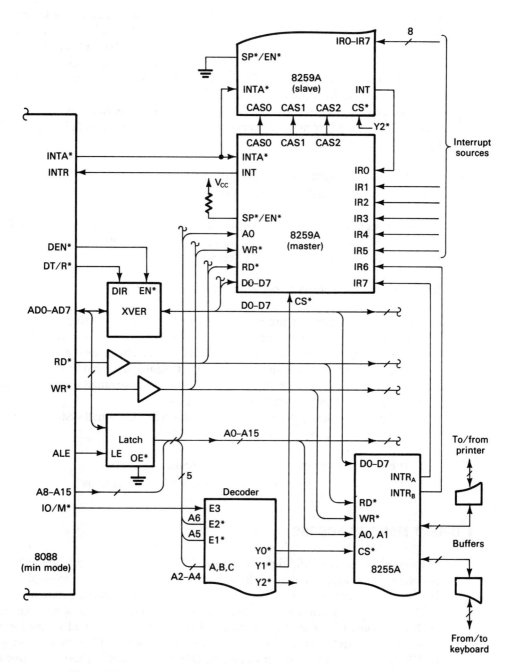

Figure 5-21. Example of an I/O interface employing the 8259A programmable interrupt controller.

interrupt levels. The SP^*/EN^* (slave program/enable) input of the lower 8259A is tied to a high, placing the device in master mode. The same input of the upper one is grounded, placing it in slave mode. Only the INT output of the master connects to the $INTR$ input of the CPU. The INT output of the slave connects to the $IR0$ input of the master. This gives the highest priority to interrupt sources connecting to the IR inputs of the slave 8259A.

For selection of the two 8259As we need two separate chip select signals. They are generated by an octal decoder. Recall from Section 5.2 that the 8255A PPI provides for interrupt purposes:

1. The $INTR_A$ signal on behalf of the printer.
2. The $INTR_B$ signal on behalf of the keyboard.

These two signals drive inputs $IR7$ and $IR6$ of the master, respectively. Of all 15 available IR lines, these have the lowest priority. Notice that otherwise, the original programmed I/O interface remains the same.

Interrupt-Driven versus Programmed I/O

The basic disadvantage of programmed I/O is the nonproductive consumption of CPU time for device status checking. Such overheads could be reduced by scheduling status scanning over longer time intervals, which, however, may cause the I/O device to wait and thus slow down I/O. Besides, an input device may not be able to wait for long. For example, if a keyboard is not scanned frequently enough, some of the keyed-in characters may be lost.

Yet programmed I/O deserves consideration in some small system applications where CPU time might not be a problem:

1. It eliminates the external interrupt circuits.
2. It simplifies the development of associated I/O programs.

5.4 DIRECT MEMORY ACCESS

Although conserving CPU time, interrupt-driven I/O is not always adequate. The problems arise when dealing with high-speed I/O devices. For example, a CPU is not able to keep up with the speed of a hard disk transferring data at a rate of 1 MB/s. In this section we examine the I/O technique which is appropriate for such situations: direct memory access I/O (DMA I/O). We will follow the same order we did with the other two I/O techniques. First we will discuss the principles of DMA and how we go about designing DMA interfaces. Then, we move on to DMA controllers and how to apply them in the design of such interfaces. We start with an overview contrasting the three basic I/O techniques.

Usually I/O data are organized into blocks and they are processed as such. Take, for instance, the case of input data. All bytes comprising a data block must be accumulated in memory before the CPU processes that block. Similarly, the CPU prepares in memory a full block of data prior to transmitting to an output device any word of that block. DMA eliminates CPU involvement in the transfer of each and every data word of a block. Unlike programmed and interrupt-driven I/O, data are not stored in a CPU register on their way to/from memory. Instead, the I/O interface reads output data directly from memory and writes input data directly into it. This is pictured in Figure 5-22 which contrasts DMA with the two other I/O techniques.

Observe the similarity between programmed and interrupt-driven I/O. In both cases information flows the same way. The only difference is that interrupt-driven I/O employs the interrupt lines to request service from the CPU. Note from Figure 5-22(c) that in DMA I/O, data flow directly to/from memory. The CPU still maintains overall control by means of commands to both the I/O device and its interface. However, it no longer controls data transfers on a byte-by-byte basis. Status information now indicates readiness of the I/O device to transfer another block rather than an individual byte (or word). The DMA interface connects to the CPU interrupt lines as well. This permits us to draw the CPU's attention upon completion of a block transfer or readiness for another one. Unlike the two other interfaces, the DMA interface also connects to the DMA interface lines of the CPU. It is through these lines that the CPU requests bus mastership for data transfers to/from memory.

DMA in Microcomputers

In Chapters 2 and 3 we had the opportunity to deal with the external interface lines of μPs. Among them were the lines associated with DMA. In this section we review the typical structuring of such lines in μPs. Then, we examine the sequence of events associated with DMA operations.

Typically, a μP is equipped with two DMA lines (see Figure 5-23). The first one is usually called a **bus request (BR)** or **HOLD line**. It is through this line that I/O devices place requests for the CPU bus. (Remember, the CPU bus is normally under control of the CPU.) Before passing bus control to an I/O device the CPU must

1. Complete any bus cycle that may be currently in progress
2. Bring its output lines to a floating state

When this is accomplished, the CPU proceeds to acknowledge the bus request. It does so via a second DMA line named **bus grant (BG)** or **hold acknowledge (HLDA) line**. From here on, the I/O device has full control of the CPU bus. It then proceeds to generate its own read/write cycles. After transferring the required

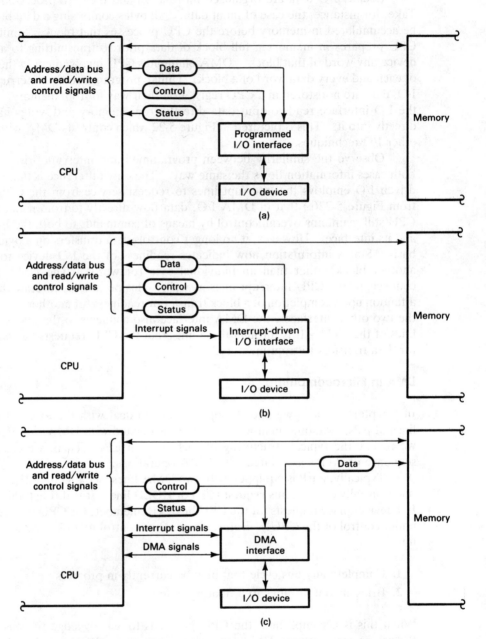

Figure 5-22. Information flow for different types of I/O. (a) Programmed I/O. (b) Interrupt-driven I/O. (c) DMA I/O.

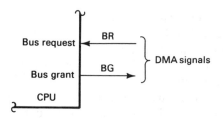

Figure 5-23. DMA signal lines of a typical microprocessor.

number of data words, the I/O device brings *BR* back to a low. Then, the CPU responds by deactivating the *BG* line. Bus control is once again returned to the CPU.

How do we initiate a data (block) transfer in DMA? How does the DMA interface know the addresses of memory locations where the data are to be written or read from? The steps involved in initiating (and thereafter controlling) a DMA block transfer are depicted in the flow diagram of Figure 5-24. We will examine each step following the order in which they are numbered.

1. First of all, the CPU reads the status of the I/O device. It has to make sure that this device is in a position to accept commands for a data transfer. Status may be read via an (ordinary) I/O port, just like the two other I/O techniques we dealt with thus far.

2. If status checking reveals a nonready state, the CPU abandons its attempt to initiate a block transfer. Instead, it jumps to an error routine to determine the cause. If the device is in a ready state, the CPU proceeds to the next step.

3. The CPU sends to the I/O device the appropriate command(s). For example, if a data block is to be read from a disk, such commands must specify that this is a read operation. Also, where on disk is the data block to be found.

4. In the course of a data block transfer there is no involvement of the CPU. Consequently, the CPU must provide to the DMA interface sufficient information so that it can carry the read/write operations on its own. Basically this information consists of a **starting address** and a **word count**. The starting address specifies to the DMA interface the memory address at which the first data word is to be written or read. Memory addresses for subsequent data words are generated by incrementing or decrementing the current memory address. This is done in accordance with the "direction" specified by the CPU. In other words, a data block is expected to occupy contiguous memory locations. The word count indicates (to the DMA interface) how many data words are to be transferred. After transmitting the above parameters, the CPU issues to the DMA interface a start command.

5. At this point the CPU withdraws to whatever other tasks it may have. All responsibility for the data block transfer is left to the DMA interface. Now the latter monitors the I/O device to find out when it is ready for the first

data transfer. Take, for instance, the case of a DMA transaction which involves transferring a data block from a disk. The DMA interface waits until the disk indicates that the first data byte has arrived. Then it proceeds to request bus mastership from the CPU. When the CPU relinquishes control of its bus, the DMA interface:

(a) Places over the address bus the starting memory address

(b) Gates the data presented by the disk over the data bus

(c) Generates the control signals—for example, WR^*—required for a memory write cycle

6. The DMA interface decrements the word count by 1. This way it keeps track of the number of transferred words. Then it prepares the memory address of the location in which the next word is to be written (or read from). To do this, it simply increments (or decrements) the starting address.

7. At this point the DMA interface examines the word count. If greater than zero, it loops back to step 5 to transfer the next word. A zero count is indicative of the fact that the number of specified words has been transferred. Consequently, the DMA interface stops any further transfers. At the same time it disables BR to relinquish bus mastership and generates an interrupt. In response to the interrupt, the CPU checks the status of the DMA interface. There it finds the indication that the data block transfer was completed successfully. Beyond this point the CPU may send new commands to the I/O device and its interface for another block transfer. Otherwise, the DMA interface enters an idle mode.

In the preceding discussion we assumed that the DMA interface gains bus mastership prior to the start of a block transfer and that it maintains the bus until the whole block is transferred to/from the I/O device. Indeed this is necessary when the I/O device is capable of transferring data at a very high rate. Why? Recall that after placing a bus request, the DMA interface has to wait until the current bus cycle is over (Section 2.6.2). Besides, bus mastership is not transferred instantaneously (see Figure 2-18). Thus, if the time between successive data words is not long enough, we are better off keeping the bus until the whole block is transferred. Such a DMA mode of operation is referred to as **burst mode**.

Example 5-12

The bus cycle of a CPU consists of six clock cycles. However, because of the length of the memory access time, the CPU has to insert two wait states per bus cycle. When a DMA device activates (via its interface) the BR line, it takes two clock cycles to gain bus mastership (provided there is no bus activity). For how long does such a device have to wait given a CPU clocking rate of 8 MHz? Would you use DMA in burst mode for a device having a data transfer rate of 0.75 MB/s?

Solution. First, let us assume that there is no bus cycle currently going on. A clock cycle takes 125 ns. Hence, the I/O device will wait for $2 \times 125 = 250$ ns to gain bus control. However, if a bus cycle is currently going on, the I/O device may have

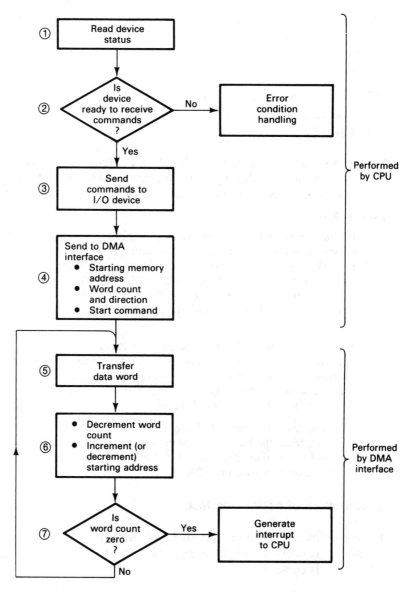

Figure 5-24. Typical sequence of events during a DMA transaction.

to wait for up to an additional $(6 + 2) \times 125 = 1000$ ns—that is, 1 μs. Therefore, the I/O device will have to wait for a time interval ranging from 250 ns to 1.25 μs. For an I/O device having the given speed we should employ DMA in burst mode.

What if the I/O device is not that fast? Consider, for instance, a system where bus cycles take 500 ns and one of the system's peripheral devices has a data rate of 50 KB/s. Here the device transfers one byte every 20 μs—that is, a time interval equivalent to 40 bus cycles. Hence, if we employ DMA in burst mode we will be wasting a considerable amount of CPU time. It is better if the DMA interface:

1. Requests the bus when it is to transfer a data word
2. Transfers the data word
3. Releases the bus

Such a mode of operation, where the device "steals" a machine cycle only when it really needs one, is called **cycle stealing** mode. This mode frees the bus between successive bus cycles, permitting its use by the CPU or other devices.

Example 5-13

Consider a system where bus cycles (whether generated by the CPU or by an I/O device) take 500 ns. Transfer of bus control in either direction—from the CPU to the I/O device or vice versa)—takes 250 ns. One of the I/O devices of the system has a data transfer rate of 50 KB/s and employs DMA I/O. Data are transferred one byte at a time. Suppose we employ DMA in burst mode. For how long would the device tie up the bus when transferring a block of 128 bytes? Repeat for cycle stealing mode.

Solution. A rate of 50 KB/s corresponds to 20 μs per byte. For 128 bytes the device takes 20 × 128 = 2560 μs—that is, 2.56 ms. To this we must add the time taken for transfer of bus control (at the beginning and the end of the block transfer). This time is comparatively small anyway (only 500 ns). Hence, in burst mode the bus will be tied up for a total of about 2.56 ms.

The time taken for transfer of one byte in cycle stealing mode is 250 + 500 + 250 = 1 μs. Since the bus is released between successive byte transfers, the CPU bus is tied up for a total of only 1 × 128 = 128 μs. Thus, cycle stealing mode will reduce bus occupancy by a factor of 20!

Organization of a DMA Interface

Having examined the principles of DMA we proceed to examine how a DMA interface is organized. Figure 5-25 pictures the hardware organization of such an interface. It consists of:

1. A device control/status part
2. A DMA control part

Functionally, the device control/status part is similar to an interrupt-driven I/O interface. It connects to the interface lines of the I/O device and those of the CPU. Notice, however, that only status and control information is exchanged with the CPU—not I/O data. The only I/O data path is to/from memory.

How does this part of the interface know the appropriate time for presentation

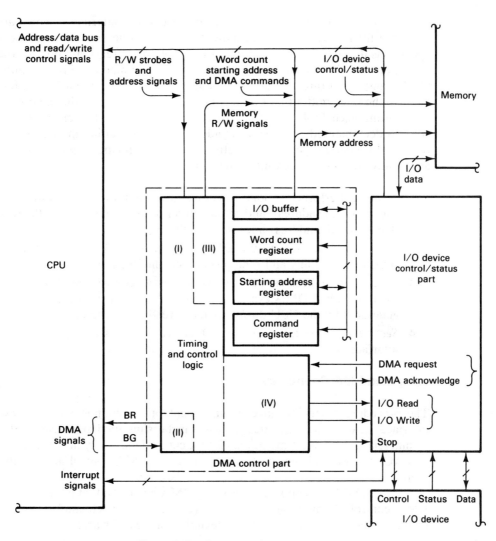

Figure 5-25. Organization of a DMA interface.

of device data to memory? Also, how does it know when to gate memory data
to the device? This is accomplished with control signals generated by the DMA
control part of the interface (*I/O Read* and *I/O Write* signals). Another control
signal (*Stop*) indicates that the whole data block has been transferred. In fact,
when this signal goes active the interface generates an interrupt, signaling the end
of the block transfer. Observe two more signal lines between the two parts of the
DMA interface: **DMA Request** and **DMA Acknowledge**. The first indicates readiness of the I/O device to provide or accept a word of data. In other words, it
signals the need for a DMA cycle on behalf of the I/O device. The second line
indicates if permission for such a cycle has been granted.

Next we examine the DMA control part of the interface. This part is responsible for generation of each individual DMA cycle and for all housekeeping operations during a block transfer. It has three main registers: one for the word count, one for the starting address, and one for commands. Prior to initiating a block transfer, all three registers are loaded by the CPU via an I/O buffer. It is through the same buffer that the starting address is gated over the memory address lines during each DMA cycle. Upon completion of each such cycle, the word count is decremented. The starting address register is either incremented or decremented (depending on the bit settings in the command register). The timing and control logic is divided into four sections.

1. *Section I:* Performs the logic functions associated with the loading of the word count, starting address, and command registers. It connects to the read/write strobe and the address lines of the CPU bus.
2. *Section II:* Interfaces to the DMA lines of the CPU. It handles the handshaking for gaining and relinquishing bus mastership.
3. *Section III:* Generates the memory read/write control signals as required for each individual DMA cycle. Bear in mind that these signals are like those generated by the CPU during memory read and write cycles.
4. *Section IV:* Interfaces to the I/O device control/status part of the DMA interface.

Integrated DMA Controllers

The preceding discussion gave us an insight of the complexity of a DMA I/O interface. Fortunately the design task can be simplified significantly thanks to commercially available (integrated) DMA controllers. A typical **DMA controller (DMAC)** provides all the functions we need for DMA control and usually many more.

Most DMACs support two or more DMA channels; that is, they can provide DMA control for multiple I/O devices (one device per channel). Some of the features which enhance further the flexibility of DMACs are:

1. Ability to support memory-to-memory block transfers
2. Operation in both burst and cycle stealing modes
3. Support of block search operations
4. Handling of variable-width data words
5. I/O-to-I/O block transfers
6. Choice of priority in the case of multiple channels

Next we discuss some of the characteristics of a typical DMA controller, the Intel 8237A DMAC.

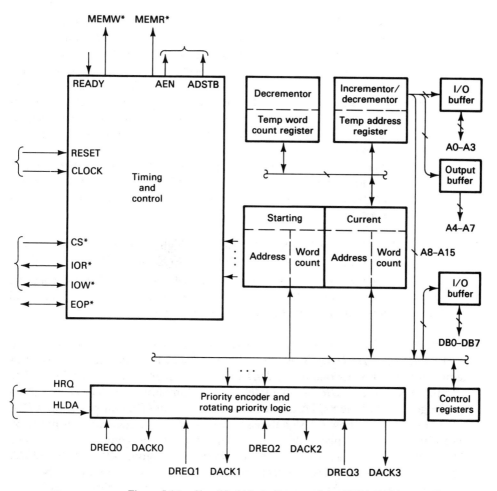

Figure 5-26. Simplified block diagram of the 8237A DMA controller.

Example of a DMAC

As an example of a DMAC we examine the 8237A. Figure 5-26 shows its simplified block diagram. The 8237A supports four DMA channels, so it needs four separate sets of word count and starting address registers. Notice how these registers are organized. For each channel, there are separate registers for storing the starting and current values of these parameters. In addition, there is a common temporary register for each parameter.

Prior to initiating a DMA cycle for a channel, the 8237A stores in the temporary registers the current values of the parameters of that channel. The contents of the temporary address register represent the memory address for that channel.

They flow out of the 8237A via the buffers shown on the upper right-hand side of Figure 5-26. Address bits A8–A15 are presented over the *DB0–DB7* lines. These bits must be stored in an external latch using the *ADSTB* (address strobe) signal provided by the 8237A for this purpose. Following completion of a DMA cycle the contents of the word count register are decremented. Those of the temporary address register are either incremented or decremented. Subsequently, these up-dated values are stored in the respective channel registers holding the current values of the channel parameters. All parameter registers are 16 bits long. Hence, the 8237A can handle blocks as large as 64 KB.

For each channel there is a separate pair of *DREQ* (DMA request) and *DACK* (DMA acknowledge) lines. Requests can be serviced employing either a fixed or a rotating priority scheme. The selection is made through one of the bits of the command register.

1. *Fixed Priority Scheme:* The 8237A assigns the highest priority to *DREQ0* and progressively lower priorities to *DREQ1*, *DREQ2*, and *DREQ3*.
2. *Rotating Priority Scheme:* As soon as a channel is serviced, it is assigned the lowest priority. Hence, this scheme provides equal chance of service to all four channels (and thereby the devices attaching to them).

See from Figure 5-26 that the priority logic block is associated with two additional signals: *HRQ* and *HLDA*. The *HRQ* (hold request) line goes active as soon as the priority logic honors one of the *DREQ*s. Consequently, *HRQ* can be used to drive the bus request (*BR*) input of the CPU. Similarly, the *HLDA* (hold ac-knowledge) input of the 8237A connects to the bus grant (*BG*) output of the CPU.

Let us examine now the signals associated with the timing and control block. Lines *IOR** and *IOW** play a dual role. When the 8237A is engaged in an active (DMA) cycle, they act as *I/O Read* and *I/O Write* (see Figure 5-25). If the 8237A is in an idle cycle (no DMA activity), they can be used as read/write strobe lines for internal registers. Another bidirectional line is *EOP** (end of process). As an output line it functions like the *Stop* line of Figure 5-25. As an input, it permits an external signal to terminate a block transfer regardless of the stage in which such a transfer might be. *CLOCK* is the clock input (the DMA data transfer rate of the 8237A is determined from the frequency of its clock). *MEMR** (memory read) and *MEMW** (memory write) correspond to the *RD** and *WR** lines of a CPU (remember that during a DMA cycle, a DMAC controls the memory the same way a CPU does). *AEN* (address enable) provides an auxiliary signal for enabling of the external 8-bit latch containing address bits A8–A15.

When the chip select (*CS**) input of the 8237A is activated, address lines A0–A3 serve as means to select one of the on-chip registers. Data read from, or written into, these registers are presented over the *DB0–DB7* lines. Such oper-ations are, of course, performed only when the 8237A is in an idle cycle. The *DB0–DB7* bus is also utilized during memory-to-memory block transfers. Such transfers take two cycles. During the first cycle, the 8237A transfers one byte from memory into an internal register.   Then, in a following cycle, it transfers the byte from the internal register to the destination memory address.   Finally, the 8237A has a status register indicating if a channel has a pending DMA request, or if it has completed the desired data block transfer.

Next we list some of the programmable characteristics of the 8237A (as determined by loading its control registers appropriately).

1. *Type of Data Transfer:* That is, memory-to-memory versus ordinary DMA cycles.
2. *Priority Scheme:* Selection of fixed or rotating priority in the servicing of the four DMA channels.
3. *Direction of Data Transfers:* Memory to I/O device or I/O device to memory.
4. *Address Generation:* Generation of the next memory address either by incrementing the current address or by decrementing it.
5. *Auto-initialization:* This feature concerns the automatic reloading of the starting address and word count registers with the respective starting values.   The reloading starts when *EOP** goes active (assuming we have selected the channel for operation in this mode).   This mode allows data to be transferred time and again to/from the same block of memory addresses.   Though it sounds peculiar, this can be very useful in certain applications.   CRT refreshing represents such an example (see Chapter 6).   If we set up a channel in this mode, refresh operations can go on without CPU involvement.
6. *Mode of Data Transfers:* In addition to cycle stealing and burst mode, the 8237A allows a **demand transfer mode**.   Its difference from the burst mode is that the 8237A stops any further DMA cycles and releases the bus as soon as *DREQ* goes inactive.   However, DMA cycles resume as soon as the I/O device reactivates *DREQ*.   Eventually, data transfers are terminated when the specified word count is reached.
7. *Cascade Mode:* This mode supports cascading of 8237As for accommodation of more than four DMA channels.   When an 8237A is programmed for such an operating mode, its *DREQ/DACK* lines can be connected to the *HRQ/ HLDA* lines of another 8237A.
8. *Active DREQ and DACK Levels:* The active levels on the DMA request and acknowledge lines can be defined to be either highs or lows.

Example 5-14

Examination of the timing diagrams of the 8237A indicates that once we start a block transfer it takes three clock cycles per DMA cycle.   During such a cycle the 8237A transfers one byte of information between memory and I/O device.   Suppose we clock the 8237A at a rate of 5 MHz.   How long does it take per byte transfer?   What would be the maximum attainable data transfer rate?

Assume that memory is not fast enough and we have to insert two wait states per DMA cycle.   What will be the actual data transfer rate?

Solution. A clock cycle of the 8237A takes 200 ns. Hence, a byte transfer takes 3 $\times$ 200 = 600 ns. The maximum data transfer rate we can achieve in the course of a block transfer will be 1/0.6 MB/s—that is, about 1.6 MB/s.

If the memory cycle time is longer than 600 ns, we have to insert wait states through manipulation of the *READY* line of the 8237A. In other words, we must slow down DMA cycles. For example, insertion of two wait states per DMA cycle will lengthen the latter to (3 + 2) $\times$ 200 = 1000 ns, or 1 μs. As a result, the data transfer rate would drop to 1 MB/s.

Example 5-15

Assume that in the system dealt with in Example 5-14 a memory cycle takes 750 ns. To what value could we reduce the clocking rate of the DMAC without effect on the attainable data transfer rate?

Solution. A DMA cycle could be as long as 750 ns and still have no need for insertion of wait states. Such a length would correspond to a clock period of 750/3 = 250 ns, which in turn corresponds to a clock frequency of 4 MHz. This approach would eliminate the circuitry associated with wait state insertion and also reduce power dissipation.

Example 5-16

A DMAC serves four (receive-only) telecommunication links (one per DMA channel) having a speed of 64 Kb/s. Would you operate the DMAC in burst mode or in cycle stealing mode? What priority scheme would you employ for service of the DMA channels?

Solution. Here the I/O devices are the links themselves. A rate of 64 Kb/s corresponds to 8 KB/s—that is, one byte every 125 μs over each link. Burst mode is out of the question since data arrive continuously and thus the DMAC would not give the CPU any chance to use the bus. Therefore, we should operate in cycle stealing mode. Over a period of 125 μs the DMAC would have to perform at most four byte transfers. Even if we assume 2 μs per byte transfer, that would leave plenty of bus time for the CPU (125 − 2 $\times$ 4 = 117 μs).

Since all four links have the same data rate, we should give them the same opportunity of service. That means selection of a rotating priority scheme. The higher the data transfer rate over the links, the more important the selection of such a priority scheme.

Design Example with a DMAC

Next we see how we would go about designing a DMA interface with the 8237A. The CPU is an 8088 and is configured in minimum mode. We assume use of the separate I/O address space of the 8088 for I/O operations.

A decoding circuit is needed for generation of the CS^* signal for the 8237A. This can be accomplished with an octal decoder generating CS^* signals for the controllers of the system (Figure 5-27). The decoded addresses are I/O addresses. A second decoding circuit is required for generation of the IOR^* and IOW^* strobes.

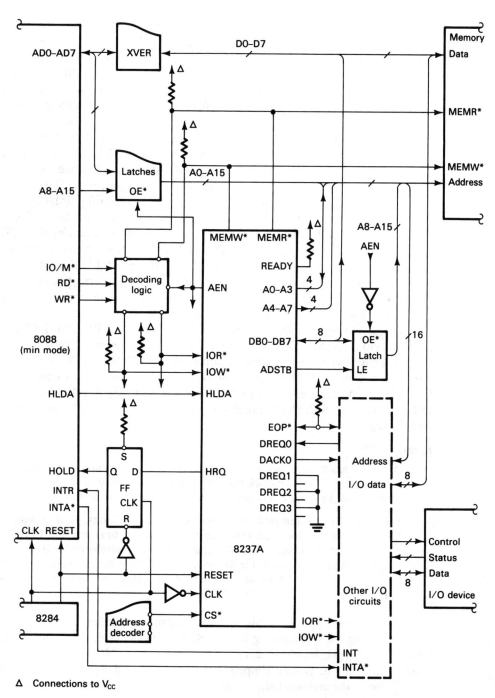

Figure 5-27. Example of an I/O interface using the 8237A DMA controller.

Recall that these are used when the CPU reads or writes information into internal registers of the 8237A. The decoded signals are IO/M^*, RD^*, and WR^*. When IO/M^* is a high, this decoder may activate either IOR^* or IOW^*. When IO/M^* is a low, it may generate either a memory read strobe ($MEMR^*$) or a memory write strobe ($MEMW^*$). However, during a DMA cycle all four strobe lines must be under control of the DMAC. Therefore, during such cycles the decoding logic must be disabled. For this purpose we can use the AEN signal provided by the 8237A. AEN can also be used to disable the (ordinary) address latches.

By employing the AEN signal this way we ensure that, during DMA cycles, all four strobe lines are controlled by the DMAC only. (Notice these lines are wire-ORed with the respective outputs of the second decoder). The address lines (toward memory) are also under control of the DMAC during DMA cycles. Address lines $A0$–$A7$ are driven from the synonymous outputs of the 8237A. Lines $A8$–$A15$ are driven from an external latch. This latch is loaded by the 8237A via its $DB0$–$DB7$ bus and is enabled by the AEN signal. The ability to disable other circuits (which connect to the bus) is key to the design of a DMA interface. For lines driven directly by the CPU there need be no concern, because the CPU automatically brings its outputs to a high impedance state during DMA cycles. But, when this is not the case, we must design for it.

In our example we have chosen to drive both the CPU and the DMAC by the same clock signal. Our next concern is how to drive the $HOLD$ input of the CPU, specifically, the setup time requirements for $HOLD$. These requirements specify how long $HOLD$ should be stable prior to a low-to-high transition of the CPU clock. A solution to this problem is using a D-type flip-flop for sampling of HRQ on a low-to-high clock transition. This secures plenty of setup time for the $HOLD$ signal.

Example 5-17

Assume a clock frequency of 8 MHz and a $HOLD$ setup time requirement of 30 ns (see Figure 5-27). The clock-to-output propagation delay of the FF is 25 ns. Determine how long our safety margin is as far as $HOLD$ setup time goes.

Solution. HRQ is sampled on low-to-high clock transitions. Let us assume HRQ has been at a high for some time (satisfying the setup time needs of FF) when such a clock transition occurs. The Q output of FF (and thereby $HOLD$) goes active 25 ns later. A clock period is 125 ns long, so the $HOLD$ input is sampled by the CPU another $125 - 25 = 100$ ns later. Since the $HOLD$ setup time requirement is 30 ns, our safety margin is $100 - 30 = 70$ ns.

Another assumption in this design is that memory is fast enough to complete its cycle during the normal length of an 8237A DMA cycle. Otherwise we would have to stretch the length of each DMA cycle. The $DREQ$ lines of the unused channels are tied to ground (implying the 8237A is initialized to treat a high on a $DREQ$ line as the active level). Notice also that the high-order address lines $A16$–

A19 of the CPU are ignored.   By being able to specify a 16-bit address, the DMAC can transfer data to/from any memory location in the range of 0 to 64K.

What if we had to be capable of transferring data to/from locations in the address range of 0 to 1M?   This could be accomplished by means of one additional latch.   The new latch might be loaded by the CPU when the DMAC is initialized with new block transfer parameters.   Then, by enabling the output of the latch with AEN we could specify to memory a full 20-bit address.

DMA versus Interrupt-Driven I/O

Interrupt-driven I/O is far better than programmed I/O because it eliminates the CPU time wasted for I/O device status scanning.   However, interrupt processing itself takes CPU time.   So, if interrupts are very frequent, the CPU ends up consuming a significant fraction of its time for their processing.

Example 5-18

Consider a system employing interrupt-driven I/O for a particular I/O device which transfers data at an average rate of 8 KB/s on a continuous basis (such a "device" could be a telecommunications link).   Interrupt processing takes about 100 μs (that is, the time to jump to the ISR, execute it, and return to the main program).   Determine what fraction of the CPU time is consumed by this I/O device.

Solution.   On the average, the device transfers only one byte over a period of 1/0.008 = 125 μs.   Yet the CPU has to consume 100 μs for processing of the associated interrupt—that is, 100/125 = 0.8, or 80 percent of its time.   So the time taken for servicing of the I/O device would hardly spare CPU time for other tasks.

If the I/O device is equipped with a data block buffer, we may interrupt the CPU only on a per block basis.   This can reduce interrupt processing times considerably.

Example 5-19

Assume the device of Example 5-18 has two 16-byte buffers and interrupts the CPU as soon as one of the buffers is filled.   Now the CPU is interrupted only once per 16 × 0.125 = 2 ms.   Naturally interrupt processing takes longer, since the ISR must transfer 16 bytes.   While executing the ISR the CPU takes about 8 μs for the transfer of each byte.   Calculate the fraction of CPU time consumed for I/O device service.

Solution.   Over a period of 2 ms there is one interrupt.   The processing time associated with one such interrupt is now 100 + (8 × 15) = 220 μs.   This represents 0.22/2 = 0.11—that is, 11 percent of the CPU's time.

The above approach yields even better results if the CPU is equipped with block I/O or repeat type of I/O instructions.   This permits the associated ISR to transfer a whole block by executing repeatedly the very same instruction—hence, further reduction of interrupt processing time.

Example 5-20

The CPU we considered in the two previous examples is equipped with a repeat type I/O instruction. This permits the associated ISR to transfer each byte of a block within only 2 μs. What fraction of the CPU's time is now consumed for I/O device service?

Solution. In Example 5-19, the ISR was transferring each byte of a block by executing a software loop consisting of several instructions. These instructions were transferring each byte in a CPU register and from there on to memory or I/O device (depending on the direction of the transfer). Each instruction of the loop had to be fetched and executed separately. However, the repeat type of instruction eliminates the need for such a software loop. Now, the ISR fetches that instruction only once and executes it repeatedly until all 16 bytes are transferred. Hence the interrupt processing time is reduced by $16 \times 6 = 96$ μs. The consumed fraction of CPU time over an interval of 2 ms is $(0.22 - 0.096) / 2 = 0.062$, that is, 6.2 percent. This represents an improvement factor of almost 2.

DMA allows further reduction of interrupt processing time. The ISR need only initialize the DMA interface prior to transferring a block, with, for example, a new starting memory address and a new word count. Data are transferred without any involvement of the CPU (and thereby the ISR). Each transfer takes one DMA cycle, which is generally equivalent to only one memory cycle. Besides, DMA may be the only choice when the CPU is not capable of keeping up with the data transfer rate of an I/O device. On the other hand, DMA introduces extra complexity (especially in terms of hardware). Consequently, it should not be used unjustifiably. Next we summarize the three key considerations in the design of a DMA interface.

t is time between DMA Cycles

1. *Length of a DMA Cycle:* The data transfer rate is determined by the length of a DMA cycle. The higher the DMAC clocking rate, the shorter the DMA cycle. However, unless memory is fast enough, high DMAC clocking rates do not help.

t < Bus Cycle
Don't even consider cycle stealing

2. *Burst Mode versus Cycle Stealing:* An important criterion is the time interval between two successive DMA cycles. Unless this interval allows the CPU to perform at least one bus cycle of its own, cycle stealing is not even worth considering. When determining this interval, you should take into account the time required for passing bus mastership between CPU and DMA interface.

3. *Impact on Response to Interrupts:* The CPU gives DMA requests the highest priority, so that DMA transfers delay response to interrupts regardless of their priority. Such delays are longer in burst mode where the CPU is locked off the bus until the whole block is transferred.   In the course of choosing data block lengths you must take into consideration the interrupt response time requirements of the particular application.

5.5 I/O SUPPORT DEVICES

At this point we have concluded our discussion of the three basic I/O techniques employed in μCs (and computers in general).   Our next objective is to examine devices used in the design of specific kinds of I/O.   These devices concern:

- Serial communication
- Visual displays

Before we do so, we discuss a device supporting certain I/O-related functions such as **counting** and **timing**.

5.5.1 Programmable Timers

Very often the CPU must take certain actions at timed intervals.   For example, it might be necessary to scan the status of a keyboard every 100 ms (programmed I/O).   Similarly, in a multitasking system it may be necessary to suspend the execution of a task for a specified amount of time.   Such actions may be timed by software means—that is, by executing a program loop a specific number of times. The major problem with this approach is the extra burden in terms of CPU time. For this reason, timed intervals are usually generated by hardware rather than software means.   This is accomplished using presettable counters which are loaded by the CPU with the appropriate contents and are subsequently decremented at some clocking rate.   When the counter contents reach zero, the CPU is interrupted and in this way is informed that the desired time interval has elapsed.

The circuitry required for the design of an interval counter includes several MSI counters, as well as some decoding logic for the loading of the counters.   The design task is greatly simplified with integrated programmable interval timers. Typically, a **programmable interval timer (PIT)** provides three or more independent counters and also allows additional modes of operation, enhancing its flexibility. They may be used for:

1. Event counting
2. Time measurement
3. The generation of pulses having programmable timing characteristics
4. The design of real-time clocks and other applications.

Example of a Programmable Interval Timer

Figure 5-28 illustrates the block diagram of a typical PIT—the Intel 8254. The main element of each counter block is a 16-bit presettable synchronous down counter. In addition, each such block includes registers, latches, a status register/latch, and some control logic. The registers serve the presetting of the down counters. The latches serve the reading of the counter contents by the CPU (via the internal bus of the 8254). Among other information, the status byte indicates the state of the *OUT* line and the null count flag of the respective counter.

The three counters of the 8254 are independent. They can be programmed to operate in six different modes. The programming of each counter is done in two steps. The first step is to load the control word register to indicate

1. The counter the control word is intended for
2. The sequence in which the selected counter is to be read or written during the subsequent step (that is, which of the two bytes, or, if both)
3. The desired mode of operation for that counter
4. Whether counting is to be done in binary or in BCD (binary coded decimal)

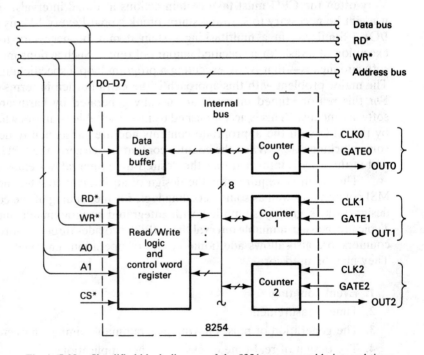

Figure 5-28. Simplified block diagram of the 8254 programmable interval timer.

The second step involves writing the desired initial count into the selected counter. A list of the six operating modes permitted for each counter follows.

Interrupt on terminal count (mode 0)

An initial count (say N) is loaded into a counter. Then, on each subsequent clock pulse, the count is decremented by 1. The only condition is that the $GATE$ input of that counter is maintained at a high. Otherwise the process of decrementation is inhibited. As the counter keeps decrementing, its OUT line remains at a low until the count becomes zero. Thereafter, OUT goes to a high and stays so until the counter is again programmed. The low-to-high transition of the OUT signal can be used for generation of an interrupt—hence, the name of this mode.

Example 5-21

The CPU of a system scans an I/O device every 10 ms. The scanning is triggered through an interrupt generated by means of an 8254. What should be the initial count, given the 8254 is clocked at the rate of 2 MHz?

Solution. The period of the clock is 0.5 μs. Thus, 10 ms corresponds to 10000 / 0.5 = 20000 clock pulses. Consequently, the respective counter of the PIT should be loaded with the binary equivalent of 20000.

Hardware retriggerable one-shot (mode 1)

In this mode, $GATE$ plays the role of a trigger. OUT is initially at a high. One clock cycle after the counter is triggered it goes to a low. Thereafter, OUT remains so until the count gets to zero. However, the counter can be retriggered through the $GATE$ input (without having to reinitialize its contents).

Rate generator (mode 2)

When an 8254 counter is programmed in this mode, it acts as a divide-by-N counter. OUT is normally at a high. When the initial count (N) is decremented down to a 1, OUT goes to a low for one clock cycle. Then it goes back to a high, and the counter is automatically reloaded with the initial count N. In other words, OUT will be pulsing periodically every N clock cycles. This mode finds applications in the design of real-time clocks.

Square wave mode (mode 3)

This one is somewhat similar to mode 2. OUT is again initially at a high. It goes to a low as soon as the initial count N is decremented by one half. If N is odd, OUT goes to a low after $(N + 1)/2$ clock cycles. Hence, the counter generates a square (or close to a square) wave. This mode is useful in the design of serial communication ports (see Section 5.5.2).

Software triggered strobe (mode 4)

When a counter is programmed in this mode, *OUT* stays at a high until the initial count is decremented to a zero. At that time, *OUT* goes to a low for a duration of one clock cycle, after which it again switches to a high. The cycle ends at this point (until a new initial count is loaded). However, if a new initial count is loaded before the present one expires, the counter ignores its previous state and starts from the new count—that is, the sequence is retriggerable. This mode allows generation of strobes under software control.

Hardware triggered strobe (mode 5)

This last mode is similar to mode 4, but the difference is that the timing sequence is triggered when *GATE* goes from a low to a high. Now we can generate strobes under hardware control.

Design Example

Figure 5-29 pictures an application example of the 8254 PIT. We assume an 8088-based system. The CPU is configured in minimum mode. An 8284 clock generator provides a 5 MHz clock to the CPU. For the PIT we use the *PCLK* output whose rate is half of that provided to the CPU.

The assumed application concerns an I/O port which must be scanned every 100 ms, as, for instance, a port serving a keyboard. The approach we take is using the 8254 to count 100 ms time intervals. Each time such an interval elapses, an interrupt is to be generated to the CPU.

First, let us examine how far we can go with a single counter. Since such a counter is 16 bits long and the *PCLK* period is 400 ns, we can handle time intervals up to only 400×64000 ns long—that is, up to 25.6 ms. Thus we need to divide down the frequency of the clock. This can be accomplished with a second counter which is essentially employed as a prescaler. In Figure 5-29 we employ counter 0 as such. This counter is programmed to operate in square wave mode. Its output (*OUT0*) feeds the clock input of another counter (counter 1). For example, if the initial value loaded into counter 0 is 2500, counter 1 will be clocked every 400×2500 ns, that is, every 1 ms. As a result, counter 1 may count intervals up to 10 s long (assuming counting in BCD).

For counter 1 we select mode 0 (interrupt on terminal count mode). If counter 0 is loaded with 2500, then counter 1 must be loaded with 100. Its output (*OUT1*) connects to one of the interrupt request inputs of an 8259A PIC. At the end of the 100 ms interval, the latter sees the low-to-high transition over its *IR*1

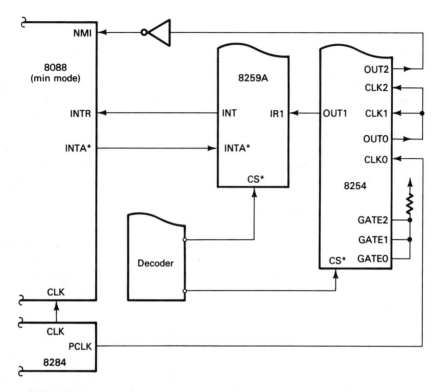

Figure 5-29. Example of timed interrupt generation circuit using the 8254 programmable interval timer.

line. From there on, it leads the CPU to the service routine, which is to scan the aforementioned I/O port. Besides its other tasks, this routine must initiate the counting for the next 100 ms interval. For this purpose it loads a new initial count into counter 1.

The reader must not confuse such timed interrupts with interrupt-driven I/O, because the I/O port itself has no interrupt capability. A timed interrupt simply reminds the CPU that it is time to check the readiness of that I/O port again. However, it has no way of knowing if the port does in fact need attention.

A watchdog timer

Besides timed interrupts, Figure 5-29 shows how we can go about implementing a **watchdog timer**. Such a timer can be used to determine if the CPU is in an undesired (possibly endless) loop. A CPU may end up in such a state because of some software or hardware error. Examples are a noise spike which caused inversion of a single bit or an undetected memory error. Sometimes a timer of this kind is called a **sanity timer**.

In Figure 5-29 the watchdog timer is implemented by counter 2, which is also clocked from *OUT0*. The idea is to have the CPU retrigger the counter before reaching a zero count, so that under normal conditions, the watchdog timer will never cause an interrupt. An interrupt is generated only if the CPU is "lost" and has not come back to retrigger the counter. For this counter we select the software triggered mode and an initial count of, say, 1000. Unless retriggered by the CPU, *OUT2* will go to a low after 1 s. What then? In our example we use the pulse generated over *OUT2* to cause a nonmaskable interrupt. This can lead the CPU to a ROM-resident routine which attempts to restart the system. Another common approach is using the pulse generated by the timer for activation of the reset input of the CPU.

5.5.2 Serial Communication

All cases of data transfers we dealt with so far have one thing in common. The bits comprising a data word were transferred in parallel. Take, for instance, the design pictured in Figure 5-13. All eight bits of a character are transferred to the printer at the same time over eight separate data lines. This brings up a number of questions:

1. Is the parallel scheme the only way of transferring information?
2. What if the two points are far away from each other—for example, two μCs separated by thousands of miles? In this case, transferring information in parallel (over many signal wires) is certainly out of the question.

Fortunately there is an alternative to the parallel scheme, an alternative that is widely used and is our subject in this section. It is commonly called **serial communication**.

In **serial I/O**, data are transferred over a single signal line on a one-bit-at-a-time basis. This simplifies interconnections with I/O devices, but at the expense of lowering data transfer rates. Yet, the resulting rates are adequate for many I/O devices. Indeed, keyboard/display terminals and character printers are very often equipped with serial interfaces. Figure 5-30(a) depicts how such an I/O device attaches to a CPU. Both ends are equipped with serial interfaces. Among other functions the latter perform the required parallel-to-serial and serial-to-parallel data conversions. Another way of referring to this configuration is to say that the I/O device connects to the CPU through a **serial I/O port**.

Serial I/O becomes the only choice when a system must communicate with remote terminals or other remote systems. In this case, communication is accomplished through a data network which is either local (spanning a distance of say 500 m) or geographically dispersed. It may also be accomplished through the public telephone network, using ordinary telephone lines. A serial port, though, does not connect directly to the telephone network, because the telephone network

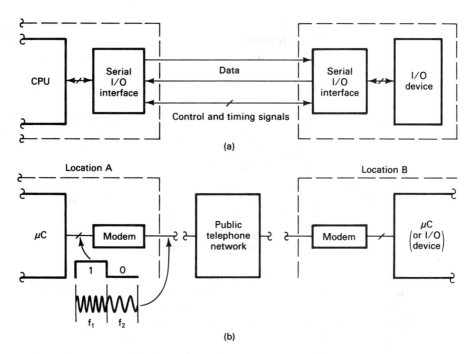

Figure 5-30. Communication through serial I/O ports. (a) Direct communication between CPU and an I/O device via a serial port. (b) Serial communication between a μC and an I/O device (or another μC) via the public telephone network.

was designed for analog voice—not digital data. Instead, the connection is made via a modulator/demodulator known as a **modem**.

A modem uses the digital data to modulate an (analog) carrier signal. The resulting signal is then transmitted in the same way as voice signals are. At the other end, another modem demodulates received signals and retrieves the original digital data. Figure 5-30(b) pictures the case of communication via the public telephone network. Common two-wire dial-up (otherwise called switched) lines may support transmission rates of up to 4800 b/s. Leased telephone lines are usually four-wire ones and may support up to 9600 b/s. Furthermore, depending on the employed modem, stations A and B may be able to communicate in

1. Only one direction at a time (half duplex communication)
2. Both directions simultaneously (full duplex communication)

A commonly employed modulation technique is **frequency-shift keying (FSK)**. This technique amounts to modifying the frequency of the carrier signal according to the logic levels of the transmitted data. Observe, for instance, the frequency of the carrier signal at the output of the modem in Figure 5-30(b). It is higher during the transmission of a 1 ($f_1 > f_2$). Other modulation techniques are **phase modulation** and **amplitude modulation**, as well as certain combinations of the three. Some modems are equipped with a pad which can be coupled acoustically to a common telephone handset. Such an approach provides portability but limits data rates to about 300 b/s.

The subject of serial communication raises a long series of questions. For example, given that data are transmitted over a single line, how do we know which bit is which? What signals are involved in a serial interface? What voltage levels are employed? How far can we go without a modem? How about speed? What options do we have as far as interface circuits go? How do we go about designing such interfaces? What about LSI/VLSI components for this purpose? This is the kind of topics we deal with in the remaining part of this section.

Asynchronous and Synchronous Communication

How does a receiving serial port know where a data word starts and where it stops? How does it know the instances it must sample the line in order to detect an arriving 1 or 0? These and many other issues are resolved by using well-defined sets of rules known as **protocols**. Generally, information is transmitted serially either asynchronously or synchronously.

In **asynchronous communication** data words are transmitted independently of each other. Also, the time intervals between successive data words may vary. A data word is usually referred to as a character. It consists of up to eight data bits and possibly a parity bit. Two additional bits are used to "bracket" each character: a **start bit** and a **stop bit**. Optionally one may use 1.5 or two stop bits. For example, the format shown in Figure 5-31(a) employs two stop bits per character. In this one, each character consists of seven data bits. There is also a parity bit.

As seen from Figure 5-31(a), the duration of the idle time intervals between successive character transmissions varies. In fact, while idle, the voltage level remains at a high. The start bit is a low and serves to prepare the receiver for the reception of the data bits that are to follow. The stop bit(s) brings the line back to a high. Thereafter follows the start bit for the next character, or an idle period during which the line voltage continues to be at a high. One of the drawbacks of asynchronous communication is its comparatively large overhead (in terms of start and stop bits). Also, since the clock of the receiver is not synchronized by the transmitter, transmission at rates higher than 9600 b/s becomes very problematic. Yet the asynchronous approach is used very widely, especially for low-speed peripherals where the volume of transmitted data is relatively small and the required transmission speed modest.

Example 5-22

Calculate the overhead associated with the format of Figure 5-31(a). Suppose this format is employed for data transmission at the speed of 1200 b/s. What will the transmission rate be in terms of characters per second (cps)?

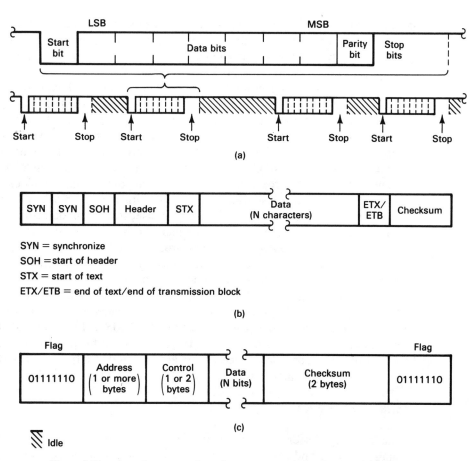

Figure 5-31. Asynchronous and synchronous transmission formats. (a) Example of an asynchronous transmission format with seven data bits, one parity bit, and two stop bits. (b) Frame format of the bisync character-oriented protocol. (c) Frame format of the HDLC bit-oriented protocol.

Solution. Each character consists of a total of 11 bits. From the latter, only seven are data bits. Hence the overhead amounts to $4/11 = 0.36$, that is, 36 percent. Since each character requires transmission of 11 bits, the transmission rate in terms of characters will be up to $1200/11 = 109$ cps.

In **synchronous communication** data are not transmitted on a character-by-character basis. They are transmitted in blocks. Figures 5-31(b) and (c) illustrate examples of synchronous transmission formats. In both formats the data field represents a block of data supplemented with additional (overhead) information to form a so-called **frame**. Such an approach typically reduces the overhead per character to a few percent. Synchronous communication can support high data rates by keeping the receiver in sync with the transmitter. Usually this is accomplished by encoding the data such that they contain more signal transitions than ordinary binary data do and maintaining transmission during idle time between successive frames. On the other hand, synchronous communication introduces more complexity at both ends of the channel. Consequently it is used only when the required transmission rates justify its complexity.

Let us now examine more closely the two examples of synchronous transmission formats. Figure 5-31(b) shows the frame format of the IBM bisynchronous (**bisync**) protocol. A frame starts with two SYN (synchronize) characters. They are followed by an SOH (start of header) character and a header field, which provides to the receiver addressing and control information. The data field contains an integral number of characters. It is bracketted between an STX (start of text) and an ETX (end of text) character. ETB (end of transmission block) replaces ETX when sending the last frame associated with a large block of data. The checksum field is two characters long and is used for error detection purposes. Synchronous protocols of this kind, in which the building blocks of a frame are characters, are called **character-oriented protocols (COP)**. One of the problems with such protocols is that if we are to send bit-oriented information—for example, graphics—we have to subdivide and pack it into characters.

The problems associated with COPs are overcome by **bit-oriented protocols (BOP)**. Figure 5-31(c) shows the frame format of such a protocol—the HDLC (high-level data link control) protocol specified by the ISO (International Standards Organization). A frame starts and ends with a special bit pattern named a flag. This pattern represents the only control character used in a frame. The data field has a variable length specified in terms of bits rather than characters.

Interface Standards

Thus far we have seen the format in which we transmit serial data. However, nothing has been said about the signals involved when we do so. Going back to Figure 5-30(a), we see that the set of I/O interface lines of a serial port includes:

1. One data line for each direction of transmission
2. A number of additional lines for control and timing purposes

When communicating via the public telephone network, we employ the very same set of interface lines to connect to the modem. From there on, the data are transmitted over a telephone line by means of analog signals. The μC (or I/O device) which transmits/receives data via a serial I/O port is called **data terminal equipment (DTE)**. The modem (and generally the equipment through which we connect to a network) is called **data circuit-terminating equipment (DCE)**. The need for compatibility among the equipment connecting to networks motivated the development of pertinent interface standards. A most widely employed standard for communication between a DTE and a DCE is the **EIA RS-232C** (Electronic Industries Association recommended standard 232C).

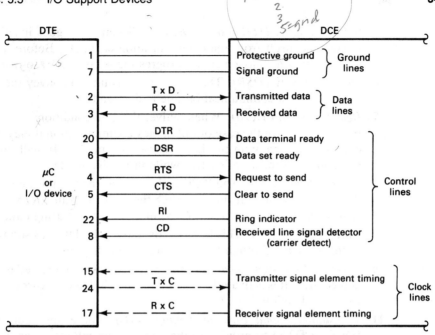

Figure 5-32.   A subset of the interface lines specified in the EIA RS-232C standard.

EIA RS-232C

The RS-232C interface standard defines a total of 20 lines.   Figure 5-32 shows those usually employed in the implementation of serial I/O ports.   In fact, very often an even smaller subset of lines is employed.   The numbers indicated on the DTE side are pin numbers of the 25-pin connector specified in the RS-232C standard (Figure 5-32).   Shown also are the mnemonics used in practice for the signals carried by these interface lines.   A brief description of the functional characteristics of each line follows.

1. *Protective Ground:* Each end of this line is electrically bonded to the respective chassis ground.
2. *Signal Ground:* This line establishes a common ground reference for all signal lines between DTE and DCE.
3. *Transmitted Data (TxD):* The DTE uses this line to transmit data to the DCE. The data are formatted in accordance with a particular asynchronous or synchronous transmission protocol.
4. *Received Data (RxD):* The DTE receives data from the DCE via this line.
5. *Data Terminal Ready (DTR):* The DTE activates this line for indication of its in-service status to the DCE.   Subsequently, the DCE connects itself to the communication channel (toward the network) and maintains the connec-

tion as long as *DTR* remains active. When *DTR* goes inactive, the DCE disconnects itself from the communication channel. Before doing so, however, it waits for any currently progressing transmission to complete.

6. *Date Set Ready (DSR):* The DCE uses this line to convey the fact that it is connected to a communication line and is ready.

7. *Request to Send (RTS):* When active, this line conditions the DCE for data transmission. In the case of full duplex communication it may be kept active constantly to maintain the DCE in transmit mode. In half duplex communication, *RTS* must be inactive while in receive mode.

8. *Clear to Send (CTS):* The DCE activates this line to indicate its readiness for data transmission. It does so after the DTE activates *RTS*. Note that all four lines (*DTR, DSR, RTS, CTS*) must be active during data transmission.

9. *Ring Indicator (RI):* This line is activated by the DCE as soon as it receives a ringing signal through the communication channel.

10. *Received Line Signal Detector (CD):* This line is also referred to as the carrier detect line. It is activated by the DCE when it detects a carrier signal suitable for demodulation.

11. *Transmitter Signal Element Timing (TxC):* These lines permit either side (DCE or DTE) to provide to the other a transmit clock for synchronization purposes. Such an arrangement becomes necessary in the case of synchronous communication.

12. *Receiver Signal Element Timing (RxC):* The DCE provides via this line a receive clock to the DTE for synchronization. It is used in the case of synchronous communication.

What if we connect directly two serial ports as pictured in Figure 5-30(a)? In general, the required number of lines is a subset of those just listed. In fact, for some simple applications we could do with as few as four lines (that is, *TxD*, *RxD*, and the two ground lines).

How about electrical characteristics? First of all, the voltage levels for a low must be in the range of -3 V to -25 V. Those for a high must be in the range of $+3$ V to $+25$ V. However, logic levels are not defined the same way for all signal lines. For the two data lines (*TxD*, *RxD*) a low is defined as a 1 and a high as a 0. For the rest of the interface signals it is the other way around. The RS-232C standard supports a maximum data rate of 20 Kb/s over cables up to 50 ft long.

EIA RS-449

A new standard permits higher data rates and longer cable lengths. It is designated as **RS-449** and defines a total of 30 interface lines. Most of the signals specified in RS-232C are preserved. However RS-449 adds new signals allowing other types of functions such as testing. The connector is also different.

Actually, RS-449 defines only the functional and mechanical aspects of the serial interface. The electrical aspects are defined in two separate standards: the **RS-422A** and the **RS-423A**. Both require line drivers capable of handling long transmission lines. Voltage levels for a low are -3.6 V to -6 V. Those for a high must be $+3.6$ V to $+6$ V. The difference between RS-422A and RS-423A is that the former specifies balanced line drivers, and the latter specifies unbalanced—that is, single-ended—ones. Consequently, when electrical characteristics comply to RS-422A, RS-449 can support higher data rates and cable lengths. For example, RS-422A may allow a data rate of 2 Mb/s over a 200 ft cable. RS-423A would permit only up to 140 Kb/s.

Note that RS-449 was defined with RS-232C compatibility in mind. With appropriate provisions it is possible to design RS-449 compatible equipment which can communicate with equipment conforming to the older RS-232C standard. See EIA Industrial Electronics Bulletin No. 12 for application notes concerning interconnection between interface circuits using RS-449 and RS-232C.

Interface Circuits

Before considering the overall design of a serial I/O port, we examine the circuits connecting directly to the serial interface lines. Such circuits include both receiving circuits and driving circuits. Receiving circuits convert the signals received over the interface lines to ordinary (TTL) logic levels. Driving circuits do the reverse. Since the signal levels employed in both interface standards are not ordinary (TTL) levels, these circuits are not standard logic circuits. We start with RS-232C interface circuits.

Interface circuits for RS-232C

The conversion of TTL voltage levels to RS-232C levels (and vice versa) is not a trivial task but it is greatly simplified thanks to the availability of special drivers and receivers. These devices were designed to meet the specific electrical requirements defined in RS-232C.

An example of an RS-232C compatible driver is the Motorola MC1488 quad driver. The corresponding quad receiver for this driver is the MC1489L. Typically, RS-232C drivers require a $+12$ V and a -12 V supply voltage. Receivers require only $+5$ V. Figure 5-33(a) pictures a single interface line driven by one of the four driving circuits of an MC1488. The same line is terminated by one of the four receiving circuits of an MC1489L.

Do we need any external components? The answer is yes. For example, in order to reduce radiated emission to neighboring circuits, RS-232C specifies a **slew rate** of less than 30 V/μs. The idea is to slow down signal transitions and thereby reduce crosstalk to other circuits. Unless the cable presents to the drivers an adequate amount of capacitance, we have to add an external capacitor (see capacitor C_1). Receivers may involve external components too. See, for example,

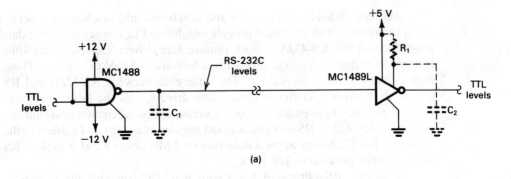

(a)

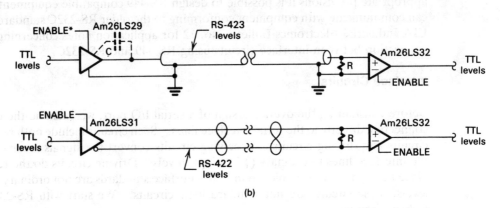

(b)

Figure 5-33. Examples of serial interface circuits for: (a) RS-232C, and (b) RS-422A and RS-423A.

the resistor (R_1) and capacitor (C_2) connecting to the so-called external response control pin of the MC1489L. Such an external resistor may be used to shift the input threshold of the receiver and thus increase noise immunity. C_2 filters noise spikes and thus enhances noise immunity further.

Example 5-23

The signal at the output of the driver swings between -11.75 V and $+11.75$ V [Figure 5-33(a)]. Transitions (in either direction) are almost linear and take 0.5 μs. Do signal transitions meet the RS-232C restriction on slew rate?

In order to meet the slew rate requirements of RS-232C, we decide to add an external capacitor (C_1). What should be its approximate value, given the driver supplies a constant current of about 10 mA?

Solution. During a transition the output voltage varies by a total of $2 \times 11.75 = 23.5$ V. The slew rate is $23.5/0.5 = 47$ V/μs. Hence, signal transitions do not meet the pertinent RS-232C requirement.

The required capacitance can be determined from the relation $q = CV$ where q, V

are the charge and the voltage across a capacitor C, respectively. Taking the derivatives of both sides (in terms of time) we obtain $dq/dt = C(dV/dt)$, or $i = C(dV/dt)$ where i is the current. Equating dV/dt to 30 V/µs and substituting, we get $C = (10/30) \times 10^{-9}$ F, or about 330 pF. If we are to meet the requirement, the driver must see at its output a total capacitance of at least 330 pF. The actual capacitance seen by the driver is calculated from the same relation by substituting 47 V/µs for dV/dt. The result is about 210 pF. This capacitance is contributed mainly by the cable. Thus, in order to meet the slew rate requirement of RS-232C, we must add an external capacitor of at least 330 − 210 = 120 pF.

Interface circuits for RS-449

Similar types of interface circuits are available for RS-422A and RS-423A. Figure 5-33(b) shows three such devices as examples. The first is an AMD Am26LS29 quad single-ended driver conforming to the requirements of RS-423A. It requires a +5 V and a −5 V supply voltage and has tri-state outputs. Each driving circuit of the quad device has a separate slew rate control pin. This provides the means to suppress crosstalk to other interface lines of the cable. It is accomplished by connecting a capacitor of the appropriate value between the slew rate control pin and the output pin of the individual driver. All four drivers of the quad device share a common enable input which allows their outputs to be brought to a floating state. This permits connection of multiple drivers to the same transmission line.

The Am26LS29 of Figure 5-33(b) drives a coaxial cable terminated by an Am26LS32 differential receiver, which is also a quad device. It is intended for both RS-422A and RS-423A. Like the driver, it has an enable input and tri-state outputs. However, it requires only +5 V. Resistor R serves as a terminating resistor for the transmission line. Finally, the Am26LS31 is a quad differential driver intended for RS-422A. It requires only a +5 V supply and is capable of driving twisted-pair and parallel-wire lines terminated at 100 Ω.

Designing Serial I/O Ports

The design principles of a serial I/O port are fairly similar to those of a parallel I/O port. We still need input and output data registers, a status register, and a control register (see Figure 5-1). However, the design of serial I/O port circuits is more involved because of the additional functions they must perform. Such additional functions include:

1. Conversion of the parallel data (sent by the CPU) into a serial bit stream. This is accomplished with a parallel-in/serial-out shift register which is clocked at the appropriate rate.

2. Conversion of the serial data received over the interface lines of the serial port into parallel data for input to the CPU. This is accomplished with a serial-in/parallel-out shift register which is again clocked at the appropriate rate.

3. Generation of a clock signal. In the case of asynchronous communication, such a signal may be generated by simply subdividing the CPU clock frequency. The situation is more complicated in synchronous communication where such a clock must be derived from information received from the other end.

4. Generation of the control signals required by the employed serial interface standard, as well as processing the control signals received from the other end.

5. Conversion to the signal levels required by the employed standard and conversion of received signals to ordinary logic levels.

6. Functions required by the particular protocol we use. Take, for example, the case of asynchronous communication. Data arriving over the serial interface lines include start bits, stop bits, and so on. These bits must be extracted and discarded since the CPU is interested only in actual data. The reverse is required in the opposite direction. That is, before transmitting CPU data we must insert a start bit and one or more stop bits. Such functions become far more complex in the case of synchronous communication protocols.

These additional tasks may increase the total number of required SSI/MSI components to 100 or more. Yet there should be no major concern thanks to integrated serial communication controllers.

Serial Communication Controllers

The design of serial ports is simplified drastically by using LSI/VLSI devices known as **serial communication controllers (SCCs)**, provided you employ one of the popular protocols for which such devices are available. SCCs perform all of the functions we just listed above and (usually) many more. SCCs differ in many ways.

1. *Protocols:* The classes of supported protocols vary from SCC to SCC. For example, a relatively simple controller may support just asynchronous communication. A complex one may support all three classes of protocols—that is, asynchronous, character-oriented, and bit-oriented protocols. Also, SCCs may differ in the number of functions they provide on behalf of a protocol. Such a function, for instance, is the transmission of flag patterns during idle time intervals in BOPs. Unless provided by the SCC, this function will have to be performed by the CPU through software. Furthermore, an SCC may or may not have the flexibility of handling variations within a protocol. For example, some SCCs can handle only the bisync COP pictured in Figure 5-31(b). Others can handle monosync COPs as well (that is, COPs employing only one SYN character per frame).

2. *Data Rates:* First, SCCs supporting asynchronous communication. In general, they are capable of operating over the entire range of speeds employed

in asynchronous communication (0 to 9600 b/s). In SCCs supporting synchronous communication, the maximum rate varies. Some devices permit rates of many Mb/s. Very often the data rate is referred to as the **baud rate**, which actually refers to the number of transmitted code elements per second. However, in the case of binary coding (1s and 0s), baud and bit rates are equal. Baud rates are programmable. They are derived from clock signals which are either supplied externally or generated on-chip (*TxC*, *RxC*). The associated circuitry is often known as a **baud rate generator**. Some manufacturers offer such circuitry in a separate device.

3. *Synchronization:* This becomes an issue in synchronous communication. The SCC must be provided with a receive clock (*RxC*) from its respective DCE (synchronous modems provide such a clock). Some SCCs require a transmit clock (*TxC*) as well. Others give the option of either providing or being provided with a *TxC* clock. Alternatively, an SCC may include on-chip circuits for extraction of the clock from incoming data.

4. *Number of Channels:* Certain SCCs are able to support two channels. Moreover, they may permit each to be configured independently as far as protocols and data rates go.

5. *Supported Modem Control Signals:* Many SCCs do not support all the interface signals shown in Figure 5-32. For most applications, this does not represent a problem, but some may require most or all of these signals. For example, if a system has to be able to answer (automatically) incoming calls for data transfers, it needs the *RI* (ring indicator) signal.

6. *Data Encoding/Decoding:* Binary data are not always encoded into voltage levels the familiar way we know in ordinary logic. Prior to their transmission they may be encoded using some other scheme, for example, NRZ or NRZI. An SCC may or may not include on-chip circuitry for special encoding/decoding schemes.

7. *Special Features:* Such features may, for instance, serve test purposes. Examples are **local loop-back** and **auto-echoing** which refers to the ability of an SCC to transmit on the *TxD* line the very same data it receives over the *RxD* line. In local loop-back mode, the SCC does not transmit any data over the *TxD* line. Instead, the data are looped back internally as if they were ordinary received data.

8. *Interfacing to the CPU:* An SCC is usually compatible with a particular family of CPUs. Some include on-chip circuitry for interfacing to the interrupt and DMA lines of the CPU.

Example of a Serial Communication Controller

Next we examine in some detail a specific SCC—the Western Digital WD1983. This device is a single-channel asynchronous SCC. Figure 5-34 illustrates its organization.

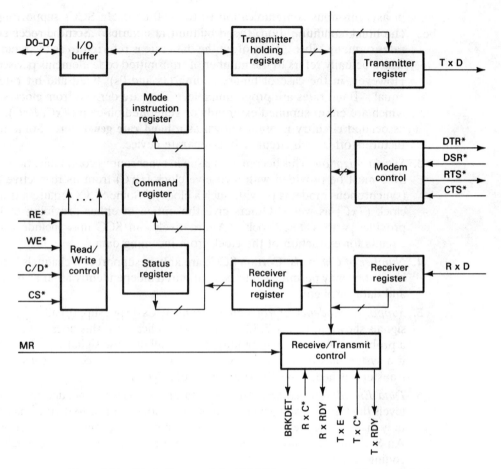

Figure 5-34. Block diagram of the WD1983 asynchronous serial communication controller.

On the left we see the usual signal lines driven by the CPU for selection and access to internal registers. *RE** (read enable) and *WE** (write enable) correspond to the read/write strobe lines we have seen in other controllers. Similarly, *MR* (master reset) corresponds to the *RESET* line. *C/D** (control/data) connects to the least significant address line. It is used by the CPU to indicate whether a control/status or a data register is to be accessed. The information loaded by the CPU in the mode instruction register specifies to the WD1983 which specific asynchronous communication format is to be used—that is, the number of data bits per character, the number of stop bits, and so on.

Let us examine now the lines associated with the receive/transmit control block. The *BRKDET* (break detect) output goes active when the WD1983 receives a string of 0s equal to the total length of a character (including start and stop bits). To see what purpose this serves go back to Figure 5-31(a). Note that during idle periods data lines stay at a high.   There is no limit to how long an idle period can be.   The break condition can be used by the transmitter to alert the receiver that data transmission is to resume.   *RxC** and *TxC** are the receiver and transmitter clock inputs.   *RxRDY* (receiver ready) goes active when an assembled character is transferred from the receiver register to the receiver holding register.   Then, after the CPU reads the new character, *RxRDY* goes back to a low.   The *TxE* (transmit empty) line goes active when the current character is fully transmitted and the transmitter holding register has not yet been loaded with a new character. On the other hand, *TxRDY* (transmit ready) indicates the transmitter holding register can be loaded with a new character.

The remaining lines (on the right in Figure 5-34) connect to the modem (or generally the DCE).   Notice these lines are a subset of the RS-232C lines shown in Figure 5-32.   The WD1983 permits transmission only when the *CTS** (clear to send) input is active.   However, the meaning of the *RTS**, *DTR**, and *DSR** lines is left to the software.   The state of the first two reflects the settings of two specific bits in the command register.   The state of the third is simply provided to the CPU as part of status information.

The CPU loads the mode instruction register at initialization time.   The loaded bit pattern defines the desired character format.   Figure 5-35(a) depicts how the WD1983 interprets the contents of the mode instruction register.   In addition to specifying fully the character format, this register selects the **baud rate factor**.   In other words, it indicates whether the transmit/receive rates are to be equal to the *TxC**/*RxC** clock frequencies or a particular fraction of them.

When a character is to be sent via the serial I/O port, the CPU loads into the transmitter holding register only the data bits.   Then, when its transmitter is ready, the WD1983 transfers the data bits from the transmitter holding register to the transmitter register.   At this point the WD1983 adds the start bit, parity (if any), and the required stop bits.   Subsequently, it transmits the full character over the *TxD* line one bit at a time.   The same steps are involved in the receive direction except that the sequence is reversed.   Unlike the transmitter register which is a parallel-in/serial-out shift register, the receiver register is a serial-in/parallel-out one.   After accumulating in the receiver register a full character, the WD1983 checks the parity (if any).   Then, it transmits to the receiver holding register only the data bits.   It is from this register that the CPU reads the received character. Transmission and reception can proceed in parallel.   Hence, the WD1983 supports full duplex communication.

Figure 5-35(b) illustrates the format of the command word.   The command register provides to the CPU the means of

1. Enabling/disabling transmission or reception
2. Switching the states of the *DTR** and *RTS** lines
3. Resetting any outstanding error conditions
4. Generating an (internal) initialization signal
5. Instructing the WD1983 to transmit (via the *TxD* line) a break character

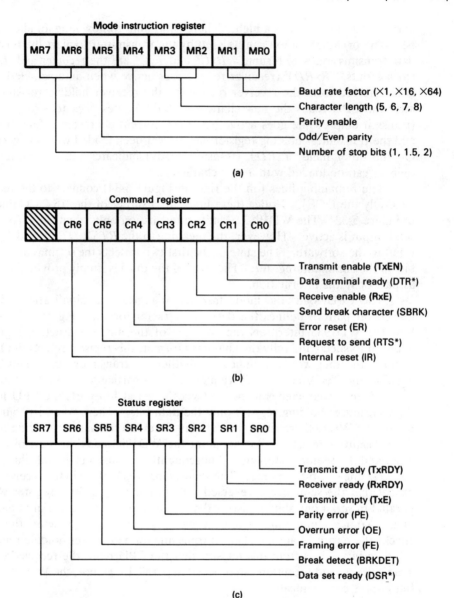

Figure 5-35. Control and status word formats of the WD1983. (a) Mode instruction word format. (b) Command word format. (c) Status word format.

The status register reflects the state of five of the external interface lines (*TxRDY, RxRDY, TxE, BRKDET*, and *DSR**). It also indicates detection of any errors having to do with parity, overruns, and character framing. The parity error bit is set when the WD1983 detects incorrect parity in the received character.

Likewise, the **framing error** bit is set when the stop bit(s) at the end of the received character are invalid. **Overruns** refer to the case where the CPU did not read a character from the receiver holding register on time (that is, before the next character became available from the receiver register).

Example 5-24

Suppose we clock the WD1983 externally at a baud rate of 38.4 KHz (RxC^* and TxC^* inputs). The device has been initialized for a baud rate factor of $\times$ 16. When, at the latest, should a received character be read by the CPU if we are to prevent overruns? Assume the WD1983 has been initialized such that a character includes eight data bits, parity, and two stop bits.

Solution. Since the baud rate factor is $\times$ 16 the actual operating rate of the device is 38,400/16 = 2400 b/s. Each character consists of a total of 12 bits. Hence the character rate is 2400/12 = 200 cps (at maximum). This in turn means that successive characters could be as close as 1/200 = 0.005 s—that is, 5 ms from each other. Hence, once notified of a received character, the CPU should read it within the next 5 ms. Otherwise there is a risk of overruns.

Design Example

Figure 5-36 shows an application example for the WD1983. First of all we need a baud rate generator for provision of the transmit and receive clocks. An alternative solution would be using a programmable timer (see, for instance, the square wave mode of operation of the 8254 in Section 5.5.1). The frequencies of the TxC^* and RxC^* clocks, in conjunction with the programmed baud rate factor, determine the bit rates for transmission and reception. These rates must have the same nominal values as those employed by the DTE attached at the other end of the serial communication channel. However, no synchronization is required. The receiver simply monitors the incoming serial data for detection of the start bit. Thereafter, it synchronizes the sampling of the remaining character bits to the start bit. The maximum number of character bits following a start bit is only 11, so the accumulated distortion is tolerable as long as bit rates remain relatively low. Contrast this with the case of synchronous communication, in which the number of bits between the SYN characters or the flags can be very large and thus the accumulated distortion would be intolerable.

Our next concern is the I/O technique for reading and writing data characters in the WD1983. In this example we assume there is already an 8259A interrupt controller for other I/O devices. Hence, we decide to use two of its spare interrupt request inputs (say, $IR3$, $IR4$) for the SCC. The interrupting signals are $RxRDY$ and $TxRDY$. When the CPU recognizes an interrupt caused through the $IR4$ input, it accesses the receiver holding register to read the newly arrived character. Similarly, when recognizing an interrupt through $IR3$ it goes on to load the next character into the transmitter holding register. Alternatively, we might have ORed $RxRDY$ and $TxRDY$ to drive only one input of the 8259A.

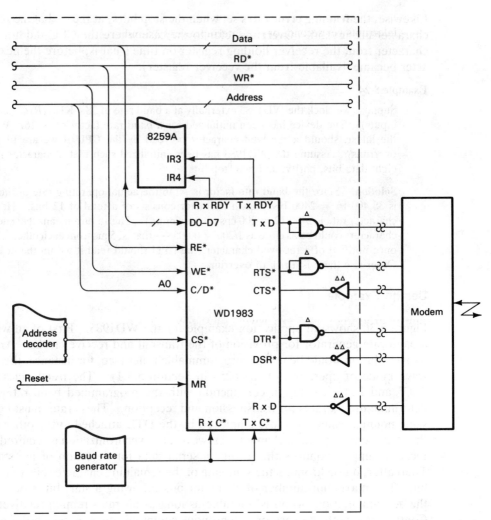

△ TTL to RS-232C level converter (1488 or equivalent)
△△ RS-232C to TTL level converter (1489 or equivalent)

Figure 5-36. Example of a serial I/O interface employing the WD1983.

Example 5-25

The SCC of Figure 5-36 operates at a rate of 2400 b/s. There is a total of 12 bits per character. What is the maximum rate at which the SCC would interrupt the CPU? Determine the average rate of CPU interruptions given the average utilization of the communication channel is only 0.2.

Solution. From the given bit rate and format we deduce a maximum of 2400/12 = 200 cps—that is, one character every 5 ms. In full duplex communication this applies to each direction. Hence, the rate of interruptions by the SCC can be as high as 400 interrupts per second, or one interrupt every 2.5 ms.

Under the given conditions the average character rate is reduced to $400 \times 0.2 = 80$ interrupts per second.

Example 5-26

How would you go about using programmed I/O for the SCC of Figure 5-36?

Solution. The CPU would simply read the status register of the SCC at regular intervals to determine if a new character is available for input and so on. The decision would be based on the state of the RxRDY and TxRDY status bits. In fact, for the receiver, we might choose to use *BRKDET* as an interrupt signal initiating the status scans. This would save CPU time during long idle intervals.

The serial data lines, and those for modem control, interface to the DCE, which in our example is a modem. We assume that our port is RS-232C compatible, so drivers and receivers could be MC1488s and MC1489Ls, respectively. Note that it took only four devices to implement the discussed I/O port: the SCC, a baud rate generator, an RS-232C compatible quad driver, and an RS-232C compatible quad receiver if we consider that the address decoder and the interrupt controller are not used exclusively by the WD1983.

5.5.3 Visual Indicators and Display Modules

Most often it is desirable to convey certain kinds of information visually. For example, the CPU may turn on a lamp to indicate detection of some error condition. Similarly, such an indicator may serve to convey whether the CPU is in a run or halt state. Apart from the occurrence of single events, we may want to display numbers or even messages. Take, for instance, an application involving manual entry of numeric data. During this process it is highly desirable that the system provide a visual display of what has already been entered.

This section deals with those devices that enable visual display of information. We are interested in their principles and operational characteristics and in how to go about designing the associated interface circuits for control of such devices by the CPU. We start with the simplest of all: visual indicators.

Visual Indicators

Usually, visual indicators are implemented by **light emitting diodes (LEDs)**. Like common diodes, LEDs are P-N junction semiconductor devices. They have, however, the special property of emitting light. This occurs under forward bias conditions when electrons and holes recombine. LED forward voltages (V_F) are typically about 2 V. The required forward current (I_F) is usually less than 15 mA. Thus, it is possible to drive them with standard logic circuits. Figure 5-37(a) shows such a case where the driver could be, for instance, a 7404 inverter. As a matter

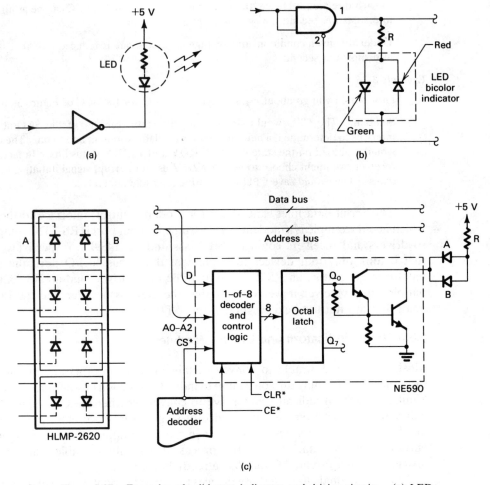

Figure 5-37. Examples of solid-state indicators and driving circuits. (a) LED driven by a common TTL inverter. (b) LED bicolor indicator driven by a differential driver. (c) HP HLMP-2620 LED light bar and the NE590 addressable peripheral driver.

of fact, the so-called low current LEDs require forward currents as low as 2 mA. In any case, the forward current is determined by a series **current-limiting resistor**. Some LEDs incorporate an integral current-limiting resistor to eliminate the need for an external one.

Example 5-27

Consider an LED with a V_F of 2 V and an I_F of 10 mA. The device is driven by a TTL inverter in a way similar to the one pictured in Figure 5-37(a). Determine the value of the required series resistor given that the saturation voltage (V_{CE}) across the output of the inverter is about 0.3 V.

Solution. The value of the current-limiting series resistor is determined from the expression $R = (V_{cc} - V_F - V_{CE}) / I_F$, where V_{cc} is the supply voltage. Substituting the numeric values we have $R = (5 - 2 - 0.3) / 0.01 = 270\ \Omega$.

The LED is on only when the input of the inverter is at a high. At this point, the output of the inverter is at a low, acting as a current sink. When the inverter input is at a low, its output is at a high of approximately 3.5 volts, so the LED stays off.

LEDs are available in red, green, and other colors. Some manufacturers combine two LEDs of different colors in a dual in-line package (DIP) to form a **bicolor indicator**. This case is illustrated in Figure 5-37(b). Now we need a driver capable of reversing the voltage polarity across the two LEDs. Such a characteristic is inherent in differential drivers whose outputs are always in opposite states. When the input of the driver of Figure 5-37(b) is at a high, output 1 is at a high and output 2 at a low. Under these conditions the indicator will be green because only the green indicator is forward biased. When the input of the driver is switched to a low, the states of outputs 1 and 2 are reversed. As a result, the indicator turns red. The so-called **light bars** are combinations of four or more LEDs. Such devices serve the implementation of multiple indicators. Figure 5-37(c) shows a device combining eight red color LEDs in a 16-pin DIP for implementation of four indicators. Unlike single LEDs, light bars provide larger and brighter indicators permitting attachment of legends as well.

How does a CPU control the state of a visual indicator? Going back to Figure 5-6 we see that LEDs may be connected directly to the output of some addressable latch. What if the latch cannot provide the required current drive? In such cases the LEDs connect to the latch via a buffer. When an excessive current drive is necessary, you may consider using darlington transistor arrays (such arrays of up to seven darlington pairs are available in DIPs). The same buffering considerations apply when indicators are driven through port lines of an I/O interface controller.

To facilitate designs with multiple indicators some manufacturers combine in a single device an addressable latch, buffers, and other circuitry. Figure 5-37(c) shows as an example the Signetics NE590 addressable peripheral driver. This device combines a decoder, an octal latch, and eight darlington transistor pairs. It connects to one of the lines of the (CPU) data bus and to three address lines which provide the means of identifying which particular bit of the latch is to be set or reset. Such a device could accommodate, for instance, two of the light bars shown in Figure 5-37(c). Regardless of how they are driven, visual indicators are always handled by the CPU the direct I/O way.

Display Modules

Display modules serve to output numeric, alphanumeric, and even graphic information. In its simplest form a module displays a single numeric digit. It can be mounted on a standard IC socket. The other side of the spectrum concerns mod-

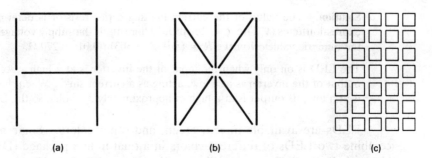

Figure 5-38. Numeric and alphanumeric character fonts. (a) Seven-segment font for numeric characters. (b) Sixteen-segment font for numeric and (upper case) alphabetic characters. (c) 5 × 7 dot matrix for numeric and alphabetic characters (upper and lower case).

ules capable of displaying many lines of alphanumeric information. These ones may include driving circuits and even power supplies. They may mount on the front panel of a system or even be treated as separate subsystems. However, when the amount of information to be displayed is large—for example, 20 lines of 80 characters each—we resort to CRT displays, which are larger, more complex subsystems and are treated as computer peripherals (see Chapter 6).

First, let us discuss the principles of character formation. Although there is a variety of module types and fonts, the basic principle is the same: Each character position consists of an array of display elements. A particular character is formed by activating the appropriate combination of display elements. For example, Figure 5-38(a) shows a **seven-segment character font** employed for display of numeric symbols. By activating the appropriate set of segments, this simple font allows formation of any numeric symbol and a small number of alphabetic ones.

The **16-segment font** shown in Figure 5-38(b) accommodates:

- Numeric symbols
- Upper case alphabetic symbols
- Special symbols

and can support a 64-character set. To support a larger character set, such as the ASCII 96-character one, we need more segments. Usually, however, we resort to a **dot matrix font** instead. Figure 5-38(c) illustrates a 5 × 7 dot matrix font. A display module may include a few additional segments (or dots) for special purposes such as decimal points.

Here are some of the factors you should consider when selecting a display module.

1. Information content. This depends on the employed character set and the total number of displayable characters.

2. **Character size.** Character sizes vary from a small fraction of an inch to several inches. The choice should be made on the basis of the reading distance associated with a particular application.

3. **Power consumption and supply voltages.**

4. **Color and brightness.**

5. **Overall physical size, interface characteristics, cost, and so on.**

Some of the listed characteristics depend on the kind of technology employed in the implementation of the segments or dots. In the remaining part of this section we examine display modules based on:

- LEDs
- Liquid crystals
- Other technologies

LED Displays

In LED display modules, the segments (or dots) are produced by means of light emitting diodes. Such modules may provide one or more characters. Usually they are end-stackable to facilitate formation of larger displays. Their size is small (and often compatible with standard DIPs) for easy mounting on a circuit board. A variety of devices is available for driving LED display modules. In fact some can drive multicharacter modules.

Example of a driver for numeric displays

Figure 5-39 shows an example of such a device—the Teledyne TSC 700A decoder/driver. This device can handle up to four seven-segment LED displays having a common anode. Here we assume it interfaces to the CPU through an 8255 I/O interface controller. Note from Figure 5-39 that the TSC 700A has a separate select line for each digit and four data input lines. Consequently we need an 8-bit port for its control.

Suppose the CPU is to display a new value in the most significant bit position. To accomplish this, it places on the *PB0–PB3* lines the BCD code corresponding to the new value. It also sets to a high *PB7* for selection of the left-most digit. When this happens, the TSC 700A enables the decoder of the left-most digit which maps the presented BCD code into a 7-bit binary pattern. This pattern is then strobed into the respective 7-bit data latch for activation of the corresponding segment drivers. Thereafter the contents of the latch remain unchanged until updated by the CPU again. The brightness control input permits control of the on-resistance of the segment drivers and thereby segment brightness. A common potentiometer may serve this purpose.

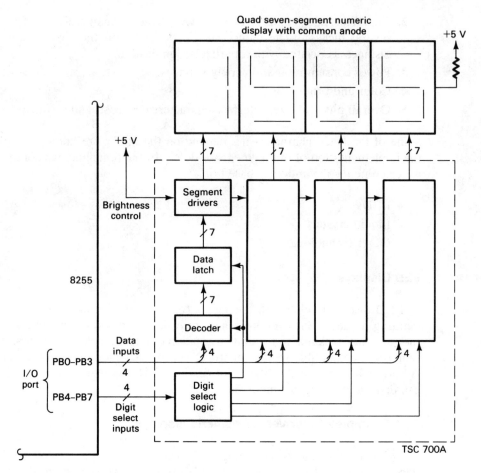

Figure 5-39. Example of a seven-segment display driver controlled via a parallel I/O port.

Multiplexing

In the preceding example the total number of segments is 28. However, consider the case of an eight-character alphanumeric display employing a 16-segment font. The total number of segments is now 128! If we were to use the same approach we would need many drivers and a large number of interconnections. This problem motivated the use of multiplexing in the driving of multicharacter displays. Multiplexing allows character modules to time-share a common set of segment drivers. Hence, it simplifies the situation drastically. An example will demonstrate how multiplexed driving works.

Example of a driver for alphanumeric displays

Figure 5-40 illustrates the simplified block diagram of the Intercil ICM7243A display driver. Thanks to multiplexing, this device can handle (small common cathode) eight-character alphanumeric displays. Observe that the total number of segment drivers is only 17 (16 plus one for the decimal point). Instead, there are eight character select lines (one per character). The ICM7243A activates the character select lines sequentially on a one-at-a-time basis. Therefore the segments of each character are driven only for 12.5 percent of the time. LED displays are especially suitable for multiplexing because their luminous intensity varies almost linearly with the driving current. By using higher currents we can compensate for the fact that the segments of each character are not driven continuously.

The ICM7243A employs an 8×6 bit RAM storing the 6-bit ASCII character codes of the eight characters it handles. A free-running oscillator advances con-

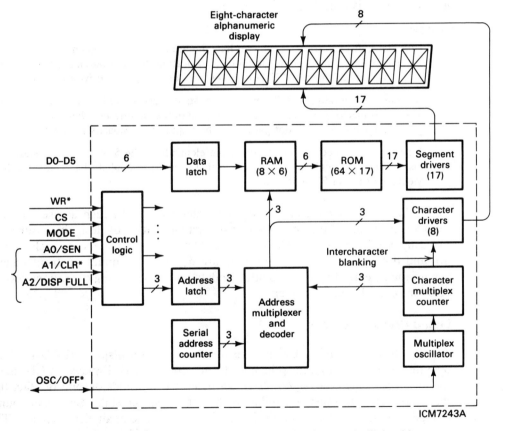

Figure 5-40. Example of an eight-character alphanumeric display driver.

tinuously the character multiplex counter whose contents activate via the address multiplexer one of the eight character drivers. At the same time, the contents of the character multiplex counter are presented to the RAM as an address. The character code read from the RAM is then translated (through a 64 × 17 ROM) into the respective 17-bit pattern. It is this pattern which controls the state of the segment drivers. Prior to advancing to the next character, the multiplex counter disables all character drivers for an interval of about 10 μs. The idea is to eliminate the **ghosting effect** produced during the transition from one character to another. Character codes are written by the CPU in the RAM either randomly or sequentially. The write mode is controlled through the control lines seen on the left in Figure 5-40. The same lines permit control of the frequency of the internal oscillator, among other things.

Multiplexing is also the favored technique when it comes to alphanumeric displays employing dot matrix fonts. Indeed, the number of elements per character in such displays is even larger.

Example 5-28

Consider a display driver capable of handling up to 20 characters employing a 5 × 7 dot matrix font. Suppose the driver employs a ROM for translation purposes. What is the capacity of the ROM? How many lines are needed to drive the display?

Solution. Generally, 5 × 7 dot matrix fonts can accommodate a 96-character set. The ROM has to be capable of decoding each of the 96 different character codes into the corresponding 5 × 7 dot pattern. The required bit capacity is then 96 × 35.

First of all we need 35 lines to drive the elements of the 5 × 7 dot matrices. We also need one select line per character—that is, an additional 20 character select lines yielding a total of 55 signal lines.

What if you need a display of many characters? In such a case you may consider using an off-the-shelf display subsystem instead of designing your own. Typically, such display subsystems support 32 or more characters and include control and driving circuits. Usually they are designed to mount on front panels. Some provide extra functions facilitating data entry and editing operations such as deletion of a selected character.

Liquid Crystal Displays

Another type of popular displays are the **liquid crystal displays (LCDs)**. They operate on entirely different principles from those of LED displays. LCDs make use of special organic compounds which behave like liquids despite the fact that their molecular structure is similar to that of a solid crystal. Such compounds change their light transmission properties in the presence of an electric field. This is precisely what provides the basis for information display.

In the so-called **nematic LCDs** the liquid crystals are sealed between two glass plates which are in turn sandwiched between two plastic films capable of polarizing light.   To see how it operates, let us consider the approach in which a reflective material is placed behind the rear polarizer.   In the absence of an electric field, ambient light passes through the described assembly and is simply reflected back. However, the situation changes if any elements of the display are subjected to an appropriate electric field, in which case the ambient light will be absorbed and the elements will appear dark.   In other words, characters will appear dark against a light-reflecting (usually silver) background.   By changing the orientation of the two polarizers it is possible to construct an LCD that does the reverse—that is, displays characters as light-reflecting areas against a dark background.

The so-called **dichroic LCDs** employ a different technique.   Instead of po-larizers, liquid crystals are combined with a special dichroic dye.   In this case, absence of an electric field causes absorption of certain wavelengths.   However, display elements subjected to an electric field do not exhibit such spectral absorp-tion.   Hence displayed characters will appear colorless on a colored background.

A major disadvantage of LCDs is that they required AC voltages because application of an electric field in one direction, results in electrolytic phenomena, which shorten their life.   The required voltage levels are generally low, however. For example, nematic LCDs require 2 to 5 V (rms values) and are usually operated at a frequency of 30 to 50 Hz.   Another disadvantage is that, since they do not generate light, they cannot be read in the dark.   Two advantages are that

1. LCDs need very low current drives.   This is a direct consequence of the principles of their operation.   For example, nematic LCDs require currents amounting to no more than several $\mu A/in^2$.   This, in conjunction with their low operating voltages, means very low power consumption, so LCDs are ideal for portable and other battery-operated systems.

2. LCDs are readable in direct sunlight (while LED displays are not).

The capacities of commercially available LCD modules vary from a few nu-meric characters to many lines of alphanumeric (or even graphic) information. There are also multicharacter drivers analogous to those we have seen for LED displays.   The main difference is that such drivers include additional circuits for generation of the necessary AC voltage waveforms.   An alternative to designing your own LCD display is using an off-the-shelf LCD subsystem.   Such subsystems have capabilities similar to those we have seen for LEDs.   Again, they should be considered seriously when the number of displayed characters is large.

Other Types of Displays

Though not as widely employed, there are several other technologies for infor-mation display, including gas discharge and vacuum fluorescent displays.   Both require voltages higher than those of standard logic families.   Normally they are available as self-contained display subsystems (including control/drive electronics and power supplies). They are mainly intended for applications involving the display of substantial amounts of information.

A **gas discharge display** consists of a gas "envelope" formed between two parallel glass plates. These plates accommodate the anode and cathode conductors implementing the desired character font. For example, in seven-segment gas discharge displays there is one anode and seven cathodes per numeric character. In other words, a cathode plays the role of a segment. A cathode is turned on by applying a sufficiently high voltage between itself and the anode. This ionizes the gas and generates a bright light around the selected cathode. For example, in the case of neon gas, the ionization voltage is around 170 V. The generated light is orange. The need for such a high voltage represents a drawback for this type of display.

Vacuum fluorescent displays (VFD) are somewhat similar to the old vacuum triode. They too use cathode filaments, control grids, and anodes. The difference is that each anode consists of many segments (whose number depends on the character font). Besides, each anode is coated with a fluorescent material. A display element is turned on by applying the appropriate voltages on the grid and the corresponding anode segment. In this way, electrons produced by the cathode flow through the grid and hit the selected anode segment. The energy of the electrons agitates the phosphoric coating which emits a blue-green light. VFDs require an additional supply of about 6 V for their heating filaments. On the other hand, they have the advantage of lower anode voltages (typically 10 to 40 V). Some commercially available drivers have been designed to withstand anode voltages as high as 40 V and hence can drive VFDs directly.

5.6 MICROCOMPUTER BUSES

With this discussion of the basic I/O support devices, we conclude our presentation of input/output. In fact, at this point, we have examined all sections of a μC except peripherals. Looking at Figure 5-41, let us review in brief each of these sections:

1. *CPU* (*Chapter 2*): This section represents the CPU itself. It amounts to a single μP device.
2. *CPU Support Circuits* (*Chapter 3*): It includes CPU support circuits such as:
   (a) A clock generator
   (b) Bus buffers and (possibly) address latches
   (c) Bus transceivers
   (d) A reset circuit
   (e) A wait state generation circuit
3. *Memory* (*Chapter 4*): The main components of this section are RAMs and read-only memory devices. It also includes memory support components such as address decoders and dynamic memory controllers.

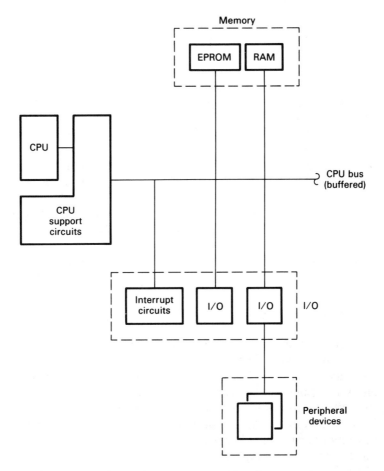

Figure 5-41.   Functional block diagram of a microcomputer system.

4. *I/O* (*Chapter 5*): This section is shown to consist of three parts. First, there are interrupt circuits which usually amount to a single programmable interrupt controller. They serve interrupts generated by peripheral devices and other interrupt sources such as timers. The second part (on the right of the interrupt circuits block) represents I/O circuits which do not relate to peripheral devices—for example, I/O circuits interfacing to switches and visual indicators. The third (and last) part of the I/O section represents I/O circuits interfacing to peripherals. Typically, it includes I/O interface controllers, buffers for the I/O port lines, and terminating resistors. It may also include circuits for one or more serial ports for devices such as character printers or terminals.

In all of this, however, we have ignored the physical aspects of the design. In fact, our design examples have assumed that memory and I/O circuits connect to the (buffered) CPU bus. The implication was that the CPU and all such circuits are accommodated on the same circuit board. This may indeed be the case in small μC systems, such as one based on an 8-bit CPU equipped with 8 KB of ROM and 64 KB of RAM. This system may also include some low-speed peripherals such as a keyboard, a character printer, and a CRT display. Here our circuitry amounts to two parallel I/O ports (for the keyboard and the printer) and one serial port (for the CRT). It is thus possible to place all components associated with CPU, memory, and I/O on a single circuit board. The three peripherals can connect to the circuit board by means of edge connectors or by means of connectors plugging into board-mounted connector sockets.

On the other hand, consider a large μC system based on a 32-bit CPU with 64 KB of ROM and 4 MB of RAM, with a few low-speed peripherals and some high-speed ones (a disk, a magnetic tape unit, and a high-speed printer, for example). Now we may need several boards for accommodation of all the circuits of the system. This in turn raises a number of questions:

- How do we partition the circuitry among boards?
- How do we interconnect the boards?

Need for a higher level bus

For partitioning of the circuits among boards we should employ the general criteria discussed in Section 1.4. These criteria suggest placing on one board the CPU and its support circuits, as well as any circuits interfacing directly to the CPU and serving many other parts of the system—as, for instance, interrupt circuits. We will refer to this board as the CPU board (Figure 5-42). Memory and I/O are implemented on separate boards (**memory boards** and **I/O boards**). The amount of memory or I/O circuitry placed on these boards depends (among other factors) on the size of the employed circuit board. Furthermore, I/O circuits could be distributed among I/O boards on the basis of their complexity. For example, one I/O board may be dedicated to all slow peripherals using programmed and interrupt-driven I/O. Another I/O board may be dedicated to DMA and other complex I/O control circuits required for disk and tape units.

What kind of interconnection scheme should we employ among the CPU, memory, and I/O boards? As with partitioning, the main criterion is the minimization of interconnections among the circuit boards (Section 1.4). It turns out that this criterion is satisfied best by employing a common set of signal lines for interboard communication. At first it looks like all we have to do is extend the (buffered) CPU bus to the rest of the circuit boards. Doing just that, however, would not be adequate. What we need is a higher level bus which includes (in addition to other CPU bus signals):

1. Multiple interrupt request lines serving the I/O boards
2. Bus control signals for priority resolution when two or more circuit boards contend for bus mastership

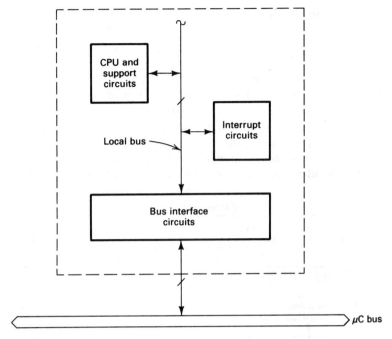

Figure 5-42.   Block diagram of a typical CPU board.

Such a bus is commonly known as a **microcomputer (μC) bus.**   Very often it is also referred to as a **system bus.**   In contrast, the CPU bus (on the CPU board) is called a **local bus** (see Figure 5-42).   Note that in addition to the above extra signals a μC bus may also provide more data transfer control signals.   The latter are derived on the CPU board by decoding appropriate CPU signals.   The idea is to economize decoding circuitry on the rest of the circuit boards.   For example, a μC bus may provide separate read/write strobes for memory and I/O.

Bus interface circuits

Going back to the CPU board, we realize the need for circuits buffering the local (CPU) bus from the μC bus (Figure 5-42).   These bus interface circuits:

1. Provide the extra driving capability required by the (physically longer) μC bus.

2. Insulate the local bus from the μC bus.   Such insulation permits the two buses to carry on data transfers in parallel and independently of each other. It is advantageous when the CPU board includes local (on-board) memory. For example, an I/O and a memory board could exchange data while the CPU fetches instructions from its local memory.

3. Generate the signals employed for control of the μC bus (priority resolution for bus mastership).

Example of a bus-based μC

Figure 5-43 pictures a microcomputer system organized around a μC bus. Besides the CPU board, this system includes two memory boards and many I/O boards. All boards interconnect via the μC bus. The CPU board also connects to visual indicators and some switches, both of which are mounted on the front panel of the system. The indicators display the present state of the system (running, halted, waiting), and the switches serve power on/off, system initialization, manual starting/stopping of progrm execution, and so on.

The I/O boards include a speech synthesizing board, a serial communication board providing multiple serial I/O ports, an analog I/O board, and a number of

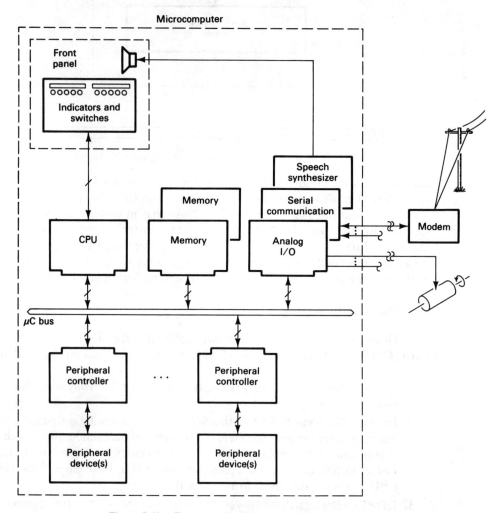

Figure 5-43. Example of a bus-based microcomputer system.

peripheral controllers.   Each of the latter handles one or more peripheral devices, depending on the complexity of such devices.

Some other advantages and drawbacks

Bus interface circuits become necessary for memory and I/O boards too, so organizing a system around a μC bus means increased component and other costs. On the other hand, the bus approach facilitates system modularity and thereby yields a number of advantages (see also Section 1.4):

1. Permits use of the same boards in multiple products (as long as such products employ the same μC bus).
2. Permits expansion of a system's capabilities by adding new types of boards or by redesigning certain of the existing ones.   This is more economical than redesigning the entire system.
3. Makes system maintenance easier.

How do we implement a μC bus?   What signal lines are involved?   How do we control interrupts over a μC bus?   Who is in control of the bus?   How?   What about standards for such buses?   How do we go about interfacing to a μC bus? What problems do we face in the course of designing and using μC buses?   How do we go about solving such problems?   These are the kind of topics we will be dealing with in the remaining part of this section.

Structure of a μC Bus

In Section 1.3 we looked at how electronic systems are packaged (see Figure 1-6). We saw that printed circuit boards (PCBs) are plugged into connectors which are mounted on another board called a backplane.   The backplane provides the interconnections among the PCBs it accommodates.   It also distributes power to all boards.   Since a μC bus serves to interconnect the boards of a μC system, it is implemented right on the backplane itself.   Figure 5-44(a) pictures such a backplane.

The signal lines are etched on the backplane and run across from connector to connector.   They interconnect corresponding pins of the connectors and thereby distribute the μC bus to all circuit boards.   An often used practice is etching the traces carrying the bus signals and the supply voltages on one side, and dedicating the other side to a **ground plane**.   The objective is to minimize noise (see Section 4.1.1 for noise problems on printed circuit boards).

In general, the total number of bus lines is in the range of 50 to 100.   Figure 5-44(b) pictures the bus lines grouped on the basis of the functions they perform. Turning back to Figure 2-3, you can see that these groups are exactly the same as the groups of external interface lines in a typical CPU.   This, of course, is not surprising since the types of functions we must be able to perform over a μC bus

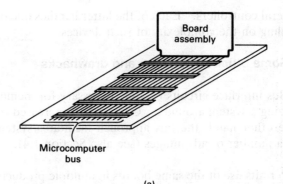

(a)

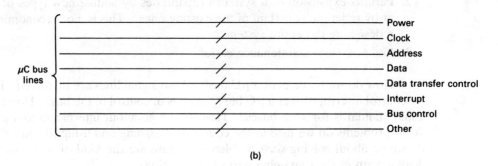

(b)

Figure 5-44. (a) Microcomputer bus lines etched on a backplane (or motherboard). (b) Types of signal lines in a typical microcomputer bus.

are the same as those we do over a CPU bus. However, while the groups are the same, the individual lines of corresponding groups do not necessarily perform identical functions. This will become clear as we discuss each group of lines separately.

1. *Power Lines:* This group includes a number of lines for $+5$ V and a few lines for some other voltages (usually $+12$ and -12 V). It also includes many ground lines.

2. *Clock Lines:* The (master) clock is usually generated on the CPU board. It is distributed to the rest of the boards through a clock line. Another line may carry a different clock signal intended for special use—for example, for advancing counters or timers.

3. *Address Lines:* The number of address lines determines how large the address space of the μC system is. Typically this number is between 20 and 32.

4. *Data Lines:* μC buses do not usually multiplex address and data signals (as CPUs often do), so there is a separate set of bus lines for data. Their number may be 8, 16, or even 32. The width of the data bus determines how many

transceivers we need.   Consequently, it impacts on the complexity of the bus interface circuits needed on each of the circuit boards.

5. *Data Transfer Control Lines:* This group carries the read/write strobes and a signal analogous to the *READY* signal of a CPU.   It may also carry an address strobe.

6. *Interrupt Lines:* Compared to CPUs, μC buses dedicate a larger number of lines to interrupts.   Typically there are about eight interrupt request lines and an interrupt acknowledge line.   The interrupt request lines correspond to the synonymous input lines of a programmable interrupt controller which is usually part of the CPU board.

7. *Bus Control Lines:* These lines serve to transfer μC bus mastership.   Bus mastership may be transferred temporarily from the CPU board to a (DMA) I/O board (or possibly another CPU board).

8. *Other Lines:* The remaining lines of a μC bus are used for initialization, indication of status conditions, and other miscellaneous purposes.

Next we examine some of the schemes employed for interrupts and bus arbitration in μC buses.

Interrupts over a μC Bus

When an I/O board needs CPU attention, it causes an interrupt through the interrupt lines of the μC bus.   This may be accomplished either with the nonvectored approach or with the vectored one.   The two schemes are illustrated in Figure 5-45.   Before examining each of these typical approaches, we consider the bus "master" and bus "slave" labels seen in the figure.

The name **bus master** is used for circuit boards capable of gaining bus mastership.   Such are CPU boards and I/O boards equipped with DMA capability. Once they gain bus mastership, these boards proceed to perform their own data transfers over the μC bus.   In contrast, **bus slaves** cannot acquire the μC bus. They simply monitor the address lines and respond to control signals generated by masters.   What if a slave needs the attention of a master?   In this case it proceeds to cause an interrupt via the interrupt request lines of the μC bus.

Figure 5-45(a) depicts one of the schemes a slave may employ for this purpose. Notice that each slave is strapped to one of the interrupt request lines ($INT0^*$– $INTn^*$) of the μC bus.   When its interrupt request flip-flop is set, the slave activates the respective interrupt request bus line.   From there on, it causes activation of the master's interrupt control logic.   This approach permits direct identification of the requesting slave.   Could we possibly strap two or more slaves to the very same interrupt request line?   The answer is yes.   In fact, this becomes a necessity when the number of interrupting boards exceeds the number of interrupt request lines of the bus.   To facilitate such wire-ORing of interrupt requests, $INT0^*$– $INTn^*$ lines are usually driven by open collector circuits.   (Note the pull-up re-

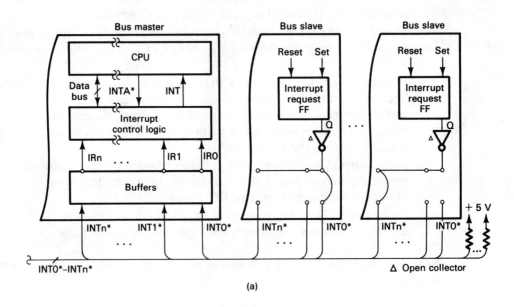

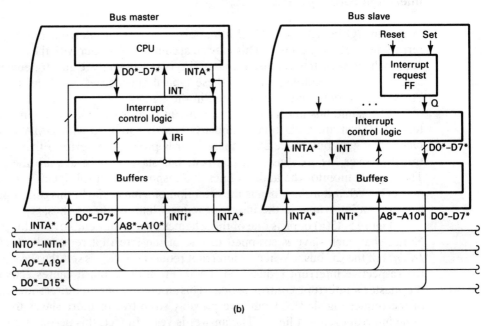

Figure 5-45.   Typical interrupt schemes employed in microcomputer buses.   (a) Non-bus-vectored interrupts.   (b) Bus-vectored interrupts.

sistors on the right side of the last slave.) When such is the case, the CPU cannot determine immediately who caused the interrupt. It can do so, however, after examining the status of the slaves sharing that particular interrupt request line. The point is that in neither case does the slave provide an interrupt vector to the CPU. This justifies why this scheme is called a **non-bus-vectored** interrupt scheme.

What if a slave has two or more interrupt sources? For example, a slave board may be accommodating several interrupt-driven I/O ports. Our options are:

1. After the interrupt, read the status of the slave. From this, the CPU could determine which particular event (at the slave) caused the current interrupt.

2. Allocate to the slave two or more interrupt request lines (say one per I/O port).

Both solutions have serious problems. The first one does not permit the CPU to jump directly to the service routine of the interrupting I/O port, so it lacks efficiency. The second one wastes interrupt request lines we may need in the future for system expansion.

A better alternative is provided by the scheme pictured in Figure 5-45(b). Observe that the slave now has its own interrupt control logic. Also, it connects to the interrupt acknowledge line ($INTA^*$) of the bus. The sequence of events goes as follows:

1. The slave activates the interrupt request line it is strapped to ($INTi^*$). No other slave is strapped to this request line. Hence, the CPU identifies this slave directly. What the CPU does not know, though, is which particular source of the slave caused the current interrupt. To find out, it proceeds to the next step.

2. The CPU activates the $INTA^*$ line. At the same time it places on the address lines a code identifying this particular slave. In Figure 5-45(b) we employ address lines $A8^*$–$A10^*$. Hence, the CPU would be able to identify up to eight such slaves.

3. The slave board recognizes its address, but it does not proceed further. It waits for a second $INTA^*$

4. When the CPU sends the second $INTA^*$, the slave places on the data lines of the μC bus a vector which then leads the CPU to the service routine of the interrupting source. That is, the slave employs vectors to identify to the CPU which of its interrupt sources caused an interrupt (for example, which of its I/O ports).

This scheme is referred to as a **bus-vectored** interrupt scheme. Clearly, it is far more powerful than the first scheme we discussed. On the other hand, it requires equipping the slave with interrupt control logic.

Bus Arbitration

What if two or more masters contend for bus mastership? How is it decided which of the contending parts is to obtain the µC bus? This is accomplished by means of **bus arbitration lines.** These lines belong to the group of bus control lines.

A popular approach is employing two arbitration lines for priority resolution:

1. A bus priority in (*BPRN**) input line
2. A bus priority out (*BPRO**) output line

When active, *BPRN** indicates to a master that none of the higher priority masters is competing for the µC bus. If our particular master wants to gain bus mastership, it drives *BPRO** to a high to prevent lower priority masters from doing so. Otherwise, it activates *BPRO**, indicating to the next lower priority master that it may proceed to obtain the bus (if it needs to). Having two such lines makes possible priority resolution in a number of ways.

Figure 5-46(a) depicts how we can resolve priority serially by interconnecting the masters in a daisy chain fashion. The master on the left is the highest priority one. Its *BPRN** input is strapped to the ground (and is thereby always active). Consequently it can proceed to gain bus mastership any time, provided of course, the bus is at present nonbusy. However, if it does not need the bus, it keeps its *BPRO** output line to a low. This permits the next (lower priority) master to have its chance, and so on. Such a technique is called a **serial priority resolving technique.** Notice it requires no external components. On the other hand, it has serious limitations due to the propagation delays associated with it.

Figure 5-46(b) pictures a **parallel priority resolving technique**. Once again we use the *BPRN** lines. However, instead of *BPRO** we use the *BREQ** (bus request) lines. As you see, this technique necessitates external logic. The *BREQ** outputs of all masters are fed to a priority encoder. Recall that such devices place on their output lines a 3-bit code corresponding to the highest priority currently active input. For this application it means that the code will indicate the highest priority master currently requesting the bus. The 3-bit code is then decoded by an octal decoder which drives to a low only the *BPRN** input of that master, so the latter proceeds to obtain the bus while the rest of the competing masters wait. The parallel priority resolving technique overcomes the limitations of the serial one. We will come back to this subject shortly.

µC Bus Standards

Many µC manufacturers design their systems according to already defined µC buses. Such buses were introduced and are supported by groups of manufacturers. Some are even industry-standard. The specifications of these buses define their

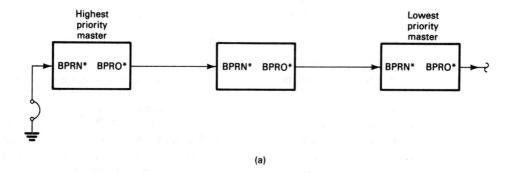

(a)

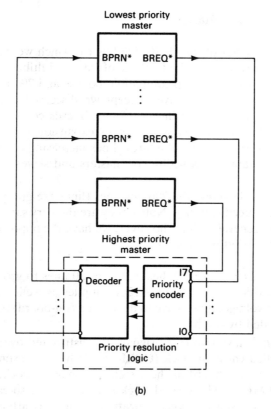

(b)

Figure 5-46. Bus arbitration techniques.   (a) Serial priority resolving technique.
(b) Parallel priority resolving technique.

functional, electrical, and mechanical characteristics. Included among the mechanical characteristics are:

1. The dimensions of the circuit boards
2. The types of connectors
3. Connector pin assignment and, in some cases, even connector spacing

Figure 5-47 pictures some of the main characteristics of two popular μC buses. The first is an approved IEEE standard known as the **IEEE-796 μC bus standard**. The second one is the **VME bus**. Notice that both allow variations in the address and data widths. In fact, the VME bus supports both single and double size circuit boards. Next we examine in more detail the μC bus defined in the IEEE-796 standard.

IEEE-796 μC Bus Standard

The characteristics of the IEEE-796 bus (to which we will be referring simply as the 796 bus) are very much like those of Intel's Multibus. It is supported by many manufacturers offering 796-compatible boards and 796-based products. The 796 bus employs the master/slave concept we discussed previously. As seen from Figure 5-47, it defines 86 lines. Circuit boards connect to the bus through the edge indicated by P1. Edge P2 serves expansion purposes (for example, it accommodates four additional address lines increasing the total address width from 20 to 24). Data access widths for masters and slaves can be either eight, or 16 bits wide.

Figure 5-48 shows the 796 bus lines (lines are grouped somewhat differently in the IEEE specification). Notice they are the very same groups of lines we listed for buses in general. Here, however, we have the opportunity to see what specific signals are carried by each group.

1. *Power Lines:* The 796 bus dedicates 20 lines to ground and supply voltages. It provides for $+12$ and -12 V supplies as well. If a board requires some other voltage, it will have to be derived (on-board) from the standard voltages provided by the bus.
2. *Clock Lines:* Two clock signals are distributed over the bus. The first one is called **constant clock (CCLK*)**. It has a constant frequency and can be used by any board of the system as a master clock. Its nominal frequency is 10 MHz. The second clock line carries the so-called **bus clock (BCLK*)** which is used for synchronization of the bus arbitration logic. It may be slowed down, single-stepped, or even stopped. The important thing to note is that both clocks are generated by one (and only one) source within the μC system.
3. *Address Lines:* The 796 bus provides separate address spaces for memory and

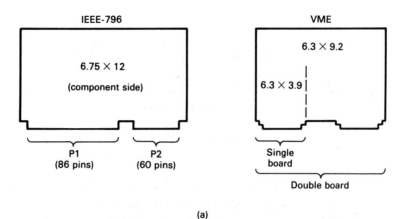

(a)

	IEEE-796	VME Bus
Number of pins	86	96
Address width	20/24	16/24/32
Data width	8/16	8/16/32
Bus type	Non-multiplexed	Non-multiplexed
Interrupt levels	8	7
Bus arbitration scheme	Serial or parallel	Serial or parallel

(b)

Figure 5-47. Main characteristics of two widely used μC buses. (a) Board dimensions for the IEEE-796 and VME buses. (b) Other characteristics of the same buses. Indicated dimensions are in inches.

I/O. All 24 address lines can be employed for memory addressing. Hence the memory address space amounts to 16 MB. On the other hand, an I/O address can be either eight or 16 bits long, so the I/O address space may be as large as 64 KB.

4. *Data Lines:* Data lines ($D0^*$–$D15^*$) are bidirectional. They can be used for both 8- and 16-bit transfers.

5. *Data Transfer Control Lines:* Different read/write strobes are provided for memory and I/O. These strobes are generated only by masters and are called

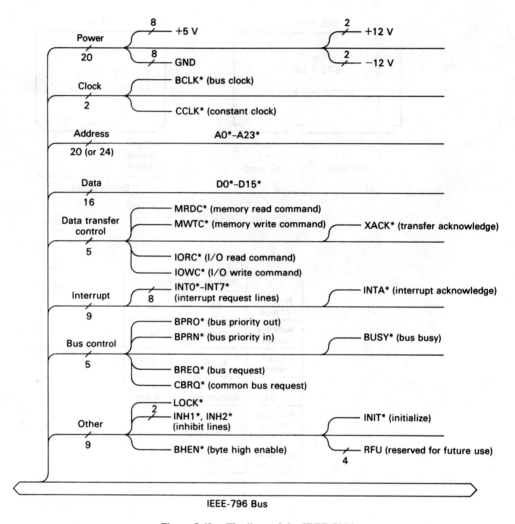

Figure 5-48. The lines of the IEEE-796 bus.

command signals. How does a slave respond to a read/write strobe? The response signal is named *XACK** (transfer acknowledge). A slave activates this line when the associated data transfer cycle is complete.

6. *Interrupt Lines:* This group consists of eight interrupt request lines (*INT0*–INT7**) and an interrupt acknowledge line (*INTA**). These lines permit implementation of either one of the two schemes pictured in Figure 5-45.

7. *Bus Control Lines:* Two of these lines serve bus arbitration purposes (*BPRN** and *BPRO**). They can be used to resolve priority either serially or in parallel (see Figure 5-46). When a master needs the bus, it activates the bus request

($BREQ^*$) line.   After gaining bus mastership it brings the bus busy ($BUSY^*$) line to a low, which prevents other masters from gaining the bus until released by the current master.   Besides $BREQ^*$, there is a "common" bus request line ($CBRQ^*$), which is intended for lower priority masters.   They may use it to indicate to the current master that they need the bus (higher priority ones can do so through $BPRN^*$).   Thus, when the current bus master completes its bus transfers, it releases the bus only if $CBRQ^*$ is active.   Otherwise, it keeps holding the bus for future use.   The idea is to eliminate the overheads associated with (unnecessary) release and regaining of the bus. $BREQ^*$ cannot be used to indicate if another master needs the bus because it is maintained in an active state by the current master while holding the bus. All bus control signals of the 796 bus are synchronized by the bus clock ($BCLK^*$) signal.

8. *Other Lines:* This last group includes:
   (a) A $LOCK^*$ line
   (b) Two inhibit lines ($INH1^*$, $INH2^*$)
   (c) A byte high enable line ($BHEN^*$) line
   (d) An initialization line ($INIT^*$)
   (e) Four reserved lines

   $LOCK^*$ serves the same purposes the synonymous line of the 8088/8086 does. The inhibit lines provide the means of assigning the same memory address space to different memory devices.   For example, proper manipulation of these lines would allow a ROM slave to occupy part of the address space of a RAM slave. $BHEN^*$ becomes useful in systems having 16-bit memory boards.   It is used for access to the upper byte of a 16-bit word. $INIT^*$ is a master reset signal and is usually activated prior to starting the system.   It may be generated by means of a front panel switch or by some master(s).

Master/slave interconnection example

Let us now use an example to see how circuit boards interconnect through the 796 bus.   Our example involves a bus master (say, a CPU board) and one representative from each type of slave—that is, a memory slave and an I/O slave. Assume the access width of the master and the two slaves is 16 bits.

Figure 5-49(a) indicates which signals are employed by each board.   Starting from the top:

1. The constant clock is generated by the master.   It is available to both slaves.
2. Address lines connect to both slaves.   However, the I/O slave need only connect to the 16 low-order address lines.
3. All three boards connect to the bidirectional data lines of the bus.
4. Command signals—that is, read/write strobes—are generated only by the

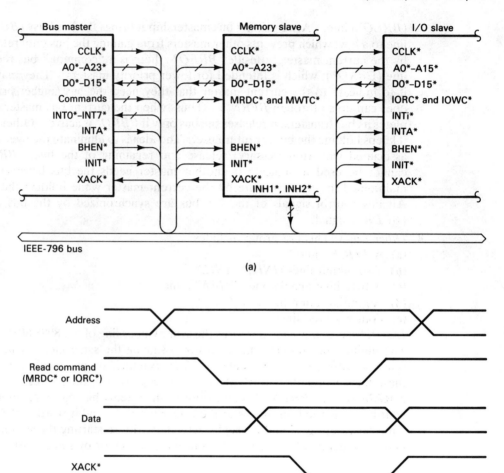

Figure 5-49. Bus master/slave interconnections and timing relationships in the IEEE-796 bus. (a) Bus lines interconnecting a bus master with a memory slave and an I/O slave. (b) Read cycle timing.

master. The memory slave connects only to the *MRDC** (memory read command) and *MWTC** (memory write command) lines. Similarly, the I/O slave connects only to the *IORC** (I/O read command) and *IOWC** (I/O write command) lines.

5. Only the I/O slave connects to the interrupt lines of the bus. *INTi** represents one of the eight interrupt request lines of the bus. On the other hand, the memory slave connects to the inhibit lines of the bus.

6. The *BHEN** and *INIT** signals are generated by the master. Both are utilized by the two slaves.

7. Both slaves connect to the *XACK** (transfer acknowledge) input of the master.

Bus cycle timing

The 796 bus specifies the timing relationships associated with all types of bus operations. Figure 5-49(b) shows as an example the timing for a read cycle. Remember there is no address strobe line. The master, however, must ensure an address setup time of at least 50 ns prior to activating a command line. After sensing activation of the command line, the addressed slave proceeds to retrieve the data from the specified location (or port). Subsequently, it places the data over the data lines of the bus and drives *XACK** to a low. The master takes notice of the event, reads the presented data, and drives the read command line back to a high, which causes the slave to deactivate the *XACK** line. This completes the read cycle. Such a handshaking sequence is reminiscent of the one employed by some CPUs, such as the 68000.

The 796 bus is asynchronous in the sense that there is no time constraint as to when a slave must respond over the *XACK** line. In fact, once a read or write cycle starts, a master will wait indefinitely until *XACK** is activated. What if some malfunction prevents a particular slave from responding, or what if the master has attempted to address a nonexisting memory location? Either case would cause the bus cycle to go on forever. As a result, the entire system would be driven to a lockup. Such situations can be prevented by equipping the master with a **timeout circuit**. The idea is to have the master terminate a bus cycle by itself when slaves do not respond within some preset time interval.

Example 5-29

Describe how you would go about designing a timeout circuit with a programmable timer. How would you employ such a circuit to terminate abnormally long cycles in the case of a 796 bus?

Solution. Let us assume an 8254 programmable interval timer. Going back to Section 5.5.1, we realize that the mode most suitable for this application is mode 1— that is, the hardware retriggerable one-shot mode. Consequently, we must program the 8254 so that one of its counters (say, counter 1) operates in this mode. We must also load counter 1 at initialization time with the appropriate count. For example, assume we want bus cycles to terminate after 1 ms and the *CCLK** is 10 MHz. Then counter 1 should be loaded with the binary equivalent of 10000 (why?). In mode 1, *GATE*1 plays the role of a trigger. The idea is to trigger the timer at the beginning of each bus cycle—that is, as soon as any of the command signals goes active. We might NAND all command signals and drive *GATE*1 with the resulting signal or (even better) drive *GATE*1 with some internal signal of the master which goes to a high when a new bus cycle starts. Under normal conditions, the timer is retriggered before

*OUT*1 goes high. However, if a bus cycle exceeds 1 ms, *GATE*1 will be at a high during the transition of *OUT*1 from a low to a high. This condition can be used to generate an "artificial" *XACK** at the master, as well as an interrupt, so that the CPU can take notice of the event.

Interfacing to the 796 Bus

How do we go about designing bus interface circuits? How complex is the design task? The complexity of such circuits depends on the particular bus we are interfacing to and on whether the associated board is a master or a slave. Interfacing becomes more involved in the case of bus masters since they have to be capable of generating almost all bus signals. In contrast, slaves do not have to interface to bus control and to all interrupt lines. Moreover, they need not have the ability to generate all data transfer control signals. Next we discuss the circuits involved in the interfacing of a master and a slave to the 796 bus.

Bus interface for a master

Most critical is the design of the bus arbitration circuits (Figure 5-50). These circuits generate the timing sequences required for obtaining and releasing the bus. They do so on the basis of the CPU and bus signals they monitor. When in control of the bus, these circuits enable the tri-state drivers of command and address lines (*AEN** signal). It is only then that the master can inject addresses and read/write strobes in the bus.

Another important part of the interface is the command decoding circuits. Their function is to monitor the data transfer (and other) signals carried over the CPU bus and transform them into 796 command signals. Notice that they also generate the *INTA** bus signal and some other internally used ones such as the *DEN* (data enable) signal which enables/disables the data bus transceivers. The remaining interface circuits of the master include the data bus transceivers, the address drivers, and the generator of the bus clocks.

What if a master accommodates on its board some slave section as well? For example, a CPU board might include on-board RAM which must be accessible by other masters. In such cases the master has to be capable of receiving addresses and of generating *XACK** signals for other masters (see the asterisked arrowheads in Figure 5-50).

Some manufacturers offer specialized devices for interfacing of particular CPU families to certain buses. An example of such a device is the Intel 8289 bus arbiter. This device simplifies the design of the bus arbitration circuits when the master employs an 8088 or an 8086. Similarly, the Intel 8288 bus controller converts 8088/8086 bus signals into 796 command signals and thus simplifies the design of the command decoding circuits for masters based on 8088/8086 CPUs.

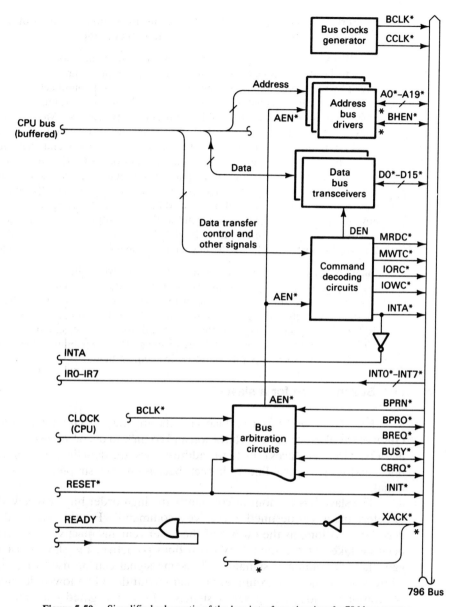

Figure 5-50.   Simplified schematic of the bus interface circuits of a 796 bus master.

Example 5-30

The 8289 bus arbiter is designed to perform bus arbitration on behalf of an 8086- or an 8088-based master.   It connects to all five bus control lines shown in Figure 5-48. Assume a number of 8289s chained as shown in Figure 5-46(a) for priority resolution in a serial fashion.   Each 8289 performs bus arbitration on behalf of a bus master. It is located on the circuit board implementing that particular master.

The *BPRN** signal is sampled on the falling edge of the bus clock (*BCLK**).   In fact, it has to be stable 15 ns (at minimum) prior to sampling time.   Assume the master served by the arbiter requested the bus and *BPRN** was found active when sampled. Then, the 8289 deactivates its *BPRO** 40 ns later (at maximum).   Now *BPRO** propagates down the chain to disable all lower priority masters.   Meanwhile our master waits for the next falling edge of *BCLK**.   When it arrives, our master checks the *BUSY** line of the 796 bus.   If inactive, it drives it to a low and goes on to use the bus.   However, if active, it waits to check again one *BCLK** cycle later.   What if (in the meantime) the arbiter of a higher priority master activates its *BPRO** output as a result of a bus request?   The requirement here is that *BPRO** must reach our master on time to disable it before the next falling edge of *BCLK** arrives.   Determine how many masters we can chain given the *BPRO** output of an inhibited master goes inactive 25 ns (at maximum) after its *BPRN** input does.   Allow an additional 3 ns for propagation delays along the bus, and assume an 8 MHz clock signal for *BCLK**.

Solution.   The worst case delays are experienced when the *BPRO** signal from the higher priority master has to propagate through the entire chain; that is, when our master happens to be the last one in the chain, and the contending higher priority master is actually the highest priority one.   Then, the number of chainable masters is $2 + [125 - (40 + 3)] / 25$; that is, 5.   For example, we could accommodate the CPU board and up to four I/O boards having DMA capability.   For more masters, we have to resort to a parallel priority resolving scheme.

Bus interface for a slave

For slaves, the bus interface circuits are much simpler (see Figure 5-51). Observe the absence of bus arbitration and command decoding circuits.   The slave, an I/O device, interfaces only to the address lines, the data lines, one of the interrupt lines, and some control lines.   In fact, because it is so simple, it is shown in more detail.

The slave has to monitor constantly the high-order bits of received addresses to determine if it is destined to receive a command.   For this, we need an address decoder.   As long as the output of the latter remains inactive, no further actions need be taken at the slave.   When it does go active, the slave must proceed to gate the I/O command signals.   The same signal can be used to enable further address decoding—for example, another circuit decoding low-order addresses for generation of (local) chip select signals.   From the gated command signals we derive the read/write strobes for local operations at this slave.

Our I/O slave is assumed to be a 16-bit one.   Consequently it must connect to all 16 data lines of the 796 bus.   An I/O operation may involve transfer of a low byte over the *D0**–*D7** bus lines or transfer of a 16-bit word over the *D0**–*D15** bus lines.   However, in addition to these two modes, the 796 specification requires the capability of transferring a high byte over the *D0**–*D7** bus lines. To do this we need an extra bus transceiver between the local high-order data lines

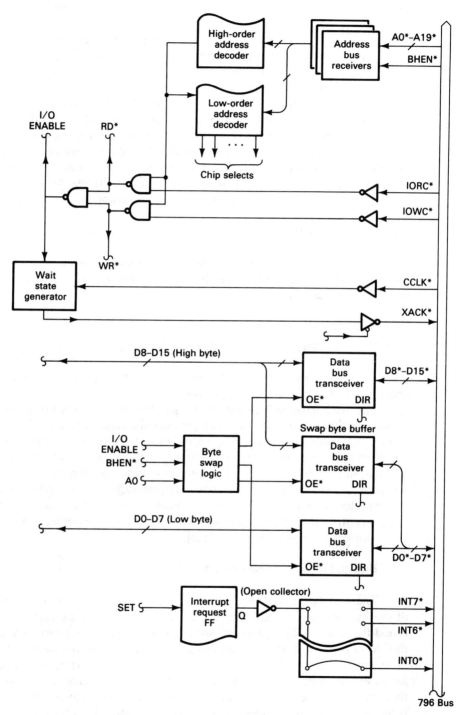

Figure 5-51. Simplified schematic of the bus interface circuits of a 796 bus slave.

and the $D0^* - D7^*$ lines of the 796 bus. A circuit performing this kind of operation is often referred to as a **swap byte buffer** (Figure 5-51). The decision as to which of the three data bus transceivers is to be enabled must be made on the basis of the states of the $BHEN^*$ and $A0^*$ signals.

At a certain point the slave must respond to the master via the $XACK^*$ bus line. This can be accomplished by means of a wait state generator triggered by the local read/write strobes. Notice that in this example the slave employs the simple non-bus-vectored interrupt scheme. The slave board connects to all eight interrupt request lines of the 796 bus. However, only one of them ($INT0^*$) is actually strapped to the on-board circuits. This sort of strapping arrangement is employed in practice for greater flexibility in interrupt priority assignments.

Bus Noise Problems

Thus far we have examined how μC buses are structured, what signals they involve, and what bus interface circuits are about. Yet we have not dealt with fundamental questions such as:

- How long can a μC bus be?
- How fast can we transmit information through it?

As we will see, the answers to these questions go hand in hand with noise and other nasty phenomena of the real world.

The backplane implementing the μC bus is itself a printed circuit board. Consequently most of the noise concerns we discussed in Section 4.1.1 apply to it as well. A ground plane again becomes key to keeping noise down. Besides, the bus must include many ground (and supply voltage) lines. These lines should be assigned so that they correspond to connector ends. Such remedies are not always adequate, however, because bus lines are generally longer. Also they run close and parallel to each other, and the currents needed to drive the large bus capacitances contribute further to the problem. All these increase transmission line and other noise effects [see Figure 4-11(a)].

Bus delays and their effects

The signals injected in the bus by circuit boards propagate toward the ends of the bus and are reflected back. Usually we refer to the elapsed time as the **round-trip delay**. The effects of such signal reflections depend on the length of this delay relative to the rise/fall times of the original signal (note the comments on ringing in Section 4.1.1). If round-trip delays are shorter, the reflected waveforms arrive prior to the completion of the original signal transitions. Hence, there is little concern. However, if it is the other way around, we have a serious problem. Now, such reflections may cause (among other effects) false transitions in receiving circuits.

Example 5-31

The velocity of a signal along an unloaded transmission line can be approximated through the relation $v = 1/\sqrt{LC_1}$. L and C_1 are the distributed inductance and distributed capacitance of the line, respectively. From this formula we deduce that the propagation time along an unloaded transmission line of length d is $T_1 = d\sqrt{LC_1}$. Consider a (backplane-etched) μC bus where each bus line has a distributed capacitance of 2 pF/in. and a distributed inductance of 0.02 μH/in. Suppose we drive one end of a bus line from a low to a high. After how long we will "see" the transition at the other end if the bus is 16 in. long? How long is the round-trip delay?

Solution. Substitution of the numeric values in the given expression yields $T_1 = 16\sqrt{2 \times 10^{-8} \times 2 \times 10^{-12}}$, or $T_1 = 3.2$ ns. The round-trip delay is twice as long; that is, 6.4 ns.

Example 5-32

If we load a transmission line with an additional (lumped) capacitance of C_2 per unit length, the propagation time T_1 increases to $T_2 = d\sqrt{LC_1}\sqrt{1 + (C_2/C_1)}$. Assume we load the μC bus of the previous example with 20 equally spaced boards. Each board contributes to the bus load about 13 pF of capacitance. What round-trip delays would you expect? Would you anticipate any problems if some of the bus lines carry signals having rise times of about 10 ns?

Solution. The value of C_2 is $(20 \times 13)/16$ pF/in., or about 16 pF/in. Substituting in the given expression we have $T_2 = 3.2\sqrt{1 + (16/2)}$, or $T_2 = 9.6$ ns. The round-trip delay is then $2 \times 9.6 = 19.2$ ns. Actually, this value holds for boards occupying end slots (worst case value). The rest of the boards will be experiencing shorter delays (depending on the backplane slot they occupy). Yet the calculated value is about twice as large as the given rise time. We must therefore expect very serious problems.

Bus termination

Fortunately such unwanted signal reflections can be prevented. In fact in the case of a uniform transmission line they can be eliminated. This is accomplished by terminating the line with a resistor whose value is equal to that of its **characteristic impedance** Z_0. For backplane-etched μC bus lines, Z_0 is usually in the range of 90 to 120 Ω. A common approach to terminating a bus line is using one resistor to V_{cc} and one to ground (Figure 5-52). The resistor values are chosen such that their parallel combination yields a resistance close to the value of Z_0. When a signal line is not driven by a bus driver, these resistors serve as voltage dividers. They maintain the signal line at a high. Hence their values must be chosen with this additional consideration in mind.

Example 5-33

What is the equivalent terminating resistance for the line pictured in Figure 5-52? At what voltage level is the line maintained during signal inactivity?

Solution. In the AC equivalent circuit (where DC voltage sources are shorted), the

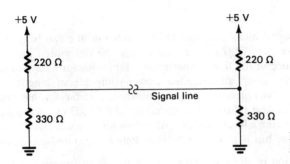

Figure 5-52. Bus signal line terminated at both ends.

resistors connecting to each end of the line are indeed in parallel, so the equivalent terminating resistance is $(220 \times 330) / (220 + 330) \ \Omega$; that is, $132 \ \Omega$. This value is close enough to the characteristic impedance of an etched signal line. Although reflections will not be eliminated, they will be reduced drastically. During signal inactivity, the signal line will be maintained at $(5 \times 330) / (220 + 330) = 3$ V.

In reality a bus line is not uniform because of the load introduced along its length by the backplane connectors and the plugged-in circuit boards. Such loading modifies the characteristics of the bus line and reduces the value of the termination resistance.

Example 5-34

If we assume uniform loading we may determine the characteristic impedance of a loaded bus line from the expression $Z = Z_0 / \sqrt{1 + (C_2 / C_1)}$. Z_0 is the characteristic impedance of the line when unloaded. C_1 and C_2 are the distributed and (lumped) load capacitances per unit length, respectively. Consider the bus of Example 5-32. By what factor is the characteristic impedance of bus lines reduced when loaded?

Solution. Substitution of the values of capacitances yields $Z = Z_0 / \sqrt{1 + 16/2}$, or $Z = Z_0 / 3$. This result is indicative of the very significant reduction of the characteristic impedance of a line under load conditions. Naturally, low terminating resistances necessitate higher currents from the bus drivers. That in turn means higher power dissipation and increased bus noise due to crosstalk and other factors. So, in practice, we terminate bus lines with resistances higher than those calculated from the above expression (usually with values in the vicinity of Z_0). In other words, we settle to reducing rather than eliminating signal reflections.

Should we terminate all bus lines like the one pictured in Figure 5-52? Not necessarily, provided

1. Signal transitions are long enough compared to round-trip delays.
2. The built-in time margins allow for decay of ringing prior to signal sampling. Such is usually the case with address and data signals.

As a consequence we may have to employ the two-resistor approach only for clock lines. For lines driven by tri-state and open collector circuits, we may simply use pull-up resistors. Moreover, if the source of the clocks is very close to one end of the bus, it may suffice to terminate the bus only at the far end. Anyhow, terminating resistors are either soldered directly on the backplane, or they are accommodated on small boards plugging into the end slots of the backplane.

Crosstalk

The induction of unwanted signals from one signal line to another is commonly known as **crosstalk**. Such parasitic signals are due to the capacitive and inductive coupling between adjacent signal lines (see Problem 4-16). The two signal lines may represent etched lines on a circuit board, etched bus lines on a backplane, or two common wires. Crosstalk increases with the length of the lines, their physical proximity, and the speed of signal transitions. The magnitude of the induced noise in the case of bus lines can be severe.

Example 5-35

Let us consider two adjacent, properly terminated bus lines. Let us further assume that one of them is driven from one of its ends. The crosstalk noise induced into the nondriven line consists of two components. The first one is called **near-end crosstalk**. Its amplitude (V_{NEC}) is maximum at the end close to the driven point and is given by $V_{NEC} = d(CZ_0 + M/Z_0)\,(\Delta V/t)\,/\,2$, where

d is the length of the bus line

C is the coupling capacitance between the two lines

Z_0 is the characteristic impedance of each line

M is the mutual inductance between the two lines

ΔV is the voltage difference between a low and a high

t is equal to the rise/fall time of the signal injected into the driven line, or to the round-trip delay of the bus (whichever is longer)

The second component is called **far-end crosstalk**. Its amplitude (V_{FEC}) is maximum at the far end of the nondriven line and is given by $V_{FEC} = d(CZ_0 - M/Z_0)(\Delta V/t)\,/\,2$, where t is the rise/fall time of the signal injected into the driven line. Notice from these formulas that V_{NEC} has the same polarity with the signal generating it. V_{FEC}, however, may have either polarity. Another thing to note is that the induced crosstalk spikes can be much higher (than the values calculated from these expressions) when many neighboring bus lines switch simultaneously.

Discuss why crosstalk can be a serious problem in μC buses (and buses in general).

Solution.   First of all, the length of bus lines is usually longer than that of signal lines etched on circuit boards. For example, a μC bus may be 1.5 ft long. The degree of coupling between two adjacent signal lines is also high in μC buses because etched backplane lines run parallel and are very close to each other. $\Delta V/t$ represents the speed of signal transitions. It is key to achieving high-speed data transfers over a bus and is therefore generally high.

The noise resulting from crosstalk can be reduced to tolerable levels by

1. Keeping the bus short.
2. Avoiding high-speed signal transitions (when unnecessary). Bus drivers must be capable of charging/discharging bus capacitances fast enough. Otherwise, rise/fall times will be excessively long. As a result, bus cycles will be longer, reducing bus throughput. On the other hand, bus drivers should not be faster than needed. This helps crosstalk reduction.
3. Giving special treatment to the lines carrying the clock, strobes, and certain other control signals. For example, clock rise/fall times have to be short, so clock lines are a potential source of crosstalk. At the same time, it is critical to protect clock lines from crosstalk induced from other sources. Both goals can be achieved by isolating the clock lines from the rest. We may, for instance, use wider spacing between them and adjacent lines and/or sandwich them between ground lines. Such lines should also be kept away from groups of lines that are likely to switch simultaneously—that is, data and address lines.

Example 5-36 Consider a system whose μC bus is implemented on a 12-in. backplane. The bus clock is 5 MHz. Suppose we are to employ the same μC bus in a new system where product requirements dictate higher bus throughput. After some analysis we determine that the new system requires an 8 MHz bus clock. In fact, as a consequence, rise/fall times of the bus signals must be shortened by about 50 percent. To what length should we limit the bus of the new product if crosstalk noise is to remain the same?

Solution. Bus lengths and rise/fall times affect V_{NEC} and V_{FEC} the same way (Example 5-35)—that is, both increase linearly with the length of a bus (d) and vary inversely with rise/fall times (t). Let us represent the bus signal rise/fall times of the existing product by t_1. If the new bus is to experience the same level of crosstalk noise, its length (d_2) must satisfy the relation $d_2 / (0.5t_1) = 12/t_1$. We can thus deduce that $d_2 = 6$ in. Hence the length of the μC bus must be reduced by one half.

Tradeoffs and Other Design Considerations

Having examined the noise problems we face in μC buses, we are now in a position to discuss design tradeoffs. First, our objectives when designing a μC bus. It should be

1. Supportive of all types of bus functions required for present and expected future products.
2. Well-defined in terms of bus signal set and bus cycle timing relationships. (The simpler and the smaller the number of lines, the better.)
3. Long enough for accommodation of the number of anticipated circuit boards.

4. Fast (in terms of the number of bus cycles it can perform per second).

5. Reliable.

6. Cost effective.

Usually, a μC bus is intended for a family of products rather than a single one. To make this possible we have to take into account future needs (objective 1). For example, the first product may be based on a single master and thereby does not involve bus arbitration. Yet we should provide for such functions if the next product is to support multiple masters (I/O boards with DMA, for instance). Circuit boards themselves should be designed with future needs in mind. This may not help the cost effectiveness of a specific product. It does, however, ensure long-term usability of the circuit boards and therefore future savings.

Often a designer is tempted to derive the signals of the μC bus by simply buffering those of the CPU bus. This approach will not help in establishing a flexible μC bus in the long run, however. While it may economize CPU board circuitry, it does not necessarily simplify the bus interface circuits required on the other boards. For example, bus interfacing might be simplified by providing over the bus certain signals which are derived through decoding on the CPU board. The set of signals which is to comprise the μC bus must, therefore, be thought of carefully (objective 2). In fact, bus design should go hand in hand with the design of circuit boards, not tacked on as an afterthought.

The speed of a bus depends on how fast bus drivers can charge/discharge bus capacitances. That in turn depends on

- How long the bus is (distributed capacitance)
- The input capacitance presented by bus receivers
- The number of circuit boards plugged in the bus
- The current-driving capabilities of the bus drivers

Thus, reaching the desired bus speed involves tradeoffs among the listed factors. In the course of doing so, one must consider the impact of the length of the bus on noise. Besides, bus speed has noise and power dissipation impacts. This means tradeoffs with reliability.

Example 5-37

Discuss the type of bus-driving circuits required in a typical μC bus.

Solution. Most bus lines, such as address, data, and read/write strobes, can be driven by any one of the bus masters. However, only one master can drive them at any particular time. These and other lines of a similar nature are driven by tri-state drivers. Other lines—such as interrupt request and possibly bus request lines—may be activated at the same time by two or more signal sources, which means that they require open collector drivers. Finally, some other lines are always driven by the same circuits. Such are the clock lines which are usually driven by ordinary (totem pole) TTL drivers.

Bus reliability is very much a function of proper bus termination and bus noise. System performance can be further enhanced by detecting and reporting to the CPU (or other bus masters) bus errors. Here again we have to make tradeoffs with cost.

Custom versus standardized μC buses

The task of defining, testing, and documenting your own bus can be quite substantial, especially in the case of high-speed μC buses where the definitions of timing sequences and time margins become very critical. To this end, you may find it valuable to use the specification of one of the standardized buses as a reference. As an alternative you may decide to employ an already existing (or even standardized) μC bus. (Prior to doing so, make sure you discuss with the bus specifier the existence of any legal implications.) In either case, keep in mind the bus organization of the CPU you plan to use. The complexity of bus interface circuits is very dependent on the differences between the μC bus and the CPU bus.

There is another advantage in selecting one of the widely used μC buses, namely, the availability of a large variety of compatible circuit boards, as well as other system components such as backplanes, chassis, and software packages.

5.7 DESIGN EXAMPLES

This section concludes the chapter on I/O with some additional design examples. Our first example deals with worst case timing analysis of I/O cycles. The second example will give us the opportunity to see how we design the interrupt circuitry of a CPU employing a set of priority encoding lines. The last example involves a CPU implementing on-chip interrupt, DMA, and other I/O interface logic.

I/O Timing Analysis

In Section 4.5 we discussed the timing analysis of memory cycles. Timing analysis of I/O cycles is not done any differently. As a matter of fact, when I/O and memory share a common address space, cycle timing is identical. Moreover, this is usually true even when a CPU has separate address spaces for memory and I/O. Take, for instance, the circuit shown in Figure 5-21. There the 8088 uses I/O timing sequences to read and write into internal registers of the 8259A interrupt controller. Such I/O sequences, however, are identical to those used for memory.

Let us consider the case of I/O write cycle timing for the circuit of Figure 5-21. Our goal is to determine whether the 8088 and the 8259A are compatible under worst case conditions. Figure 5-53(a) shows the write cycle timing sequence generated by the 8088. The sequencing requirements of the 8259A for such a

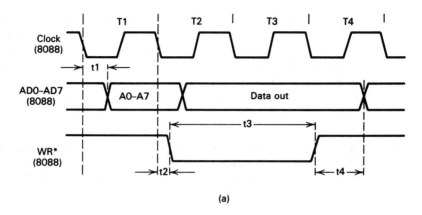

(a)

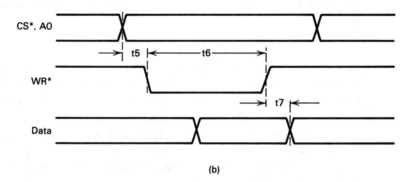

(b)

Figure 5-53. (a) Write cycle timing of the 8088.   (b) Write timing sequence of the 8259A programmable interrupt controller.

cycle are pictured in Figure 5-53(b).   The assumed values for the timing parameters indicated in Figure 5-53 are (in ns):

Parameter	Minimum	Maximum
$t1$	15	110
$t2$	10	110
$t3$	$2T-60$	
$t4$	$T-30$	
$t5$	0	
$t6$	290	
$t7$	0	

T represents the period of the CPU clock.

1. *Address and CS* Setup Time.* The value of parameter $t5$ indicates that WR^* should not go active (at the input of the 8259A) before CS^* is activated and $A0$ settles. CS^* is delayed more than $A0$ since its signal path includes an address decoder, so only CS^* setup time margins need be examined. We will use the leading edge of $T1$ as a reference point. Under worst case conditions, CS^* will go active after a time interval of:

$$t1_{(MAX)} + 20 + 40$$

where 20 and 40 represent the maximum propagation delays through the address latch and the address decoder, respectively. On the other hand, the earliest time WR^* can go active (at the input of the 8259A) is:

$$T + t2_{(MIN)} + 5$$

where 5 ns is the assumed value of the minimum delay via the buffering gate along the WR^* path. Hence, the worst case time margin between CS^* and WR^* will be:

$$T + t2_{(MIN)} - t1_{(MAX)} - 55 = T - 155.$$

This expression indicates that the time margin in question is a function of the CPU clock frequency. For example, if the latter is 5 MHz, the CS^* setup time requirement of the 8259A is met with a margin of at least 45 ns.

2. *Write Pulse Width:* The 8259A requires a write pulse width of at least 290 ns (minimum value of $t6$). On the other hand, the one generated by the CPU is at least $2T - 60$ ns wide. Once again there is dependence on the clocking rate. For example, if the frequency of the clock is 5 MHz, this requirement is met with a margin of 50 ns.

3. *Data Hold After Write:* Data presented to the 8259A must remain stable until its WR^* input goes back to a high (minimum value of $t7$). This requirement is met easily since:

   (a) The CPU guarantees stable data for at least $T - 30$ ns after switching WR^* to a high.
   (b) The delay experienced by data through the transceiver is longer than that experienced by WR^*.

Example 5-38

Consider the discussed CS^* setup time requirement of the 8259A interrupt controller. To what value could we increase the CPU clocking rate and still meet it? What if we clock the CPU above the calculated rate? What solution would you suggest?

Solution. Equating the expression $T - 155$ to zero, we obtain 6.45 MHz. Beyond this clocking frequency the requirement is not met (under worst case conditions). One solution is delaying arrival of WR^* at the synonymous input of the 8259A. This can be accomplished by using additional circuit elements along its path, for example, one or more 74LS04 inverters.

Example 5-39

Suppose our timing analysis had revealed a failure to meet the worst case write pulse width requirement of the 8259A. What solution would you propose?

Solution. The width of the WR^* pulse (generated by the CPU) can be lengthened with wait state insertion. Each inserted wait state will extend the pulse width by T (the period of the clock). The employed wait state generator could be triggered with CS^*.

CPU with Priority Encoding Interrupt Lines

Throughout this chapter we have seen interrupt circuit design examples for CPUs employing a single maskable and a single nonmaskable interrupt line. Here we will do so for the 68000. Recall the 68000 has a common set of priority encoding lines for both maskable and nonmaskable interrupts. The interrupt circuitry of our 68000-based example system is shown (in simplified form) in Figure 5-54. Notice that the schematic includes address decoding circuits and a control/status register. The former serve presentation of an example of address space allocation, and the latter gives us the opportunity to discuss what a system control/status register is about.

Interrupt circuits

The 68000 has a set of three interrupt priority level lines ($IPL0-IPL2$). Their state is continuously compared against a 3-bit mask contained in the CPU status register. These lines encode the priority level of the interrupting device. Level 7 has the highest priority. Such a scheme does not necessitate an interrupt controller. Instead all we need is a priority encoder prioritizing the interrupt requests of the various interrupt sources.

The 68000 does not have an interrupt acknowledge line. The only way to find out when such a cycle takes place is to decode its $FC0-FC2$ status lines. An interrupt acknowledge cycle is indicated by a 111 code on the $FC0-FC2$ lines. In the course of such a cycle the 68000 places on address lines $A1-A3$ a priority code which identifies the device whose interrupt is being acknowledged. At this point we have two alternatives:

1. Decode (on the CPU board) only the $FC0-FC2$ status lines, not the $A1-A3$ address lines. In other words, generate a common interrupt acknowledge signal ($IACK^*$) for all devices. This signal is distributed to all interrupting devices. At the same time, each device decodes address bits $A1-A3$ to find out if the acknowledgment is for its own interrupt.

2. Decode address lines $A1-A3$ as well—that is, generate individual $IACK^*$ signals on behalf of devices.

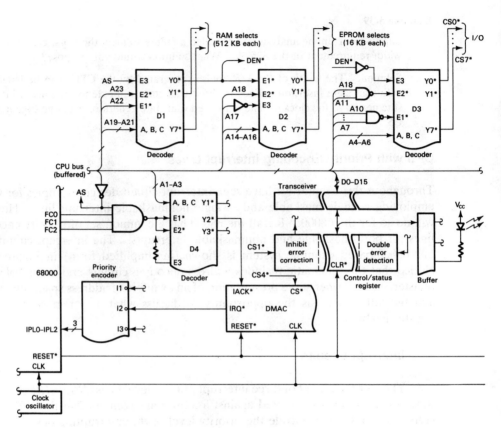

Figure 5-54. 68000 CPU with a control and status register, address decoding, and interrupt circuitry.

The first approach simplifies the interconnection problem since we need only distribute a single *IACK** signal. On the other hand, we need decoding circuits for *A1–A3* at each device. The second approach saves decoding circuits at the devices but does require distribution of all individual *IACK**s.

Our example employs the second approach. An octal decoder is used to generate up to seven *IACK**s. The decoder is enabled when *AS* (the address strobe) is active and status lines carry the code 111. Figure 5-54 illustrates only one interrupting device—a DMAC (direct memory access controller). The *IACK** input of the DMAC connects to the *Y2** output of the decoder, so the DMAC is provided with its own private interrupt acknowledge signal.

Address space allocation

Let us assume our 68000-based system is to accommodate at minimum:

- Four memory boards of 512 KB each

- 64 KB of read-only memory implemented with 16K × 8 EPROMs and starting at address zero
- Six I/O controllers (requiring chip select signals) and 256K byte addresses for I/O

Prior to designing the address decoding circuitry we sketch an **address space map** (Figure 5-55). Such a map helps in the design of the decoding circuits and is included in the specification of the system.

Read-only memory is assigned the bottom 128K addresses. I/O is assigned the next three consecutive 128K blocks of addresses—that is, addresses 128K–512K. Chip-select signals (CSs) are to be generated by decoding I/O addresses. Use of addresses close to the 512K boundary for CSs makes decoding easier. The rest of the address space (from 512K and up) can be assigned to RAM.

One decoder is needed to identify to which 512K block an address belongs. Output $Y0^*$ will indicate an address falling in the 0–512K range. Hence, it must be used to enable the read-only memory and CS decoders. The rest of the outputs of this decoder—that is, $Y1^*$ to $Y7^*$— can serve as select signals for the 512 KB memory boards. The required number of read-only memory devices and CSs suggest that all we need is two additional (octal) decoders. Consequently, the required decoding circuitry can be designed with three octal decoders (see Figure 5-54):

1. Decoder D1 is enabled by the CPU address strobe (AS^*) whenever the two most significant address bits (A22 and A23) are at a low. Therefore, only byte addresses 0–4M are employed. Address bits A19–A21 are decoded

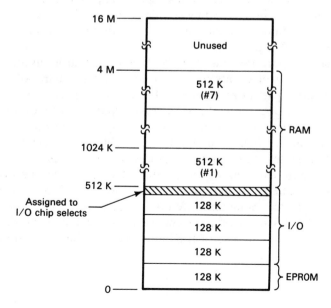

Figure 5-55. Example of an address space map.

for identification of one out of eight 512K blocks of addresses. Since only the bottom 512K addresses are not used for RAM, this decoder provides *CS* signals for up to seven memory boards.

2. Decoder D2 generates the *CS* signals for EPROMs. Since it is to decode addresses in the range of 0–128K, it must be enabled when:

   (a) Output $Y0^*$ of decoder D1 is active (indicating an address in the range 0–512K)

   (b) Address bits A17 and A18 are both at a low (indicating addresses 0–128K of the bottom 512K block)

   The decoded bits are A14–A16. Each output of decoder D2 can serve to select one 16K × 8 EPROM. Hence, we can handle a total of 128 KB of read-only memory.

3. Decoder D3 generates up to eight *CS* signals for selection of I/O controllers. It is enabled when

   (a) Output $Y0^*$ of decoder D1 is active

   (b) Address bits A7–A18 are at a high

   In other words, for I/O chip selection purposes, we use the top 128 byte addresses of the space allocated to I/O. Each generated *CS* signal corresponds to 16 byte addresses. This is usually adequate for most I/O controllers.

System control/status register

The remaining part of the schematic (Figure 5-54) concerns a control/status register (CSR). Such a register is implemented very often on the CPU board. It should not be confused, however, with the status register implemented on-chip with the CPU which includes flag bits indicating certain events within the CPU as, for instance, an overflow condition and control bits set by the program in order to enable certain modes of CPU operation.

The CSR serves similar purposes but at the system level; that is, its status part is employed for indication of events having to do with other parts of the system. Likewise, its control part provides the CPU with the means to enable/disable certain modes of system operation. Such a status bit could be one indicating occurrence of an uncorrectable double memory error. An example of a CSR control bit might be one which, when set by the CPU, disables error correction. This can be very useful in the testing of circuitry associated with EDAC.

The CSR of Figure 5-54 connects to the (buffered) CPU bus via its own transceiver. The CSR is treated just like another I/O port (or I/O controller) having its own chip select signal. Sometimes we do not settle for simply making system status available to the CPU—we may also choose to display status conditions by means of LEDs. Such is the purpose of the buffer seen on the right side of the schematic.

CPU with On-Chip I/O Interface Logic

Some of the μPs we discussed in Chapter 3 are available in enhanced versions. Such versions include on-chip memory interface circuits and I/O control logic. Representative examples are the Intel 80188 and 80186. These devices are enhanced versions of the 8088 and 8086, respectively. Both include on-chip

- Decoding circuits for generation of chip select signals for memory and peripheral controllers
- Clock circuits
- An interrupt controller
- A DMA controller
- Programmable timers

That, of course, eliminates a number of external components and thereby simplifies the design task. We will demonstrate this through the 80188.

First, let us examine the external interface lines of the 80188. Figure 5-56 shows its block diagram in simplified form. The broken-line box represents the circuitry associated with an ordinary 8088 (section I). The rest of the blocks represent the additional circuits provided in the 80188 (section II). Most of the interface lines associated with section I are identical to those we have seen in Figure 3-2 for the 8088. The differences are:

1. There is no *IO/M** line (since the device decodes on-chip memory and I/O addresses).
2. Instead of minimum and maximum modes, the 80188 has a regular mode and a queue status mode, which is enabled by grounding the *RD*/QSMD** line.
3. Two (instead of one) ready lines (*SRDY* and *ARDY*) provide greater flexibility. Which one we use depends on whether the ready signal has been synchronized (externally) to the CPU clock or not.
4. Instead of a single reset line there is a Reset In line (*RES**) and a Reset Out line (*RESET*).

However, the 80188 has many additional interface lines. These are the lines associated with the functional blocks of section II. The block at the top-right performs functions similar to those of an 8259A programmable interrupt controller. *INT0–INT3* play the role of maskable interrupt request lines. *NMI* is used for nonmaskable interrupt requests. Two of the interrupt request lines can be configured (by software) to act as interrupt acknowledge lines. The next block downwards is a programmable DMA controller. It is equipped with two DMA channels. *DRQ*0 and *DRQ*1 are the DMA request inputs for these two channels. Three

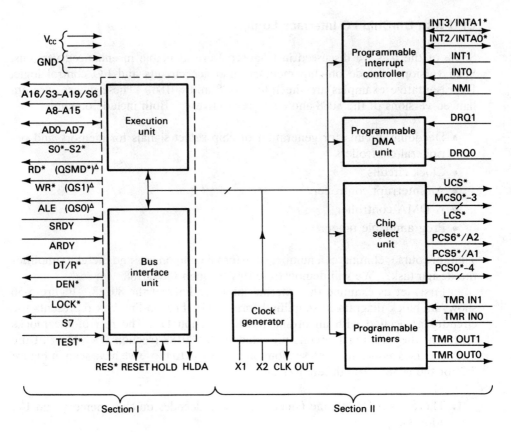

Figure 5-56. Simplified block diagram of the 80188 CPU.

lines are associated with the on-chip clock generator—two for connections to an external crystal and one for a clock output intended for external devices.

Now, the chip select unit. This one generates:

- Six chip select signals for memory devices
- Seven chip select signals for peripheral controllers

Each of these chip select (*CS*) signals is activated whenever the CPU addresses a specific block of contiguous locations. The boundaries of such blocks are programmable (to a certain extent). The *CS* lines intended for memory include:

1. A *UCS** (upper memory *CS*) line
2. Four mid-range *CS* lines (*MCS*0*–3)
3. An *LCS** (lower memory *CS*) line

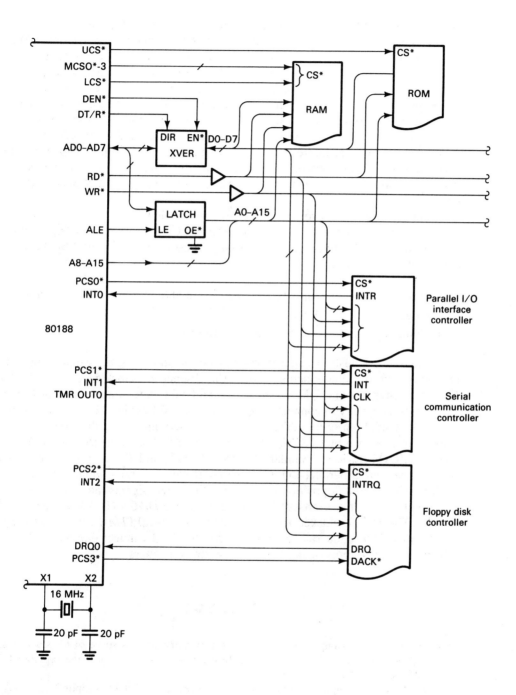

Figure 5-57.   Example of 80188 interfacing to memory and I/O controllers.

Upper memory is usually implemented with ROM storing the initialization program. Lower memory stores interrupt vector tables, among other items. Mid-range memory is generally RAM storing programs and data. The scheme is somewhat different for the *PCS0*–6* (peripheral *CS*) signals. Here only a single base address (belonging to either the memory address space or the I/O address space) can be programmed. Then each of the seven PCS signals corresponds to one of seven contiguous blocks of 128 bytes (each) above that base address. Note that lines *PCS5** and *PCS6** may also be programmed to carry address bits A1 and A2, respectively. Another interesting feature of the chip select unit is that it can be programmed to ignore either one or both ready inputs, as well as to insert a programmable number of wait states. This is possible for each *CS* signal individually.

Finally, the 80188 provides three programmable timers. Two of them can be used to count external events, interrupt the CPU after reaching a certain count, and so on. The third is used for internal purposes. It is triggered by the CPU clock. Its uses include:

- Generation of interrupts (after a programmable number of clock periods)
- Generation of DMA requests
- Counting of pulses for the two other timers

Figure 5-57 illustrates an application example indicating the gained simplicity in terms of external components. Notice the absence of a clock generator, address decoders, interrupt and DMA controllers, and wait state generators. In fact, it becomes unnecessary to connect to the high-order address lines (*A16–A19*) of the CPU. Instead, high-order address bits are decoded on-chip by the 80188. *UCS** is used for selection of a ROM. *LCS** and *MCS0*-3* serve selection of different banks of RAM devices. Similarly *PCS0**, *PCS1**, and *PCS2** provide the chip select signals for a parallel I/O interface controller, a serial communication controller (SCC), and a floppy disk controller. The select signals can play other roles too. Note, for instance, that *PCS3** serves here as a *DACK* (DMA acknowledge) signal. The SCC is clocked from the output of timer 0 (*TMR OUT* 0) and that saves an external baud rate generator. *INT0–INT2* connect directly to the interrupt request outputs of the three peripheral controllers.

PROBLEMS

5-1. I/O Port Addressing. An 8-bit μP has a memory address space of 64 KB and an I/O address space of 256 bytes. A designer decides to use only the separate I/O address space for I/O purposes.

(a) How many input and how many output ports can this CPU support?

(b) Suppose each I/O port must serve both input and output. How many I/O ports can be implemented?

(c) Assume that all we need is eight I/O ports. Show how you would take advantage of this fact to simplify I/O address decoding.

(d) Assume we need a total of 16 I/O ports. Show how we should choose port addresses so that I/O address decoding can be accomplished with only two 74LS138 octal decoders—that is, no gates, inverters, or other circuits.

5-2. I/O Port Addressing. A particular system is based on a 16-bit CPU and has two I/O devices. The first device has three status and four control lines. The second one has six status lines and five control lines.

(a) How many 8-bit I/O ports do we need for status reading and control of each device? What is the total number of I/O addresses needed?

(b) Is it possible to use a single 16-bit-wide I/O port for both devices? How?

(c) Assume the second device has only two status lines and four control lines. Determine the minimum number of needed I/O port addresses.

5-3. Memory-Mapped I/O. A CPU has a four MB common address space for both memory and I/O. It is to be used in an application where memory capacity will never exceed 2 MB.

(a) How would you divide the address space between memory and I/O so that the distinction between memory and I/O addresses (by the hardware) becomes very simple?

(b) Assume we need a separate select signal for each 256 KB of memory. Show how you would generate the memory select signals.

5-4. Direct I/O. A μC-based instrument has eight modes of operation. Operating modes are selected by means of an eight-position rotary switch. The CPU employs direct I/O to "sense" (on a periodic basis) the position of the switch. Subsequently, it takes the appropriate actions applying to the selected mode of operation. The CPU has a 64 KB I/O address space and an IO/M^* line indicating whether a cycle involves memory or I/O. You are asked to design the interface circuits required between the switch and the buffered (demultiplexed) bus of the CPU. Include the address decoding circuits, assuming the I/O port of the switch has been assigned I/O address 4096.

5-5. Insertion of Wait States in I/O Cycles. Consider a CPU with I/O write timing similar to the one shown in Figure 5-53(a) and an I/O device having write cycle timing waveforms like those of Figure 5-53(b). The CPU data sheets guarantee a write strobe pulse width of $2T - 60$ ns (where T is the period of the clock). On the other hand, the I/O device requires this pulse width to be no less than 340 ns.

(a) How many wait states should we insert per I/O cycle if the CPU is clocked at a rate of 8 MHz?

(b) Repeat if the clock frequency is reduced to 6.25 MHz.

(c) To what value should we reduce the clocking rate so that wait state insertion is no longer necessary?

5-6. Ordinary versus Memory-Mapped I/O. Sometimes I/O devices are equipped with memory buffers accommodating blocks of data. Such a buffer may be filled (or emptied) by the CPU with data from its own memory. Iterative types of instructions are very effective in speeding up such transfers. The problem is that many CPUs do not have iterative I/O instructions. For example, the 8086 has iterative instructions only for memory-to-memory transfers. Yet if we employ memory-mapped I/O we can capitalize on them.

(a) Assume an 8086-based system employing the separate I/O address space for data transfers to/from a device equipped with a 128-byte buffer. A data block is transferred by executing a program loop using the "input" or "output" instructions of the 8086. The program loop transfers one 16-bit word per iteration and takes 50 clock cycles to execute. Determine how long it takes to transfer a 128-byte block of data given a CPU clocking rate of 5 MHz.

(b) Suppose we employ memory-mapped I/O instead. Now we have the option to use the "move string" instruction which takes only 17 clock cycles per word. Calculate the factor by which data transfers are sped up (on a percent basis).

(c) The I/O device buffer is loaded with new data 200 times per second. What fraction of the CPU time is consumed for transfers to/from this device? Calculate this for the systems discussed in parts (a) and (b) above.

(d) The I/O device buffer is loaded only once per second. Does it really matter if we use a program loop or a string processing instruction?

5-7. Polled Interrupts. Some CPUs are not capable of handling vectored interrupts. When the single interrupt request line of such a CPU is activated, the CPU jumps to a fixed memory address. Through the latter, the CPU finds its way to a common ISR (interrupt service routine). The ISR reads the status of the highest priority I/O device to find out if it is the one requesting service. If this is not the case the ISR proceeds to examine the status of the immediately lower priority device, and so on, until the source of the interrupt is located. Then, the CPU jumps to another routine which services that particular device. Such an interrupt scheme is known as polled interrupts. Unlike vectored interrupts, it does not require external interrupt circuits. Each interrupt source is simply driving the common interrupt request line of the CPU via an open collector circuit. On the other hand, it increases interrupt processing overheads and slows down CPU response to interrupts.

(a) Consider a system employing polled interrupts and having a total of eight interrupting devices. After jumping to the common ISR the CPU takes 10 μs to read and examine the status of each device. How much time is wasted for polling when the lowest priority device causes an interrupt? (Assume no pending interrupts.)

(b) Suppose the rate at which interrupts are generated is the same for all eight devices. What is the average length of time wasted for device polling? (Assume, again, no pending interrupts.)

5-8. Response Time to an Interrupt. A designer wants to determine how long it takes to get to the ISR of the highest priority device. From the CPU users manual and discussions with software engineers, the designer accumulated the data listed in Figure P5-8. These data concern the duration of the various tasks associated with interrupt processing (in terms of clock cycles). With this information at hand and the fact that the CPU is clocked at a rate of 5 MHz, answer the questions that follow.

(a) Determine the worst case response time to an interrupt of the highest priority (ignore any interrupts that might be pending; response time is the time taken to get to the ISR).

(b) In what range will response times vary for the highest priority interrupts?

(c) The probabilities that the current instruction cycle needs 20, ten, or six clock cycles to complete (when an interrupt occurs) are 20, 30, and 50 percent, respectively. Calculate the average response time to an interrupt.

5-9. Interrupt Processing Overheads. A particular system takes (on the average) 30 μs

TASK	DURATION
• Completion of the longest instruction	50
• Activation of the CPU interrupt request input by the external interrupt circuits following generation of an interrupt by an I/O device	2
• Interrupt acknowledgement and reading of the interrupt vector from I/O device	16
• Saving of the contents of CPU registers in the stack and other housekeeping operations	60
• Getting to the beginning of the ISR through the interrupt vector	52

Figure P5-8.

to get to the pertinent ISR afer the interrupt is honored. On the average, an ISR takes 150 μs to execute. However, servicing of an I/O device actually takes 135 μs. The remaining 15 μs are taken up with restoring the contents of the CPU registers and for other operations associated with returning to the interrupted program.

(a) Determine (in percent) the total overhead associated with an interrupt, considering that the only productive time is the time consumed for device servicing.

(b) Measurements on the real system indicate an average of 750 interrupts per second. Calculate what fraction of CPU time is spent on interrupts.

5-10. Impact of Data Block Transfers on Interrupt Response Times. Noninterruptible data block transfers can have a serious impact on interrupt response times. As a first example consider a string processing type of instruction moving a block of data from a set of consecutive memory (or I/O) locations to some other memory (or I/O) area. Unless the CPU is designed to allow interruption of the execution of such instructions, no interrupt can be acknowledged until the entire data block is transferred. As a second example consider a DMA block transfer. Here, again, no interrupt can be acknowledged until the DMA device returns control of the bus to the CPU. So, if interrupt response times are critical in your application, you may have to restrict the allowable length of such transfers.

In order to appreciate the interrupt delays introduced by noninterruptible block transfers, consider a system where DMA devices are operating at the rate of 2 MB/s. The CPU of the same system has a string processing instruction which is noninterruptible. This instruction takes 15 clock cycles for the transfer of each 16-bit word.

(a) The CPU uses the above instruction to fill a 128-byte I/O device buffer. By how long could such transfers increase interrupt response times? The CPU is clocked at a rate of 5 MHz.

(b) The data blocks transferred by some of the DMA devices of this system are up to 256 bytes long. What could be the impact of a single DMA block transfer on interrupt response times?

(c) Suppose interrupts must be acknowledged within 64 μs at the latest. To what length should you limit the lengths of the data blocks in order to meet this requirement? Calculate this for both types of transfers discussed above [questions (a) and (b)]. Ignore the time taken for completion of the current instruction.

5-11. Insertion of Wait States in DMA Cycles. One of the key characteristics of a DMAC (direct memory access controller) is the speed at which it can transfer data to/from memory. However, the actual DMA speed is also a function of memory speed. In fact, very often it is necessary to slow down the DMAC such that memory can keep up with it. How do we slow down a DMAC?—either by reducing its clocking rate or by inserting wait states. Take, for example, the 8237A DMAC. Like the 8088/ 8086 CPUs, its read and write cycles consist of four states, and the duration of each state is equal to the period of its own clock. The 8237A samples its *READY* input while in state *T*3 and inserts one wait state if at a low. Thereafter it keeps inserting more wait states until *READY* goes to a high.

(a) Assume that memory is faster than the DMAC. What is the maximum possible rate of DMA transfers if the DMAC is clocked at a rate of 4 MHz?

(b) When clocked at 4 MHz, the DMAC guarantees a read strobe pulse width of 220 ns. However, memory requires this parameter to be 350 ns (at minimum). How many wait states do we have to insert in each DMA read cycle? What is the resulting DMA transfer rate?

(c) The pertinent data sheets guarantee the read strobe pulse width to be $T - 30$ (where T is the period of the DMAC clock). Can we meet the memory pulse width requirement without using wait states? To what value should we lower the clocking rate of the DMAC to meet this requirement?

5-12. Passing Bus Mastership Between CPU and a DMAC. When a device is ready for a DMA transfer, it generates a DMA request to the DMAC. Then the DMAC activates the bus request (BR) line of the CPU to request control of the bus. The elapsed time, until the CPU responds with a bus grant (BG), depends not only on the particular CPU but also on what the CPU is doing at the time the DMAC places its request. For example, if the CPU is engaged in a bus cycle, it will wait for its completion and then grant the bus. Here we will assume that the bus is granted within two (CPU) clock cycles. Similarly, when the DMAC drops the BR signal, the CPU does not drop BG immediately. It does so within about two (CPU) clock cycles. Assume it takes the DMAC four clock cycles per DMA cycle and that both CPU and DMAC use a 5 MHz clock.

(a) How long does it take to transfer 64 bytes if we operate the DMAC in cycle stealing mode? Include the time for gaining and releasing the bus.

(b) Repeat for burst mode of operation.

(c) What fraction of the calculated values represents overhead?

5-13. Cycle Stealing versus Burst Mode in DMA. Consider a system in which gaining or releasing the bus takes two clock cycles. The time to do a byte transfer (once the DMAC is in control of the bus) is equal to six clock periods. Both CPU and DMAC use a 4 MHz clock. A peripheral I/O device provides data in blocks of 128 bytes with consecutive bytes coming at a rate of one every 20 μs.

(a) The DMAC is operated in burst mode. For how long is the CPU prevented from using its bus during a 128-byte block transfer? What fraction of this time is wasted unnecessarily?

(b) Repeat if the DMAC is operated in cycle stealing mode.

(c) Suppose the CPU is equipped with an instruction queue. Is there any chance it might be doing productive work for some appreciable portion of the time it waits to regain the bus? Answer this for both burst and cycle stealing modes.

(d) Which DMA mode would you choose if the I/O device provides consecutive bytes at the rate of one every 2.5 μs?

5-14. Programmed versus Interrupt-Driven I/O. A low-speed I/O device provides (at most) one byte of information every 100 ms. The device is scanned by the CPU regularly every about 50 ms (programmed I/O). Some analysis indicates that each time the CPU scans the device it consumes about 20 μs of its time. Besides, it has been determined that on the average the device provides only one byte per second. Calculate the improvement ratio (in terms of CPU time) if we equip the I/O device with interrupt capability. Assume the interrupt service routine and associated overheads amount to 40 μs.

5-15. Interrupt-Driven I/O versus DMA. An I/O device is capable of accepting one byte of data every 100 μs. The data are transferred to the device in blocks of 256 bytes. Initially we consider designing the system such that the device will cause an interrupt whenever it is ready to accept another byte of data. It is estimated that servicing of each interrupt will take a total of about 40 μs.

   (a) What will be the improvement ratio (in terms of CPU time) if we employ DMA in the cycle stealing mode and interrupt the CPU only after transferring the whole block? Assume a total of 2 μs to gain the bus, transfer a byte, and return bus control to the CPU. Also assume that the CPU does no productive work while its bus is tied up.

   (b) Suppose that such 256-byte blocks are transferred to the device at an average rate of one every 2 seconds. What fraction of CPU time is consumed for device service when employing interrupt-driven I/O?

   (c) Assume blocks are transferred at a rate of 20 per second. What fraction of CPU time we will economize if we employ DMA?

5-16. Timing Loops. Sometimes we have to generate time delays of specified lengths in order to time certain actions of a running program. Take, for instance, the case of an electromechanical device with one or more motors. After turning a particular motor on we may have to wait before instructing the device to perform another task in order to allow the motor to reach full speed. Such time delays may, of course, be generated with programmable timers. Another approach is to use a program loop whose execution time can be calculated from those of the individual instructions. A specific time delay is then produced by executing the time loop an appropriate number of times. This approach deserves consideration when the μP is dedicated to controlling the device.

   (a) From the user's manual of your CPU you find out the execution time of each instruction of the loop (in terms of clock cycles). Then, by summing up, you calculate that the loop takes 80 clock cycles to execute. How many times would you have to execute the loop if you are to generate a time delay of 1 ms? Assume clocking of the CPU at 8 MHz.

   (b) How would you generate a 250-μs-wide pulse over one of the lines of an output port?

   (c) Suppose you upgrade a system with a 10 MHz version of the CPU. What will the new execution time of the timing loop be? What do you have to adjust (as far as timing loops go) if you are to prevent timing problems in part (b)?

5-17. Programmable Timers. Preferably, time delays are generated by hardware rather than software means (see Problem 5-16). Usually, this is accomplished with programmable timers. In addition to eliminating direct involvement of the CPU, these timers offer many other helpful functions. Consider a system using an 8254 programmable interval timer (PIT). The timer is clocked at a rate of 2 MHz.

(a) What initial contents would you load into counter 1 if you are to use it for generation of interrupts timed at 1 ms intervals? What is the longest time interval you can count with this counter in BCD mode?

(b) Assume your system is attached to a network. You are about to send a message to some other system and wish to measure how long it takes to get a response back. Describe how one could perform such a measurement by means of an 8254.

(c) What is the longest time interval you can measure with an 8254? (Express it in terms of its clocking frequency f.)

5-18. RS-232C Interface Standard. A design engineer tests a newly designed RS-232C interface to determine if it meets the 30 V/μs slew rate. The oscilloscope indicates that the voltage levels are -12 and $+12$ V and that signal transitions are approximately linear. Subsequently the designer measures the durations of signal transitions and finds that transitions from $+12$ to -12 V take about 0.8 μs. Those from -12 to $+12$ V take only 0.5 μs.

(a) Does the interface under test satisfy the slew rate requirement of the RS-232C standard?

(b) The designer consults the data sheets of the employed drivers and finds out that during transitions from a low to a high the drivers supply a constant current of 10 mA. Determine the approximate value of the capacitor you have to connect at the output of each driver in order to meet the 30 V/μs slew rate requirement.

(c) What is the duration of a transition from -12 to $+12$ V after connecting such a capacitor at the output of each driver?

(d) Generally, rise times are measured between the 10 percent and 90 percent points of a transition. Calculate the rise times of the interface signals with and without the above capacitors.

5-19. RS-449 Interface Standard. The RS-449 standard allows cables up to 4000 ft long. However, the maximum allowable cable length depends on the transmission rate. For example, if our transmission rate is only 50 Kb/s, and we use properly terminated 24 AWG twisted-pair cable, we may indeed go that far. On the other hand, if the transmission rate is 1 Mb/s, the maximum allowable cable length will be only around 300 ft.

(a) What is the main reason justifying the dependence of the maximum allowable cable length on the transmission rate? (Hint: Rise and fall times must not exceed one half of the nominal duration of a pulse.)

(b) When employing the RS-423A, the maximum allowable cable length does not depend only on the transmission rate. It also depends on the shape of the signal waveforms. For example, all other parameters being equal, linear waveshaping permits cables more than twice as long as those allowed with exponential waveshaping. This is because crosstalk noise depends on the maximum value of dV/dt during signal transitions (see Problem 4-16; also Section 5.6). So the crosstalk noise generated by two signals can be different even when transitions take the same amount of time for both signals. Crosstalk noise increases with the length of the cable too. Hence, if a particular waveform contributes more noise, we must use shorter cables to keep such noise at a tolerable level. Consider an exponential and a linear waveform taking the same amount of time to reach the 90 percent level of a high from a low. Prove that for the exponential waveform the value of dV/dt is more than twice that of the linear one.

5-20. Asynchronous Serial Communication. An asynchronous serial communication controller (SCC) is programmed for a character length of seven bits, odd parity, and one stop bit. The transmission rate is 1200 b/s.

(a) Illustrate the overall character format (including start and stop bits).

(b) Up to how many characters can be transmitted per second?

(c) The system is designed such that the SCC causes an interrupt whenever ready to accept or deliver another character. At what rate will the CPU be interrupted if we communicate in full duplex mode?

(d) Our system exchanges with some other system two 64-character-long blocks per second (on the average). The servicing of an SCC interrupt takes a total of about 83 μs. Determine (on a percent basis) what fraction of CPU time is consumed for serial I/O.

5-21. Synchronous Serial Communication. A system is equipped with two synchronous serial communication ports operating in full duplex mode. The transmission rate for both (bidirectional) channels is 9600 b/s. Each frame of information is 1064 bits long and carries 128 bytes of data.

(a) The SCC is programmed such that it interrupts the CPU every time it is ready to accept or provide another byte of data. At what rate will the SCC interrupt the CPU while receiving a frame? What if the SCC deals simultaneously with one frame per direction of each channel?

(b) It is estimated that interrupt servicing (for each data byte) takes a total of about 50 μs and that the composite traffic (over both ports) amounts to about 25 frames/s. What fraction of its time does the CPU spend servicing the SCC?

(c) Assume that we are using DMA and that the CPU is still interrupted once per frame. However, the data are transferred to/from memory by a four-channel DMAC. In cycle stealing mode, each DMA cycle takes 1 μs (including bus control transfer overheads). It is also estimated that during such transfers there is a 20 percent chance the CPU may stay idle waiting for the DMAC to release the bus. What portion of the CPU time is now taken by operations associated with the SCC? Assume the same interrupt service time and composite traffic data given in the previous question.

(d) Suppose the transmission rate of each channel is 64 Kb/s. Is there any chance of being able to employ interrupt-driven I/O the way we did in questions (a) and (b)?

(e) Repeat question (c) for the rate of 64 Kb/s.

5-22. LED Driving. A designer uses a standard TTL inverter to drive an LED indicator which has a forward voltage drop of 2 V for a recommended forward current of 15 mA.

(a) What should the value of the series resistor be if we are to drive the LED as recommended by its manufacturer? Assume 0.3 V for the saturation voltage at the output of the inverter.

(b) Consider the circuit shown in Figure 5-37(c) which drives one section of an LED light bar. The manufacturer specifies that the forward voltage drop can be calculated by multiplying the forward current with 50 Ω and adding 1.6 V. What should the value of resistor R be? Assume for each diode a forward current of 20 mA and a saturation voltage of 0.16 V at the output of the driver.

5-23. LED Test Circuits. A μC-based medical instrument is to employ LEDs for indication of certain critical events. Because of the dangerous consequences resulting from a faulty LED (or a faulty LED driver), it is decided to monitor on a continuous basis each LED and its associated driver. If any of them fails, then an interrupt is to be generated to the CPU. Design the monitoring circuits to satisfy the described requirements for three LEDs.

5-24. Bus Design. Going back to Figure 5-47(b), we see that both the 796 bus and the VME bus are nonmultiplexed. In fact, this is the case with many μC buses.

(a) Does this increase the number of bus lines?

(b) Does it increase the complexity of the bus interface circuits at the slaves?

(c) With all other factors being equal, does it allow higher bus speeds?

(d) Why do μC buses employ generally negative logic for interrupt and certain other signals?

5-25. Bus Delays. A (backplane-etched) μC bus has a distributed capacitance of 2 pF/in. and a distributed inductance of 0.02 μH/in.

(a) At what speed do signals propagate over the bus when it is unloaded? Compare the signal speed to that of light.

(b) Suppose we drive one end of the bus from a low to a high. After how long we will "see" the transition at the other end if the bus is 10 in. long?

(c) The backplane provides 20 equally spaced board slots (that is, 0.5 in. board-to-board spacing). The capacitance presented to each line by the connector and the bus driving/receiving circuits of each board is 8 pF. Repeat part (b) given the backplane is fully populated.

5-26. Signal Reflections in μC Buses. Consider the bus described in Problem 5-25. Assume that the rise/fall times of the signals injected into the signal lines by the bus drivers are about 5 ns.

(a) Would you be concerned about signal reflections if the bus is very lightly loaded?

(b) What if the backplane is fully populated as in question (c) of Problem 5-25?

(c) Suppose we plug the CPU board in slot 1 and all other slots are occupied by slave boards. Which of the slave boards will experience the longest duration of ringing?

5-27. Bus Termination. Consider the bus termination scheme pictured in Figure 5-52. Assume a saturation voltage of 0.3 V for the bus drivers.

(a) What should the current sinking capability of the bus drivers (at minimum) be?

(b) How much power is dissipated in each pull-up resistor while the line is at a low?

5-28. Bus Termination. The equivalent termination resistance of the terminating two-resistor networks in Figure 5-52 is about 130 Ω. Suppose we drop the pull-down resistors and replace each resistor pair by a single 130 Ω pull-up resistor.

(a) By what amount will the current sinking capability of the bus drivers have to increase?

(b) How about the power dissipated in each pull-up resistor?

5-29. Bus Termination. Consider a 10 in.-long μC bus having a characteristic impedance of 120 Ω when unloaded. The bus has a distributed capacitance of 2 pF/in. and a uniform capacitive load of 16 pF/in.

(a) What termination resistance (Z) would eliminate completely reflections at the ends of the bus?

(b) Assume we employ the two-resistor network approach of Figure 5-52. For what values of the pull-up and pull-down resistors will we be able to eliminate reflections at both ends of the bus? Take into account that when a line is at a high, these resistors must maintain a voltage of 3 V.

(c) Determine the required current sinking capability of the bus drivers assuming a saturation voltage of 0.3 V. How much power is dissipated in each pull-up resistor?

(d) Such high currents increase power dissipation, noise, and the cost of the drivers themselves. Consequently, we decide to use the resistor values shown in Figure 5-52. These resistors yield an equivalent termination resistance (Z_1) of about 130 Ω. As a result of this compromise, reflections at the two ends of a signal line are not completely eliminated. The ratio between the amplitude of the reflected waveform (at the end of the line) and the amplitude of the arriving waveform is called the reflection coefficient. It can be determined from the relation $K = (Z_1 - Z) / (Z_1 + Z)$. Calculate the reflection coefficient under the above conditions.

(e) As an improvement, a designer suggests connecting a diode between each signal line and a constant voltage source of 0.7 V. What kind of improvement can we achieve with such diodes?

5-30. Crosstalk Noise. Crosstalk noise can be reduced by slowing down signal transitions. In fact, some commercially available bus transceivers are designed to provide slow signal transitions for this purpose. For example, a particular bus transceiver switches in either direction within about 15 ns. This is much longer than the 3 ns switching time of an ordinary Schottky driver.

(a) Determine the percent reduction in crosstalk noise amplitude when using the above transceiver instead of a driver whose output signal has a 3 ns rise/fall time. Assume the same output voltage swing for both devices.

(b) When it comes to clock lines, our options are limited because clock edges must generally be sharp. Why?

5-31. Bus Receivers. For bus receivers we need high input impedance in order to reduce bus loading and signal reflections along the bus. In addition, the receiving circuits of commercial bus transceivers are often equipped with low-pass RC filters at their inputs. Such a filter consists of a series resistor and a capacitor connecting between the receiver input and ground. The filter serves noise rejection purposes. Consider a bus receiver having a threshold of 1.7 V. Assume its input filter has an RC time constant of 30 ns.

(a) Suppose a positive-going noise spike arrives while the signal level at the receiver input is 0.2 V. Upon arrival of the noise spike, the input capacitor C starts charging through R. The outcome depends on the amplitude and the duration of the spike. These two characteristics determine whether C will reach 1.7 V or not while the spike lasts. Would a 2.5-V-high, 20-ns-wide square noise pulse be rejected by the receiver?

(b) A negative-going noise spike arrives while the signal level at the input of the receiver is at 2.7 V. Assume again (for simplicity) that the shape of such spikes is square and also that their amplitude does not exceed 2 V. How wide a noise pulse is guaranteed to be rejected by the receiver?

(c) What delays does the filter introduce during normal signal transitions from 0.2 V to 2.7 V and vice versa? Disregard rise and fall times.

5-32. Phantom Interrupts. While debugging a new μC system, a designer finds out that the CPU consumes an unexpectedly large fraction of its time handling interrupts. As a first step the designer disables all maskable interrupts and determines that the CPU is not interrupted now at all. The project engineer suspects the cause of the problem

and suggests disabling all interrupting devices instead.   After doing so, the designer
finds out that the CPU is still spending a substantial amount of time handling interrupts.

(a) What do you suspect as a probable cause, given none of the interrupting devices
is malfunctioning?

(b) After further investigation the designer determines that one of the interrupt request lines of the µC bus is very noisy.   In fact, this occurs whenever certain data
patterns are transmitted over the data lines of the bus.   Subsequent inspection
of the backplane shows that the noisy interrupt request line is adjacent to a group
of eight data lines.   What is the cause of the noise?   Why is it associated with
data patterns?

(c) What remedies would you suggest so that system debugging can continue?

(d) The designer observes that there is an unused pin between the pin corresponding
to the noisy interrupt line and those carrying the eight data bits.   What change
would you make in the layout of the backplane to rectify the problem permanently?
The solution should not impose any changes on the circuit boards themselves.

(e) Suppose that after disabling all maskable interrupts the designer had found that
the problem persists.   What would you suspect as a probable cause?

(f) How would you go about detecting and reporting such "phantom" interrupts
through the interrupt service routines?

5-33. Bus Arbitration.   Consider the system discussed in Example 5-30 where bus priorities
are resolved serially.

(a) To what value do you have to reduce the frequency of the $BCLK^*$ in order to
make possible chaining of up to six masters?

(b) What is the penalty?

5-34. Bus Arbitration.   The requirement to resolve priority within one period of $BCLK^*$
does not constrain only the serial priority resolving scheme—it also constrains the
parallel priority resolving scheme.   Going back to Figure 5-46(b), we see that in the
parallel priority resolving scheme we use the $BREQ^*$ outputs of the arbiters instead
of $BPRO^*$.   Following a request by its master, the bus arbiter activates its $BREQ^*$
output shortly after the next falling edge of the clock.   In the case of the 8289 bus
arbiter, this time is 35 ns (at maximum).   Here the timing constraint is that the priority
resolution logic must sort things out fast enough such that the $BPRN^*$ inputs of all
arbiters settle at least 15 ns prior to the next falling edge of $BCLK^*$ (see Example
5-30).

(a) How long a delay could we tolerate through the priority resolution logic if we use
an 8 MHz bus clock?   Allow 5 ns for propagation delays along the signal paths
between the priority resolution circuits and the arbiters.

(b) Suppose the priority resolution circuits introduce a delay longer than that calculated in the previous question.   What course of action would you take?

5-35. Bus Timeout.   Consider a system whose µC bus is based on the 796 standard.

(a) Suppose the master is based on a 68000 µP.   Which CPU input would you control
with the $XACK^*$ signal of the bus?

(b) How about a master based on an 8086 µP?

(c) It is decided to implement a timeout circuit (see Example 5-29).   Which signal
would you employ to trigger such a circuit in the case of a 68000-based master?

(d) Repeat the previous question for the case of an 8086-based master.

6

PERIPHERALS

In Chapter 5 we dealt with the techniques employed for entering and obtaining information from a processor. We have seen that information flows between processor and the outside world via parallel and/or serial I/O ports. It may also flow directly between memory and the outside world via DMA channels. However, very little was said about the devices connecting at the other side of such ports and channels. It is these devices that permit us to communicate with machines. They are known as **I/O peripheral devices**, or simply **I/O peripherals**. Without them we cannot enter in the system commands, programs, or data. Neither can we obtain the results of the execution of commands and programs.

Another major limitation of the systems we discussed thus far concerns memory. Where do we store information when we run out of memory space? Such information may include programs and large amounts of data. Naturally, memory capacity is not limited only by the size of the address space. It is also limited by cost. Besides, programs that are not often used by the CPU need not be resident in memory all the time. Instead, they could be stored externally and brought into memory only when needed. Even if we could fit everything in memory we may still have a problem because of the volatility of RAM devices. This problem is a serious one. Usually, the only information stored in read-only memory is the system loader and perhaps certain diagnostic program. Thus, a power failure causes a loss of all other programs and data. On the other hand, power backup is neither economical nor practical. What we really need is some nonvolatile (external) means of storing information at a reasonable cost. Storage devices, or **storage peripherals**, satisfy this need.

I/O peripherals and storage peripherals are collectively referred to as pe-

ripherals. They are the subject of this last chapter. First we overview μC peripherals and discuss the approaches employed in the design of their control circuits.
Then we discuss four common types of peripherals. They are:

- Keyboards (for input)
- CRT displays (for output)
- Printers (for output)
- Floppy disks (for storage)

We are primarily interested in the control circuits required for each of these peripherals. However, prior to examining such circuits we need to understand how
a peripheral operates. Consequently, for each peripheral, we start with the principles of its operation. In the course of examining control circuits we will have
the opportunity to deal with integrated peripheral controllers. We will also discuss
design examples illustrating the issues involved in attaching peripherals to a system.

6.1 OVERVIEW OF μC PERIPHERALS

Generally, peripherals are electrical or electromechanical assemblies. They are
either free-standing or mounted in the same enclosure with other parts of a μC
system such as the CPU board, the power supply, and so on. The performance
of a μC system depends very much on the characteristics of its peripherals. At
the same time, peripherals may represent the largest part of the total cost of a μC
system.

   Peripherals interface to a CPU the same way I/O devices in general do. For
example, the basic I/O functions discussed in Section 5.1 hold for peripherals as
well (see Figure 5-1). In fact, in Section 5.2 we used as I/O device examples two
simple peripherals: a keyboard and a character printer. Figure 5-8 illustrates how
we would go about designing the I/O interface circuits for these two peripherals
with common logic circuits, and Figure 5-13 shows how we can accomplish the
same task with an I/O interface controller. In Figure 5-21 we enhanced the interface controller with interrupt capabilities for implementation of interrupt-driven
I/O. Furthermore, what we picture as an I/O device in the DMA interface diagrams
of Figures 5-25 and 5-27 could (again) be a peripheral. However, we have not
dealt with the circuits controlling the internal operations of a peripheral—for
example, the circuits controlling the motion of various motors within a printer.
We will refer to these circuits collectively as **peripheral controllers**.

   Where do we accommodate the peripheral controller?

   1. Very often the controller is part of the peripheral itself, as indicated in Figures
      6-1(a) and (b). The interface between the peripheral and the CPU board
      may be either parallel or serial. In the serial case, shown in Figure 6-1(b),

the peripheral connects to the CPU via a serial communication controller (SCC). This approach is used often for low-speed peripherals. The employed mode of communication is usually asynchronous.

2. The peripheral controller may be implemented on a small daughter board. Such a board may then plug into sockets which are mounted on the CPU board. The daughter board may accommodate (in addition to peripheral control circuits) the I/O interface circuitry. Hence, it may connect directly to the CPU bus.

3. We may choose to implement a peripheral controller on a full size board. This case is pictured in Figure 6-1(c). If our system is designed around a μC bus, the peripheral controller plugs directly into the μC bus, as for example, in Figure 5-43. Would such a board play the role of a bus master or a bus slave? The answer depends on whether it is capable of performing DMA transfers or not. When a peripheral controller does not have DMA capability, it constitutes a bus slave. If our system does not employ a μC bus, the peripheral controller connects to the CPU board. This may be accomplished through backplane-etched connections or a (generally short) cable. The full-size board approach is usually employed for complex peripheral controllers such as those for disks. Such controllers are often designed to control two or more peripherals—for example, up to four disks.

Integrated peripheral controllers

Interfacing to a CPU a peripheral which is already equipped with a controller is a fairly straightforward task (Figure 5-13). Designing a peripheral controller is a much more serious one. Fortunately, such designs can be simplified by using special LSI/VLSI devices which are also named peripheral controllers. There are two types of such LSI/VLSI devices:

1. *Dedicated Peripheral Controllers:* These are specialized devices intended for control of some specific types of peripherals. Examples are keyboard controllers and CRT controllers.

2. *Universal Peripheral Controllers:* These are general-purpose devices. In fact, they are very similar to μC chips consisting of a CPU, RAM, ROM or EPROM, I/O ports, timers, and so on. The idea is to store in the on-chip ROM (or EPROM) appropriate program loops. These loops, in conjunction with the timers, generate the timing sequences required for control of a particular peripheral. In other words, this approach necessitates development of the proper firmware. Normally, it is used when a suitable dedicated controller is not available for our particular peripheral. An example of a universal peripheral controller is the Motorola MC68120 "intelligent peripheral controller." This device includes on-chip 2 KB of ROM, 128 bytes of RAM, a set of 23 I/O lines, and so on.

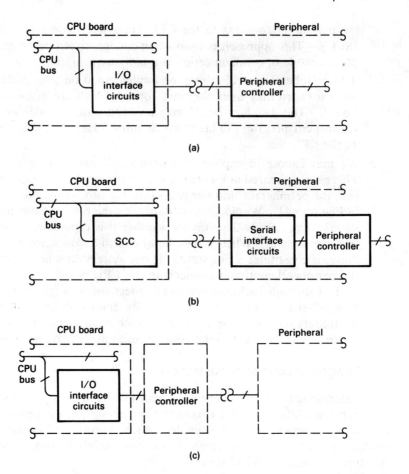

Figure 6-1. Alternatives in interfacing peripherals and accommodating peripheral controllers. (a) The peripheral controller is an integral part of the peripheral and connects to the CPU via a parallel I/O interface. The latter may include, in addition to I/O ports, DMA circuits. (b) Besides the peripheral controller, the peripheral includes serial interface circuits such that communication with the CPU is accomplished via a serial I/O port. (c) The peripheral controller is implemented on a separate board.

Whether dedicated or universal, peripheral controllers economize CPU time because they perform many functions which otherwise would have to be performed by the main CPU. For this reason they are often referred to as **slave processors**. As a matter of fact we may choose to use a dedicated I/O processor to which the main CPU delegates the control of a group of peripherals. This approach is especially attractive in large μC systems where peripherals may consume a large fraction of CPU time.

Next we examine the principles of operation and the control circuits of keyboards. No further attention is to be given to physical partitioning—that is, whether the peripheral controller is implemented on the CPU board, a separate board, or it is an integral part of the peripheral device.

6.2 KEYBOARDS

Keyboards are the most widely employed type of input peripherals. A keyboard consists of an array of labeled **keyswitches** arranged in a typewriter-like fashion. When one of its keyswitches (or simply keys) is depressed, the keyboard generates a unique binary code. It is from this code that the CPU identifies which key was depressed.

Very often a keyboard is combined with an output peripheral into a single unit called a **terminal**. Examples are CRT (or video) terminals consisting of a keyboard and a CRT display. In such terminals the output peripheral plays an additional role—that is, it serves to display the programs and data entered through the keyboard.

What coding schemes do we employ in keyboards? What kind of symbols do they code? What type of device is a keyswitch? How about the circuits involved in a keyboard? How do they communicate with the CPU? Are there any special controllers for keyboards? How do we apply them in the design and interfacing of keyboards? These are the topics we deal with in this section. We start with the coding schemes.

ASCII Code

One of the most common keyboard coding schemes is the **ASCII code** (American Standard Code for Information Interchange). Figure 6-2(a) shows the 7-bit ASCII code. The coded symbols include

1. The letters of the alphabet
2. Numerals
3. Special symbols for punctuation and so forth

The remaining 34 codes are employed for control functions such as:

- Back space (BS)
- Line feed (LF)
- Carriage return (CR)
- Functions associated with remote communication

b7 b6 b5 (most significant) →				Bits	COLUMN →	$^0_0{}_0$ / 0	$^0_0{}_1$ / 1	$^0_1{}_0$ / 2	$^0_1{}_1$ / 3	$^1_0{}_0$ / 4	$^1_0{}_1$ / 5	$^1_1{}_0$ / 6	$^1_1{}_1$ / 7
b4 ↓	b3 ↓	b2 ↓	b1 ↓		ROW ↓	0	1	2	3	4	5	6	7
0	0	0	0		0	NUL	DLE	SP	0	@	P		p
0	0	0	1		1	SOH	DC1	!	1	A	Q	a	q
0	0	1	0		2	STX	DC2	"	2	B	R	b	r
0	0	1	1		3	ETX	DC3	#	3	C	S	c	s
0	1	0	0		4	EOT	DC4	$	4	D	T	d	t
0	1	0	1		5	ENQ	NAK	%	5	E	U	e	u
0	1	1	0		6	ACK	SYN	&	6	F	V	f	v
0	1	1	1		7	BEL	ETB	'	7	G	W	g	w
1	0	0	0		8	BS	CAN	(	8	H	X	h	x
1	0	0	1		9	HT	EM	)	9	I	Y	i	y
1	0	1	0		10	LF	SUB	*	:	J	Z	j	z
1	0	1	1		11	VT	ESC	+	;	K	[	k	{
1	1	0	0		12	FF	FS	,	<	L	\	l	¦
1	1	0	1		13	CR	GS	—	=	M	]	m	}
1	1	1	0		14	SO	RS	.	>	N	^	n	~
1	1	1	1		15	SI	US	/	?	O	—	o	DEL

(a)

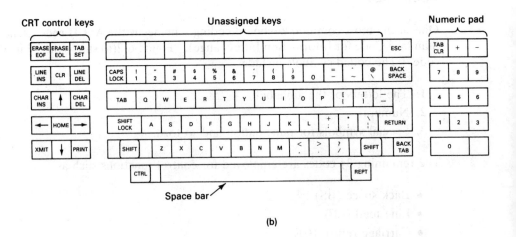

(b)

Figure 6-2. (a) ASCII code. (b) Example of a keyboard including a numeric pad and a cluster of control keys for a CRT display.

The codes assigned to control functions are those corresponding to SP, DEL, and the first two columns of the ASCII table shown in Figure 6-2(a).

Notice from Figure 6-2(a) that the 7-bit codes for lower and upper case alphabetic characters differ only in the value of bit b6, which is always a 1 for lower case characters. For upper case characters it has the value of 0. For example, the ASCII code for "p" is 1110000, while the one for "P" is 1010000. Thus we may use the same key for both, provided that for upper case letters we depress some other key, forcing b6 to a 0. Keyboards do indeed provide such a key. It is called the **SHIFT key**. This approach is used widely for other symbols as well.

The required number of keys can be reduced further by using an extra key called the **CONTROL key**, which forces b7 to a 0 when depressed. Although it is quite desirable, key reduction must be done with caution. Otherwise, the operation of the keyboard may become very involved. In fact, very often, keyboards dedicate two or more keys to the same symbol (or function) for convenience of operation.

Example of a Keyboard

The keyboard pictured in Figure 6-2(b) is a MICRO SWITCH 103SD30 series. First, let us examine the main section of the array. It consists of keys for alphanumeric and other special symbols. Four modes of operation are provided in this particular keyboard:

1. *Ordinary (Unshifted) Mode:* Depression of one of the keys generates the ASCII code corresponding to the lower case symbol. For example, depression of the Q key generates the ASCII code for "q." Similarly, depression of the !/1 key generates the ASCII code for "1."

2. *Shift Mode:* Suppose we depress one of the two SHIFT keys while doing so for an ordinary key. Then, the keyboard generates the code corresponding to the upper case symbol. For example, instead of the codes for "q" and "1," the keyboard generates those for "Q" and "!." Besides the two SHIFT keys, this keyboard provides a **SHIFT LOCK key**, which is an alternate action key. It allows the operator to lock the keyboard in shift mode until one of the SHIFT keys is depressed and released again.

3. *Control Mode:* Certain (ordinary) keys generate control codes if we depress the CTRL (control) key at the same time.

4. *Capitals Lock Mode:* The 103SD30 permits a fourth mode of operation which is enabled through the alternate action **CAPS LOCK key**. While in this mode, the alphabetic keys generate the codes corresponding to upper case letters regardless of the state of SHIFT keys.

Although control codes can be generated while in control mode, this keyboard dedicates five keys of its main section to frequently used control functions such as RETURN, BACK SPACE, and TAB. When depressed, these keys generate the respective control code regardless of the state of the SHIFT and CTRL keys. The same holds true for the unassigned keys which are intended for **user-defined functions**. Finally, there is a **REPT (repeat) key**. When depressed, it enables repeated generation of the character code for the currently depressed symbol key. In other words, the keyboard generates successive character strobes as if the symbol key were depressed and released repeatedly.

Let us now see the other two clusters of keys (seen on the left and right sides of the main section). The cluster on the right consists of numeric (and certain other) keys. It is usually referred to as a **numeric pad**. The cluster on the left provides keys for CRT control (see Section 6.3). It includes keys for editing purposes, such as line insertion or deletion, and keys for cursor control (movement of the cursor horizontally, vertically, or to its home position). Such control keys are required when the keyboard is part of a CRT terminal where the CRT displays the information we enter through the keyboard. Note that the codes generated by these keys are not affected by the SHIFT, CTRL, and CAPS LOCK keys. The same is true for the keys of the numeric pad. This fact, plus the separation of these keys from the main section of the keyboard, is intended to facilitate input of numeric data.

What if the total number of control codes exceeds 34? We have just seen, for instance, that a CRT necessitates additional control codes. The solution is simply to add one more code bit b8 (8-bit ASCII). Another widely employed 8-bit code is the IBM EBCDIC (Extended Binary Coded Decimal Interchange Code).

Keyswitches

The basic element of every keyboard is the keyswitch. Keyswitches are classified into **contacting** and **noncontacting** ones. An example of a contacting keyswitch is the **mechanical keyswitch** illustrated in Figure 6-3(a). When force is applied to the keytop, the plunger pushes the movable contact against the fixed contact and closes the circuit between the two terminals of the switch. When the key is released, the return spring forces the plunger upwards and the circuit opens again. Figure 6-3(b) pictures the so-called crosspoint contact arrangement employed in some mechanical keyswitches. The right angle crossing and the shape of the contacting arms are chosen for greater reliability. Mechanical keyswitches mount individually on a printed board to form a keyboard array.

Figure 6-3(c) depicts the principles of a **membrane-based contacting keyswitch**. Here the entire set of the keyswitches of a keyboard is implemented on a single assembly, which consists of two flexible polyester (or other appropriate material) sheets and an insulating layer sandwiched between them. The whole assembly is then sealed around its outside edges and is mounted on a printed board. The two membrane sheets accommodate the circuit layers which terminate on two contacts

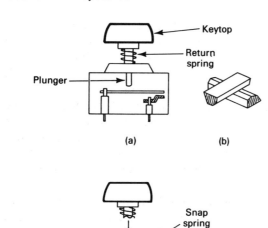

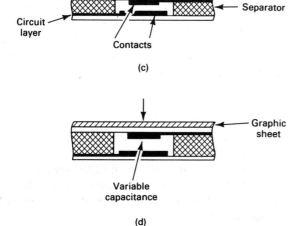

Figure 6-3. Some of the types of keyswitches employed in keyboards. (a) Mechanical keyswitch. (b) Crosspoint contact in a mechanical keyswitch. (c) Membrane switch with dome playing the role of a snap spring. (d) Capacitive switch.

for each switch. When the top of the upper membrane sheet is pressed, the two contacts close the respective circuit through the hole cut into the insulating layer. When pressure is removed, the upper membrane returns to its normal position because of its elasticity.

Depending on the magnitude of the motion involved, contacting membrane keyswitches are categorized into

1. Limited-travel or no-travel keyswitches
2. Full-travel keyswitches

The former are also known as micromotion or **touch-sensitive** keyswitches and are usually employed in applications requiring a sealed front panel. Symbol legends and any other graphics are printed beneath the translucent touch surface and are thus immune to wearing. Full-travel keyboards include for each keyswitch a key, a plunger, and a return spring. The objective is to create the feel of a typewriter-like keyboard and thereby increase the productivity of the operator. Both types of membrane-based contacting keyswitches can be equipped with metal domes which click down and then snap back providing tactile feedback for operator satisfaction. Because of the way they are constructed, membrane-based contacting keyboards are more economical than those employing discrete mechanical switches. They are also less sensitive to vibration and, thanks to their sealed construction, more immune to environmental conditions (moisture, dust, contamination, and so on).

The problem with contacting keyboards of all types is that switch contacts wear out gradually. This in turn affects the reliability and life of keyswitches. Longer lives—on the order of 100 millions of operations—are achieved with non-contacting keyswitches. A main representative of this class are **capacitive keyswitches** like the one pictured in Figure 6-3(d). Notice that this switch is also membrane-based. However, instead of contacts it employs two pads forming a capacitor. When the upper membrane is pressed, the two pads get closer to each other. Hence, the capacitance of the capacitor they form increases. This change constitutes the basis for detecting a key depression.

Keyboard Controllers

How does the CPU sense closure of a keyswitch? In Chapter 5 we saw that switch settings can be monitored by dedicating to each switch one line of an input port (see Figure 5-6). Such an approach becomes inefficient in the case of keyboards, however, because of the large number of switches we are dealing with. For example, a 64-keyswitch keyboard would require eight 8-bit input ports and more than 64 wires for interfacing to the CPU.

A more efficient scheme is employing an X-Y interconnection matrix. The idea is to connect each switch to one of the rows and one of the columns of the matrix. Then, we ground successively each of the rows and examine which (if any) of the columns is at ground voltage. As an example let us consider the case of 64 mechanical keyswitches. Figure 6-4 depicts an 8×8 interconnection matrix for the latter. Notice that each column is maintained at a high via a pull-up resistor to V_{cc}. Now let us assume the switch at point P is depressed and that we apply a low to the uppermost row. You can see that this will pull the right-most column to a low. However, this will not happen when we apply a low to any other row. Hence we have a means of detecting depression of key P (and any other key).

Row lines can be driven to a low via output ports. That is, they constitute output lines from the CPU side. Column lines are treated by the CPU as input lines. They connect to input ports. In the 64-keyswitch example, all we need is one 8-bit output port and one 8-bit input port. Monitoring of switch closures is

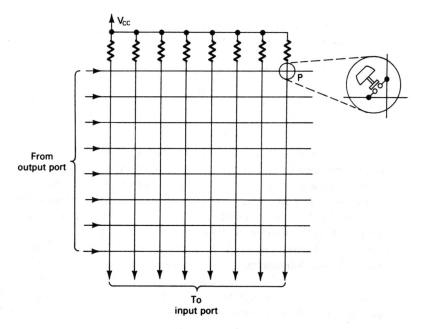

Figure 6-4.   An 8 × 8 keyboard matrix.

accomplished by scanning the matrix periodically. The steps (for the matrix of Figure 6-4) are:

1. The CPU sets (via the output port) the top row line to a low.
2. Subsequently, the CPU reads through the input port the states of the column lines. The objective is to determine which of the column lines (if any) is at a low.
3. If one of the column lines is found to be at a low, the CPU goes to a memory-resident table. This table contains the codes for all keyswitches. The CPU uses the row/column coordinates of the depressed switch to locate the respective code.
4. If none of the columns is found to be at a low, the CPU resets the top row back to a high. Then, it sets the next row to a low and goes on to repeat the described process.
5. After scanning all eight rows, the CPU goes away to work on some other task. Later on (say after 20 ms), it comes back to scan the matrix again.

Example 6-1

Consider an array of 128 keyswitches organized into an 8 × 16 matrix. How many I/O ports are needed for its handling? Suppose it takes 2.5 μs to change the state of the lines of an 8-bit output port and another 2.5 μs to read and check the lines of an input port. How long does it take to scan the entire keyswitch array once?

Solution. One 8-bit output port will suffice for control of the states of the row lines. Since there is a total of 16 columns, we need two 8-bit input ports.

The time required to set a row line to a low and to read/check the states of all 16 columns is $2.5 + 2 \times 2.5 = 7.5$ μs. Hence, scanning of the entire array takes $8 \times 7.5 = 60$ μs.

How about nonsymbol keys like SHIFT, CONTROL, and so on? Such keys are not included in the matrix. Instead, they connect to separate input port lines. Their states are read by the CPU after detecting a switch closure, and they are then used to determine the respective character code. If our keyboard is equipped with a REPEAT key, we need one more dedicated input line. While the REPEAT line is active, the CPU must treat the currently depressed symbol key as if it were depressed/released repeatedly at a certain rate. Moreover, our CPU may have to deal with **switch bouncing**. This is a serious problem when the keyboard employs mechanical keyswitches. Also, the CPU may have to deal with situations resulting from depression of a key before releasing a previously depressed one. This means that the CPU must be capable of

- Avoiding errors when a second key is depressed prior to releasing the first one
- Dealing with the second key after the first one has been released

Such a capability is referred to as **two-key rollover (2-KRO)**. When it extends to more than two keys, it is called **N-key rollover (N-KRO)**.

All these tasks represent a considerable burden for the CPU. This however need not be the case thanks to integrated keyboard controllers. Typically such controllers perform all functions required for a keyboard plus more. When a key is depressed, they simply provide over the CPU data bus the respective character code. As usual, they are programmable for greater flexibility. As an example we will discuss the Signetics SC2671 "programmable keyboard and communications controller."

Example of a Keyboard Controller

Figure 6-5 shows the block diagram of a keyboard controller, the SC2671. It consists of

1. A keyboard control section (keyboard encoder)
2. An asynchronous serial communication control section (asynchronous SCC)
3. Bus logic for interfacing to the CPU

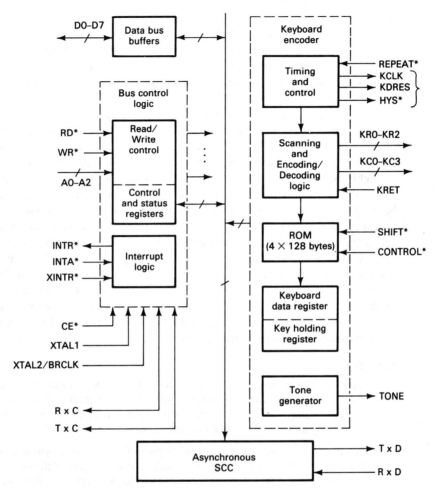

Figure 6-5. Simplified block diagram of the SC2671 programmable keyboard and communications controller.

Lines *XTAL*1 and *XTAL2/BRCLK* connect the on-chip baud rate generator to an external crystal. In addition to serving the SCC, the baud rate generator provides clocking to the keyboard encoder. When we wish to use an external clock instead, that clock is connected to the *XTAL2/BRCLK* input. The *RxC*, *TxC*, *RxD*, and *TxD* lines are for the SCC. With the exception of *XINTR**, the remaining lines seen on the left-hand side connect to the CPU bus. The *XINTR** (external interrupt request) line allows another (external) device to share the on-chip interrupt control logic with the keyboard encoder and the SCC.

All other lines are used for keyboard purposes. The *REPEAT** input is provided for keyboards equipped with a REPEAT key. When the latter is depressed, the encoder generates the code of the currently depressed key about 15 times per second.   The SC2671 is intended for both contacting and capacitive keyboards.   In fact, lines *KCLK* (keyboard clock), *KDRES* (key detect reset), and *HYS** (hysteresis output) are used exclusively for capacitive keyboards.   They control the analog circuits which convert the capacitance changes resulting from key depressions into ordinary TTL logic levels.

The SC2671 can scan keyswitch matrices as large as 8×16.   However, in order to economize pins, row and column lines are encoded into three and four lines, respectively.   These are the *KR0–KR2* (keyboard row scan) and *KC0–KC3* (keyboard column scan) lines.   They are decoded externally for selection of one of eight rows and one of 16 columns.   *KRET* (key return) is activated by the external circuits whenever a scanned switch is found to be closed.   The device can be programmed to scan either an 8×16 matrix or an 8×10 one.   Two scanning rates are allowed for each.   In the case of an 8×16 matrix, for instance, we can select the scanning period of the whole matrix to be either 10 ms or 2.5 ms.

What about **debouncing** (when employing mechanical keyswitches)?   How does a keyboard controller know that a switch closure is now stable and can be recorded?   The solution is simply to wait until bouncing dies out.   So when the SC2671 detects closure of a particular keyswitch, it does not record it immediately. Instead, it remembers to verify the fact one scanning period later.   Consequently, the time allowance for debouncing is determined from the selected scanning period.

Example 6-2

Suppose you employ an SC2671 for control of an 8×16 keyswitch array and you program the device for a 2.5 ms scanning period.   What time allowance does it provide for debouncing?   What if the employed mechanical keyswitches are known to bounce for as long as 4 ms right after they are depressed or released?

Solution.   First, assume a keyswitch happens to be scanned right after its depression. Since the SC2671 waits for one scanning period, the keyswitch is allowed 2.5 ms for debouncing.   On the other hand, if the keyswitch happens to be depressed immediately after a scan, the closure is not recorded until 5 ms later, so the time allowance for debouncing will vary between 2.5 and 5 ms.

If the keyswitches are known to be bouncing for as long as 4 ms, we must select a 10-ms scanning period.   This will provide a time interval of at least 10 ms for debouncing.

After verification, the SC2671 combines the row/column coordinates of the depressed key with the states of the SHIFT and CONTROL keys to locate the code in an on-chip ROM.   Notice the size of the ROM is 4×128 bytes.   This is to allow (through the SHIFT and CONTROL keys) selection of one out of four codes per key.   These include the ASCII codes plus additional ones.   Subsequently, the character code is transferred to the key-holding register for reading by the CPU.   What if a previous character is still waiting in the key-holding register? In such cases the new character is transferred into the keyboard data register.

The SC2671 can also operate in a nonencoded mode.   In this mode the SC2671 bypasses the ROM. Instead, it sends to the CPU the row/column address of the key (and the states of the SHIFT and CONTROL keys). In other words, the choice of the code is left to the CPU. Finally, the *TONE* line provides a square wave of programmable frequency and duration.

Design Example

Next we see how we could go about controlling a keyswitch array with an SC2671 controller. We assume keyswitches of the contacting type.

First of all we need a 4-to-16 decoder for the *KC0–KC3* lines of the SC2671 controller. The decoder activates accordingly one of the 16 column lines of the keyswitch array (the SC2671 selects one column at a time and looks at the rows rather than the other way around). We also need an 8-to-1 multiplexer for the row signals. Its select inputs must be connected to the *KR0–KR2* lines of the SC2671 (Figure 6-6). The output of the multiplexer can serve as a *KRET* (key return) signal; that is, if the examined row is at a low, the output of the multiplexer goes to a high, activating the *KRET*.

What if we were dealing with capacitive keyswitches? Here we use the *KCLK* (about 400 KHz) to enable/disable the 4-to-16 decoder and thereby gate the *KC0–KC3* signals. This is essentially equivalent to applying a square wave to the selected column. Also, we have to replace the 8-to-1 digital multiplexer with an analog one whose output now feeds an analog detector. If the scanned capacitive keyswitch is depressed, the series capacitance between the selected column and the examined row is larger. As a result, the amplitude of the square wave seen by the analog detector is higher and its output switches to a high. This signal, in turn, can be used for activation of the *KRET* input of the SC2671. The analog detector is controlled by the *KDRES* and *HYS** signals we saw before.

Keyboard Selection and Other Design Considerations

Keyboards providing a variety of options are available from many manufacturers who very often offer custom design capability. Such offerings range from keyboard assemblies consisting of a mere array of wired keyswitches (without electronics) to complete easy-to-interface keyboards. Let us put aside for the moment the electronic circuits and consider the selection criteria for the keyswitch array:

1. *Type of Keyswitch:* The reliability, life, and cost characteristics of a keyboard depend primarily on the type of the chosen keyswitch. It is also the keyswitch that determines how well our keyboard will perform under adverse conditions (shock, vibration, temperature, and humidity and exposure to dust, vapors, liquids, and contaminants).

2. *Motional Characteristics:* The required actuation force, the profile, travel, and tactile feedback affect **ergonomics**—that is, ease of operation and therefore throughput.

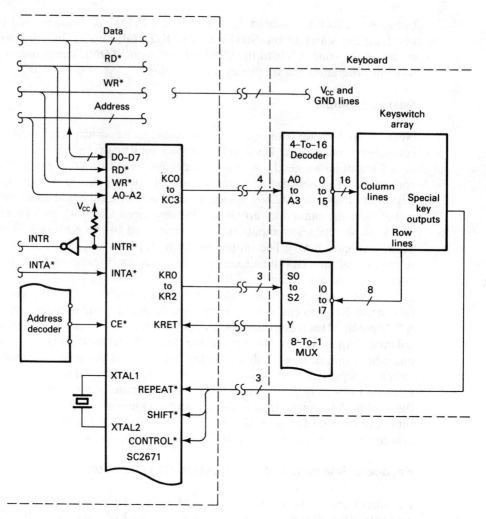

Figure 6-6. Design example employing the SC2671 programmable keyboard and communications controller.

3. *Number of Keys and Their Legends:* Some of the questions to consider are whether there should be separate keypads for numeric and control keys. How many SHIFT keys? Should there be keys for special application-oriented functions? Relegendable unassigned keys?

4. *Position of the Keys:* The relative positions of the keys within the array affect speed and accuracy of operation. For the same reason one may, for instance, consider using oversize keytops for certain symbols or functions.

5. *Other Factors:* Ergonomics also depend on other factors such as key spacing, array style (stepped, slopped, and so on), keytop shape and finish, and color, among others.

Usually the keyboard control ciruits and the keyswitch array share a common printed board. What if the keyboard is not (structurally) integrated with its associated terminal or system? Then the control circuits are accommodated on the keyboard. In such cases the keyboard is referred to as a **detached keyboard**. For detached keyboards you should consider serial communication with the CPU. This simplifies cabling and makes the length of the cable to the rest of the system less critical.

For most applications it is advisable to purchase a complete keyboard rather than to design your own control circuits. Such keyboards are available with and without an enclosure. Known as **encoded keyboards**, their interface lines typically include eight data lines and a strobe line indicating the availability of a character code. There is a choice of options concerning:

- Character codes
- Number of modes
- Key rollover
- Audio feedback with each strobe
- Parity (carried over a 9th data line)
- Level or pulse strobe
- Type of interface logic
- Type of connector

Off-the-shelf complete keyboards are interfaced easily to the CPU via I/O ports employing either polled or interrupt-driven I/O (see Figures 5-13 and 5-21). Whether purchasing or designing a keyboard, you must give special attention to

1. Susceptibility to external noise
2. Its protection from static electricity (via a direct discharge path)

6.3 CRT DISPLAYS

Cathode-ray tube (CRT) displays allow display of large amounts of information, and are used widely as output peripherals. A CRT display may be an integral part of a μC system. It may also be combined with a keyboard into a terminal, commonly known as a **CRT terminal** or **video terminal** [Figure 6-7(a)]. Usually, CRT terminals communicate with the CPU serially.

CRT terminals are very suitable for interactive communication with humans. Besides its ordinary output role, the CRT serves to display commands, programs, and data entered via the keyboard. It can display alphanumeric information, graphics, or both, as seen in Figure 6-7(b).

In some applications—notably those associated with personal computers— we may use an ordinary TV set for information display. The signal is fed to the

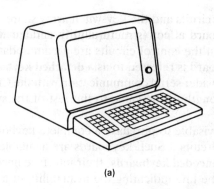

(a)

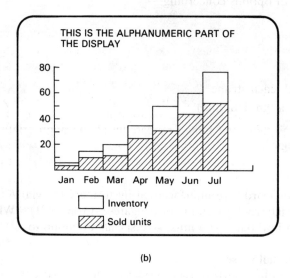

(b)

Figure 6-7. (a) A CRT terminal. (b) Display of alphanumeric (text) and graphics on a CRT screen.

antenna of the TV set via an RF modulator tuned to the frequency of some unused TV channel. Usually though, we employ a **TV (or video) monitor** which is similar to a common TV set except for the lack of RF (and often sound) circuits. These monitors are similar to the TV monitors employed in closed circuit TV and other applications. The higher bandwidth of TV monitors, in conjunction with the elimination of RF circuit stages, allows better quality displays. Thus the design of a CRT display amounts to:

1. Selecting an off-the-shelf TV monitor
2. Designing the display circuits to convert digital information into signals suitable for the TV monitor

This section addresses both tasks for character (or alphanumeric) CRT displays. First, we have to understand the principles of operation of a TV monitor.

We are primarily interested in the electrical characteristics of the signal(s) we must feed to it and in those characteristics affecting the quantity and quality of the information we can display. From these we deduce the criteria for selecting a TV monitor. Our next topic is the design principles of display circuits—that is, how we go about displaying alphanumeric characters on a CRT screen—a process commonly known as character generation. After discussing character generation, we examine integrated CRT controllers. We are interested in the kinds of functions they provide and how to apply them in the design of practical CRT display circuits. The section concludes with an overview of design considerations applying to CRT display circuits.

TV Monitors

Let us first see what a **monochrome**—that is, **black-and-white**—**monitor** consists of. Figure 6-8(a) pictures the block diagram of such a monitor. The basic part is a cathode-ray tube (CRT) which includes an "electron gun" producing a beam of electrons. When the beam passes through the magnetic field of the yoke (mounted on the neck of the CRT) it is deflected. Then it strikes the phosphor layer (coated on the inner side of the screen) which illuminates accordingly. The screen maintains a full picture by refreshing the image repeatedly at the appropriate rate. Most TV monitors employ the same raster scan technique used in common TV sets; that is, the beam scans across and down the screen, causing selected points to turn on or off. The deflection signals are generated by two oscillators. Both oscillators are synchronized by means of externally generated signals: *HSYNC* (horizontal synchronization) and *VSYNC* (vertical synchronization) signals. The *VIDEO* input signal controls the intensity of the electron beam and thereby the illumination of the picture elements displayed on the screen. TV monitors are powered either from AC or from DC (typically 12 or 24 VDC).

    Color TV monitors have a similar organization. However, they employ one electron gun for each of the three primary colors, red, green, and blue. Figure 6-8(b) illustrates the principles of the so-called in-line color TV monitor. It is so named because the three electron guns are positioned along a line. The three beams are directed through a slotted metal shadow. Then they strike the alternating stripes of red, green, and blue phosphors on the screen. The same approach is used in color TV sets because of its low cost.

    Better quality color monitors employ the so-called precision-in-line (PIL) or delta-delta arrangements. In both cases the metal shadow mask has round holes. The distance between neighboring holes is referred to as the **pitch** and determines (in conjunction with other factors) the resolution of a monitor. Now the phosphors are organized into triads of red, green, and blue dots. The dots are so closely spaced that we see a mixture of colors. The difference between these two approaches is that in the delta-delta case the three guns are arranged in a triangle. Regardless of what approach they may employ, color TV monitors have a separate *VIDEO* input for each color.

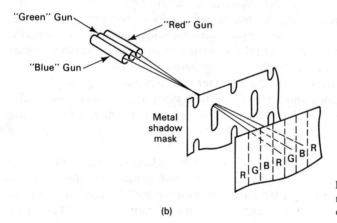

(a)

(b)

Figure 6-8. (a) Block diagram of a TV monitor. (b) Generation of a color display using three in-line electron guns.

Screen scanning

To understand how we can display characters we must first understand how the beam(s) scans the screen. Figure 6-9(a) illustrates one of the common scanning schemes. The electron beam starts from the top left corner and moves horizontally (from left to right) across the screen. After completing the first horizontal scan (see top solid line), it returns to the left edge of the screen to perform a second scan. Meanwhile the beam has been gradually deflected (by the vertical deflection current) downward by some small amount. Hence, the second horizontal scan starts from a different point of the screen. Following the second horizontal scan,

Horizontal
retrace

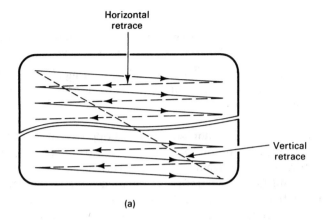

(a)

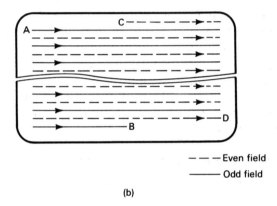

— — — Even field

———— Odd field

(b)

Figure 6-9. Scan lines (raster) in a TV monitor. (a) Noninterlaced. (b) Interlaced.

the beam performs a third one, and so on, until it reaches the bottom right corner of the screen. At this point we say that the beam completed a **vertical scan**, or a **vertical sweep**. Another way of expressing this is to say that the beam has displayed one **frame**. The scan lines are often referred to collectively as **raster**. This scanning technique is itself referred to as **raster scanning**. Next, the beam returns to the top left corner of the screen to repeat the described process for a fresh frame. Refreshing becomes necessary because of the volatile nature of the phosphor-generated images.

At what rate is the screen refreshed? Typically the refresh rate is chosen to be equal to the AC power frequency—that is, either 60 or 50 frames per second in order to avoid "beating" with the AC power frequency (which would cause weaving of the displayed information). A rate of 60 frames/s corresponds to a time interval of 16.67 ms per frame. Typically, though, only 15.42 ms are consumed per vertical scan. The remaining 1.25 ms are consumed by the vertical return, also known as **vertical retrace**.

Example 6-3

Assume a horizontal scan takes about 53.5 μs and a horizontal return (or horizontal retrace) about 10 μs. What is the total number of scan lines per frame?

Solution. The total duration of a horizontal scan, including retracing, is 53.5 + 10 = 63.5 μs. A vertical scan lasts for 15.42 ms or 15420 μs. This provides time for 15420/63.5—that is, about 242—scan lines.

This type of raster scanning is called **noninterlaced**, as opposed to the **interlaced** raster scanning illustrated in Figure 6-9(b). In this type of raster scanning the beam performs two vertical scans per frame. The first vertical scan starts from point A and is known as an **odd field**. When the beam reaches the right edge of the screen it returns to the left side to perform the second horizontal scan of the odd field (see second solid line from the top). The scanning along the solid lines continues until the beam reaches point B. Then the beam jumps to point C to start the second vertical scan known as an **even field**. This one proceeds along the dashed lines until reaching point D. Subsequently, the beam jumps back to point A to start the odd field of another frame.

Because of the greater number of scan lines, interlacing permits better resolution. On the other hand, what we refresh now (at the rate of 60 or 50 Hz) is fields—not frames. The frame refresh rate is halved. Hence, the potential for flicker increases. This problem can be solved by using phosphors having longer persistence. Such a solution has two drawbacks, however:

1. It increases the "smearing" effect generated by moving images.
2. It makes the CRT more expensive.

Common TV sets employ interlacing to enhance picture details (525 lines per frame or 262.5 lines per field).

Timing

Going back to Figure 6-8(a), we see that a monochrome TV monitor requires:

1. Horizontal and vertical sync (synchronization) pulses
2. A video signal

For simplicity we will assume that the video signal is composed of equal height pulses. In other words, we assume a single level of intensity. Our objective is to examine the timing relationships between sync pulses and video pulses.

Figure 6-10(a) depicts the approximate timing relationship between horizontal sync pulses and video pulses. Sync pulses are not necessarily part of the signal carrying the video pulses. They are simply shown together for simplicity. A

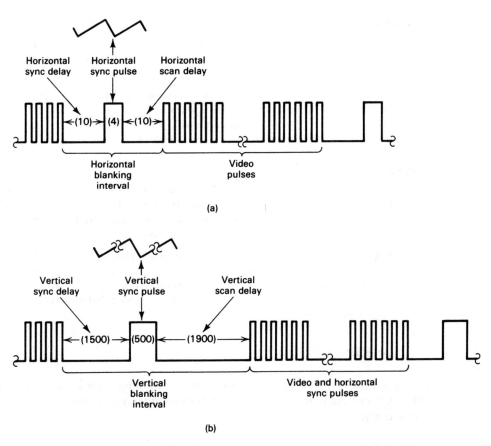

Figure 6-10. Synchronization pulse timing in a TV monitor. (a) Relation of horizontal sync pulses to video pulses. (b) Relation of vertical sync pulses to video pulses. Parenthesized numbers indicate durations in microseconds.

horizontal sync pulse is supplied externally in the course of the horizontal retrace. The width of the pulse is usually 4–30 μs. Observe the (typically) 10 μs margin on both sides of the pulse. These delays are introduced on purpose. The idea is to avoid displaying anything near the edges of the scan lines where distortion due to nonlinearities of the horizontal deflection waveforms becomes significant. Thus, during the whole period indicated as **horizontal blanking interval**, the *VIDEO* input must be externally disabled.

A similar situation holds for vertical sync pulses as can be seen in Figure 6-10(b). Time durations are, of course, much longer. For example, vertical sync pulse widths are usually in the range of 50–1500 μs. The discussed timing relationships apply to color TV monitors as well. However, such monitors have three separate *VIDEO* inputs: one for red, one for green, and one for blue.

Example 6-4

Assume the horizontal sync pulse width and the delay times shown in Figure 6-10(a). A horizontal scan takes 53.5 μs and its retrace 10 μs. What fraction of a horizontal line is usable for display purposes?

Solution. The horizontal scanning period (including retracing) is 63.5 μs. However, the horizontal blanking interval has a duration of $10 + 4 + 10 = 24$ μs. Hence, only $63.5 - 24 = 39.5$ μs are actually usable for information display. This represents a fraction of only 39.5/63.5—that is, 62.2 percent.

Example 6-5

Assume the vertical sync pulse width and delay times shown in Figure 6-10(b). The frame refresh rate is 60 frames/s. What fraction of frame time is wasted as a result of the vertical blanking interval? How many scan lines are usable given the period of the horizontal deflection oscillator is 63.6 μs?

Solution. The vertical blanking interval lasts for $1500 + 500 + 1900 = 3900$ μs, or 3.9 ms. A frame takes 1/60 s, or 16.67 ms. Thus, a fraction of 3.9/16.67, or 23.4 percent, is wasted. The frame time corresponds to a total of 16666.7/63.6 = 262 scan lines. Yet only (16.67 − 3.9)/0.0636—that is, about 200 of them—are usable for display purposes.

Selection criteria

In general, TV monitors allow vertical scanning rates in the range of 47–63 Hz. Other than that, the characteristics of commercial monitors vary (and so does their cost):

1. Would a monochrome monitor satisfy the requirements of your application? If a **color** monitor is preferred, would the extra cost be justifiable?

2. A monitor may operate in noninterlaced **mode**, interlaced mode, or both. Earlier in this section we saw that interlacing has its advantages but also its potential problems.

3. What **size**? Screen sizes vary from 5 to 25 in. They are usually expressed in terms of the length of the screen diagonal.

4. What **resolution** is needed? Resolution determines the amount of information we can display on the screen at a satisfactory quality. It is expressed as a product of two factors. These factors represent the resolution of the monitor in the horizontal and vertical directions.

   (a) Horizontal resolution is determined from the number of distinguishable dots we can display along a scan line. This number depends on the bandwidth of the monitor, which is typically in the range of 15–30 MHz (while that of a common TV set is only 6 MHz). It also depends on the usable portion of each scan line. For example, in a common TV set we may have to use only two-thirds of each scan line.   In a high-quality monitor the usable portion can be as high as 90 percent.

(b) Vertical resolution is determined from the number of distinguishable dots along a vertical axis.   This number depends on the number of scan lines per frame—that is, on the horizontal scanning rate.   This rate varies from 15 KHz (which is the rate employed by common TV sets) to around 30 KHz.   The above definition assumes that the beam's spot size and spot profile do not become a limiting factor before the number of scan lines does.   (Spot profile is a measure of the energy distribution throughout a spot on the screen.)

For color monitors there is one additional factor to consider: pitch.   In fact, it is pitch that prevents color monitors from having as high a resolution as those achievable with monochrome monitors.   In addition, the resolution, as perceived by the operator, will also be (in all cases) a function of the screen size.

5. How about input signals?   Some monitors provide an input for **composite video**; that is, *HSYNC*, *VSYNC*, and *VIDEO* signals need not be fed via separate inputs.   Instead they are combined in accordance with a television standard and are fed to the monitor via a single input.   This option necessitates some extra circuitry.   On the other hand, it simplifies the wiring between display circuits and monitor.

Example 6-6

Why does the horizontal resolution of a TV monitor depend on its bandwidth?

Solution.   Let us assume that information is displayed by turning the beam on/off on a selective basis—that is, at a single level of intensity.   Going back to Figure 6-10, we realize that each video pulse corresponds to a dot position on the screen.   The closer the video pulses to each other, the more dot positions per scan line.   However, this is not enough.   Video pulses must be adequately sharp so that two successive dots can be distinguished from each other.   That in turn depends on the bandwidth of the monitor's video amplifier.

Example 6-7

A particular TV monitor can operate in both noninterlaced and interlaced modes. Its vertical and horizontal scanning rates are 60 Hz and 15.9 KHz, respectively.   Determine its vertical resolution given that only about 80 percent of the scan lines are usable.

Solution.   The vertical scanning rate corresponds to a frame time of 16.667 ms.   From the horizontal scanning rate we calculate that a scan line and its retrace amount to $1/(15.9 \times 10^3)$ s, or 62.9 μs, so the total number of scan lines per frame is 16667/62.9—that is, about 265.   However, since only 80 percent of the lines are usable, the vertical resolution is $265 \times 0.8 = 212$ scan lines.   This result holds for noninterlaced mode.   If we operate the monitor in interlaced mode, we will have about that many lines per field (rather than per frame). Hence, the vertical resolution will be about 2 × 212 = 424 lines.

TV monitors are often classified on the basis of their resolution into low, medium, and high quality. Typically, low-quality monitors have resolutions on the order of 250 × 250. Normally they are used only in character displays of as many as 64 characters per character row. (In a common TV set this number is usually less than 32.) Medium-quality monitors have resolutions on the order of 500 × 500 and are used for both characters and graphics. High-quality monitors, having resolutions of 1000 × 1000 and beyond, can be justified only in graphics.

Character Generation

At this point we know what a TV monitor is and what we have to consider in the course of selecting one. Our next step involves the design principles of the display circuits, as reflected in the block diagram of Figure 6-11. First, how do we form a character on the screen?

Character formation

CRT displays of the raster scan type employ dot matrix fonts. In Figure 6-11 we picture the formation of letter "Z" by means of a 5 × 7 dot matrix font [see also Figure 5-38(c)]. At the beginning of the first scan line, the beam is turned on via the *VIDEO* input five times. This forms the top line of dots for the letter "Z." Then, as the beam sweeps along the first scan line, it forms the first line of dots for the second character, and so on. After reaching the last character position (at the right edge of the screen), the beam is retraced. Subsequently, it starts sweeping along the second scan line. Now the beam forms the second row of dots for the top row of characters. Notice that for the letter "Z" it turns on only once. The process continues until forming the seventh line of dots for the top row of characters. During the next several scan lines we display no information at all (for spacing purposes). Then we start forming the second row of characters.

After forming the last row of characters the beam is retraced back to the top scan line. From there on, it repeats the entire process we have described all over again. In other words, it starts a new frame to refresh the display. Otherwise, the displayed characters would disappear within very short time because of the limited persistence of the phosphor.

Example 6-8

A TV monitor has a vertical resolution of 400 lines. The monitor is used to display characters in a 5 × 7 font. Up to how many rows of characters can we display? Assume that the spacing between consecutive character rows is equivalent to three scan lines.

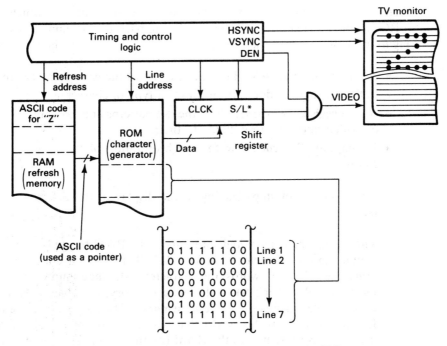

Figure 6-11.   Principles of character generation on a CRT screen.

Solution.   Each character row takes a total of $7 + 3 = 10$ scan lines (including inter-row spacing).   Hence, we can display up to $400/10 = 40$ character rows.

Example 6-9

Consider the TV monitor of Example 6-8.   What should its horizontal resolution be if we are to be capable of displaying up to 80 characters per row?   Assume inter-character spacing along a character row is equivalent to one dot.

Solution.   In the horizontal direction, each character requires five dots for its formation and one for spacing—that is, a total of six dots.   To display 80 characters along a character row, we need a total of $6 \times 80 = 480$ distinguishable dots.

Thus, the monitor in question must have an overall resolution of at least 480×400. The total number of displayable characters (when employing a 5×7 font) is $40 \times 80 = 3200$.

The character generator

At first it looks as if we will have to store in memory the data corresponding to the dot pattern of each character.   Actually, what the CPU stores in memory is simply the codes of the characters we are to display.   Each character code is then utilized as a pointer to locate the respective "dot pattern," which is stored in a ROM called a **character generator**. Going back to the simplified schematic of Figure 6-11, we see that the display circuitry consists of four main parts:

- **RAM**, storing the (ASCII or other) codes of the characters we are to display
- **ROM**, storing the dot pattern for each type of character
- A **shift register**, which serializes the dot patterns and transmits to the monitor the video pulses corresponding to them
- **Timing and Control Logic** for synchronization of the monitor and overall control

The sequence of steps leading to the display of the first row of characters follows:

1. The timing and control logic presents to the RAM the address of the location containing the character code for "Z." This RAM is not necessarily a separate one. In other words, the character codes may simply be stored in main memory. Whether part of the main memory, or separate, it is very often called **display memory** or **refresh memory**. The name *refresh* stems from the fact that it is from this RAM that data are refreshed (frame after frame). The address presented to the RAM (by the timing and control logic) is itself called **refresh address**. The same logic generates the **line address**, which is presented to the ROM. It indicates which line of dots is being displayed within a character row. At present, it is an all-0s address indicating to the ROM that the first line of dots is to be displayed.

2. The character code retrieved from the RAM is treated by the ROM as an address. It is used to locate the set of locations containing the dot pattern for "Z." Since the line address is currently all 0s, the ROM retrieves the dot data for line 1 of letter "Z." A 1 in the dot data corresponds to a dot— that is, to the beam being on.

3. Now the timing and control logic drives the S/L^* (shift/load) input of an 8-bit shift register to a low. The objective is to store in the register the dot data read from the ROM—that is, 01111100.

4. The S/L^* input of the shift register is brought back to a high. Then the timing and control logic starts clocking the dot data out of the register one bit at a time. When a 1 is shifted out, the electron beam turns on, generating an illuminating dot on the screen. Notice the gating of dot data by the *DEN* (display enable) signal. *DEN* goes, and stays, at a low during the horizontal and vertical blanking intervals. In this way we ensure that the beam remains off during such intervals.

5. Meanwhile, the timing and control logic advances the refresh address by 1. What will be accessed now is the code of the second character—that is, the

one to be displayed next to "Z." At this point steps 2 to 4 are repeated for the second character.

6. Step 5 is repeated for the rest of the characters of the first row. When this is accomplished, we are done with the first line of dots for all characters of the first row.

7. The timing and control logic advances the line address by 1 and again presents to the RAM the refresh address for letter "Z." Hence, the ROM loads into the shift register the second line of dot data (00000100). The result is generation of the second line of dots for "Z." Next, the refresh address is advanced for display of the second line of dots for the other characters—that is, the second, third, and subsequent characters.

8. After generating the second line of dots for all characters, the line address is advanced by 1. This time we generate the third line of dots for all characters. Similarly, the process is repeated for generation of the fourth line of dots, and so on.

Screen format

The number of characters we can display per row, in conjunction with the number of rows per screen, defines the **screen format**. For example, a 32 × 16 screen format means that we can display up to 16 rows of characters, each of which can be up to 32 characters long. Incidentally, this particular format is very common when employing a TV set for display purposes. Examples of other screen formats are 64 × 32 and 80 × 24. Given a fixed resolution, the screen format depends on

- The character font we employ
- The spacing between characters (horizontally and vertically)

The 5 × 7 font we have seen accommodates both upper and lower case letters. Such a compact font has two disadvantages, however; first, it does not permit formation of certain special symbols. Second, the characters it accommodates are not very readable. These problems can be solved with a 7 × 9 font. In fact, for very high-quality displays we may even employ a 9 × 13 one. Naturally, these (denser) fonts limit the total number of characters we can display on the screen.

Example 6-10

Consider a low-quality TV monitor having a resolution of 250 × 250. Determine the maximum number of characters we can display on the screen when employing a 5 × 7 font. Assume that intercharacter spacings are one dot horizontally and three dots vertically.

Solution. With a 5 × 7 font, each row of characters takes a total of 7 + 3 = 10 scan lines—that is, ten dots in the vertical direction. Hence, we can display up to

250/10 = 25 character rows. Horizontally we need six dots per character. Consequently, we can fit up to 250/6, that is, 41 characters per row. The total number of
characters we can display on the screen is 41 × 25 = 1025.

Example 6-11

Repeat Example 6-10 for a 7 × 9 font.

Solution. In the case of a 7 × 9 font, each character row takes a total of 9 + 3 =
12 dots. The number of character rows per screen is now 250/12, that is, 20. Similarly,
the number of characters per row is 250/8, that is, 31. Thus, the total number of
characters per screen is reduced to 31 × 20 = 620.

Example 6-12

Assume you are designing a CRT display which is to employ a 7 × 9 font and a 64
× 32 screen format. Intercharacter spacings are as in Example 6-10. What should
be the resolution of the selected monitor (at minimum)?

Solution. In the horizontal direction each character takes eight dots. For 64 characters we need 8 × 64 = 512 dots. Hence, we need a horizontal resolution of at
least 512. In the vertical direction we need 12 scan lines per character row. For 32
rows we need 12 × 32 = 384 scan lines. Actually, the last (32nd) character row
does not necessitate spacing, so the vertical resolution could be as low as 384 − 3 =
381. These results indicate need of a medium-quality monitor having a resolution of
at least 512 × 381.

Timing and control

The design of the display circuits depends very much on the chosen screen
format and font. To see this, let us assume a 32 × 16 screen format and a 5 ×
7 font. Figure 6-12 shows the block diagram of the display circuits and allows us
to see what the timing and control circuits consist of.

Observe that although we employ a 5 × 7 font each character is constructed
within a 7 × 10 block in order to allow for intercharacter spacing. In other words,
columns 1 and 7 are not used for information display purposes. They provide a
two-dot-wide intercharacter spacing in the horizontal direction. Similarly, (dot)
lines 1, 9, and 10 provide a three-dot-wide spacing between character rows.

As seen from Figure 6-12, the timing and control logic includes a clock. This
clock shifts the dot data out of the shift register and is often known as the **dot
clock**. The same clock serves for generation of refresh addresses, line addresses,
and the shift/load signal. These signals are derived by a chain of counters:

1. The **dot counter** counts seven dots and then advances the next counter which
   contributes the low-order bits of a refresh address. Thus the output of the
   dot counter determines the rate at which characters are refreshed. For this
   reason, it is referred to as the **character clock**. The same signal is used to

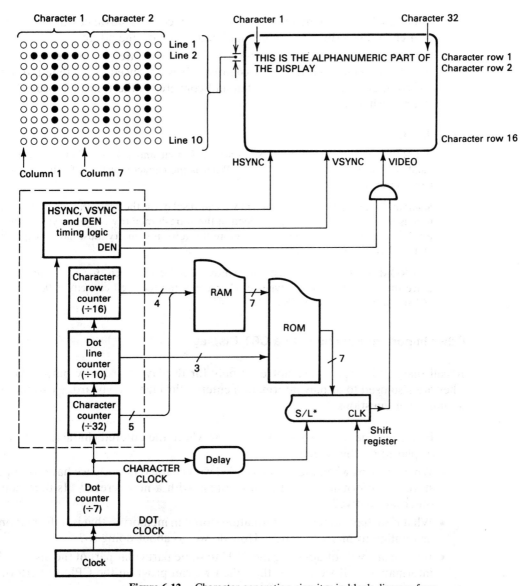

Figure 6-12.   Character generation circuitry in block diagram form.

load new dot data in the shift register.   It is, however, delayed to allow sufficient time for RAM and ROM accesses.

2. The **character counter** is advanced by the character clock.   It is a divide-by-32 counter keeping track of the characters within a character row and contributes the five low-order bits of a refresh address.

3. After reaching a count of 32, the character counter advances the **dot line counter**, a divide-by-10 counter that keeps track of line addresses.

4. The last counter keeps track of the character row we are currently displaying. Hence, the name **character row counter**. It is advanced every time the dot line counter reaches a count of ten and contributes the four high-order bits of a refresh address.

Example 6-13

A CRT display employs an 80 × 24 screen format and a 7 × 9 font. The total number of displayable symbols is 96. What is the capacity of the refresh memory? How about the ROM?

Solution. The number of characters we can display on the screen at any particular time is 80 × 24 = 1920. All we need in the refresh memory is a one-byte location for the code of each character. Therefore the refresh memory must have a capacity of 1920 bytes (about 2 KB).

The ROM has to store at least nine words, of seven bits each, for every character. Since there are 96 different types of characters, the required capacity is 96 × 9 = 864 seven-bit words (or 6048 bits).

Other Important Functions in a CRT Display

Recall that CRT displays are not used only for display of ordinary output data. They are also used to display information entered through a keyboard. This raises a number of questions:

- How does the keyboard operator know where the entered character is to be displayed on the screen?
- What happens when the screen is filled with characters? Do we have to stop, store the information, and then continue with a new screen? Is there any other alternative?
- What if we have to search information stored in memory—that is, information amounting to many screens? How do we go about doing so?
- Is there any way of directing the CPU to some particular part of the displayed information? If we can do that, then we can program the CPU to perform some specific function whenever such pointing is done.

We will examine how these functions are accomplished in a CRT display.

The cursor

Generally, CRT displays provide some means indicating where the character being entered is to be displayed. Such means are commonly known as a **cursor**.

A cursor may be implemented in various ways.   For example, in Figure 6-12 we could implement the cursor:

1. As an underline (by using dot line 9 or dot line 10, which are not employed for character formation)
2. As an overline (by using dot line 1)
3. As a box (by using dot lines 1 and 9 in conjunction with dot columns 1 and 7)

Furthermore, a character display may be designed to turn the cursor on and off at some fixed rate.   This provides a **blinking cursor**.   Usually, the cursor on/off frequency is 30 Hz.

The character we are to enter from the keyboard always takes the current position of the cursor, which then advances automatically to the next character position on the screen.   In addition to this capability, a CRT display must allow (1) movement of the cursor by one character position in any direction and (2) movement to the first character position on the screen (home position).   These functions are accomplished via the cursor control keys of the keyboard.   They facilitate editing prior to transmitting the displayed information to the CPU.   A cursor might be employed for marking purposes, as well—for example, to indicate which part of the displayed information is to be erased, sent to the CPU, or protected.

Scrolling

It is desirable to be able to shift characters off the top of the screen while new ones are coming in from the bottom (and vice versa).   This sort of function is called **scrolling**.   When performed on a page rather than a character row basis, it is referred to as **paging**.   Here all of the displayed information is shifted off screen and a new page is displayed.   Such a mode implies that refresh memory is large enough to hold at least several pages at a time.   A character display may also be designed to scroll up automatically when we finish entering information in the bottom character row.   In this case the cursor jumps back to the beginning of the bottom character row.   Then, a new row of characters can be entered.

The light pen

Pointing to a particular displayed item can be accomplished with a **light pen**, which works by means of a light sensor.

1. The light pen is pressed against the screen.
2. When the electron beam passes through the area pointed to by the light pen, light emission peaks.   This triggers the light pen which generates a pulse to the CRT control circuits.

3. After receiving the pulse, the CRT control circuits take notice of the coordinates of the beam (in terms of the corresponding refresh address). Then they generate an interrupt to the CPU.

4. On the basis of the furnished coordinates, the CPU takes the appropriate actions through an interrupt service routine.

For example, the CPU may respond by displaying a new page of information concerning the item pointed to by the light pen. Or, it may move a certain displayed item to some other area of the screen.

Character Display Controllers

The need for the functions we just discussed complicates further the design of the display circuits. However, integrated controllers reduce once again the magnitude of the design task. At minimum, a typical **character display controller** replaces the timing circuits shown within a dashed box in Figure 6-12. Usually, though, they provide circuits for interfacing to the CPU and for other functions such as cursor generation and control. Most are programmable so that they can accommodate different fonts and timing characteristics for the sync pulses. Next we discuss in brief the Motorola MC6845 "CRT controller" (CRTC).

Example of an Integrated Character Display Controller

Figure 6-13 illustrates a simplified block diagram of the MC6845 CRT controller we will be discussing as an example. On the left we see the lines interfacing to the CPU. E plays the role of a data strobe. RS is used for on-chip register selection purposes. All lines seen on the right are for CRT control purposes. HS and VS carry the horizontal and vertical sync signals. DE is the display enable signal. The 14 refresh address lines ($MA0-MA13$) permit up to 16 KB of refresh memory. On the other hand, there are five outputs ($RA0-RA4$) for line addresses, so it is possible to have up to 32 dot lines per character block. The MC6845 supports a wide range of character fonts, character block sizes, and timing characteristics for the HS, VS, and DE signals. This is accomplished by means of programmable on-chip registers.

Additional registers permit definition of the cursor in terms of any number of consecutive dot lines. Take, for example, the cursor shown in Figure 6-13(b). It is obtained by defining that the cursor starts and ends on line 10. The one pictured in Figure 6-13(c) is obtained by defining line 1 as the start and line 4 as the end. Another (14-bit) register permits cursor positioning anywhere within the refresh memory. Consequently, scrolling can be performed without loss of the cursor. It is also possible to inhibit display of the cursor or to have a blinking one. The MC6845 provides the video pulses that correspond to the cursor via the $CURSOR$ output line seen in Figure 6-13(a). Finally, there is a "**start address register**" indicating to the MC6845 from which refresh address it should start each

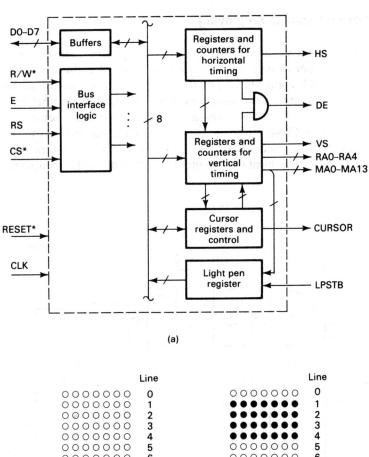

(a)

Figure 6-13.   The MC6845 CRT controller (CRTC).   (a) Simplified block diagram.   (b) Single-line cursor.   (c) Multi-line cursor.

new frame, so that scrolling is accomplished by simply loading this 14-bit register accordingly.

The *LPSTB* (light pen strobe) signal is intended for light pen support. When activated, *LPSTB* loads the current refresh address into the **light pen register**. This address is then read by the CPU, which determines the proper course of action.

Design Example Employing a CRT Controller

At this point we have discussed the principles of character displays and the basic functions performed by the display circuits. We also saw an example of an integrated CRT controller. Let us now see how we would go about designing the display circuits. Our design example is based on the MC6845 CRT controller. We assume a 7 × 9 font and a 9 × 12 size for character blocks.

    The MC6845 must connect to the CPU bus for its own control. However, this CPU is not necessarily the main CPU of the µC system. In the case of a CRT terminal it is the **local CPU**—that is, a µP dedicated to controlling the CRT display

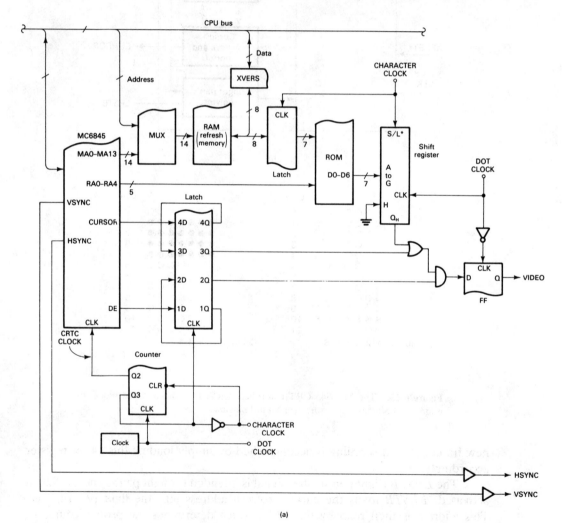

(a)

Figure 6-14. Design example employing the MC6845 for CRT control.

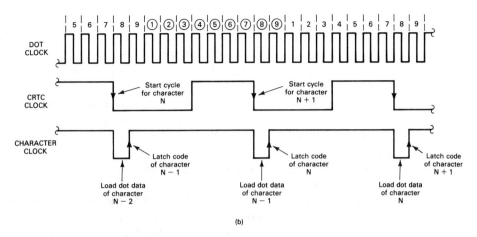

Figure 6-14. (cont.)

and its associated keyboard.   Such a local CPU in turn is slaved to the main one. The two CPUs exchange information via a serial I/O port.   In either case, the MC6845 has to share the refresh memory with the CPU which decides what information is to be displayed.   Such information is then stored by the CPU in the refresh memory.   From there, it is accessed by the MC6845 which controls the display functions as instructed by the CPU.   This means we have to multiplex CPU addresses with the refresh addresses generated by the MC6845 and also that the data lines of the refresh RAM must connect to those of the CPU as well, as indicated in Figure 6-14(a).   For the implementation of the refresh RAM we have two choices: We can use separate devices for the refresh memory, or we can assign some section of the main memory (of the CPU) for display purposes.   Usually, the choice is a separate refresh RAM.   As we will see shortly, this approach reduces the degree of contention between CPU and CRT controller when accessing memory.

Our next concern is the dot clock.   We need a crystal-controlled oscillator. The (assumed) 7×9 font and the 9×12 block size, suggest a divide-by-9 counter for generation of the character clock.   One way of implementing this counter is by using a 4-bit binary counter having a synchronous clear (CLR) input.   Notice how the character clock pulse is generated in Figure 6-14(a).   The leading edge of the eighth $DOT CLOCK$ pulse brings $Q3$ to a high and thereby $CHARACTER CLOCK$ and CLR to a low.   Then, on the leading edge of the ninth $DOT CLOCK$ pulse, the counter resets and $CHARACTER CLOCK$ goes back to a high.   It remains so until another eight $DOT CLOCK$ pulses, as illustrated in Figure 6-14(b).

The period of the signal used for clocking of the MC6845 controller is the same as that of $CHARACTER CLOCK$.   This signal is derived from the $Q2$ output of the counter and is not as asymmetrical as $CHARACTER CLOCK$ (see $CRTC$

CLOCK).   The MC6845 starts a new cycle (advancing the refresh address, and so on). on the high-to-low transition of *CRTC CLOCK*.   Ten *DOT CLOCK* periods later, the character code retrieved from the RAM is stored in an 8-bit latch. Subsequently, after another eight *DOT CLOCK* periods, the data corresponding to the addressed dot line are latched in the shift register.

How about character spacing within a character row?   Since we employ a 7 × 9 font, there are seven data bits per dot line.   The shift register is an 8-bit one, so if we ground its most significant data input, we ensure one-dot spacing between characters.   An additional one-dot spacing is generated while *CHARACTER CLOCK* is at a low (eighth *DOT CLOCK* period), because at that time the shift register is in load rather than shift mode.

The MC6845 generates the *DE* and *CURSOR* signals at about the same time it advances its refresh address outputs.   Hence, both signals must be delayed by two *CHARACTER CLOCK* periods.   In Figure 6-14(a) we employ a second latch for this purpose.   How do we generate the *VIDEO* signal?   First of all we have to OR the dot data shifted out of the register with those of the cursor.   Secondly, we must gate them with the *DE* signal.   The resulting signal is used to set/reset a flip-flop whose output constitutes the *VIDEO* signal.

Example 6-14

The TV monitor used in the design shown in Figure 6-14 has a horizontal resolution of 360.   It is also known that the usable fraction of a scan line lasts for 50 μs.   Up to how many characters can we possibly display per row?   What should the frequency of the *DOT CLOCK* be?   How about the *CHARACTER CLOCK* and the *CRTC CLOCK*?

Solution.   Each character takes a block of 9 × 12 dots (including spacing).   As far as horizontal resolution goes, we can display up to 360/9 = 40 characters per row. The required *DOT CLOCK* frequency is 360/50 = 7.2 MHz.   Both the *CHARACTER CLOCK* and the *CRTC CLOCK* have a frequency of 7.2/9 = 0.8 MHz.

Video Attributes

The type of functions we dealt with so far are considered basic to a CRT display. However, these functions are not adequate for some applications that may require a way of drawing the operator's attention to a selected segment(s) of the displayed information.   This can be accomplished with video attributes such as **character blinking** or **blanking**, **underlining**, and **reverse video**.

Activation of the underline attribute causes the display of an underline beneath the character.   The width of the underline is equal to that of a character block.   Thus, if we specify underlining for consecutive characters, a continuous underline appears under the respective character string.

The reverse video attribute causes inversion of the dot data associated with a character.   Take for instance the case where characters are normally displayed as white on a gray background.   Reverse video will make a character appear as gray on a white background.   Another video attribute known as **highlighting** produces a third variant.   For example, a character could be displayed as white on a black background.

Video attributes are themselves stored in RAM.   As a result, they increase the size of the memory we need for display purposes.   Assume, for instance, that we store the video attributes of a character at the byte address next to the one containing the code of that character.   This would double the size of the display memory.   If we dedicate one bit per attribute, this scheme permits up to eight attributes per character.

The point is that usually we specify the same video attribute for a block of consecutive (rather than single) characters.   Hence, we need to store the attribute only once.   The idea is to

1. Fetch from display memory the attribute data
2. Store them in a latch
3. Display the following characters accordingly until another byte of attribute data is encountered in the display memory

How would we differentiate character codes from attribute data?   In the case of 7-bit-long character codes, we can employ the unused eighth bit of a byte as an indicator.   Another approach is to increase the width of the display memory such that both character code and attributes fit in the same word.

Example 6-15

Consider a CRT display equipped with video attribute capability.   It is estimated that, on the average, video attributes are used every 100 characters and that, when specified, such attributes involve a string of about 15 characters.   By what portion has the refresh memory capacity increased because of the video attributes?   Assume a total of 128 displayable symbols.

Solution.   Character codes are 7-bit long.   Hence, we can use the eighth bit as an indicator of a video attribute change.   It is only then that we need one byte to store the applicable attributes.   Whenever such attributes are used, there are two changes: one at the beginning of the associated character string and one at the end of it.   The first change involves the fact that we turn the attributes on, and the second, that we turn the attributes off.   In other words, all we need is two bytes every 100 characters.   This amounts to a display memory capacity increase of only 2 percent.

Besides the extra memory we need additional logic, which transforms the original dot data according to the specified attributes.   Fortunately such circuits are integrated into devices known as **video attribute controllers** (**VACs**).   A typical VAC integrates the shift register (needed for the serialization of the dot data) as well.   As a result it further simplifies the design of display circuits.   Some manufacturers offer a CRT controller and a VAC as a compatible chip set. The character generator (ROM) may be either part of the VAC or a separate chip of the set.

Example of a Video Attribute Controller

To see how a VAC functions we examine the Signetics SC2670/SC2672/SC2673 CRT control chip set which includes such a device. This chip set consists of:

- The SC2672 "programmable video timing controller"
- The SC2670 "display character and graphics generator"
- The SC2673 video attributes controller

Figure 6-15 shows the signal lines associated with each of these devices and how they can be employed for character generation and CRT control.

The SC2672 generates timing signals for the refresh RAM, the TV monitor, and the other two members of the chip set. $CTRL1-CTRL3$ are handshaking signals whose meaning depends on the mode employed for data transfers to the refresh RAM. (We will see more on this subject shortly.) Lines $DA0-DA13$ (display address) carry refresh addresses for the RAM. However, when $BLANK$ (which plays the role of a display disable signal) is active, these lines carry line addresses and other control signals. $CCLK^*$ is the character clock input. The SC2672 can be programmed to provide over the $VSYNC/CSYNC$ line either a $VSYNC$ signal or a **composite sync** ($CSYNC$) signal.

The character codes read from the RAM are fed to the $CA0-CA6$ (character address) inputs of the SC2670, which then retrieves the dot data corresponding to the dot line specified over its $LA0-LA3$ inputs. The $CSTROBE$ (character strobe) input is fed the character clock signal generated by the SC2673 VAC. GM determines whether the SC2670 is to work in character mode or in graphics mode. The SCD (selected character disable) permits blanking of selected characters.

Now, the SC2673 VAC. The character clock is generated from an externally supplied dot clock ($DCLK$). Video attributes are read from the RAM and are latched by the VAC on the falling edge of $CCLK^*$. The following input signals are furnished by the SC2672 and relate also to video attributes:

1. UL *(underline):* Indicates which dot line is to be used for the underline attribute.
2. $BLINK:$ This signal permits selection of one of two possible blinking rates.
3. LL *(last line):* Indicates the last scan line of each character row.

On the basis of the video attributes and the indications just noted, the VAC processes the dot data for generation of the $VIDEO$ signal, which is actually a three-level signal that provides two levels of intensity (gray and white). Aside

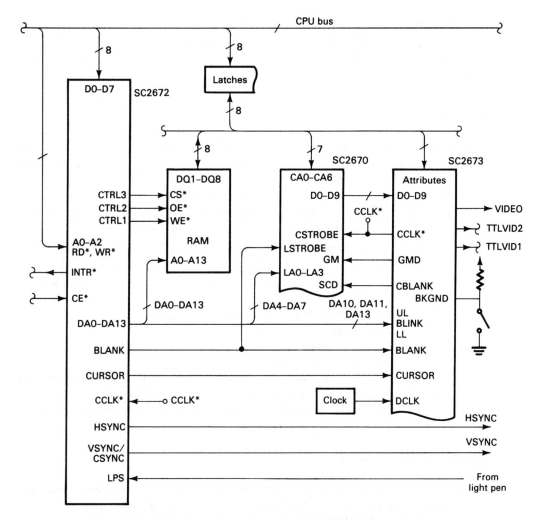

Figure 6-15.   Design example employing the 2670/2672/2673 chip set for character generation and CRT control.

from this, the SC2673 provides TTL video signals over lines *TTLVID*1 and *TTLVID*2. These two signals may be decoded to produce:

- Gray on black
- White on black
- Gray on white
- Black on white

Finally, input *BKGND* (background) permits choice of a light or dark background.

Notice the design simplicity gained when employing such a CRT control chip set. In fact, such chip sets permit implementation of all the control circuits of a CRT terminal (including local CPU, serial interface, and keyboard control circuits) with as few as 15 devices.

Some CRT control chips provide features beyond those we have discussed thus far:

1. *Soft (or Smooth) Scrolling:* Permits scrolling on a scan line (rather than character row) basis. The result is a more gradual scrolling of the displayed text which is easier to follow with the eyes.
2. *Split Screen:* Allows partitioning of the screen into regions referred to as **windows**. The latter can be scrolled and operated upon independently as if they were separate full screens—hence, the name **virtual screens**.
3. *Color Attributes:* Some VACs are capable of handling color attributes. For example, they offer the choice of many background and foreground colors.
4. *Other:* Other useful characteristics often provided by CRT control chips include:
   (a) On-chip implementation of character row buffers
   (b) DMA capabilities
   (c) Double-height/double-width characters
   (d) Programmable scrolling rates
   (e) Proportional spacing (similar to that of a proportionally spaced printer)
   (f) Soft font support (that is, dynamically reloadable fonts)
   (g) Ability to shift a character such that it appears as a superscript or as a subscript

Design Considerations

Before concluding this section we consider solutions to the problem of **memory contention**. Then we review the decisions faced by the designer in the course of developing a CRT display.

The memory contention problem

The refresh (or display) memory must be accessible to both CPU and display controller. The CPU writes in refresh memory the new information we are to display—for example, a new character just entered via the keyboard or a wholly new page we want to examine. On the other hand, the display controller reads the refresh memory repeatedly in order to refresh the screen. Inevitably, this leads to contention. How can we reduce—or possibly eliminate—such contention for the display memory?

Let us first consider the case where the display memory is separate from main memory. Here the CPU accesses the display memory via address multiplexers and bus transceivers, as shown in Figure 6-14, or possibly via an independent access port.   Our alternatives are:

1. *Give the CPU Higher Priority:* This approach reduces CPU delays.   The problem is that while the CPU is accessing the display memory, the controller is unable to keep on refreshing the screen.   This may lead to noticeable flicker in the display.

2. *Allow Access by the CPU only During Retracing:* We might, for instance, AND the (inverted) display enable signal with the display memory chip select signal and then use the resulting signal to drive the CPU *READY* line.   Such an approach prevents contention altogether.   However, it means long waiting times for the CPU.

3. *Use Faster Memory Devices:* We can make the display memory fast enough so that we can complete two accesses during a period of the character clock— one for the display controller and one for the CPU.   Faster memory devices are of course more expensive.

Example 6-16

A CRT display employs an 80 × 24 display format.   The vertical blanking interval is about 3.5 milliseconds.   Suppose we allow CPU access to the display memory only during such intervals.   How long would the CPU have to wait for such an access? How many pages would the CPU be able to transfer to the display memory during a vertical blanking interval?   Assume a 900-ns-per-byte transfer rate and a vertical scanning rate of 60 Hz.   The display memory is separate from main memory.

Solution.   The frame time is 1/60 s, or 16.67 ms.   However, only 16.67 − 3.5 = 13.17 ms are actually consumed for screen refreshing.   If the CPU attempts an access to the display memory just as the CRT controller starts screen refreshing, it will experience a worst case delay of 13.17 ms.

One page corresponds to 80 × 24 = 1920 characters.   Therefore, it takes 1920 × 0.9 = 1728 μs for its transfer.   During a vertical blanking interval the CPU will be able to transfer up to 3500/1728 pages—that is, about two pages.

What if the display memory is part of the main memory?   Now the CPU has to contend with the display controller not only when it writes new information in the display section of the memory, but also when it accesses memory for other reasons—that is, during the execution of other tasks.   The result is a high degree of contention.   For example, terminals employing this approach are usually limited to transmission rates of no more than 2400 baud.   When higher transmission rates are required, or when the main CPU directly controls the display circuits, this approach is unacceptable.

Example 6-17

A CRT display employs an 80 × 24 format and a 7 × 9 font.   How many times is the refresh memory accessed by the CRT controller during a refresh cycle?   Assume the refresh memory is part of the main memory and has a cycle time of 600 ns. Calculate its average utilization by the CRT controller given a screen refresh rate of 60 Hz.

Solution. First we consider a character row. During each of the nine scan lines (used for character formation), the CRT controller must access the memory 80 times. Thus, the number of accesses corresponding to a character row is $9 \times 80 = 720$. Since there are 24 character rows, the total number of accesses per screen refresh cycle is $24 \times 720 = 17280$. This corresponds to a memory busy time of $17280 \times 0.6 = 10368$ µs, or about 10.37 ms. Consequently, average memory utilization by the CRT controller amounts to 10.37/16.67—that is, 62.2 percent. That leaves the CPU with less than 40 percent for access to instructions and data.

A very effective solution is using a **row buffer**. The idea is to fill the buffer prior to (or during) the first scan line of a character row. Then no more memory accesses are required until we go to the next character row. Very often, CRT controllers implement on-chip one or two such row buffers. Two row buffers are, of course, better since we can fill one while displaying the contents of the other. The situation improves further if row buffers are filled via DMA. In fact, we may choose to do so in short bursts of, say, four characters for even distribution of memory accesses by the CRT controller.

Example 6-18

Consider again the CRT display of Example 6-17. By what factor could we reduce the number of memory accesses if we employ a row buffer? How about memory utilization?

Solution. The number of memory accesses per screen refresh cycle is reduced by a factor of nine. Memory utilization is reduced (by the same factor) down to 62.2/9 —that is, 6.9 percent. The row buffer would have to be 80 bytes long.

Early decisions

The design of a CRT display depends very much on whether the display will be an integral part of your µC system or part of a terminal. A terminal is controlled by its own local µP. It communicates with the µC system over a serial channel employing one of the pertinent interface standards such as RS-232C. Transmission rates are usually in the range of 110–9600 baud. They should be selectable for greater flexibility.

The choice of the CRT control chip (or chip set) is driven by the requirements concerning:

- Screen format
- Character set and font
- Color and other video attributes
- Other features such as split screen, scrolling, and so on

The capacity of the display memory depends on these requirements and also on whether we are to maintain in the display memory a single page or multiple pages.

The same requirements determine the choice of the TV monitor (refer to the selection criteria noted in the early part of this section). Other factors to be considered are packaging, power (AC or DC), and luminance under given ambient conditions. In applications involving prolonged operation of the CRT display by operators, we must consider ergonomics, which relates to viewing comfort for prevention of eye fatigue. In general, such considerations point to the selection of a small size screen, provided the displayed information can still be read clearly by the operator. Besides, a small size screen has the advantage of greater luminance and is easier to package. Other characteristics influencing ergonomics are resolution, luminance, flicker, color of the phosphor, size of the displayed elements, the ability to tilt and swivel the TV monitor, and so on.

If your system is based on one of the standard μC buses there is an advantage. You have the choice of selecting a compatible off-the-shelf board(s) for your CRT display needs. Moreover, you may consider selection of an off-the-shelf CRT terminal instead of putting together or designing your own. This approach is very appropriate when the number of units is not very large.

6.4 PRINTERS

Another common output peripheral is the printer. Unlike a CRT, a printer provides a permanent (hard copy) record we can read and analyze at a later time. The information is presented to the printer by the CPU in terms of binary codes. Each such code identifies to the printer which symbol is to be printed. The employed coding scheme is usually based on the ASCII code [see Figure 6-2(a)].

Typically, printers are able to identify either 64 or 96 ASCII codes. When equipped with a 64 ASCII character set, a printer is capable of printing upper case alphabetic symbols, numerals, and special symbols such as those for punctuation (columns 2 to 5 of the ASCII code table). A printer equipped with a 96 ASCII character set can print (in addition) lower case alphabetic symbols plus some other special symbols (columns 2 to 7 of the ASCII code table).

Sometimes printers are combined with keyboards into printing terminals. When such a terminal includes circuits for remote communication, it is referred to as a **teleprinter**. The character set of a teleprinter includes codes for communication control functions (columns 0 and 1 of the ASCII code table).

In general, a printer is designed for tabletop operation, as in Figure 6-16, or for mounting on a pedestal as a stand-alone unit. Printers are classified into

1. *Character Printers:* They print one character at a time as the print mechanism moves horizontally across the paper. Because characters are printed along a line serially, one after another, such printers are often called serial printers (not to be confused with serial communication).

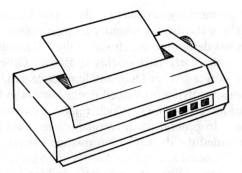

Figure 6-16. A character printer designed for tabletop operation.

2. *Line Printers:* They print characters along a line in a parallel fashion. Thus, printing of a page takes place on a one-line-at-a-time basis.

Printers belonging to either class may be of the **impact** or **nonimpact** type. In impact printers the print mechanism strikes the paper physically through an inked ribbon as in a typewriter. In nonimpact printers, there is no direct or indirect contact between print mechanism and paper.

On the basis of the approach employed for character formation, printers may also be categorized into

1. *Solid Font Printers:* They produce "fully formed" characters like those of a typewriter.

2. *Dot Matrix Printers:* They form characters by means of dot patterns.

This section is about printers. First we examine in brief the types of available printers and the principles of some representative printing mechanisms. Then we deal with the associated circuits. We are interested in the kinds of control circuits needed in a printer, how a typical printer interfaces to a CPU, and the I/O techniques employed when transferring print data. Before concluding the section, we discuss how to go about selecting a printer from the large variety of commercially available ones.

Character Printers

An example of a solid font character printer of the impact type is the **daisy wheel** printer. Figure 6-17(a) depicts how printing is accomplished in such a printer. The type element resembles a daisy whose "petals" carry the character font. One or two characters are embossed at the end of each petal. When a character is to be printed, the printer circuits compare its code with that of the character corresponding to the current position of the wheel. Then, on the basis of the difference, the wheel is advanced to bring the desired character into printing position. A hammer is subsequently activated which strikes the respective petal. Now, the

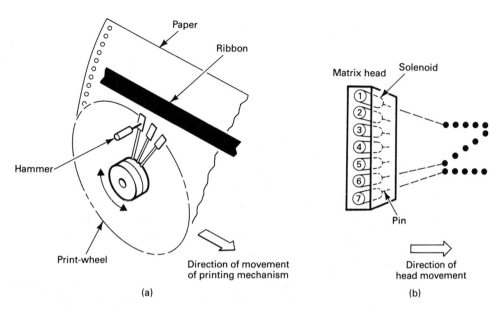

Figure 6-17.   Principles of operation of two types of character printers.   (a) Daisy wheel printing mechanism.   (b) Wire matrix print head.

daisy wheel is advanced horizontally to the next character position, and the above process is repeated.   The speed of such printers is typically 30–55 cps (characters per second).   They are used in applications demanding "letter quality (LQ)" printing.

Another family of character printers of the impact type are **matrix** printers. Here the printing mechanism amounts to a "print head" consisting of a set of small solenoids which strike metal wires (or pins) arranged in one or more columns. The principles of character formation are similar to those we have seen in CRT displays, except that now the character generator supplies dot data on a one-column-at-a-time (not row at a time) basis.   Column data simultaneously activate the appropriate set of solenoids.   Then the print head moves on horizontally by a small increment to print the next column, and so on.   Figure 6-17(b) illustrates a simple seven-wire print head for printing of characters employing a 5 × 7 font. Even with far more complex fonts, the printing quality is inappropriate for some applications.   On the other hand, matrix printers are more suitable for graphics.

How about nonimpact character printers?   Such printers also utilize the matrix approach to character formation, and they have the advantage of not requiring ribbons.   However, they cannot produce multiple copies.   They include:

- *Ink jet printers* forming characters by projecting tiny droplets of ink onto paper.   They have speeds in the range of 20–1000 cps and operate quietly. Some support resolutions as high as 120 × 120 dots/in.² (for graphics) and even multiple colors.

- *Thermal printers* having the advantage of portability and very quiet operation. However, they require special paper and are not as fast (30–120 cps).
- *Electrostatic printers* capable of printing faster than all previous types (160–2000 cps). Unfortunately, they also need special paper.

Line Printers

A representative solid font line printer of the impact type is the **band printer**. Figure 6-18 depicts the principles of a typical one. The images of the characters are engraved or etched on a thin, stainless steel band, rotating by means of two pulleys. Behind the paper there is a bank of print hammers. The circuits activating the hammers are synchronized by timing marks which are also etched on the band. Now assume the character passing in front of a print position corresponds to that stored in the respective position of the (printer) line buffer. Then the respective hammer is activated, pushing the paper and the ribbon against the band.

The belt carries multiple images of the character set, so several characters arrive simultaneously under the correct hammers. As a result, a line is printed within a fraction of the time taken by a full rotation of the belt. Band printers usually have speeds in the range of 300–1500 lines per minute (LPM). They (and line printers in general) print 132 characters per line. Typically, they are used in applications involving high volumes of printed output (program listings, test data, and so on). Some band printers can sustain duty cycles amounting to many hours of operation per day.

Line printing can be accomplished with matrix technology too. Such line printers employ a "print comb" stretching across the width of the paper. The comb consists of 132 wires and an equal number of small solenoids. Characters are printed one row at a time while the comb is oscillating.

Nonimpact line printers include thermal and electrostatic devices with speeds in the range of 300–18000 LPM. They do, however, require special paper and a toning process. Another type of high speed, nonimpact printer is the **laser** or

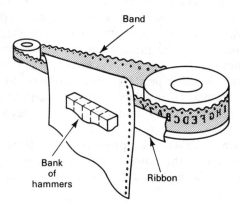

Figure 6-18. Principles of operation of a band printer.

xerographic printer. These printers are capable of producing "presentation quality" printouts for both text and graphics. When a printer can print many pages per minute it is often called a **page printer**.

Printer Control and Interfacing

At this point we have some general background on printing mechanisms and the types of available printers. Our next subject concerns circuits. First, let us consider briefly the circuits needed for control of a printer:

1. Unlike keyboards and CRTs, printers have mechanical parts whose motion must be controlled electrically. A typical printer has at minimum:
   (a) One motor for paper feeding
   (b) Two or more solenoids for hammer activation and ribbon advancing
2. In addition to controlling such electromechanical devices, we need circuits to monitor occurrence of certain conditions. Examples of the latter are paper out, ribbon out, and cover open. These conditions are sensed by means of limit switches and other types of sensors.
3. We also need circuits to monitor the state of manually operated panel switches and drive panel indicators. Typically, a printer has a *power* switch, an *on-line/off-line* switch, a *line feed* switch, and a *top-of-form* switch. While in off-line mode, the last two switches allow us to advance the paper manually in increments of one line or one "form." Usually the panel indicators include a *power on* indicator, an *on-line* indicator, a *ready* indicator, and one or more indicators for error conditions such as parity errors and buffer overflow.

Figure 6-19 shows, as an example, the simplified schematic of a daisy wheel printer. Note on the right the circuits controlling the printing mechanism. The print wheel motor is controlled by a dedicated microcontroller employing a closed loop. This microcontroller is slaved to the supervisory μP on the left. It executes the complex algorithms required for control of the print wheel motor. An identical approach is used for control of the carriage motor which moves the print wheel horizontally across the paper. The I/O interface controller provides input ports for the alarm lines and the panel switches. It is also through this controller that the supervisory μP drives the paper feed motor, the hammer and ribbon solenoids, and the panel indicators.

How about the supervisory μP? This one plays the role of a local CPU slaved to the main CPU of our μC system. A small size RAM—say, 1 KB—is used to store one or more character lines and to implement various registers. Programs are stored in a ROM, for example an 8 KB one. The ROM-based programs include not only those operating the printer, but also diagnostics. Some printers provide multiple levels of diagnostics. Execution of the latter may be triggered from a panel switch, the main CPU, or the supervisory μP. Not shown in Figure 6-19 are various support circuits such as the clock, timers, and decoding logic.

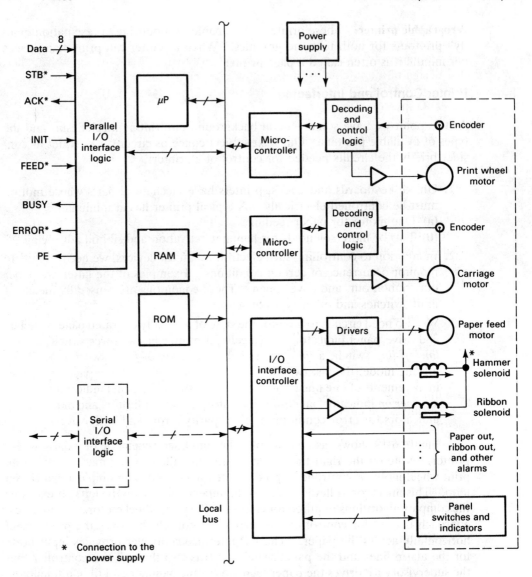

Figure 6-19. Simplified block diagram of a daisy wheel character printer.

Do we always need multiple μPs and/or microcontrollers in a printer? Certainly not. This depends on both the complexity of the printing mechanism and the capabilities of the employed μP or microcontroller. For example, the control circuits of matrix and thermal printers are less complex than those of daisy wheel ones. Similarly, if the μP is fast enough it may be able to control directly the printing mechanism and still keep up with all other tasks. How about integrated printer controllers? Some manufacturers offer controllers designed specifically for matrix printers. Usually, however, printer control circuits are based on universal peripheral controllers or even general-purpose μPs. However, off-the-shelf printers are generally equipped with all the required control circuits. Consequently, the design task amounts to simply interfacing the printer to your system.

I/O interface lines

How does a printer communicate with the main CPU? This is accomplished either via a serial (usually RS-232C compatible) interface or via a parallel interface. Recall, for example, the parallel interface of our simple character printer from Section 5.2 (Figure 5-13).

An example of a widely employed printer interface is the Centronics parallel interface. Figure 6-19 pictures the signal lines of this interface. Print data are sent to the printer over an 8-bit-wide data bus on a one-character-at-a-time basis. Optionally, each character code may be accompanied by a parity bit. Placement of valid data over the bus is indicated by the *STB** (strobe) signal. After storing the character, the printer activates the *ACK** (acknowledge) line. Hence, the CPU is informed of its readiness to accept the next character.

Besides the two data transfer control lines, there are two other control lines, one for initialization (*INIT*) and one for paper feeding (*FEED**). The rest of the lines carry status signals to the main CPU. *BUSY* indicates the printer is busy printing previously sent characters. When active, *PE* indicates detection of a parity error. *ERROR** serves to indicate occurrence of some other error (or alarm) condition.

Printers are often capable of executing commands. Such commands are sent by the main CPU over the data bus. The distinction between ordinary data and commands is accomplished by means of **escape (ESC) codes** (refer to the ASCII code table in Figure 6-2). Whenever the CPU sends an ESC code, the printer interprets the immediately following code as a command. Such a command may specify the size of the margins, the amount by which the paper advances for each line feed, the desired font, and so on.

I/O interface design

If the printer is equipped with a serial interface, then the main CPU communicates with it via a serial I/O port (see, for instance Figure 5-36). This port may be implemented either on the CPU board or on some other circuit board of the μC system. Data transfers can be accomplished with any of the I/O techniques we have seen in Chapter 5—subject to the considerations discussed in Sections 5.3 and 5.4. A serial interface has the advantage of allowing longer distances from the CPU or even remoting via a modem. For example, with RS-232C the distance can be up to 50 ft. In contrast, a parallel interface generally limits cable lengths to 10–15 ft.

Yet a parallel interface permits higher data transfer rates. It may also reduce (main) CPU overheads significantly. Assume, for instance, we are using interrupt-driven I/O. In the case of a serial interface, like the one shown in Figure 5-36, the main CPU is interrupted every time the printer is ready for a new character. On the other hand, in the case of a parallel interface, we need interrupt the CPU only when the printer buffer must be filled again, assuming, of course, that the printer is equipped with a buffer for one or more character lines. If a printer has a single-character buffer, the rate of interrupts would be the same for both cases.

Example 6-19

Consider an 80-column printer equipped with a single-line buffer. The printer is equipped with an RS-232C interface. I/O is interrupt-driven as in the design example shown in Figure 5-36. How many times does the printer interrupt the CPU for each printed line? Repeat assuming a Centronics-like interface. How would you interrupt the CPU in this case?

Solution. The printer interrupts the CPU every time it is ready to accept a new character—that is, 80 times for each printed line.

After printing the contents of its buffer, the printer drives *BUSY* back to a low. This transition can be used to cause a CPU interrupt. After getting to the interrupt service routine, we start transmitting characters one after another until the buffer is filled. Thus, the CPU is interrupted only once per printed line.

The larger the buffer of the printer, the less frequent the interrupts to the CPU. If we employ DMA, CPU involvement is further reduced. Moreover, with DMA and a sufficiently large printer buffer, the chances of slowing down printing because of higher priority tasks become very small. See the printer interface design examples in Sections 5.2 and 5.3. Note that the *PNC* (print new character) and *RDY* lines of the printer we dealt with there correspond to the *STB** and *ACK** lines of Figure 6-19.

Remember that the cable carrying the parallel interface signals to/from the printer should be:

- Either a twisted-pair cable (with one wire of each pair grounded), or
- A flat cable (with every other conductor grounded)

All signals must be buffered on both sides of the cable. Depending on the length of the cable, you may also have to terminate them (see Section 5.2 and Figure 5-13). Many of the considerations we discussed for μC buses in Section 5.6 apply here as well.

Printer Selection Criteria

Selecting a printer from the large variety of commercial ones is not a trivial task. Yet certain requirements of your application may point to a specific class of printers. For example, suppose your application requires multiple copies. Then your choice

is limited to impact type of printers.   The need for high quality would narrow
down your choice further to solid font printers, and so on.   The characteristics of
key importance are:

1. *Speed:* Very often, speed is expressed as the rate at which characters are
   printed along a line.   However, such a measure does not take into consideration the time taken for paper feeding or capabilities increasing the effective
   speed of the printer such as **bidirectional printing** and **slewing**.   Slewing refers
   to the ability of a printer to advance paper at an accelerated rate when
   consecutive lines are left blank.   For character printers, slewing applies horizontally as well.   Here the printer may accelerate the carriage when consecutive character positions are to be left blank. So it is more appropriate to
   consider the throughput of a printer in terms of average number of printed
   lines per minute.

2. *Output:* Quality requirements will dictate whether matrix printers should be
   considered at all.   However, quality depends also on other factors such as:
   (a) Horizontal and vertical alignment
   (b) Correct registration of printed characters
   How about character set and font?   Do you need multiple font capability for
   greater flexibility?   Other characteristics of importance are:
   (a) Line length (generally 80 or 132 columns)
   (b) Line spacing (usually six or eight lines per inch)
   (c) Character spacing.   Ten characters per inch is considered standard.
   Nevertheless, some printers permit denser spacing—for example, 15 characters per inch—or even **proportional spacing**, in which characters are
   not allocated equal spaces.   Instead the space allocated to each character
   varies with its width.   Text is considered more readable when characters
   are spaced proportionally.

3. *Paper Handling:* There are many factors when it comes to paper handling
   capabilities:
   (a) Would the printer require special paper?
   (b) Does it produce multiple copies, and up to how many?
   (c) What paper widths does it accommodate?   Most printers handle standard
   8.5-in.-wide paper.   Some can handle larger or even variable widths.
   (d) How about paper feeding?   Some printers employ the common typewriter
   approach.   There paper is held by friction against the platen and moves
   as the platen turns.   This simple approach makes paper alignment problematic.   Usually it is employed only in low speed printers.   Good paper
   alignment can be achieved with a pin platen feed mechanism.   Here both
   sides of the platen are equipped with pins.   The pins engage the holes
   punched close to the edges of the paper.   Good alignment can also be
   achieved with a pin tractor feed mechanism.   Now the pins are carried
   on two tractors driven by motors.   This approach has the advantage of
   allowing variable paper widths by adjusting the distance between the two

tractors. If your application involves preprinted forms, you may consider a feature known as a **vertical format unit** (VFU). This one permits a printer to skip preprogrammed numbers of lines and slew to the next print position, which, of course, increases throughput. Other features associated with paper handling include adjustable form thickness control, form length selection, automatic insertion of single-sheet paper, and so on.

4. *Reliability:* In printers (and generally all electromechanical devices), reliability represents a critical factor. Depending on the printer, the MTBF may vary from several hundred to over 1000 hours. Maintenance costs can be substantial. In fact such costs and those for supplies, including paper, should be factored into initial purchase costs. From these, one could derive the so-called cost of ownership over the expected life of the printer.

5. *Other Considerations:* Besides cost there are other factors such as ribbon type and life, buffer size, availability of diagnostics, and color capability. Also, acoustic noise, dimensions, weight, and environmental and power requirements. If you need graphic output, the selected printer must satisfy additional requirements concerning resolution and so on.

6.5 FLOPPY DISKS

All three peripherals we discussed so far are I/O peripherals. Recall, however, that there are also storage peripherals. Such peripherals provide space for storage beyond the main memory. Moreover, they retain information even when power is turned off.

The storage peripheral we examine belongs to the family of magnetic disks so named because the storage medium consists of a disk coated (or plated) with some sort of magnetic material. Retrieval and recording of information is accomplished by means of a **read/write head**. The head moves directly to the appropriate position without having to access data stored in in-between positions. For this reason, disks are often referred to as **direct access storage devices**. Disks are categorized into **flexible** (or **floppy**) **disks** and **hard disks**. Floppy disks are relatively inexpensive, modest-performance storage devices. They employ a thin, flexible, plastic-based medium resembling a phonograph record. For protection, the medium comes enclosed permanently in a rectangular jacket. From here on, we will refer to the medium and its associated protective jacket as a **diskette**. In hard disks, which provide higher performance at a higher cost, the medium is constructed from aluminum.

Figure 6-20(a) shows what a typical floppy disk looks like. In the front you see a rectangular opening for insertion and removal of the diskette. After inserting the diskette we push the load button (top right) which positions the diskette appropriately on a rotating spindle. Pushing the same button again, allows disengagement of the diskette for removal. The visual indicator (top left) shows whether

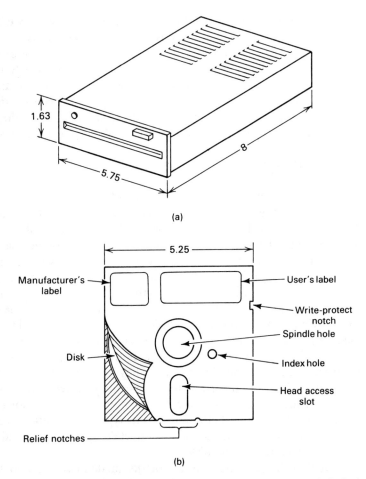

Figure 6-20.   (a) A typical 5.25-inch floppy disk (all dimensions are in inches). (b) Structure of a 5.25-inch diskette.

the device is currently involved in a read/write access or not (activity light).   The diskette is usually rotated at either 300 or 360 rpm (rotations per minute).

Despite their modest performance, floppy disks are very popular because of

1. Their very low cost
2. The removability of the storage medium

In fact, diskettes are highly portable and can be sent through ordinary mail.   Typically, floppy disks are used in small μC systems for system loading and for storage of data and/or infrequently used programs.   In large μC systems they are used often as a backup to hard disks.

How do we record 1s and 0s on a diskette? How do we organize recorded data? What other information must be recorded and why? These are our first topic in this section. Once we deal with the principles, we examine how floppy disks work and their main characteristics. We are primarily interested in their capacity and access speed. Then we discuss the control circuits needed and integrated floppy disk controllers. The reliability of a storage device is always of concern. In fact, in floppy disks, error rates can be fairly high. We will see how we can prevent such errors and how we go about detecting those that occur.

Basic Principles

Figure 6-20(b) depicts some structural details of a diskette. Notice that the front side of one of the corners of the jacket is shown lifted to make visible the disk. The inner sides of the jacket are lined with a nonwoven fabric which protects the medium from abrasion. At the same time, this fabric acts as a wiping surface, keeping the disk clean. This function of the jacket is extremely important because during an access the read/write head is in direct contact with the medium. Engagement with the rotating spindle is through the **spindle hole** at the center.

Both jacket and medium have an **index hole**, which provides a reference point for locating information on the disk. Contact of the read/write head with the medium is accomplished through a jacket cutout called the **head access slot** or **head window**. The two relief notches at the bottom edge protect the diskette from the extra stress near the head window. They also serve as positioning guides when the diskette is inserted for loading. The **write-protect notch** allows us to inhibit write operations as desired. We will see how this is done shortly. A label on the upper left side of the diskette indicates its type, classification, and other data from its manufacturer. A second label is attached by the user for identification of the information stored on the diskette.

Although the entire surface of the medium may be coated with magnetic material, we do not actually utilize the entire surface. Instead information is recorded only along a number of concentric discrete **tracks**. Tracks have widths of, say, 0.005 in. They are separated with **guard bands** where no information is recorded. Figure 6-21 illustrates the case of a diskette having 77 tracks. They are numbered from 00 (outermost track) to 76 (innermost track). Observe that tracks are confined between the edge of the disk and the index hole. Naturally, the amount of data we can store depends (among other factors) on how close the tracks are to each other. The latter is called **track density**. It is expressed in terms of the number of tracks per inch (TPI) along a radius of the disk. To read or record information:

1. The read/write (R/W) head is moved radially over the head window until positioned over the desired track.
2. The R/W head and medium are brought in contact to accomplish the read or write operation.

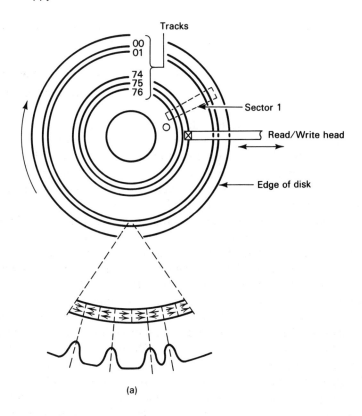

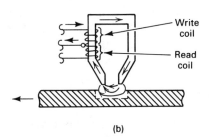

Figure 6-21. (a) Organization of recorded information on a floppy disk. (b) Example of a read/write head.

Magnetic recording

What is the underlying mechanism for information recording? Imagine each track subdivided into a large number of segments as shown in Figure 6-21(a). Each such segment constitutes an independent magnetizable region. Now, assume that as a particular segment passes under the R/W head, we apply through the head a magnetic field. Then, the magnetic particles of that region are forced to orient themselves in one of two distinct directions along an axis. The axis may be:

- Parallel to the surface of the disk as in Figure 6-21 (**longitudinal recording**)
- Perpendicular to the surface of the disk (**perpendicular recording**)

In either case, the two distinct directions of magnetization provide the key to distinguishing a 1 from a 0, but this is not done in a direct way. For example, in the so-called **NRZI** (nonreturn-to-zero inverted) recording scheme, 1s are represented by means of flux reversals between adjacent regions. Assume, for instance, that the left-most of the eight regions shown in Figure 6-21(a) is already magnetized in a left-to-right direction. To record a 1 we reverse the direction of the magnetic field so that the next region is magnetized in a right-to-left direction. Subsequently, if we were to record a 0 we would magnetize the third region in a right-to-left direction. Figure 6-21(a) pictures the read signal generated during a read operation when the eight regions are magnetized as shown. Observe that a pulse (for a 1) is produced only when there are flux reversals between adjacent regions. Otherwise, the recorded bit is assumed to be a 0.

How do we control the direction of the magnetizing field during a write operation? This is determined by the direction of the current through the write coil of the head [see Figure 6-21(b)]. During read operations the R/W head plays a passive role. Now, no signals are applied to the write coil. Instead, we monitor the signal provided by the head at its read coil terminals. This signal consists of voltage pulses which are induced across the read coil whenever the head encounters a flux reversal between adjacent regions. Besides the read/write operations, we also need to confine the width of the magnetized regions so that they do not spread beyond the nominal width of a track. This is accomplished with an **erase head** which is part of the overall head assembly. One approach to erasing is to employ an erase head which follows to the side of the R/W head and "clips" the edges of the magnetized regions according to the specified track width.

Encoding techniques

By now it should be clear how we detect flux reversals and thereby read 1s. The problem is that 0s are not associated with flux reversals and thus are not detectable. What we need to know is when we should interpret the lack of a signal across the read coil as a 0—in other words, knowing the time instances we should expect a bit. This can be accomplished by recording on the medium clock pulses (in addition to data). During reading, the clock pulses provide a time reference indicating when we should expect a data bit.

As an example we illustrate the **FM encoding technique** shown in Figure 6-22(a). FM (frequency modulation) is a very simple encoding technique usually employed in single-density floppy disks. As seen, clock pulses and data bits are

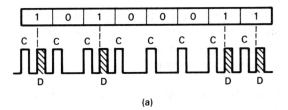

(a)

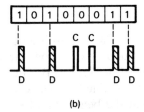

(b)

Figure 6-22. Two common data encoding schemes employed in floppy disks. (a) Frequency modulation (FM) encoding scheme. (b) Modified frequency modulation (MFM) encoding scheme. C indicates clock pulses, D indicates data pulses.

interleaved. The leading edges of clock pulses define the boundaries of the **bit cells**. A single data bit (1 or 0) is written at the center of each bit cell. The name of this technique stems from the fact that the data modulate the frequency of the pulses. A 0 corresponds to one pulse per bit cell, and a 1 corresponds to two pulses per bit cell. The problem with the FM technique is that one half of the possible flux reversals are wasted for clock pulses.

What if we employ a clock whose frequency is equal to that in which we encounter bit cells? Such a clock could then be synchronized by the pulses generated whenever we detect a flux reversal. This approach would certainly eliminate the problem of wasting flux reversals, but if flux reversals do not occur frequently enough (as in the case of consecutive 0s), we lose synchronization. That in turn would mean losing track of the boundaries of bit cells. Thus it is still necessary to record on the medium clock pulses, but not on a regular basis, however. An example of an encoding technique employing this approach is the **MFM** (**modified frequency modulation**) technique. Here clock pulses are recorded only when adjacent bit cells contain 0s. As seen from Figure 6-22(b), data bits are again written at the center of the cells. However, a clock pulse is recorded only when the previous and present cells contain 0s. Now we have no more than one flux reversal per bit cell, so that bit cells can be twice as small. The MFM technique is employed widely in double-density floppy disks.

Sectoring of the Diskette

The size of the bit cells determines how densely we can store data along a track. In other words, it determines the **bit density**, which is expressed in bits per inch. Since outer tracks are longer, we can store more data on them, although normally we do not. Instead all tracks are divided into an equal number of segments (say

26) named **sectors**.   Each of the sectors stores the same amount of information. This approach is used for convenience, even though it wastes some storage capacity.

Unlike memory, information is not read and written on a byte or word basis. Information is instead handled on a sector basis:

1. If a block of information exceeds the capacity of a sector, it is simply written in two or more sectors.
2. If it is smaller than the capacity of a sector, the unused part of that sector is filled with 0s.

How do we locate the desired sector after positioning the R/W head over a track?   The way this is accomplished depends on how the diskette is sectored. Some floppy disks employ **hard-sectored** diskettes.   Besides the index hole, such diskettes have one extra hole at the beginning of each sector (typically a total of either 16 or 32).   The index hole is at the beginning of sector 1, so a particular sector is identified by counting the number of holes following the index hole.

Floppy disks usually employ **soft-sectoring**.   This approach necessitates formatting the diskette prior to its use; that is, subdividing each track into sectors, writing an identification number (ID) at the beginning of each sector, and so on. Soft sectoring has the advantage of permitting sector size selection by software means.   For example, we may divide each track into:

- 26 sectors of 128 bytes each
- 15 sectors of 256 bytes each
- eight sectors of 512 bytes each

On the other hand (as we see next), formatting reduces significantly the amount of usable storage capacity.

Diskette Formatting

A diskette is formatted (or initialized) by a program.   This program subdivides (in the logical sense) each track into sectors.   Formatting involves the writing of special information on all tracks.   Each track is formatted from beginning to end without interruption.The ends of a track are defined through the index hole which generates one pulse for each rotation of the diskette.

However, not all the tracks are formatted for ordinary data storage.   For example, one track may be reserved for writing information identifying the data sets stored on the diskette.   Such a track is called an **index track**.   Similarly, one or more tracks may be left aside as **alternate tracks**—that is, for future replacement of ordinary data tracks that may fail because of "bad spots," for example.   The replacement can be done by reinitializing the diskette.   For a better understanding of what diskette formatting is about we will discuss the industry standard format employed in 8-inch floppies.

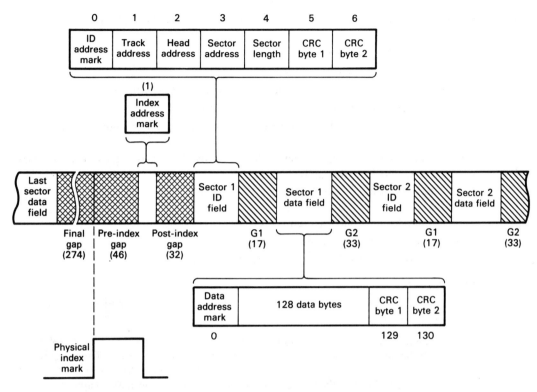

Figure 6-23. Example of a physical data format for soft-sectored diskettes. Parenthesized numbers indicate the length of each field in bytes.

This format allocates the 77 tracks of an 8-inch diskette as follows:

- Track 00 is reserved for indexing purposes.
- Tracks 01 to 73 are used for data storage (data tracks).
- Tracks 74 and 75 play the role of alternate tracks.
- Track 76 is unassigned (spare).

Figure 6-23 depicts how data tracks are formatted. The reference point is the index hole pulse. Following the leading edge of this pulse, there is a *pre-index gap* where the formatting program stores certain specific bit patterns. Next is the *index address mark* which stores an 8-bit pattern identifying the beginning of a track. A *post-index gap* follows before track sectorization starts.

From there on, a track is subdivided into equal size sectors consisting of

1. A *sector ID* field
2. A 17-byte-long gap (G1)
3. A 131-byte-long *sector data* field
4. Another 33-byte-long gap (G2)

Notice in Figure 6-23 how the seven bytes of the sector ID field are allocated:

- The *ID address mark* is a fixed pattern.
- *Track address* identifies that track.
- The *head address* and *sector length* fields are filled with 0s.
- *Sector address* identifies a particular sector.
- The two remaining bytes store the checksum (CRC) of bytes 0 to 4.

CRC stands for **cyclic redundancy code** and is used for error detection purposes. We will come back to this subject later.

The data field of each sector is composed of

- A *data address mark* (fixed pattern)
- Space for 128 bytes of data
- Two bytes for the checksum of the whole field

Example 6-20

Determine what portion of the capacity allocated to each sector in Figure 6-23 is usable for storing data.

Solution.   The total capacity allocated to a sector is $7 + 17 + 131 + 33 = 188$ bytes. From this, only 128 bytes are actually usable for storage purposes. This is equivalent to $128/188 = 0.68$, or 68 percent. Thus, when it comes to disk capacities, it is important to know if the figures concern formatted or unformatted capacity.

Each of the 128 bytes of data is stored serially with its most significant bit first. Why the gaps? First, they provide time allowance for switching from read mode to write mode. Secondly, they compensate for rotational speed and other manufacturing tolerances and thereby make possible diskette interchangeability— that is, data written on a diskette by one floppy disk can be read by another.

Floppy Disk Drives

With the principles behind us, we proceed to the next step, namely, to examine how a floppy disk operates as a whole, what its I/O interface signals are, how we can determine its capacity and access time, and the types of commercially available floppies and some of their characteristics.

Floppy disks are electromechanical devices much like printers.

1. They too include mechanical parts whose motion must be controlled electrically. A typical floppy has
   (a) A motor for rotation of the diskette
   (b) A (stepping) motor for positioning of the head

2. In addition to controlling these motors we need two positioning detectors:
   (a) One for the index hole
   (b) One for detection of the fact that the head reached the outermost track (track 00)
   A third detector (consisting of an LED/photodetector pair) is used to determine whether the write-protect notch is covered (taped) or not. If taped, then write operations on that particular diskette are inhibited.
3. We also need read/write circuits for the R/W head. The read circuits amplify the signal induced into the read coil of the R/W head during a read operation. The write circuits derive (from the data we want to record) the signals driving the write and erase coils of the head.

All the circuits, motors, and other mechanical parts just mentioned are accommodated in a common enclosure. They are referred to collectively as a **floppy disk drive (FDD)**. As an example, we show in Figure 6-24 the basic parts of a 5.25-inch FDD.

Typically, the diskette is rotated by a 12 VDC motor at a speed of 300 (or 360) rpm. Constant speed is maintained by monitoring the speed of the motor and regulating the driving signal accordingly. When the FDD receives a read or write command it proceeds as follows:

1. It turns the (spindle) drive motor on for rotation of the diskette.
2. The stepping motor starts moving the R/W head through some mechanism (such as a lead screw) from track to track.
3. After positioning the head over the desired track the FDD waits for some time interval known as **head settling time**.
4. The circuits locate the desired sector and perform the read or write operation.
5. After completion of the read or write operation, the FDD turns the drive motor off.

Not all FDDs operate this way. Some (including 8-inch ones) employ AC motors rotating the diskette continuously. In order to avoid excessive wear of the media, such FDDs do not keep the head in contact with the diskette all the time. Instead the head is loaded (that is, brought in contact with the media) only after the desired track is located. Then, following completion of the read or write operation, the head is unloaded.

I/O interface lines

Our typical FDD has four status lines (see bottom left in Figure 6-24). Three of them reflect the status of the signals generated by the three detectors we just discussed. The *READY* status line indicates readiness of the FDD to initiate a read/write operation. For example, this line may not go active until the diskette reaches the nominal rotational speed.

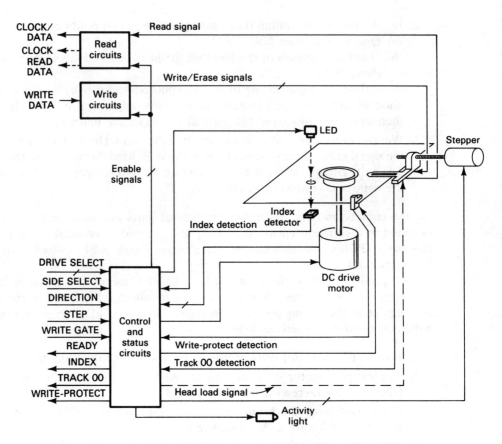

Figure 6-24.   Block diagram of a 5.25-inch floppy disk drive.

The set of I/O interface lines includes five or more lines for control of the FDD:

1. *DRIVE SELECT:* There are two or more such lines. They play the role of address lines when multiple FDDs are controlled by a common controller.

2. *SIDE SELECT:* This line is intended for FDDs capable of handling double-sided diskettes, in which both sides of the medium are usable. Such FDDs have a separate R/W head for each side.

3. *DIRECTION:* The state of this line indicates to the FDD the direction in which it must move the head when a step pulse arrives—that is, whether it should move the head inward or outward from the present position.

4. *STEP:* This line carries the step pulses advancing the head positioning mechanism.

5. *WRITE GATE:* This line plays essentially the role of a write enable line.

How about data and clock lines? The data we are to record arrive over the *WRITE DATA* line (top left in Figure 6-24). After conditioning, they are supplemented with the appropriate clock pulses for recording. Typically, a FDD provides read data and clock pulses over a single line (*CLOCK/DATA*) line. Some include circuitry for separation of the clock from the data (see the broken lines for *CLOCK* and *READ DATA*).

Capacity

Most important among the characteristics of a storage device is its capacity. The capacity of a FDD is determined from that of the diskette(s) it has been designed to handle and is measured in bytes. The capacity of a diskette depends on its

- Physical size
- Track density
- Bit density

These characteristics determine the total number of tracks and how many bits we can store per track.

Example 6-21

The media of a FDD have 77 tracks per surface and employ a recording density of 3268 bits per inch (bpi). The radius of the innermost track is 2 in. Calculate the total storage capacity assuming single-sided diskettes. Repeat for a density of 6536, assuming double-sided media.

Solution. The length of the innermost track is about $2 \times 3.14 \times 2 = 12.56$ in. Hence we can store on it up to about $3268 \times 12.56 = 41046$ bits, or 5.13 KB. Since we store on outer tracks the same amount we do on the innermost one, the total capacity of a single-sided diskette is $77 \times 5.13 = 395$ KB.

With the twice as high bit density, we can store on a surface $2 \times 395 = 790$ KB. Consequently, the capacity of a double-sided diskette is $2 \times 790 = 1580$ KB or about 1.6 MB.

However, as we have already indicated, the usable capacity of an FDD depends also on the sectoring approach and the format we employ.

Example 6-22

The total capacity of a single density 8-inch FDD is 382 KB. The total number of tracks is 77. Determine its usable capacity assuming hard sectoring into 32 sectors of 128 bytes each. Repeat your calculations assuming soft sectoring into 26 sectors of 128 bytes each.

Solution. Each track provides $32 \times 128 = 4096$ bytes of usable capacity, so the total usable capacity is 77×4096 bytes, or about 315 KB. With soft sectoring, the usable (formatted) capacity of the FDD drops to $77 \times 26 \times 128$ bytes, or about 256 KB.

When it comes to double-sided diskettes we define (in addition to sectors and tracks) a third entity—the cylinder. A cylinder consists of two corresponding top and bottom tracks. For example, track 50 of the top surface and track 50 of the bottom surface form cylinder 50. Thus, the number of cylinders is equal to the number of tracks per surface.

Access time

How fast can we locate the sector from which we want to read (or write) data? The time taken to do so includes at least three components:

1. *Seek Time:* First of all, the head must be stepped from its present position to the track where the desired sector is. In a typical FDD this is accomplished one step at a time. Assume, for instance, the head is positioned at present over track 40 and we want to read sector 10 of track 60. To do so we step the head to track 41, then 42, and so on until reaching track 60. The time it takes to locate the desired track is called **seek time**. It is clear that seek time depends on the position of the sought track relative to the present position of the head. However, it can be determined that its average value is equal to $Nt/3$ (see Problem 6-17). N is the number of tracks per surface, and t is the time taken to advance the head from one track to the next (track-to-track time).

2. *Head Settling Time:* After reaching the sought track, the head requires some time **interval to settle**.

3. *Latency Time:* Once settled, the head is ready to start reading (or writing) the sector. If the beginning of the desired sector happens to be passing under the head at that time, reading (or writing) starts immediately. Otherwise, the head must wait. This waiting time is called **latency time**. Its average value is equal to one half the time taken for a full rotation of the diskette.

The sum of the average values of these three components determines the **average access time** of a FDD.

Example 6-23

A FDD rotates the diskette at 300 rpm. Calculate the maximum and average latency times, and determine the average seek time assuming there are 77 tracks and a track-to-track time of 3 ms.

Solution. A full rotation of the diskette takes $60/300 = 0.2$ s, or 200 ms. The maximum possible value of the latency time will be just as long. On the average, the latency time will be $200/2 = 100$ ms. The average seek time is $(77 \times 3)/3 = 77$ ms.

If the diskette is not already rotating, we have to take into consideration an additional factor, namely, the time taken by the drive motor to reach its nominal speed after it is turned on.

Example 6-24

Determine the average access time for the FDD of Example 6-23 given a head settling time of 13 ms. Assume the diskette is already rotating at nominal speed.

Repeat the calculations given a 50 percent chance the diskette is already rotating. When turned on, the drive motor takes 220 ms to reach nominal speed.

Solution. The average access time of the FDD is $77 + 100 + 13 = 190$ ms.

The average access time must be increased by $0.50 \times 220 = 110$ ms. Thus, the new value is $190 + 110 = 300$ ms. Note that this additional factor does not exist in FDDs in which the drive motor is operating all the time. On the other hand, such floppies require a typical head load time of 15 ms.

Once the beginning of a sector comes under the head, data are read (or written) serially one bit at a time. The speed at which this is done determines the **data transfer rate** of a FDD.

Example 6-25

Calculate the data transfer rates for the FDD of Example 6-21. Assume a rotational speed of 300 rpm. How long does it take to read one byte of data once the desired sector is located?

Solution. In the single-density case a track stores 41046 bits. The diskette makes a full rotation in $60/300 = 0.2$ s. Therefore, the data rate is $41046/0.2$ b/s, or about 200 Kb/s. For double-density the data rate is twice as large.

To read or write one bit requires $0.2/41046$ s, or about 5 μs. Hence, one byte takes $8 \times 5 = 40$ μs. With double density this time is reduced to 20 μs.

Classification of FDDs

FDDs are classified on the basis of the physical dimensions of their diskettes into

- 8-inch FDDs
- 5.25-inch FDDs (known as **minifloppies**)
- 3.25-inch FDDs (known as **microfloppies**)

The diameter of the employed diskette determines the width of the FDD. Thus, it becomes a determining factor of its overall size. Typical sizes (in terms of height, width, depth) are:

- $4.6 \times 9.5 \times 14$ (8-inch floppies)

- $3\frac{3}{8} \times 5\frac{3}{4} \times 8$ (minifloppies)
- $1.62 \times 4 \times 6$ (microfloppies)

Note that some manufacturers offer "half-height" versions as well.

Floppy Disk Controllers

For control of a FDD we need a significant amount of circuitry (between the CPU and the FDD). Fortunately, the magnitude of the design task is reduced drastically with the use of an **integrated floppy disk controller** (**FDC**). The type of functions performed by a FDC will become apparent while discussing the simplified block diagram of such a device (see Figure 6-25).

The disk drive status/control interface logic monitors the status lines of the FDD and generates all signals for its control. In doing so, it takes into consideration the contents of the four registers seen at the top of the diagram and, in some cases, those of the data register as well. The functions of the four registers are as follows:

1. The **command register** contains the CPU command we are to execute or are currently executing. Examples of typical commands are:
   (a) Seek (for positioning of the head over a specified track)
   (b) Read sector
   (c) Write sector
   (d) Write track (for formatting purposes)
2. The **status register** reflects the state of the FDD following execution of a command—for example, not ready, write-protected, occurrence of an error, detection of the index hole or track 00, and so on.
3. The **sector register** is loaded by the CPU with the address of the sector we are to access.
4. The **track register** contains the number of the track over which the head is currently positioned. Initially, when the FDC is reset, the control logic positions the head over track 00 and clears this register. From there on, the contents of the track register are modified as follows:
   (a) They are incremented by 1 for every step of the head inwards.
   (b) They are decremented by 1 for every step outwards.
   So, the FDC knows the position of the head at any time.

Now let us see how the FDC would go about executing a seek command. Assume the drive motor is already up to speed and that the CPU has placed the desired track number in the data register and the seek command in the command register. First, the FDC compares the contents of the data register to those of the track register. It does so in order to determine the direction in which it should step the head. Then it starts generating (on its own) step pulses to the FDD. Meanwhile

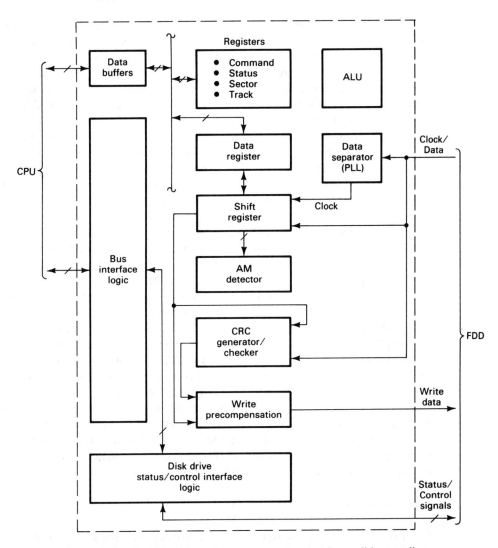

Figure 6-25. Simplified block diagram of an integrated floppy disk controller.

it continues to do two things: (1) update the head position in the track register, and (2) compare the contents of the data register to those of the track register. When these data match, the FDC stops generating step pulses.   It then waits for a time interval adequate for head settling and finally generates an interrupt to the CPU to indicate the seek command has been executed.

Since a FDD may not provide separate *CLOCK* and *READ DATA* outputs, the FDC has a **data separator** for this purpose.   The data separator examines composite *CLOCK/DATA* pulses and clocks a shift register only at time intervals corresponding to data bit positions.   It employs a **phase-locked loop (PLL)** consisting of a **voltage-controlled oscillator** and a **phase comparator**. This approach allows the data separator to keep track of interpulse time interval variations in the stream of CLOCK/DATA pulses. Data bytes are transferred from the shift register to the data register. From there on, they are transferred to the CPU. The CRC generator/checker serves to detect errors (we will see how shortly), and the AM (address mark) detector monitors the bits of information accumulated in the shift register for detection of index, ID, and data address marks.

Next, let us see how the FDC goes about writing a data byte on the diskette. Assume this byte has already been placed in the data register by the CPU. First, the byte is transferred from the data register to the shift register. Subsequently, bits are shifted out serially to both the CRC generator/checker and the **write precompensation** block. The first derives the CRC bytes stored in the data field of each sector, and the second adds to the data bits clock bits. It also shifts all bits to compensate for the **bit shift** experienced during reading. Then it sends them to the FDD. Bit shift effects—due to the partial overlapping of consecutive clock/data pulses—increase with bit densities. The result is shifting of the peak of each pulse as if the respective bit were recorded off the center of a bit cell.

How does the FDC proceed into reading a sector after execution of a seek command? Recall that the FDC interrupts the CPU after executing a seek command. Next the CPU places in the sector register the address of the desired sector. It also places in the command register the code for the read sector command. From this point on, the FDC monitors the ID fields of the sectors passing under the head. That is, it compares their sector address bytes to the one contained in the sector register. These comparisons are performed by an ALU (arithmetic and logic unit), which is also useful for incrementation/decrementation of registers in the course of other disk operations. When a match is detected, the FDC proceeds to read and send to the CPU the data stored in the data field of that sector. Before doing so, however, it checks for correctness the information stored in the sector ID field. Next we discuss how CRC works.

Error Detection

Error detection in storage devices is as important as error detection in memories. In both cases the motivation is the same: to preserve system and data integrity. Yet the employed techniques are different, mainly for the following reasons:

1. In storage devices, the nature of the error-causing processes are different. Errors tend to occur in bursts rather than on a single-bit basis. For example, a bad spot on the surface of the medium may corrupt several or even many neighboring bits. Similarly, a noise spike is likely to affect more than one of the bits transmitted serially to/from a disk. The effects of such spikes depend on their widths relative to bit durations.

2. Unlike memories, disks do not access information in parallel (in terms of bytes or words). They deal with serial information in terms of blocks.

The bursty nature of errors makes parity schemes very inappropriate. With one parity bit per block, for instance, we would have only a 50 percent chance of detecting a burst of errors within a block.

Fortunately there is a family of error-checking codes which are very efficient in the case of error bursts. They are known as **polynomial codes** or **cyclic redundancy codes (CRC)**. The term *polynomial* stems from the fact that such codes treat bit strings as representations of polynomials having coefficients of either 0 or 1. For example, the polynomial corresponding to the bit sequence 10100101 is $x^7 + x^5 + x^2 + 1$.

While a block is being transmitted to the storage device, we divide its polynomial representation by another predetermined polynomial; called a **generator polynomial**. The division is done modulo 2—that is, it amounts to shifts and EXOR (exclusive or) operations. All we are really interested in is the remainder of the division. If we append this remainder to the original block, it makes the composite polynomial divisible by the generator polynomial.

When that block is read from the storage device, we divide its respective composite polynomial by the same generator polynomial. Now the remainder should be zero. Any nonzero remainder indicates detection of an error(s). Incidentally, recall that such codes are also employed in serial communication where information is also transmitted in blocks (see Section 5.5.2).

CRC generation/checking can be implemented with a shift register and feedback loops via EXOR gates. The order of the chosen generator polynomial determines how long the register should be. The feedback loops correspond to bit positions with nonzero coefficients in the generator polynomial. Such an implementation permits doing the division while transmitting the information serially. The contents of the register at the conclusion of the transmission of the original block represent the remainder of the division, called **checksum**. The checksum is shifted out to the storage device right behind the original block. When reading, we pass through the shift register both the original block and its checksum. At the conclusion of the transfer the contents of the shift register should be zero. The CRC circuits may be part of an integrated disk controller or, in the case of serial communication, part of a serial communication controller. Besides, there are commercially available devices called **CRC generators/checkers**.

What if CRC checking during a disk read operation indicates an error? The usual approach is to retry reading that sector. If successful, the error is considered a soft one. Soft errors are generally due to noise. In floppies they are typically on the order of 1 in 10^9 bits. What if the error persists after a predetermined number of retries? In this case it is declared a hard error. Usually hard errors are due to surface defects in the media (bad spots). They are on the order of 1 in 10^{12} bits. In this case, one solution is replacing the bad track with an alternate one.

Another source of errors (besides noise and media defects) is surface contaminants. Such particles may limit the amplitude of recorded bits to the degree that those bits will not be sensed during reading. Errors can also be the result of operating beyond the environmental range specified by the manufacturer. For disks, the temperature range is typically 10 °C to 45 °C. The relative humidity range is 20 to 80 percent. Finally, in disks we may deal with so-called **seek errors** (typically one in 10^6 seeks). These errors result from positioning the head over the wrong track. Recovery from a seek error can be accomplished by going back to track 00 and retrying positioning over the desired track.

Example of an Integrated FDC

Figure 6-26 pictures an application example of an integrated FDC—the Western Digital WD2795 "floppy disk formatter controller."

Observe that with the exception of the *DSEL* (drive select) signal, the WD2795 provides all control signals of the FDD illustrated in Figure 6-24 and accommodates all status lines as well. The *DSEL* signal is generated by an address decoder (see Figure 6-26).

The WD2795 provides a number of additional lines for greater flexibility:

- The head load (*HLD*) signal is intended for those FDDs that need one. An external, one-shot circuit determines the duration of this signal through the head load timing (*HLT*) input of the WD2795.
- Line 5*/8 selects the appropriate frequency of the on-chip voltage-controlled oscillator for accommodation of both 8-inch and 5.25-inch FDDs.
- The WD2795 can handle double densities as well. Density selection is done through the *DDEN** (double density enable) input.

Line *TG*43 (track greater than 43) indicates that the head is positioned on one of the inner tracks beyond track 43. In Figure 6-26 this line connects to the *ENP* (enable write precompensation) input of the WD2795. (Remember that bit densities along tracks increase as we move inward.) Lines *PUMP*, *VCO*, *RPW*, and *WPW* permit adjustment of the center frequency and other characteristics of the voltage-controlled oscillator (VCO). They also control the amount of delay introduced for write precompensation purposes. *TEST** is used in conjunction with these lines to facilitate adjustments.

The remaining lines connect to the CPU bus and CPU-related circuits. *DRQ* (data request) indicates that the FDC is ready to accept/provide the next byte of data. *INTRQ* (interrupt request) is activated whenever any command has been fully executed.

For more flexibility the WD2795 allows programmable stepping rates and sector lengths. Other characteristics typical of integrated FDCs are its ability to

- Read, write, or search multiple sectors
- Handle multiple FDDs

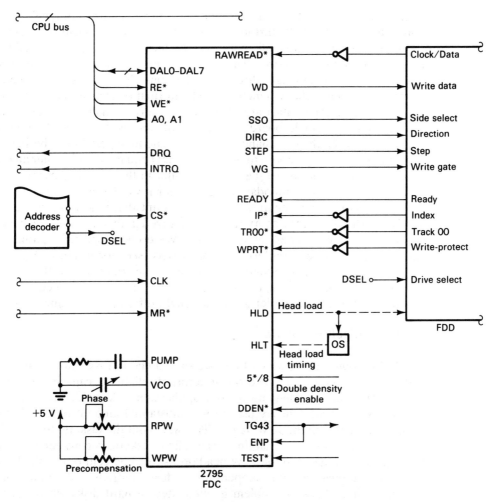

Figure 6-26. Example of an integrated floppy disk controller.

Design Considerations

Execution of a command by a FDD takes a relatively long time. A seek, for instance, may take 200 ms or more. Thus, interrupting the CPU after executing a command is not a problem. However, data cannot be dealt with in this fashion. Since we are dealing with 1 byte every 32 (or less) μs, interrupt-driven I/O is very inappropriate. The proper choice is DMA. As a matter of fact, we should operate the DMA controller in cycle-stealing mode so that the CPU is given the chance to use the bus between successive byte transfers (see Section 5.4).

An integrated FDC simplifies the design task greatly. However, in some applications it may be necessary to equip the controller with additional capabilities in order to deload the CPU further. You may, for instance, include a sector buffer or employ a local μP to handle control of all local operations associated with file management and other tasks. The idea is to relieve the main CPU from having to send commands and data directly to the controller. Instead the main CPU informs the local μP where in memory such information can be found. Controllers with this sort of capabilities are also commercially available. Usually they are implemented on a single board and are compatible with one of the popular μC buses. Very often they can handle hard disks and tape peripherals besides FDDs. Furthermore, you may choose to purchase a FDD equipped with either an ordinary or an intelligent—that is, μP-based—controller in the same enclosure.

Where do we accommodate the controller if we design our own? One way is to implement it on a separate board and mount that board in the enclosure of the FDD. Because of the short distances involved in this case, interfacing to/from the FDD circuitry is somewhat simplified. We do not need terminating resistors and may not even need buffering of the signals (see, for instance, Figure 6-26). Another way is to accommodate the circuits of the controller on the CPU board or some other board external to the FDD. In such cases we need to apply the guidelines we discussed earlier as far as signal buffering and termination go.

FDD selection criteria

Before considering which FDD we should choose, we must ensure that the modest performance of floppy disks (in terms of reliability, capacity, access speed, and so on) is indeed adequate for our application. A major problem is that a diskette cannot sustain heavy usage for a substantial amount of time because of its direct contact with the R/W head. This wears out the diskette to the point that read signals become quite marginal. Usually a diskette is considered worn when the read signal induced in the R/W head drops to 80 percent of its initial (normal) value. In a typical case this happens after a few hundreds of thousands of passes per track. This kind of problem is eliminated in hard disks where there is no contact between the R/W head and the medium.

Once we decide to use a floppy disk, we have to consider such additional criteria as

1. *Capacity:* The required capacity does not necessarily narrow down the choice to a specific size diskette. Recall that capacity is also a function of bit and track densities. Microfloppies, for instance, permit higher track densities. This becomes possible because (due to its smaller size) the medium undergoes less expansion/contraction with temperature and humidity changes. Thus track positions do not vary as much as they do in larger diskettes.

2. *Physical Size:* This may point to a particular class of FDDs. For example, if small overall system size—and possibly portability—is a must, we should consider selection of one of the microfloppies.

3. *Media Interchangeability:* This can be a problem especially in the case of 5.25-inch FDDs. In general, the latter are standardized as far as physical dimensions, interface signals, connectors, and so forth. Their media are soft-sectored, with each track divided into 16 sectors. Yet they do not employ a standard format. However, even when employing a standard format, as in the case of 8-inch FDDs, there can be problems. Necessary (though not sufficient) conditions are that the FDDs (between which we will be interchanging diskettes):

(a) Have the same rotational speeds

(b) Employ compatible recording techniques

If these conditions are satisfied, then soft-sectored diskettes written by one FDD may be readable by another. (Some preprocessing may be required if the employed file structures are incompatible.)

4. *Reliability:* This factor depends on both the media and the FDD itself. A typical FDD has an MTBF of the order of 2000 POH (power on hours). The drive motor can be a major contributor to failures and thus it is preferable to have it off while the FDD is not being used by the CPU.

5. *Average Access Time:* Typically, access time is on the order of a few hundreds of milliseconds, but it varies considerably among FDDs. Some applications are not sensitive to this factor.

6. *Other:* Cost, of course, can be a key factor, but certain other characteristics that may permit a more hostile environment are noteworthy. For example, microdiskettes are more rugged. They are enclosed in hard jackets which are equipped with a shutter covering the head access slot when the microdiskette is not in the FDD. As a result, microfloppies are better equipped for operation in industrial environments.

The weight given to each of these criteria depends on the particular application. For example, capacity is very important in a word processing application. On the other hand, in a large system where the FDD may simply be used for operating system loading we would be more concerned about reliability.

PROBLEMS

6-1. Entry Errors in Keyboards. N-key rollover does not prevent another type of errors known as "phantom key" errors. These occur when three simultaneously depressed keyswitches happen to be positioned rectangularly within the keyboard matrix. Consider, for instance, the 4 × 4 array of mechanical keyswitches shown in Figure P6-1. If keys K, L, and P happen to be depressed at the same time, an electrical path is established between row 2 and column 4 (see broken line). Now as soon as the keyboard controller applies a low to row 2 and scans the columns, it detects that column 4 is at a low; that is, it detects the very same condition encountered when key

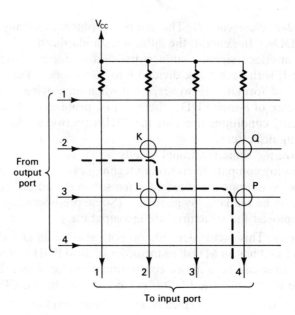

Figure P6-1.

Q (alone) is depressed.   As a result, the controller proceeds to generate (falsely) the code for Q.

(a) A possible solution to phantom key errors is using isolation diodes.   Show how you would connect such diodes to the keyboard matrix.   What is the main problem with this solution?

(b) Some manufacturers eliminate phantom key errors by means of software routines executed by an on-board μP or μC chip.   Describe how you would go about detecting phantom key errors with a software routine.

6-2. Usable Portion of Frame Time in a TV Monitor.   A TV monitor has a vertical scanning rate of 60 Hz.   The vertical and horizontal blanking intervals are 1.25 ms and 12.5 μs, respectively.

(a) How long is the frame time?

(b) What fraction of the frame time is actually usable for display purposes, given that the horizontal scanning rate is 16.2 KHz?

(c) What is the total number of scan lines per frame?   How many of them are usable?

(d) Why are the blanking intervals chosen to be generally longer than the respective retrace times?

6-3. Medium Quality Monitor.   A TV monitor has a 60 Hz frame refresh rate and a horizontal scanning frequency of 33720 Hz.

(a) Up to how many scan lines could it possibly provide per frame?

(b) Suppose we use this monitor in an application requiring a resolution of 512 $\times$ 512.   How many scan lines correpond to the vertical blanking interval?   What is the duration of this interval?

(c) How long is the usable portion of a scan line (in terms of time) given that we waste only 4 μs for horizontal blanking?

(d) What would the dot clock frequency be?

6-4. Character and Dot Clock Rates. Consider an alphanumeric CRT display employing a 7 × 9 character font and a 9 × 12 character block. The display format is 80 × 24. The vertical and horizontal scanning rates are 60 and 18000 Hz, respectively.
  (a) How many usable scan lines do we need?
  (b) Usually, the horizontal blanking time is chosen to be an integral number of periods of the character clock. Here we assume it corresponds to 20 periods of the character clock. Determine the length of the usable portion of a scan line (in terms of time).
  (c) What is the frequency of the character clock?
  (d) How about the frequency of the dot clock?
  (e) The vertical blanking interval is itself chosen to be an integral number of scan line periods. Verify that this is indeed true. What would you vary slightly if it was not?

6-5. Display Memory Access Time. Consider the display discussed in Problem 6-4. How fast should the display RAM and the ROM be in order to support a character refresh rate of 1.8 MHz? Assume an organization similar to the one pictured in Figure 6-12.

6-6. Character Display Design. Figure 6-14 illustrates a design example employing the MC6845 for CRT control.
  (a) Notice that the shift register is clocked with the dot clock. However, the output flip-flop (FF) is clocked with the inverted dot clock. Why?
  (b) What maximum cycle time would you tolerate for the refresh memory? How about the ROM? Assume an 8-MHz dot clock.

6-7. Display Memory Access Modes. Figure 6-15 shows a design example employing the 2670/2672/2673 chip set for CRT control. Here the display RAM is not directly accessible to the CPU. Instead CPU accesses are indirect via latches acting as an I/O port. For example, to write a new character in the display RAM, the CPU
  • Writes that character in the input latch
  • Sends to the 2672 the associated address
  • Checks the status of the 2672
  • Issues a write command to the 2672, which copies the character from the input latch into the display RAM

However, in order to avoid visual disturbances of the displayed information, the 2672 does so only during blanking intervals. This approach is often referred to as an "intelligent buffer" mode. Clearly, such a mode eliminates contention problems and requires very little in terms of hardware components. The problem is that it takes a substantial amount of CPU time, and the display of a new page takes a long time.

Assume the CPU sends new data to the display RAM only during vertical blanking intervals and each character transfer takes 7.8 µs. Calculate how long it takes the CPU to send a new page. Assume a SRAM-based display memory and the values shown for the listed display parameters:
  • Screen format: 80 × 24
  • Vertical blanking interval: 1.5 ms
  • Frame refresh rate: 60 Hz

6-8. Row Buffering Mode. Another display memory access mode supported by the 2672 is the so-called row buffering mode (see Figure 6-15 and Problem 6-7). That is, during the first scan line of a character row (when no data are displayed on the screen), the 2672 fills the row buffer from memory (via DMA). Thereafter, no data transfers are necessary until finishing the display of the fetched character row. This scheme has the advantage of reducing contention greatly when the display memory is part of the main memory. However, it requires more hardware than the scheme discussed in Problem 6-7.

(a) Identify the additional componentry required for implementation of such a scheme.

(b) Suppose the row buffer cannot be filled completely during the first scan line (due to contention with other bus users and/or to slow memory). Consequently you decide to employ two row buffers. Now the time interval we have available for buffer fill-up is longer. By what factor did it increase relative to the single row buffer case? Assume a 7 × 9 font and one scan line for spacing purposes.

6-9. Display Memory Access Modes. In addition to the modes discussed in Problems 6-7 and 6-8, the 2672 supports a third mode named "shared buffering" mode. Now the display memory is accessed by the CPU directly in a fashion similar to the one pictured in Figure 6-14. Although it is implemented by separate devices, the display memory address space is part of the main memory address space. Prior to initiating an access, the CPU informs the 2672 of its intent. Subsequently, the 2672 grants the display address and data buses, and blanks the screen. Such a mode is very convenient for the CPU, but the disadvantage is that it temporarily disrupts the display.

(a) On which characteristic(s) of the employed TV monitor does the impact of such disruptions depend?

(b) The 2672 supports a "transparent buffering" mode as well. The latter is similar to the shared mode, except the CPU is granted access to the display memory only during blanking intervals. Calculate how long it takes the CPU to send a new page in this mode. Use the parameter values assumed in Problem 6-7 with the exception of the duration of a character transfer which is now 780 ns.

(c) Suppose we employ a shared buffering mode, except that accesses by the CPU and the CRT controller are interleaved. For example, during the first half of a character clock period, the display RAM can be accessed only by the CRT controller. During the second half, it becomes available only to the CPU. Assume the character clock rate is 2 MHz. What is the maximum memory cycle time you would tolerate if you were to implement such a scheme?

6-10. Character Printer. A μC system is equipped with a CRT display employing an 80 × 24 screen format. After examining a (screen) page we have the option of requesting a hard copy, which is printed while examining the next page.

(a) Assume a character printer having a single-character buffer and an average speed of 100 cps. After printing a character, the printer interrupts the CPU which sends the next character within 5 ms (on the average). How long does it take to print one page?

(b) Repeat your calculations assuming the printer is equipped with a two-character buffer.

6-11. Line Printer. Assume the system discussed in Problem 6-10 is equipped with a nonimpact type line printer instead. This line printer has a single-line buffer and an average speed of 9600 LPM. After printing a line, the printer generates an interrupt to the CPU, which, on the average, responds within about 4.2 ms and starts sending the characters of the next line at the rate of 100000 cps.

(a) How long does it take to print a (screen) page?

(b) What fraction of CPU time is consumed for printer servicing during the printout of a page? Assume interrupt service overheads amount to about 200 μs.

(c) Suppose the printer is equipped with a full-page buffer filled through DMA at a rate of 1 MB/s. Page printing starts only after the buffer is filled completely. Repeat the two previous questions assuming the same interrupt response and overhead times (except the printer is now interrupting only after printing a page to obtain the starting address of the next page).

6-12. Data Rate of a Disk. Prove that the data rate (R) of a magnetic (floppy or hard) disk can be determined from the expression

$$R = (2\pi rd) / L$$

where
r is the radius of the innermost track
d is the recording density on the innermost track
L is the time taken for a full rotation of the disk

6-13. Variation of Recording Density with Track Diameter. Derive an expression for the recording density of track i in terms of the radius (r) and recording density (d) of the innermost track. Assume the magnetic disk has a track density of D tracks per inch.

6-14. Storage Capacity of a Floppy Disk. A two-sided diskette rotates at 360 rpm. Once the desired sector is located, data are provided/accepted at a rate of 500 Kb/s. Determine its storage capacity in kilobytes given a total of 135 tracks per surface.

6-15. Floppy Disk Latency and Seek Times. A floppy disk drive rotates the diskette at 360 rpm and has a track-to-track time of 3 ms. The employed diskettes have a total of 77 tracks per surface.

(a) Determine the minimum, maximum, and average values of the latency time.

(b) Repeat the previous question for the seek time.

6-16. Average Access Time of a Floppy Disk. A floppy disk drive has a track-to-track time of 3 ms and rotates the diskette at 360 rpm. The employed diskettes have a total of 135 tracks per surface.

(a) Calculate the average access time given a head settling time of 15 ms.

(b) Suppose we use 50 consecutive tracks only. What will be the effective average access time seing by the CPU?

6-17. Average Seek Time of a Disk. Prove that the average seek time of a disk is $[(N + 1)t]$ / 3 (and thus can be very closely approximated by $Nt/3$), where N is the number of tracks per surface and t is the track-to-track time. Assume that head positioning is accomplished by stepping from each track to the adjacent one until the desired track is located.

6-18. Sector Transfer Time. A floppy disk drive rotates its diskette at 300 rpm. The employed diskettes are soft-sectored into 26 sectors having data fields of 128 bytes.

(a) Calculate how long it takes to read the data stored in a sector (after locating it) given a data transfer rate of 200 Kb/s.

(b) We are about to read a block of data stored in four consecutive sectors of a track. Assume the beginning of the first sector of the block is already under the R/W head. Calculate (approximately) how long it will take to read the whole block.

6-19. Availability of Disk Data to the CPU. The access time of a disk represents the time taken from the moment the controller initiates a seek operation until the head is positioned over the beginning of the desired sector. Thus, in order to determine how

long it takes to make available to the CPU a block of data, we must add
- The time taken by the controller to execute a READ command.
- The time taken to transfer the data from the disk to the controller and, from there on, to the CPU (or its memory).

Assume hard-sectored diskettes sectored into 32 sectors of 128 bytes each. The rotational speed is 300 rpm.

   (a) The floppy disk controller has a single-sector buffer. How long does it take to fill it from the disk after the desired sector is located?

   (b) After receiving the desired sector data, the controller performs error checking. Then it transfers the data to CPU memory via a DMA channel operating in burst mode at the rate of 2 MB/s. Calculate the time interval elapsed from the moment the controller starts execution of a READ command until the sector is fully transferred to memory. Assume 500 μs for the execution of a READ sector command by the controller and an average disk access time of 203.2 ms.

6-20. μC System with Floppy Disk and CRT. The peripherals of a small μC system include:
- A keyboard
- A CRT displaying alphanumerics in an 80 × 24 screen format
- A floppy disk

During a read/write operation the disk provides/accepts one byte of data every 16 μs. Its controller has a single-character buffer. Both the CRT controller and the floppy disk controller transfer data to/from memory via an 8237A DMAC (see Section 5.4) which is clocked at a rate of 2 MHz. As a matter of fact, the CRT is refreshed directly from (main) memory at a rate of 60 Hz.

   (a) For what fraction of time is the CPU locked out of its bus due to CRT refresh operations? Assume the CRT has a row buffer and that each byte transfer takes four clock cycles. Disregard bus mastership transfer overheads.

   (b) In which mode would you operate the DMA channel serving the floppy disk? Why? Which of the two DMA channels should be assigned higher priority?

6-21. μC System with Floppy Disk and CRT. Consider again the μC system discussed in Problem 6-20.

   (a) In what size blocks would you have to transfer refresh data in order to prevent floppy disk data overruns?

   (b) For which peripheral device would you take advantage of the autoinitialization feature of the 8237A? Why?

6-22. Transfer of a File Stored on Multiple Tracks. Consider a file occupying sequential sectors over four consecutive tracks of a floppy disk. The floppy disk has a track-to-track time of 3 ms and a head settling time of 17 ms. The diskette is rotated at 300 rpm. Determine how long it takes the disk drive to read the entire file after positioning and settling of the head over the very first sector.

6-23. File Transfer. Consider a disk drive like the one discussed in Problem 6-22. The employed diskettes use a format based on 16 sectors. A particular file occupies one full track and two consecutive sectors of the adjacent track.

   (a) Calculate how long it takes to read the entire file after positioning and settling of the head over the first sector of the file.

   (b) How would you go about minimizing the file access time?

6-24. Driving of Peripheral Cables. The noise considerations discussed in Chapters 4 and 5 apply just as well to the cables interconnecting a CPU and its peripherals. In fact,

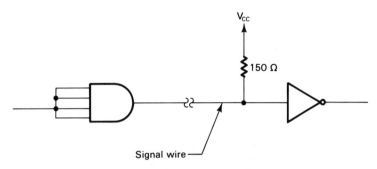

Figure P6-24.

noise is now more severe since the length of such cables is usually much longer than the length of an etched printed board trace or the length of a μC bus. For example, in the case of stand-alone peripherals, cables are typically 10 to 15 ft long. Peripheral cables may be either flat or round.

(a) Explain why, in the case of a flat cable, it is a good practice to ground every other conductor. Which signals should be definitely "sandwiched" between grounded conductors?

(b) Consider a printer connecting to the CPU via a 10-ft round cable. Discuss why the round cable should be providing one twisted pair (rather than a single wire) for each signal.

Figure P6-24 illustrates a very common approach to driving a peripheral cable. The cable driver is an open collector gate whose pull-up resistor is placed at the other end of the signal line.

(c) In general, the required current-sinking capability of a cable driver increases with the length of the cable. Why?

(d) Explain why the pull-up resistor is placed at the far end of the signal line.

6-25. Termination of Peripheral Cables. The need for proper termination of signal lines increases further the current-sinking requirements of cable drivers (see Problem 6-24).

(a) To see this, assume a cable driver having a saturation voltage of 0.2 V and a TTL receiver (Figure P6-24). The value of the pull-up resistor is 150 Ω. How much current does the driver sink when the signal line is at a low?

(b) Suppose we control with a single disk controller several disk drives interconnected in a daisy chain fashion. Explain why we should terminate the signals at the disk drive connecting to the far end of the chain.

REFERENCES

ADVANCED MICRO DEVICES. *AmZ8000 User's Manual*. Sunnyvale, Calif.: Advanced Micro Devices, Inc., 1981.

———. *MOS Microprocessors and Peripherals Data Book*. Sunnyvale, Calif.: Advanced Micro Devices, Inc., 1985.

———. *Bipolar Microprocessor Logic and Interface Data Book*. Sunnyvale, Calif.: Advanced Micro Devices, Inc., 1985.

BLAKESLEE, THOMAS R. *Digital Design with Standard MSI & LSI*, 2nd ed. New York: John Wiley & Sons, Inc., 1979.

ELECTRONIC INDUSTRIES ASSOCIATION. *Standard RS-232-C*. Washington, D.C.: Electronic Industries Association, August, 1969.

———. *Standard RS-449*. Washington, D.C.: Electronic Industries Association, November, 1977.

———. *Application Notes on Interconnection Between Interface Circuits Using RS-449 and RS-232-C*. Washington, D.C.: Electronic Industries Association, November, 1977.

———. *Standard RS-422-A*. Washington, D.C.: Electronic Industries Association, December, 1978.

———. *Standard RS-423-A*. Washington, D.C.: Electronic Industries Association, December, 1978.

HEWLETT PACKARD. *Optoelectronics Designer's Catalog*. Palo Alto, Calif.: Hewlett Packard, 1986.

INSTITUTE OF ELECTRICAL AND ELECTRONICS ENGINEERS. *IEEE Standard Microcomputer System Bus (IEEE Std 796-1983)*. New York: The Institute of Electrical and Electronics Engineers, Inc., 1983.

INTEL. *Multibus Specification*. Santa Clara, Calif.: Intel Corp., 1978.

———. *Components Data Catalog*. Santa Clara, Calif.: Intel Corp., 1982.

———. *Memory Components Handbook*. Santa Clara, Calif.: Intel Corp., 1983.

———. *Microprocessor and Peripheral Handbook*. Santa Clara, Calif.: Intel Corp., 1983.

———. *80386 High Performance Microprocessor with Integrated Memory Management*. Santa Clara, Calif.: Intel Corp., 1985.

INTERSIL. *CMOS Data Book*. Cupertino, Calif.: Intersil, 1984.

MICROSWITCH. *Microcomputer-based Hall Effect Intelligent Keyboard; 103SD30 Series*, Product Specification. Freeport, Il.: Microswitch, 1981.

MOTOROLA SEMICONDUCTOR PRODUCTS. *The MC68010 Virtual Memory Processor*, Product Specification. Austin, Texas: Motorola Semiconductor Products, Inc., 1982.

———. *MC68000 16-Bit Microprocessor*, Product Specification. Austin, Texas: Motorola Semiconductor Products, Inc., 1983.

———. *MC68020 Technical Summary*. Austin, Texas: Motorola Semiconductor Products, Inc., 1984.

———. *Single-Chip Microcomputer Data Manual*. Austin, Texas: Motorola Semiconductor Products, Inc., 1984.

NATIONAL SEMICONDUCTOR. *NS32032-6, NS32032-10 High Performance Microprocessors*. Santa Clara, Calif.: National Semiconductor Corp., 1984.

PEATMAN, JOHN B. *Digital Hardware Design*. New York: McGraw-Hill, 1980.

SEIKO INSTRUMENTS. *LCD Technical Manual*. Torrance, Calif.: Seiko Instruments USA, Inc., 1981.

SIGNETICS. *MOS Microprocessor Data Manual*. Sunnyvale, Calif.: Signetics Corp., 1982.

TANENBAUM, ANDREW S. *Structured Computer Organization*, 2nd ed. Englewood Cliffs, N.J.: Prentice-Hall, Inc., 1984.

TEXAS INSTRUMENTS. *The TTL Data Book*. Dallas, Texas: Texas Instruments Inc., 1985.

———. *MOS Memory Data Book*. Dallas, Texas: Texas Instruments Inc., 1984.

TOCCI, RONALD J., LESTER P. LASKOWSKI. *Microprocessors and Microcomputers*, 2nd ed. Englewood Cliffs, N.J.: Prentice-Hall, Inc., 1982.

WESTERN DIGITAL. *Components Handbook*. Irvine, Calif.: Western Digital Corp., 1983.

ZILOG. *Z8000 Technical Manual*. Cupertino, Calif.: Zilog Inc., 1979.

ZILOG. *1982/83 Data Book*. Cupertino, Calif.: Zilog Inc., 1982.

TRADEMARKS

INDEX

A

Access time, 179
Address:
  bus, 28–29
  decoding, 247–49, 400–402
  displacement, 42
  logical, 230–33
  mapping, 231
  offset, 107
  physical, 107, 230–33
  refresh, (*see* CRT display)
  segment, 107
  translation, 230
  virtual (*see* Virtual memory)
Address/data bus, 71
  demultiplexing, 71, 162
Address space, 29, 281
  allocation, 400–402
  map, 401
Addressing:
  linear, 130, 230
  modes, 39–44
  segmented, 108, 230

Advanced Micro Devices:
  Am2960, 226–29
Architecture, 18, 94
Arithmetic/logic unit (ALU), 2,
  24–25
ASCII code, 421–24
Asynchronous communication (*see
  also* Serial communication), 344

B

Backplane, 9, 373
Barrel shifter, 139
Battery backup, 206–7, 262
Block I/O, 293
Block transfer mode, 51
Bus (*see also* Microcomputer):
  advantages, 373
  arbitration, 378
  asynchronous, 127
  buffers, 163–64
  characteristic impedance, 391
  control lines, 34
  custom versus standard, 396